HITCH-HIKER'S GUID

KEN WELSH was born in Au
RAAF and working as a staff
for Europe, where he still liv
the road he conceived the idea
Europe, which has been in print for twenty-four years and is considered 'the road-bum's bible'. Though married with three children, he remains an insatiable traveller, paying his way with his work as a professional photographer. He estimates that during the last twenty-seven years he has travelled over six hundred thousand miles. Ken Welsh is also the author or photographer, or both, of six travel books about Spain and one on Malta, and has published five novels.

KATIE WOOD is a name familiar to most British back-packers. In the last decade her *Europe by Train* and *Cheap Sleep* guides (published by HarperCollins) have become bestselling travellers' bibles for those on a tight budget.

An established travel journalist and broadcaster, Katie has taken on the task of ensuring that the *Hitch-hiker's Guide* receives the attention it requires to keep it up to date now that Ken is living in Spain and therefore unable to play the hands-on role that he used to. Living in Perth-shire, Scotland, and with more than eighty countries, thirty-five guides and a string of freelance commissions including TV travel programmes in Scotland under her belt, she's well qualified to add her tuppence worth to the world of hitching.

HITCH-HIKER'S GUIDE TO EUROPE

How to see Europe by the skin of your teeth

Revised and updated for 1996

KEN WELSH AND KATIE WOOD

Researcher
Rupert Cocke

HarperCollins*Publishers*

HarperCollinsPaperbacks
An imprint of HarperCollins *Publishers*
77–85 Fulham Palace Road,
Hammersmith, London W6 8JB

First published by Fontana 1983
This edition published 1996
9 8 7 6 5 4 3 2 1

First published in Great Britain by
Pan Books Ltd 1971

ISBN 0 00 638691 1

Set in Linotron Meridien and Linotron Frutiger by
Rowland Phototypesetting Ltd
Bury St Edmunds, Suffolk

Printed in Great Britain by
HarperCollinsManufacturing Glasgow

For Ann, who came too.
And for Ben, who came also.
And for Marcos and Carina.

CONTENTS

INTRODUCTION

This book is designed to show you how to get around Europe for about £100 a week – cheaper, if you're tough enough.

Although it's called *Hitch-hiker's Guide* and is aimed at people on a hitch-hiking budget, van and car travellers will also find it useful because it lists facts which someone with his own wheels can use just as well as someone who's moving around on temporarily borrowed wheels.

For every guidebook that is written, three-quarters of its readers can do better than it. That's because they are guidebooks and not at all holy. This book is no exception. And it's certainly not sacred.

Hitch-hiker's Guide gives you a rundown on Europe, Scandinavia, Eastern Europe, the Middle East, and North Africa, telling you some of what there is to see and enjoy and giving you an indication of what it would normally cost. But I haven't experienced it *all*. There's lots more and plenty of it will be better than the stuff listed.

I ask those wandering souls who have already covered their first ten thousand miles on the road to skip the section which deals with the practical aspects of hitch-hiking. It certainly wasn't written for them.

INVITATION

If you find a deal in eating and sleeping, or a way of saving money in any of the major cities covered in *Hitch-hiker's Guide* you are invited to send your find to us care of the publishers. Your hint and credit will be included in the relevant chapter.

Write to: Ken Welsh & Katie Wood,
Hitch-hiker's Guide to Europe,
c/o HarperCollinsPaperbacks,
77–85 Fulham Palace Road,
Hammersmith, London W6 8JB

Thanks . . .
. . . to all hitchers who have responded to my invitation and written in with reams of interesting tips. Mail was so heavy during 1994–95 it was impossible to answer letters personally. So thanks to everyone, and thanks again. Keep those letters coming.

Special thanks for assistance in preparing the *Hitch-hiker's Guide* are owed to: David Isaacs, Noreen Wells, Isla Stone, Peter Stone, Allen Harbinson, Shaun Harbinson, Lynn Kersh, Ginney Ashton, Thea Braam and Maria Colaluca – all good truckers.

Special contributors . . .
Robert A. H. Prins
Jon Banks
Gerard van Weele
Sarah Monroe
Will Thompson
Olly Davies
Edda Eiriksdottir

HITCHER STUFF

Definitions for hitchers
'*Hitch-hike*: travel by begging lifts from passing motor vehicles. (Fifteenth century, of obscure origin: partly synonymous with Scots *hotch*, move by jerks)' – *The Concise Oxford Dictionary.*

'*Hitch-hike*: to travel by getting free automobile rides and sometimes by walking between rides' – *The Random House Dictionary of the English Language* (unabridged edition).

'*Wander*: rove, stroll, go from country to country or from place to place without settled route or destination' – *The Concise Oxford Dictionary.*

Opinions for hitchers
'When I see so many young people thumbing lifts these days I feel depressed. Have they no pride at all? I can't imagine anything more humiliating than standing at the roadside like a tramp, begging. I always thought that the great thing about young people today was their high principles, independence and determination to make a better job of the world than their predecessors did. But I just can't equate that picture of healthy, intelligent young people, with the deplorable one of cringing, cadging hitch-hikers swarming the roads in their thousands' – *opinion in the letters column of a women's magazine.*

Guilt for hitchers
(Speaking of books commonly stolen from public libraries). Mr Chris Heaton, library manager, said: 'Travel Guides are also popular – books such as *The Hitch-hiker's Guide to Europe . . .' – reported by Robert Shrimsley in his article 'Chapter and Verse on Book Thieves' in* The Daily Telegraph, *October 1991.*

Records for hitchers
The career record for hitch-hiking accepted by *The Guinness Book of Records* is now held by Bill Heid of Allen Park, Michigan, USA who since 1964 has obtained free rides totalling 673,200 kilometres, or 418,300 miles. To back his record, Bill submitted details of departure points, destinations, times of departure, times of arrival, miles covered and even his personal ratings of the trips. I mean, this is serious stuff, right?

Are there aspirants for Bill Heid's title amongst *Hitcher-hiker's Guide* readers? Will one of you back your claim by dumping a kilo of trip info on my desk around 1999? I'll stay tuned!

To take the *Guinness* career hitch-hiking record away from Bill, you would need to supply:

1. An accurate log with details of your travels (routes, distances, times, etc.)
2. Signed statements of authentication by two independent persons of some standing in the community, including contact addresses and telephone numbers, confirming that they believe your log is accurate.
3. If possible, independent corroboration in the form of newspaper cuttings and colour transparencies or photographs of you hitching.

You could present the record claim directly to *The Guinness Book of Records* or send it to me. I have an agreement with them that I will pass claims on.

Each year readers write in with their record attempts in the following categories of hitching:

1. Longest hitch in one vehicle (excluding aeroplanes and ships).
2. Most miles hitched in any 12-month period.
3. Most miles hitched in any 24-hour period.
4. Slowest hitch between two points (include distance, time and brief reason for slowness).
5. The world's craziest lift.

1. (Longest hitch in one vehicle) The new winner in this category is *L. J. Gordon of Western Australia,* who started from Whitepark Bay Youth Hostel in Northern Ireland, where four Americans in a Combi Van gave him a lift through Ireland, Scotland, England, Wales, France, Andorra and into Spain. They covered an astonishing 4441.90 miles before parting company.

   Honourable mention must go to *Robert Prins of De Bilt, Netherlands.* Robert hitched from Platamon in Greece to Driebergen in the Netherlands, 1555 miles.
2. (Most miles in any 12-month period) *Mike Wakefield of Retford, Nottingham, UK,* hitched a staggering 30,500 miles covering most of East and West Europe.
3. (Most miles in any 24-hour period) *Fred Roberts of Clapham in London* raced a friend from Prague to London in just under 24 hours, door to door. We decided to include this amazing hitch even though he cheated a little: Fred paid £10 for a ferry to Calais.

4. (Slowest hitch between two points) The half-mile journey taking 45 minutes by *Ruth Cleece, Preston, Lancashire, UK,* on a steam-roller is still tops, but honourable mention must go to *William Innes, Aberdeen, Scotland,* who bagged a lift on a milkfloat on 'collection' day and took $4^1/_2$ hours to travel 2 miles from North London to the start of the M1.
5. (World's craziest lift) *Dick of Stourbridge, West Midlands,* got a lift in an amphibious troop carrier in Zimbabwe.

Can you better these efforts? If so, let's hear from you. No testimonies are needed. Just tell me the facts. No prizes. Just brief glory.

Limericks for hitchers

There was a young hitcher named Bright
Who travelled much faster than light;
He went out one day
Thumbed in a relative way
And got home the previous night.
– with apologies to the late Prof. A. H. Reginald Butler FRS

A hitcher living in Staines
Is inventing with infinite pains
A new type of thumb
Which he hopes when it's done
Will travel him faster than planes.

A glamorous hitch-hiking neighbour
Rattled her socialist sabre:
Till she hitched a ride
with a midwife from Hyde
Now she knows a lot more about Labour!
Adam Brady, Wales

Graffiti for hitchers

'Eurail, we hitch!' – *Patrick Hine, Oxford, England*

'Orange: such a beautiful place you can't leave it!' – *spotted by Mike Waldie of Shenfield, England, on the sliproad by the Orange péage, France*

'A hitch in time saves a fucking long walk!' – *scrawled on the railings at the autopista entrance near Gerona, Spain*

'Sandra L. is one slick hitch bitch . . .'
and beneath that

'She goes slumming it in Lamborghinis . . .'
and beneath that
'So would you if you were built like her . . .'
and beneath that
'This is male chauvinistic rubbish!'
and beneath that
'Bullshit. Sandra's my girlfriend.' Signed, Lois.
– seen on the A11, near Norwich, England

'Rucksacks suck!' *– seen near Frankfurt, Germany, by Robert T. Duncan, Aberdeen, Scotland*

'Chuck bricks – that stops the bastards!' *– seen near Barcelona, Spain, by Keith Harvey, Haywards Heath, UK*

'Never give up – next thing you know you'll be voting' *– contributed by Yid, Flensburg, Germany*

'If God had meant us to hitch-hike, he would have given us bigger thumbs' *– contributed by Doug Bissell, UK*

'Better a terrible ride than an easy walk' *– seen near Göteborg, by 'Slow' Archie, Netherlands*

'Don't spit – you might need it' *– seen one hot summer in Spain, by Paul Hinckley, Birmingham, UK*

'Hope you like the view because you've got plenty of time to see it' *– seen at Stillhorn services, Hamburg, by Mark Naisbitt, Darlington, UK*

'Welcome to the Black Hole – nothing leaves here, not even night' *– seen near Warrington, by Mike Eal, Solihull, UK*

'Reality is just a frozen possibility' *– spotted by Steve Mulrooney of NSW, Australia*

'Well, it looks like I won't reach Istanbul by lunchtime . . .' *– seen in Paris by Tom Eke of Norfolk, UK*

'He who looks to the past too much was born far too late' *– spotted in Zeeland by Gerard van Weele, Pretoria, South Africa*

Any more hitcher limericks, or hitcher graffiti? Send them in and I'll try to include more examples in the next edition. Include your name and address for a credit, and in the case of hitcher graffiti, where you saw it.

Quotes for hitchers

'When you get there, there's no there' – *Gertrude Stein* (1874–1946)

Q: 'What *are* you rebelling against?'
A: 'Wadda ya got?' – *Marlon Brando* in *The Wild One*

'What is the answer?' (*I was silent*)
'In that case, what is the question?' – *last words,* from *Alice B. Toklas, What is Remembered,* by *Gertrude Stein*

'The more corrupt the state, the more numerous the laws' – *Tacitus* (55?–130?)

'I am one individual on a small planet in a little solar system in one of the galaxies' – *Roberto Assagioli*

'The race advances only by the extra achievement of the individual. You are the individual' – *Charles Towne*

'A fanatic is one who goes through life with his mouth open and his mind closed' – *Dr Lawrence J. Peter*

'To enjoy freedom we have to control ourselves' – *Virginia Woolf*

'Freedom is nothing else but a chance to be better' – *Albert Camus*

'The journey of a thousand miles starts with a single step' – *Traditional Japanese saying*

'It's not worth while to go around the world to count the cats of Zanzibar' – *Henry David Thoreau* (1817–62)

'Travel, in the younger sort, is a part of education; in the elder, a part of experience. He that travelleth into a country before he hath some entrance into the language, goeth to school, and not to travel' – *Francis Bacon* (1561–1626)

'The use of travelling is to regulate imagination by reality, and instead of thinking how things may be, to see them as they are' – *Samuel Johnson* (1709–84)

'The denunciation of the young is a necessary part of the hygiene of older people' – *Logan Pearsall Smith*

'To travel hopefully is a better thing than to arrive . . .'

'Give me the young man who has brains enough to make a fool of himself . . .'

'For my part, I travel not to go anywhere, but to go. I travel for travel's sake. The great affair is to move' – *Robert Louis Stevenson* (1850–94)

'You will do foolish things, but do them with enthusiasm' – *Colette* (1873–1954)

'Adventure is something you seek for pleasure . . . but experience is what really happens to you in the long run, the truth that finally takes you over' – *Katherine Anne Porter* (1890–1980)

'If you don't risk anything, you risk even more' – *Erica Jong*

'I do want to get rich, but I never want to do what there is to do to get rich' – *Gertrude Stein*

'He travels fastest who travels alone' – *Rudyard Kipling*

'Every absurdity has a champion to defend it' – *Oliver Goldsmith*

'He who is impatient waits twice' – *Mack McGinnis*

'An adventure is an inconvenience rightly considered. An inconvenience is an adventure wrongly considered' – *G. K. Chesterton*

'Life as a hitcher is like being a pubic hair on a bog seat! Sooner or later you get pissed off' – *Wally Hughes*

'As long as I keep moving I won't need a place to stay' – from '*Motorcycle Mama*' by *Neil Young*.

'There are three types of travellers:
those who make things happen;
those who watch things happen;
those who wonder what happened.'
Sent by Chan Hing Fai, Hong Kong

The sky is grey the ground damp,
My pack is heavy and my legs have cramp,

My boots sodden my feet blistered
My hair ragged my face twisted,
With the discomfort
This journey's brought,
And I wonder what the Hell I'm doing,
The crazy goals that I'm pursuing,
And then a motor turns on to the roadside,
Lugging baggage, I climb inside.

The driver smiles –'Grim day,'
Fastening seatbelts we drive away.
– *Andrew Dunwoodie*

Poetry for hitchers

There is no solace on earth for
us – for such as we –
Who search for a hidden city we
shall never see.
Only the road and the dawn, the sun,
the wind and the rain,
And watch-fires under stars, and sleep
and the road again.

'The ideal start would consist of a clean slate inscribed with just two words – *knowledge and reason . . .*' – *John Wyndham* (submitted by 'Jock the Hulk', alias *Jim Condron*)

Books for hitchers

Here's a list of books useful to hitch-hikers. Some are American editions and hard to find in Europe; some are out of print and will only be found in public libraries or secondhand book stores. To assist you in locating titles, I've included the date the book was first published:

A Traveller's Guide to Health – A Guide to Prevention, Diagnosis and Cure for Travellers and Explorers by Lt Col James M. Adam, RAMC. Sphere Books, 30–32 Gray's Inn Road, London WC1X 8JL, UK, in association with the Royal Geographical Society (1968).

Africa for the Hitchhiker by Fin Biering-Sœrensen and Torben Jœrgensen. Bramsen and Hjort, 12 Vestergade, DK-1456 Copenhagen K, Denmark (1974).

Alternative England and Wales, published by Nicholas Saunders, 65 Edith Grove, London SW10, UK (1975).

Alternative London, edited by Georganne Downes with Kathy Holme and Max Handley. Otherwise Press. Distributed by Gower House, Croft Road, Aldershot, Hampshire, GU11 3HR, UK. This incredible book on how to use London was first published by Nicholas Saunders in 1970. Georganne publishes it now and you can find the tome in most decent bookshops.

Asia for the Hitchhiker by Mik Schultz. Bramsen and Hjort, 12 Vestergade, DK-1456 Copenhagen K, Denmark (1972).

Asia Overland – A Practical Economy-Minded Guide to the Exotic Wonders of the East by Dan Spitzer and Marzi Schorin. The Stonehill Publishing Company, 10 East 40th Street, New York, NY 10016, USA (1978).

The Asian Highway – The Complete Overland Guide from Europe to Australia by Jack Jackson and Ellen Crampton. Angus and Robertson, 77–85 Fulham Palace Road, London W6 8JB, UK (1979).

Auf Achse – Tips für unterwegs by Jürgen Bischoff. Bund-Verlag GmbH, Köln, Germany. German-speakers will find this book full of real hitcher stuff. Jürgen spent a long, long time on the road and once published a regular hitcher's letter called *On the Road*. He also wrote many Hitchers' Tips and Comments for previous editions of the *Hitch-hiker's Guide to Europe*.

Backpacking by Peter Lumley. Teach Yourself Books, St Paul's House, Warwick Lane, London EC4P 4AH, UK (1974).

The Book of Survival by Anthony Greenbank. Signet, New American Library, 1633 Broadway, New York, NY 10019, USA (1970).

The Complete Traveller by Joan Bakewell. Hamlyn Paperbacks, Bridge House, 69 London Road, Twickenham, Middlesex, TW1 3SB, UK (1977).

Hitch-Hiker's Manual – Britain by Simon Calder. Vacation-Work Publications, 9 Park End Street, Oxford, UK (1979). A cheap, slim volume with lots of good info on getting around Britain, but last updated in 1985: there have been a few changes since then, so try to check all info locally.

Hitch-Hiker's Manual – Europe by Simon Calder, Colin Brown and Roger Brown. Vacation-Work Publications, 9 Park End Street, Oxford, UK (1980). Cheap, and not much bulkier than the book above. Info on getting out of over 100 cities, the vast majority of which still holds good. But, again, not updated since 1985, so try to check your facts locally.

The Hitchhiker's Road Book – A Guide to Traveling by Thumb in Europe by Jeff Kennedy and David E. Greenberg. Doubleday and Company, Inc., 245 Park Avenue, New York, NY 10167, USA (1972).

Hitch-hiking in Europe – An Informal Guidebook by Ed Buryn. Hannah Associates, PO Box 31123, San Francisco 94131, USA (1969). This is the first hitcher's guidebook I know of. Ed had published his while I was still gathering info together for mine, which first appeared in 1971. My copy is autographed by the man himself. Extremely rare.

In Strangest Europe – A Cabinet of Curiosities, Rarities and Monsters by Peter Ratazzi. The Mitre Press, Sardinia House, Kingsway, London WC2, UK (1968). Weird facts about Europe, and weirder destinations.

International Youth Hostels Handbook, Volume 1 (Europe and Mediterranean) and *Volume 2 (Africa, America, Asia and Australasia)* published annually by IYHF Copies obtainable at 14 Southampton Street, London WC2E 7HY, or in the SYHA Shop, 161 Warrender Park Road, Edinburgh.

Kibbutz Volunteer, Vacation-Work, 9 Park End Street, Oxford, UK (1978).

Latin America for the Hitchhiker by Mik Schultz. Bramsen and Hjort, 12 Vestergade, DK-1456 Copenhagen K, Denmark (1974).

Nicholson's London Guide, Robert Nicholson Publications Ltd, 77–85 Fulham Palace Road, London, W6 8JB, UK. For me, it's the best pocket guide to London on the market. Great value for money. Updated regularly.

Rule of Thumb – A Hitchhiker's Handbook to Europe, North Africa and the East by Paul Coopersmith. A Fireside Book, Simon and Schuster, 1230 Avenue of the Americas, New York, NY 10020, USA (1973).

Seven League Boots – the story of my seven-year hitch-hike around the world by Wendy Myers. Hodder and Stoughton (1969). The title explains it all. Hard to find now, but worth the hunt.

Stay Alive in the Desert by K. E. M. Melville. The Jerboa Press. No address in book, but printed by Grafiche Trevisan, Castelfranco Veneto, Italy (1970).

The Student Book edited by Klaus Boehm and Nick Wellings. Papermac, 4 Little Essex Street, London WC2. Updated regularly. If you're bombing around trying to figure out just what to study when lack of funds finally forces you home, this 'applicant's guide to universities, polytechnics and UK colleges' will help. Six hundred pages of easily assimilated info on study courses from accountancy to zoology.

Summer Jobs Abroad edited by David Woodworth. Vacation-Work, 9 Park End Street, Oxford, UK. Published annually.

The Traveller's Handbook edited by Ingrid Cranfield. A Futura book published in association with WEXAS International Ltd. Seven hundred pages of every sort of information about every form of travel, including expeditions.

Traveller's Survival Kit Europe by Roger Brown, revised by Simon

Calder. Vacation-Work, 9 Park End Street, Oxford, UK (1976).

Traveller's Survival Kit to the East by Nigel Clarke. Vacation-Work, 9 Park End Street, Oxford, UK (1979).

Vagabonding in Europe and North Africa by Ed Buryn. Random House Inc., 201 East 50th Street, New York, NY 10022 and The Bookworks, 1409 Fifth Street, Berkeley, California 94710, USA (1971). Ed's second, much more substantial book went through several printings. You might find a secondhand copy if you're lucky.

Wandering – A Walker's Guide to the Mountain Trails of Europe by Ruth Rudner. Photographs by James Goldsmith. The Dial Press, 750 Third Avenue, New York, NY 10017, USA (1972).

Whole World Handbook – A Guide to Study, Work and Travel Abroad by Marjorie Adoff Cohen, revised and edited by Margaret E. Sherman, of the Council on International Educational Exchange. Elsevier-Dutton Publishing Co. Inc., 2 Park Avenue, New York, NY 10016, USA. Published annually.

Work Your Way Around the World by Susan Griffith. Vacation-Work, 9 Park End Street, Oxford, UK. Yet another first-rate tome from Vacation-Work, and to the best of my knowledge the *definitive* book of its type. Three hundred-plus pages stuffed with facts and ideas on working all over the world.

Guidebook series

Lonely Planet, Devonshire House, 12 Barley Mow Passage, Chiswick, London W4 4PH. (tel. 0181 742 3161 – mail-order enquiries only). The Shoestring Guides cover whole regions (South-east Asia, Africa or Eastern Europe, for example), while the Travel Survival Kits provide information on specific countries. A quarterly newsletter is also available.

The Rough Guides, Rough Guides Ltd, 149 Kennington Lane, London, SE11 4EZ. Volumes available covering most European countries, plus several guides devoted to major cities such as Berlin and Prague.

Let's Go Guides, Elsevier-Dutton Publishing Co., 2 Park Avenue, New York, NY 10016, USA. Various titles covering Europe, Asia and the USA, aimed at the budget traveller.

Hachette World Guides, Hachette, 79 Boulevard Saint-Germain, Paris, France. In-depth cultural guides covering Europe, North Africa and the Middle East. Heavy to carry and very expensive, but well worth having the book covering your favourite country.

Michelin Green Guides, The Dickens Press, 4 Upper Thames Street, London EC4, UK. Cover countries, areas and capital cities. Strong on what to see. Excellent city maps.

Berlitz Travel Guides, Editions Berlitz, 1 Avenue des Jordils, 1000

Lausanne 6, Switzerland. Cover over fifty world-wide destinations. Reasonably priced, pocket-sized, all-colour photography.

The most your pound is worth

at the date of going to press

Algeria	37.90 dinars	Lebanon	2480 pounds
Austria	17.45 schillings	Libya	0.41 dinars
Belgium	51.15 francs	Luxembourg	51.15 francs
Bulgaria	7.40 leva	Malta	0.57 pounds
Cyprus	0.75 pounds	Morocco	13.87 dirhans
Czech Republic	40.70 koruna	Netherlands	2.78 guilders
Denmark	9.76 kroner	Norway	10.80 kroner
Egypt	4.96 pounds	Poland	32,800 Zloty
Finland	8.08 markkaa	Portugal	255 escudos
France	8.48 francs	Romania	2430 leu
Germany	2.48 deutschmarks	Russia	2625 roubles
Greece	365 drachma	Slovakia	48.39 kporuna
Hungary	150 forints	Slovenia	198 tolar
Iceland	105 krona	Spain	202 pesetas
Iran	2574 rials	Sweden	11.60 kronor
Iraq	0.43 dinar	Switzerland	2.08 francs
Ireland	1.03 punts	Syria	38.40 pounds
Israel	4.36 shekels	Tunisia	1.53 dinar
Italy	2400 lira	Turkey	45,280 lira
Jordan	1.03 dinar		

● **Warning!** Prices will inevitably change between the time the research was completed and the time this book hits the shelves, so all prices have been upped by a bit more than they might be expected to rise, taking into account inflation in the various countries. In Eastern Europe and the Middle East you may actually find the prices lower than those quoted here for the simple reason that, despite spiralling inflation in the countries of those regions, hard currencies invariably hold their value (at least) against the soft currencies. Even so, prices anywhere (but especially in Western Europe) may rise above the figure given here – think of all the Brits who found about 20% wiped off their spending power virtually overnight in 1992. So be prepared . . . even as little as another £30–40 can make all the difference.

1 · ON THE ROAD

Once upon a time – well it was only eighty years ago – a young man with a romantic head could disappear into the wilderness of his dreams to seek his fortune and become a man of the world.

These days jumbo-jets have made us all men of the world – if we can find the air fare – and the seeking of fortunes starts more often than not in the London School of Economics or in the dollar-shaped halls of learning of American business schools. You don't stake claims any more if you want to make a fortune, you buy shares; and you don't disappear into the wilderness because the wilderness has been turned into real-estate.

Sometimes you can sense all this closing in on you and you know you have to escape. You must get right away and there ain't no more slow boats to China, and if there were you'd have to belong to the Seamen's Union before you could get aboard. But you have to get away and the place you can go is on the road, the infinite miles of tarmac and pot-holes which criss-cross the world, the magic ribbon which can lead to a thousand other worlds.

Get on the road and sometimes you get the feeling of what a non-computerized planet must have been like – or rather, what it was like when people *used* machines and didn't *depend* on them. Get on the road and the press-button-something-happens syndrome disappears. The action-reaction principle doesn't apply on the road, unless you count a car not stopping as a reaction to a thumb in the air. On the road you enter the world of pure chance, a world where mathematical equations mean nothing. Because the tenth car doesn't stop doesn't mean that the eleventh will. On the road you are in a world where time passes without the aid of a clock. On the road you even have time to think.

You wake up in the morning – be it in some cheap hotel or in a sleeping bag beneath a tree in a field – and you get up and have breakfast if you can afford it and then make your way to the road; and the only thing you know for sure is that you *don't* know where you'll be that night. That's a strange feeling the first time it dawns on you.

The thing is that the road takes you. You can't dictate to the road. If you do you might as well be in a train. Hitch-hiking is the art of wondering what will happen to you between your starting point and your destination and taking from everything that *does* happen everything that you can.

And unless you really have to go somewhere, a destination is not all that important. You can set out from London to go to Rome and end up in Lisbon and what the hell? Rome will still be there next time around. And if there isn't any next time? Well, you've seen Lisbon – and it's a nice city.

Hitching is more than anything else an attitude to travel, not just a means of getting from point A to point B. If you look upon it purely as a means of getting to where you want to go, you'll probably get very bored very quickly. Hitch-hiking is a cumulative experience, a never-ending happening of unknown factors which contribute, with a little luck, to a memory of what real travelling is all about – not just the chance to say that you've been to a place, but the feeling that at one time, somewhere, even if only for an instant, you felt like you had become a part of the land through which you travelled.

Hitch-hiking involves you. It fulfils that need for occasional fast-forward movement which seems to be built into the mind of the 20th-century wanderer – a sense of the looming miles ahead being slashed aside by the roar of a powerful motor – and, at the same time, it deposits you five, six, seven times a day into the guts of a lonely landscape where the atavistic man who survives in some of us can be briefly at home. And by the very nature of the game it is impossible to avoid the citizens of the country through which you are moving. You become, in effect, a mechanized Marco Polo.

That's the bright side of the game, but there's a dark side too, and it comes when you're twenty-seven miles from nowhere in the middle of a black night with rain drenching you and when you have no tent and no cover. It comes when you're sick, it comes when you're tired. Mostly it comes when loneliness hits you like a dart and you've got to be with people and in a light place, a warm place. It comes when it's like that and the cars won't stop and those that do don't seem to be making up the distance between where you are and where you need to be.

It's when the dark side comes that you discover something about who you are, because the hitch-hiker who moves alone is with himself for a long, long time each day – and not many of us are used to that.

What you do when the dark side comes depends on who you are. Some people invest their remaining money in a train ticket for home and, for them, that's the best thing. Other people just wait for something better to happen and it usually does. And some people just keep on moving, which is what it's all about.

The warning, for what it's worth, is given; you pay for what you get and the longer the road the bigger the toll because hitching can be hard travelling.

Mostly, though, it's good travelling, and a hundred miles split between walking, riding pillion on a motorbike, bouncing on the tray of a huge semi or sitting comfortably in the back of a Mercedes – a hundred miles covered like that on the little-travelled side roads of Morocco or in the hard mountainous terrain of Greece will give you more memories (and bruises) than any sports-jacketed tourist will find as he slumbers in the relax-back aeroplane seat of an air-conditioned bus trying to figure in his travel-fuzzed mind which day it is in his twenty-one countries in twenty-one days super-fantastic luxury tour of the world.

Hitchers' Tips and Comments . . .

A taster for anyone dubious about undertaking a first hitch trip in Europe: try reading *A Hitch in Time* by Ian Rodger in combination with the *Hitch-hiker's Guide*. Enough to give any prospective traveller itchy feet! (*A Hitch in Time: Recollection of a Journey* – by Ian Rodger; published by Hutchinson 1966.)

JOHN HOAD, EASTBOURNE, ENGLAND

I'd never been abroad until I read your book – boy, you've got a lot to answer for!

STEVE, HECKMONDWIKE, ENGLAND

Thank you for inspiring me to travel.

LOIUISE BROMLEY, NEWTON-LE-WILLOWS, ENGLAND

Books for hitch-hikers and travellers in general:

Travels with Lizbeth by Lars Eigner (Bloomsbury). Doesn't specifically deal with hitch-hiking but more with trying to survive as a homeless person in the US. However, it does contain a chapter detailing how to make a living out of dumpsters.

Travelling Two Continents – A Thousand Miles from Nowhere by Graham Coster (Viking). This book tells the story of two 'organized' hitching trips the author made to Moscow and through the USA.

ROBERT A. H. PRINS, IPSWICH, ENGLAND

For free maps of towns and cities, try the car-hire places.

JOHN MEHERS, CARDIFF, WALES

2 · HOW TO HITCH

Hitch-hiking is a sport. It's like a motorized version of snakes and ladders, except that instead of throwing dice on to the board and automatically moving, you throw a thumb into the air and more often than not don't move.

As with all sports, hitch-hiking has its mythical heroes. You hear stories of guys who can dress like something out of *Mad Max*, stand by the side of the road without moving a muscle and take their choice of the cars which screech to a halt in regimental lines on either side of them; cars which not only give them lifts, but which detour thirty, forty or fifty miles out of their way to land the magic men at a stated destination.

And you hear of others who can pick the car they want out of an approaching bunch and always make it stop; and it's always a big Citroën or a Porsche, and its owner always buys them a meal at an expensive restaurant.

It's a fact that if you're a good-looking woman hitching alone you can make this happen. I know a girl who came clear across Germany in one day and never stepped into anything lowlier than a Mercedes. She was also propositioned twice, middle-aged German businessmen being as fast, if not as smooth, as their chariots.

But if you're not a magic man, or if you don't have long blonde hair, you're left with the problem of stopping cars. The only thing on your side when you stand by the road and put up your thumb is that *some* drivers pick up hitchers. Sooner or later one of them will stop – though you shouldn't count on it. You might go the whole day without a ride and then get twelve the next day. What you must do then, is try and raise the odds in your favour and to do that there are some basic things which can be considered.

APPEARANCE These days not many people in Europe have anything against those of us who don't look like we've just stepped out of an office, so there are no worries there. But if you think of the problem in terms of how many people will willingly stop and talk to you if you approach them in the street while you're wearing fancy-dress costume and when you haven't bathed for twenty-three days, you get a perspective on how many cars are going to stop for some dirty crusty thumbing them from the side of the road. The majority of people who will be picking you up will be ordinary suburban types. Their own kids might look like you, but they are 'nice kids'. Look like a nice kid and you can skid around pretty fast.

LUGGAGE Carry as little as possible. Try and keep it down to just your frame-pack, or at the most, one hand item as well. I know plenty of people who have hitched carrying a frame-pack, suitcase, camera bag and portable typewriter, but it's not a good general rule. A lot of cars won't stop because they simply don't have room for your luggage.

ROAD TACTICS This is the most important thing of all and while plenty of experienced hitchers might argue that you can get away with any sort of appearance because people *want* to pick up hippies, punks or crusties for a kick, or that if a driver wants to stop to help you on your way he's not going to worry about extra pieces of luggage, they'll agree unanimously that you have to choose your thumbing position carefully.

First (and most obviously, though it's horrifying how many fools do it), *don't hitch on a bend*. There are three reasons. One, it's deadly. Cars cut through bends and you can get killed. Two, drivers are concentrating too much on the problem of getting through the bend to be worried about anyone trying to stop them from the side of the road. Three, even if the driver was stupid enough to want to stop on a bend, the law forbids him to do so.

Second, *choose your road edge carefully*. Drivers aren't inclined to stop in the middle of the road – it's too dangerous – so you must pick a position, when possible, which has a nice safe edge for them to run off on to, and the more of their car they can get off the road when they stop the more they like it. And the smoother the area the better. Drivers don't like running off into mud, or pot-holes, or into a puddle of water when they don't know how deep it is.

Third, *when you're trying for a ride, try properly*. My experience has been that I get rides when I'm standing up and looking like I want to go somewhere. You might get one when you're lying on the ground with your feet up on your pack, lazily devouring a bottle of wine, with a daisy stuck behind your ear and nonchalantly waving your free hand up above the grass, but the odds are right against you.

HOW TO CONQUER BOREDOM Half an hour or more without a ride can leave you feeling a little lost. It's not so bad if you're with a companion – especially one of the opposite sex – but if you're alone you can start suffering from terminal boredom.

If you're into Zen or yoga then time is the air around you and you have no problem. If you've got a decent novel, things are OK. Paper and pencil lets you catch up on letters back home or allows you to make paper aeroplanes complete with military markings.

Standard side-of-the-road games, equally suitable for one or more people, include hurling stones at specified targets (hurl at leisure, spin and hurl, five hurls in ten seconds, etc.), golf, played with a suitable stick and assorted round stones (across the road on the full counts as a hole in one), tin-can football (hard on the boots), breath-holding, and standing on one foot.

One driver reports pulling up beside two gentlemen of the road who were in the middle of a push-up competition. He offered them a ride but they informed him that the loser was buying dinner and asked if he could wait a moment. The driver – patient type – watched in fascination as the two hitchers battled it out. The loser fell on his nose after the forty-seventh push-up, while the winner did five more just for the hell of it. The hitchers later told him that they held the competition every day.

HOW TO WAVE THE CAR DOWN My technique depends upon my constitution. Normally I use my thumb – always my right thumb regardless of which side of the road I'm on – but when I'm feeling a little poetic I sometimes change to a regal, floating wave of my whole hand which, if the driver happens to be feeling in the same mood, seems to work wonders. And then, of course, there's the old two-finger wave, which, if the car doesn't stop, can be continued in one sweeping movement upwards to tell any rear-view-mirror observer that you're suggesting up him for the money or sending him on his way with peace. (Once, in Spain, a field worker watched my thumb technique with interest for quite some time. Eventually he enquired if I was trying to stop a car. I said I was, that I was going to Granada. He said I was doing it all wrong and when the next car came, wandered out into the middle of the road waving his hand like a policeman's halt signal. The car stopped and he lined up a ride for me. Not that the driver seemed too impressed with it all.) How *you* do it is your problem, but there's one trick you might try. Always smile, and always latch right on to the driver's eyes as he approaches and don't stop staring or smiling. You can psych some of them into stopping!

COUNTRY IDENTIFICATION This is purely a matter of choice. I've done one trip with the international AUS for Australia attached to my pack and two cars stopped specifically because the drivers had relatives in Sydney. The question is, how many cars *didn't* stop because of it? Lots of people carry small flags or national emblems and one friend of mine went through Europe like a rocket, dressed in a suit and carrying a small suitcase with a notice attached which simply read 'US student'. Perhaps you can approach the problem in terms of international political opinion. Try and figure how popular your country is in Europe before you mount a sign.

DESTINATION PLACARDS These are used by most hitchers purely as last resorts after a rotten day's hitching. You find an old piece of cardboard or paper and print in large letters the name of the city you're heading for. Generally you can't tell how successful the idea is, so it's a matter of choice. I do think a destination placard is worth considering, for instance, on the German autobahns. The only places you're legally allowed to hitch or walk on these, or any other super-highways, are at the entrance and exit roads and, because of the ring-road systems, a car heading north might only be doing so to get to an exit road to take him south. Which can cause the temporarily northbound car driver to decide not to stop for what looks like a northbound hitcher who, in fact, happens to want to go the same way as the soon-to-be-southbound car. (Get it?) German students seem to make a lot of use of placards for that reason.

WHAT RIDES TO TAKE Providing a driver isn't obviously bombed out of his mind, my rule is to take any car that stops which has its bonnet pointed even vaguely in the direction I want to go. I work on the simple premise that if the ride is only for five miles, I'm going to be five miles closer to my destination and the next car I want might be sooner or later coming out of a side road we pass during that short drive. Some hitchers prefer to refuse the small rides in the hope that they'll eventually catch the big one. To me, that's like throwing away ten cents in the hope that you'll find twenty-five.

WHEN A CAR STOPS A lot of drivers who have stopped for you are nevertheless in a hell of a hurry. Most drivers pull up fifty or a hundred yards beyond you. Never risk losing a ride by wandering to them. Run. Grab your bag and move! When you get to the car, just wish the driver a good day in his own language (if possible) and then tell him where you're going. If you can't pronounce the name of the town have a map ready to pull out and point at. From then on, whatever the driver says, just answer *oui, si, ja* or *yes* as the case may be. It doesn't matter what the driver has said – 'I'm going to Kassel', 'I'm in a hurry', 'It'll be a slow trip' – *yes* is the one word which is the nearest thing to an answer. And keep smiling. Your one objective is to get into the car. Once rolling you can work out a way of finding exactly how far the driver is going.

FAST DRIVERS If you make the mistake of getting in with a fast one who you reckon is taking you both on a one-way ride (and it happens just about every trip), politely indicate that you want out. If he won't or doesn't understand what you're trying to say, be a little more obvious and a little less polite and make sounds which suggest you're about to throw up all over his upholstery. That usually drives the point home. And perhaps saves your life.

FAST DRIVERS OTHER TYPE Occasionally, through no fault of their own, lady hitchers find themselves being attacked by guys who give them a ride. What to do? If it's one man it's not so bad. At least he has to stop the car first, and if he stops it in a suspicious place you've got a lead on what might be about to happen. In that case a simple 'no' (politely offered) will probably work. If it doesn't and he's obviously not a psycho type, you can try putting on a sick act, telling him you're having your period, that you're pregnant, that you've just had a bad operation or that you've got some dreaded venereal disease. If he *is* a psycho type you've got problems and about all you can do is keep talking until you can see a way out. If there's more than one guy there's not a great deal you can do about it. Screaming will probably get you roughed up pretty bad, fighting back, pulling out the old hat-pin or kneeing somebody in the balls will have the same result. (The knee works OK with one guy, but make sure your aim is good and you get him first try.) Best advice to offer is this: if you are a lady hitcher then travel with a second person. If you must travel alone, just make sure you're on the Pill.

THE LANGUAGE PROBLEM A lot of timid souls I know tell me that they could never hitch-hike in a foreign country because they just wouldn't know how to handle the language barrier. Well, the excuse is understandable, but it's a pretty sad one. One of the first things any hitch-hiker learns is that lack of language is no barrier to simple friendly communication. English-speaking people who say they don't know one word of a foreign language are either stupid or have no imagination. To start with, *imagination, communication* and most other words which end in *ion* in English are roughly the same in Spanish, French and Italian – they're just pronounced a little differently. And how many people don't know the meaning of *au revoir*, or *vino*, or *grazie*, or *Fraülein*? The point I am trying to make is that anyone who speaks English automatically has a stock of words in other languages he can draw on either because they are the same words, or they have entered the English language through popular usage, or because they figure prominently in films and books. Of course he mightn't be able to pronounce them correctly, but at least he has them and it doesn't take too many words to find out someone's name, what they do, where they're going, or if they're married and have kids. And that's the sort of small talk you find yourself indulging in when you're zipping down the highways of Europe and when you don't have a mutual language with the driver.

If you happen to speak a second language you're in business, not just because many Europeans speak at least one other language after their own, but because people who speak two languages, even if they aren't mutual, know enough about word association to be able to make some sort of conversation.

But many Europeans do speak English and when you get rides with them, that's when hitch-hiking comes into its own. On a good day you might be picked up by half a dozen cars with each of the drivers speaking a little English. Those drivers will usually be a cross-section of their society – young, old, rich, and poor – and from them you can glean a first-hand word picture of their country's attitudes and feelings.

If you don't have a mutual language with your host, don't worry about it. If you try to communicate and he's not interested in playing word games, just practise sitting without talking. If the tension seems to be building (and it often does), break it by offering a cigarette or something to chew – it nearly always works.

As a generalization, I've found that the better educated and/or more affluent my host, the easier it's been for me to talk with him even if he doesn't speak English. I say it as a generalization because I've had some great rides with truckies – particularly Arabs – without exchanging a single word. And it was from rides like those that I learned that communication is not only a matter of utterances, but a willingness to share the pleasures (or discomforts) of a situation. At that basic level, things can get boring but, if it's the only level you have, you learn to make the most of it.

GETTING IN AND OUT OF A CITY This is the biggest bugbear of any hitcher. Towns and small cities aren't so bad because you can walk in or out of them in less than an hour. But try walking out of Paris or London! If your ride has let you off in the suburbs of a big city and you want to go to the centre, you can try to hitch, but the odds are right against you. People in a suburban traffic stream usually don't have the chance to stop for you even if they want to. I've managed to hitch in the suburbs of medium-sized cities, but I've never had any luck in the big capitals. If you don't have any money, then obviously you'll have to walk and try to hitch, but the only real answer is to take a train or bus. You'll save yourself a couple of hours of hard work and a lot of energy.

The only way to get out of a really big city, as far as I'm concerned, is to take a train to the nearest small village outside the city limits.

This might cost a pound or so, but it's quick and puts you straight on the road you want and away from the traffic-congested areas. And on a long walk out of a city – maybe two or three hours – you usually end up spending £1 or more anyway on drinks and food to keep you going. You can only walk by so many French *pâtisseries* before you break down and step inside!

FINDING A ROOM European cities and towns are nearly always six or seven centuries old at least, and this rather obvious fact gives the clue as to how to find the cheapest rooms in a strange city. The majority of large towns and cities were built either on rivers or ports for purposes of trade and communication, around a castle which was built for the defence of an area, or around a church which was the religious seat of a parish. The old sections then, and the cheapest, are often around a castle, a cathedral, or on the river, or around the port area.

This doesn't apply so much to very large cities which continually instigate building programmes to clear such areas, but more in the smaller cities. Lisbon is an example of a city with a cheap 'castle area'. Paris used to be an example of a city with a cheap 'river area'. (The Île de la Cité was reputedly the first settled area of Paris. The Marais, supposed to have been the second settled area, is now one of the cheapest places in the city.) Restaurants in these areas are generally very cheap as well.

In villages and towns you can find reasonably priced rooms in private houses. These normally cost about the same as a cheap hotel room except, being part of someone's home, they are usually cleaner and better value for money. If you want one of these but can't spot a 'Room Free' sign, ask at the local bar.

Special note: when you visit a city covered in the *Hitch-hiker's Guide* with a **Where to sleep** section, and decide to try one of my recommendations rather than taking pot luck hunting around, you may find it worth investing a few pence in a phone call. Wherever possible I've listed the hostel or hotel phone number beside the address; thus you can check, before you go to the address, that they have a room free, that their prices haven't gone up since this new edition was published and, also, that they are open. Many student hostels close at various times during the year and, because closing dates can vary from year to year, it's hard to make the listings in this book absolutely accurate. A quick phone call could save a lot of trouble (and bus fare money).

TRAVEL ALONE OR IN COMPANY? This is an old argument amongst veteran hitchers. Opinions break down like this: men travel fastest by themselves, but not as fast as a woman by herself. Two women travel faster than two men, but a mixed couple travels faster than any other pair.

Many drivers are wary of picking up more than one person, especially if they're men. Travelling alone is the ideal, anyway, because when you're by yourself you move at precisely your own speed – you don't have to worry about your partner's fitness or their inclination to go two hundred miles out of their way to catch an exhibition of Russian icon art in Geneva.

A lone woman will travel very fast, but it mightn't be pleasant travelling – lots of wolves drive cars. I'm not Moses the Lawgiver, but I think girls are crazy to hitch by themselves. Think of all those stalwart gentlemen willing to accompany you, ladies. And if that doesn't appeal, remember that two girls are safer than one and the chances of catching a ride don't drop dramatically.

A man and a woman together is the ideal combination if you must travel in company. You don't get lonely on the road or off the road, and you still get plenty of rides. Another real advantage of travelling as a couple is that you can share double hotel rooms and cut the cost per head considerably.

To try hitching in the company of *more* than one other person is crazy.

HITCHING AT NIGHT This is a curly one. Some people swear by night hitching. Others swear about it. Some people say they can always get to where they're going at night. Others say drivers just won't pick them up and, although occasionally I've had to move at night and done OK, I think of all the times I tried but didn't get anywhere, and agree that it's a slow game. Anyway, you miss the countryside.

If you like the idea of night hitching or find it necessary to make a night-time journey, the following hints are handy. First, try to get under a light (obvious) and try to pick a light which will allow the driver to see that it's safe for him to pull off the side of the road. Second, try for an all-night service station where you can, if necessary, wander over to stopped cars and ask if they can help you on your way. Third, if you are stuck somewhere without light, for God's sake find a straight stretch of road where cars can catch you in their beam from a fair distance; and carry a white handkerchief or a white something to help them spot you. If you've driven a car at night, you'll understand the sense of that.

HITCH-HIKERS AND THE POLICE If you listen long enough to some of the road-talk around Europe you start getting the idea that cops devote most of their energy to hassling hitch-hikers. But before you finally make up your mind, take a good look at who's doing the talking.

Cops often stop you and ask to see your passport. They blow you up for hitching on an autobahn instead of from the entrance. They tell you to stop eating your lunch on the municipal grass (grass is for looking at, *not* sitting on!). They wake you up and tell you to piss off out of public parks. They ask to see your rail ticket when they notice you loitering in a lovely warm railway station at three in the morning.

That's usually all they do. Some of those things might be stupid – like so what, you're asleep under the mayor's favourite oak tree – but you have to be pretty uptight to think a cop is hassling you if he asks you politely (and *most* of them are polite) to abide by some bylaw he's being paid to enforce.

Thing is, of course, that a lot of people who consider themselves very cool are so uptight that their eyeballs are popping. A cop asks them to do something, they start screaming and next thing the cop is frisking them for drugs, asking how much money they've got, wanting to see their return ticket to country of origin and all the rest of it.

Take someone with more authority than you and rub them up the wrong way and odds are you'll have trouble on your hands. Cops are no exception. Be nice to the police, ladies and gentlemen, and they'll be nice to you. But when you get way down south and too far east, don't take my word for it.

HITCH-HIKERS AND IMMIGRATION OFFICIALS Every so often it happens that some hitcher trying to cross a border is asked to produce a substantial amount of money (substantial from a hitch-hiker's point of view) to prove he can support himself in the country he wants to enter. This is something that happens from time to time all over the world.

In Italy, Spain, Greece and other Mediterranean countries it tends to happen most during summer when a lot of people are on the road and the authorities are cracking down on genuine, nasty-type bums. These countries do have problems in summer. Organized gangs from all over Europe descend on holiday resorts to mug, rob and plunder the visiting tourist population.

In Germany, Denmark and other northern countries you may be asked to produce money or proof of being able to support yourself at any time, depending on the whim of the immigration official you approach.

In England, non-British travellers can strike trouble at Heathrow or Gatwick airports where officials regularly ask where you intend staying, the purpose of your visit, whether you are solvent and whether you have an outward-bound ticket.

There's not much you can do if you strike trouble at an airport, but when you're on the road at a frontier post you can at least start things off in your favour – provided you're not approaching a country where people of your nationality require a special visa, and you don't have it.

1 Remember that like the police mentioned earlier, immigration officials are only people doing their job, and are not inherently nasty or out to cause hitch-hikers trouble (yeah, right, there *are* exceptions!).
2 Before approaching an immigration post, make yourself look as respectable as it is possible for a road bum to be. Put on a clean shirt or blouse. Comb your hair. Clean your teeth. Brush your shoes. Ditch your hash. Remember – the object is to disguise yourself.
3 At the post, stay as inconspicuous as possible. Don't jump the queue. Don't flatten little old ladies with your pack. Don't play musical instruments or portable radios. Don't be amorous with your partner (particularly if your partner is of the same sex). Don't fart, scratch your balls or be otherwise uncouth.
4 After approaching the official, place your passport in front of him. Don't throw it. Say *good morning, buenos días,* or *guten Tag* as the case may be. Call him *sir, señor,* or *mein Herr.* Don't refer to him as pal, mate, buddy, man or cock. Answer his questions civilly, agreeing with him where possible. Smile politely all the time.
5 If all this works and you get your stamp, thank the official politely in his own language, retire quietly, get the hell away from the frontier before he changes his mind, and revert to your true personality.
6 If all the above doesn't work and you don't get your stamp, under no circumstances break or kick things, make dire threats or start bellowing that the official is a dumbhead, a jerk, a dago bastard or a lousy shit. Nod your head understandingly, look disappointed and concerned, and with downcast eyes retreat from whence you came. Hide behind a bush for eight hours and try again when the official's tour of duty is over and his replacement has relieved him. This time you'll probably make it.

Mainly, hitching is a matter of persevering. Keep the thumb up. Keep working. You hear of hitchers striking bad luck and moving slowly but you rarely hear of a hitcher who knows his business not getting to where he wants to go.

● **International car identification letters** It's a good idea to learn a few identification letters. Especially useful when you're hanging around roadside cafés searching out a likely truck to take you on your way. Also interesting to know the nationality or diplomatic status of the guy who didn't pick you up as his tail-end disappears in a cloud of dust down the highway.

A Austria
AND Andorra
AUS Australia
B Belgium
BG Bulgaria
BR Brazil
C Cuba
CC Consular Corps
CD Diplomatic Corps
CDN Canada
CH Switzerland
CO Colombia
Cs Czechoslovakia
CY Cyprus
D Germany
DK Denmark
DZ Algeria
EIR Ireland
EQ Ecuador
ET Egypt
F France
FL Liechtenstein
GB Great Britain
GBZ Gibraltar
GR Greece
H Hungary
I Italy
Il Israel
IR Iran
IRQ Iraq
IS Iceland
L Luxembourg
M Morocco
MC Monaco
MEX Mexico
N Norway
NL Netherlands
NZ New Zealand
P Portugal
PL Poland
PR Peru
R Romania
Ra Argentina
RCH Chile
RL Lebanon
S Sweden
SF Finland
TR Turkey
U Uruguay
USA United States of America
V Vatican
ZA South Africa

Hitchers' Tips and Comments . . .

I note that you think it 'crazy' to hitch in numbers greater than two. I'd like to inform you that I have just arrived back from a holiday in which there were three of us – two females, one male. We travelled through Belgium, Luxembourg, Germany, Austria (Yugoslavia by train), Greece, Italy and Switzerland. The longest period we had to wait for a lift was 1.5 hours. Our luggage was also far from minimal as we had set out in a car which broke down in Ashford, Kent! CHRISTINE WADE, SOUTHAMPTON, ENGLAND

Re your statement that it's crazy to hitch with more than two, I disagree. I have hitched all over in a threesome (all girls). I even know of a friend who was out walking with about twelve when they were offered a lift in a laundry van. Beat that!
WENDY FOULDS, ORPINGTON, ENGLAND

I can't. K.W.

Great book! A 'no wordy crap' tour of Europe!

Here's some stuff. Re country identification, I reckon I can attribute 50% of my rides to the Union Jack plastered on to my pack.

Useful to know that in Europe 'hitching' is known as 'auto-stop'.

If one is desperate, and in the company of other desperados, it's possible to book a motel for two and occupy it with, say, six. Works out pretty cheap!

A useful end-of-season trick is to go to offices of international car-hire firms (except Hertz) and see if they need any cars returned to base – for instance, from Copenhagen to Amsterdam. Sometimes you'll get the job and you get paid expenses for your efforts. Good way of travelling. MIKE FEENEY, HASLOW, ENGLAND

About carrying flags. It's worked for me. I've hitched all year with an Alaskan flag on my pack and drivers have stopped and picked me up to find out what country the flag belongs to.

DAVID FREMON, PALATINE, USA

Here are a few tips: Union Jack attached to my pack got me at least half my rides in France recently – but it should be removable just in case. A torch is an essential item if you're camping or hoping to sleep in churches (which I have done successfully). Definitely agree with you that 'high' packs are more practical than 'wide' packs. Try getting a 'wide' into a 2CV Citroën!

PAUL HOUGHTON, BRISTOL, ENGLAND

Advise others to travel with someone else and not go off alone. I did and regretted it – I was as lonely as hell!

WALTER STILES HOYT, BRISTOL, USA

What's this about W. S. Hoyt getting lonely? Everyone can talk to themselves. PETER NASH, CHELMSFORD, ENGLAND

I agree with Pete Nash. What's more, talking to yourself is sometimes the only way you can get into a decent conversation!

ANDY CITIZEN OF THE WORLD, LONDON, ENGLAND

I've taken to praying to cars on my knees. Works wonders if you're not too proud and can manage a brave smile.

TIMMY MALLETT, ALTRINCHAM, ENGLAND

Hitching in threes is quite feasible, and fairly easy. One man and two girls can travel as fast as two men. The largest number of people with whom I've hitched and got a lift is 14.

SIMON CALDER, UNIVERSITY OF WARWICK GOLDEN THUMB CLUB

For those who can't afford hotels in the big cities, it's worth a few bob to lay the pack up in the left-luggage at the main station and see the sights with just a bedroll and washing gear.

MARCEL THOMAS, HORNDEAN, ENGLAND

A further comment on the score of women hitch-hiking alone: if there are two or more gentlemen in the car which stops, unless one has very good reasons for thinking otherwise, the answer is obviously 'no'.

BETH PARKER, NEUENKIRCHEN, WEST GERMANY

I bought and learnt to play a small musical instrument, a flageolet (glorified tin whistle), and when no vehicles are in sight I sit down and start tooting away. Passes the time away successfully. Good gimmick for starting conversation with any local, too.

MICKEY HOHEL, PLYMOUTH, ENGLAND

I've been hitching, mostly in Germany and Austria, the last two summer holidays and I found my greatest asset for getting lifts was the wearing of a kilt.

Some drivers stopped out of curiosity, others were bent double with laughter by the time they stopped, but since they always gave me a lift, this didn't bother me in the slightest.

So if you've got a Scottish connection, get yourself a kilt!

ANDY DEANS, FIFE, SCOTLAND

The thing about dressing up in what are grossly expensive national costumes in the mode of a kilt is that it offers hitch-hikers from Scotland an increased chance of grabbing that incredibly interesting feature of drivers – their attention.

'JOCK THE HULK', ALIAS JIM CONDRON, HAMILTON, SCOTLAND

Try some yoga. Read a book. Write a letter to ma. Construct paper planes. Throw stones. Play golf with a stick'n'stones. Football with a tin can. Hold your breath. Stand on one foot. For godzakes! *What* is that kindergarten stuff? And is *that* what people levitate themselves off their asses and creep'n crawl abroad for?

PASI PUNNONEN, SAVONLINNA, FINLAND

Hold up a card with PLEASE! written in the local language. You get a smile if nothing else. BERNARD JENNINGS, BRISBANE, AUSTRALIA

I used a card saying ANYWHERE! Boy, did I hit some wild places.

F. J. GOODING, BIRMINGHAM, ENGLAND

I'm a great believer in signs. I don't mean signs that say 'Amsterdam' or 'Antwerpen', but things like 'I don't bite!', 'I wash!' etc.

MIKE PLUMMER, SEAVIEW, ISLE OF WIGHT

Having hitched as a student, and now a car owner and giver of lifts, I was very interested in the *Hitch-hiker's Guide to Europe*.

I feel you don't say enough about the importance of hitchers earning hitch-hiking a good name. One bad impression leaves one sour driver and one less who'll pick up the next hitcher. Dirty clothes and dirty boots means a soiled car. Also, dear hitch-hiker, earn your keep, tell us where you've been and what you've seen, otherwise you're more boring than the stereo-cassette player.

I only pick up clean, interesting looking hitch-hikers, who are presentable and who will be good travelling companions – not out-of-work dustmen. In a word, 'get professional' and make yourself pick-upable. C. N. C. PETERS, WEST HAGLEY, ENGLAND

OK you bums, you heard the man. Out with the tuxedos! K.W.

Two friends hitched from London to Bristol with a sign saying *Moscow*. While talking about signs, remember that when hitching in the southern hemisphere, all signs should be held upside down.

KARLOS VAN PEE, BRISTOL, ENGLAND

I think maps, or good knowledge of an area are essential for fast hitching. Just because someone isn't going exactly where you want to go is no reason to turn down a lift. I often reach my destination swiftly by approaching it from a completely unexpected direction. Flexibility is essential. ALASTAIR SIMPSON, HATFIELD, UK

The overwhelming advantage of youth hostels, in my opinion, is that they act as a forum for swapping info and moneysaving ideas between travellers. Especially useful for first-time hitchers during their first weeks on the road. ALAN THATCHER, NEW ZEALAND

I met a hitcher who'd had all his gear stolen by a driver who gave him a lift. The driver had put the hitcher's pack in the boot. When the hitcher reached his destination the driver stopped and the hitcher got out and walked to the boot. Then the driver simply took off with this hitcher's kit. On consideration, you have to admit, this could happen at any time! The only way I can see around it is that if the driver insists on putting your rucksack in the boot, when you stop you ask him for the keys and tell him *you'll* get the pack out.

JOHN PILKINGTON, BRISTOL, UK

How to stop yourself from getting bored on a lonely road – practise eating spaghetti out of a frisbee with a Swiss army knife.

JOHN PILKINGTON, BRISTOL, UK

I hold my destination placard upside down, and when helpful drivers frantically gesture, I flip it over to show I KNOW written on the other side. ASHOK GUPTA, DELHI, INDIA

Whenever you hitch in Holland always use a destination placard. The Netherlands is such a full, small country, with such an incredible cobweb of roads that most people won't stop to pick you up if they don't know where you're going. With a placard, hitching isn't too bad here. GYS DE GRAAFF, BREDA, HOLLAND

Tricks I've used with great success are to hold up a placard with my destination spelled wrong, or to hold the sign upside down. Human nature being what it is, people stop to point out the error, and in I jump! JOHN RIORDAN, VINDERUP, DENMARK

When hitching in the UK I use a placard which says, TEST YOUR BRAKES! Works wonders! Also, remember, if you're in a car or truck with CB radio, try using it to line up your next ride. Finally, if you're having no luck and you're bored, paper and pen comes in handy. You can write long, dull letters to the *Hitcher's Guide*.

DOUG BISSELL, 'THE CLYDESIDE REBEL', GLASGOW, SCOTLAND

Nobody likes the idea of a soaking wet stranger messing up his brand new car. So, when it's raining, get under cover and try to *look* dry.

THEO VAN DRUNEN, OOSTERHOUT, HOLLAND

Did Norway to Italy by thumb with the *Hitcher's Guide*, but ended up with one hell of a neckache from looking behind for cars as I walked. Simple solution – fit an adjustable bicycle mirror to the top of the rucksack and, hey presto, you've got a panoramic view of all that's coming from behind without moving a muscle. The mirror can be folded away along the length of the bag when not in use.

MICHAEL MCLINDEN, HARLOW, UK

Tramping around cities for days on end and walking the roads between lifts is very hard on the feet and blisters are a problem. I advise anyone new to the game to rub the soles of their feet with surgical spirit for a couple of weeks before leaving home. This toughens them up. PAUL HINCKLEY, BIRMINGHAM, UK

Secret of getting rides with trucks is to go to truck-stops, roadside cafés, etc., and *ask*! You'll get a lot of knockbacks, but there's enough good guys around who'll take you aboard. What's more, at the end of their run they often get you aboard a friend's truck to keep you moving. It's unreasonable to expect a guy to stop a 32-ton juggernaut on the road when he sees a hitcher. It costs him time and it's *dangerous*. IAN SMITH, LIPHOOK, ENGLAND

When crossing borders, anyone carrying dope should, as a matter of principle, leave the car he's hitched a ride in and cross on foot. More chance of getting caught? Yes. But if you're caught in the car with the stuff, the driver who's been good enough to pick you up can be in big trouble. IAN, ENGLAND

When hitching at night try wearing a reflective band on your hitching wrist. Apart from being a great safety device it also helps get lifts as motorists tend to slow down when they see it.

AIDAN MURRAY, ATHLORE, ENGLAND

Many stations have lock-up lockers. Who wants to lug a backpack around when sightseeing? And anyway, many places won't let you in with them, especially museums and churches.

MARI DOYLE, GODALMING, SURREY, UK

Your book has a lot of good tips but I do wish you would do something about your ridiculous attitude towards 'lady' (sic) hitchers. Why is your book full of hints for heterosexual males? Boring . . .

FIONA GRAPH, LONDON, UK

The Hitcher's Guide *is full of hints for everyone. If I suggest a place where hitchers may find company, I'm referring to all hitchers – male and female heterosexuals, homosexuals and lesbians. As to my ridiculous attitude towards 'lady' hitchers ('lady' is synonymous with 'woman', 'girl' or 'female', and it doesn't matter which word I use, I'll still be criticized by a minority of ladies – women – girls – females), I can assure you that it is not meant to be patronizing. Lady hitchers can, and do, get into very nasty situations particularly when travelling alone. And these situations are caused by men – boys – males who are definitely not 'gentlemen'. I have to stand by my ridiculous attitude.* K.W.

Carrying your national flag biases fellow countrymen towards you but can bias foreigners against you. To overcome the problem, have a flag by your side and hold it up whenever you see a car from your own country. SIMON WADSWORTH, SHIPLEY, WEST YORKSHIRE, UK

I've got many rides wearing an army jacket and a crew cut. Many people have stopped because they thought I was in the forces.

WALLY HUGHES, MUNICH, WEST GERMANY

Good places for catching lifts are at large supermarkets where lorries arrive and leave from almost everywhere.

PETER WALSH, TRURO, CORNWALL, UK

'*Los Angeles*: Traffic on the motorway in Hollywood ground to a dreadful halt. Brakes screeched and bumpers crashed as drivers tried in vain to avoid piling into cars which had inexplicably slowed down. The reason was up ahead. A female hitch-hiker, tired of thumbing a lift without success, had started a striptease. By the time police arrived, her charms had worked. The hitch-hiker was gone and the disappointed policemen were left to sort out the muddle.' – *seen in the* Scottish Sunday Express. ALAN GIBSON, GLASGOW, SCOTLAND

Practice makes perfect: Two friends and I spent many weekends experimenting with approaches and techniques. These include poise, in-car manners and equipment that can be comfortably carried. Don't attempt to hitch all of Europe without any preparation. Try a few weekend hitches to the nearest large town and back. Even a 'day-return hitch' is valuable experience.

If rides are seriously slow and you are with a couple of friends try this: stand in a huddle with one of you holding a placard, one of you pointing to the word, and one of you holding your arms out in a 'well, what do you think?' sort of pose. If you all smile and look like you are having fun cars will stop.

Don't listen to personal stereos in the car: the driver assumes that you are anti-social and that if you can afford a walkman's batteries, you can afford a bus! I should know.

Don't complain about the driver's taste in music. Instead tap a finger in time. If you like their music, they like you.

When the driver lets you out (assuming it's not pissing down), have the courtesy to wave the driver off. We saw lots of hitchers just get out and run without even a 'thank you'. That stinks – say thanks. RICH SADLER, EAST YORKSHIRE

Where possible try to keep up personal hygiene when hitching. There's nothing worse for a driver than having a stinking hitch-hiker fouling up their car. JAMES DEVLIN, DUMBARTON, SCOTLAND

To get out of a large, sprawling city try large engineering works or construction sites. There are always semi-trailers and trucks delivering and collecting. DAVE AITKEN, AYR, SCOTLAND

Lay-bys and roadside restaurants (services) are ideal for picking up lifts. You catch people coming out nice and relaxed after having enjoyed a meal. You can actually choose your transport by walking round the parked trucks and spotting the company's address on the side of the cab. If they are empty, then they are returning home.

TAM MATJEK, LINLITHGOW, SCOTLAND

I am a driver, and the only way I would stop on a trunk road is at a lay-by. But never, ever, would I pick up a hitch-hiker at night. If I happen to call into a lay-by at night, I won't open my doors or windows for anyone. 'DRIVER', PORTSMOUTH, ENGLAND

Waving a packet of cigarettes can help get a lift. For instance in Turkey cigarettes, especially Marlboro, are very popular (I hope everyone doesn't rush out and buy entire stocks of Marlboro otherwise the Turks will soon lose their taste for them!).

VINCE O'NEILL, CLYDEBANK, SCOTLAND

3 · WHAT IT WILL COST AND HOW TO GET IT CHEAPER

The beauty about a hitch-trip is that you can make it on precisely the budget you have. Some people have done it for nothing, working their way everywhere and relying on hand-outs from others.

Basically, though, there are three grades of hitch-hiking, each with its own cost structure, and they are discussed below.

1 HOLE-IN-THE-WALL HITCHING This is for the hitcher on the tightest imaginable budget. It's a rough way of travelling, but preferable to not travelling. It involves *always* sleeping out, *always* buying and preparing your own food, *always* visiting museums and galleries on half-price days and *always* sightseeing on foot. It means that you *must* walk into and out of cities, that you *must* carry a tent and that you *must* carry some sort of cooking pannikin. The weekly cost structure for this sort of travelling breaks down something like this:

nil	bed
£5.00	main meal with leftovers for breakfast
£2.40	tobacco and/or coffee
£7.40	a day or £51.80 a week

Add a round figure of £21 a week for fares and sightseeing and for this most basic and foot-weary way of moving it will cost only around £73 *a week*! (And you'll be pretty fit at the end of it all.)

2 HOSTEL HITCHING This is the normal way of travelling for those with an average bank roll. It involves sleeping out whenever the weather is good to save your money, sleeping in hostels, dormitories or dirt cheap hotels when the weather is bad or when you're in the city, eating at hostels or cafeterias, and generally making full use of student and hostel facilities wherever you go. Costs should be approximately:

£7.00	bed
£6.60	main meal
£1.20	breakfast (fruit or bread)
£2.40	tobacco and/or coffee
£17.20	a day or £ 120.40 a week

Add, let's say, £48 per week for ferry fares, sightseeing, bus or train fares around and out of cities and you have, for what is an average hitch-hiking budget, about £170 *per week.*

3 HOTEL HITCHING This, without a doubt, is the best way to do it if you can afford it. For the money you can have the privilege of sleeping in a cheap hotel without the bug of curfews which plague hostel hitchers. You also eat at least one good meal a day in a cheap restaurant. Moving this way you're completely your own man, dependent on no one and subject to no rules or regulations. But it costs. Below is a realistic price structure:

£15.00	bed
£5.50	main meal
£1.20	breakfast (fruit, bread or inclusive hotel breakfast)
£2.40	tobacco and/or coffee
£24.10	a day or £168.79 a week

Add, let's say, £68 per week for ferry fares and a general good time, and for the most luxurious and enjoyable way of hitching it costs you £237 *a week.*

HOW TO GET IT CHEAPER When you're travelling on a hitcher's budget every cent counts. You have a certain amount of money and that money must get you around your route. Tricks to make your roll last as long as possible are important. Here are a few.

INTERNATIONAL STUDENT IDENTITY CARDS These things are invaluable. In many countries they will get you into museums, galleries, monuments and theatres at half-price – and that can save you a *hell* of a lot of money. In Paris, for instance, some central cinemas were offering 25% reductions to holders of student cards as we went to press.

Obtain these cards, or the information on how to buy one, from your college or university. Britons, or foreign students in Britain, who require an International Student Identity Card, should contact:

The London Student Travel Bureau, 52 Grosvenor Gardens, London SW1W 0AG (tel: 0171 730 8111).

In some countries card-holders are offered reduced air fares between international cities. In the UK, students and under-26s should check out the cheap charter deals offered by Campus Travel. Nowadays though, you can usually manage to escape paying the full fare anyway, regardless of age. To give a few examples: as this book goes to press, a scheduled return air fare London–Málaga–London costs about £200; London–Zurich–London about £220 and Glasgow–Faro–Glasgow about £240. But, if you scour the travel pages of newspapers and check out possibilities at local travel agents it's possible to find flights on all these routes in the £80–120 range.

YOUTH HOSTELS There are three main disadvantages about youth hostels. First, they are often so far out of town it takes you an hour or two to locate and get to them; second, they have curfews which are usually strictly enforced, and third, they have a completely institutional flavour about them (though in fairness it must be added that some of the new hostels are superbly designed and extremely well administered). The advantages of hostels are equally obvious. They guarantee you a clean bed for a very reasonable fee and they supply (in some countries) excellent meals for a fraction of what they would cost outside. And married couples will be pleased to know that if there is plenty of free space in the hostels (usually only during or towards the off-season) the staff will do their best to put you in a room together. In fact, off-season hostelling (when you can find them open) is great fun. You end up getting hotel conditions for half the price you'd pay in an hotel.

There are over 4,000 Hostelling International (HI) hostels in 44 countries throughout the world, a large number of which are in Europe. There is no maximum age limit at HI hostels except in Bavaria, southern Germany, where only those aged under 27 are admitted. However, priority will always be given to members aged under 30 if beds are filling up fast.

The *average* cost of an HI youth hostel in Europe is about £6, though you might not agree with that figure if you confine your touring to the major tourist cities such as Venice, Berlin and London, because then you're looking at paying £10–£16 a night on average. The *average* cost of a meal is £4 – and a good meal at that. Cooking facilities are available in many hostels if you want to cut costs even further by preparing your own food.

Full information on the location of all HI hostels can be found in the two volumes of the *Hostelling International Handbook.* Volume 1 deals with hostels in Europe and the Mediterranean area, Volume 2 with hostels in other parts of the world. They cost about £4 each and can be obtained through any national hostel association.

The cost of becoming a Hostelling International member through your national youth hostels association is extremely cheap in view of what you gain by membership.

Addresses to contact regarding membership of Hostelling International are:

UNITED KINGDOM

Youth Hostels Association Association of England and Wales, Trevelyan House, 8 St Stephen's Hill, St Albans, Herts AL1 2DY (tel. 01727 55215).

Scottish Youth Hostels Association, 7 Glebe Crescent, Stirling FK8 2JA (tel. 01786 51181).

Youth Hostel Association of Northern Ireland, 56 Bradbury Place, Belfast BT7 1RU (tel. 01232 324733).

REPUBLIC OF IRELAND

An Óige, 61 Mountjoy Street, Dublin 7 (tel. 01 304555).

UNITED STATES

PO Box 37613, Washington DC 20013–7613.

CANADA

1600 James Naismith Drive, Gloucester, Ontario K1B 5N4.

AUSTRALIA

60 Mary Street, Surry Hills, 2010 NSW.

NEW ZEALAND

PO Box 436, 28 Worcester Street, Christchurch.

SOUTH AFRICA

PO 4402, Cape Town.

You can cut basic living costs by better than a half if you're a member of Hostelling International. So, if you think you can put up with the disadvantages mentioned, join!

As well as HI hostels you will often have the option of staying in an independent hostel. These are particularly widespread in Ireland, The Netherlands, Belgium and Greece. Prices are usually on a rough par with local HI hostels – where they aren't, expect much lower standards. The one main advantage independent hostels have over HI hostels is that they rarely have early curfews.

● **Warning!** Guard your stuff well in all hostels. There's a lot being ripped off. Leave valuables at the desk (if they have facilities) or take them with you. Careful of your watch when you take it off to shower!

FREE MAPS AND LITERATURE These days there is no need to buy maps of European countries. Most national tourist agencies will supply them for free if you ask. Failing that, service stations in many countries offer free maps. These maps aren't as good as Michelin or Hallwag, but then they don't cost a pound apiece. They're certainly good enough to help you find your way between the major cities and points of interest.

Don't be afraid to ask for literature, either. Tourist offices have tons of it and it's there for only one reason – to give away. City maps, descriptions of the sights, just about any information you can imagine. But tourist offices are funny. They rarely give until they're asked. So ask. Nicely.

WHAT TO BUY WHERE You can save the odd pound or dollar by being aware of which countries sell which items cheaper than other countries and stocking up before you cross borders.

For instance, buy cigarettes on ferry-boats crossing international waters (where they are duty-free) or in Belgium, Luxembourg or Spain which are the three cheapest countries in Europe for tobacco. Even if you don't smoke you should always buy your quota for resale. If, for example, you carry 10 packets of cigarettes from Spain to Denmark where they are about five times the price, then even by selling them at half the normal Danish price you should make sufficient profit to keep you on the road for an extra day. The same goes for bottles of spirits. Always buy your quota if you think you can sell it across the border at a profit. (This is especially true if you are heading from the UK, Germany or Poland into Scandinavia.)

Anyone thinking of camping out would do well to stock up with instant coffee in England before crossing to the Continent where, in many countries, it is more than twice as expensive. And the same goes for tea drinkers.

Hitchers with worn-out boots can buy the cheapest boots in Europe in the Czech Republic, Slovakia or Poland. Those with worn-out clothes can find the best bargains in new clothes at sales in Germany or England. Those who want secondhand boots or clothes should head for the flea markets in any of the big cities. Amsterdam, Paris, Madrid, London, Rome all have big open-air markets where you can buy anything cheap if you haggle long enough.

SOMETIMES CHEAPER TO BUY A TICKET If you're in a big hurry to go somewhere for a specific reason, remember that it's sometimes cheaper to buy a bus or train ticket than to hitch. For instance, in Turkey, if you're in a hurry, buses are much cheaper than hitching. Sometimes it's even cheaper to *fly* than to hitch if you get a charter flight.

TRAVELLERS' CHEQUES When you set out on your hitch-trip you'll probably have a fair wad of money. The safest way to carry it is in travellers' cheques which can be cashed just about anywhere in the world. The cheques cost a small amount to buy and you must pay a small commission when you cash them, but if you happen to lose your wallet or it gets stolen, you can make arrangements to cancel those cheques by going straight to a bank.

RESTAURANTS Only go into restaurants (or bars) where you can check the price list first. Many restaurants – most notoriously in London and Rome – have 'hidden' costs such as so-called 'service' and 'cover' charges, as well as extra charges for everything from vegetables to VAT, which can add as much as 40% to your bill. Always check! Stick with pubs, workers' cafés and chain restaurants. Normally, in these places, you pay the price you see on the menu.

HOTELS When you ask the price of a room and you are told, do not accept immediately. Try the downcast-face act and ask gently if there isn't a somewhat cheaper room in the house, for instance, on the top floor. It's surprising the number of times, especially in France, when you'll be offered something a fraction cheaper.

There are dozens of little ways of saving on your expenses. Always be on the lookout for them – youth hostels are where you hear of many – and when you discover them pass the word around. Help others travel cheaper, too!

● **Warning!** If you want to buy a camera, radio, cassette recorder, etc., it's best to wait until you get to Switzerland or Germany where such things are cheaper. Better yet, wait until you reach a duty-free port or airport. But this is the warning . . . some so-called duty-free ports and airports offer very bad deals on certain items. For instance, I have seen cameras at London's Heathrow airport with higher price-tags than you can find in a good discount store right in the centre of town. Don't be fooled by the words 'tax-free' or 'duty-free'. Check out prices.

● **For van vagabonds only** You're approaching a border and there's plenty of room for fuel in your tank. Do you tank up now, or across the border? It's worth doing a bit of research into petrol/diesel prices in the countries you'll be driving through as it can save you a fair bit of cash. For instance, a trip to the pumps in little Luxembourg is easier on the pocket than in any of its three bigger neighbours. For an up-to-date guide to petrol/diesel prices around Europe contact: Royal Automobile Club (Foreign Touring Department), 49 Pall Mall, London SW1 5JG

● Drivers should also know that in some countries (e.g. Italy)

tourists can buy petrol coupons at the frontier which offer discounts.

- Remember, also, to nurse ailing vehicles into cheaper countries where workers' wages are considerably less than in the north and where motor repairs can be a lot cheaper.

Hitchers' Tips and Comments . . .

Wherever possible buy American Express travellers' cheques. Not only are they the most widely accepted, but you can change them commission free at American Express offices in some of the major cities. DANNY PHILLIPS, DROGHEDA, IRELAND

If you're going to be hitching solely (or even mainly) in a major West European country, consider buying travellers' cheques in that country's currency. That way you need only pay one commission in Britain as there is always one major bank in that country which will cash them without taking a commission.

PAUL DARLING, CONWY, WALES

On my last two trips to the Continent I discovered that the only places which would change money and travellers' cheques on Saturday nights, Sundays or public holidays were bureaux at railway stations, airports or hotels. Also, it's worth noting that most places will only exchange travellers' cheques from the most prominent world banks or travel agents. Anyone carrying cheques from minor banks can have trouble. SUE PYLE, GEELONG, AUSTRALIA

True enough, especially in outback areas. Perhaps best to stick to big names like Cook's and American Express. Also, I've noticed that trying to get rid of lesser-known currencies – like Australian dollars – is like trying to give away rocks . . . no one is interested. K.W.

Thanks to Sue Pyle for her advice. *But,* arrive early at railway stations – even queue in advance – or you face horrendous queues. The exchange at Gare du Nord, Paris, on a Sunday is mobbed.

JULIA BUTT, GLASGOW, SCOTLAND

Try the hypermarkets on the outskirts of French cities where you can buy enough for a picnic meal dead cheap.

STEVE IRELAND, BELFAST, N. IRELAND

You find these giant supermarkets outside Spanish cities, too. I've seen them between Málaga and Torremolinos and between Alicante and San Juan. At least 25% cheaper than in the cities. K.W.

If you get stuck in the rain at night near parked trucks, check with drivers until you find an empty truck and ask if you can sleep in the back. Sometimes works and it gives you a dry night's kip. Happy hitching. PHIL HARDY, LEICESTER, ENGLAND

When I'm travelling anywhere in Europe, and it's time to sleep, I simply go to the nearest apartment block, press somebody's bell, then when the door opens, go in, go down instead of up, hide out under the stairs and roll out my sleeping bag. I'm always up and away by 8 a.m. to miss janitors, stair washers, etc.

DANNY LONG, SAFFRON WALDEN, ENGLAND

An International Camping Carnet will get you discounts in many European camping grounds. ALAN THATCHER, NEW ZEALAND

In France, Italy and Spain, always stand at the bar when taking coffee or drinks. If you sit down you get thumped with a whacking great service charge. ALAN THATCHER, NEW ZEALAND

Most bars have three price structures. As Alan says, it's cheapest to drink standing at the bar; sitting at a table inside is more expensive; sitting at a table outside on the terrace is more expensive again.

K.W.

Couple of tips for fellow hitchers. If you *must* travel by train, always travel at night – it's cheaper and you save more money by having somewhere to sleep. And if you fly anywhere always keep the disposable cup and cutlery you get with meals – handy camping implements.

'JOCK THE HULK', ALIAS JIM CONDRON, EAST KILBRIDE, SCOTLAND

On the Newhaven–Dieppe ferry route I found I could save over 50% of the fare by buying a *same day return*, instead of a one-way ticket! But you have to hide your luggage until after you get the ticket so you *look* like a day-tripper. At the other end you can give the return part of your ticket to some hitcher who looks like she/he needs it.

CATHY JURGEN, EDINBURGH, SCOTLAND

If crossing the Channel from Dover, Folkestone, etc., keep your eyes open for special cheapy returns. These can be half the normal single fare. HINSH, GLASGOW, SCOTLAND

The English newspapers regularly do special offers of £1 for day trips on the ferries to France. From Oostende try and find a Belgian to help you out by buying a day return ticket to Ramsgate. It'll save you a packet on the usual single fare.

MARK HILL, LONDON, ENGLAND

When changing money, check if there is a flat rate of commission on transactions, e.g. $1. If so, find a few likely looking souls and change all your money in one go, thus making the commission proportionately less than if the money was changed in several transactions. IAN, ENGLAND

You make the hole-in-the-wall hitcher sound like a superhuman toughguy. It helps if you are, but anyone who can carry a tent can get by on the budget you suggest. There are advantages to hitching hole-in-the-wall style, too: you *never* have to worry about finding a bed in cities. City campsites are never full up like hostels. Further, you can recover some of your campsite costs because better off campers and caravaners often give you food, particularly when they're on their way back home.

JON GLANVILLE AND MARTIN ELSTON, BRISTOL, UK

Free Channel crossing: Yes, it can be done by getting a ride with a trucker and being signed on as his co-driver, but there are a few things that should be said: most truckers get blinkered vision the closer to the channel ports they get. They are tired, late, hungry etc. and don't want to stop again until they get into that lorry park. So hitching just outside ports can make for a very long day. Better to hitch at the last service station or autobahn roadhouse before the port. From London to Dover Farthing Corner M2 (East) between exit 4 and 5, train to Rainham and walk 2 miles south. Out of Germany from Köln on route 4 make a sign for Aachen, Belgian border at Vetschan.

Once you get someone to stop, even if the trucker cannot give you a free trip (Company rules, mate!), ask him to take you as far as the lorry park because getting through the dock gate is half the battle. Arrival offices have a canteen, TV room etc. where truckers can wait to board the ferries. This is the place to take a low profile and ask for a lift across. Don't spend too long walking around with your pack on your back in case an official calls the police. You must get a ride before the trucker presents his paperwork, some can put your name down as second driver. Once on board the truckers sometimes ask if you want the mate's meal ticket to eat in the truckers' canteen (£3 for a mega meal!). Well worth buying him a beer. Many drivers help you find a ride on the other side if they are not going your way. These guys all know each other. If you have to buy your own ticket on the ferry, go to the truckers' canteen anyway and try setting up a ride on the other side. After a meal and a beer, the idea of company across the country seems better.

Once across, the only problem with trucks is that they are slow. Drivers must stop every so many hours and cannot run on Sunday in many countries.

Note: Hitching out of ports can be bad. Ostend–Zeebrugge is OK but Calais and Dover are the pits. Be warned.

DAVE COLLARD, CANTERBURY

While hitching to Amsterdam in aid of charity we were told by a truck driver that they are no longer allowed to take a passenger across the channel free of charge, so don't get caught short of cash at the channel ports.

SIMON, SWANSEA, WALES

4 · WHAT TO TAKE

The only sure thing that's going to happen on a hitch-hike trip is that you will get sick of lugging your pack around. It's an unavoidable millstone which is always too heavy.

Some hitchers are very aware of this and it's not unusual to see people wandering around Europe with a hold-all which has scarcely the capacity of an airline bag. When you figure it, all you basically need, apart from the clothes on your back, is a toothbrush, a change of socks and underwear, and a spare shirt. But that's pretty rough travelling and, for myself, if I'm hitting the road for anything longer than a couple of weeks, I like to carry enough stuff to keep me comfortable and reasonably clean throughout any situation I'm likely to encounter.

Any list of what to take on a trip – as with any other suggestion in this book – can only be a guideline to a plan you might finally adopt for yourself. The two lists which follow soon are based on what my wife and I carry when we set out.

The first thing you need, of course, is a pack. The only type worth considering, in my opinion, is a frame-pack with some sort of adjustable system which allows you to vary the tension strap, which sits just above your buttocks, so that a load, no matter what its weight, can be kept from digging into your spine. The shoulder-straps, also, should be adjustable so that you can find the most comfortable carrying position and they should be made of leather, rather than the cheaper webbing material, because the latter tends to crease and become very uncomfortable.

Examine the shoulder-straps thoroughly before buying because, if you're carrying any sort of load, it's your shoulders which will take the bashing for the first few days until you get fit. Some more expensive packs have canvas-encased sponge-rubber strips sewn to the inside of the strap. These are great. You can fit them on to a cheaper pack yourself.

Another important point to consider when buying is that there are 'wide packs' and 'high packs', meaning that the volume of the pack, when filled to capacity, comes either from the width or from the height. I favour the high pack because it's easier to carry through crowded streets without slaughtering people and, more important, it's less trouble to get through the door of a small car.

If your budget doesn't run to sleeping in cheap hostels, you'll need a sleeping bag. (Even if you're sleeping in hostels, which charge a small fee for the use of bedding, you can save money by having your own bag.) The bag you should buy is the best you can afford for the conditions you expect to meet. If you've any sense you won't be considering sleeping out in anything close to freezing and therefore you *do not* need something like Hillary took to Everest. Any good camping shop should be able to give you a rundown on what is available. The minimum requirements are that the bag will keep you comfortable at freezing point, that it is reasonably water-resistant and that it is light.

If you take a sleeping bag, then you need something to lay it on – a groundsheet of some kind. Don't buy a regular groundsheet because they cost money and weigh a couple of pounds. The best thing – and for free if you look around – is a six feet by four feet sheet of heavy-duty plastic (like factories encase new mattresses in) which is light, disposable and easily replaceable, and which doubles perfectly as a poncho if you're caught in the rain.

If you're a hole-in-the-wall hitcher (which means that to make your money last you have to sleep out every night and always prepare your own meals) then it might be worth investing in a lightweight inflatable air-mattress. You'll curse the extra weight by day, but bless the comfort it offers you by night. (Remember to take a puncture repair outfit along with the mattress!) If you reckon your shoulders can stand it, you might consider taking the midget stove that the Gaz people make. You can buy refills in just about every European country. (Spain is the cheapest country I've found for refills.) It's cheaper to make fires, but also more hassle, especially if you're thinking you'd like a quick cup of coffee.

Suggested men's list

passport and money
photocopies of passport, driver's licence, ID card, tickets, etc. (Keep separate from originals and use them if originals get lost or stolen)
6 passport-size photographs
photocopy of prescription for glasses/contact lenses
good pair of light boots plus spare laces (you'll be walking quite a few miles a day)
sandals for city wear when you're resting up
2 pairs of trousers
2 shirts (drip-dry)
1 good jacket with plenty of pockets
2 changes of underwear
2 pairs of socks
3 handkerchiefs
sweater
toilet bag containing:
toothbrush and paste

small bar of soap (use other people's where possible)
toilet paper (most toilets on the Continent seem to be without it – stolen by hitch-hikers, no doubt)
nail scissors and file
sticking plaster (for blistered feet – very handy during first week)
half-dozen aspirin tablets
condoms (they can be hard to find in certain countries, or illegal, or both)
dozen anti-diarrhoea tablets
needle and cotton
pocket knife (doubles as eating knife and fork)
spoon
plastic cup
combination bottle-opener, corkscrew and can-opener (simplest type possible or it won't work)
notebook, pen and envelopes
reading matter
spare box of matches
maps of areas to be travelled through
if under 18 years old, a letter from parents or guardian stating that their permission has been granted for you to travel and hitch-hike alone

Suggested women's list
passport and money
photocopies of passport, driver's licence, ID card, tickets, etc. (Keep separate from originals and use them if originals get lost or stolen)
6 passport-size photographs
photocopy of prescription for glasses/contact lenses
good pair of tough shoes or light boots plus spare laces
sandals for city wear
2 pairs of slacks or jeans
3 blouses (drip-dry)
1 light crushproof, drip-dry dress
3 changes of underwear
3 pairs of socks
3 handkerchiefs
sweater
toilet bag containing:
toothbrush and paste
small bar of soap
toilet paper
small pair of scissors and nailfile
sticking plaster

half-dozen aspirin tablets
condoms and other contraceptives (they can be hard to find in certain countries, or illegal, or both)
dozen anti-diarrhoea tablets
couple of sanitary towels or tampons (which can be hard to find if you're stuck in small southern European and North African villages; same goes for the Pill. Take them with you)
needle and cotton
pocket knife (doubles as eating knife and fork)
spoon
plastic cup
combination bottle-opener, corkscrew and can-opener
notebook, pen and envelopes
reading matter
spare box of matches
maps of areas to be travelled through
if under 18 years old, a letter from parents or guardian stating that their permission has been granted for you to travel and hitch-hike alone

Those lists, depending on your sense of proportion, will seem impossibly long and stupid or the exact opposite. If the latter, you can only be warned that every extra pound you carry in your pack will be like lugging around dumb-bells. Don't be tempted to put in too much else. If you are, try to dispense with some other item. For instance, if you see the necessity for an extra shirt, try *not* to see the necessity for sandals.

Reading matter is something I was trapped into taking on my first hitch-trip. I figured I'd have plenty of time to catch up on some stuff I wanted to read and took six paperbacks. Well, I had plenty of time all right – on some Portuguese back-roads – but I never got around to reading three of the titles because I'd given them away after the first day. Plus I was wishing to God I'd left half my clothes home and had managed to subdue my camera-bug to the extent where I'd taken a Kodak Instamatic instead of the heavy SLR I use.

(One item I *do* carry, mainly because it dispenses with several others, is a Swiss army knife. They are advertised as pocket workshops and it is an accurate description. The one I have has two blades, a screwdriver, a bottle-opener, a tin-opener, a corkscrew, a punch, a pair of scissors and a miniature wood saw which is strong and sharp enough to cut small branches for campfire kindling. I've lost count of the number of things I've managed to do with it when I've been on the road. There's a super *de luxe* version, incidentally, which even has a pair of tweezers and a plastic toothpick.)

Best rule is to pack only what you absolutely need and then get ruthless and dispense with about 20% of it. Remember that you'll probably pick up odd bits and pieces to take home and you'll need room in the pack – and the strength to carry them.

The tougher you are before you set out, the more you're going to like yourself when you're slap in the middle of what you just know is going to be a rideless day. One of those days when the only place you're about to go is where you get around to walking to!

● **Lifesaver** When I'm heading into colder climes – and that can mean just about anywhere in Europe during winter, including Spain, Italy and Greece – I've taken to carrying a heavy, woollen knitted scarf. I know this goes against everything I've written regarding bulk and weight, but I've found that the scarf has more value than an extra sweater when you're stuck on the road in an icy wind. You can wear it around your neck, open it up and cover half your upper body with it, wear it around your ears and head or wrap it around your face Arab-style. A scarf can be a lifesaver. Think about it. (But don't blame me if the sun shines the whole way and you never have to use it!)

Hitchers' Tips and Comments . . .

If your budget stretches to it, try 'sportsman's blankets' (sometimes called 'space blankets'). Indestructible, light-weight, plastic-backed foil sheets that reflect body heat and have many uses: blanket, poncho, windbreak, groundsheet. Also, when on long stretches in the backwoods, a water bottle is worth its weight in gold.

KELLEY AND GAIL, MUSWELL HILL, LONDON

A few things I think a traveller should carry, but which you don't mention: International Driver's Licence, so you can help out drivers on long hauls; mini-radios, which can help conquer boredom on the road; clothes-washing materials, like a small ball of plastic string and a couple of pegs. DANIEL KIDREN, HENZLIGGER, ISRAEL

For cheap, comfortable sleeping, try a hammock. Do it in style, lads!

B. J. BROCK, EAST ST KILDA, VICTORIA, AUSTRALIA

Useful additions to the *Guide's* list might be: a light plastic water bottle; one pair of woollen gloves – it gets damn cold in Switzerland even in September – a luxury well worth including; large felt-pen marker for quick, easy destination placards; assorted Tupperware food containers (tops double as plates); plus, if you live in the UK, as much cheap food as you can carry – it will save pounds in the first week on the Continent. JOHN HOAD, EASTBOURNE, ENGLAND

I strongly recommend getting hold of a 'survival bag'. I bought mine in an Army & Navy store. The bag, made by Karrimor, is plastic, and designed so you can put your sleeping bag and luggage in it. Really keeps you dry. I've used mine for a year and it's still OK. As for Swiss army knives, I've had two ripped off. They've got everything else on them – why not a burglar alarm? DAVE P., LEEDS, ENGLAND

One of the smartest things I did was carry a Xerox copy of the first page of my passport, and extra photos. It saved me a lot of time and expense in phone calls when my passport was ripped off in Yugoslavia. Try cashing a travellers' cheque without a passport!

JIM HENDERSON, REGINA, CANADA

A useful addition to my pack has been a couple of plastic refillable cigarette lighters. They sell in Britain for about £1, give 2,000–3,000 lights, and will work when it's wet or there's a strong wind. They have an adjustable flame which gives a blowtorch effect and will light even damp kindling. ADRIAN PARK, PRESTON, ENGLAND

If you want to carry a plate, take a frisbee instead. Great plate, yet useful for roadside games. MIKE WALDIE, SHENFIELD, ENGLAND

We were amused by Mike Waldie's comment about frisbees, but a better idea is to take a metal plate which you can use as a frying pan, a cooking pot lid *and* a frisbee!

JON GLANVILLE AND MARTIN ELSTON, BRISTOL, UK

If you're heading into cold areas, take a plain-coloured towel, then it can double up as a scarf. I can't recall ever having needed a scarf and towel simultaneously. KEVIN BILKE, SOUTHAMPTON, UK

Scandinavian Airlines (SAS) give away free 'pen portraits' of all major cities. These booklets cover tourist attractions, places to eat and stay (usually way above a hitcher's budget), plus other handy things to know like shopping hours, Tourist Information Centre addresses, etc. Also an inner-city map. Pick them up at SAS offices.

JOHN STRACHAN, TOOWOOMBA, AUSTRALIA

Instead of buying Karrymat rolls to sleep on, or other registered makes, go to an industrial supply place and ask for a sheet of 'Plasters Oats' cut to the required size. It's the same condensed foam you buy in the camping shops but about half-price.

MIKE AND SUE, LEICESTER, UK

I always carry several short lengths of string. It serves as clothesline and replacement bootlaces, and once I was able to use it to repair a slash in the side of my pack. TOMMY HAIG, LONDON, UK

Keep matches, salt, pepper, etc., dry in 35mm film cans.
IAN BAMBURY, GREAT BOOKHAM, UK

A better buy than Gaz stoves is a paraffin stove. It's heavier and a bit more expensive to buy but it's much more economical. You can even burn diesel in it, although this turns your pots black.
NIGEL CLAYTON, SOUTH AFRICA

An insulating pad such as Karrymat provides warmth, dryness, adequate comfort and protects your bag from rough ground. A cheap, compact, brightly-coloured cagoule keeps you warm in wind or rain and makes you more visible by the roadside. Freezer bags and tinfoil are great for carrying and cooking food in. Insulating tape, safety pins and thick rubber bands are useful for running repairs. Consider a second water bottle if you like wine. Packs with an *internal* frame are more comfortable and compact than the traditional framesack, and cheaper. PAUL, LONDON, UK

Sunglasses worth carrying, especially in Mediterranean area, North Africa or if you're heading into snow country. Keep on trucking! DANNY DE DUDE, STANISLAUS, CALIFORNIA, USA

Take a compass. Don't laugh: you don't need anything more elaborate than the type that comes out of a Christmas cracker but mine has saved me endless hassles in city streets. I never go to any town of which I have less than intimate knowledge without mine. It's been particularly useful in cities like London where much of the travelling may be done by underground railway: have you never come out of a strange tube station and wondered which way to go?
STEPHEN MORGAN, POOLE, DORSET, UK

Ski belts available at all sports shops are marvellous for carrying valuables as they're bigger than purses, so take passports as well as a notebook, etc. (easier than fumbling in rucksacks and safer).

Losing a passport is a lot of hassle as we found out. Worth having a visitor's passport (one year duration) as well as full passport if you're on a long trip. Needless to add – keep them separate!
JULIA BUTT, GLASGOW, SCOTLAND

I found a plastic bin liner very useful when sleeping out on a wet night. Stick your pack in it and your gear stays dry.
TIM MEADS, NR NORWICH, UK

A fishing line has always been a must for me. Not only can you sit out in the wilds beside some river willing the fish to bite, but it also makes ideal thread for repairs of clothes etc. Easy to obtain anywhere and a lot stronger than cotton.

DICK, STOURBRIDGE, WEST MIDLANDS

Very handy for quick repairs to packs, tents, shoes, or anything that has to hold for a while, is so-called Gaffertape: silver or black. We have even repaired a 2CV with it. ANNA LISS, AMSTERDAM

I always carry a lightweight cyclists' cape for two reasons. One, it is a means of keeping both your body and your pack dry, and two, it serves admirably as a portaloo. It provides excellent privacy should you need a crap in a place where cover is thin on the ground. Spread some paper or whatever on the ground, put on the cape, squat à la Middle East, and. . . PETER COLLINS, MANCHESTER, ENGLAND

One of the handiest items to take is dental floss. It can be used to repair bags and even tent poles, apart from using it on your teeth.

TOM CORCORRAN, DUBLIN, IRELAND

Pack two or three cheap gas lighters, plus a box of waterproof matches. JAMES COYLE, LIVERPOOL, ENGLAND

For safety, carry a whistle. OK, you can't knock anyone out with it, but you might scare them off.

LOUISE BROMLEY, NEWTON-LE-WILLOWS, ENGLAND

5 · HOW TO SURVIVE

If you're down and out for food, remember that the cheapest buys are always in the markets. In-season fruit will never cost you more than 25p apiece and if you're that broke you can find bruised pieces which the stallholder will probably give you. Also check the floors where you can often find edible wastage. Just cut out the bad sections and give what's left a wash under running water and you're all right.

Chinese restaurants – and just about every city in Europe has them – always serve plain boiled rice. Not the tastiest of dishes, but at 90p a bowl it's cheap, and if you splatter it liberally with the free soy sauce you can get it down.

Every country in Europe knows about chips. A big plate of these – and make it obvious that you need them! – won't cost more than 90p and they'll hold you together until you can figure something out.

Salvation Army and other religious organizations often have free soup kitchens. To locate them ask fellow hitchers or, in an emergency, ask the police. Don't freeload on them! Only use them if you have no alternative.

Bananas, apart from being nutritious, are about the most filling item weight-for-weight that you can buy. Two bananas and a small loaf of bread will keep you going all day. Cost? Around 65p.

In country areas, try the old tramp trick. Approach farmers or house-owners, explain the problem as best you can and offer to do an hour's work for a good feed. You'll get a lot of knockbacks, but there are enough good people around to agree to such a simple bargain.

When you're a long way from home and the money's getting low you nearly always have to start cooking for yourself. This is not so bad if you balance your diet – though the whole deal tends to get a little boring after a while. I find that in such emergencies it's possible to eat fairly well for £2.50 a day, by eating only one meal and watching what I buy. The following list is an example of the type of hot, nutritious meal you can prepare:

couple of potatoes (bake them in the campfire ashes)
couple of eggs (boil in a tin can)
one or two sausages (barbecue them on the end of a stick or piece of wire)
loaf of bread (toast it)

couple of pieces of fruit (try stewed apple or mashed banana on toast)
coffee (boil water in tin can)

The two basic condiments that help make a meal worth eating are sugar and salt. Salt is cheap anywhere, sugar not so cheap. Don't be afraid to go into a shop and ask for only 100 grammes of sugar. It's enough to last a dozen cups of coffee. (But don't worry if you don't have any. Eating sugar is only a habit and your body operates better without. Mostly, sugar just rots your teeth.)

Fire-making isn't hard. The 'pyramid'-type fire is the easiest. You put small sticks and any old paper you can find in the middle and then build larger sticks in a pyramid shape over them, making sure you leave plenty of room for the fire to breathe. Try to put a low wall of large rocks on the down-wind side of the fire – it reflects heat back into the fire and it's something of a safety measure. Always, of course, cover the fireplace with dirt and trample on it before you leave.

SLEEPING If you're a hole-in-the-wall or hostel hitcher you'll have a sleeping bag with you. You must have one to sleep out in Europe. The nights can get chilly even in summer.

Sleeping out on good nights is no problem. You just sack down. Rainy nights are when you're in trouble and want to head for the nearest hotel or hostel. But if you have no money, what do you do?

In the country

If you're carrying a tent you can hole up in that, but if you haven't you must start improvising. Plastic wrapping material is the stuff – if you can find enough of it. You need enough to cover your sleeping bag completely and it has to be broad enough so that with the aid of a stick you can erect a miniature tent over your head.

You can sleep in the rain with a groundsheet and sleeping bag, but even waterproof bags (unless they are very expensive models) tend to forget their maker's claims and sog up. Two nights of rain spells the ruin of most bags unless you have the chance to dry them out properly.

If you don't have a tent, then your choice of action is limited. Bridges and culverts are good bets. Animal shelters in the fields are OK if you can get one to yourself without the company of a cow. Failing that, approach a farmer for permission to sleep in one of his outbuildings. Some will let you, some won't. (Southern Ireland is the place for that. I know many hitchers who have not only been given permission to sleep in the hayloft, but have been supplied with blankets *plus* breakfast the next morning!)

In the city

In towns and cities you have more chance of finding a dry place to sleep. There are railway stations, which are nearly always impossible to sleep in, but which at least are warm and where also, more often than not, you meet other people to talk to. (Of course, if you don't have a ticket for a train departing the next day you stand a good chance of being booted right back into the cold, cold night, but with luck you'll get by.) There are churches (particularly in France) which are sometimes left open. There are sites with half-constructed buildings which offer superb shelter (and the occasional watchdog to keep you on your toes). There are street foyers to large office buildings where you can at least find a corner in which to squat out of the wind. There are Salvation Army type relief places, the addresses of which you can get from fellow hitchers or from the police. And finally, particularly in smaller towns or city suburbs where the police are more easy-going, you can always beg the loan of a cell for the night. It's been done before, though for me that'd be the absolute last resort!

● **Warning!** Sleeping out alone in cities is extremely dangerous. (See letters by Hugh Darlington, Clive Gill and Hugh Dunne at the end of this chapter, and other letters elsewhere in the book.) There are too many stories like this for it to be a joke. It's happening all the time. And it's not just things getting stolen. There's often violence involved and I've met more than one girl who has either been raped or just managed to fight her way out.

Sometimes, because of the money problem, you just have to sleep out, so what to do?

Ideally, get with a group of people so that thieves will think twice about trying to sneak up to the camp. If you have to sleep alone, conceal yourself as well as you can (you should, anyway, to avoid visits from police, park guards and nightwatchmen). Always keep your passport, papers, money and travellers' cheques on your person, or at least in your sleeping bag. Finally, if you're by yourself, keep a dirty great stick handy by your sleeping bag.

If you're ever attacked – be it at night, as the result of a ride you've hitched, in a bar, anywhere – remember that the surest way of saving your skin is to run like hell and forget all about being a hero.

If you're cornered and you have to fight, fight dirty. Anyone who is attacking you will presumably have no hesitation in laying you out and you have to fight on those terms. Unless you're a trained boxer or at least a brown belt martial arts man, forget all about fancy holds and uppercuts. Only experts can defend themselves scientifically. Fight like an animal – go for your opponent's eyes, throat, plexus, genitals and knees – and *get out* of the vicinity.

If you are attacked by several opponents and can't escape, you've got big problems on your hands. Safest thing is to give them everything you've got. That way you *might* save yourself a beating. If you're convinced they're going to bash you even if you hand over your stuff, or if you decide to give it a go, the odds of you winning are slim. But with considerable luck you might be able to break through them and get room to run (and if you've got your money and passport on your person the loss of your pack isn't so important).

If you go down and you know there's no way you can get up again, all that's left is to save yourself from as much damage as you can. Lie on your belly to protect your crotch and get your arms up to protect your head. That leaves your kidneys and back exposed, but there's nothing else you can do; except play dead.

And, of course, during the brawl – whether you're fighting one man or five – scream at the top of your voice for help. You *might* get some.

MEDICAL The worst thing that can happen on the road is that you might get ill. If you're moving with someone, it isn't so bad – you've got moral support. But just one day alone on the road when you're physically ill can be hell. You feel like you're never going to make your destination.

The only thing you can do is keep moving and if it's some ordinary little thing which any doctor can fix, stop off at the nearest village, search around and find someone who can speak your language (bars and cafés or the police station) and enlist their aid to help you out. If you find you can't pay the doctor, all you can do is give him your name and address and promise him that you'll send him the money when you have some. If he won't buy that you might have to give him something as collateral. Give him anything except your passport! Most doctors, though, like most people, aren't going to strike a rotten bargain if they see you can't pay.

SEX ON THE ROAD I hope you get plenty and I hope you enjoy it. But I'm obliged to point out 'the problem', right? Anyone who has wandered around the old city in Warsaw will have seen young AIDS victims begging for money for food and medicine. AIDS is rampant in many Eastern European countries, in Africa, in the Caribbean, It's also in London, Paris and any other place you like to name. AIDS is a killer. It's sad, sad, sad, but a person indulging in their first sexual experience could contract AIDS. Men: wear a condom during sexual intercourse. Women: make your partner wear a condom during sexual intercourse. If you and your partner have experienced a series of casual encounters and are now enjoying a more permanent relationship you might like to have a doctor make tests before you both decide to forget the rubbers.

DRUGS ON THE ROAD I'll recommend sex to anyone, but not drugs. However, if you are into drugs never be tempted to use a needle twice. And *never, but never, never* share a needle with someone. You would risk infection, including even AIDS infection. In most countries it is an offence to buy or sell drugs. In many countries it is an offence to carry or use drugs. Some penalties will ruin your life for a long time to come. If you are into drugs never, please, never carry drugs across borders. (I need to keep all the readers I can!) If you need help to get off drugs, there are many organizations willing to help you. They exist in all western European capital cities and in many provincial cities as well. Tourist offices, youth organizations, ministers of religion, hospital staff, private doctors and police departments will help you get in touch with people qualified to give you help and support.

NEEDLES Several readers have written about the problem of needles. In Eastern Europe, North Africa and some countries in the Middle East medical supplies can be hard to come by and needles may be re-used without being properly sterilized. The result of getting a shot to combat one problem could land you with another worse than the first. The answer would be to take a few syringes and needles of your own (2cc and 5cc syringes should cover most problems but, of course, check with a doctor or a qualified nurse or chemist before you buy). But this obvious answer might land you with some obvious problems if you are ever searched at customs. How you solve this one I do not know. In some countries, you will be able to buy syringes and needles in a chemist shop, in other countries they will not be in stock.

Diabetic hitchers who must inject regularly should consider carrying a letter from their doctor (in a couple of languages if possible) along with their medical supplies. The letter should detail the illness and treatment at both a layman's and a professional level so that it can be immediately understood by, first, customs or police officials or, if they decide to check things further, by their medical staff.

APPENDICITIS is one of the most dangerous things that can hit you while you're on the road. If it should happen when you're in a city, present yourself to the nearest tourist information office and convince them to take it over from there. (Play it sicker than you are if you have to, because they'll be able to get you to a decent hospital faster than you can yourself.) If you're out in the country, get yourself to the nearest town or village and let the police take over. Wherever you are, the best rule for something as serious as appendicitis is to somehow put yourself in the hands of a person or organization that has the facilities to act for you while you rest. If you can get straight to a hospital, well and good, but they usually take some time to locate and it is important that you should move as little as possible. The effort you'll put into flagging down a ride, if you're on the road, is going to take all the strength you can afford.

A SPRAINED ANKLE is something which can quite easily happen to you on the road. What you must do is bind it tightly and keep off it as much as possible. It may mean holing up in a hostel or somewhere for a few days. While resting you can bathe it in hot water. If you even vaguely suspect it might be more than a sprain, hobble along to the nearest chemist and let him take a look. That way you get a qualified opinion for nothing. If he thinks it is something more serious, *then* you can spend money at the doctor's.

Remember that whatever you think you might have, providing it's not obviously serious, a chemist can give you an opinion and prescribe simple drugs and medicines much cheaper than a doctor will.

DIARRHOEA is something which will attack just about every hitcher if he stays on the road long enough or does enough trips. For that reason I always carry a couple of dozen tablets which a doctor friend once prescribed for me. They are the sort of tablet you take *after* you get the attack. There are other prescriptions you can take to fortify your intestines *before* you go into an area (like Morocco or Turkey) where you might pick up a bug. Talk to a chemist before you start on your trip. Take something with you – it's worth the effort.

If, however, you are on the road and are suddenly stricken there's nothing you can do but wait it out. Eat as little as possible – dry biscuits and black tea without sugar seem OK – and rest.

(A friend of mine once got an attack in Algeria. He was in the middle of nowhere and he reckons he was in a bad way. He had no paper except one book which he hadn't read. He tells of sitting on the side of the road, frantically reading page after page so he'd have a backlog of paper to see him through his next attack. The book? Richard Aldington's *Death of a Hero*.)

If you're convinced your stomach will give out when you hit the wilder regions there are a couple of things you can do to lessen the chances of complete tragedy . . . Don't drink tap water but stick to bottled drinks like local mineral water, beer or Coca-Cola. Don't eat uncooked vegetables and only eat fruit which you peel, like oranges and bananas. (Human dung is used as fertilizer in some Arab and Eastern countries.) Eat only meat which is well cooked. (Long cooking won't save you if the meat is bad before it's cooked, but at least it'll destroy any lurking kitchen germs.)

TOOTHACHE Of all the things you can get on the road, is probably the least dangerous and yet the hardest to live with. The methods of holding the pain down while you get yourself to a dentist are legion. My favourite is to buy a bottle of whisky or cognac and to hold mouthfuls of the stuff over the offending tooth. Each mouthful usually holds the pain down for five minutes or more. It's a nice way of handling the problem if you can afford the luxury, and after a couple of hours you're so pissed you don't give a damn about anything anyway. Mouthfuls of cold water held over the tooth sometimes help for very brief periods of time. All you can do is stay sane until you reach a dentist. (See Evan Jones's letter at the end of this chapter.)

THE BLACK MARKET is rife everywhere in Eastern Europe and some parts of North Africa and the Middle East. The mighty dollar is king – with the German mark and Swiss franc nudging the throne. Yes, you can make money on the black market, but remember that exchanging money on it is illegal.

If you *are* tempted remember, too, that some professional money changers are determined to cheat you. One hint of possible trouble comes when one money changer offers you three or four percent more than others. Out of date notes mixed with current notes are one way of getting at you.

Another is the folded note trick. The guy says he'll give you two thousand thingos for twenty dollars and if he's a right hander he holds his wad flat in his left hand with his thumb over the middle of the pile and makes a big show of counting out twenty one hundred thingo notes. He peels them off and gives them to you. You've *watched* him count them, right? But when *you* count them there are only eighteen notes – two of which he folded in half so that he counted them twice. You're down, he's up and long gone.

Basic rules for playing the black market are: (1) be very sure of *that day's* bank rate so you can judge if you want to risk exchanging illegally; (2) check four or five money changers to get an idea of what *that day's* going street rate is; (3) beware of anyone who offers a substantial percentage above the street rate; (4) try and pick a man to change with rather than let him pick you. Try and pick someone you have watched make several exchange deals. This is to lessen the chances of being approached by a plain-clothes authority; (5) make your deal somewhere where the guy has to put each note down flat so he can't pull the 'old note' or 'folded note' stunts; (6) never let a money changer (or anyone for that matter) see your whole wad; (7) remember that in some countries to change local currency back into foreign currency you must have exchange slips from banks or hotels, so make sure the slips you do have reasonably justify the amount of cash the average hitcher would have spent during their stay.

SELLING BLOOD Blood is one thing that everyone has and which plenty of people need, and in several areas in Europe it is possible to sell it at rates which vary from £1.50–£4.80 a half-litre (about a pint). The biggest markets are, at the moment, in Greece, Turkey and Spain. Whether they will remain the markets is another question. Information on which countries and which hospitals in those countries are buying can always be picked up on the road from other hitchers and in youth hostels. The facts are continually changing so I am not listing any places here.

The idea of selling rather than *giving* blood may be repugnant to plenty of people and I agree, but this chapter is to do with survival, and selling your blood is a more honourable way of making a dollar than some others I can think of.

If you decide you have to hawk your blood, keep a very close watch on what is happening to you, particularly if you're in some out-of-the-way-type country and some backwoods hospital. Be very sure, for instance, that the needle is a fresh one straight from the sealed wrapper, and make sure they don't take more than half a litre from you. When you leave the hospital go and sit in a café or bar and have a coffee and something to eat and generally relax for half an hour. *And don't, under any circumstances, give blood more than once a month!*

SELLING AND PAWNING OTHER THINGS It's remarkable the number of people you meet on the road who will moan, 'Christ, I'm stony broke.' And sitting on their wrists is a £25 watch. It reminds you of the motorist who dies of thirst in the desert because he forgets to moisten his lips from the water in his car radiator.

Most big cities have pawn shops and even if you can't find one there are plenty of other shops which will buy your gear. Sleeping bags, tents, cameras, watches, wallets, rings, even haversacks (bundle your stuff into something else) are all items which are easy to sell, although you'll only get a fraction of what you paid for them. Youth hostels are great places to unload tents and sleeping bags to people looking for a bargain. You'll also get a better price there than you will from a shop or outdoor market. (At outdoor markets set up your own pavement stall – but be ready to scoot when the inspector comes and make sure you don't set up on a local's pitch.)

In effect, you're never really down and out until you're down to the clothes on your back and your boots. And a good pair of boots are worth a few dollars to anyone!

Survival is purely a matter of common sense and imagination. Use both and there's no problem.

● **Money belts** When you're on the road you can afford to lose everything except your passport, money and any return tickets you have. You should always keep those three items on your person wherever you go. A good way to do this is to buy one of those old-fashioned money belts, or make one from light canvas or suede. A cheaper alternative is to sew a deep pocket on to the *inside* of your trousers. If you do that, just make sure you don't move too far away from your trousers.

Hitchers' Tips and Comments . . .

Re your invitation to offer information . . . The buy of my life has been a small gas burner. They're light, compact and foolproof. Refills are cheap and give you a good week's cooking. A pan and a plate and you're set for a feed anywhere. If you can take the weight, a kilo of spuds and onions doesn't go astray either.

Here's a good recipe. Vegetable stew. Use a packet soup for a base, boil up spuds, onions, carrots, salami – anything that looks a fair thing – and eat with plenty of bread. It's not the best eating in the world but it's a lot better than starving to death and I've had some nights that have changed my life sitting around the burner in cheap pensions with a bit of good company.

FRANK SCAHILL, PUNCHBOWL, AUSTRALIA

Dear Sir: Stuff the *Hitch-hiker's Guide to Europe*. I've had three copies ripped off in hostels in as many months!

PETER LANE, LONDON

Don't leave cameras, radios, etc., in hostel rooms. My mini-radio was lifted in Rome. Check them in at desk.

MIKE FEENEY, HASLOW, ENGLAND

It's worth a mention that people who wear glasses should always carry a spare pair with them.

DAVE WILLIAMS, BIRMINGHAM, ENGLAND

It's probably worth carrying your optician's prescription with you, too. K.W.

You have plenty of instructions on how to keep dry (plastic bags, etc.) but have made no mention about protection from the sun. Sunburn can be one of the most distressing and painful afflictions to affect the hitcher. So how about a hat and sunglasses and a light, plastic tube of barrier cream?

And how about a packet of vitamin pills to keep the pecker up when food is scarce? DR IVY GARNHAM, HARARE, ZIMBABWE

Lomotil pills are the best cure for diarrhoea.

UNSIGNED, SOUTH KENSINGTON, LONDON

Watch out for national holidays all over Europe. You can get stuck without bread because you can't cash your travellers' cheques or pawn things. You can change money at the big hotels, but the rates are a bloody rip-off.

Last summer I took along a tube of Steratabs, which are water sterilizing tablets, and also seem to have a gut reinforcing effect after a couple of weeks' use. (Very handy in North Africa.)

Definitely forget about dossing out in a big Spanish town. I got a truncheon in the ribs one night. Stations, subways, everything is patrolled. If you sleep sitting upright on a park bench you're OK (preferably with your eyes open!). Watch out for the 5 a.m. high-pressure street hosing all over Europe.

CLIVE GILL, BIRCHINGTON, ENGLAND

If you need food really bad, pick a big and busy self-service place. Join the line and just buy a cup of coffee. When you pass the cash register pick a table where three or four people have just left after a big meal, sit down and get stuck into their leftovers.

PAUL RUSH, SAN FRANCISCO, USA

I write as a fellow traveller who has found the *Hitch-hiker's Guide* most useful. I did, however, come unstuck and will give you a brief account of my fortune and misfortune. I left England with the intention of hitching to Istanbul and then taking the overland route through the East to Australia. My second lift landed me in Paris for two days and then I made a château near Orleans where I stayed for a further seventeen days. I hitched in Spain for a couple of weeks and then back to Marseilles and asked at the dock about a boat for Italy and was immediately put in touch with a guy delivering a brand new yacht to Genoa – three days on the Med with all expenses paid!

I finally ended up in Rome (after Venice), having spent six fantastic weeks travelling on a minimum budget, having met the kindest and most generous people imaginable. I then referred to your book and headed for the Borghese Gardens where I crashed out in my sleeping bag for free. I woke at four in the morning to find my pack had been stolen. It contained my entire kit, including my addresses, diary, maps, books and all the hints I had collected from people *en route*. Also my contact lenses and worst of all . . . my *trousers*! Fortunately I had my wallet and travellers' cheques in my sleeping bag and my passport and papers in a bag around my neck.

I met a Belgian a couple of days later who, in the same park, had been forced to hand over his pack to a bunch of thugs on the threat of his life. I ask you to suggest that people don't crash out alone in Italian parks! HUGH DARLINGTON, OXFORD, ENGLAND

PS My copy of the *Hitcher's Guide* was in the bag. Got a spare one?

Selling blood in Greece, you've got to be over 21 – they check your passport for all particulars. DAVE MARTILL, LEICESTER, ENGLAND

Check out coin return slots. Telephones are an obvious place, but also in the endless banks of automatic lockers in airline terminals. Best place to panhandle is at an international airport. Hit US tourists returning home for the odd foreign coins they got stuck with and couldn't change back into dollars.

LEN TOWER, BAY SHORE, NEW YORK

Great places for sleeping rough are football stadiums and sports grounds. They are usually easy to enter and it's not necessary to be up and away too early in the morning. I've also had good kips in grounds beside open-air swimming pools. For late autumn and winter when nights are freezing try underground car parks (easy once you slip by the attendant) and under the stairs in foyers of office and apartment blocks.

DANNY LONG, SAFFRON WALDEN, ESSEX, ENGLAND

I sold some blood in Spain, but if you have any North African stamps in your passport it's no deal.

I always buy plenty of packet soup before leaving on a big hitch. Mixed with macaroni or rice it really sticks to the ribs. Follow that with bread and cheese and coffee and you can tackle Mt Everest!

DENNIS CLUBB, BLETCHLEY, ENGLAND

If you're stuck in coastal towns on the Continent and can't find the price of a hotel, try the Missions to Seamen. These are really for seamen, but most of the padres in charge are kind-hearted blokes and many let you kip on a couch in the TV lounge.

J. P. RIDLEY, FALKIRK, SCOTLAND

If you are crashing out (roughing it) take something for the mosquito bites – 'cause whatever you do these crazy goddamn creatures get you.

CAPT'N CLEM, BRISTOL, ENGLAND

In cold weather try the old tramp trick of keeping warm by putting two thicknesses of old newspaper between your shirt and jumper.

C. J. MAJOR, CAMBRIDGE, ENGLAND

Easy money: collect empty Coke bottles from dirt bins or especially along beaches and claim the deposit. I know someone who kept himself for six weeks in Torremolinos, Spain, this way.

LESLEY KOUNTAFF, SOUTH AFRICA

One of the most useful items I packed was some fishing tackle. Just some line, a few hooks and float – nice way of passing time on any coastline, lake or river in Europe. Camping rough it provides food or even offers an afternoon's pleasure while waiting for a ferry ride somewhere.

What I've often resorted to (e.g., hitched from Athens to Luxembourg city with *no* negotiable money) is going into bakeries in the morning and asking for yesterday's leftovers. Often got a fresh loaf; often got yesterday's pastries. Was rarely refused totally.

ROGER BROWN, AUTHOR OF *TRAVELLER'S SURVIVAL KIT EUROPE*
Published by Vacation-Work, Oxford

Roger: Great book! K.W.

Stay clear of Persian drivers if possible – we crashed outside Munich after several heart attacks. They are far worse than the Belgians.

JONAH, NEATH, SOUTH WALES

I had all my luggage ripped off from a *locked* left-luggage locker in Gare du Nord, Paris – on the last day luckily. Fortunately it was insured and I've been able to replace it all with better stuff – except the photos which are the only thing I regret losing.

DAVE, SOUTHAMPTON, ENGLAND

For those who get their *Hitcher's Guide* ripped off – try a plain paper cover!

MARCEL THOMAS, HORNDEAN, ENGLAND

Spain is still good for selling blood, but you must weigh over 55 kg otherwise they won't take it.

UNSIGNED

A few lines to all would-be travellers going camping or hiking abroad. To cover you for medical care write to your local Social Security for an E111. This is an exemption form for medical costs abroad. MISS E. REED, PETERBOROUGH, ENGLAND

I understand that Britons carrying this form in EC countries don't have to pay for medical services. Brits should check at their Social Security office. K.W.

Medical Insurance form E111 is *not* available to students – only those paying National Insurance, or unemployed, or under 19!
AVRIL HORTON, LEEDS, UK

For Brits only: when applying for form E111 from the Social Security, ask for leaflets SA 28 and SA 30. These tell you which countries have reciprocal health agreements with Britain, and thus where you can get treatment free or at reduced cost.
ALAN BARLOW, CHEADLE, UK

One thing you don't seem to mention is travel insurance. Luggage, money, medical and personal accident can all be covered with a good company very cheaply. S. DERRICK, SOUTHAMPTON, ENGLAND

Appearance: I try to save a clean shirt (at least) for the journey home and keep my face, hands and nails clean if I'm broke. Then I *look* OK even if I stink. BERNARD JENNINGS, BRISBANE, AUSTRALIA

For toothache: even better than booze is a packet of dried cloves available from most chemists or health food shops. Just let them dissolve over the offending tooth and the ache vanishes. Warning: don't chew them or have more than two at a time, unless you want a hole burnt in your throat. SIMON BARRY, ISLE OF MAN, GB

Your advice about knocking on farm doors for food works. I did that in Germany, after being dropped off on an autobahn, and even though they didn't speak English and I don't speak German, I got food and blankets for the night.
ALAN SMITH, SUNDERLAND, ENGLAND

If you do this, remember to offer to do an hour or so's work the next day. It keeps the image up. K.W.

If you need tomato sauce or mustard for home cooking visit self-service restaurants with a plastic bag. THRIFTY, ISRAEL

Plainclothes cops mix in cafés, bars and discos all over Europe whenever city fathers decide to do a 'clean-up'. They're after smokers and other 'undesirables'. Watch it! J.D., NOTTING HILL, LONDON

I read it in your book, and I've been warned a thousand times – 'beware of thieves in Italy'. One always thinks, it can't happen to me! I was parked outside a youth hostel in Rome for ten minutes. When I returned to the car, I found it had been broken into. My jacket, money, radio and camera had been pinched. I'd like to warn fellow travellers to be that extra bit careful whilst travelling in Italy.

GARY SOGOT, JOHANNESBURG, SOUTH AFRICA

These things don't happen only in Italy. They happen elsewhere, too. Never let your gear out of your sight. Never leave anything of value in your van. Look at it this way: your pack with clothes, camera and the rest of your stuff is worth maybe one hundred, two hundred pounds. Would you leave two hundred quid's worth of bank notes on a bus-stop floor while you went for a coffee? Or on the front seat of your van? These thieves don't see a rucksack or a camera – they don't need rucksacks or cameras. They just see money sitting there waiting to be ripped off. K.W.

Consume plenty of vitamin C. It'll save you from lots of minor ailments. C. D. COOK NEW ZEALANDER, LONDON, ENGLAND

Vitamin C is particularly important in the daily diet. You find good quantities of this vitamin in brussels sprouts, parsley, cabbage, cauliflower, oranges, lemons, mandarins, silverbeet, etc., so look for these fruits and vegetables when you shop in markets. Because money circumstances so often force you to eat badly when you're on the road, I reckon Dr Ivy Garnham (see page 62) hits it on the button when she says take along a pack of vitamin pills. Look for a pill that contains both vitamins and minerals. Avoid junk food whenever possible. If you have a choice between a hamburger joint and a workers' café offering good, simple food, take the latter every time. Junk food wrecks you. K.W.

If you're on the road and you walk by a garbage tip or rubbish dump, get your ass in there. People throw away really good stuff. I once found a chair I sold to a junk shop for enough money to buy me food for a day. It was tough hitching to get the chair back to town, but at least I got to sit on it while waiting for a ride. Roll on baby.

STEVE L. MANNHEIM, LOS ANGELES, UNITED STATES

If you're sleeping out in a city it's advisable to leave your gear in a locker in the main railway station. This lessens the risk of robbery (though it doesn't guarantee it). If you enter a park at night with a pack on your back, you'll attract the attention of muggers.

HUGH DUNNE, DUBLIN, IRELAND

For males only. If you fall on hard times in Israel, it's worth knowing that most big hospitals have sperm banks. If you can overcome your embarrassment, and also pass a blood test, you can earn around £5 sterling per contribution. RAY TOUT, ISRAEL

John Radcliffe Hospital in Oxford (next door to Somerville College on Woodstock Rd) gives £5 for donations to their sperm bank most times of the year. Check the student newspaper, *Cherwell*, where they actually advertise! A. MILLER, CARDIFF, UK

Anyone know if European hospitals seek contributions for sperm banks? K.W

A Eurocheque card (and your cheque book, of course) can be very handy in case of an emergency in Western Europe. You can't normally get money on the card, but you can buy air and boat tickets. Remember, if you lose the card and the cheque book you're giving a forger the licence to do you for a lot of cash.

NIGEL ROBERTS, PRESCOTT, ENGLAND

Pavement drawings are a way of making a few coins anywhere in the world. If you can't draw, find some abandoned picture on the pavement and touch it up. You should earn something off the tourists. But keep an eye open for the original artist!

JEZ, HEMEL HEMPSTEAD, ENGLAND

If you're stuck for a place to sleep in a large city, try the national departure lounge of the main airport.

PAUL DOWRICK, ANDOVER, ENGLAND

Good toilet facilities, but very expensive meals and coffee. Take your own food. K.W.

My funds were running low in Corfu and I was thinking of heading for home when I heard someone in a bar say they were desperate for a haircut. I'd never cut hair before, but I took a chance. It worked out OK (thank God) so I became a hairdresser charging 100 drachmas a trim. My new-found skill kept me on the island another month. JANET PAWLTER, CHELMSFORD, UK

Forget the Mediterranean coasts in July and August unless you enjoy fighting your way through millions of tourists and spending hours looking for rooms and then paying rip-off prices. Go to Scandinavia, Scotland or Timbuktu, but don't go to the Algarve, the Costa del Sol, the Riviera, or Greece, etc. If you *must*, be warned, take a tent. It will save you a hell of a lot of money and time.

ALAN THATCHER, NEW ZEALAND

Big supermarkets, department stores, etc., often have good, clean toilets with *hot water*! Don't hesitate to discreetly take advantage, though don't go as far as two guys I saw in the Corte Ingles store in Málaga, Spain. Rucksacks and gear all over the floor, dirty plates and clothes soaking in sinks, and them stark naked soaping themselves all over. Nuff to give us bums a bad name.

JERRY JAKES, PLYMOUTH, UK

Dehydrated packet food is light, doesn't take much space and is reasonably cheap. Just add water and heat for a while on a small gas burner. Use small single portion packets from camping shops. With bread it's a good meal. ANDREW PRICE, TORQUAY, UK

I think fresh food is always better than dehydrated food, but if you decide to go that route it would be cheaper to buy the food in large commercial packs like those used by restaurants. With a group of friends splitting costs you could save as much as 50%. K.W.

I agree totally with *Andrew Price* of *Torquay*. If you buy a packet of dried food (*Scout Shop*, £1.05), count up the gas (say 20p), plus bread and greens (reduced price goods) you have a good meal for under £2. Who wants to lug big commercial packs around if you are travelling on your lonesome? VINCE O'NEILL, CLYDEBANK, SCOTLAND

Eat muesli, the type without sugar that you buy from health stores. Pour milk or juice over it. A cupful at breakfast will keep your stomach happy until it's time for dinner. Also, it's extremely nutritious. PAUL HENNING, HILLSBOROUGH, FLORIDA, USA

I've made money on the road during the Christmas season by painting Christmas scenes on café windows with poster paints. It's easier to do than it sounds. Buy a kid's colouring book with Christmas scenes, rip out a suitable page and tape it on the *outside* of the window. Back inside you trace a black outline of the picture and colour it in. By the way, my present well-thumbed *Hitcher's Guide* has been heavily used despite the plain brown paper cover which reads *Terra Firma Classicus*. I can leave it lying around in hostels and no one so much as opens it, much less thinks of nicking it.

JOHN RIORDAN, VINDERUP, DENMARK

Liked John Riordan's tip about calling his copy of the Hitcher's Guide *Terra Firma Classicus*. Mine now reads the same with 'Essays on the Early Latin Classics' by K. W. Welsh. Nobody even touches it.

MARK NAISBITT, DARLINGTON, DURHAM, UK

To stop condensation in survival bags punch small holes on top: small enough to keep rain out, big enough to let air in.

PATRICK FITZGERALD, SOUTH LOPHAM, ENGLAND

You can get ample pickings from fish markets along the Mediterranean coast. Go to the quaysides after the stalls have closed down and you'll find plenty of fish lying around. OK, they may look dirty, but give them a quick wash in the sea and you've got yourself a free meal. JOHN TIGHT-FIST MORTON, AMERSHAM, ENGLAND

When short of cash anywhere in Scandinavia, a highly nutritious and affordable commodity is tinned mackerel or sardines. Also, many shops sell bananas and apples at a reduced price because they're bruised. Day-old bread can also be bought cheap.

JEFF MOORE, ENGLAND

When looking for a place to crash, keep an eye out for bandstands. They provide perfect cover. PHILIP ATTWOOL, ORPINGTON, KENT

About thieving in hostels: it's not just obvious valuables like cameras or radios that disappear. Some people will nick *anything*, like towels or clothing hanging on radiators to dry. Some hostels provide lockers but these shouldn't be regarded as absolutely secure. A girl with a set of skeleton keys was caught red-handed in a Munich hostel helping herself to cameras. Italy in particular seems to be bad for thieving so don't ever turn your back on your gear or it might not be there when you turn round again.

All French wine bottles with stars around the neck have deposits and can be cashed in. ALAN BARLOW, CHEADLE, UK

Nostalgia made me pick up your book and leaf through it. Without making a fetish of hitch-hiking I did it for a few years when I first arrived in England (from New Zealand) because I couldn't afford to travel there any other way and was quite literally dazzled by Europe.

What strikes me about your book is the emphasis given to your hitch-hiker being 'ripped off' by Europeans and yet you proceed to give space to people proclaiming ways and means of 'ripping off' these same Europeans. I don't in fact wish to be holier than thou, but I can't see anything admirable about defrauding foreign public transport systems; or exploiting the loneliness of migrant workers by abusing, in my view, their hospitality. I should think that the average hitch-hiker today is a good deal better off than the average migrant worker.

To say that your book is offensive is probably pitching it a little high as I'm sure a lot of the tips in it, places to stay, restaurants, etc., are very useful. It's just a great pity that you are encouraging a brand of rather unpleasant, parasitic travellers. H.D., LONDON

For one pound just nip into one of the following railway stations: Venice, Toulouse, Basel and Hamburg. You can take your pack into the cubicle and spend a good 15 minutes soaking.

MARI DOYLE, GODALMING, SURREY, UK

Need a bath or wash? Motorway service areas in France and Belgium have showers for truckers. Warm water and free. Desperate for a kip? You can crash in them, too, but don't make your bed until 11 p.m. when it's quiet. The cleaners will wake you at 6.

A. P. KIK, MIDDLESBROUGH, TEESSIDE, UK

Learn to play a musical instrument, such as the flute or trumpet, and busk your way around Europe. In Munich I played the flute for two hours one rainy night in the city centre and made £20!

PETE THE FREAK, LONDON

Travel soap, the concentrated detergent that you buy in tubes, is worth taking. Also soya mince in granules which can be bought at health food shops, and only needs water and a stock cube to flavour. It keeps well, and doesn't take up much space.

DOUGLAS NUNN, EDINBURGH, SCOTLAND

Wherever you stay remember to sleep with cash, travellers' cheques and passport inside your sleeping bag and not in your rucksack or trouser pockets, even if these are by the side of your bed. It's the best way to avoid being ripped off. RICHARD BARKER, LEEDS, UK

A chemist in E. Turkey recommended me to try black tea (no sugar), boiled eggs and peaches for a case of chronic diarrhoea. It worked wonders. Peaches contain pectin which settles your intestines and helps bind you up. ISABEL MORRIS, SUSSEX, UK

Toothache is a thing of the past. Many chemists sell special packs consisting of painkillers and hard wax to fill the hole. They work! On my last trip I plugged a bad tooth with one of these and it lasted for 5 days before I got to a dentist. Not a twinge!

EVAN M. JONES, SUNDERLAND, UK

The best and cheapest cure for sunburn is a tomato! Cut one in half and gently rub over affected area – it works wonders.

PAUL HINCKLEY, BIRMINGHAM, UK

If you use a left-luggage locker in a bus or railway station don't forget to ask what time it closes. I didn't and ended up almost freezing to death in a churchyard in Zurich.

DAVE LAIDLAW, EDINBURGH, SCOTLAND

It is worth noting that if you are a camper and have the bad luck to arrive at a site after 10.30 p.m., try in vain to raise the guardian from his slumbers, and have an urgent engagement compelling you to leave before 7 a.m., you are unfortunately unable to pay your night's sleep, hot shower and drinking water!

JULIAN CANN, LANCASTER, UK

FOOD: Instant mashed potato. Easy to make, you don't even need boiling water, possible to season with almost everything, and keeps forever.

SLEEPING OUT: From the south of Holland through to Belgium, France, Italy and Spain, you'll find tiny roadside chapels where you can sleep dry watched over by the Virgin Mary. Sometimes you'll find a candle or flowers in them; if you're very lucky, fresh fruit or bread. Remember though, they mark the spot where something has happened in the past, so don't leave a mess in them but rather a fresh bunch of field flowers in the morning, and apologize profusely if ever caught by worshippers!

health: When hitching down south in the hot sun, always protect your head and drink, drink, drink!

Get a tetanus jab before you set off. It's a bother having to get one for some reason (rusty fences, animal bites) when you're on the road, as it stiffens your leg and interferes with your walking.

ANNA LISS, AMSTERDAM

Sport stadiums are a good spot for roughing it. If you look closely, there will always be an easy way of entering. After all, how do the locals sneak in? GERARD VAN WEELE, PRETORIA, SOUTH AFRICA

Rules for hitchers

Patience isn't a virtue, it's a necessity

Flexibility is essential

Better hitch than never

Never take more than you need when living off the land

Always accept meals if offered: it might seem rude and can offend if you don't

If it's raining or cold, accept any ride at all

VINCENT CROOK, HUNTINGDON, ENGLAND

If you're dossing out in cold weather, you've got to stay as warm as possible. Most heat loss is through your head, so wear a warm hat. Wear as many layers as possible (including newspaper under your clothes) and zip your sleeping bag right up and put a survival bag over the top. Get down in a ditch or somewhere that isn't exposed, and keep your head covered all night. Booze and hash make you feel the cold worse.

Good luck!

SARAH MONROE, CITIZEN OF THE WORLD

6 · THE BRITISH ISLES AND IRELAND

Most Australians and North Americans use England as the base for their European trip for one of two reasons – one sound and the other unfashionable. The sound one is that if you can get the correct papers (see chapter on **Working in Europe**) you have more chance of working in England than in any other European country. The second reason, the unfashionable one, is that England remains in a manner of speaking the object of an Oedipus complex. It's the Motherland and even if most of her sons have long since left, via means of secession, revolution and diplomacy, or have just wandered off uninterested, she still offers the solution to the most puzzling question of all: where did our families come from?

Plenty of people find the answer a little disappointing. The tiny island crammed with over 56,000,000 people is hardly the green field of yesteryear which grandmothers and grandfathers back in the old ex-colonies talk about so fondly. England can present a mean face. Many of her people rarely see whatever green fields are left because they can't afford the train fare. Her gasping cities are grimed and blackened by industry. Too many Britons are literally fighting for survival amidst overpopulation. It's not unusual to find city children who have never seen a cow, much less the cow in its green field. And that sad observation is, of course, as true of New York as it is of London.

But have no fears. London is a great city and a load of fun, even if it never did swing with quite the momentum *Time* magazine would have liked to believe, or if Antonioni's *Blow-Up* turned out to be as much a blueprint for London to fashion itself by as London ever was an inspiration for the movie. But it's all fun if you can enter into London's idea of fun which, along with its dance clubs and cinemas and thousand lifestyles is also the place where you try to convince yourself that your 10 × 10, dirty-floored bed-sit is the next best thing to a palace (in London it is, unless Daddy is supplying you with a nice fat allowance each week); and that the solid wall of bus, lorry, car and train fumes which you breathe is as healthy as the next cubic mile of poison. And not to mention the noise. Take a walk in Hyde Park one day, around midday. Stroll a hundred yards in from Park Lane and stop amongst the green silence and listen to the dragon of sound flowing around beyond you.

But when you finally leave the big city, there *are* places you can go on that tiny island. One of them is northern Scotland, way up in the damp Highlands where you can walk for hours and never see a person and where the only noise is that of continuously falling rain – clean rain – and where the smell is of pure air and not of nearly pure carbon monoxide.

And then, just a little way across the water is Ireland, especially southern Ireland where the people are just a fraction wild and where the landscape is a fraction wilder, and nearly as beautiful as the people. Southern Ireland, like northern Scotland, is a place you can absorb, which you can let run over and into you – not like the Midlands in England where even though you may be living it up and enjoying yourself you have to keep it all at arm's distance in case it kills you with an overdose of claustrophobia.

But don't get me wrong. Dirty, cancerous, black-faced London is one of the most exciting and one of the greatest cities in the world and you may find that the diminishing green countryside of which it is capital harbours more than a handful of memories for you.

England

population	46,956,000
size	50,053 square miles
capital	London, population 6,767,000
government	Constitutional monarchy
religion	Protestant
language	English, with very little of anything else spoken or understood
currency	*Pound Sterling* (£) One *pound* equals 100 *pence*. Coins of 1, 2, 5, 10, 20, 50 *pence*, and £1. Notes of 5, 10, 20 and 50 *pounds*

England is stacked with sights to see. But where to start? From London, a trip into the south and south-east is a great introduction to Britain. Some 20 miles south of the capital is the town of **Westerham** and near it is **Chartwell**, the country home of the late Sir Winston Churchill (open March to October) where you can see a collection of the statesman's paintings, the study where he wrote many of his books, and amongst many other things, the famous wall which he built with his own hands and which looks exactly like a wall.

Heading further south is the village of **Battle**, one of the crucial landmarks of English history, for it was here that in 1066 the Battle of Hastings was fought. An abbey was built on the site by William the Conqueror after the conflict.

1. N.W. Highlands
2. Grampians
3. Southern Uplands
4. Cheviots
5. Pennines
6. Cambrian Mountains
7. Cotswolds
8. Dartmoor
9. Mourne Mountains
10. Wicklow Mountains
ATLANTIC OCEAN
NORTH SEA
IRISH SEA
SCOTLAND
N. IRELAND
EIRE
WALES
ENGLAND
FRANCE
CHANNEL ISLANDS
John o'Groats
Thurso
Ullapool
Gairloch
L. Maree
Loch Ness
Inverness
Balmoral
Braemar
Fort William
Mallaig
Ben Nevis
Glen Coe
Dundee
Loch Lomond
Crieff
Glasgow
Stirling
Edinburgh
Clyde
Abbotsford
Melrose
Ayr
Jedburgh
Selkirk
Alloway
Carter Bar
Dumfries
Hadrians Wall
Stranraer
Londonderry
Carrick Fergus
Larne
Donegal
Belfast
Sligo
Carlisle
Newcastle
Durham
Keswick
Lake Windermere
Haworth
Blackpool
Manchester
Liverpool
Grimsby
Lincoln
Galway
Liffey
Dublin
Conway
Chester
Trent
Caernarvon
Bangor
Nottingham
Limerick
Kilkenny
Adare
Cashel
Tralee
Clonmel
Killarney
Blarney
Cork
Harlech
Birmingham
Aberystwyth
Kenilworth
Warwick
Norwich
Stratford-upon-Avon
Cardigan
Abergavenny
Stow-on-the-Wold
Severn
St. David's
Carmarthen
Monmouth
Oxford
Thames
London
Cardiff
Bristol
Windsor
Bath
Westerham
Canterbury
Amesbury
Stonehenge
Dover
Winchester
Battle
Salisbury
Hastings
Portsmouth
Chichester
Brighton
Lands End
0 50 100 Miles
0 50 100 km

Canterbury, on the A2 if you're heading to Dover on your way to the Continent, is worth a stopover for its cathedral. It's a classic and famous as the scene of Thomas à Becket's assassination in 1170. The city's worth a look, too.

Heading west along the coast through **Rye, Winchelsea** and **Hastings**, and then along the South Downs through **Brighton** (one of England's most popular seaside resorts), you eventually come to the old walled cathedral city of **Chichester**. Next is **Portsmouth** where, in the naval dockyards, you can see Nelson's flagship the *Victory* in dry dock. You can board the 180-year-old ship and look over all its decks. Very near HMS *Victory* is the *Mary Rose*, Henry VIII's warship that sank in The Solent in 1545 and was raised in 1982. Also in Portsmouth is the house in which Charles Dickens was born. It is now a Dickens museum.

A little to the north is **Winchester**, ancient capital of Saxon England and famed for its superb Norman cathedral.

Salisbury is yet another city with an outstanding cathedral. It and the Close which sit on the river Avon make for one of the most often painted and photographed scenes in all the British Isles. By following the pretty road through Woodford, along the Avon, you join the A303 at **Amesbury** and you're within a couple of miles of **Stonehenge**, the mysterious stone circle possibly connected with the druids of ancient Britain. Stonehenge is worth the visit, but because of past vandalism the monument is roped off, and can only be seen from a distance. (If you want to wander among megalithic stones take the A345 north to **Marlborough** and then the A4 to **Avebury**, a picturesque village encircled by two sets of standing stones.) Also in this area (if you have spare cash for the admission fee) is **Longleat**, home of the Marquess of Bath, yet another titled gent of England who has to make ends meet by turning his family seat into a profit machine. The marquess does it by having lions and other wild animals roaming in his grounds.

While the quickest way to **Devon** and **Cornwall** is via the M5, the best way to hitch (and it's a most beautiful route) is via the A30. In **Exeter**, see the cathedral, ancient buildings and what is left of the Roman walls. The M5 and A38 trunk route will take you rapidly down to **Dartmoor** and Cornwall, but if you have time take the slower, northern route A39 through beautiful **Exmoor** and along the spectacular **north Devon coast**. Cornwall has an even grander coastline on the north, stormswept by the Atlantic, and a more peaceful but equally lovely subtropical south coast. While in the area don't miss **Glastonbury** (legend says that this is Avalon, resting place of King Arthur and the Knights of the Round Table). Visit Glastonbury Tor and see the ancient Zodiac pattern set out in the surrounding fields. The beautiful cathedral city of **Wells** is also worth a visit if time is plentiful, as is the **Cheddar Gorge**.

Whilst in the West Country, do not miss **Bristol**, England's greatest medieval port, with its wealth of history and interest. And see **Bath**, with its Georgian architecture and Roman baths, a city renowned for its spa where you can take the piping hot natural waters. From Bristol on the A466 you pass **Tintern Abbey** and then it's up the beautiful **Wye Valley** to **Monmouth**, passing the **Forest of Dean** which still has oaks planted by Nelson in case England ever ran out of wood for her ships!

Starting from London again, you can head out to **Windsor** with its huge castle which is still used by the British Royal Family (you can wander in the grounds and the castle when the Royal Family are not in residence) and nearby **Eton** – where there is a school on whose playing-fields (some people would like to believe) the battle of Waterloo was won.

Cambridge can now be reached by the M11 from London – named from a bridge which crossed the river Cam in ancient days – and since the 13th century one of England's great seats of learning. Peterhouse College was founded in 1284. Prominent Britons who were educated at Cambridge included Newton, Darwin, Macaulay, Milton and Byron. See King's College Chapel and, just beyond, a classic English scene, green slopes leading down to the river Cam where punters drift in peaceful waters.

From Cambridge it's the A11 to **Norwich** with its Castle Museum complex, cathedral, and medieval streets. It is also the gateway to the **Norfolk Broads**, a popular destination for boating holidays, and it's worth the effort to try hitching boats to picturesque Broads villages like **Potter Higham** or to the east coast resort of **Great Yarmouth**.

South-west sits another of England's great educational institutions and Cambridge's famous rival, **Oxford**, which has been a student centre since the 12th century. Have a look at Magdalene College and Merton College (founded in 1264), walk down the High Street (so *very* English), see Christ Church which was founded by Cardinal Wolsey and try and get in to see the very important Bodleian Library which contains 3,000,000 volumes and 50,000 manuscripts.

Continuing north on the A34 you are skirting the **Cotswolds**. Short detours will take you through quaint villages with such outlandish names as **Stow-on-the-Wold, Chipping Norton**, and **Shipton-under-Wychwood**, until you finally reach **Stratford-upon-Avon** – Shakespeare country. Shakespeare's birthplace is worth a visit but watch out for rip-offs. Anything around the main attractions will be expensive and street vendors should be avoided.

In the town (if you can fight your way through the busloads of tourists) you can see Shakespeare's birthplace, Anne Hathaway's Cottage (she was the playwright's wife), Hall's Croft where Shakespeare's daughter lived, and three miles out of town is Mary Arden's House – she having been his mother. All of these places are worth seeing if you're at all interested in Shakespeare or Elizabethan architecture. Two other places to visit are Holy Trinity Church where the man was baptized and where he is buried and the Royal Shakespeare Theatre where from March to January performances of his plays are held. Booking is usually well in advance if any well-known actor like Alan Howard is playing. To be thoroughly English in Stratford, try hiring a punt and poling yourself around the river for an hour or two.

Just eight miles north of Stratford is **Warwick**. The castle, though expensive, is in my opinion well worth the visit. Warwick Castle recently sold off many of its treasures so it might not be such good value for money as it was in the past. And five miles further north is **Kenilworth** with the ruins of the castle which Sir Walter Scott wrote about. The jousting grounds outside the walls make a nice camping area if you're at all romantically inclined.

From Kenilworth you are on your way to **Worcester** and **Hereford** and the remote and unspoiled Welsh Border country.

But you may prefer cities and their associations, in which case from Kenilworth you move on through **Coventry**. North of Coventry is **Birmingham**, England's second largest city. It's your classic urban jungle, but contains a wealth of theatres, galleries, museums, and nightlife. From Birmingham take the M6 and M54 to **Telford**, where Abraham Darby first used coke to smelt iron in the 1700s and so began the Industrial Revolution. The event is commemorated both by the preservation of the world's first iron bridge and in the **Ironbridge Museum**.

Back on the M6 your next stop could be **Stoke-on-Trent**, home of the pottery industry. Stoke, too, is something of an urban mess but the Wedgwood Village, Gladstone Pottery Museum, Chatterly Whitfield Mining Museum, and City Museum are worth a visit for those interested in such things. From Stoke the M6 goes north and the A54 leads to the **Peak District National Park**, containing lovely, lonely moorland and hills, and old mineworkings now open to visitors.

Peak District towns like the spa centre of **Buxton** are worth visiting. South to **Nottingham**, the city around which the legendary Robin Hood is said to have operated. There's scarcely anything left of Sherwood Forest these days, but if you care to travel out to

Edwinstowe you can see the church where they say Robin married the Maid Marian. Nottingham Castle, from where the Sheriff hatched his plans against Robin, is now a museum and art gallery. Two of England's oldest public inns are in Nottingham – the Trip to Jerusalem (12th century) and the Salutation Inn (13th century). Those interested in theatre should have a look at what is becoming one of England's best, the Nottingham Playhouse.

East from Nottingham, the A46 takes you to the underrated city of **Lincoln**, dominated by a spectacular cathedral which houses one of the few remaining copies of the Magna Carta, and surrounded by Roman and medieval remains.

The route north takes you through the ancient counties of **Yorkshire** via the M1, or **Lancashire** via the M6. Both are heavily industrialized but offer masses to see and do, excellent motorway links, lovely surrounding countryside and, above all, some of the friendliest folk in England.

The M1 will take you to **Sheffield**, a city famous for its steel and cutlery industry, sitting amongst the lovely rolling moorland of South Yorkshire. Among many sites of interest, visit the Worsburg Mill Museum at nearby **Barnsley**, and Abbeydale Industrial Hamlet, Conisbrough Castle and Roche Abbey near Sheffield itself. The M1 takes you through West Yorkshire to **Leeds** with its fine medieval remains and a certain lingering Victorian splendour. At **Halifax** (on the M62), set in the lovely Calderdale Valley, visit the nearby Shibden Hall Folk Museum. Camera freaks will enjoy **Bradford**'s National Photographic Museum. The A650 will take you north to **Keighley** and then to **Haworth**, famed as Brontë country, where the extraordinary Misses Brontë lived in the local parsonage and wrote *Jane Eyre* and *Wuthering Heights*.

North of Haworth you reach the **Yorkshire Dales National Park**. Hitching here may be slow, but it will be peaceful and you'll enjoy great scenery. Best route is the A684 through the heart of **Wensleydale**. If you have time, check out picturesque villages like **Sedburgh**, and **Hawes** with its **Hardrow Force** waterfall.

To the east lies **York**, which embraces nearly twenty centuries of history, and remains England's most medieval looking city. Four gates still open through the three miles of Roman walls which girdle the city. Visit the incredible York Minster which took 250 years to build and still dominates the city. Unfortunately it was badly damaged by a fire a few years ago, but restoration work has been carried out. Don't miss the 2500 square feet of stained glass which comprise the Great East Window. Photographers will love the lurching buildings in streets with names like Whip-ma-Whop-ma-Gate, the Shambles and Goodramgate. See also the Castle Folk Museum, housed in an old prison, which features reconstructions of York streets, and the National Railway Museum where you can board the *City of Truro*, the first 100-mph train in England. Also in York is the **Jorvik Centre**, a Viking city uncovered by archaeologists. Well worth a visit, but there is an entrance charge.

York is surrounded by some lovely old towns, including **Beverley** and **Harrogate**. South of Ripon stand the ruins of **Fountains Abbey**, once among the largest in Europe until Henry VIII fell out with the pope! Next try the **North Yorkshire Moors National Park**, where you can walk on rugged Rosedale moor or visit the ruins of **Rievaulx Abbey**. The abbey is set in a magical valley where you can wander in peace and forget the world a while. East again takes you to **Pickering** with its castle and the North York Moors Steam Railway, and then to the east coast.

Heading north on the A1(M) you reach **Durham**, an important medieval city dominated by a magnificent Norman cathedral. It also offers a host of other attractions for the culture vulture: a castle, the Gulbenkian Museum and the County Durham Open-air Museum.

North yet again on the same route and you find **Newcastle**, with its warm, hospitable people (Geordies), speaking the most unintelligible dialect in these islands! Asking directions *can* be confusing. You might get the reply: 'Gan reet doon this lonnen', i.e., 'Go straight down this long road'; or someone might say 'Howay, mar' which means 'Come on, friend'; 'nee' means 'no'; 'neet' is 'night'; 'summick' is 'something' and so on, everything spoken in a lovely deep lilting accent. The city displays a wealth of attractions: Roman sites, galleries and museums are all easily reached by a cheap and efficient metro system. Of special interest to culture addicts is the Shakespeare season at the Theatre Royal. The Royal Shakespeare Company takes all its productions (four each from Stratford and London) to Newcastle for two weeks each year in February and March).

Further north on the A68 and you are in wild Northumberland where the introspective can walk alone for hours in the **Border Forest Park** and the Cheviot Hills, before crossing into Scotland.

The other route is the M6. Follow this and you can choose from two of the most important cities in England, **Manchester** and **Liverpool**. Manchester is England's northern capital and it shows. Here you'll find excellent theatres (including the famed Royal Exchange), three first-rate galleries, famous libraries, and museums covering subjects like Air and Space, Industry and Transport, and the history of the city. The city also boasts splendid Victorian architecture, including a stupendous Gothic town hall.

Liverpool, too, has a lot to offer. Great buildings like the Town Hall and the Liver Building, the Walker and Sudley galleries and two superb cathedrals are worth visiting. No football freak should miss the opportunity of visiting the stadiums of Anfield (Liverpool) or Old Trafford (Manchester United) – an unforgettable experience.

South of Liverpool is **Chester**, a great town for a whiff of the Middle Ages. Two miles of walls enclose the city and its streets are riddled with architectural leftovers from medieval times. The city was known to the Romans as Deva and in the Grosvenor Museum is an excellent collection of Roman artifacts. The Chester Zoo is famous for its pachyderms.

Next stop is **Lancashire**. The M6 will take you to **Lancaster** and then to the **Trough of Bowland**, an area of moorland and forest, wild and lonely enough to blow the city grime from your hair.

North-west again and you're in the English Lake District, a spectacular and beautiful area, very easy to take after the smog and bustle of the great industrial cities of the Midlands. Here there is a lot to see in a small space and if you are an English literature fan a trip along the A591 will take you by **Lake Windermere** and along to the tiny village of **Grasmere**. It was here that William Wordsworth lived for many years in Dove Cottage which is now the Wordsworth Museum. The poet is buried in the Grasmere churchyard. After Wordsworth moved out of Dove Cottage, Thomas De Quincey (*Confessions of an Opium-eater*) – perhaps the first turned-on Englishman – set up house there for twenty years. **Keswick**, just a dozen miles further on, is a town in which Lamb, Keats, Shelley, Scott, Carlyle, Tennyson and Ruskin all stayed at one time or another.

The southern lakes get very crowded in summer, so if you want to experience a little of what Wordsworth was about then head for less visited northern lakes like **Crummock Water** and **Buttermere**. A word of warning: sea beaches in the area have been polluted by discharges from the Sellafield (Windscale) nuclear plant.

Carlisle, a city of 71,000, boasts an 11th-century cathedral, a museum featuring Roman remains, and a castle in which Mary, Queen of Scots was imprisoned in 1568. From here also, you can find your way out to **Hadrian's Wall** – although a better place to see it is near the village of **Wall** just north of **Hexham** which is on the A69.

North of the Roman wall and you've made Scotland.

● **Annual events and customs** England is a great country for celebrating its own history and customs. It seems that just about every village and town has some celebration some time in the year. For full details of what's happening where and when, you'll have to check at tourist offices, but here's a sample of the type of thing to look for: *Pancake Day Race* at Olney, Buckinghamshire, on Shrove Tuesday (February or early March). *Cheese Rolling* at Cheltenham, Gloucestershire, in June. *Brick Throwing and Rollingpin Throwing Contest* at Stroud, Gloucestershire, in July (this is an international event amongst Strouds from England, Australia, Canada, and the USA). *Shakespeare Birthday Celebrations* in April and *Shakespeare Season of Plays* at Stratford-upon-Avon, Warwickshire, from March to January. *Bottle Kicking and Hare Pie Scrambling* at Hallaton, Leicestershire, at Easter. *Manchester to Blackpool Veteran and Vintage Car Run*, in June. *Southport Music Festival* at Southport, Merseyside, in September and October. *Wassailing the Apple Trees* at Carhampton, Somerset, in January. *The Hot Penny Ceremony* at Honiton, Devon, in July. *Annual Carnival and Rolling of the Tar Barrels* in November, at Ottery St Mary, Devon. *East Kent Morris Men Hop Hoodening Tour of Kent*, in September. *Isle of Thanet Ploughing Match* at Margate, Kent, in October. *Bonfire Celebrations* at Lewes, East Sussex, in October. *The Appleby Horse Fair* at Appleby, Cumbria, in June, which is a gathering of gypsies for a horse fair. *Guy Fawkes Celebrations* all over the country in November. *Oxford v Cambridge University Boat Race* from Putney to Mortlake every March or early April.

● **Cigarettes** Tobacco and alcohol are tremendously expensive in England, so if you're a smoker and you're entering the country, don't forget to pick up your maximum quota of everything from duty-free shops on ships or at airports. These shops will have lists posted telling how much you are allowed to import free of tax.

● **Hitching in England** Hitching is OK except around the tremendously congested and built-up areas. It's best to clear those by bus or train – but one tip, when in big cities (and this applies all over Europe), is to go to the central markets very early in the morning, say 4 or 5 a.m., and try to pick up a ride from the scores of lorry drivers who have delivered produce. They'll be heading home in every direction. You can pick up some long, long lifts. Hitching is fast on the big highways. It's much, much slower on the small roads and considerably more pleasant, too. No hitching is permitted on motorways, only on entrance and exit roads, and at service stations – very fast.

● **The Islands of the British Isles** For information write to the following addresses:

Isle of Wight Southern Tourist Board, Town Hall Centre, Leigh Road, Eastleigh, Hampshire.

Jersey Tourist Information Bureau, Weighbridge, St Helier.
Guernsey Information Bureau, PO Box 23, St Peter Port.
Orkney Islands Tourist Association Information Centre, Kirkwall.
Isle of Skye Tourist Association at Meall House, Portree, Isle of Skye.
Isle of Man Tourist Board at 13 Victoria Street, Douglas.
Isle of Arran Tourist Information Centre, The Pier, Brodick, Isle of Arran, KA27 8AU, Scotland.

● **Money savers** If you anticipate doing a lot of sightseeing around the British Isles it's well worth buying special passes which are available. One allows you to visit all sites administered by the government including musts like the Tower of London and Stonehenge. Another, more expensive, gains you entry to all of those plus many of the National Trust properties around the country. The Open-to-View ticket is available from the Tourist Information Centre at Victoria Station Forecourt, and from the British Tourist Authority. For full information, write to the British tourist office in your country.

● **Van vagabonds** If you feel like hiring some wheels for a week or two on the road, the cheapest way you can do it is by hiring a Dormobile. In fact, if you can get together with, say, four other people you can probably drive cheaper than you can hitch! Considering that four bodies can sleep in the van (take it in turns to sleep in the annexe tent) and that you can cook on the premises, it works out pretty cheap. (Of course, if you're planning on van vagabonding for more than two weeks you're better off buying a beat-up heap so you can sell it later and recover some of the money.) The only problem with Dormobiles is that the minimum age for insurance is 25, 'unless people are able to transfer their own vehicle policy to the satisfaction of the Hire Operator'. (Whatever that means.)

London: where to sleep

The main areas for cheap accommodation in London are Earls Court, Notting Hill Gate, Kensington, Bayswater, Fulham, Shepherd's Bush and Willesden, and also those areas of North and South London which are easily reached by bus or the Underground ('tube').

If you've arrived unprepared, your best bet is to take instant accommodation for one or two days in any cheap B&B (bed and breakfast) hotel near your station, then find cheaper or more permanent accommodation by the following methods:

The **London Tourist Board and Convention Bureau** at 26 Grosvenor Gardens, SW1 (tel: 0171 730 3488) has a list of low-priced and emergency accommodation, which can be obtained on the spot or by writing in advance. They also publish *the* most valuable book on accommodation, entitled *Where to Stay in London*, which is updated every year, and can be obtained in most central London bookshops. This indispensable book gives details of all recommended hostels, flats (apartments), bed-sits, B&B houses and emergency accommodation in the city, including phone numbers and prices per night or week. An absolute must!

The **Tourist Information Centre** at Victoria Station Forecourt (tel: 0171 730 3488), open 9 a.m.–7 p.m., and the **British Travel Centre** at 12 Regent Street, W1 (tel: 0171 730 3400), open 9 a.m.–6.30 p.m., will supply information about hotel and student accommodation.

You could also try the **Piccadilly Advice Centre**, 100 Shaftesbury Avenue, W1 (tel: 0171 434 3773).

If you're in serious trouble, **Alone In London** (tel: 0171 278 4224) will help with emergency shelter, longer accommodation, and even emotional problems relating to homelessness.

For serious room-hunting, and particularly if you intend to stay in London for any length of time, it's worth checking out the 'Accommodation' lists in *Time Out* and *City Limits* magazines, or the London *Evening Standard*.

Beds in the hostels run by the Youth Hostels Association (England and Wales) cost £6–£18 for B&B – usually towards the upper end of the price scale in London. You won't get past the door without a Hostelling International membership card. For a full list of English and Welsh hostels, contact the Head Office of the Youth Hostels Association (England and Wales) at Trevelyan House, 8 St Stephen's Hill, St Albans, Hertfordshire AL1 2DY (tel: 01727 845047), or visit the YHA shop in London (see Addresses below).

Remember, also, to check noticeboards in the windows of shops in the area you want.

It's also worth buying a copy of *The A to Z Atlas of London* published by Geographers. This 270-page book is indispensable for finding your way around the 30,000-odd streets of London and its environs. The free Underground map supplied at tube stations is the weapon needed to tackle the 250 or more Underground stops.

Hostelling International Hostels:

City of London Hostel, 36 Carter Lane (tel: 0171 236 4965).
Earls Court Hostel, 38 Bolton Gardens (tel: 0171 373 7083).
Hampstead Heath Hostel, 4 Wellgarth Road (tel: 0181 458 9054).
Highgate Hostel, Highgate West Hill, Highgate (tel: 0181 340 1831).
King George VI Memorial Hostel, Holland House, Holland Walk, Kensington (tel: 0171 937 0748).
Rotherhithe Hostel, Salter Road (tel: 0171 232 2114).
Oxford Street Hostel, 14 Noel Street (tel: 0171 734 1618).

Other hostels/student accommodation:

The Salvation Army Hostel for Men, 18 Gt Peter Street, SW1 (tel: 0171 222 1546) and at 259 Waterloo Road, SE1 (tel: 0171 928 4591).
The Salvation Army Hostel for Women (Hopetown), 60 Old Montague Street, London E1 (tel: 0171 247 1004).
Superior Hotel, 191 Queens Gate, London SW7 (tel: 0171 584 3019). Also known as The Albert Hotel. 'Run by young people for young people.' Good facilities. Great location.
Talbot Hotel, Talbot Square (tel: 0171 402 7202).
International Student House, 229 Great Portland Street (tel: 0171 631 3223).
Alliance Club, Newington Green (tel: 0171 226 6085). Men only.
Budget Hotel, 17 Courtfield Gardens, Earls Court, London SW5 (tel: 0171 370 3991). Near Earls Court station. Single rooms, some with own bathroom.
YWCA and **YMCA** For complete information write to YWCA, National Offices, 52 Cornmarket Street, Oxford, OX1 38J (tel: 01865 726110) or to YMCA, YMCA National Council, 640 Forest Road, E17 3DZ (tel: 0181 520 5599). There are YWCA hostels at:
Central Club, 16 Great Russell Street, London WC1 (tel: 0171 580 4827).
Alexandra Residential Club, 4 Lloyd Street, London WC1 (tel: 0171 278 8625); also at 2 Devonshire Street, London W1 (tel: 0171 580 5323); and at 2 Weymouth Street, London W1 (tel: 0171 580 6011).
Ashley House, 14 Endsleigh Gardens, London WC1 (tel: 0171 387 3378).
Victoria, 32 Warwick Square, London SW1 (tel: 0171 834 1096)
Park House, 227 Earls Court Road, London SW5 (tel: 0171 373 2851).

There are YMCA hostels at:
YMCA, 112 Great Russell Street, London WC1 (tel: 0171 636 8616).

The Barbican YMCA, Fann Street, London EC2 (tel: 0171 628 0697).
The German YMCA, Lancaster Hall Hotel, 35 Craven Terrace, London W2 (tel: 0171 723 9276).
The Indian Student YMCA, 41 Fitzroy Square, London W1 (tel: 0171 387 0411).
Waltham Forest YMCA, 642 Forest Road, London E17 (tel: 0181 520 0931).
King George's House YMCA, Stockwell Road, London SW9 (tel: 0171 274 7861).
Hornsey YMCA, 184 Tottenham Lane, London N8 (tel: 0181 340 2345).
Wimbledon YMCA, 200 The Broadway, London SW19 (tel: 0181 542 9055).

Doubles for under £35 are rare in London's hotels, as are singles for under £25. Try the following:

Kensbridge Hotel, 31 Elvaston Place (tel: 0171 589 6265).
Royal Hotel, Woburn Place (tel: 0171 636 8401).
Oxford Hotel, 11 Craven Terrace (tel: 0171 262 9608).
Hotel Melita, 76 Fordwych Road (tel: 0181 452 1583).
Howard Hotel, 64 Princes Square (tel: 0171 727 6062).

Write to the **International Students House**, 229 Great Portland Street, London W1 (tel: 0171 631 3223), who have rooms at their residences in Great Portland Street and 10 York Terrace East, NW1. Also **London Accommodation Centre**, 22 Wardour Street, W1 (tel: 0171 287 6315).

If you have your own tent, try **Hackney Camping**, Millfields Road (tel: 0181 985 7656). £5 per night (tent included). Open mid June–late Aug. Take the Underground to Liverpool Street, then bus 22A to Mandeville Street. The site is on the other side of the canal. Also the **Lee Valley Campsite**, Sewarstone Road, Chingford (tel: 0181 529 5698). £5.50 per person (tent included). Open Easter–Oct. Underground to Walthamstow Central, then bus 505 or 215. **Tent City**, Old Oak Common Lane, East Acton (tel: 0181 310 2233) has 400 beds in huge tents, as well as camping space. £5.50 per person. Free baggage storage, which can save you a fair bit of cash in London. Underground to East Acton, then bus 12 or 52A.

For sleeping rough, there are plenty of hide-away spots in Hyde Park or Kensington Gardens. The police make checks, but these are very big parks. Also, the city is dotted with greens and churchyards (as are most big cities) where you can kip down if you're quick enough getting out of sight and quiet enough after you do.

MIND (the national mental health charity) says that up to 40% of people roughing it in London are schizophrenia sufferers who have no one to care for them and nowhere to go. They are victims of a government policy to close down mental hospitals. They are on the streets because the street is their only home. If you are sleeping rough you may come in contact with them.

The *Oxford Dictionary* definition of schizophrenia is: 'Mental disease marked by disconnection between thoughts, feelings and actions'. The word means 'splitting of the mind'. Scribner's *New American Pocket Medical Dictionary* says that the three elements common to all cases of the disease are 'a shallowness of emotional life; an inappropriateness of emotion; unrealistic thinking'.

Schizophrenia exhibits itself in different forms: some sufferers are withdrawn, cannot respond emotionally or practically to a situation; some hallucinate and suffer delusions of persecution or grandeur; some will not talk and will sit or stand in a position for a long time and then perhaps do something completely unpredictable like wave their arms about or scream.

If you run into these people when you are dossing out remember that they are ill, not evil. Sometimes their behaviour can be disturbing so you may prefer to move on, but as a group they are no more violent than any other. So don't be frightened. Try and spend a few minutes with them, share a sandwich, pass on an old magazine – or just give them a kind word. (*Special thanks to Jim Condron of Hamilton, Scotland, for prompting me to write a few words about this problem K.W.*)

● **Warning!** Travellers arriving at Victoria Station by train, *avoid the hostel agents*. Some of these touts try to con you into vans, then drive you off to some woe-begotten flea-pit. If you need help, ask the Tourist Information Centre staff at Victoria. They dress in uniforms, but they're OK people. They have lists of cheap, decent places to stay. Just insist that you want somewhere *really* cheap. The tout warning applies to Liverpool Street, too, but that station has no TIC office.

London: where to eat

A good filling meal in London can still be had as cheaply as anywhere in Europe – as long as you're careful and avoid the obvious tourist restaurants. The usual chain restaurants abound – Wimpy,

McDonald's, Burger King, Pizzaland or Pizza Hut (neither of which should be confused with places like Pizza Express, which are upmarket and expensive) and Kentucky Fried Chicken. But workers' cafés and pubs – and there are plenty of them – are without doubt the cheapest places to eat decent food, if you avoid 'tourist' pubs. A good café or pub meal can still be bought for between £3 and £5 – and if you're *really* living on the cheap, remember that cafés, pubs and sandwich bars offer a wide range of nutritious sandwiches for slightly under or well over £1, depending on the filling.

In all big cities, wherever you find a big concentration of offices and office workers, you find a proliferation of cheap eating spots. In London, in these areas, you can eat as cheaply as anywhere in Europe. Examples:

The Stockpots: There are three of these in London and they offer very good food at a very good price. Addresses are: 40 Panton Street, SW1; 273 King's Road, SW3 and 6 Basil Street, SW3. **The Chelsea Kitchen** at 98 King's Road, SW3, is run by the same people.

Spreads Sandwich Bar & Restaurant at No. 15 and the **Brasilia Café** at No. 7 are only two of the half dozen excellent cheap sit-down or take-away food places in the lively New Row, just off St Martin's Lane, where Charing Cross Road runs into Trafalgar Square, WC2.

Gaby's Continental Deli and Sandwich Bar at the corner of St Martin's Court and Charing Cross Road remains one of the West End's oldest and cheapest good restaurants (café prices) – and it's surrounded by the take-away sandwich bars that are a hallmark of the West End and City in general.

The Round Table in St Martin's Court itself (see above) remains a good 'old-fashioned' pub amidst the modernist glitter of this part of the West End, as is **The Green Man & French Horn** in St Martin's Lane.

Valoti Restaurant at 154 Shaftesbury Avenue, off Cambridge Circus, is another long-established family-run restaurant where the meals are cheap and good. Opposite the MGM cinema.

The **New Piccadilly Restaurant** is at 8 Denman Street, W1, where Shaftesbury Avenue meets Piccadilly Circus. Remarkably, it survives in a street filled with high-priced 'tourist' restaurants – doubtless because it still serves great food at café prices.

Jimmy's Café is an odd name for the cheapest Greek restaurant in Soho (though most 'Greek' dishes are served with chips!), located on the corner of Frith and Old Compton Street, W1.

Pho (Saint Michel) Snack Bar at the Wardour Street end of Lisle

Street, in Chinatown, WC2, serves cheap take-away or sit-down meals. It's located between the equally cheap **Hung Ky** Vietnamese and Chinese take-away and the lively **Falcon Pub**, which also serves cheap food in a colourful atmosphere.

Chan May Mai at 25 Lisle Street is basic, cheap and popular with local Chinese. A few doors up is the **Man Lee Hong**, serving the cheapest Chinese in town. All of Chinatown is worth checking out for good, cheap food in a lively, exotic area.

Ludgate Restaurant & Sandwich Bar in New Bridge Street, at Ludgate Circus, EC4, has survived the exodus of journalists from Fleet Street and still serves excellent cheap meals.

Mick's Café at 148 Fleet Street has also survived the loss of its printer/journalist clientele and remains rough-and-ready and cheap, as do most of the old pubs in this former 'street of sin'.

Jones Dairy at 24 Tudor Street (off Whitefriars Street, facing Mick's Café) is a fancy name for a café that serves good old British 'tucker' at knock-down prices.

New vegetarian restaurants are springing up all the time, but the best and most reasonable is the **Cranks Health Food Restaurant** chain, which has restaurants at 8 Marshall Street, W1; 17–18 Great Newport Street, W1; 9–11 Tottenham Street, W1 (not Tottenham Court Road!); and 11 The Market (Piazza), Covent Garden.

Most of the workers' cafés (not to be confused with the newly fashionable 'café-brasseries', which look expensive, and are!) in the West End, the City, and especially the outlying areas of North and South London still serve substantial meals for under £5. A feed of take-away fish'n'chips can be had nearly anywhere in London (apart from the tourist traps) for about £2.90, while Greek and Chinese take-aways are now almost as popular for their exceptional value.

There are thousands of pubs in London and a fair proportion of them sell food of one kind or another at lunchtime. Some might only offer snacks like sandwiches or sausages, others put on proper hot meals. The point is that pub food offers one of the best deals to be had in London. Check with people in your area for the pubs which offer the best value for money.

If you take a bed-sit and decide to do your own cooking, the cheapest places to buy supplies are in major supermarkets, such as Sainsbury's, Tesco's and Budgen's. The small 'corner' shops, which still survive, are more personal, but more expensive.

London: what to see and do

TOWER OF LONDON at Tower Hill. Entrance charge. Great if you're a history fan. Ten centuries of England staring you right in the face. See the Crown Jewels (extra charge), the armoury, the rooms where Raleigh was imprisoned, the site of the old chopping block, and lots more.

If you pay you can also explore the hydraulic works inside Tower Bridge (with museum, illustrated history, and magnificent views of London and the river Thames). By crossing the bridge itself (Tower Bridge Road) and entering Symon's Wharf, or by taking a cheap boat trip from Tower Dock, you can visit HMS *Belfast*, the famous Second World War battle cruiser.

ST KATHERINE'S DOCKS beside the Tower of London first harboured ships in 1827. The docks are now restored, and in them you can see the Maritime Trust Collection of Historic Ships. Particularly beautiful is the three-masted schooner *Kathleen and May*, built in 1900. Across the bridge is Butler's Wharf and the Design Museum.

THE MONUMENT in Monument Street. Cheapest way to get a good view of London. The column, which is 202 feet high and was erected the same number of feet from where the Great Fire of London started in Pudding Lane in 1666, was designed by Wren. You can climb to the top for a small fee.

ST PAUL'S CATHEDRAL on Ludgate Hill. Costs to enter, and more to go into the upper galleries. Worth paying, though, because from the Golden Ball on the top (only one person can enter the ball at a time) you get a great view. You can also look straight down through a glass panel a couple of hundred feet to the cathedral floor. All sorts of people buried in the crypt.

THE BARBICAN Culture vultures and architecture freaks will be in their element at the Barbican Centre. Officially opened in 1982, this £150 million arts and conference complex boasts a concert hall (home of the London Symphony Orchestra), a theatre (London base for the Royal Shakespeare Company), three cinemas, an art gallery geared to visiting exhibitions, a library, two exhibition halls and a massive conference area. Next door to the Centre is the Guildhall School of Music and Drama. Watch the press for details of special events at the Centre.

WESTMINSTER ABBEY in Parliament Square. Beautiful building

founded in 1042 and serving as a burial ground for some of England's greatest. Poetry fans should look over Poets' Corner.

SPEAKERS' CORNER at Hyde Park, Marble Arch. Free. Any fine Sunday from around 2 p.m. Great place to let off steam, meet people, hear some really crazy people sounding off and (occasionally) to hear some clever speeches. Heckling is the order of the day.

BRITISH MUSEUM in Great Russell Street. A complete display of just about anything you're interested in. This must be the most complete summing up of the human race in existence.

VICTORIA & ALBERT MUSEUM, NATURAL HISTORY MUSEUM, SCIENCE AND GEOLOGICAL MUSEUMS All are accessible via a series of clearly marked underground tunnels spreading out from South Kensington Underground station. Art, architecture, furniture, fashions, fossils, reconstructed dinosaurs, minerals, steam engines and space craft – if it isn't at the British Museum, it will be in one of these museums, all conveniently grouped together. Give at least a day to cover them all – but check opening and closing times, which can vary. All charge for admission.

MUSEUM OF LONDON at London Wall, EC2, tells the story of London from prehistoric times until today. Closed Mondays.

NATIONAL GALLERY in Trafalgar Square. Great collection. Just about everyone is represented. Fantastic collection of Rembrandt. And just around the corner, in Charing Cross Road, is the National Portrait Gallery.

TATE GALLERY on Millbank. Modern stuff, mostly. Superb collection of Blakes and The Clore Gallery housing Turners. Good retrospective exhibitions every now and again (which usually cost, but are worth it).

CHURCHILL'S CABINET ROOMS near Horseguards. Great visit for modern history freaks. See the underground 'bunker' from which Churchill directed the Second World War. Everything is exactly as it was when he left it in 1945. The map room, the cabinet room, his bedroom, etc.

MADAME TUSSAUD'S in Marylebone Road (Baker Street Underground). Costs to get in; admission fee includes 'Spirit of London' ride. Huge display of waxwork figures, historical and contemporary, goodies and baddies. Some of the politicians seem more business-like in wax than they act in real life. Downstairs is the Chamber of Horrors. The waxworks were started when Madame Tussaud arrived in London in 1802 with models of the heads of guillotined victims of the French Revolution.

LONDON PLANETARIUM next door to Tussaud's in Marylebone Road. Admission charge. If you're an Arthur C. Clarke fan, it's great stuff. Also LASERIUM – rock and pop.

HOUSES OF PARLIAMENT by Westminster Bridge. The public is permitted to sit in on debates at the House of Commons. If you are doubtful about the efficacy of the English political system, you should try to listen to at least one debate. Queue at St Stephen's Entrance.

THE CENTRAL CRIMINAL COURT (known as the Old Bailey) in Newgate Street, on the site of the famous Old Newgate Prison. Free entry to the public galleries to hear court in session. Best to arrive around 10 a.m. No cameras. No children.

COVENT GARDEN the site of the vegetable and flower market which served central London's needs from the 17th century until the 1970s, is now a tourist shopping area (with prices to match) housed within the original, restored halls. But, you don't have to spend money. Wander around and absorb the atmosphere. See the London Transport Museum, lodged within the old Flower Market (fee); St Paul's church in the Piazza, designed by Inigo Jones, completed in 1633, and featured in *My Fair Lady*; the craft stalls in the North Hall; and best of all, the truly amazing London buskers (musicians, singers, magicians, acrobats, comedians, escape artists) who offer you entertainment every day (but particularly on Sunday mornings) for whatever small coin you care to throw their way.

THEATRE MUSEUM in the old Flower Market, Covent Garden. This is the National Museum of the performing arts in Britain.

BUCKINGHAM PALACE the Mall. Now open to the public. Official London home of Her Majesty the Queen. (She has several other homes, as well.) See the Changing of the Guard at 11.30 a.m. (Alternate days in winter.)

FREE BAND CONCERTS at Victoria Embankment Gardens, St James's Park and Regent's Park. Around 12.30 p.m. in summer. They've never heard of an electric guitar, but they try hard. For full details of a variety of free or nearly free outdoor entertainment, including summer Shakespeare productions in Regent's Park, ring the London Tourist Board and Convention Bureau (tel: 0171 730 3488).

TRAFALGAR SQUARE Good place to rest your aching feet. Site of the Nelson Monument (more widely known as Nelson's Column) and always filled with people who loll around the two ornamental fountains or feed the thousands of pigeons circling overhead. On one side of the square is ST MARTIN-IN-THE-FIELDS, the famous church with a crypt in which derelicts were once looked after, but which now houses a candlelit, self-service restaurant and wine bar (check the stone flags of the floor!), a Visitors' Centre and bookshop, and the London Brass-Rubbing Centre. Off another side of the square is the entrance to the MALL, which leads to BUCKINGHAM PALACE. Opposite the NATIONAL GALLERY is WHITEHALL, maybe *the* most famous street in the world; it leads down past GREAT SCOTLAND YARD, the ADMIRALTY, the WAR OFFICE, HORSEGUARDS (always guarded by two mounted members of the colourful Household Cavalry), and DOWNING STREET, containing the official residences of the Prime Minister and the Chancellor of the Exchequer. Keep walking past the Ministry of Defence and you will soon come to the CENOTAPH, which soars up from Whitehall, and PARLIAMENT SQUARE, where you will find BIG BEN, the HOUSES OF PARLIAMENT, WESTMINSTER ABBEY and the GUILDHALL. Now you know why it's considered to be one of *the* great streets in the world!

PICCADILLY CIRCUS with the statue of Eros in the centre, is considered to be the centre of London's West End and *the* place to watch people go by. The Circus itself is notable for the TROCADERO and LONDON PAVILION. The former is an enormous 'leisure' complex that includes touristy shops, THE GUINNESS WORLD OF RECORDS exhibition, the LONDON EXPERIENCE exhibition (admission charges for both), and FOOD STREET, in the basement, where you can buy reasonably priced, self-service, 'fast' oriental food (Malaysian, Chinese, Japanese, Thai, etc.). The latter is a glittering shopping complex that includes Rock Circus ('bionic performances of the Immortals of Rock') and the Rock Island Diner, which is a surprisingly cheap 'American'-style restaurant. You'll either love it or hate it!

Radiating out from Piccadilly Circus like the spokes of a wheel are PICCADILLY, which contains the famous Hatchards bookshop, the Fortnum & Mason store, with its liveried doormen and (on occasion) horse-drawn carriage out front, and the Ritz hotel; REGENT STREET, a wide boulevard of elegant architecture, shops and travel companies, leading up to OXFORD CIRCUS; the short, busy thoroughfares, LOWER REGENT STREET and the HAYMARKET, contain theatres, cinemas and cheap eateries and both lead down towards Trafalgar Square (see above); SHAFTESBURY AVENUE, known as the 'theatre' avenue, which, apart from its theatres and restaurants, has SOHO on one side and CHINATOWN on the other; and finally, the short, frantically busy COVENTRY STREET, which leads into:

LEICESTER SQUARE Not to be missed – particularly in the evening! If Piccadilly Circus (see above) is the centre of London's West End by day, Leicester Square is its hub when darkness falls. The equivalent of New York's Times Square, but without quite so much sleaze (watch out for pickpockets, teenage drug-dealers and alcoholics, though). Leicester Square is bounded on three sides by London's most frequented and expensive cinemas, and is otherwise packed with pubs, clubs, discos and restaurants. At the end of Coventry Street is the HIPPODROME, one of the city's most famous nightclubs.

SOUTH BANK On the south bank of the Thames River (Waterloo Underground or take the spectacular walk across Charing Cross Bridge), a sprawling complex houses the ROYAL FESTIVAL HALL (often free concerts in the busy foyer); the QUEEN ELIZABETH HALL and the PURCELL ROOM (classical concerts and recitals); the HAYWARD GALLERY, for modern art; the NATIONAL THEATRE, which contains the Olivier Theatre, the Lyttleton Theatre and the Cottesloe Theatre and often has free entertainment in its various lobbies; and maybe most fun of all, the NATIONAL FILM THEATRE, with its two cinemas, restaurant, bar, bookshops and, particularly, MOMI, or the MUSEUM OF THE MOVING IMAGE, which is a spectacular exhibition on the history of the cinema. It costs, but it's worth it.

MUSIC Every kind of music imaginable is available in London. Best for their music listings are the magazines *Time Out* and *City Limits*. London is the dance capital of the world. Every weekend top DJs play to huge crowds at clubs like THE MINISTRY OF SOUND (103 Gaunt Street; Underground: Elephant & Castle) and CLUB UK (Buckhold Road, nr Wandsworth station). Entry is pricey and most clubs have strict dress codes – ring for details before you go – but the London club scene will be the highlight of any trip to Europe.

For opera and ballet try the ROYAL OPERA HOUSE (cheap seats in the gallery) in Bow Street (Covent Garden Underground); the COLISEUM in St Martin's Lane (Charing Cross Underground), or the SADLER'S WELLS THEATRE in Rosebery Avenue, Islington (Angel Underground). Classical concerts are given at the ROYAL FESTIVAL

HALL (which often has free performances in the foyer, notably on weekends) on the South Bank (Waterloo Underground or walk across Charing Cross Bridge); the ROYAL ALBERT HALL (where the famous 'Proms' take place and which also stages pop concerts) in Kensington Gore (nearest Underground is Kensington High Street, though lots of buses stop on the doorstep); and the relatively new BARBICAN ARTS CENTRE at the Barbican. Best for rock, country and pop are the ROCK GARDEN, the Piazza, (Covent Garden Underground); the MARQUEE at 105 Charing Cross Road (Tottenham Court Road Underground); and for Country and Western buffs, the MEAN FIDDLER in the High Street, Harlesden (Willesden Junction Underground). No music lover should miss a visit to the VIRGIN MEGASTORE (Oxford Street, at Tottenham Court Road Underground), where, at least once or twice a week, rock groups go to sign records or make pop videos. This record store is so big you could spend a whole day there (which is why it has a restaurant upstairs) and further along Oxford Street, heading towards Oxford Circus, is its hottest competitor, HMV RECORDS, where pop 'happenings' also take place every week.

MARKETS: PORTOBELLO ROAD (go to Notting Hill Gate and ask from there). Antiques one end, then fruit and vegetables beyond that. Most people stop there. Keep walking. The junk section beyond is where you find the bargains. Good place to pick up secondhand clothes and shoes if you need them. Don't take the first price. Never buy in a shop, even in the 'gear' shops. It's cheaper on the street. Best day, Saturday – or Friday morning if you just want to check the junk section. PETTICOAT LANE, Middlesex Street, E1. Huge outdoor market every Sunday morning. OK and worth seeing but packed with tourists. For a better market continue up Bishopsgate to BRICK LANE. Nearby are endless streets and alleys packed with junk of every description. Sundays only. Closes at 1 p.m. Up in this area you'll be pleased to know you're in Jack the Ripper land. Check London Tourist Board and Convention Bureau for free guides to London's markets.

SOHO is, more or less, the area bounded by Charing Cross Road, Oxford Street, Wardour Street and Shaftesbury Avenue. It was once London's 'red light' district, its square mile of sin, but has been cleaned up in the past few years. While it still has its fair share of fun parlours, strip joints, blue-movie houses and prostitutes (most of them to be found at the crossroads of Brewer Street, Rupert Street and Walker's Court), it is still a colourful mixture of cheap cafés, expensive restaurants, good pubs, and interesting locals. CHINA-

TOWN, which remains authentically Chinese (with many excellent and often cheap Chinese restaurants, see **Where to eat**) is just the other side of Shaftesbury Avenue.

THEATRES Sitting in the gods (the gallery) is usually the cheapest way to view London theatre, though some theatres have standing room for students. The National, the Aldwych, the RSC at the Barbican, and the Royal Court are four which consistently present good plays with good actors. At the Theatre Ticket Booth in Leicester Square you can buy 'leftover' theatre tickets at half-price (plus a small service charge) *on the day of the performance*. The Booth is open from Monday through Saturday from 12–2 p.m. for matinée performances and from 2.30–6.30 p.m. for evening performances. Check *Time Out* for details of lunchtime and fringe theatre.

PUBS Most of the London pubs are now open all day, every day except Sunday (when they close for the afternoon) but some still stick to the old opening times of 11 a.m.–3 p.m., and 5.30–11 p.m. No list could begin to do justice to the huge variety of London pubs, but try **Kings Arms**, Shepherd Market, W1; **The Shepherd's Head**, Carnaby Street, W1; **Museum Tavern** (opposite the British Museum), 49 Great Russell Street, WC1; or any of the 'older' pubs in Soho, Covent Garden or St Martin's Lane. Slightly further out, you can't go wrong with **Dickens Inn**, St Katherine's Docks, E1; **The City Barge** at 27 Strand-on-the-Green, Chiswick, W4; **Prospect of Whitby** at 57 Wapping Wall, E1; **Sun in Splendour** at 7 Portobello Road, W11; **Dirty Dick's**, at the top of Petticoat Lane, or most of the pubs of Islington or historic Hampstead, NW3. Back in town, an absolute must is the **Ye Olde Cheshire Cheese** in Fleet Street or the **Black Friars** at Blackfriars Underground station, both in EC1. These and other 'Grub Street' pubs are liveliest during the working week, even though the journalists no longer work and play there.

CINEMAS West End prices are now out of this world – about £7 to £9 for a decent seat, though the prices are reduced all day Monday and first performance weekdays, and the Prince Charles in Leicester Place only charges £1.20! The 'independent' cinemas just outside the West End, therefore easy to get to, are the **Screen on the Green** (Angel Underground), the **Screen on the Hill** (Belsize Park Underground), the **Everyman** (Hampstead Underground), the **Ritzy** (Brixton Underground) and the **Scala** (King's Cross). All of these are not only much cheaper, but offer terrific double bills and special all-night programmes where the audience is often as entertaining as the movies – particularly at the **Scala**! The most comprehensive guides to these cinemas are in the magazines *Time Out* and *City Limits*.

RIVER TRIP A nice (if expensive) way of seeing certain sights is by river launch up or down the Thames, from Westminster or Charing Cross piers. Head eastwards for the Tower of London and, further on, the historic town of Greenwich (The Royal Naval College, the Observatory, Chichester's *Gypsy Moth*, and the *Cutty Sark*), and the spectacular Thames Barrier; or go west to Kew (for Kew Gardens, Richmond and Hampton Court). Water buses and narrow-boat tours also operate on the REGENT'S CANAL but since their times and dates of operation are so erratic, it's best to check them out through the tourist offices or *Time Out* and *City Limits*.

LONDON ZOO A great collection and well worth the visit – if you can afford it. One interesting feature is the Moonlight Hall where night and day are reversed so that you can see nocturnal animals and birds alert and awake in the middle of the day. For an extra charge you can see the excellent London Zoo Aquarium complete with man-eating sharks, stingrays and what-have-you's. At Regent's Park, NW1 (Camden Town Underground, then up Parkway).

Meetings, discussions, ins and outs of what's happening, etc.

Several publications tell you all you need to know. The best magazines for a complete rundown of everything happening in London in just about every field of interest are *Time Out* and *City Limits*. Art, music, cinema (including every film on in London that week), demonstrations – you name it, these magazines have got it. Indispensable, especially if you're only in town a short time.

Other publications which really give value for money are Nicholson's *London Guide Book* which includes city maps, Underground maps, bus routes, cheap eating, cheap sleeping and lots more. *Alternative London*, edited by Georganne Downes, is far and away the best book ever written on how to live in London. Downes examines every aspect of living in the big city, starting with getting somewhere to live and giving hints on how to furnish it cheaply, then moving on through food cults, London markets, the mystical scene, sex, drugs, and on and on for a couple of hundred pages. If you can't cut your living costs by a third after studying Downes' book (and this one!) you can count yourself stupid.

Project London was a dropout booklet distributed free in 1969. It was banned because of some of the frankly silly and dangerous crap it contained. It remains, though, one of the most fascinating documents ever written on how to survive in a big city for practically nothing. Richard Neville's book, *Playpower* (Paladin), reprints much of the booklet.

Free newspapers and magazines are given away at the entrances of many Underground stations. Most are aimed at secretaries seeking work, but they contain good general articles and information. Daily newspapers can be collected free and often in mint condition from the rubbish bins in the stations or the seats of the trains. Cinemas and bookshops also offer free magazines relating to their respective subjects.

Problems

If you strike hard times in London, there are plenty of organizations which will help you out. **Alone in London** (tel: 0171 278 4224), also mentioned under **Where to sleep**, specializes in the problems of young people and, if they can't help you themselves, will put you in touch with someone who can.

The Samaritans offer 'confidential ears and advice' to anyone who is lonely, depressed or in trouble. Open 24 hours a day at 46 Marshall Street, W1 (tel: 0171 734 2800). **Release** (tel: 0171 377 5905) provides free legal advice to people who have been arrested. They specialize in drugs and have a 24-hour telephone service. The **London Rape Crisis Centre** (tel: 0171 837 1600) has a telephone line open 24 hours a day, every day, with confidential advice. **The Terrence Higgins Trust** (tel: 0171 242 1010), open from 7 a.m.–10 p.m. Monday to Friday, 3–10 p.m. Saturday and Sunday, offers a helpline and counselling service for anyone worried about AIDS.

Transport in London

There are two ways of moving around London by public transport. Buses and the 'tube' or Underground. Prices depend on how far you want to go, but best bets are the one-day or one-week Travel Cards, which allow unlimited travel by bus or tube to most inner city areas any time *after* 9.30 a.m. A one-day Travel Card costs (at time of going to press) £2.90 and a one-week Travel Card £18.80. For other city travel bargains (and those that take you out of the city) check the up-to-date information brochures obtainable from the London Transport information kiosks in the main Underground and rail stations.

Bicycles can be hired from a number of outlets. Count on paying at least £7 for a day's hire, though daily rates can drop for longer rentals. Also be ready to cough up a deposit of £40–£50 for your machine. Contact: Mountain Bike and Ski, 18 Gillingham Street,

SW1 (tel: 0171 834 8933, Victoria Underground station); Kensington Cycling Centre, 69 Golborne Road, W10 (tel: 0181 960 0444, Ladbroke Grove Underground); Bell Street Bikes, 73 Bell Street, NW1 (tel: 0171 724 0456, Edgware Road Underground); and On Your Bike, 22 Duke Street Hill, SE1 (tel: 0171 378 6669, London Bridge or Monument Underground stations).

Student discounts
There is a tremendous amount to be gained from student discounts all over Great Britain and Ireland. Museums, galleries, concerts, cinemas, restaurants, bars, dry cleaning, cameras, tape recorders, typewriters, watches and clothing are just some of the places and items you can enter at a reduced rate, or buy at a discount, if you belong to the magic club. If you are eligible, you can obtain an International Student Identity Card from any student travel operator. Main ones are: STA Travel, 117 Euston Road, NW1 or 748–56 Old Brompton Rd, SW7.

Addresses

Main post office (for poste restante) at King Edward Street, London EC1, and 22–8 William IV Street, Trafalgar Square.

American Express at 6 Haymarket, London SW1 (tel: 0171 930 4411).

London Student Travel Bureau at 52 Grosvenor Gardens, London SW1W OAG (tel: 0171 730 3402).

British Tourist Authority at 12 Regent Street, London SW1 (tel: 0171 730 3400).

London Tourist Board Information Centres at 26 Grosvenor Gardens, London SW1 (tel: 0171 824 8844, credit card holders only); Victoria Station Forecourt; Selfridges store (in Oxford Street), ground floor; Harrods store (Knightsbridge), fourth floor; at Heathrow Airport; and, in summer, at the Tower of London.

US Embassy at 24 Grosvenor Square, London W1 (tel: 0171 499 9000).

Youth Hostels Association Shop 14 Southampton Street, WC2 (tel: 0171 836 8541).

Hitchers' Tips and Comments . . .

LONDON: Many markets, for instance Camden Market and Petticoat Lane, always need people to hand out flyers, and so do junk food places and bars, but then you have to look a little bit smarter than for the markets (they don't care what you look like). Not great money, but a quid and a half per hour at least.

ANNA LISS, AMSTERDAM

The best place to stand when hitching out of London heading north: pick up the M1 at Brent Cross. Heading west pick up the M4 at Hammersmith or Gunnersbury. All 3 junctions are a short walk of a tube station. Forget about the M25. THE LAUGHING GNOME

Going south from Liverpool, avoid Junctions 6, 7 and 8. We waited 12 hours before we got a lift. Going north to Liverpool the M6 is slightly easier to get a lift if you are heading towards Gloucester. M5 northbound is dead sound for lifts. We waited for only 20 minutes and ended up getting to Runcorn.

DAVID GRIFFITH & PETER PAYNE, LIVERPOOL

Don't sleep rough near or inside main line railway stations, i.e. King's Cross. Not only is there a possibility of explosive devices going off, but there are police and rail security bods patrolling regularly.

OSSIE, NSW

For good eating at good prices, try YHA Carter Lane, near St Pauls. Good tucker! Also you can make very good contacts. Can't say too much, but if after you had your meal, you went for a kip in the downstairs lounge, it was not your fault that you could not wake up till next morning! KIWI, SOUTH ISLAND

To get out of London, take a tube. But first get a map of the Underground and you'll find it helps then to compare with your road map.

JOE SEMPLE, YORK

If you require some work for a spell in London, and you are fluent in several languages (English helps!) contact YHA or YMCA headquarters. YMCA at 640, Forest Road, (tel: 0181 520 5599) YHA at 14 Southampton Street, Covent Garden (tel: 0181 836 1036). You can only ask! MICHELLE DUMAS, MONTPELIER

Before attempting to sleep rough, make sure you have a four-season bag. It means you can get your day clothes off at night. The difference it makes to a sensitive nose is amazing – particularly when hitching. JOE O'DONNEL, CORK

The best deal of all in Britain and Ireland is Slatterys bus to/from London – to/from Dublin. From gate 20 at Victoria Station, London you can get the bus to Dublin for £10 (leaving a.m.) and £14 (leaving p.m.) This incredible price includes the Holyhead/Dublin ferry. Absolutely unbeatable! No point in hitching.

If trying to hitch the ferry from England/Wales to Ireland (Eire) it is possible on most routes where truck drivers can carry a passenger. However, Dublin/Liverpool/Dublin is freight only, so don't waste your time. TOM CORCORRAN, GLASNEVIN, DUBLIN

A point of interest, and perhaps warning, to would-be sleeping rough contenders in England. Bristol has the biggest sleeping rough population in Britain. PADDY O'HARE, WARRENPOINT

Wales

population	2,700,000
size	8,000 square miles
capital	Cardiff, population 260,000
government	Constitutional monarchy
religion	Protestant
language	Welsh and English
currency	Same as England

Best way into Wales is across the tremendous **Severn Bridge** just outside Bristol. If you continue on to **Monmouth** and then turn west along the A40 to **Abergavenny** where you meet up with the A465, you can travel through some of the strangest country in the British Isles. Luxurious green valleys, once scarred by black cuts of coal mines – villages which from the distance seem to be gentle and fairytale-like turn out to be places of cold brick coated with the black dust of the mines.

Cardiff, down on the coast, is the capital of the country. Sights to see include the National Museum of Wales, the Welsh Folk Museum (this is at St Fagan's, four miles out of town) where typically Welsh buildings have been reconstructed to give the visitor an idea of the rural architecture of the country, and Cardiff Castle. Cardiff Castle is just one of more than 150 in Wales. The Welsh Tourist Office claim that their country has more castles per square mile than any other country in Europe.

Dylan Thomas fans will want to drop in on the village of **Laugharne** which is on a side road off the A49 just outside **Carmar-**

then. The poet lived a good deal of his life in the village and is buried there.

St David's, on the A487, has the dubious distinction of being the smallest city in the British Isles. Its population of 1,650 supports a cathedral and the ruins of a bishop's palace.

On the river **Teifi**, which reaches the sea at **Cardigan**, you might be lucky enough to spot a fisherman in a coracle. These wicker-basket boats are the earliest form of water transport known to man except for the log.

Heading north along the coast you reach **Aberystwyth**, an important university town, while further north again is **Harlech** with its famous castle. North again, takes you to another castle town, this time **Caernarvon**, traditional site of the investiture of the Prince of Wales. It happened to Prince Charles in the summer of 1969 with due pomp and ceremony. Certain strata of the Welsh population – those interested in breaking ties with England – were not impressed. Hitchers wanting more information on that subject can probably find it amongst the students at Aberystwyth.

Just outside **Bangor**, which has a Museum of Welsh Antiquities, is a village with only one claim to fame. It's called: *Llanfairpwllgwyngyllgogerychwyrndrobwllllantysiliogogogoch*. The main street isn't as long as the name. For wanderers new to Wales, the word is a fair introduction to the Welsh language.

Heading back towards England along the A55, there's at least one more worthwhile stop and that's at **Conway** which is a pleasant enough town with yet another famous castle. The A5 passes through beautiful Snowdonia National Park.

Hitchers' Tips and Comments . . .

WALES: You haven't mentioned Machynlleth at all. Just up the road from Machynlleth is Llangwern Quarry and the Centre of Alternative Technology (phone Machynlleth 2400). Lots of interesting people.

ANNA LISS, AMSTERDAM

Scotland

population	5,200,000
size	30,414 square miles
capital	Edinburgh, population 453,000
government	Constitutional monarchy
religion	Protestant
language	English; Gaelic is spoken in the Western Isles and north western mainland
currency	Same currency as England, although the three Scottish banks also issue their own banknotes (including £100 notes which are not issued in England). Both English and Scottish notes are accepted throughout Scotland

Scotland is best approached by the A68 where the border is crossed at **Carter Bar** (1,300 feet up). The southern upland towns of **Jedburgh**, **Melrose**, **Kelso** (all with ruined abbeys), **Hawick**, **Selkirk** and **Galashiels** (home of Sir Walter Scott) are well worth seeing.

Alternatively, if you are coming from Newcastle, take the A1 along the coast, but this is generally slower for hitching although picturesque.

You will probably be heading for **Edinburgh**, well worth a few days' stay as one of the most beautiful cities in Europe. The best time to visit is late August when the famous Edinburgh International Festival is in full swing and the city is literally bursting with life. Accommodation can be a problem then, although there are plenty of parks in the city centre where sleeping rough should be possible (but don't try Calton Hill or Princes Street Gardens as you are liable to get hassled).

North of Edinburgh, after crossing the big Forth Road Bridge, you can join up with the M90 to Perth then the A85 which will take you through to **Dundee**. The city is nothing spectacular, but nearby, at a place called **Glamis**, is one of the better castles in Scotland.

Scotland is a place where you can enjoy the countryside – particularly the famous Highlands. In these heather-covered hills you will recognize the colours of the traditional tartans and you will notice a sense of spaciousness which you can't find elsewhere in the British Isles. Scotland is half the size of England, but with only one-tenth the population.

To get the full flavour of this Highland Scotland, probably the best route you can take is north from Dundee up through **Spittal of Glenshee** and **Devil's Elbow** to **Braemar**, which is the big centre for the Royal Highland Gathering, with caber-tossing and hammer-throwing. This takes place on the first Saturday in September each year. Just a little further on is **Balmoral Castle**, still used by the British Royal Family for summer holidays. The Dee River, which runs through the Royal Estate, is well stocked with trout if you care to indulge in a little high-class poaching. Follow the river down to the sea and you come to **Aberdeen**, the self-proclaimed oil capital of Europe. Accommodation can be expensive as a result, so try and stay out of town, but it is worth a visit nonetheless. Despite the oil wealth, the city has escaped too much development and thanks to the granite buildings looks remarkably clean.

Further north at **Huntly** you can join up with the A96 which curves around the coast towards **Inverness**, a pleasant town with a cathedral and a museum containing relics of the Jacobites. It's known as the Highland Capital and sits at the northern end of **Loch Ness**, home of the monster which has been seen by *everyone* in Scotland except the scientists. Just outside Inverness is **Culloden**, site of the famous battle of 1746 when Bonnie Prince Charlie's Jacobites were defeated by the Hanoverians. You can visit a small museum housed in a contemporary farm dwelling, and see the memorials of the various clans. If you make it on a drizzly day (you probably will), you'll get a real feeling of how the moor must have been on the day of the battle.

From Inverness, if time is short, the A9 south has recently been upgraded and is excellent for hitching. It takes you through the **Spey Valley** and the famous resort of **Aviemore**, then further south **Pitlochry** and **Perth**.

But if you have the time, go north again and you're heading for **John o' Groats**, the northern counterpart of England's Land's End. The towns of **Wick** and **Thurso** are interesting and quite different from towns in the south.

Orkney and **Shetland** From Scrabster by Thurso you can catch the ferry to **Stromness** and the Orkney Isles, rugged, wild and beautiful, with no trees. The islands abound with prehistoric and Viking ruins, the most notable being the preserved Neolithic village at **Skara Brae**.

To get to the Shetland Isles, Britain's northernmost land, you have to take the ferry from Aberdeen, a longish trip. But it is worth it when you get there – buy some of their unique knitwear!

If you take the western route back south, you'll be travelling through some of the loneliest country outside northern Scandinavia. It's the real moor country with peat bogs and little else. I remember passing through one 'town' which consisted of a signpost, one house, one hotel, and then another signpost. How the two establishments supported each other is a difficult question to answer. The whole area is beautiful if you enjoy a little loneliness. Be warned that the hitching can get really bad between **Tongue** and **Ullapool**.

South of Ullapool and you're in the land of mountains and lochs – the best part of the Western Highlands. See the tropical gardens (yes, tropical!) at **Inverewe** and then continue through **Gairloch** and alongside **Loch Maree**, perhaps the loveliest of all the lochs.

At **Kyle of Lochalsh** or **Mallaig** you can catch the ferry to **Skye**, the most beautiful of all the Scottish isles. The further from the mainland you go, the more remote and beautiful the island becomes. If you feel really adventurous, cross over to the **Outer Hebrides**, wild, wild islands facing the Atlantic. The Scottish isles are strictly, almost fiercely, religious, so nothing at all moves on a Sunday – and I mean nothing. No trains, buses or cars, and even walking is frowned upon, so do all your travelling by Saturday. Back on the mainland, the road south continues through uninterrupted and outstanding scenery until you come to **Fort William** which is on Loch Linnhe and backed by the 4,406-foot Ben Nevis mountain. Twenty miles further south again and you're at **Glencoe**, scene of the massacre of 1692.

Down the A82 and A84, through a whole lot of nice country and you arrive in **Stirling**, historically one of the most important towns in Scotland. Have a look at Stirling Castle, ex-home of the Royal Mint, and a great visit. A couple of miles north are the ruins of **Cambuskenneth Abbey**, while south is **Bannockburn**, scene of the battle where Robert the Bruce defeated King Edward in 1314.

The next city you come to is **Glasgow**, where it's worth spending a few days visiting the Art Gallery, Museum of Transport, and the 12th-century cathedral. Also have a look at Provand's Lordship, the oldest house in the city, dating from 1471. With two universities (Watt, of steam-engine fame, attended Glasgow University) the city is a good place to meet people.

South of Glasgow on the A77, is **Ayr**, and a couple of miles outside is **Alloway**, birthplace of Scotland's favourite poet, Robbie Burns. The cottage in which he was born in 1759 is now a completely restored monument. Inside you can see original manuscripts, letters, and objects associated with Burns.

Stranraer is where you can jump a ferry for Northern Ireland (see **Northern Ireland**). East along the A75 and you come to **Castle Douglas** with the huge Threave Castle nearby. Then you come to **Dumfries** where Burns died in 1796 and is buried. Then, just before you cross back into England, you come to **Gretna Green**, once famous around the world as the place to which young people ran off to get married.

● **Highland Games** Main places for Highland Games are Fort William, Dunoon, Crieff, Glenfinnan, Edinburgh, Aboyne and Braemar, although almost every town in the Highlands will have its own games meeting. Generally they are held in July, August and September and feature the famous caber toss as well as traditional dancing and music. Ask the Scottish Tourist Board for dates.

● **Edinburgh festival** The famous International Festival of Music and Drama is held every year in the second half of August and the first week of September.

Edinburgh: where to sleep

A bed in Edinburgh costs about £10 in a youth hostel, £12–£14 in one of the cheaper B&Bs or guest houses. You'll need a Hostelling International membership card to use the hostels operated by the Scottish Youth Hostels Association (SYHA). Accommodation becomes difficult to find during the Edinburgh Festival in August.

SYHA hostels:
Bruntsfield Hostel, 7 Bruntsfield Crescent (tel: 0131 337 1120).
Eglinton Hostel, 18 Eglinton Crescent (tel: 0131 337 1120).
Other hostels:
High Street Hostel, 8 Blackfriars Street (tel: 0131 557 3984).
Belford Youth Hostel, Belford Road (tel: 0131 225 6209). In a converted church.
Iolaire, 14 Argyle Place (tel: 0131 667 9991).
Christian Alliance Frances Kinnaird Hostel, 14 Coates Crescent (tel: 0131 225 3608). Women only.

Student accommodation:
With prices starting around £20 for singles, a room in a student residence during the summer vacation (July–Sept.) is no longer the bargain it was a few years ago. Ask the Tourist Office about possibilities in this line if you're interested.

Edinburgh is full of guest houses and bed-and-breakfasts. The best places to try are Mayfield and Bruntsfield. For help in finding a cheap place try the **Edinburgh Marketing Service**, Waverley Market, 3 Princes Street (tel: 0131 557 1700). For sleeping rough, take a bus out to Holyrood Park.

Edinburgh: where to eat

Two pounds should handle any hunger problems. And remember, as in London, if you're ever really broke, you can survive very well (survive, though scarcely thrive) on fish'n'chips.

The YWCA and YMCA both serve well-priced meals. (Addresses in **Where to sleep**.) If you like to make lunch your main meal of the day you can have good feeds at any number of pubs and small restaurants for around £3–£4. Try:

SYHA Hostel, 18 Eglinton Crescent. The three-course dinner served to guests is excellent value.
Milnes Bar at 35 Hanover Street.
Sandwiches at Rose Street. Good chip butties for 75p.
Students' Union at 9 Chambers Street. Open July through October. Dinner served (very cheap) 5–7 p.m.
Wayfarer Café (Gino Iannone) at 53 Clerk Street. Good cheap food.
Cantina at Rose Street, Good Mexican food, low prices.
Lothian Restaurant at 16 Drummond Street. Cheap curry meals.
Phuket-Penang at 176 Rose Street. Malaysian & Thai meals.

Edinburgh: what to see and do

THE CASTLE The huge military complex which dominates Edinburgh. Entrance charge. Good place for overall view of what is a beautiful city.

JOHN KNOX'S HOUSE at the foot of High Street. Entrance charge. Closed on Sundays.

NATIONAL GALLERY OF SCOTLAND on the Mound. No entrance fee. Some good stuff.

THE OLD TOWN This is the area between the castle rock and Holyrood House. It's the old quarter of Edinburgh which settled itself around the protective castle. Holyrood House was the home of several Scottish sovereigns, including Mary Queen of Scots. You can still see the room where Rizzio, her Italian secretary (and possibly lover) was murdered before her eyes in 1566.

DEACON BRODIE'S TAVERN at the corner of Bank and High Streets is a little touristy, but you can meet some good types there. Deacon

Brodie was the evil man who inspired R. L. Stevenson to write *Dr Jekyll and Mr Hyde*. Prices OK.

THE TRAVERSE THEATRE CLUB is a sort of pub-cum-theatre-cum-art-gallery. Membership fee. Worth visiting to meet people and for general good talk.

CAS ROCK at West Port. Live music. Good crowd.

ALTERNATIVE EDINBURGH If you're going to be in town for an extended stay you'll get some good tips on breadline living if you buy *Alternative Edinburgh*, published by the University Student Publications Board, 1 Buccleuch Place, Edinburgh. It has chapters on eating, sleeping, seeing Edinburgh for nothing, etc.

Transport in Edinburgh

The bus service is the main means of public transport. It will take you everywhere.

Addresses

Main post office (for poste restante) at corner of Waterloo Place and North Bridge.

American Express at 139 Princes Street (tel: 0131 225 7881).

Edinburgh University Students' Association at Bristo Square (tel: 0131 667 0214).

Scottish Tourist Board at 23 Ravelston Terrace, Edinburgh 4 (tel: 0131 332 2433). Postal and phone enquiries only.

City of Edinburgh Tourist Information Centre at Waverley Bridge, by the station (tel: 0131 226 6591 for info; 225 8821 for accommodation).

SYHA Shop at 161 Warrender Park Road.

US Consulate at 3 Regent Terrace (tel: 0131 556 8315).

Glasgow: where to sleep

The **Greater Glasgow Tourist Information Centre** at 35 St Vincent Place (tel: 0141 204 4400) offers excellent free maps of the city (in Edinburgh they charge £1) plus a very comprehensive *Official Quick Guide* – also free (Edinburgh's equivalent costs £1.50). They also provide an efficient room-finding service – again free (or £3 cheaper than in Edinburgh, to look at it another way). Incredibly, Glasgow doesn't have a campsite!

Hostels:

SYHA Hostel, 7/8 Park Terrace (tel: 0141 332 3004).
Glasgow Backpackers Hostel, Kelvin Lodge, 8 Park Circus (tel: 0141 332 5412).
YMCA Aparthotel, David Naismith Court, 33 Petershill Drive (tel: 0141 558 6166). Singles from £15. Special weekly rates.

B&Bs and guest houses:

Mrs M. Williamson, 15 Kintillo Drive (tel: 0141 959 1874).
Mrs C. McArdle, 171 Mount Annan Drive (tel: 0141 632 0671).
Brown's Guesthouse, 2 Onslow Drive (tel: 0141 544 6797).
Mr & Mrs J. Shearer, 2 Avdie Place (tel: 0141 632 0644).

Glasgow: where to eat

Friendly cafés, bistros, pubs and first-class restaurants offer excellent hospitality to suit all pockets. The same rule applies as in every other major city: seek out the university halls of residence (Glasgow has three universities: Strathclyde, Caledonian and Glasgow University) for around these you will find an abundance of good, cheap eating places.

The Blythswood at 97 Hope Street (opp. Central Hotel) Glasgow. 11 a.m.–6 p.m.
Buzby & Co, 100 George Street, Glasgow.
Cafe Oriental, 223 High Street, Glasgow.
Sylvesters Lounge, 358 Argyle Street, Glasgow.
Alhambra Inn, cnr Wellington/Waterloo Street, Glasgow.
Toby Jug, Waterloo Street, Glasgow (opp Central Station).
Glasgow School of Art: Students Association, 168 Renfrew Street, Glasgow. Show your student card.
Quarter Gill Restaurant, cnr Hyndland/Dumbarton Road, Partick, Glasgow.
Multi-Cultural Centre (next door to St Aloysius RC Church) 21 Rose Street, Glasgow.

Glasgow: what to see and do

As a leading holiday destination, Greater Glasgow combines the thrill of one of Europe's most exciting cultural capitals and an unmistakable Scottish charm. The skyline is a mixture of architectural gems, from the 12th-century Cathedral to the unmistakable Art Noveau designs of Charles Rennie Mackintosh.

ART GALLERY & MUSEUM in Kelvingrove. Contains fascinating displays on Natural History, Archaeology, History and Ethnography, and Britain's finest civic collection of British and European paintings.

BURRELL COLLECTION in Pollok Country Park. This unique collection has more than 8,000 items and includes exhibits from the ancient world, oriental art, paintings (especially 19th-century French art), furniture, carpets, ceramics, tapestries and stained glass.

UNIVERSITY OF GLASGOW Founded in 1451, and boasting a long line of achievers ranging from the economist Adam Smith to the scientist Lord Kelvin, the University is one of Glasgow's major tourist attractions. The Visitor Centre offers video displays and 'hands-on' information systems, plus guided tours. Overlooking Kelvingrove Park, the campus contains a host of important buildings and some of the city's top museums: the HUNTERIAN ART GALLERY houses works by Chardin, Rembrandt, Koninck and Whistler, along with a collection of 15,000 prints; the Mackintosh House forms part of the complex. The HUNTERIAN MUSEUM features geological, archaeological and ethnographic displays, an exhibition on the history of Glasgow University, plus William Hunter's world-famous coin cabinet.

MCLELLAN GALLERIES Built in 1854, these exhibition galleries on Sauchiehall Street have now been completely refurbished and provide an important venue for temporary art exhibitions.

PEOPLE'S PALACE This museum, which stands on historic Glasgow Green, tells the story of Glasgow from 1175 to the present day. Learn about the city's rich industrial heritage and the legacy left behind by the Suffragettes, trade unions and labour movements.

PROVAND'S LORDSHIP, Castle Street. The oldest house in Glasgow (built 1471). Displays include the 16th-century room of the chaplain of the Hospital of St Nicholas and a fine collection of 17th-century furniture.

THE TENEMENT HOUSE, Buccleuch Street is a time capsule of living conditions in a Glasgow tenement during the early part of the 20th century.

MUSEUM OF TRANSPORT, Kelvin Hall. Including a reproduction of 1938 Glasgow street scene, complete with cinema and subway station, this museum also features a walk-in motor car showroom with cars from the 1930s up to the present day and a comprehensive display of model ships in the 'Clyde Room'. Other exhibits include Glasgow trams and buses; Scottish-built cars; fire engines; horse-drawn vehicles; motorcycles and railway locomotives.

GLASGOW CATHEDRAL Castle Street. Established by St Mungo, the patron saint of Glasgow, the Cathedral dates in parts from the 12th century and is an outstanding example of Gothic architecture.

ST ANDREW'S RC CATHEDRAL Clyde Street. A good example of Gothic architecture with an 1816 'College Chapel' façade and a plaster-vaulted interior.

CITY TOURS Daily tours of Glasgow's main attractions may be booked at the Strathclyde Buses Travel Centre from Apr.–Oct. From May–Sept. it is possible to cruise the Firth of Clyde aboard the historic paddle-steamer Waverley (tours start from the Waverley Terminal, Anderston Quay).

SHOPPING Glasgow offers great shopping from the chic (but also very expensive) Prince's Square and St Enoch's Shopping Mall to the more down-to-earth and affordable BARRAS – Glasgow's traditional street market, where you can shop for almost anything from a needle to an anchor at knock-down prices. Best on a Saturday or Sunday after 10 a.m.

CULTURE In addition to the **Scottish Opera**, **Scottish Ballet** and the **Royal Scottish Orchestra** (plus the new concert hall near Buchanan Street bus station), this dynamic city is home to a number of leading Scottish arts companies who present quality programmes throughout the year. Annual festivals include *Mayfest* and the *Glasgow International Jazz Festival*.

For information on the arts – dance, music, theatre, opera – call 'What's On' (tel: 0141 204 4400), or contact the excellent **Tourist Information Centre** at St Vincent Place. There you will be provided with a range of brochures and literature to make your stay in Glasgow and surrounding districts worthwhile.

Transport in Glasgow

By Air: Glasgow International Airport in Renfrew District is just 15 minutes from the city centre and is among Britain's busiest.

By Rail: Greater Glasgow is a key link in the nationwide rail network. There are hourly high speed Intercity rail services to and from London with a journey time of 5 hours, and fast services from the rest of the UK.

By Road: There are direct motorway links with all major UK cities. But to get a good hitch, get out of Greater Glasgow.

Getting Around: Travelling within Glasgow could not be easier. There is an extensive network of Scotrail suburban services, a wide range of public bus services and an excellent Underground service. But the best bet is to get travel information right from the horse's mouth – the Travel Centre in St Enoch Square, right in the city centre. They will give you all information about cheap rates, Zone-cards, Day Trippers, plus specials on the Underground.

Addresses

Main Post Office 1–5 George Square, Glasgow (tel: 0141 242 4336).

American Express at 115 Hope Street, Glasgow (tel: 0141 226 3077).

Greater Glasgow Tourist Information Centre at 35 St Vincent Place, Glasgow (tel: 0141 248 7491).

American Express 24-hour traveller's cheque refund claims, tel: 0141 0800 521313.

Canadian Consul, 151 St Vincent Street, Glasgow (tel: 0141 221 4415).

German Consulate, 144 West George Street, Glasgow (tel: 0141 331 2811).

Spanish Consulate, 389 Argyle Street, Glasgow (tel: 0141 221 6943).

Swedish Consul, 228 Clyde Street, Glasgow (tel: 0141 221 0605).

Netherlands Consulate, 102 Hope Street, Glasgow (tel: 0141 221 0605).

Hitchers' Tips and Comments . . .

When hitching in Scotland, before leaving the country make sure you trade all your Scottish pounds for English pounds. On the Continent they don't want to know. I only had twenty Scottish pounds left once in Germany, and I starved for two days before I found a bank that would change them. ALAN, BROCKVILLE, CANADA

You can have similar troubles, particularly in small banks, with Gibraltar pounds, Maltese pounds, Australian dollars, most Middle Eastern, North African and all ex-Communist currencies. K.W.

A visit to Skye is a good way to close the Knoydart gap on the west coast. Sail from Mallaig to Armadale in south-west Skye, proceed to Kyleakin and cross by ferry to mainland Kyle of Lochalsh.

MOYNA GARDNER, GLASGOW, SCOTLAND

Dossing in Edinburgh: Advise hitchers not to try Princes Street Gardens. Too open, and the town's authorities do not care for 'budget' tourists in full view of the 'large-wad' variety. Best bets are University's George Square and New Town's Queen Street Gardens. Both have good cover and are located in quiet, non-policed, student areas but close enough to the main sites. Outstanding Edinburgh pubs include Bannerman's (live music midweek) and Sneeky Pete's (great juke-box) in the Cowgate. MICHAEL GRAHAM, SCOTLAND

Don't go on a ferry to the Orkney Islands. Ask fishermen for a lift, or offer them a small sum to take you aboard as a passenger.

PATRICK FITZGERALD, SOUTH LOPHAM, ENGLAND

Northern Ireland

population	1,500,000
size	5,452 square miles
capital	Belfast, population 425,000
government	Constitutional monarchy
religion	Protestant and Roman Catholic
language	English
currency	Same as England, although Northern Irish banks also issue their own banknotes. In theory these should be accepted throughout the UK; in practice they can be difficult to get rid of in shops and pubs on the mainland

Northern Ireland looks set to become a very popular tourist destination if the current ceasefire holds.

Crossing to Northern Ireland is done cheapest by jumping the ferry in **Stranraer** (Scotland) and crossing to **Larne** which is just a few miles north of Belfast. Other routes are from Liverpool (England) to Belfast; and Cairnryan (Scotland) to Belfast.

The main points of interest are the capital, Belfast, the ancient city of Londonderry, and the incomparable Giant's Causeway.

Belfast is a city of markets. Smithfield is the big one. It's open every weekday and sells whatever you want to buy. Chichester Street, May Street and Oxford Street are three others, but they mostly sell food. Friday is the day at May Street and Chichester Street when they hold the junk market, somewhat reminiscent of London's Portobello Road, but not as touristy.

Buildings worth looking over include City Hall and Queens University. The Museum and Art Gallery are OK to wander through, but a better display is at the Ulster Folk Museum which gives you a good idea of what Irish life was like in centuries past. It's located eight miles from Belfast on the A2 Belfast-Bangor road and is built along the same lines as the big open-air museum at Skansen in Sweden. (See **Scandinavia, Finland and Iceland**.) While you're out that way you can see **Stormont**, until 1972 the seat of the British government in Northern Ireland.

Carrickfergus, on the coast between Belfast and Larne, is a lobster-fishing port and the site of a big Norman castle. Gory story attached to the castle tells that during a siege, which came as the result of a war with Scotland, the garrison was so badly starved that they ate thirty Scottish prisoners. These days Carrickfergusians prefer seafood.

You reach the **Giant's Causeway** via the A2, following it up through Larne and **Ballycastle**. The Causeway is one of *the* natural wonders of the world. It's a weird formation of basalt rock which was caused by volcanic action millions of years ago. At least that's how scientists tell it. The legendary explanation of the creation of the Causeway makes more sense. It tells that a gigantic Irishman, Finn MacCool, heard of a Scottish giant Finn Gall and decided to fight him to find out who was the better man. So he built the Causeway and walked over to Scotland. He found Gall's house and entered. He found Mrs Gall sewing and saw a huge body sleeping on a bed. He asked if it was her husband and she said her husband was out and that the sleeping figure was her two-year-old son – at which MacCool lost his cool and hurtled back to Ireland scared out of his wits at the thought of how big Finn Gall must be. They say he ripped up the Causeway as he returned so that Gall couldn't come over and get him. And that explains why there's so little of it left.

Londonderry, 40-odd miles further on from the Causeway, is the second city of Northern Ireland and the one most laden with history. It was founded with the building of an abbey in AD 540 and has been a magnet for strife ever since. Before the year 1200 it had been attacked by Danes and Normans and burned seven times. In 1556 it was the headquarters of a rebellion and destroyed by a huge explosion from the city ammunition magazines. In 1608 it was burned again. And then in 1689 a terrible siege which lasted 105 days resulted in the death of 7,000 defenders. The city walls, which saw much of this, date from the 1600s and (incredibly!) are preserved intact. At St Columb's Cathedral you can see relics of the great siege, and the modern Guild Hall contains other objects related to the city's past.

To the south, as far as scenery is concerned, there is plenty of it and it is beautiful. **County Down** offers a lot. I suggest that you get out of Belfast by bus and get onto the A7 or A22 and then hitch to **Downpatrick**. This area, known as **St Patrick's Vale, Land of Legend**, is steeped in history and mythology. To the south it is bounded by a coastline which stretches from the shores of **Carlingford Lough** (Loch) to **Strangford Lough**, a haven for birds (the flying kind!) and wildlife.

Inland, its boundaries are marked by towns such as **Newry** which has much to offer the visitor. Its reputation as one of the best shopping towns in N. Ireland is such that shoppers from Eire cross the border to shop in Newry. Bargains are to be found at the variety market Thursdays and Saturdays. **Newcastle**, the biggest seaside resort in the area, has the majestic Mountains of Mourne as a backdrop. For the sports-minded hiker, particularly those keen on water sports, Newcastle has lots to offer, as do Cranfield, Killowen, Rostrevor and Warrenpoint. If you are apprehensive about hitch-hiking in this part of the country, then take a train or a bus to Newry. But try not to miss this lovely part of Northern Ireland. When you get to Newry, it is only a short distance to the very pleasant town of **Warrenpoint**.

The town lies on the northern side of beautiful **Carlingford Lough**. Some great water cruises can be made from Warrenpoint marina. The Lough nestles between the rugged **Mountains of Mourne** (which will always sweep down to the sea!) and the high hills of **Cooley**.

● **Warning!** In this country it's not a good idea to loudmouth your political or religious views.

Hitchers' Tips and Comments . . .

Travelling in the North isn't that much more dangerous than elsewhere in Europe so long as you don't express strong views on the situation. I wouldn't recommend sleeping out in Ulster but, if you must, avoid the cities, towns and sensitive border areas.

STEVE IRELAND, BELFAST, N. IRELAND

Ninety per cent of Ulster is very safe and normal – and beautiful. Also, Ulster people are far more interested in you as a traveller than are their southern counterparts. Before setting out, read the papers and listen to the news. Find out the current trouble spots and avoid them.

HELEN SNIVELY, DUBLIN

If you're in Newcastle, try the 'Beverly' bed and breakfast at 72 Tollymore Road (tel: 013967 22018). I thought it was a fantastic deal.

BODGIE, MELBOURNE, AUSTRALIA

Ireland (Eire)

population	3,549,000
size	27,137 square miles
capital	Dublin, population 1,000,000
government	Parliamentary democracy
religion	Predominantly Roman Catholic
language	English and Irish
currency	*punt* (Irish pound – IR£). One *punt* equals 100 *pence*. Coins of 1, 2, 5, 10, 20, 50p and IR£1. Notes of IR£1, 5, 10, 20, 50, 100

For me, the Republic of Ireland is more interesting than the North. The people are more relaxed and perhaps that is why the countryside seems more beautiful. And there's much more to see. To get to the South, you can cross over from the North with scarcely any formalities. Or, if you're crossing over from England, the ferry routes are as follows: Liverpool (England) to Dublin, Holyhead (Wales) to Dun Laoghaire, Fishguard (Wales) to Rosslare, Holyhead (Wales) to Dublin, Pembroke (Wales) to Rosslare.

The Irish have a saying, 'Everyone is an Irishman and those that ain't are wishin' that they were.' If you check down the list of the top twenty names in Ireland (see p. 124), you'll see how many of us *do* have Irish blood in the family. This strange fact derives from the exodus of the Irish from their country to escape the great famine of the early 1800s and the desolation which followed it. In less than eighty years the population dropped from eight to four million, and many of those four million expatriates went to America and the British colonies and took with them not only their family names but also the names of their towns which have become household words in the English language: Limerick, Killarney, Tipperary, Blarney, Galway, Cork – and plenty of others.

Tiny **Kilkenny** (population 9,500) is known as the capital of medieval Ireland. See the beautiful 13th-century castle with its fine collection of manuscripts. The old castle stables house the Kilkenny Design Workshops which aren't open to the public, but there is a permanent exhibition and shop where you can see the best Ireland has to offer in textiles, silver, ceramics and glass. St Canice's Cathedral and the Dominican church also date from the 13th century. Towards the end of August, Kilkenny stages an Arts Week featuring concerts, lunchtime recitals, poetry readings and exhibitions. Well worth a visit if you are in the area and so inclined.

The **Dunmore Cave**, seven miles from Kilkenny on the Castlecomer road, is a fascinating example of a natural cavern formed in limestone. In AD 928, 1,000 people who had hidden in the cave were slaughtered by the Vikings. The cave is fitted with special lighting and viewing galleries.

Cashel, between Kilkenny and Tipperary, is, after **Tara**, which is six miles south of Navan in County Meath, the most important historical site in Southern Ireland. Tara, in ancient times, was the capital of Ireland and the seat of the Irish kings. However, little remains to be seen today and it's scarcely worth the visit unless you're an archaeology or history crank. At Cashel, though, there is plenty to see. It's a town of 2,500 people dominated by the dramatic Rock of Cashel, a 200-foot-high outcrop of limestone crowned by ruins. The town was the seat of the Munster kings from AD 370–1101 and also a place where St Patrick preached. It's said that it was in Cashel that he used the shamrock as an illustration of the doctrine of the Trinity, thus establishing for ever the national symbol of Ireland. On the rock you can see a round tower dating from the 12th century, the cathedral, the hall of the Vicars Choral, and King Cormac's Chapel. (A story tells that the first cathedral on the site was burned down in 1495 by the Earl of Kildare. The Earl later apologized and explained to Henry VII that he'd done so because he'd thought the archbishop was inside.)

Cork is the second city of Ireland and perhaps one of her prettiest. Best things to see are the streets around the quays (it's a riverside city), and Christ the King Church, an outstanding piece of modern architecture designed by an American, Barry Byrne of Chicago. The School of Art contains good examples of modern Irish painting.

Five miles out of Cork is **Blarney**, a tiny village of less than 1,200 people. The town boasts a fine old castle, and on the outside wall of the highest tower is the world-famous Blarney Stone; £3 buys you the privilege of performing a contortionist act to kiss the stone and, the deed being done, you are blessed for ever with 'the gift of the gab'.

Wandering up through Killarney, by **Dingle Bay** to **Tralee** you reach the village of **Adare** (11 miles south of Limerick). The exact origins of Adare are unknown but it has survived, at least, since the reign of Henry II, when it was occupied by the Anglo-Normans. Even so, its population is still only 550. The point about Adare is that it's a perfect place to rest up a day or two, providing you like peace and quiet. Many travellers claim the village is Ireland's prettiest. Sights to see in and around Adare include the ruins of the Trinitarian Abbey and the Augustinian Priory; the Franciscan Friary and Desmond Castle which dates from the 13th century. If you can hustle up some tackle, try the first-rate brown trout fishing on the Maigue River.

The city of **Limerick** is more famous for the making of fine lace than the invention of dirty verse. See King John's Castle (one of the castle's five towers is used twice weekly during the summer months as the setting for evenings of Irish entertainment) and St John's Cathedral. The 280-foot spire is the highest in Ireland. In the old city Exchange (only the front wall remains) there was a pedestal known as the 'Nail' where merchants paid their debts – from which came the expression 'paying on the nail'. The nail in question can be seen at the Limerick Museum.

Galway, a city of 37,835, sitting on the famous bay of the same name, is a pleasant place with a long history. The Church of St Nicholas dating from 1320 is said to have been visited by Columbus on his way out to the Americas. Lynch's castle dates from the same year and was the mansion of a city judge, part of whose story is told in a skull and crossbone memorial erected in the Old Jail: 'This memorial of the stern and unbending justice of the chief magistrate of this City, James Lynch Fitzstephen, elected mayor AD 1493, who condemned and executed his own guilty son, Walter, on this spot.'

Galway, once described as the most Irish of all Irish cities, is a good place to catch Gaelic sports. The Pearse Stadium is where you can see hurling or gaelic football. Feis Ceol an Iarthair – a festival of Irish music, dance and drama with competitions for various age groups – is held annually in late October/November. And if you're in town between June and October, don't miss the salmon at Salmon Weir Bridge, over the river Corrib. Near Galway is **Gort** where you can visit the house of Lady Gregory who was a great friend of W. B. Yeats, Shaw, Synge and O'Casey. There is still a beech tree in the grounds into which they all carved their initials.

From Galway you can hop a ferry or boat to the lovely **Aran Islands**, home of the famous sweaters. These beautiful islands are where John Millington Synge went when he wanted to find his Irish 'roots', which provided the inspiration for his magnificent play, *Playboy of the Western World*.

Alternatively, head north from Galway through beautiful **Connemara** – even the name sounds beautiful – to Ireland's wild and wonderful west, **County Mayo**. Mayo is the largest of Ireland's counties and the least populated. You can wander for hours without seeing another human being. The town of **Westport** is a great place to use as a base. From here you can reach lovely **Achill Island** off the west coast where the mighty Atlantic breaks on the shore. The locals will tell you that the next parish west is New York.

From Westport head north to the village of **Killala**, where the French invasion force that landed during the Napoleonic Wars inspired Thomas Flanaghan's bestseller, *The Year of the French*.

North again takes you through **Ballina** and the Ox Mountains to **Sligo** – Yeats country. Ireland's greatest poet spent much of his life here and is buried in **Drumcliff** churchyard under his beloved **Ben Bulben** mountain. The area offers miles of lovely scenery: try **Rosses Point** and **Mullaghmore** on Donegal Bay as well as the lovely green **Dartry Mountains**.

North yet again and you reach **Donegal** with its marvellous **Blue Stack** mountains and rugged scenery. The coastline around **Dungloe** and **Ardara** is particularly spectacular.

Don't ignore Ireland's Midlands. The lakes and the rolling green fields are as peaceful as you'll find anywhere. Try following the banks of the **River Shannon** (at over 300 miles the longest in these islands) along the N4 and N6 through **Athlone**. Boat hitching is possible. Visit the Shannon loughs like **Lough Ree** or **Lough Derg**.

If you have entered Eire from Newry, try to hitch into **Dundalk**. The small town is only 13 miles from Newry and worth a look. The traveller will notice the lack of 'apprehension' amongst the locals, which is perhaps more in evidence on the other side of the border. If you have time during your stay in Dundalk, you will find the area is a good base for exploring, particularly around the **Cooley Penninsula**.

From Dundalk you could do several things. Grab a hitch straight to Dublin, or stop off at **Drogheda**, which is only 25 miles north of Dublin on the N1. The town is situated on the estuary of the **River Boyne**. It was a meeting place of Ireland's medieval parliaments. The town was sacked in 1649 after a siege by Cromwell, Lord Protector of England and most of the 2,000 defenders were massacred. The handful of survivors were shipped to the West Indies. Drogheda surrendered to the British again in 1690 after William of Orange defeated James II at the Battle of the Boyne. In St Peters Church is preserved the head of Saint Oliver Plunkett, Archbishop of Armagh and Primate of all Ireland from 1669. He was executed at Tyburn in London in 1681 after being implicated in the fictictious popish plot to murder Charles II. Things to see around Drogheda include the site of the Battle of the Boyne, and the abbeys of Mellifont and Monasterboice. The latter is known for its collection of stone crosses, especially the 10th-century Muiredach's Cross which is among Ireland's finest.

● **Horse-drawn caravan travelling** For a small group with a little time to spare, hiring a four-berth horse-drawn caravan and covering a leisurely ten miles or so a day can make for a wonderfully relaxing time. A few years back this was as good a deal as hitching and hostelling, bearing in mind that you can sleep and do all your cooking in the caravan. Unfortunately, the increasing popularity of horse-drawn caravans means that they are no longer a bargain. Nowadays you're looking at paying £550 a week in summer, and you have to leave a deposit of about £200. If you're keen, try contacting the addresses below:

Blarney Romany Caravans, Blarney, Co. Cork (tel: (021) 85700).
Ocean Breeze Horse Caravans, Harbour View, Kilbrittain, Co. Cork (tel: (023) 49731/49626).
Slattery's Horse-drawn Caravans, Slattery's Travel Agency, Tralee, Co. Kerry (tel: (066) 21722).
Dieter Clissmann Horse-drawn Caravans, Carrigmore, Wicklow (tel: (0404) 8188).

● **Trace your ancestors** If you think your family is Irish and you want to trace some relatives or find out more about your ancestors, then your visit to Ireland is the ideal time to do it. The Irish Tourist Board will send you a free pamphlet on the subject if you write to them but, in the meantime, here are some basic facts you should attempt to find out before you leave home: (*a*) the full name of your emigrant ancestor; (*b*) any background information as to his trade or social standing; (*c*) his religion; (*d*) the name of the county and town from which he came. With that information you have a good chance of finding out something about your family.

Just in case you're wondering if you *do* have Irish ancestors, here are the top twenty surnames in Ireland listed in order of frequency of occurrence:

Murphy	O'Brien	Reilly	Kennedy
Kelly	Byrne	Doyle	Lynch
Sullivan	Ryan	McCarthy	Murray
Walsh	Connor	Gallagher	Quinn
Smith	O'Neill	Doherty	Stewart

Dublin: where to sleep

For full information on all accommodation, ask at the **USIT**, Aston Quay, O'Connell Bridge, Dublin 2 (tel: 679 8833), or contact **Dublin Tourism** at 14 Upper O'Connell Street, Dublin (tel: 747 733).

Count on paying £10 for a hostel bed. During the university summer vacation singles in student residences go for about £15, about the same as you're likely to pay in one of the cheaper B&Bs.

Hostelling International hostels:

Dublin International Youth Hostel, 61 Mountjoy Street (tel: 301 766).

69–70 Harcourt Street (tel: 750 430). 24 June–24 Aug. only.

Scoil Lorcáin, Monkstown (tel: 284 4655). 24 June–24 Aug. only. Far from the centre.

Other hostels:

Marlborough Hostel, 81 Marlborough Street (tel: 874 7629/874 7812).

Avalon House, 55 Aungier Street (tel: 475 0001).

Isaac's (The Dublin Tourist Hostel), 2–4 Frenchman's Lane (tel: 749 321/363 877).

The Young Traveller, St Mary's Place (tel: 305 000).

Goin' My Way/Cardijn House, 15 Talbot Street (tel: 878 8484/ 874 1720).

Student accommodation:

Dublin City University, Glasnevin (tel: 704 5000). 14 June–24 Sept.

The University of Dublin, Belfield (tel: 269 7696). 22 June–21 Sept.

Sleeping rough in Phoenix Park is illegal and unsafe. Sleep out in recognized camping grounds or in private grounds with the agreement of the owners.

Dublin: where to eat

You can make a good meal in Dublin town for around the £3.50 mark. Remember that, like the British, the Irish have a big thing about fish'n'chips. You can gorge yourself stupid on them for about £2.50.

The Buttery Snack area at Trinity College. A student haunt. Cheap.
Stag's Head at 1 Dame Court. Lunch is served between 12 and 2 p.m. It's big, it's hot, and the price is just fine! Good place for main meal of the day.
Bewleys Cafés Ltd at 10–12 Westmorland Street, 78–9 Grafton Street and 12–13 South Great Georges Street.
The Coffee Inn at 6 South Anne Street.
Mornington House at 62–3 Marlborough Street, Dublin (tel: 745128). Meals from £1.50; 4-course dinner £4.45. Great value.

Many hotels in Ireland and the British Isles offer counter-lunches and dinners. Pub lunches usually cost from about £3 and are filling enough to count as the main meal of the day.

Dublin: what to see and do

DUBLIN CASTLE in Castle Street. Thirteenth century. Hangout of the English until they were removed (ask in any pub for details of the removal). Entrance charge to see the State Apartments. CITY HALL adjoins the castle.

THE GENERAL POST OFFICE in O'Connell Street was the headquarters of the Irish Volunteers during the insurrection of 1916. It was destroyed during the fighting but is now rebuilt.

THE CUSTOM HOUSE at Custom House Quay is the city's finest piece of architecture. Destroyed during the War of Independence, but restored to its former Georgian elegance.

GUINNESS BREWERY at St James Gate is the home of the famous 'drop'. You're welcome to visit between 10 a.m. and 4.30 p.m. Monday to Friday to see a film of its operation – and sample the product. See the Brewery Museum.

THE NATIONAL MUSEUM at Kildare Street. Fine collection of Irish antiquities. Closed Mondays.

THE HUGH LANE MUNICIPAL GALLERY OF MODERN ART at Parnell Square. A fine collection of modern Irish works. Admission free.

NATIONAL GALLERY at Merrion Square West. Collection of old masters. Admission free.

TRINITY COLLEGE LIBRARY at Trinity College Green contains over two and a half million volumes, plus manuscripts. Don't miss *The Book of Kells*, considered one of the world's most beautiful illuminated manuscripts.

THE JOYCEAN MUSEUM at the Martello Tower houses manuscripts, photographs, etc., relating to Ireland's greatest writer. Take a Number 8 bus from O'Connell Bridge and get off at Sandycove.

ST MICHAN'S CHURCH in Church Street offers a somewhat unusual sight. In the vaults are bodies which have lain for centuries without decay. You can see these and, if you want, shake hands with a gentleman known as the 'crusader'. (Vaults closed on Sundays.)

ST PATRICK'S CATHEDRAL in St Patrick's Street. Fine old building dating back to the 12th century. Jonathan Swift (*Gulliver's Travels*) was Dean of St Patrick's from 1713 to 1745. Fans can see his tomb.

PHOENIX PARK is an ideal venue for a pleasant day's wandering. You can watch horse-racing at the racecourse for free if you can find a way in, for over £2 if you're rich enough to pay (the admission charge is halved for holders of student cards). You can visit the zoo, one of the oldest in Europe. With a bit of luck you might find some Gaelic football. With extra luck you'll find plenty of attractive people wandering around, especially Saturday afternoons and Sundays.

MOORE STREET MARKET Best place in Dublin to get an idea of what the Irish are really like. Great stuff and free. Saturday morning is best.

KILMAINHAM JAIL If you're interested in modern Irish history take buses 23, 51, 51A, 78 or 79 out to Kilmainham on a Sunday afternoon or between 10 a.m.–12 p.m. and 2.30–4 p.m. on Wednesdays. You get a guided tour through the cradle of the modern Irish revolutionary spirit. It was here that those who signed the proclamation of the Easter Week Rising of 1916 were executed. The last political prisoner to be released from the jail (in 1924) was Eamon de Valera, the late President of Ireland.

PUBS **Davy Byrne's** at 21 Duke Street was one of James Joyce's haunts; it's now a good place to meet young Dubliners. **The Brazen Head**, the oldest pub in Dublin, is situated close to Christchurch Cathedral; traditional folk groups meet here regularly. **Mulligan's** in Poolbeg Street is a good rough pub in the Irish tradition. **O'Donoghue's** at 15 Merrion Row is a place where would-be-if-they-could-be folk groups meet to try themselves on the customers. **The Baggot Inn**, Baggot Street, features live entertainment every night (reasonable entrance charge). **Lincoln's Inn**, 18 Lincoln Place, is where the Trinity College mob drink and talk.

Transport in Dublin

There are various bus and bus/rail passes available for the city's transport network. For full details go to the Dublin Bus office at 59 O'Connell Street (tel: 873 4222/872 0000).

Student and under-26 discounts

USIT at Aston Quay, O'Connell Bridge (tel: 679 8833) have a wealth of information on reduced international and domestic travel, and on various cards which give discounts at local shops, restaurants, cinemas and theatres.

Addresses

Main post office (for poste restante) at O'Connell Street, Dublin.
American Express at 116 Grafton Street, Dublin (tel: 77 28 74).
USIT, Aston Quay, O'Connell Bridge, Dublin 2 (tel: 679 8833).
Tourist Information Office at 14 Upper O'Connell Street, Dublin (tel: 74 77 33).
British Embassy at 33 Merrion Road, Dublin 4 (tel: 269 52 11).
US Embassy at 42 Elgin Road, Ballsbridge, Dublin (tel: 687 122).

Hitchers' Tips and Comments . . .

Sleeping rough in Dublin's Phoenix Park is not to be recommended. If the police don't throw you out, the army will.

D. G. MULVEY, DUBLIN, IRELAND

Re sleeping rough in Dublin's Phoenix Park. If the police don't get you, gangs might. You're safer dossing out in the countryside. Take a city bus to the end of the line and walk a bit (try No. 44B, 65, 31 or 60). HELEN SNIVELY, DUBLIN, IRELAND

For dossing out around small Irish villages try the local primary schools (called 'national schools'). You can always spot them by the 'children crossing' signs. There's usually somewhere flat to pitch a tent, running water on an outdoor tap, often toilet facilities and always a schoolyard shelter to get you through a wet night. On weekday mornings get out well before nine o'clock.

AIDAN MURRAY, ATHLORE, ENGLAND

To avoid paying on the ferry from Dublin to Holyhead (Wales), hitch a ride from outside the harbour. Drivers shipping their cars pay the price for the car and two passengers, so you can confirm a free passage across with the driver.

K. M. FITCHET, JOHANNESBURG, SOUTH AFRICA

A Jazz festival is held in Cork during the last weekend in October – one of the largest in Europe. P. SISK, CORK

7 · WESTERN EUROPE

Europe can never bore you. It stretches 2,400 miles north to south, 3,000 miles east to west and contains some 35 different states. Its highest elevation, Mount Elbrus in the ex-Soviet Union, rises 18,481 feet, its lowest, the Caspian Sea, also in the ex-Soviet Union, plunges 92 feet below sea-level. Its highest recorded temperature was at Sevilla in Spain with 124 °F and its lowest was –61° at Ust-Tsilma in Russia.

But the people are the thing. With its 650,000,000 citizens stacked 150 to the square mile, it is the most densely populated continent on the planet. You may never manage to remember which city the Forum is in or the gallery in which you saw the *Mona Lisa*, but you will certainly remember the city in which someone did you a good turn.

You meet hitchers on the road when you're heading, for instance, towards Austria and you ask if they've come from there. They tell you, sure. You say, what's it like? And they tell you that they met this guy in a bar and he bought them a drink and then went 40 miles out of his way to get them on to the road they wanted. So you ask what Vienna is like and they tell you there was this young kid in the marketplace who stole apples for them and that a cop came and chased the kid off and then pinched an apple for himself and started talking about his son who was hitching down in Africa.

You ask good travellers about a country and they never wax romantic about green fields or snow-capped mountains. They tell you about people. And everyone has a country in Europe they like best because of how the people were with them and everyone has a country they like least because they couldn't understand the people. There are 4,063,000 square miles filled with people.

What you will want to do in Europe depends on who you are. If history is your line, you can pursue history until it runs out your ears. If you're an artist, you can visit so many of the world's great galleries that you'll go cross-eyed. If you're a person with an ordinary job and a few months off to wander the hundreds of thousands of miles of European roads, then that's OK, too, because you can dip and choose as the mood takes you, without feeling the pressure of having to visit that city or see such and such a gallery.

If you can wander in Europe with just the vaguest idea of your route and enough money in your pocket and enough time up your sleeve to go as the road takes you, then you're lucky.

And there's nothing more to say, because Europe will say it all itself. Enjoy.

France

population	56,160,000
size	543,965 square kilometres
capital	Paris, population 10,825,000
government	Republic
religion	Predominantly Catholic
language	French
currency	*Franc* (F) One *franc* equals 100 *centimes*. Coins of 5, 10, 20, 50 *centimes*, and 1, 2, 5, 10 *francs*. Notes of 20, 50, 100, 500 *francs*

From England, about the cheapest way into France (or on to the Continent) is by the hovercraft service which runs between Ramsgate and Calais and Dover and Boulogne. Full-time students who are under 26 years of age and who have a student card can claim a substantial discount. Other main routes are Dover–Calais, Southampton–Cherbourg, Newhaven–Dieppe, Southampton–Le Havre. Dover boats also go to Zeebrugge and Ostend in Belgium. Check out the price of day returns; on certain routes they are cheaper than a single – cheaper still if you manage to sell the return half when you reach your destination port.

St Malo, an old walled seaport badly bombed in the latter days of the war, but beautifully restored, and **Dinan**, inland on the river Rance, a citadel town with a medieval castle, are both beautiful, impressive, and well worth seeing. In Brittany, of the many colourful seaports, **Morlaix**, **Concarneau** and **Lézardrieux** are perhaps the most outstanding, while **Carnac** is a must for prehistory buffs. Its 300 menhirs and dolmens (that's standing stones for the uninitiated), spread over 4 km and aligned for sunrise at solstices and equinox, date from Neolithic times and offer an even greater spectacle than Stonehenge.

If you're heading straight for **Paris**, you might want to stop in at **Rouen**, the capital of Normandy. An old, old city, it retains an ancient look with timber-framed houses (actually only 18th century) and huge Gothic structures dating from the 12th to the 16th centuries. The Fine Arts Museum contains a fine collection of work from the French schools, including a good display of Impressionists. Buildings worth looking at include the gigantic Notre-Dame Cathedral and the Church of Saint Ouen. See also the Great Clock on Rue du Gros-Horloge. Its workings date from 1389. The Place du Vieux-Marché is the public square in which Joan of Arc was burned at the stake on 30 May 1431.

Around Paris, there are at least three places worth a visit.

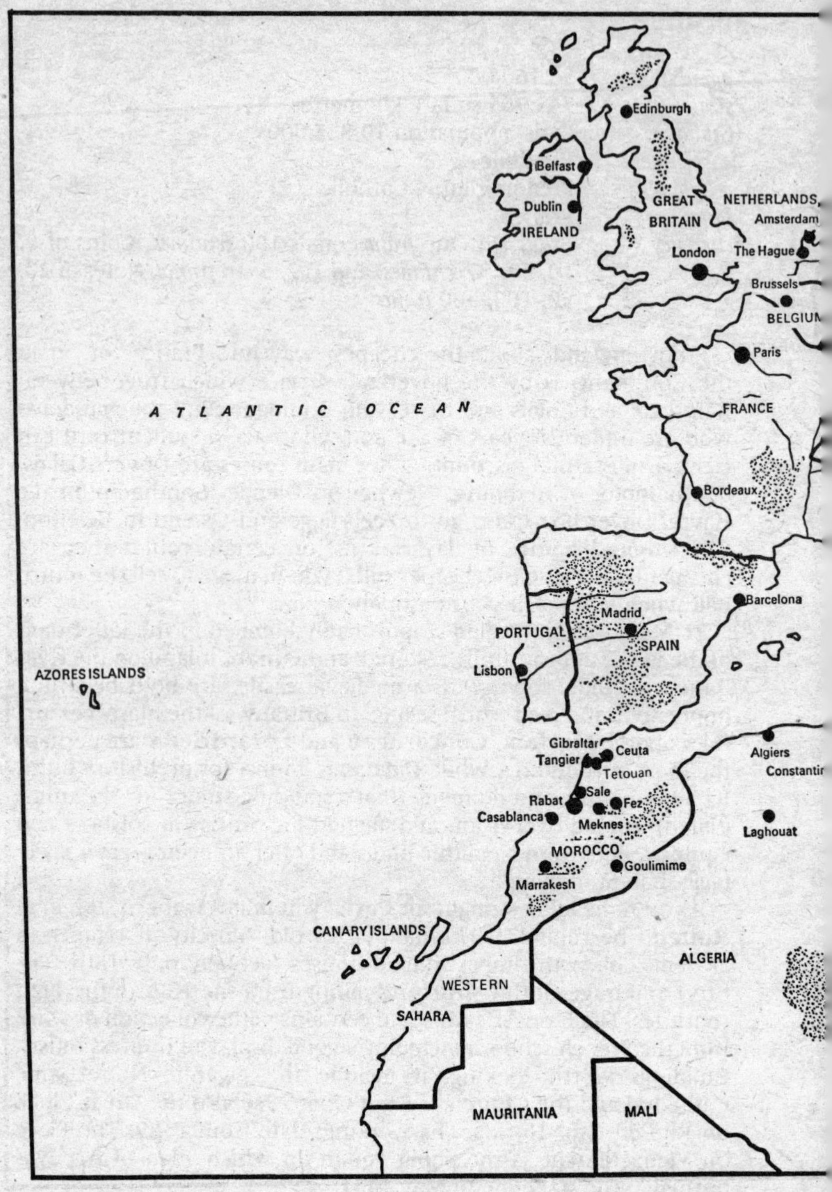
Edinburgh
Belfast
Dublin
IRELAND
GREAT
BRITAIN
NETHERLANDS
Amsterdam
London
The Hague
Brussels
BELGIUM
Paris
ATLANTIC OCEAN
FRANCE
Bordeaux
Barcelona
Madrid
PORTUGAL
SPAIN
Lisbon
AZORES ISLANDS
Gibraltar
Ceuta
Tangier
Tetouan
Algiers
Constantin
Rabat
Sale
Fez
Casablanca
Meknes
Laghouat
MOROCCO
Goulimime
Marrakesh
CANARY ISLANDS
ALGERIA
WESTERN
SAHARA
MAURITANIA
MALI

SWEDEN
DENMARK
Copenhagen
Moscow
Gdansk
U S S R
Hanover
Berlin
POLAND
Warsaw
GERMANY
Bonn
Kiev
Prague
Krakow
Brno
LUXEMBOURG
CZECHOSLOVAKIA
Vienna
Bratislava
Budapest
Miskolc
Bern
Zurich
AUSTRIA
RUMANIA
Rostov
Graz
HUNGARY
Clug
SWITZERLAND
L. Balaton
Zagreb
Deva
Brasov
Milan
Belgrade
Bucharest
ITALY
YUGOSLAVIA
Split
BULGARIA
Varna
BLACK SEA
Dubrovnik
Nessebur
Plovdiv
Sofia
Rome
ALBANIA
Istanbul
Naples
Ankara
GREECE
TURKEY
Athens
Souk-el-Arba
Tunis
MEDITERRANEAN SEA.
Sousse
Monastir
Kairouan
El Djem
SYRIA
LEBANON
Beirut
Damascus
IRAQ
Djerba Is.
TUNISIA
Jerusalem
JORDAN
Tripoli
Benghazi
Tobruk
ISRAEL
Cairo
Ghadames
LIBYA
EGYPT
SAUDI ARABIA
Aswan
RED SEA
Tamanrasset
NIGER
CHAD
SUDAN

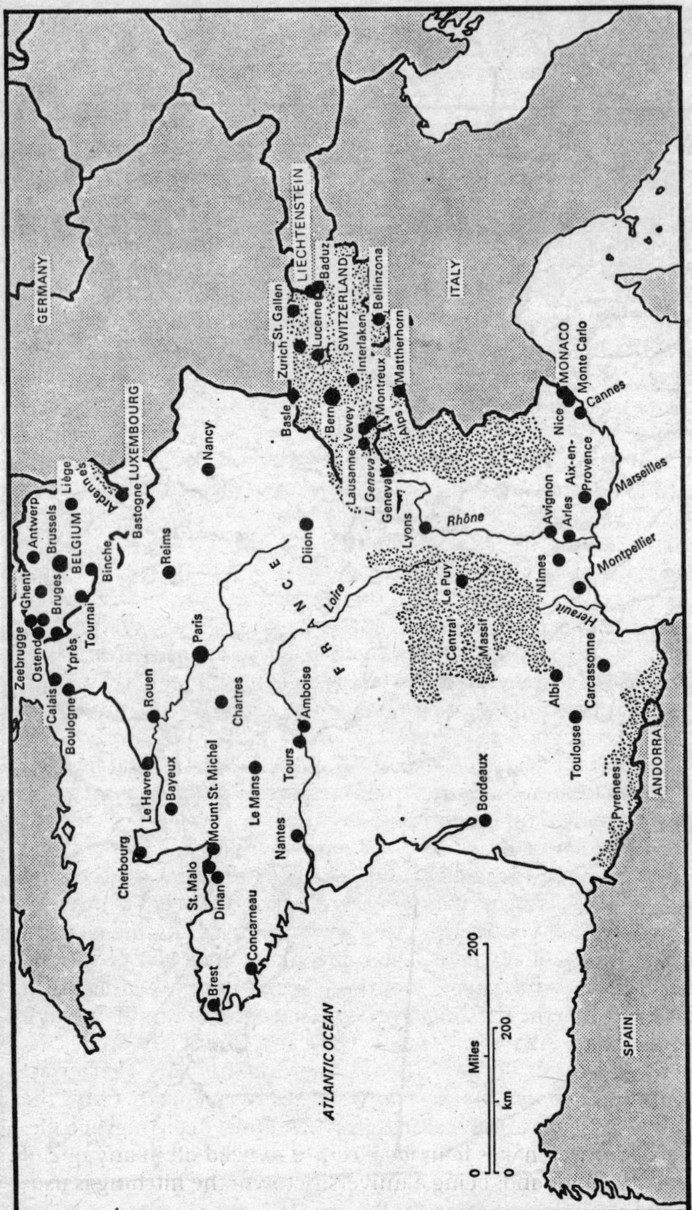
GERMANY
LUXEMBOURG
LIECHTENSTEIN
SWITZERLAND
ITALY
MONACO
BELGIUM
F R A N C E
ANDORRA
SPAIN
ATLANTIC OCEAN
Zeebrugge
Ostend
Ghent
Antwerp
Bruges
Brussels
Liège
Ypres
Tournai
Binche
Calais
Boulogne
Ardennes
Bastogne
Reims
Nancy
Paris
Rouen
Le Havre
Bayeux
Cherbourg
Mount St. Michel
St. Malo
Dinan
Brest
Concarneau
Chartres
Le Mans
Tours
Amboise
Nantes
Dijon
Loire
Basle
Zurich
St. Gallen
Lucerne
Baduz
Bern
Interlaken
Bellinzona
Vevey
Lausanne
Montreux
Mattherhorn
Alps
L. Geneva
Geneva
Lyons
Rhône
Le Puy
Central Massif
Bordeaux
Avignon
Arles
Nimes
Aix-en-Provence
Marseilles
Nice
Monte Carlo
Cannes
Montpellier
Herault
Albi
Carcassonne
Toulouse
Pyrenees
Miles
0
200
km
0
200

Chartres is the home of the 700-year-old Cathedral of Notre-Dame (they're all called that – it means 'Our Lady') which Rodin the sculptor described as the 'Acropolis of Christendom'. The 371-foot-high structure can be seen from Montmartre, in Paris, on a clear day. And that's 90 km away. The church took 200 years to build and its 137 stained-glass windows cover an area of 25,000 square feet. See also the house known as 'Picasiette' which is decorated with pieces of broken china set into cement. The work, which took 36 years and 29,000 hours, is a mosaic of Chartres itself.

Fontainebleau, 60 km south of Paris, is the site of the palace of the French kings. Begun in the 12th century it was continually added to. You can go through various royal apartments, including Marie Antoinette's.

Versailles is only 20 km out of the capital. On this trip you can see the palace of Louis XIV (the famous Sun King) and La Malmaison, home of Napoleon and Josephine.

Back in Normandy again, **Bayeux** is an old Norman town with yet another cathedral of Notre-Dame. See the famed Bayeux tapestry, 225 feet long, dating from the 11th century and depicting the Norman conquest of England.

Near Bayeux, on the coast, is the site of the 1944 D-Day landings. You can visit the beaches – **Utah, Omaha, Gold, Juno** and **Sword**. Plenty of things to see connected with the battle, including a museum of the invasion at the tiny village of **Arromanches**.

Mont St Michel is claimed to be the eighth wonder of the world. Built on an island linked to the mainland by a road, the 12th-century fortified town topped by its huge monastery looks quite unreal. And in springtime the *Grande Marée*, the big tide, comes rolling in from the English Channel at better than 16 km an hour, covering the road and completely surrounding the rock with water.

Pushing down to Tours, you go through **Le Mans**, scene of the big international car-racing events. **Tours**, a medium-sized city of around 100,000, is an old commercial centre and of no great interest. But from there, if you're interested, you can head into the château country of the Loire Valley. There are more than 120 of the old fortress homes in the valley, the most spectacular of them being at **Amboise** (catch the *son et lumière* if you have the time and money), **Chenonceaux, Azay-le-Rideau, Ussé** and **Cheverny**.

Orléans, further up the Loire, is where Joan of Arc got her act together and, as well as the many statues of her in the city, the cathedral has a series of stained-glass windows depicting her life. Orléans' location makes it an ideal centre to head off in any one of several directions and, being a university town, the hitching is usually good.

Hitching eastward through Auxerre and **Avallon**, a small medieval town with ramparts overlooking the Cousin Valley, you enter Burgundy. **Dijon**, ancient capital of the Dukes of Burgundy, has plenty to offer. The ducal palace houses the Museum of Fine Arts, which is reckoned to have one of France's finest collections. The city is renowned as a gastronomic centre and a walk through streets crammed with *pâtisseries* and bistros does wonders for the appetite. If you work up a thirst too, don't despair. Burgundy is paradise for wine fans, especially since many famous vineyards (Gevrey-Chambertin, Nuits-St-Georges, and Volnay) offer *dégustations* – free tastings. Connoisseurs sip, swill and spit out the wine, but there is nothing wrong in simply drinking it.

Beaune, on the road to Lyons, has two unusual museums in its medieval centre. The 15th-century hospital (still in use, with nurses in medieval uniform) houses a museum of medical instruments while, just along the road, the Wine Museum traces the history of wine making. The enormous wooden wine presses have to be seen to be believed.

Lyons, with more than half a million people, is the gateway city to the south. Founded in 43 BC it has a lot to offer. To start with there are twenty-two museums. Try the Museum of Fine Arts for Gauguin's *Who are we? Whence do we come? Whither are we going?* – just a sample of what you can find there. The Museum of the History of Lyons is a fascinating visual presentation of what happens to a city during twenty centuries. The Museum of the French Resistance speaks for itself. On the Hill of Fourvière, which was the city centre in Roman times, you can see a Roman theatre and the remains of a temple. The main theatre seated 10,000 people. The Gothic church of St Jean is surrounded by some of Lyons' oldest streets where many 14th- and 15th-century houses are still standing.

South of Lyons and a few kilometres west of the Rhône Valley is **Le Puy**. This weird city is a place of strange, steep, narrow streets and is surrounded by volcanic pinnacles. The Chapel of St Michel d'Aiguille sits on top of a 250-foot volcanic needle. The cathedral of Notre-Dame de Puy has a façade of multi-coloured lava. Homely lady hitchers may be interested to know that Le Puy is world famous for its lace and that its Crozatier Museum contains a selection of same.

South of Le Puy, where the N86 joins with the N113 is **Nîmes**, the oldest Roman city in France. Roman ruins everywhere, including the huge Nîmes arena. The hitching can be pretty tough in this congested area, particularly in summer, though students heading for the university city of **Montpellier** help out a lot. Montpellier is a young people's town, with plenty going on. Try to take in the enormous Saturday morning flea market, where you're likely to meet kindred spirits. Browse for bargains or, if short of cash, find a space, sit down, and sell something – anything – it's that kind of place.

Inland from Montpellier you travel through **Hérault**, the largest wine-producing area in the world. You see hectare after hectare of vineyards stretched out on every side.

There are at least two cities in this province worth visiting: **Albi** because of its Lautrec Museum which contains the largest collection of Lautrecs in the world – some 500 paintings and sketches, right from the first the artist ever made – and, south of Albi, **Carcassonne**, one of Europe's most memorable landmarks. The old medieval **Cité** remains intact and completely walled. From the distance it looks like some gigantic 20th Century-Fox movie lot. Within the walls you get a complete picture of what life was like eight or nine centuries ago. The road south of Carcassonne leads to **Andorra** (see **Luxembourg and the Small Countries**).

Over the other side of the Rhône you have **Avignon**, the papal seat from 1309 to 1403. See the Palace of the Popes and dozens of other monuments from that period. **Arles**, south of Avignon, is where Van Gogh lived and worked. **Aix-en-Provence**, where Cézanne worked, was founded by the Romans in 123 BC as a thermal resort.

South of Arles lies the **Camargue**, a vast marshy area famed for its white horses, black fighting bulls, and pink flamingos. **Aigues-Mortes**, a 13th-century Crusader city, rises spectacularly from the marshes. Its walls, nearly 2 km long, still intact and boasting twenty towers, give a great view of the flatlands. The white pyramids you see in the distance are stockpiles from the local saltmines. Nearby **Stes-Maries-de-la-Mer** is the gypsy equivalent of Mecca. Every May they come from all over the world to pay homage to Sarah, their patron. Don't miss this incredible spectacle if you are in the area at the right time.

Marseilles, the big port of southern France, is the country's oldest city, dating from 600 BC when it was founded by the Phoenicians. Much of the old city was destroyed in the Second World War, but there are still plenty of good areas to wander in. Around the Vieux-Port are some of Europe's grottiest and most interesting streets. Out in the bay stands the **Château d'If** from where Alexandre Dumas' fictional Count of Monte Cristo made his dramatic escape. If you want to visit the château (good trip), disregard the prices on the launch operators' placards and bargain like hell. A group of people should be able to cut the price per head nearly by half.

East of Marseilles is the expensive area of the French Riviera. It may qualify as the toughest hitching route in Europe, so be prepared for short hops and long pauses. If you're heading for **Nice**, largest town on the Riviera, the autoroute may not be as pretty as the Corniche but, if time is short, it should get you there a hell of a lot quicker.

Nice's Promenade des Anglais, running along the seafront, is the stuff of travel agency posters. Soak up the atmosphere with a summer's evening stroll and, if you're flush, risk the experience of a sidewalk apéritif, then just sit back and watch the world go by. Early risers can visit the flower market which is a riot of colour and perfume. Before heading off to explore the rest of the Côte d'Azur, stock up with supplies at one of the city's hypermarkets. The food prices in small shops are considerably higher.

Cannes, which hosts the International Film Festival each May, gives you the chance to rub shoulders with the glitterati. If you need reminding that this is a rich man's town, take an envious glance at the luxury yachts crammed into the harbour. Bus-boats make frequent trips out to the **Iles des Lerins**, a group of wooded islands which give scope for a bit of *camping sauvage*. Visit the castle on Ile Ste Marguerite, where the *Man in the Iron Mask* was imprisoned.

If you fancy sunbathing with the beautiful people at **Antibes**, **St Raphael** or **St Tropez**, dress may be optional but, unless you are on a public beach, you'll be charged a hefty sum for the privilege. Prices in these chic resorts are horrendous, so buskers and sketch artists might like to try and recoup their losses by trying their luck with the jet set, the yacht set and the army of would-be's if they could-be's. St Tropez, originally made famous by artists, should prove the most fruitful.

Less exclusive (i.e. cheaper) resorts, with better beaches, can be found further west at **Cavalaire** or **Le Lavandou**. Lavandou, named after the lavender that grows in the surrounding hills, still retains the atmosphere of the fishing village it once was. Here, as in the rest of France, campers should seek out the municipal camping, which is cheaper than most of the commercial counterparts.

For a change of scenery, an interesting trip is up to the **Cañon du Verdon**, north from Nice. Billed as Europe's answer to the Grand Canyon, it's great backpacking country and makes a change from the overcrowded coast. (Male hitchers with female companions, beware. The route through the hills takes you into **Grasse**, the perfume-making town, where you'll be invited to tour the factories, sniff the products – and buy!)

The miles of sandy beaches, stretching from the Camargue to the Spanish border, make this the poor man's Riviera. Wind-surfing is the big sport here and the annual championships are a colourful spectacle at **Sète**, France's second largest port on the Mediterranean. Sète, which is situated on a strip of land between the sea and the vast lagoon of the Etang de Thau, and with canals connecting the two, is sometimes called the Venice of France. The town has scores of seafood restaurants and stalls. Try oysters fresh from the enormous beds in the Etang.

Béziers, which in August emulates Pamplona with a running of the bulls through the main thoroughfare, is a good stopover. Its campsite, on the banks of the river Orb, beneath the aqueduct of the Canal du Midi, and with a view of the cathedral, is a great place for meeting fellow travellers.

Southwards is the road to Spain, with the La Junquera road carrying more traffic than the Port Bou road, though the latter is prettier, taking you down the Costa Brava.

● **Rent-a-Ride** Ever get that never-gonna-get-a-ride feeling? Well, snap out of it. Your French hosts have the problem licked! You get on the phone, tell them where you're going and they get you in touch with a driver who is going your way.

Remember that hitch-hiking is forbidden on motorways (autoroutes) but not on slip-roads or at 'péages' (where motorists pay their tolls). Several French organizations will put drivers and passengers in touch with each other; so contact the representatives of the 'Fédération Nationale des Associations d'Autostop organisé' at the following addresses:

Allostop-Provoya at 84 Passage Brady, 75010 Paris (tel: 4246 00 66). Open from 9 a.m.–8 p.m.
Allostop at 5 rue Duffour-Dubergier, 33000 Bordeaux (tel: (56) 81 24 59). Open Mon.–Fri. from 3 p.m.–7 p.m.

Also, but not belonging to this association:
Dauphiné Information Jeunesse at Jardin de Ville, 38000 Grenoble (tel: (76) 87 79 04).

You will be asked to pay an annual subscription and share petrol expenses. Or if you catch French radio and mainly RTL between 9 p.m. and 12 p.m. every day except Sunday, Max Meynier will put you in touch with really 'sympas' lorry drivers with whom you can travel. His telephone number in Paris is 720 22 11 and his broadcast is called *Les Routiers sont sympas.*

● **Corsica** You can reach Corsica by ferry from Nice, Marseilles or Toulon in France, or from Genoa, Livorno and Piombino in Italy.

The island is one of the Mediterranean's largest, over 150 km long and 75 wide. And with a high average temperature throughout the year (57.4 °F average through January and February) it's as good a place as any to hole up for a few days during the winter. But be warned, it's expensive. Keep in the backstreets for eating and sleeping or you're going to get hit with jet-set prices.

If you like mountain scenery you'll be in your element, because this is a truly spectacular landscape (Mount Cinto, for instance, reaches nearly 9,000 feet!). Top towns are **Ajaccio**, **Bastia** and **Bonifacio**. **Ajaccio**, the capital, was the hometown of Corsica's most illustrious citizen: Napoleon. Visit the Maison Bonaparte, his birthplace and old family home which is now a museum. More Napoleon stuff to be seen in the Palais Fesch museum and in the Musée Napoléonien at the Town Hall. Wander around the old fishing harbour. Usually plenty of people around the cafés facing the harbour, but watch the prices. You can get stung if you aren't careful. **Bastia**'s main attraction, in my opinion, is the beautiful old town. Great if you're a back-alley man. See also the museum, once the palace of the governors of Genoa, and the port with its superluxury ocean cruisers. (Some of them may need crew, so keep your eyes open if you're looking for a job.) The old fortified town of **Bonifacio** simply must be seen to be believed. Plenty of people claim it as the prettiest of all Mediterranean ports. 'Strangest' might be a better adjective. Have a look, anyway, and decide for yourself. History and art nuts should take the chance to drop in on the Bronze Age fort at **Cucuruzzu**. It's one of the best preserved in Europe. Also see the magnificent medieval frescoes at **Sermano di Bozio** which is in the centre of the island, near the ancient capital, **Corte**.

Camping out is permitted just about anywhere on the island, and with the high cost of hotel rooms you might as well get used to the idea, but check if it's national property 'forêt domaniale'! You can camp wild or pitch a tent at an organized site at Ota, Ajaccio, Corte, Calvi or Uccaini.

● Just been dropped off on the outskirts on the *wrong* side of a big town? Keep a lookout for the big hypermarkets (Mammouth, Euro-Marché, etc.). Cheaper shopping brings people in by car from all over, so station yourself at the exit with a sign; could save a long walk.

● If you find yourself bored with the road, you could give the canals and rivers a try. There is lots of traffic and, sometimes, boat owners are glad of extra hands for the locks. You won't travel fast but there are some great rides to be had. Most of the boats are pleasure craft, but there is commercial traffic, too, including barges carrying as much as a quarter of a million litres of wine.

- The French government says it will no longer allow in British visitors without passports, so Brits should make sure their passports are in order.

Paris: where to sleep

Under the French system, prices for hotel rooms are set for each room, and this is the price you must pay regardless of whether there are one or two of you in the room. In effect this means that there are no such things as singles or doubles in French hotels, no matter what some books might say, though some hoteliers may let rooms to solo travellers at a discount. Don't expect this to happen in peak season. You can ask for a third bed to be set up in a room: this should add roughly 30% to the basic cost of the room. It's possible to find rooms in Paris for 120–140F, but you're more likely to pay 160–200F. After you've been quoted a price *always* ask if there is anything a little cheaper as proprietors, quite naturally, try to get rid of their expensive rooms first. Youth hostels in Paris cost in the region of 90–130F, a lot more than you'll pay outside the capital where prices of 40–75F are more normal. For help finding youth or student accommodation contact the **Centre d'Information et de Documentation Jeunesse** (CIDJ) at Quai Branly 101, 75015 Paris 15e or **Accueil des Jeunes en France** (AJF) who have offices at rue St Martin 119 (tel: 42778780); blvd St Michel 139 (tel: 43549586); rue du Pont Louis-Philippe 16 (tel: 42780482); and in the Gare du Nord (tel: 42858619).

Following is a list of hotels which are amongst the cheapest in the centre of Paris:

Hôtel de la Tour Eiffel at rue de l'Exposition 17 (tel: 47051475). Métro to Ecole Militaire.

Hôtel Joigny at rue Saint-Charles 8 (tel: 45793335). Métro to Bir Hakeim.

Hôtel Port-Royal at blvd du Port Royal 8 (tel: 43317006). Métro to Gobelins.

Hôtel Des Alliés at rue Berthollet 20 (tel: 43314752). Métro to Gobelins.

Hôtel Henri IV at pl. Dauphine 25 (tel: 43544453). Métro to Pont-Neuf or Cité.

Hostelling International hostels are located as follows:

'Jules Ferry' at blvd Jules Ferry 8 (tel: 43575560). Métro to République.
Le D'Artagnan at rue Vitruve 80 (tel: 43610875). Métro to Porte de Bagnolet or Porte de Montreuil.
Relais Européen de la Jeunesse at av. Robert Schumann 52, Athis Mons (tel: 64848139). RER line C to Athis Mons.
3 rue Marcel Duhamel, Arpajon (tel: 64902855). RER line C4 to Arpajon.
Cité des Sciences at rue Jean-Baptiste Clement 1 (tel: 48432411).

Other youth and student accommodation:

1er arrondissement
Centre International de Paris at rue J. J. Rousseau 20 (tel: 42368818). Métro to Louvre Rivoli or Palais Royal Musée de Louvre.
Centre International de Paris at rue du Pélican 5 (tel: 40269245). Métro to Louvre Rivoli or Palais Royal Musée de Louvre.

4e arrondissement
Hôtel des Jeunes 'Le Fauconnier' at rue du Fauconnier 11 (tel: 42742345). Métro to Pont Marie or St-Paul.
Hôtel des Jeunes Maubuisson at rue des Barres 12 (tel: 42727209). Métro to Pont Marie or St-Paul.
Hôtel des Jeunes Le Fourcy at rue de Fourcy 6 (tel: 42742345). Métro to St-Paul.

5e arrondissement
Foyer International des Etudiantes at blvd St-Michel 93 (tel: 43544963). Open to both sexes from July–Sept., girls-only the rest of the year. RER to Luxembourg.
Hôtels des Jeunes Residence Luxembourg at rue St-Jacques 270 (tel: 43250620). RER to Luxembourg.
Y&H Hostel at 80 rue Mouffetard (tel: 45350953). Métro to Place Monge.

6e arrondissement
Association des Etudiants Protestants de Paris at rue de Vaugirard 46 (tel: 46332330). RER to Luxembourg.

9e arrondissement

Union Chrétienne des Jeunes Gens (YMCA) at rue de Trévise 14 (tel: 47709094). Half-board compulsory.

11e arrondissement

Maison International des Jeunes at rue Titon 4 (tel: 43719921). Métro to Faidherbe–Chaligny.

12e arrondissement

Centre International de Séjour de Paris at av. Maurice Ravel 6 (tel: 43431901). Dorm beds are the cheapest. Métro to Porte de Vincennes.

13e arrondissement

Centre International de Séjour de Paris at blvd Kellerman 17 (tel: 45907076). Métro to Porte d'Italie.

Maison des Clubs UNESCO at rue de la Glacière 43 (tel: 43360063). For ages 16 to 25 only. Open July and August. Métro to Glacière.

14e arrondissement

Foyer International d'Accueil de Paris at rue Cabanis 30 (tel: 45898915). Half-board compulsory. Métro to Glacière.

15e arrondissement

3 Ducks Hostel at 6 place E. Pernet (tel: 48420405). Métro to Commerce.

20e arrondissement

Centre d'Accueil et d'Animation de Paris at rue Louis Lumière 46 (tel: 43612451).

To sleep rough try along the banks of the Seine beneath the Louvre. There are usually some people sleeping there. (But see Marcel Thomas' letter at the end of this section.) Other best bets are the cemeteries, with the one at Montparnasse being handy to the centre. Cops don't seem to worry rough-sleepers in Paris as long as they're quiet, though I imagine their mood varies with the political climate.

Another tip for sleeping: word has it that many of the churches in Paris are left open at night and that the priests don't mind if someone takes a pew.

To repeat: most rock bottom hotels come out at around 135F a single, but if you gang up with one or two others to take a double or triple, the per-person price drops a little.

Paris: where to eat

It's hard to find a decent meal in Paris for under 60F. For a filling, cheap restaurant meal expect to pay 85–120F, unless you are a student who can take advantage of student facilities, or a youth hosteller. For the average hitcher in Paris on a tight budget, someone who wants to stay on for a few days, it's necessary to buy food from shops and make picnic meals. But that's no hardship. A loaf of French bread, a slab of cheese and pâté, a piece of fruit and a bottle of wine will come out around 50F, and you can sit yourself down by the Seine or in the Luxembourg Gardens and it's nice enough. Invest another few francs and eat your food with a cup of coffee at a sidewalk café and it's the nicest way of eating a meal in all of Europe.

● **Student eating** There are plenty of restaurants in Paris where students can get full meals for about 60F. For a complete list of addresses and for further information contact the **Organisation pour le Tourisme Universitaire** at av. Georges Berronos 39. Métro to Port Royal, or telephone 43 29 12 88. Here are some samples from the full list:

Le Mabillon at rue Mabillon 3. Métro to Mabillon.
Le Bullier at Avenue George Berronos 39. Métro to Port Royal.
Le Centre Albert Châtelet at rue Jean Calvin 8. Métro to Censier Daubenton.
Le Mazet at rue Mazet 5. Métro to Odéon.
Le Censier at rue G. St Hilaire 31. Métro to Censier Daubenton.
Le Grand Palais at Cours la Reine. Métro to Champs-Elysées–Clemenceau.

The above are all classified as university restaurants. They are open 11.30 a.m.–2 p.m. and 6.30–8 p.m.

Le Restaurant Chartière, rue du la Faubourg 7, Montmartre.
Latin Cluny Self-Service Cafeteria at blvd St Germain 98.
La Source at blvd St Michel 76.

● **Cafeterias** Tuesdays to Saturdays only. **Galeries Lafayette** and **Au Printemps**, both on Boulevard Haussmann, which is just at the back of the Opéra (Métro to Opéra). Good meals for about 60F if you stand up. More to sit.

Just about all of the little streets on the left side (with your back to the river) of Place St Michel – like rue de la Harpe, or rue St Severin –

have cheap eating places. Head for the restaurants with the longest queues outside because those are the ones with the best meals for your money. A lot of students eat in this area and there are usually plenty of people hanging around the fountain in Place St Michel, so you'll have no trouble getting directions to the current best place.

Here are some samples where you should be able to make a decent meal for 70–80F:

Pizza Pino, rue de la Huchette 8.
Au Bon Couscous, rue Xavier Privas 7.
Le Latin, rue Xavier Privas 22.
India, rue Xavier Privas 11/b.
Le Vieux Paris, rue St Severin 9.
Grand Mandarin, rue de la Harpe 37.

Also, at the corner of rue de la Harpe and rue St Severin is the **Pâtisserie du Sud Tunisien** which has great take-away sandwiches.

Next best eating area, though not so colourful, nor with such a young crowd, is in Le Marais on the Right Bank, in the area bounded by rue de Rivoli, rue du Temple and the boulevard Beaumarchais. You should do OK with 70F in the following:

La Dame Tartine, rue Bisemiche 2.
Les Arquebusiers, rue des Arquebusiers 12.
L'Arbre aux Sabots, rue Simon Leclerc 3.

Paris: what to see and do

MUSÉE D'ORSAY at rue de Bellechasse 1, 75007. Closed on Mondays. World's greatest collection of Impressionist paintings.

LOUVRE in rue de Rivoli. Great collection of paintings and sculptures. Closed Tuesdays. Half-price on Sundays.

RODIN MUSEUM rue de Varenne 77. Entrance charge, but half-price Sundays. Rodin is considered by many to have been the greatest sculptor since Michelangelo. Closed Mondays.

EIFFEL TOWER in Champ de Mars. There are three platforms on the 1,033-foot-high tower, and it costs to go to each of them. By the time you reach the top you're in for more than 49F but you have a great view of Paris.

GEORGES POMPIDOU NATIONAL CENTRE OF ART AND CULTURE stands on the Plateau Beaubourg, bounded by rue Rambuteau and rue de Renard. Nearest Métro: Rambuteau. Open daily except Tuesday. The centre is the result of an attempt to bring together all forms of cultural expression. Thus, under one roof, you can visit the National Museum of Modern Art, featuring work by dozens of top painters including Matisse, Miró, Picasso and Chagall; the Public Information Library with one million books, films, records, slides, etc.; the Institute for Research and Coordination in Acoustics and Music; the Centre of Industrial Creation; the Children's Workshop; the Cinémathèque, which tells the entire story of motion pictures, etc. In addition, anything up to forty exhibitions and demonstrations are held each year in this fantastic building which to some is a gem of modern architecture and to others a sewer on stilts. A day pass costs around 50F. Entry free if you're under 18. Don't miss the happenings in the plaza in front. On the right day it's the best entertainment in Paris, and all free. Great place to meet people.

FREE VIEW OF PARIS from Sacré Coeur which surmounts the Butte Montmartre. (When this church was built, the architects found that the soil of the Butte was incapable of supporting the weight of the building so they had to push the foundations right through the hill. Consequently, Parisians say that if the hill were removed the church would be left standing.) In summer, young Parisians often meet on the steps of the Basilica.

MUSÉE DE CLUNY pl. Paul-Painlevé 6. Nearest Métro: St Michel. Admission charge. Open daily except Tuesdays. A collection of some 25,000 works of art including paintings, sculptures, carvings, metal work, fabrics and tapestries, ancient furniture, porcelain and glass, all housed in one of the city's most beautiful old buildings.

LUXEMBOURG GARDENS Métro to Gare du Luxembourg. Gardens (free) in which is contained the huge Luxembourg Palace which was built between 1615 and 1620 for the mother of Louis XIII. The palace was used as the headquarters of the Luftwaffe during the Second World War German occupation of Paris. Usually plenty of people wandering about the gardens if you're looking for company.

SEWERS Enter from the south end of the Pont d'Alma on the Quai Branly, near Place de la Résistance. About a 20-minute barge trip through the sewers from the Place de la Concorde to Madeleine. Check with people for ever-changing time schedules unless you're in town between May and June when trips usually take place at 2, 3, 4 and 5 p.m.

PLACE PIGALLE This was once the centre of Bohemian Paris (now MONTPARNASSE is more the place), but these days Pigalle and Boulevard de Clichy are neon-lit tourist traps, full of clubs like the famous **Moulin Rouge** (you can see the show for about 100F if you sit at the bar and hold your drink tight), third-rate strip-joints full of drooping boobies, half-baked sex shops and handbag-swinging prostitutes who case you with a smiling eye. (The pros, by the way, aren't always what they seem. Paris fuzz did a big round-up recently and found that a large percentage of the ladies were, in fact, gentlemen.) But it's a great free show and if you're lucky you'll be able to watch some expert fleecers in action against the slow-witted tourist cult.

NOTRE-DAME CATHEDRAL One of the classic sights of Paris. Worth looking through. Also try to make it up the tower for a good view. Entrance charge for the tower.

VICTOR HUGO'S HOUSE is in the beautiful Place des Vosges which is buried in the Marais area. (Just a few minutes' walk from Place de la Bastille.) Fans of the old gent – and quite a gent at that – will enjoy the pilgrimage. Those not interested in literature will probably enjoy the square anyway. It's like stepping back a couple of centuries.

NAPOLEON'S TOMB at the Hôtel des Invalides. Take the Métro to Ecole Militaire. You'll see the granite sarcophagus in the crypt. Inside are six coffins, one within the other. In the last is the Emperor. See the room which contains his personal relics, including his death mask, his hat and his sword. Don't miss the nearby ARMY MUSEUM (at the Hôtel des Invalides) which has one of the world's best collections of swords, bows, guns, cannon and other would-be problem solvers.

MONTMARTRE CEMETERY Enter from Avenue Rachel. Free. Interesting trip through a very strange scene. Some graves are crowned by monuments as big as houses which must have cost tens of thousands of francs to build. Quite unlike English or American style cemeteries. Zola is buried there, as are Stendhal, Berlioz, Offenbach, Delibes, and the son of Alexandre Dumas. The MONTPARNASSE CEMETERY is another free, weird trip. Enter on the rue Froidevaux. Famous people buried there include Saint-Saëns, de Maupassant and

Baudelaire. A third is PERE LACHAISE CEMETERY, entrance on Boulevard Menilmontant, where you can see the graves of Rossini, Balzac, Oscar Wilde, and rock star Jim Morrison.

MARKETS Free. There are several worth a visit. The BIRD MARKET at Place Louis-Lépine, open Sundays 9 a.m.–7 p.m. The CLOTHES MARKET at Carreau du Temple, open all week, except Mondays, from 8 a.m.–7.30 p.m. and on Sundays 9 a.m.–7 p.m. The FLOWER MARKET at the east side of Madeleine, open every day except Mondays, from 9 a.m.–7.30 p.m. The FLEA MARKET, the biggest in the world with open stalls and shops, at Porte de Clignancourt, open all day Saturdays, Sundays and Mondays. The STAMP MARKET at Avenue Gabriel and Avenue Marigny, open Thursdays, Saturdays, Sundays 8 a.m.–7 p.m.

THE CATACOMBS at Place Denfert-Rochereau. Small charge. Open Tuesday to Friday 2–4 p.m., Saturday and Sunday 9–11 a.m. and 2–4 p.m. Originally the catacombs may have been a Roman quarry. Back in the 1780s, the city authorities were clearing an ancient cemetery and moved the bones into the catacombs. Some workmen took it into their heads to do a little interior decorating with the skulls – and you can still see the result of their efforts. The catacombs were also used as Resistance headquarters during the war.

PLACE ST MICHEL One of the best places to meet students is at the Place St Michel in front of the fountain showing St Michel with the Devil.

LES CAVES The famous Parisian institutions where you fight the haze of cigarette smoke and drown in the music are expensive. Entrance to most is in the vicinity of 45F, the price usually including one drink and you don't have to buy another. If you do they cost 20–30F each. But you meet some great people, hear some nice music, and have a real chance of latching on to someone of the opposite sex. If you can afford it, try: CAVEAU DE LA HUCHETTE at rue de la Huchette (Métro: St Michel), or TROIS MAILLETS at 56 rue Galande (Métro: St Michel).

Transport in Paris

With many of the major sights within half an hour of each other, Paris is a good walking city. Just as well, because the Métro (the underground railway) and the bus system are expensive. If you're going to be in town any length of time buy a *carnet*. (Make sure you get second class.) Bus prices are about the same as the Métro. Rich hitchers can buy a special 4-day tourist ticket which gives unlimited travel on the Métro, plus on city and suburban buses. It's not a bad deal when you consider you can go as far afield as Versailles! Richer hitchers expecting to be in town for a week can buy a 7-day ticket at any RATP station.

Student discounts
Reductions to all state museums and galleries, to certain other museums and galleries, plus to some theatres, cinemas and clubs. Check with the Organization pour le Tourisme Universitaire (l'OTU) at 39 av. Georges Berronos. Paris 5e (tel: 4329 12 88).

Addresses

Main post office (for poste restante) at rue du Louvre 52, Paris (tel: 40 28 20 00). Open 24 hours.
American Express at rue Scribe 11, Paris 9e (tel: 47 77 77 07).
Organisation pour le Tourisme Universitaire (l'OTU) at av. George Berranos 39, Paris 5e (tel: 43 29 12 88).
Office de Tourisme de Paris at Champs-Elysées 127, 75008 Paris (tel: 47 23 61 72).
US Embassy at av. Gabriel 2, Paris (tel: 42 96 12 02).
British Embassy at rue du Faubourg Saint-Honoré 35, Paris 8e (tel: 42 66 91 42). The Emergency Consulate is at 9 av. Hoche (same telephone number as the Embassy) (métro Charles de Gaule–Etoile).

Hitchers' Tips and Comments . . .

Best time to get from Paris to the South in one hop is to be there on the day the big vacation starts (in August) and everybody leaves for their holidays. Autoroute 1 is the main line of escape. Take a bus to the main feeder just near Orly Airport. Watch that you get the dates right. There seems to be a sort of vacuum period of bad hitching for a week after the big exodus.

CLIVE GILL, BIRCHINGTON, ENGLAND

Greetings from the Fastest Thumb in the West! In Paris don't sleep on the Ile de la Cité. You'll get ripped off. Try the woods called Bois de Boulogne where there are wooden shelters to keep the rain off. Take Métro 2 to Porte Dauphine.

BERND VAHLE PHALLUS, BOCHUM, GERMANY

Camp in Paris – at the pleasant site in the Bois de Boulogne. Don't walk from the Métro station (5 km), get a suburban train from St Lazare station in central Paris to Suresnes, walk down the hill, over Pont de Suresnes and the camp site is on your left – about ten minutes' walk from the station. Suresnes station also has trains to Versailles.

SIMON CALDER, COVENTRY, ENGLAND

If camping at Suresnes you can buy very cheap food at the Chez Tang chinese café near St Lazare station before heading out to the site.

MANDY JOBBINS, NOTTINGHAM, ENGLAND

With reference to your comments on grape picking where you say 'most of the work is of very temporary nature and badly paid', I would like to recount our experience in Beaujolais (north-west of Lyons). We worked on two farms for a total of 14 days and were paid 820F each. We were woken at 6.30 a.m. for breakfast; tea or coffee and bread and jam. Work started between 7.30 a.m. and 8 a.m. and we worked until 12 noon. Sometimes there was a break in the morning of 15 minutes for bread, cheese, chocolate and a drink. Wine, water and squash were available for the asking. Lunch was a massive affair eaten in traditional French fashion with each course being eaten separately. Wine flowed like a river. Work started at 1.30 p.m. and finished between 6 and 7.30 p.m. Dinner was excellent – plenty to eat and drink. Some might regard the sleeping and toilet facilities as being rough. You slept at the farms in a bed or on the floor – most places have hot water and showers. The working day is 10 hours, rarely more. The pay was 85F per day. If it rained you didn't work and you didn't get paid but you got your bed and food. We must add that the work is hard and dirty – particularly when it's wet.

All in all it was a thoroughly enjoyable experience – you eat and drink well, can meet some pleasant and interesting people and you can save money because you have no expenses. On some farms (the ones we worked on) cigarettes were on the house. We would recommend the grape harvest (*Vendange*). Beware of organizations like the one we contacted which gave us a vineyard address and a starting date. They charged £11 each and told us they'd send us the information via a poste restante address. After much phoning and hassling we got an address but not a starting date which was important because the harvest was a month early this year.

We think that the best thing to do would be to visit an area in early September, get yourself fixed up with a farmer and drift off until the *Vendange* starts. Sometimes you can work on afterwards. Two people we know have got jobs for three months and one year – the exception rather than the rule.

GAIL PEMBERTON AND DAVID GRIFFITH, LYONS, FRANCE

I've run this letter for several editions. The wages have risen, but the basic info still holds good. Competition for jobs is getting fiercer almost every year though. K.W.

Anywhere in France if you order a coffee, make sure it's a *petit* otherwise they serve you a super de luxe version at a price to match.

In Paris for crashing rough your book suggests the banks of the Seine near the Louvre – forget it! I slept there with a fellow English guy and several others and we were wiped out at 5 in the morning by a bunch of very professional heavies.

They woke us up but we couldn't stand up. I was rolled for about £60 cash, stripped of valuables, watch, ring, etc. Even lost me Levis and travelling the Métro in underwear isn't funny! Everyone lost something so I suggest that spot gets black-listed in the next edition.

MARCEL THOMAS, HORNDEAN, ENGLAND

On Paris you failed to mention a mass of cheap hotels directly outside of the Port de Vincennes subway stop.

LYNNE HOFFMAN AND JUDITH ZORFAS, CANADA AND USA

Just south of Paris, not too far from Porte d'Orléans, is the Rungis, an enormous fresh food market. Lorries leave from there for all over Europe. CHRIS MOORE, BEDFORD, ENGLAND

If drinking wine in a bar or restaurant, emphasize *vin ordinaire*. I got ripped off for some expensive wine, and you're obliged to pay.

JOHN HEYWOOD, DEVON, ENGLAND

There was hardly a town in France that I passed through that didn't have an approved campsite. These can work out quite cheap although not as cheap as out on the road. They have several advantages; they are safe as there is always somebody about to watch your stuff; they have hot showers; and there is usually a supermarket nearby where you can get decent grub for a decent price.

PAUL LAWRENCE, BELFAST, NORTHERN IRELAND

Underneath the Louvre and Eiffel Tower Gardens always rest your head on your kit and tie your pack to your sleeping bag.

NICHOLAS M. STEVEN, SHERBORNE, ENGLAND

Need a shower in Boulogne? Use the drivers' washrooms (male and female). Hot showers, fresh water, electricity, heaters – and it's free! The drivers are cool, provided you keep the place tidy – general rule anywhere of course. Find the washrooms in the port under the flyover, about 75 metres from the main terminal.

CHRIS TAYLOR, BLACKBURN, ENGLAND

Boulogne to Paris is a really bad hitch. We managed it in 7 hours, but heard lots of tales of people taking one to three days!

BILL AND DIANA MARTINDALE, NO FIXED ABODE, ENGLAND

If you're stuck for a cheap hotel in Paris, try the backstreets around Pont Neuf. You should find a good deal and it's a convenient base, being near the Louvre and Notre-Dame.

Watch Paris street urchins. These kids approach you in the street holding a newspaper in one hand. While talking to you, the concealed hand is going through your pockets. The kids are very young but, boy, are they professional!

When leaving Paris, if you're aiming for Belgium or Holland, catch the Métro to Porte de la Chapelle. Usually lots of other hitchers waiting, so you have to do something to stand out from the crowd.

MIKE PLUMMER, SEAVIEW, ISLE OF WIGHT

For cheap digs in France, try the Foyers des Jeunes Travailleurs. There's one in most reasonable-sized towns. Also, because of the high tolls on most autoroutes in France (and Italy and Spain), many drivers prefer to use the national routes (A-class roads) for journeys less than about 200 km. Because of this, hitching may often be faster on these roads than on the autoroutes.

CHRIS MAY, SHEFFIELD, ENGLAND

To all hitchers! The autoroute entrance at Perpignan, which leads south to Barcelona, is hitcher's hell. I waited hours there, exposed to a vicious Pyrenean wind. I met many others who'd had the same trouble at the same spot. And you should've seen the exasperated scrawlings on the roadside barrier! Try not to get dumped there!

PATRICK HINE, OXFORD, ENGLAND

Patrick Hine's comments about the motorway junction at Perpignan also apply to those who want to go north. I was stuck there for a whole day in a wind so strong I had to sit down and thumb. However, the first car that came by the next day gave me a lift, but that's hitching for you.

ALAN BARLOW, CHEADLE, UK

Montpellier is a lousy hitch out on the N113. Too many hitchers. Walk a couple of kilometres to the Péage and try your luck there.

Also, I find that the Calais to Paris N1 route is overhitched. Try the N43 instead. I never saw anyone else on it.

MIKE WALDIE, SHENFIELD, ENGLAND

A warning to backpackers travelling on the Paris métro. If it's crowded and you're forced to stand, take off your rucksack and put

it in front of you where you can keep your eyes on it. Otherwise you're an easy mark for the pickpocket gangs who travel the Paris lines.
DAZ HODSON, NORTH HYKEHAM, UK

Lyons is another hitch-hiker's hell on earth. Unless you really want to see it, try not to get dumped there. Even for a single girl it means hours of walking and waiting before you get a lift out.
SANDRA ANDERSON, BALLATER, SCOTLAND

Fontainebleau and Versailles are good visits any time except July and August when you can queue up to three hours to get in! In Paris, visit La Défense, Paris' contribution to futuristic architecture. Truly fantastic to see skyscrapers painted to resemble clouds and trees.
CLAIRE BETTINGTON AND SUSAN COOPER, LEDBURY, UK

Don't camp on forested hillsides in Corsica during summer. Devastating forest fires are common on this island.
I.B., HEMEL HEMPSTEAD, UK

Anyone heading south from Strasbourg towards Lyons should ignore the autoroute and stay on the national highway. The hitching is good and the route provides some of the best scenery in all of France.
JOHN OTIS, MANKATO, MINNESOTA, USA

For cheap sleeping in Paris, go into a métro station at around 1 a.m. and wait for the attendants to lock up. They will almost always leave you alone, and you have a warm, dry kip until 5 a.m. when they open again. The only trouble is that you're locked in, so make sure that any other people trying the same thing are harmless. The town drop-outs use the métro as hotels.

In the south of France sleep on the town beaches with all the other bodies. No one bothers a group of 20 or 30 people except the police. They tend to come along around dawn and throw water at you. Forget the rail stations in the south unless you want bruised ribs.
JOHN PILKINGTON, BRISTOL, UK

When crossing into France from Spain try to get a lift that will take you beyond Bayonne (right in the south) because the area crawls with fellow hitchers. When we passed through Bayonne on the road to Bordeaux we counted about 20 hitchers who looked like they'd been there all day. Depressing sight.
JON MORE O'FARRALL, TRINITY, JERSEY, CHANNEL ISLANDS

If an articulated truck picks you up on the way to the Channel ports, the driver can take you across for nothing in the 'free seat'. The 'free seat' is covered by what is sometimes known as a 'mate's ticket'.
PAUL, LONDON, UK

Hitchers who miss the last ferry out of Calais can doss in a couple of Second World War bunkers nearby. Expect to be woken early by bait-diggers parking their mopeds in the bunkers.

STEVE RICHARDS, WARRINGTON, UK

If you care about your life don't sleep in Marseilles parks. Gangs rob rucksacks from hitchers and inter-railers. I've seen it happen.

JENS RECKMAN, ASKIM, SWEDEN

A great place to sleep is under the pillars of the Eiffel Tower. Great shelter and fairly clean. Usually some company, too – and these days you need safety in numbers. You can stay until about 9 o'clock when the tourists start arriving. No hassle from the cops, either. Boulevard de Clichy great place for meeting people during the daytime. If you're in need of a few francs, take your talents along to the Georges Pompidou Centre – you might meet with a fellow traveller and be able to put an act together. PAUL HINCKLEY, BIRMINGHAM, UK

To get out of Paris to Lille, the best place to hitch from is Porte de la Chapelle. STEPHAN HERFURTNER, KAARST, WEST GERMANY

Sleeping rough in Marseilles: try the public Jardin Emile Leclaux near the Vieux Port. Go down the grass slope off the path and conceal yourself behind trees. DUNCAN SMITH, BOURNEMOUTH, UK

Forget sleeping rough in the Bois de Boulogne. Quite a few people, including some locals, tell us that it's frequented by some very nasty male transvestite prostitutes and is therefore patrolled by rough gendarmes.

SIMON WADSWORTH, SHIPLEY, WEST YORKSHIRE, ENGLAND

Monte Carlo – walk through the tunnel, keep to the lower road, walk past the sandy beach to the next stony beach and you reach the only place to sleep rough. You often find 50 people on this beach. MARI DOYLE, GODALMING, SURREY, UK

You always give the city of Nîmes a mention. As your readers are sure to be wearers of denim, would they not like to know that that is where it first came from – de Nîmes?

MOYNA GARDNER, GLASGOW, SCOTLAND

In Paris, for those who sleep rough, Jardin des Plantes is a good place – especially around August when it is full of other people roughing it. Police check the place around 7 a.m.

NIGE AND PAUL, BATH, AVON, ENGLAND

The cops in Paris won't hassle you unless you hassle them. Always carry your passport with you and try to have at least 10F on you or you could be pulled in for vagrancy. They have a right to hold you for 48 hours without charges (garde à vue).

PAUL HINCKLEY, BIRMINGHAM, UK

Don't use the toilets just inside the entrance at Mont St Michel – free ones higher up. Don't even buy a postcard near the entrance – everything gets cheaper the closer you get to the top. And don't eat in the restaurants there – small portions and expensive.

PETER NELSON, PLANET EARTH

Lots of work and money to be made between spring and autumn. Apricot picking around Perpignan from mid-May to June. Ice cream and doughnut selling on any of the beaches on the Gulf d'Lion or Côte d'Azur from June to mid-September. Cherry picking around Avignon in June. Castrating maize (that's what they call it) around Pau in July. Grape-picking everywhere in France, starting in the south in August/September and slowly working north to end in October. If you are in any of these areas at the right time, ask around the villages, at the Town Halls (Mairie or Hôtel de Ville) for work, or ask your fellow travellers about the ice cream selling. Just stroll along the beach and ask the first seller you see who his boss is. Any fruit picking work should pay at least 27F an hour (the National Minimum Wage in France). If you're an EEC member and find yourself on really hard times in France, go to the local Town Hall and try to explain your situation. They may give you coupons which can be exchanged for bread and meat in the local shops.

DAVID LAIDLAW, SOMEWHERE IN EUROPE

Work is no longer a certainty as much of the picking is now done automatically and the remainder, by organized groups of Spaniards and Moroccans. If you can get it, and be prepared for severe backache, it is quite well paid. NICK NEWSON

Try not to get dropped at Nîmes. I spent five long hours in the company of a much-abused roadsign. Reaching a service station on the A9 from the 'wrong' side of town in order to hitch north-east or south-west is horrendous due to appalling autoroute junctions. Nîmes is second only to Lyons on the European hitchers' blacklist.

MICHAEL GRAHAM, SCOTLAND

You do mention Carcassonne in your book, but not the very worthwhile country of Aude just south of that, through to the Pyrenees. Travel through Limoux (home of the champagne of the south, the Blanquette, to be bought anywhere for very reasonable prices), Quillan, Axat, and further down the mountain way along the River Aude. You can work the Vendange there too, and the countryside is beautiful, with incredible *gorges* (rockpools) to swim in. This is the Pays

Cathare, and the remnants of this hermetically closed Protestant sect fighting Catholic oppression can be found in the huge forts and castles built up high in the mountains such as at Puilaurens.

Hitching is excellent, anyone will pick you up. There are plenty of small alternative farming communities (Nentilla near Axat); there seem to be lots of Germans living there. Go to Usson-les-Bains just down the main road from Axat, you'll be amazed to find a whole ghost village, which used to have luxury hotels in the days when people went for spa baths rather than the seaside. They are now left empty!

Locals in Aude are friendly too, especially young people. They don't speak any English but those who haven't moved to larger cities are bored shitless and welcome a foreigner – finding places to stay is easy.

Especially in this area, you'll find many *gites d'étapes*, (hikers cabins). Originally huts built for shepherds doing the *transhumance*, the long travel from high grounds to low and back again, they have become places to stay, for free or for a very small charge, for anyone on the road and looking for a place to sleep. Safe, clean and you meet lots of people. ANNA LISS, AMSTERDAM

In Paris you can dump your pack for free in the library of the Pompidou Centre. Hand it to the attendant, look slightly interested in the library, then hit the streets. But don't forget to check what time the library closes. MARK HILL, LONDON, ENGLAND

The Info-Camping chain of campsites should be avoided if you want to keep costs low. Great facilities, but expensive.

LOUISE BROMLEY, NEWTON-LE-WILLOWS, ENGLAND

In France you can get excellent maps at most petrol stations. Get the one from Total which has all the petrol stations marked. I find these maps really useful, always telling the driver to drop me at the last petrol station before he turns off the autoroute.

LARS PETER SVANE, COPENHAGEN, DENMARK

Belgium

population	10,000,100
size	30,519 square kilometres
capital	Brussels, population 1,200,000
government	Constitutional monarchy
religion	Mostly Roman Catholic
language	French, Flemish, and some German; English widely spoken
currency	*Belgian franc* (BF) One *franc* equals 100 *centimes*. Coins of 50 *centimes* and of 1, 5, 20 and 50 *francs*. Notes of 50, 100, 500, 1,000, 5,000 *francs*

Entry into Belgium from England is by ferry from Dover, Felixstowe, Folkestone or Hull to either Zeebrugge or Ostend. A jetfoil service (fast but expensive) also runs between Dover and Ostend.

Principal cities after Brussels are **Liège, Bruges, Ghent** and **Antwerp**.

Ostend is one of the country's largest seaside resorts and even though it has 88 hotels and caters to the very solid tourist types it's a rather likeable place – one day at a time. The port is nice and there are a few things to see, but don't stop there if you're pushed for time.

Bruges, just a dozen or so kilometres inland from the sea and built on canals, is one of Belgium's main art centres and amongst Europe's best-preserved medieval cities. The most important commercial city in Europe during the 13th and 14th centuries, it is now one of the most popular for tourists. See the old market square and the 275-foot high belfry with its treasure-room and 11,400 lb Triumph Bell. See the Basilica of the Holy Blood where they keep what is believed to be a drop of Christ's blood – and if you're in town on Ascension Day (Ascension Day is a moveable feast held in May) catch the famous Procession of the Holy Blood. To see paintings by Brueghel the Younger, Van Eyck and Bosch, drop into the Groeninge Museum. If you have a student card and feel like visiting each of the sixteen museums and galleries in Bruges, you can buy a special discount card from the museums.

About 45 km south of Bruges, close to the French border and the city of Lille, is **Ieper**, better known to English speakers as Ypres, the centre of the infamous Flanders Fields of the First World War. Ieper is the most obvious base for exploring the battlefields. There are plenty of reminders of the carnage in the town itself. Inscribed inside the Menin Gate are the names of the 54,896 British and Commonwealth soldiers posted missing in the Ypres Salient, and with no known grave. The Reservoir Cemetery and the smaller Ramparts Cemetery are full of row after row of white gravestones. Memories of the war apart, Ieper is actually one of the most attractive towns in the country. The massive Cloth Hall and Belfry complex dominating the main square is the most important historical secular building in Belgium. See also St Martin's Cathedral, the Templars' House, the picturesque little Tolbooth on the Vismarkt, and the very photogenic Lille Gate (*Rijselpoort*).

Ghent, 30 km down either the E5 or the N10 from Bruges, is known as the City of Flowers, and every fifth year (2000 will be the next) hosts the Ghent *Floralies*, a huge international flower show. The other four years you can visit St Bavo's Cathedral, the Castle of the Counts (see the horrifying collection of torture instruments), the Castle of Gerard the Devil (not as good as the Castle of the Counts, but it has a better name) and see the Ghent Museum of Fine Arts for a fantastic collection of Flemish paintings. Have a look, also, at Mad Meg, a 15th-century cannon, 17 feet long, and weighing 16 tons, which used to spit out stone balls weighing 750 lb.

Antwerp, the world's leading diamond centre, is not a madly exciting city to my mind, but if you're going that way, drop in and see Rubens' house where the famous artist lived and worked. The Museum Mayer Van Den Bergh has a good collection, including *Dulle Griet* by the mystical Mr Brueghel. Seagoing types might be interested in the National Maritime Museum and, talking of the sea, it's interesting to note that even though Antwerp is 75 km from the ocean it's the world's fourth largest port. It has 45 km of docks along the banks of the Scheldt River (which drains into the sea) and those docks see 50,000 barges and 10,000 oceangoing ships tie up each year. Try the barges for possible river rides. It's done quite often by hitchers who drop the hard word into the right soft ear. The port also boasts a wild nightlife.

Halfway between Antwerp and Brussels on the E10 is **Breendonk** where the Belgians have kept intact a Nazi concentration camp. Nasty to look at and a sledgehammer reminder of what 'people' are capable of doing.

Binche, between Mons and Charleroi, is the scene of one of the wildest carnivals in Europe, culminating on Shrove Tuesday – Pancake Day. Great show if you can make it; fancy dress (Peruvian), flour bombs, more booze than you've seen in your life and lots of single ladies and gentlemen guarantee that it's a swinging show. You'll probably need a full day to rest after it, so budget accordingly. There is also a Carnival Museum.

Tournai, 80 km from Brussels on the A16, is a town of 35,000 which dates from AD 275 and mainly for those interested in history and architecture. For instance, its five-steepled Romanesque church is considered one of the finest in the world, while the belfry is the oldest in the country. Of particular interest are the ancient houses which dot the city.

Bastogne, on the E46 near the Luxembourg border, is a tourist centre for the Ardennes area. It's famous as the town where, during the Battle of the Bulge, when the Germans had the American forces surrounded and sent a man under truce to ask them to surrender, the American commander answered 'Nuts', thus leaving the German translator with an untranslatable word.

Waterloo, just south of Brussels, is the battle site where Napoleon met his you-know-what. In the town's main street you can visit Wellington's headquarters and a museum, while on the battlefield itself you can see Napoleon's headquarters and other museums and memorials.

Liège is yet another of Belgium's important art cities, and if you visit don't miss the 16th-century Palace of the Prince Bishops, the Museum of Fine Arts or the Museum of Walloon Life, which concentrates on life in Liège during the past centuries.

Hitching

Hitch-hiking is OK in Belgium, though the big main highway through from Ostend to Brussels – the E40 – can sometimes prove to be a trap. However, with any luck you'll meet someone on the ferry who is taking a car over and you'll be right on your way. Be warned that the Belgians are amongst the fastest and worst drivers in the world.

Brussels: where to sleep

Expect to pay 475BF even for a dorm bed in a hostel, and as much as 1,000–1,200BF for a single in one of the cheaper hotels. Make sure VAT and 10% service fee are included.

CHAB at rue Traversière 8 (tel: 02217 01 58).
Maison Internationale de Etudiants at Chaussée de Wavre 205, Etterbeek (tel: 02 648 97 87).
Centre International des Etudiants at rue de Parme 26 (tel: 02 537 89 61). Ask for dormitory.
Cité Universitaire at av. Paul Hèger 22 (tel: 02 647 10 56). Open 1 August to 15 September.

'Sleepwell' Sleep-in at rue de la Blanchisserie 27 (near pl. Rogier) (tel: 02 218 50 50).
Hôtel Osborne at rue Bosquet 67 (tel 02 537 92 51).
Hôtel Noga at rue du Béguinage 38 (tel: 02 218 67 63).
La Potinière at rue F. Jos Navez 165 (tel: 02 242 78 73).
Hôtel Georges V at rue t'kint 23 (tel: 02 513 50 93).
Auberge de Jeunesse Bruegel at rue du Saint-Esprit 2 (tel: 02 511 04 36).
Résidence Berckmans at rue Berckmans 12 (tel: 02 537 89 48).

For help finding hotels contact the **Brussels Information Office** at rue Marché aux Herbes.

For sleeping rough there's Parc de Brussels, the Botanic Gardens or the Parc Josaphat. But be warned – the word is that Belgian police are coming down hard these days.

Brussels: where to eat

A good filling meal will cost the equivalent of 350–450BF in a cheap restaurant or perhaps less if you use student facilities or chain cafeterias.

Cité Universitaire at av. Paul Héger 22.
L'Ecole Buissonière at rue de Traversière 13. Good set menus at lunchtime.

Brussels: what to see and do

THE GRAND' PLACE This is the heart of Brussels and has been since medieval times. Originally it was a marketplace and is still used as such in the mornings. Sunday morning is the scene of a bird market. The HÔTEL DE VILLE (Town Hall) is one of the oldest and most beautiful of the buildings on the square. A few francs gets you in for a tour. Directly opposite the Hôtel de Ville is the MAISON DU ROI, a restored 16th-century building housing the Municipal Museum.

MARKETS The best of the markets are the FLEA MARKET at Place du Jeu de Balle (every day from 9 a.m.–1 p.m. – best days Saturdays and Sundays), and the OLD MARKET at Place du Grand Sablon, which sells mostly antiques (swords, furniture, rare books, etc.), open all day Saturday and also Sunday morning.

MANNEKEN-PIS in rue du Chêne, near the Grand' Place. A small statue of a small boy taking a small leak. Not really worth seeing, but like the Mermaid in Copenhagen, you gotta go and have a look.

MUSÉE D'ART ANCIEN at rue de la Régence 3. Free entrance. Tremendous collection of Flemish art. This is where you can get a head full of Bosch and Brueghel.

CLUBS Try along av. de la Toison d'Or (between Chaussée d'Ixelles and Porte Louise) for fairly cheap prices and a fairly good chance for some action.

MUSÉE DU CINÉMA at rue Baron Horta 9 in the Palais des Beaux-Arts. This is a museum of the cinema which also shows several classic movies in the original language each night. You might catch an old one you've been hunting for. There are 12,000 titles in the archives (tel: 02 513 41 55).

YOUTH INFORMATION CENTRES You can find information and advisory centres throughout the country. They will help you locate beds and meals at reasonable prices, and introduce you to youth associations, societies and clubs. The following are all in Brussels:

Infor-Jeunes rue Marché aux Herbes 27 (tel: 02 512 32 74).
SOS Jeunes Open day and night (tel: 02 736 36 36).

For addresses of youth information centres elsewhere in Belgium, ask the tourist office for a free copy of their budget holidays brochure.

Transport in Brussels
Bus and tram tickets are expensive enough, but if you're in town a few days prices will really add up. So try investing in a five-journey card or a 24-hour card. Each offers big discounts; buy them at stations.

Student discounts
Special reductions to most museums, galleries, theatres and cinemas throughout the country.

Addresses

Main post office (for poste restante) at pl. de la Monnaie, Brussels.
American Express at pl. Louise 2, Brussels.
Belgian National Tourist Office at rue Marché aux Herbes 63, Brussels (tel: 02 504 03 90).
US Embassy at blvd du Régent 27, Brussels (tel: 02 513 38 30).
British Embassy at rue Joseph II 30, Brussels (tel: 02 217 90 00).

Hitchers' Tips and Comments . . .

If you need a clean-up in Brussels, go to the services under the main station. You get a good, hot shower there for a reasonable price.
PATRICK HINE, OXFORD, ENGLAND

In Belgium and France us females can get hit up to 30p a time for using public toilets. Take advantage of cafés and hostels.
AVRIL HORTON, LEEDS, UK

To get out of Brussels, go to the central tram station and take the tram to Diamant. From Diamant it's only 200 yards to the motorway slip road which takes you south.
DOUG BISSELL, 'THE CLYDESIDE REBEL', GLASGOW, SCOTLAND

The Snuffel Sleep-In in Bruges is a cheap place to stay.
CRAIG SEATON, WORKSOP, NOTTS, ENGLAND

In Brussels, while sleeping in a small park in the city centre, we were 'accosted' by the police about 8 a.m. All they did was check our passports and send us on our way. Cooperate and smile and you'll be all right.
NIGE AND PAUL, BATH, ENGLAND

An excellent place to stay is the Boomerang Youth Hostel at Volkstraat 58, 2000 Antwerp, tel: 238 47 82. Good value, and it's only 3 minutes' walk to the main road. In Brussels I stayed at Internationale des Etudiants. Very nice place with exceptionally friendly staff. Only drawback is 12.30 a.m. curfew.
NORRIE GREER, LONDON

If hitching from the Dutch-speaking part of Belgium to Lille in France, there is no point in having a placard with 'Lille' on it. The Belgians stubbornly refuse to change from their old name for the town, which is 'Rysel' (pronounced rye-sell). All the signposts in Belgium have Rysel on them and the French name is not mentioned anywhere. Can be confusing.
GRAEME MCCRORY, DUNDEE

Graeme McCrory is well off the mark with his comments. For one you'll see signs for Lille in the French-speaking parts of the country, but more importantly there are few Flemish-speakers who would be petty enough to ignore a placard just because it had the French name for a town (and vice versa with French speakers). Nor will Flemish speakers ignore you if you address them in French as some books say, though as many of them speak excellent English you might as well ask them in English first.

STUART COWAN, GALASHIELS, SCOTLAND

Graeme McCrory of Dundee says to write Rysel instead of Lille on your card. We did, and no one stopped for ages. When someone finally did pull up she told us that people don't use that any more. Confusing!!! LOUISE BROMLEY, NEWTON-LE-WILLOWS, ENGLAND

In some cases the French and Flemish names for a town are sufficiently alike to be immediately recognizable, for example Brugge/Bruges. In other cases they are quite different: Bergen/Mons; Doornik/Tournai; Namen/Namur; Luik/Liège; Antwerpen/Anvers; Ieper/Ypres; Aken/Aix la Chapelle (the German city of Aachen). Try using both versions on your sign.

MARC VAN DER EYCKEN, VEURNE FURNÈS, BELGIUM

In Antwerpen and Gent, look for very cheap rooms above pubs. Even if you don't see a sign advertising them, many pubs have rooms available, especially outside the centre, so don't hesitate to ask. There won't be a shower and perhaps no hot water, and there'll be a scary toilet in the hall, but usually the rooms are clean and good value. We stayed in one for 250BF (about £5). If you want to try something special, order a Kriek (pronounced Creek), Lambic or Bellevue. It's ancestral beer flavoured with cherries ripening along in the vat. Gets you pissed in no time, though.

Belgian chips are the best in the world, especially with tartare sauce. Nothing to do with raw meat, it's a kind of pickle mayonnaise, well worth trying.

If you want to travel to the Netherlands, an interesting way of going is not over the motorway but from Knokke into Dutch Flanders (Zeeland). Once in Zeeland you hitch to Breskens where you catch the boat (if you're in luck you'll get a lift from someone taking his car on the ferry anyway) to Vlissingen, a fishing port.

ANNA LISS, AMSTERDAM

The Netherlands

population	15,500,000
size	33,937 square kilometres
capital	The Hague, population 500,000
government	Constitutional monarchy
religion	Protestant and Roman Catholic
language	Dutch; a lot of English spoken, especially in the cities
currency	*Guilder* (*florin*) (f) One *guilder* equals 100 *cents*. Coins of 5, 10, 25 *cents*, and of 1, $2^1/_2$ and 5 *guilders*. Notes of 5, 10, 25, 50, 100, 250, 1,000 *guilders*

After Amsterdam, the most important cities to see are Rotterdam and The Hague.

Rotterdam, with 600,000 inhabitants, is the largest port in Europe and the second largest in the world. Its 47 km of dockside are worth going down to see. Waalhaven Dock is the largest artificial harbour in the world. For a great view over the port, climb to the 383-foot high lookout on the 600-foot Euromast (if you can afford the heavy entrance charge) – but avoid the restaurant, it's expensive. The Boymans-van Beuningen Museum claims to be the richest in Holland after the Rijksmuseum in Amsterdam. If it's half as good it's doing well. For a look at a building of a different sort, try the largest one in Western Europe. The Groothandelsgebouw, or wholesaler's building, is 220 metres long, 84 wide and 43 high. In it are 300 offices, restaurant, meeting-halls, a post office, bowling alleys plus lots more, including a staff of 5,000. Another interesting feature is its 1.5 km of road – inside! – leading to various indoor parking facilities. Americans might be interested in seeing Delfshaven, embarkation point of the Pilgrim Fathers in 1620.

The Hague, just a few short kilometres up the E10 from Rotterdam, has a lot more to offer. This city of 500,000 is the seat of Holland's government and the home of the Peace Palace, the International Justice Court. See the Municipal Museum with its fine line-up of modern art, including the world's largest collection of Mondrians. Philatelists should try the Dutch Postal Museum. To see one of the most unusual (and largest) paintings in the world, drop in on the Mesdag Panorama, or for a somewhat ghoulish hour go to the Prisoner's Gate to see the collection of torture instruments.

Don't miss the miniature town of Madurodam. It's built over an area of four acres, complete with 3 km of railway track, houses, castles, churches, and even an airport, all constructed perfectly to a $^1/_{25}$th scale. Open April to September.

Near The Hague is the seaside resort of **Scheveningen**. The long,

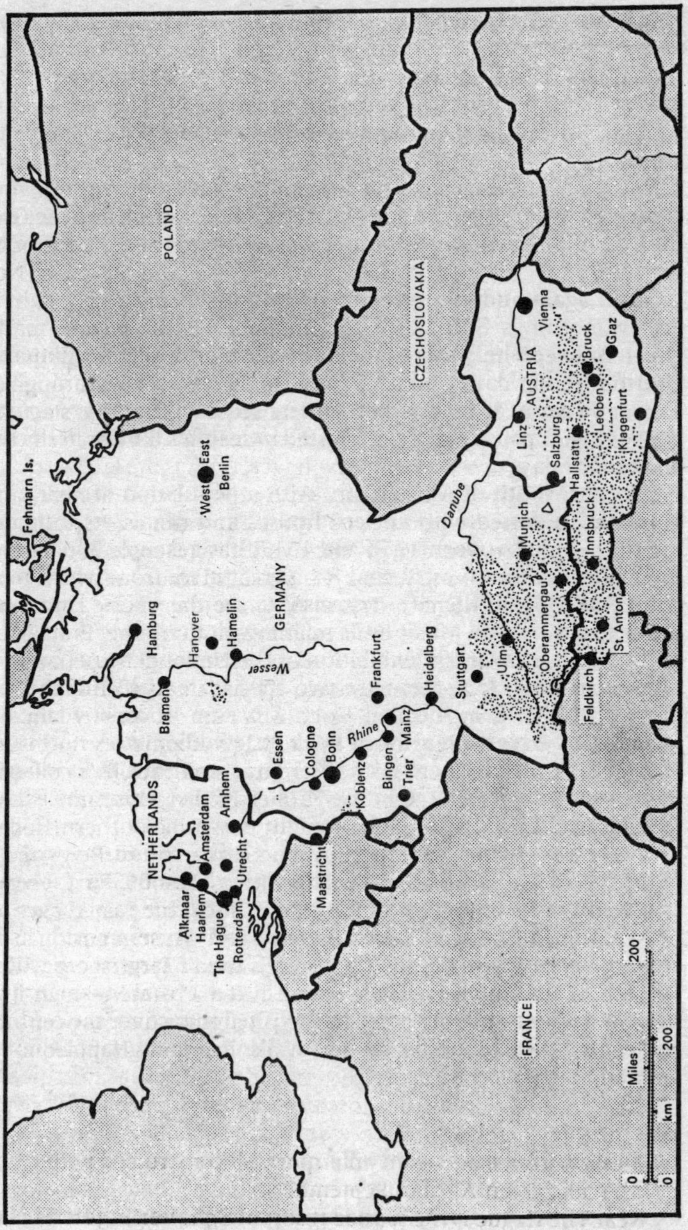
POLAND
CZECHOSLOVAKIA
GERMANY
NETHERLANDS
AUSTRIA
FRANCE
Fehmarn Is.
West
East
Berlin
Hamburg
Bremen
Hanover
Hamelin
Wesser
Alkmaar
Haarlem
Amsterdam
The Hague
Rotterdam
Utrecht
Arnhem
Maastricht
Essen
Cologne
Bonn
Koblenz
Rhine
Bingen
Trier
Mainz
Frankfurt
Heidelberg
Stuttgart
Ulm
Danube
Munich
Oberammergau
Feldkirch
St. Anton
Innsbruck
Salzburg
Hallstatt
Linz
Vienna
Leoben
Bruck
Graz
Klagenfurt
Miles
km
0
200
0
200

long beach is the ideal place to sleep while you're visiting The Hague and a marvellous place – on sunny days – to make contact with sunbathers of the opposite sex. The pier is a sideshow-type place jutting 1,200 feet out into the sea and makes for pleasant evening walking. The fishing harbour is a riot of smells just about any morning.

North of The Hague and a few kilometres from Amsterdam is **Haarlem**, where you can see the Frans Hals Museum and the Great Church of St Bavo which houses one of the largest organs in the world.

North again and you come to **Alkmaar** where the big sight on Friday mornings from April to September is the cheese market which has been held there for centuries. In peak season Alkmaar is swarming on Fridays, and you'll have to fight your way through the crowds to get near the market, far less see anything that's actually happening. If you are more interested in seeing Alkmaar itself come on another day.

Utrecht, south of Amsterdam, with a population of nearly half a million, is dotted with ancient houses and canals. Its cathedral, the Dom, built between 1254 and 1517, has a steeple 360 feet tall, the highest in the country, and it's a great place from which to get an overall view of the city. Try, also, to see the Viking ship in the Municipal Museum. Music buffs might want to try the 'From Musical Box to Barrel Organ' exhibition at the National Museum.

For Van Gogh fans there are two special treats in Holland. The first, of course, is at the Van Gogh Museum in Amsterdam. The second is at **Otterlo National Park**, a few kilometres north-west of **Arnhem**, where there is another large and excellent collection of the man's work housed in the Kröller-Müller Museum.

Maastricht, of Treaty fame, is right down in southern Holland in the enclave which juts in between Germany and Belgium. An industrial city, it is worth visiting for other reasons. First, because as a result of its geographical position, it uses three languages and has a strange mixture of Dutch, Belgian and German customs; and second, because just outside the town is the St Pietersberg with its 300 km of man-made tunnels bored into a 110-metre-high limestone hill. Thousands of people have visited them over the centuries and carved their names in the soft walls, including Napoleon, Voltaire and Sir Walter Scott.

Hitching

Hitching in Holland is generally good – you can cross the entire country in a couple of hours – but remember that if you want to travel fast you must keep to the big highways. Holland is one of the most densely populated areas in the world and it's very easy to get trapped on a village to village, town to town tour if you stay on the small roads. (Not that there's anything wrong with that if you have the time to spare!) The same rules apply on the highways as on the German autobahns – no hitching! You must grab your ride on the exit or entrance roads. Cops in white Porsches are around to make sure you do just that.

● **Tulips and windmills** There used to be 9,000 working windmills in Holland. Now, unless you know where to look, you can travel through the entire country without seeing one. The place to go is **Kinderdijk**, a few kilometres east of Rotterdam, where the largest concentration of those still remaining can be found. (During July and August the 19 mills operate on Saturdays.) The tulips can be seen at their best around mid-April to early May – acres of them. Best areas are between **Leiden** and **Haarlem**. If you specifically want to see them you should avoid the big roads and plot a route which will take you through the small villages west of the N99.

● **Hitching barges** This is becoming a more and more popular method of offbeat travel – but you must have plenty of time if you want to do a complete trip. Rotterdam is the place to start and from there you can go right through the Rhine into Switzerland. Just ask a barge captain – some will tell you to go to hell, but plenty won't. Most charge for food, some don't. If, because of the time factor, you decide you can only afford one day aboard, you'll have much less trouble finding a boat.

● **Warning!** All drugs are illegal in Holland. However, possession of small quantities of hash and grass for personal use; growing your own; buying and selling it in licensed coffee shops; consuming it in private or in coffee shops have been decriminalized. If you smoke anywhere other than in coffee shops or (discreetly) in Amsterdam parks and clubs, you could end up in trouble. Two readers have written in to say that they got busted in provincial cities.

For the best deals, try small, local coffee shops away from Amsterdam's city centre.

If you try to buy, sell, or even talk about hard drugs, you will get kicked out of the coffee shops. If you buy hard drugs on the streets you will get ripped off. If you get caught with hard drugs on you, you will get arrested.

Amsterdam: where to sleep

Sleeping prices are high in Amsterdam – even youth hostels cost f20–25 and upwards – but the blow is softened a bit when you discover that the price usually includes a breakfast guaranteed to set you on your feet for the day. Most of these breakfasts are large enough so that you can take a portion away with you and use it as a lunchtime snack. Generally, expect to pay between f50 and f100 for bed and breakfast in a hotel.

Hostelling International hostels:
'Vondelpark', Zandpad 5 (tel: 683 17 44).
'Stadsdoelen', Kloveniersburgwal 97 (tel: 624 68 32).

Other hostels:
Eben Haëzer, Bloemstrasse 179 (tel: 624 47 17). Christian hostel.
The Shelter, Barndesteeg 21–25 (tel: 625 32 30). Christian hostel.
Bob's Youth Hostel, Nieuwezijds Voorburgwal 92 (tel: 623 00 63).
Kabul, Warmoesstraat 38–42 (tel: 623 71 58).
Frisco Inn, Beurstraat 5 (tel: 620 16 10).
International Budget Hotel, Leidsegracht 76 (tel: 624 27 84).
't Ancker, De Ruijterkade 100 (tel: 622 95 60).

Cheap hotels:
Beurstraat, Beurstraat 7 (tel: 626 37 01).
Schröder, Haarlemerdijk 48b (tel: 626 62 72).
Pax, Radhuisstraat 37 (tel: 624 97 35).
Westertoren, Radhuisstraat 35b (tel: 624 46 39).
Old Nickel, Nieuwe Brugsteeg 11 (tel: 624 19 12).
Brian, Singel 69 (tel: 624 46 61).
Ronnie, Radhuisstraat 41 (tel: 624 28 21).
Rokin, Rokin 73 (tel: 626 74 56).
Casa Cara, Emmastraat 24 (tel: 662 31 35).

It's worth remembering that student hostels in the Netherlands are generally open to anyone, with or without student credentials, as long as they look *something* like a student.

Also, if you're travelling with someone, double rooms work out cheaper per person than singles.

For help with all accommodation problems, contact the VVV Amsterdam Tourist Office at Stationsplein 10 which is open all year round, 9 a.m.–5 p.m. at least, except Sundays from October–Easter when the office opens from 10 a.m.–1 p.m. only. For several years now a **Sleep-In** has operated from late June to early September at s'-Gravesandstraat 51 (tel: 694 74 44), near the Weesperplein Metro station. Prices start at f19 in dorms. The VVV has little to do with the Sleep-In which is an independent centre for youth culture and tourism (funds from the council are getting less and less). Some of those running it get paid; many are volunteers who enjoy meeting travellers from all over the world. There are several small and larger dormitories (some reserved for women only) with a total of 600 (not 800) beds. You bring along your own sleeping bag and crash out on a mattress on the floor. Cost is around f16. Great idea! Apart from just a place to crash, the Sleep-In provides concerts by local bands, theatre try-outs, workshops etc. Many of these are free for those staying in the Sleep-In and all of them are enthusiastically frequented by inhabitants of Amsterdam. In the summer, it is host to the successful 'Meet the World' festival, with a dance/music night, a rock night, an open-stage night (when anyone can perform and win a free night's kip – ideal for buskers), and a world music night. There is a restaurant offering cheap but good food (hot veggie dish for around f8), a bar, a video room where you can watch movies for free, and an information desk run by an organization called Amsterdam Calling which gives alternative and up-to-date info as well as discount vouchers for museums, excursions, boat trips and bike rent. Ask them for *Use-it*, a free newspaper published annually, featuring money-saving advice on accommodation and restaurants for travelling youth (that's you!). Also, ATAS, an initiative providing robbed or scammed tourists with a sympathetic ear, free bed, food, medical care and occasionally a ticket home is based there. (Phone 625 32 46 – but please don't take wrongful advantage!)

During the height of the season, the Sleep-In is usually completely full, but the reception desk people will ring around for you to see if there's anywhere else left to stay. Often people sleep in the garden after the bar closes, or outside the door (don't wake the neighbours!). Safer than in a park. Be nice to the personnel – they deserve it!

Sleeping rough is not a good idea: too many people get ripped off, beaten up or hassled by the police. There are youth camping grounds at: **Zeeburg**, Ijdijk (A'dam-Oost) (tel: 694 66 88). **Vliegenbos**, Meeuwenlaan 138 (A'dam-Noord) (tel: 636 88 55). (Both cost around f8.)

Amsterdam: where to eat

Beds are expensive in Amsterdam and so is food. Expect to pay as much as f18–20 for the main meal of the day in a restaurant. If you're eating breakfast away from your hotel, try a slice of *ontbijtkoek*. If you have a sweet tooth, try the deep-fried *poffertjes*.

University Restaurant Atrium, Oude Zijds, Achterburg Wall; also at Leidsestraat 106, open every day in summer until 10.30 p.m. Fixed menu f9,50.
The Chinese and Indonesian Restaurants in the Binnen Bantammerstraat near Central Station. Good filling meals. The lunchtime specials are the best deals.
Van Dobben at Korte Reguliersdwarsstraat 5–9. Sandwich shop. Cheap.
Moeders Pot at Vinkenstraat 119.
Kow Loon at Singel 498. Very cheap Oriental-type food.
Hema Department Store Cafeteria at Nieuwendijk 174.
Blauwe Hollander at Leidse Kruisstraat 28.
Restaurant Leto – Plate service at Haarlemmerdijk 114.
Haesje Claes at Nieuwe Zijds Voorburgwal 320.
Indonesian Restaurant Sukasari at Damstraat 26.
Kosmos at Prins Hendrikkade 142. Macrobiotic food at reasonable prices.

Amsterdam: what to see and do

THE STEDELIJK MUSEUM in Paulus Potterstraat is probably the greatest museum of modern art in Europe. The collections are superbly displayed and unbelievably good. De Kooning, Mondrian, Miró, Degas, Cézanne, Chagall, Picasso . . . you name it. Admission charge.

VAN GOGH MUSEUM on Museumplein. Entrance in Paulus Potterstraat. A mind-bender! Don't miss it! Closed Mondays in the winter.

THE RIJKSMUSEUM is just a couple of hundred yards from the Stedelijk. Admission charge. The museum houses a superb classical collection. Particularly strong on Rembrandt (they have his *Night Watch*). Also Vermeer, Goya, Tintoretto, Hals, Rubens, Jan Steen, etc. Closed on Mondays.

THE WATERFRONT AREA Free and fascinating. Set in amongst the streets and alleys of the Zeedijk/Nieuwmarkt area is Europe's vastest collection of bars, dives, queer-shops, clubs, cafés, and brothels. Also, be warned that the Zeedijk plays host to some of Europe's nastiest drug-pushers. No point in describing it all – just get down and have a look round about 11 at night. (Lone lady hitchers should find company before setting out to see the area at night.)

REMBRANDT'S HOUSE at Jodenbreestraat 4. Admission charge. Rembrandt lived here for twenty years. It contains a large collection of his etchings and drawings.

THE HOUSE OF ANNE FRANK at 263–5 Prinsengracht. Admission charge. This is where Anne Frank, the young Jewish girl who wrote the famous *Diary*, lived with her family in total isolation and secrecy for two years during the German occupation of the city. In 1944 the family was betrayed, the Gestapo arrested them and they were sent to a concentration camp where Anne died. The secret apartment has been preserved in its entirety. A permanent exhibition on contemporary anti-semitism is displayed in the building.

MUSEUM AMSTELKRING at Oude Zijds Voorburgwal 40 is more popularly known as 'Our Lord in the Attic'. This strange church is completely camouflaged and hidden within the top floors of several old canal houses. It was built during the Reformation when the Roman Catholics were having trouble with the authorities.

WORLD'S NARROWEST HOUSE Said the coachman to his boss, 'Sir, if only I had a house as wide as your front door.' Said the boss, 'You shall.' The result is at Singel 7 – the house of Mr Tripp's coachman.

MOVIES Shown in original language. Plenty of first-run American and English shows. Prices lower than in most capital cities.

FREE BEER! FREE FOOD! (Well almost!) The Heineken brewery at Van der Helststraat 30 gives guided tours of their establishment from June to October 9.30–11 a.m. and 1–2.30 p.m. Monday to Friday. At the end of the tour there's beer, cheese and sometimes cigarettes. All for a small fee of f2 which is donated to UNICEF.

CANAL TRIPS cost money but are a fine way of seeing Amsterdam if it's your first day there (and if you can put up with the same jokes being cracked by the same hostess in four different languages!). Trips last about an hour. You'll see the boats and advertisements near the Central Station.

FLEA MARKET at Waterlooplein. Every day, 10 a.m.–4 p.m. except Sundays. Good for secondhand clothes. If you don't mind getting up early on Saturday mornings, go to the Farmers' Market by the

Westerkerk. Fresh farm produce, made the old-fashioned way, including cheese, butter, honey, etc. Interesting to see and free samples to be had. The same place has a secondhand market on Monday mornings.

VRANKRIJK on Spuistraat 216, previously a squat, has now been bought by the inhabitants. You can't miss the garishly painted building right behind Dam Square. The bar, with the infamous Worldisco on Saturday night, has the cheapest prices in town, if not in the country (£1 for soft drinks; £1.50 for beer and wine). Reverse dress code applies here: grotty jeans, grubby T-shirts and broken shoes are the norm. Punks, hippies and the anarchist active are most welcome; indolent freeloader potheads not so. Hint: well-told, funny stories on police and customs hassle are greatly appreciated and form the best introduction to odd jobs in return for free accommodation and food.

CREA on the Turfdraagsterpad, by the Kloveniersburgwal, is the university centre for music, art and communication studies. Apart from their waterfront café, there are concerts, exhibitions, shows and videos to be seen for next to nothing.

● **Warning!** Don't ever buy hash (or any other drugs) off the street. Even if they let you 'sample' you'll be conned and you'll get ill. Furthermore, people living in this city are sick to death of street pushers, so don't make things harder on us and do yourself a favour too.

● **Health** If you get ill but aren't insured, take tram 10 to the Witte Jas (White Coat) on Wittenstraat 29 (tel: 688 1140), a collective of doctors and nurses working for free treating illegal immigrants, junkies, etc. Friendly and helpful, also with alternative medicine. First aid can be had at OLVG on Oosterparkstraat.

Transport in Amsterdam

Cheapest way to travel around is by trams, buses and metro.

Don't buy loose tickets on trams and buses, buy a Strippenkaart from a tobacco shop or post office, stamp off two strips per hour. Saves 20%. Main PT (GUB) office is next to the VVV on the Stationsplein.

For bicycle rental try Koenders, Stationsplein Oostzijde 1012AB (tel: 624 83 91).

Student discounts
Reductions to some theatres, cinemas, galleries, museums, restaurants and nightclubs. For information, contact NBBS Student Centre at Dam 17 (see below).

Addresses

Main post office (for poste restante) at Raadhuisstr and Singel 250, Amsterdam.
American Express at Damrak 66, Amsterdam (tel: 520 77 77), Mon.–Fri.: 9 a.m.–5 p.m., Sat.: 9 a.m.–12 noon, 1 p.m.–4 p.m.
NBBS (Netherlands Bureau for Foreign Student Relations) at Dam 17, Amsterdam (tel: 620 50 17).
NBBS at Rokin 38, Amsterdam (tel: 620 50 17).
Amsterdam Tourist Office (VVV) at Stationsplein 10, and Leidsestraat 106, Amsterdam (tel: 626 64 44).
US Consulate at Museumplein 19, Amsterdam (tel: 679 03 21).
British Consulate-General, Koningslaan 44, Amsterdam (tel: 676 43 43).

Hitchers' Tips and Comments . . .

You never mention Groningen; it's known as 'The Amsterdam of the North' and well worth the trip. Start hitching from the entrance to the E35 motorway outside Diemen (south-east of Amsterdam). There is a gas station there. MIKE PLUMMER, SEAVIEW, ISLE OF WIGHT

For those hitching from Amsterdam south to Germany, towards Cologne; it's much faster to go via Eindhoven, not via Arnhem.
PATRICK HINE, OXFORD, ENGLAND

Interesting and cheap hunting ground for rooms in Amsterdam is around the station and post office. An alternative to hotels and hostels is the fluctuating population of houseboats offering accommodation. ALAN THATCHER, NEW ZEALAND

Please tell your readers that they should leave their valuables in a safe locker or hand them in at reception when staying at hostels. More and more travellers are the victims of robbery and pickpockets. Too many people lose their money, and their holiday pleasure, because they keep everything on them even when they don't need it. Lady hitchers should be particularly careful if walking around with any sort of handbag. They're an easy target for snatchers.

HOSTEL WARDEN, JEUGDHERBERG 'STADSDOELEN', AMSTERDAM, HOLLAND

Many truckers going to and from Holland and Germany cross the border at Venlo. Try hitching with Venlo sign for good lift.

EVAN M. JONES, CARDIFF, WALES

I discovered special places in Amsterdam called 'Liftplaats'. To head south, east, or north-east out of Amsterdam, take tram 12 to Amstel Station. There is a Liftplaats area nearby. Such areas are set aside especially for hitchers! However, just because they are set aside for the likes of us doesn't mean they are the best places. Heading to West Germany, I waited five hours and eventually got a ride to Apeldoorn.

Groningen is nice to visit but terrible to leave. There is a horrendously complex ring road system, signs pointing in every (wrong) direction. To head into Germany, don't go to the Liftplaats area (left out of station, underneath the flyover), it's in the wrong direction. Take the bus or train to Hoogezand. From then on, it's plain sailing into Germany. MARK NAISBITT, DARLINGTON, DURHAM, UK

When in Amsterdam don't use the VVV to book a room for you as their minimum price is about f50. NORRIE GREER, LONDON

FREE FOOD: Hare Krishna on the Ruysdaelkade. If you can sit through their talk and keep your eyes open, you can dig into some very nice vegetarian food. They also do food runs in front of Central Station for tramps etc, around four o'clock in the afternoon.

CHANGE: The commercial change places, recognizable by their white or blue front and flags printed on the outside, advertise 'no commission' but their exchange rates are so lousy that you lose a lot of money. Every station in Holland has a 'Grenswisselkantoor', red front and 'GWK' sign and usually open 24 hours a day. They charge two guilder commission but their exchange rates are a lot better.

CANAL TRIPS: Better than taking canal trips in a large boat which are boring and expensive, rent a Canal Bike (Amstel 57, phone 6265574) and pedal your way across the Amsterdam waters.

BUSKING: Massive clampdown on amplified music. Stay acoustic and you're still OK. Central Station, Dam Square, Rembrandtsplein buskers and performers have certain agreements concerning times and spots, so it's safer not to crash these! Kalverstraat, Leidesplein and Nieuwedijk are free territory. ANNA LISS, AMSTERDAM

I had a fantastic time in Amsterdam. I think you under-rate Amsterdam considering how much everyone I have spoken to enjoyed it. Perhaps it's for us young ones?!

ANDREW WORALIN, PERTH, AUSTRALIA

The Zeeburg 'Youth Campsite' in Amsterdam is a total pit – don't go there! We left and went to Gaasper, the newest campsite in the city. It's really nice, and only slightly dearer than Zeeburg.

LOUISE BROMLEY, NEWTON-LE-WILLOWS, ENGLAND

The best smokes (for example, northern lights Dutch skunk and zero zero Moroccan hash) are hallucinogenic. If you get a panic attack, go somewhere quiet, breathe deeply, stay calm and drink plenty of water or orange juice. Don't forget: nobody has died from draw since two Spanish peasants laughed themselves to death in the Middle Ages!

WILL THOMPSON, LEEDS, ENGLAND

Germany

population	78,000,000
size	357,320 square kilometres
capital	Berlin, population 2,960,000
government	Federal republic
religion	All denominations
language	German; some French and English understood
currency	*Deutschmark* (DM) One *Mark* equals 100 *Pfennig*. Coins of 1, 2, 5, 10, 50 *Pfennige* and of 1, 2, 5 *Mark*. Notes of 5, 10, 20, 50, 100, 500, 1,000 *Mark*

There's a lot to see in Germany, but I'll start by mentioning something which you *can't* see unless you're in Europe in 2000. This is the famous Passion Play which is held in the village of **Oberammergau** every ten years. The play, which is performed by the villagers and which attracts crowds from all over the world, was first staged in 1634 after the village prayed that the Black Death which was ravaging Europe at that time should spare the tiny town. It did. From then on the play was performed every decade until 1934 when Hitler stopped it. It resumed in 1950.

Ulm, which is about 100 km north-west of Oberammergau, is a city of 100,000, large enough to be interesting but small enough to walk in. It's fairly representative of what you'll find in Germany. Clean, spacious, and dotted with ancient landmarks (many rebuilt since the devastation of Second World War bombing). The city, birthplace of Albert Einstein, houses a 14th-century Gothic cathedral with the highest stone church spire in the world – 528 feet.

To the west of Ulm is the beautiful **Black Forest** area – ideal for slow village to village wandering.

Heidelberg is the favourite German city of thousands of tourists. Celebrated in songs and plays it still seems to cling longingly to the memories of its past. It's the home of Germany's oldest and most famous university, founded in 1386. Visit the Red Ox, an old student inn, which was the scene of many a duelling challenge. You might also go and see the 13th-century castle which houses the Apothecary Museum and the famed Heidelberg Tun, a gigantic wine barrel which holds 221,726 litres – or about 50,000 gallons.

Heading north you reach **Frankfurt** where you can see Goethe's House and Museum and the Stadel Art Institute which displays a good collection of European paintings.

Bingen am Rhein, just west of **Mainz** (which holds a wine festival in August and September), is a wine town crowned by Klopp Castle. Climb up there for great views over the Rhine Valley.

Koblenz, at the head of the twisting, turning vineyard-lined Mosel Valley, is a city of 100,000 and another wine centre. Its big landmark is the Ehrenbreitstein Fortress. If you have time, try to catch a river barge from Koblenz which will take you down along the Mosel to **Trier** (just near the border with Luxembourg) which is the oldest town in Germany and one of the oldest in Europe. Lots of Roman ruins to see. Whether you hitch a barge or a car, the Mosel trip is worthwhile. (Also possible to find grape-picking work in this area around September.)

North-west of Koblenz is **Bonn**, former capital of the Federal Republic, birthplace of Beethoven (see his house and the museum), and home of Poppelsdorf Castle. A few kilometres further on is **Cologne** (or Köln) which was founded by the Romans in 32 BC and badly battered by the Allies in the last war. See the famous cathedral (if you can stand the sight of yet another) which dates from 1248 and is one of the largest Gothic buildings in the world.

North of Cologne is the huge industrial complex centred on **Essen**. A nightmare of converging autobahns and twisting ring-roads, for me it's one of the ugliest areas in Europe. Getting in and out of the various towns and cities without spending money is virtually impossible. It's a hitch-hiker's hell on earth.

Hameln, way away from all that and just south of **Hanover**, is a pleasant town of 60,000 which contains some of the best examples of timber-façaded houses in Germany. It was, also, the home of the legendary Pied Piper who is supposed to have led invading rats away from the town to the sound of his pipes and then, when he wasn't rewarded by the townspeople, to have caused the children to follow him in the same way. In the summer there is a Pied Piper procession through the streets every Sunday at noon.

Bremen, 63 km inland on the Weser River, is the oldest seaport in Germany. The old part of the city is great for wandering. In the 11th-century St Peter's Cathedral you can see 500-year-old mummies preserved in a lead-lined vault.

North of Bremen is **Hamburg** (population 2,000,000), which was terribly damaged in the Second World War. Her citizens have completed an amazing job of rebuilding. There are half a dozen museums worth looking through – especially the Kunst und Gewerbe which features arts and crafts dating back to the Middle Ages. But outdoing all the galleries and museums in the visitor stakes is the district of St Pauli where 300,000 souls per month go to enjoy themselves in the most up-to-date red-light district in the world. As *Time* magazine described it, you can 'swing into an underground garage, park, choose a Fräulein at a discreet *Kontakthof* (contact court), then take an elevator to one of two six-storey, modern sexscrapers named Eros Centre and Palais d'Amour. Poorer types still go to streets like Herbertstrasse, just off the Reeperbahn, where sex is dished up like ham and eggs but at a slightly higher price. If you want to explore your options for moving on from Hamburg contact the German Student Travel Service at Schluterstrasse 18 (tel: 454409).

At **Potsdam**, just 30 km south-west of Berlin, visit Schloss Sanssouci, considered a classic of German Rococo. The palace, one of four in the 600-acre Sanssouci Park, was built in 1745 by Frederick the Great. History students may be interested to visit Schloss Cecilienhof in the Neuer Garten Park where in 1945 Churchill, Stalin and Truman signed the Potsdam Agreement which contributed to the partitioning of Germany and the creation of East Germany.

Several places are worth a stop in the region of **Thuringia**. At **Eisenach**, where composer Johann Sebastian Bach was born, visit the ancient Wartburg castle. At **Saalfeld** see the castle, the town hall and visit the delicate and beautiful stalactite caves. **Erfurt**, which dates back to the 700s, is worth a day of any traveller's time. See the Church of St Severus and beside it the cathedral on the hill known as the Domberg. Stroll across the beautiful Kramerbrücke or Merchant Bridge built in 1325 and lined with 33 houses. Close by Erfurt is **Weimar**, the city in which the Weimar Republic was declared after the First World War and which was the home of the

Bauhaus school of design from 1919 until 1935 when it moved to Dessau. Weimar was Germany's intellectual centre from the late 18th and into the early 19th centuries. Liszt, Goethe and Schiller were amongst notables who lived here and the houses of each are now open as museums. See Belvedere Castle. North of Weimar the dark side of Germany can be contemplated at the Nazi concentration camp at **Buchenwald**.

About 100 km north-east of Weimar is **Leipzig** which, because of its position on trade routes, has been an important trading and economic town since the Middle Ages. The tradition continues with the Leipzig trade fairs. Bach lived and worked here, and is buried in the Thomaskirche. Next door to the church is the Bach Museum. True music lovers should also head for nearby **Halle**, birthplace of Handel. The composer's house is a museum devoted to musical instruments, some of them 400 years old.

Meissen, once home to the Saxon kings, is famous for its porcelain, which might be a difficult souvenir to lug home in a backpack. What you can safely carry away from Meissen are memories of narrow streets lined by ancient houses and the exhilarating view of the 13th-century Gothic cathedral and the 15th-century Albrechtsburg Castle which dominates the heights above the city.

Before the Second World War **Dresden** was known as the Florence of the Elbe. But during the night of 13–14 February 1945 the Allies sent 800 aircraft to destroy the city. They made four more raids with a total of over 1,500 planes up until 17 April. No one seems to know exactly why the raids were made. The result was the death of tens of thousands of people and the destruction of a city counted amongst the world's most beautiful. Many of the more important buildings have been carefully reconstructed; one that hasn't is the Frauenkirche which remains a gutted monument to the stupidities of war. Dresden was the cultural capital of the old East Germany and no wonder. Museums, galleries, orchestras, choirs, palaces and churches are its pride. See the museums in the baroque Zwinger Palace; don't miss Raphael's *Sistine Madonna* in the portrait gallery; take a glance at the Porcelain Museum which tells the story of Dresden's most famous product. Remember as you wander that the palace was almost completely destroyed in the war. An army of craftsmen took 18 years to restore it. Also check the Albertinum museum complex, particularly if you are into post-Impressionists. Take a look at the restored Semper Opera. Richard Strauss premiered some of his operas here and Wagner was just one of the theatre's distinguished conductors. Opera fans (any left out there?) should check with the tourist office about how to get the cheapest tickets (the company doesn't perform in summer). Take a long evening stroll along Brühl Terrace by the Elbe. Great place to meet locals.

From Dresden it's just one quick ride to the Czech border. Along the route to Poland are a couple of towns which merit a visit. The view you get of **Bautzen** from the roadbridge across the River Spree is one of the loveliest in Germany. One of the towers visible on the skyline is that of the town hall on the main square, beyond which stands the Dom. Be sure to look inside as this is one of only a few examples of a *Simultankirche* – a church divided up in such a manner that it can be used by both Protestant and Roman Catholic congregations. Like Pisa, Bautzen has a leaning tower, but unlike Pisa's tower the Reichenturm didn't lean from the moment it was built. It took the addition of the baroque upper part in the 18th century to cause the Reichenturm to depart from the straight and narrow. Ascend the tower for a great view over the town. See also the Witches' House down by the River Spree. This is actually an old fisherman's house, but when it alone amongst all its neighbours survived a series of fires locals assumed that the owners had special powers and so gave the house its name.

With a collection of renaissance and baroque houses unequalled anywhere else in the country, **Görlitz** has the potential to be one of Germany's prime tourist attractions, but at present there is much work afoot trying to put right the damage done by industrial pollution. Some of the best preserved buildings line the long Obermarkt, though once restored the buildings on the Unter Markt will outshine them. Just off the Unter Markt is the Biblisches Haus with its façade covered with small reliefs of biblical scenes. A more unusual sight is the Karstadt department store which is a perfect example of Jugendstil architecture. Go in even if you don't want to buy anything – there aren't many interiors like this one left in existence.

● **Happenings** Germany is filled with festivals and concerts. The famed *Munich Oktoberfest* is mentioned below. Some others to look out for are: the *Great Marksmanship Contest* at Hanover in July; the *International Fair* at Frankfurt, March and September; the *Pied Piper of Hamelin Festival* at Hamelin, June to August; the *Christmas Fair* at Nuremberg in December; the *Killing of the Dragon* at Furth-im-Wald in August; the *Bach Week* at Ansbach in July and the *European Weeks* at Passau in June and July.

● **Auer Dult** This is a fantastic flea market of both junk and antiques which is held only three times a year in Munich's Mariahilfsplatz. Approximate times are April/May, July/August and mid-October. If you're looking for an unusual souvenir from your

European trip, this'll be the place to find it. Check with German tourist office in any major city for exact dates from year to year.

- **Oktoberfest** The world-famous Munich beer festival draws thousands from all over the world – including Australians who have earned themselves a bad name in Munich ever since the year a gang of them got rat-arsed and hijacked a streetcar. These festivities last 16 days and end on the first Sunday in October. Precise details from any German tourist office.

- **Buy a ride!** In many German cities you can buy a ride in a private car to a host of destinations through Mitfahrzentrale. People driving between, say, Munich and Essen inform the company when they are going, saying they want to take a passenger to share petrol costs. The passenger pays Mitfahrzentrale a basic fee of around DM30 for fixing up the ride, and then a fee per kilometre to the driver. You can even buy insurance and pay a booking fee! It mightn't be hitching, but it's a good idea. In Munich you'll find Mitfahrzentrale at Lämmerstrasse 4 (tel: 594561). Munich also has an organization which matches up female drivers with female passengers: Frauenmitfahrzentrale at Klenzstrasse 57/b (tel: 2014690). For more informal arrangements try scouring the bulletin board at the 'Studenthaus', Leopoldstrasse 15.

- **Hitching** Important! You can only hitch on entry and exit roads to autobahns. On entry roads, you are not supposed to stand beyond the blue sign showing the white auto.

Munich: where to sleep

Outside of youth hostels, which in Germany cost around DM20, there are not many cheap beds. Youth hostels invariably provide the cheapest beds in Germany. Prices are normally around DM20, though in some of the bigger cities you're looking at DM30–35. In any other youth/student accommodation prices usually begin at about DM30, and can be as dear as hotel rooms. Note that in Munich (and throughout Bavaria) Hostelling International hostels (the first three listed below) will not accept visitors over 26. Be prepared to pay DM40–50 for a single at one of the cheaper local hotels in Munich.

YH Jugendherberge at Wendl-Dietrich Strasse 19 (tel: 13 11 56). Closed from 2 January to 1 February.

YH Jugendgästehaus München at Miesingstrasse 4 (tel: 723 6550/60).

YH Jugendherberge Burg Schwaneck at Burgweg 4–6, Pullach (about 12 km from the centre of Munich) (tel: 7 93 06 43).

Haus International (Jugendhotel) at Elisabethstrasse 87 (tel: 120060). Ask to share in five-bedded rooms.

Jugendhotel Marienberger at Goethestrasse 9 (tel: 555891).

CVJM (YMCA) Jugendgästehaus at Landwehrstrasse 13 (tel: 5521410).

Kolpinghaus St Theresa at Hanebergstrasse 8 (tel: 126050).

Haus International Jugendhotel at Elisabethstrasse 87 (tel: 120060).

Jugendlage Kapuzinerhölzl at Franz-Schrank-Strasse (tel: 1414300). U-Bahn line 1 to Rotkreuzplatz, then tram 12 (Amalienburgstrasse) to the Botanischergarten stop. A big tent with foam mattresses on the floor. The price is right – DM8 a night. Open July–Aug. – maybe! No reservations, but phone ahead to see if 'The Tent' is still in business in 1996. By the time you read this one of the great bargains in Germany may be just a memory.

For help in finding student accommodation contact the **Munich Student Travel Service** at Luisenstrasse 43, 8 München 2 (tel: 50060/207), or try the **Jugend Informationszentrum** at Paul-Heyse-Strasse 22, 8 München 2 (tel: 514106–60). For help in finding hotels head for the **Fremdenverkehrsamt** over from platform 11 in the main train station (*Hauptbahnhof*).

There are two campsites: **München-Thalkirchen** at Zentrallandstrasse 49 (tel: 7231707) and **München-Obermenzing** at Lochhausenerstrasse 59 (tel: 8112235). Both sites are open 15 March–31 Oct.

For sleeping out, try the parks on the banks of the Isar River, or the huge park up behind the Haus der Kunst. (Hitcher Hugh Dunne reports: *Think twice about sleeping out there. Police with dogs search the place each night. You might get by if you stay north of the ringroad, but it's a hell of a walk, and you're better off on the banks of the Isar.*)

Remember that as in most of the big European cities you can drop your per-person bed costs considerably by taking a double or triple room in company with others.

Munich: where to eat

It's no problem to feed yourself for around DM20 in Munich and the following list names some places where you can do just that:

Mensa Universität at Leopoldstrasse 15. Student card required.
Mensa Technische Universität at Arcisstrasse 17. Student card required.
Gastätte Engelsburg at Türkenstrasse (junction with Schellingstrasse). Good three-course lunch offers.
Cornelius Schuler Buffeteria at Bayerstrasse 13.
Herties Department Store (cafeteria) at Bahnhofsplatz.
Kaufhof Department Store (cafeteria) at Karlsplatz.
Wienerwalds (chain group). There are 48 of them in Munich, of which four are centrally located:

Leopoldstrasse 44	Herzogstrasse 25
Frauenstrasse 4	Lindwurmstrasse 48

Nordsee Restaurant at Schützenstrasse, near the Hertien Department Store.
Ratskeller at Marienplatz 8.

Munich: what to see and do

MARIENPLATZ is the centre of town. The COLUMN OF THE VIRGIN MARY (*Mariensäule*) dates from 1632 and commemorates the deliverance of Munich from the Swedes during the Thirty Years War. It stands in front of the neo-Gothic NEW TOWN HALL, the tower of which holds the GLOCKENSPIEL: animated figures on the performing clock do the usual stuff at 11 a.m. each day. Just off the square stands ST PETER'S, Munich's oldest church. From the top of the tower you can see an amazing view down into Marienplatz and FRAUENKIRCHE to the city beyond.

DEUTSCHES MUSEUM One of Europe's great museums and the largest science and technical museum in the world. Plenty of buttons to push and a bonanza for anyone who can recognize a wheel when they see one. Admission charge. Half-price with student card. On the Isarinsel.

ALTE PINAKOTHEK at Bärenstrasse 27. Featuring paintings of the 14th to 18th centuries, including some great ones. Huge collection of Rubens and works by Velázquez, El Greco, Leonardo, etc. Entrance charge, but free on Sundays.

HAUS DER KUNST at Prinzregentenstrasse 1. Fine collection of French Impressionists. Admission charge, but free on Sundays.

NEUE PINAKOTHEK at Bärenstrasse 29. Collection of 19th-century paintings.

SCHLOSS NYMPHENBURG Take the U-Bahn line 1 to Rotkreuzplatz then tram 12 to Schloss Nymphenburg. This palace was built between 1664 and 1823 as the Bavarian kings' summer residence. A huge and remarkable complex in the baroque-rococo style sitting in 500 acres of sculptured gardens. Tough entrance fee which is halved if you carry a student card. (The place was used as a setting in *Last Year in Marienbad.*)

DACHAU CONCENTRATION CAMP Take the S-Bahn to the town of Dachau, then the Dachau-Ost bus to the camp. This was Nazi Germany's first concentration camp, founded in 1933 by the SS. Over 200,000 prisoners entered its gates before it was captured in 1945. More than 30,000 of them perished in the camp.

ENGLISCHER GARTEN Huge outdoor beer garden. Great place to meet people.

BEER HALLS With southern Germany's 1,600 breweries producing about a quarter of the world's beer supply you have to enter into the spirit of the thing – and you do that in the beer halls. Entrance is free, except to certain sections where there is entertainment, and a half-litre stein costs about DM4. Try the **Hofbräuhaus** at Platzl 9 and the **Platzl** across the street. Two others worth a look-in are the **Löwenbräukeller** at Stiglmaierplatz and the **Mathäser Bier Stadt** at Bayerstrasse 5 which claims it can seat no less than 5,500 beer-swilling customers.

Transport in Munich

The Munich transport system includes trams, buses, underground trains (*U-Bahn*) and suburban electric trains (*S-Bahn*). Tickets are expensive. Cost depends on length of journey. Depending upon how much travelling you plan to do, it may be worth buying a 24-hour pass for the whole network.

Student discounts

Reduced tickets to theatres, cinemas. Reduced tickets or free entry to state-run galleries and museums. Cheaper entrance to fairs and exhibitions. For information the Munich Student Travel Service (address below).

Addresses

Main post office (for poste restante) at Munich, Postamt 32, Bahnhofplatz 1.
American Express at Munich, Promenadeplatz 6 (tel: 290900).
Munich Student Travel Service at Munich 2, Luisenstrasse 43 (tel: 523000).
Tourist Information Office at Munich, Rindermarkt 5 (tel: 23911).
British Consulate General Bürkleinstrasse 10 (tel: 211090).
American Consulate at Munich, Königinstrasse 5 (tel: 28880).

Berlin: where to sleep

The price structure is roughly the same as for Munich. Advance bookings for the Hostelling International hostels (the first three listed) should be made through: Landesverband Berlin-Brandenburg, Tempelhofer Ufer 32, W-1000 Berlin 61 (tel: 2623024).

Youth and student accommodation:
'Ernst Reuter', Hermsdorfer Damm 48 (Hermsdorf) (tel: 4041610).
Jugendgästehaus, Kluckstrasse 3 (Tiergarten) (tel: 2611097).
Jugendgästehaus am Wannsee, Badeweg 1 (junction with Kronprinzessinnenweg) (Wannsee) (tel: 8035908).
Jugendgästehaus, Feurigstrasse 63 (Schöneberg) (tel: 7815211).
Studentenhotel Berlin, Meiningerstrasse 10 (Schöneberg) (tel: 7846720).
CVJM-Haus (YMCA), Einemstrasse 10 (Wilmersdorf) (tel: 2649100).
Internationales Jugendcamp Tegel, Ziekowstrasse 161 (Tegel). Mattresses under a huge marquee. Open late June–end Aug. Under 27 only. DM10.
Bahnhofsmission in Bahnhof Zoologischer Garten. Meant for travellers who have arrived late/are departing early. No guarantee you'll get in.

Cheap hotels:
Hotel-Pension Elton, Pariserstrasse 9 (Wilmersdorf) (tel: 8836155/8836156).
Hotel-Pension Trautenau, Trautenaustrasse 14 (tel: 8613514).

Hotel-Pension Wien, Brandenburgischestrasse 37 (Wilmersdorf) (tel: 8918486).
Hotel-Pension München, Güntzelstrasse 62 (tel: 8542226).
Hotel-Pension Bialas, Carmerstrasse 16 (Charlottenburg) (tel: 3125025).

For help with student accommodation, talk to the student travel organization Artu Berliner Gesellschaft für Studenten und Jugendaustausch mbH at Berlin 12, Hardenbergstrasse 9 (tel: 310 771).

The *Verkehrsamt* people at Europa Center will sort out hotel problems for you and charge DM5 – unless they help you into hostel or student accommodation in which case it's free.

For sleeping out in Berlin it's best to move half an hour out of the city – there are a hell of a lot of police and uniforms around. Try anywhere round the Wannsee or the Grünewald – though these places are going to cost you about DM3 to reach on public transport. If you want to sleep out in the city, you should check with locals.

Three camping grounds are **Haselhorst** at Pulvermuhlenweg (tel: 334 59 55), at **Dreilinden** in Abrechts Teerofen (tel: 805 12 10) and **Kladow** at Krampnitzer Weg 111–117 (tel: 365 27 97). Open throughout the year, all are cheap and all have good facilities.

Berlin: where to eat

Same price structure as Munich.

Studentenhotel Berlin at Meiningerstrasse 10. Dinner served from 5–8 p.m. Only for groups of at least 10 people.
Kadewe Department Store at Wittenbergplatz.
Wienerwalds (chain group). Some of the more than a dozen addresses are:

Kantstrasse 17	Tauentzienstrasse 16
Schlossstrasse 82	Kurfürstendamm 90

Burger King at Kurfürstendamm 224.
Sandy Snackbar at Kurfürstendamm 20.
Mensa der Freie Universität at Habelschwerdter Allee 45. Mon.–Fri. 11.15 a.m.–2.30 p.m.
Mensa TU at Hardenbergerstrasse 34. Mon.–Fri. 11.15 a.m.–2.30 p.m.
Schipkapass at Hohenzollerndamm 185. Bohemian specialities. Good quality at reasonable prices.

Mediencafé Strada at Potsdamerstrasse 131 (tel: 2159381).

Bilka Department Store at Joachimstalerstrasse 5. The cheap, fixed-menu meal is only served until 6 p.m.

Athena Grill at Kurfürstendamm 156. A large Greek restaurant – good value for money.

Hardtke's at Meinekestrasse 27 A and B does a good, reasonably cheap three-course meal from about 1–3 p.m.

Sausage stands You can find them all around town – indeed, all around Germany. A couple of big sausages with bread for about DM4 apiece fills you up well if you're short of money.

Berlin: what to see and do

KAISER WILHELM GEDÄCHTNISKIRCHE in the Kurfürstendamm. A new and very beautiful church standing beside the war-gutted shell of the old. Berliners call the ruin the 'Hollow Tooth'.

CHECKPOINT CHARLEY used to be at Friedrichstrasse, and the site still brings back memories of the Cold War when it was a real freeze. Nearby is the MUSEUM OF THE WALL which offers vivid testimony of escapes and shooting incidents around the Wall.

DAHLEM MUSEUM at Arnimallee 23–7. This is one of Europe's greatest galleries and if you like paintings, don't miss it. All classic stuff, nothing after about 1800. Rembrandt, Brueghel, Dürer, El Greco, Goya. And it's all for free. Closed Mondays.

BERLIN ZOO beside Tiergarten. Europe's largest zoo, with more than ten thousand animals, including – in the excellent aquarium – Europe's largest collection of crocodiles. Student card gets you in cheaper.

CHARLOTTENBURG PALACE at Luisenplatz. A day's outing in itself if you're an art-lover. The 17th-century palace is the home of half a dozen galleries and museums, including the Department of Egyptian Antiquities, opposite the palace, where you can see the famous 3,300-year-old bust of Queen Nefertiti. The museums are all free but it costs to go into the palace and the mausoleum. The museum is closed on Fridays and the palace is closed on Mondays.

THE REICHSTAG BUILDING near the Brandenburg Gate, once housed Germany's Parliament. Its burning in 1933 was used by Hitler as an excuse to purge his opponents. The reconstructed building houses a photographic exhibit of German history from 1800 to the present.

BRANDENBURG GATE built in 1791, is Berlin's most famous symbol.

THE VICTORY COLUMN (*Siegessäule*), in the Grosser Stern circle on Strasse des 17 Juni, offers superb views of the city. Best to climb the nearly 300 steps *without* backpack. For another aerial view of Berlin take the lift to the observation platform of the TV tower on Alexanderplatz.

MUSEUM ISLAND (*Museumsinsel*) contains the National Gallery and several museums. If time is limited consider devoting it to the Pergamon Museum. Here you can see one of the wonders of the ancient world, the famed Altar of Zeus built in the 2nd century BC at Pergamum, Turkey and shipped from there stone by stone to Berlin by German archaeologists last century. The altar's original dimensions were 36.50 × 34.20 metres. The gigantic relief you see in the museum measures 120 × 2.30 metres. And don't miss the section of reconstructed Babylonian street along with the original Ishtar Gate which dates from 575 BC!

Transport in Berlin

The subway is the cheapest way around. There are two systems – the U-Bahn and the S-Bahn, which runs overland.

Best deal in town, though, is the Berlin-Ticket which gives you unlimited travel on all buses, the U-Bahn and S-Bahn subway lines within the city for one day. Buy it at the Berlin Public Transport Office at Potsdamerstrasse 188, or at the Zoo Station at Hardenbergplatz.

Student discounts

For details of what's available contact:

Artu Berliner Gesellschaft für Studenten und Jugendaustausch mbH at Berlin 12, Hardenbergstrasse 9 (tel: 310 466).

Addresses

Main post office (for poste restante) at Berlin 12, Postamt Berlin, Bahnhof Zoo.

American Express at Berlin, Kurfürstendamm 11 (tel: 882 75 75).

Tourist Information Office at Berlin, Europa Center, Budapesterstrasse (tel: (030) 262 60 31).

American Consulate at Berlin, Clayallee 170 (tel: 8197419).
UK Embassy at Berlin, Unter den Linden 32–4 (tel: 2202431).

Hitchers' Tips and Comments . . .

If you sleep rough on the banks of the river Neckar in central Heidelberg watch out for the rats – they're like cats!

JONAH, NEATH, SOUTH WALES

The student Mensas of most German university cities have noticeboards offering rides to almost anywhere. You get in contact with the person offering the lift and make a deal about sharing petrol expenses.

GLYN GEORGE, MERSEYSIDE, UK

Hitching out of Munich to Salzburg can be difficult, because traffic is usually heavy and fast-moving at the point where it enters the autobahn. If you're getting desperate, try this: get the S-Bahn to Starnberg and hitch down to Garmisch-Partenkirchen; from there you should easily get a lift to Innsbruck and on to Salzburg.

In large German towns you can sometimes get a free bed in an immigrant workers' hostel (if you don't mind being up and away at 5 a.m. the next morning). To pull this off you need to find a sympathetic immigrant worker, but this isn't too difficult. Many hang around railway stations and places like Munich's Marienplatz or outside the cathedral in Cologne. They're looking for someone to talk to as they have nothing to do with their time.

HUGH DUNNE, DUBLIN, IRELAND

If you're heading into Scandinavia load up on food in German supermarkets. It's much cheaper!

ANDREW PRICE, TORQUAY, UK

Avoid the Neustadter Bucht services on the A1 between Lübeck and Puttgarden. There's little traffic, but plenty of graffiti indicating it's a bad place to hitch from.

JOHN MEHERS, LEEDS, ENGLAND

Never let anybody let you off at the service station Mosel-Ost on the A61. It's a hopeless place for hitchers.

SAMULI SCHIELKE AND ANNA KULJU, TAMPERE, FINLAND

All the major towns in Germany have their own identification letters for vehicle number plates e.g. M – Munich, DD – Dresden, HB – Bremen. Using these on your sign will let you use much bigger letters than writing out a name. Most Germans are familiar with other cities' identification letters, so just ask around for those of the city you want to get to.

JOACHIM SPARWASSER, FULDA, GERMANY

An update on the price of the youth camp, Kapuzinerhölzl. It is now up to DM13. The reason: not enough hitchers making use of the facilities, which are a lot better than a lot of hostels I've seen. It might shut in the future. Come on people – support those who are out to help us! GERARD VAN WEELE, PRETORIA, SOUTH AFRICA

When you want to get clear across Germany in one day, get, at any Raststätte (Motorway Services), a small booklet that lists all of them and, as an added bonus, contains fairly decent maps of Germany. Hitch-hiking from one to the next, asking for rides, even the newest novice should have no trouble at all getting from Puttgarden in the North to Kufstein in the South in a single day. It helps significantly if you speak German. ROBERT A. H. PRINS, IPSWICH, ENGLAND

Luxembourg and the Small Countries

There exist in Europe a number of independent or semi-independent territories which are complete anachronisms. They are mini-countries which have little business existing in this hurlyburly century, but somehow survive. Most of them have fewer citizens than the Ford Motor Company has workers. The territories are Luxembourg, Monaco, Andorra, Gibraltar, San Marino, Liechtenstein and Malta.

Luxembourg with its 2,586 sq. km of territory and population of 378,400 is the largest of these. Its modern history as a Grand Duchy began in AD 963 when a nobleman took over the ruins of a Roman fort which sat on a huge rock over the Alzette River, and built it into a castle. By the 13th century the country was one of the strongest in Europe and embraced an area 500 times the size it is today. Then the empire fell and its power diminished. Because of its central location it became an axiom that whoever controlled Luxembourg controlled the Continent. As no power could tolerate another having this advantage, an agreement was made at the London Congress of 1867 which guaranteed the independence of the country and demanded that the fortress be made inoperative.

In the city of Luxembourg, with its population of 90,000, the things to see include the remains of the fortifications (the castle is known as the 'Hollow Tooth') and some of the 21 km of underground passages cut into solid rock. The fortifications, the city's 80 bridges and its cathedral, are all illuminated during the summer.

In Luxembourg cigarettes are about the cheapest in Europe outside of Spain. Good place to stock up in, especially if you're heading up north into expensive Scandinavia. Luxembourg currency (francs) has the same value as Belgian money. Note that while Belgian notes and coins circulate freely in Luxembourg, apart from a few places near the border, Luxembourgeois currency is a no-no in Belgium.

The 467 sq. km of **Andorra** sit high in the Pyrenees between France and Spain. Her 50,528 citizens speak Catalán, French and Spanish and trade in Spanish pesetas and French francs.

Legend says the country was founded by Charlemagne in AD 784. The present co-principality dates from 1278 and is under the joint suzerainty of the President of France and the Bishop of Urgel in Spain. A feudal toll is paid each year, one year to the French, the next to the Spanish. In 1968 the Bishop of Urgel received 900 pesetas in cash, plus 6 hams, 12 chickens and 24 cheeses.

After tourism, which brings in plenty of cash owing to the practically duty-free state of its shops, tobacco is one of the big businesses. Cigarettes are about the same price as in Spain. Liquor is cheaper. Petrol, if you're driving a van, is cheaper than in either France or Spain – so fill up.

In this weird little place which boasts that it is the smallest country in the world and which is locked in by 8,000-foot snow-capped peaks, they have reached one state of affairs towards which you can only wish other countries would strive. The 1969 defence budget was £2. This gross expenditure bought bullets for the police force's pistol practice and shotgun shells for the mountain gamewardens.

Hitch-hiking both in and out of the place can be hard. It's all up and down or curves and the roads are narrow. Unless you want a long, long walk, pick yourself a nice position and stay there with your thumb propped in the air.

● **Shopping** Prices are good on things like cameras, film, radios, cassettes, tapes, etc. But on decent-size purchases (say, over £15) you can still get 10–20% off by asking. The bigger the purchase the more chance of the discount, so it's worth shopping with friends and getting all the things you want on the counter at the one time so you've got better bargaining power.

Monaco with its 29,000 inhabitants stacked into an area of 1.5 sq. km on France's Côte d'Azur is a principality governed by Prince Rainier, the gentleman who was married to the late American screen actress Grace Kelly.

The Principality has been independent since 1415 and has been ruled by the Grimaldi family (of which the current prince is a member) since 1297. Many efforts have been made to destroy its independence, the most recent being in 1963 when De Gaulle blockaded the state in an effort to make it fall in line, economically, with the rest of France. Prince Rainier held out until a 90-page document was signed by both parties guaranteeing, in part, that Monaco's citizens would continue to enjoy their tax-free status.

The state makes a good half of its income from tourism. Way over a million tourists visit each year, most to soak up the sun and sample the delights of the rich Mediterranean lifestyle. Some go to play at the famous casino, all hoping that they'll be the second person to break the fabulous bank of Monte Carlo. If you want to play the wheels, good luck to you, but it's strictly for hitchers expecting an inheritance!

For such a small place (small, but it has the greatest population density in the world) there is plenty to see. Not to be missed is the fantastic Oceanographic Museum. If you expect to be hitting the area around May, check with a tourist office for the exact dates of the *Grand Prix de Monaco*, one of the most exciting races in the car-sport world. Other sights include the quite good collection of paintings in the National Museum of Fine Arts and the Prince's Palace.

Note that the hitching is slow all along this area during summer.

Gibraltar perches right on the end of the Iberian Peninsula, across the bay from Algeciras. At the moment it can be reached by air from England, by boat or by air from Tangier, Morocco, or, easiest, by simply walking across the border from La Linea in Spain.

Gib has an area of 5.8 sq. km and a population of 29,000 which makes it the second most densely populated area in Europe and the fourth in the world. Government figures count a grand total of 31 km of roads (plus 8 km of pedestrian ways) and 10,836 vehicles. According to my calculations, if every vehicle on the Rock were put in the streets each would have just a touch over four yards of road – in other words, they wouldn't fit.

The Rock is 1,398 feet high. If you feel fit, walk up. If you feel rich take the cable car from the station in the car park in front of the Rock Hotel (which would cost a hitcher about half a week's budget to stay in). Whichever way, go. On a clear day, the view from the top goes across the Atlas Mountains in Morocco. Halfway up, on Queen's Road, is where you see the famous Barbary apes – the only apes living wild in Europe – which are said to have arrived in Gibraltar by way of a secret tunnel from Africa. That may sound like rubbish, but on the other hand no skeleton of a dead ape (they live about 17 years) has ever been found. Superstition says that if the apes ever leave Gib, then the British presence will end. With typical thoroughness, the British have put the apes on garrison strength and the British Army feeds them daily rations. There are two packs, about 36 apes in all. Be warned that the beasts bite. I know. I've been bitten.

The name Gibraltar comes from the Arabic *Gibel Tarik*, or Tarik's Hill. Tarik was Tarik-ibn-Zeyad, the Moor who started the invasion of Spain near Gibraltar in AD 711. Today there are several Moorish ruins to be seen, including the castle, the wall and the baths at the Gibraltar Museum – where for a modest entrance fee you can treat yourself to a fascinating rundown on Gibraltar's history. Other sights include St Michael's Cave in which rock (so to speak) concerts are occasionally held, and the Trafalgar Cemetery in which sailors killed at the Battle of Trafalgar are buried. (Lord Nelson, killed at sea, was brought back to Gib pickled in a barrel of rum en route for his state burial in England.)

The friendly Gibraltarians boast a well-stirred blend of Genoese, Maltese, Spanish, British and Arab blood. Their temperament is somewhere between that of a Spaniard and an Englishman, though their sympathies are just about entirely English. They are bilingual in Spanish and English and interchange languages without batting an eyelid. You'll hear a lot of *Spanglish* as well, along the lines of: 'Hola, my friend, vamos a tomar un drink.'

For reasonably priced meals try the Methodist Family Restaurant halfway along Main Street. For cheap sleeping go to the TOC 'H' further along the same street. Dossers should be able to find a suitable stretch of beach around the Mediterranean side of the Rock, at Catalan Bay, but make *very* sure you don't lay down your weary bones anywhere near a military area!

Gib offers a wide range of English food, at more or less UK prices. Some items are much cheaper than in Spain. Stock up particularly on cheese (half Spanish price or less), meat, muesli, chocolate etc. In my opinion, the Lipton supermarkets on Main Street, at Marina Bay and right on the Gibraltarian-Spanish border, offer the cheapest food prices.

● **Warning!** Prices in Gib can be amongst the lowest in Europe for luxury items like cameras and tape recorders. But I've seen cameras in Main Street shop windows marked at higher prices than in the centre of London. Prices can also vary as much as 20% between different shops. Make sure you're getting value before you put your money on the counter – and bargain hard.

San Marino, completely surrounded by Italy, is the oldest state in the world, dating from the 4th century. Its official title is the Most Serene Republic of San Marino. With a population of some 23,240 and an area of 60.5 sq. km, its big industries revolve around tourism and postage stamps. Tourism brings in 1,000,000 visitors each year. The big sight is the city of San Marino itself, which sits 2,200 feet above and just inland from the Adriatic Sea. Have a look at the Rocca Fortress and the Palazzo Valloni.

Liechtenstein, sitting between Switzerland and Austria, covers an area of 160 sq. km and has a population of 25,200. It's just big (or small) enough to provide a pleasant day's walk so that you can at least say you've been through a country on foot.

The state was founded in 1719 and gained independence in 1806 after a spell as part of the Holy Roman Empire.

Vaduz, the capital, is a huge metropolis of 4,400 souls, including a prince who lives in a castle on a hill above the town. The town itself is very much tourist-oriented. It has to be because Liechtenstein is much too pleasant a place to worry much about industrialization. Postage stamps, however, are big in this tiny land and any wandering philatelists should have a look at the excellent Philately Museum in the capital. Also check over the local art gallery which has better stuff in it than you might imagine.

The Republic of Malta lies in the heart of the Mediterranean, 95 km south of Sicily and 340 km north of Libya. The archipelago consists of three main islands, Malta, Gozo and tiny Comino, which total only 316 sq. km and support a population of 349,000 which speaks Malti (one of Europe's smallest languages, a unique mix of Arabic, Italian and French), and English. The use of English as a second language by about 75% of Maltese gives hitchers immediate access to the Mediterranean culture of these islands.

Best visits reflect the complex and often bloody history which is the heritage of the tiny Roman Catholic Republic. On Malta itself, the two essential cities to roam around are the capital, Valletta, and the ex-capital, Mdina.

Valletta's origins lie in the defeat of the Knights of St John on Rhodes by Suleiman the Magnificent in the 16th century. As a result, the Knights based themselves in Malta in 1530, and after driving off the Turks during the Great Siege of 1565, Grand Master Jean Parisot de la Valette raised money to build the fortified mini-city of Valletta. Now you can walk the walls of Valletta for an overall impression of towers, forts and bastions. Visit the old Auberges, the inns once used to accommodate the Knights; many, like the Auberge de Provence which now houses the National Museum of Archaeology, are used as public buildings. See St John's Co-Cathedral, and don't miss the Grand Master's Palace which includes a fascinating armoury of medieval weapons. If you have spare cash – the cost is a matter of intricate negotiation – take a ride in a *dghajsa* (a water taxi which you can hire at Customs House wharf) and see the incredible Grand Harbour, with Valletta on one side and the 'three cities' of **Vittoriosa, Senglea** and **Cospicua** on the other. The Grand Harbour was the main target of German bombs during the second Great Siege, the 1939–45 war, when Malta was awarded the George Cross for its heroism. Nearby **Sliema** abounds in reasonably priced cafés and offers some nightlife. (Movies are shown in English!)

About 10 km from Valletta stands **Mdina**, known as the Silent City. Don't miss it. It's tiny and unpretentious, but for my money one of Europe's most exquisite architectural gems. Wander the quiet, narrow streets, visit museums, churches and the Cathedral, burn up some film on the view from Bastion Square across to **Mosta**, dominated by St Mary's church with its 122-foot-diameter dome – amongst the world's largest. At neighbouring **Rabat** visit St Paul's Grotto where the saint traditionally stayed after his shipwreck on the island, and don't miss the impressive Christian catacombs. (You'll have to stash your pack somewhere because of the narrow passages.)

Elsewhere on Malta, places with flavour include the mysterious Hypogeum cave temple cut into the rock 40 feet underground at **Paola** (an absolute must for archaeology freaks and dreamy romantics); the temple ruins at **Tarxien**, just a few hundred yards from the Hypogeum; and **Hagar Qim**, a stone circle reminiscent of Stonehenge, which sits on a cliff top with views to uninhabited Filfla Island. If you make it to Hagar Qim, on the way home you can join a boat ride to visit the **Blue Grotto**. Do it on a sunny day and before 11 a.m. That's when the sun enters the cave and the water is most luminous.

Comino is inhabited only by a few locals and guests at the island's one hotel, and not worth a visit unless you want to play Robinson Crusoe.

Gozo is reached by ferry from Valletta or from **Cirkewwa**, the port north of **Mellieha** (which boasts Malta's best beach). In contrast to Malta's barren landscape, Gozo is refreshingly green. The capital is **Victoria**, though many people still call it by its old name of **Rabat**. It stands in the centre of the island just a short distance from where the ferry berths at **Mgarr**. Best visit in Victoria involves a climb up the hill to the Citadel. It's worth the short walk. Elsewhere on the island, visit the **Ggantija Temples** dating from around 3000 BC; the **Ramla Bay** beach with its cave which legend claims is where Ulysses stayed with Calypso; the tiny fishing hamlet of **Xlendi**, now popular with tourists; and the 'inland sea' at **Dwejra**.

Buses are dirt cheap on the islands, so don't hesitate to use them when heading to out-of-the-way spots. Neither Gozo nor Malta have camping grounds, but on Gozo, particularly, you'll find some marvellous out-of-the-way beaches if you feel like roughing it for a few days.

Hitchers' Tips and Comments . . .

To get out of Andorra into Spain, the best bet is to take the St Julia bus to the end of the line, then walk to the petrol station just past town. It has a big parking lot and average waiting time for a ride out is about ten minutes. DAVID FREMON, PALATINE, USA

Andorran banks offer better exchange rates on pesetas and francs than French or Spanish banks. Also, a special note for van-travellers. When heading from Andorra into France watch out for customs spot checks anywhere between the Andorran border and Aix-le-Thermes.

T.B., CHELMSFORD, UK

Cheapest way I found to Malta was to take the ferry from Syracuse (Sicily). You can buy duty-free aboard. I found hitching on the island easy. Most cars that had any room stopped. I travelled with three other hitchers and the *four* of us got around without problems. Buses are very cheap and it's advisable to take one in the built-up areas around Valletta. If you keep away from hotels, discos and other tourist traps, prices are amongst the lowest in Europe. The Maltese are extremely generous and friendly.

CLIVE BUCKMAN, TROWBRIDGE, UK

Switzerland

population	6,673,900
size	41,293 square kilometres
capital	Berne, population 145,000
government	Federal republic
religion	Roman Catholic and Protestant
language	French, German, Italian, and the little-used Romansch are the national languages; some English spoken in cities
currency	*Swiss franc* (SFr) One *franc* equals 100 *centimes* (French) or *Rappen* (German). Coins of 5, 10, 20 and 50 *centimes* or *Rappen* and 1, 2, 5 *francs*. Notes of 10, 20, 50, 100, 500, 1,000 *francs*

Berne is the capital of Switzerland, but Zurich is the largest city and perhaps the best to wander in for a few days. After those two, the towns to visit are Geneva, Lausanne, Lucerne, Basel, and St Gallen. In the south are the big mountains which are famous the world over – Monte Rosa at 15,023 feet, Dom at 14,920 feet, Matterhorn at 14,780 feet. And there are the high alpine passes – Umbrail at 8,218 feet and Bernina at 7,643 feet – and the long, long mountain tunnels – Simplon (rail), stretching 20 km and St Gotthard (road), 15 km.

The mountains are beautiful, but when you're up that high it can be very cold so keep an eye on the weather. A good route if you're chasing snow and glaciers, is to head out from Lausanne to **Interlaken** (an out-and-out tourist town, but in a beautiful situation) and take, in turn, highways 11 and 2 down to **Bellinzona** near the Italian border. This route takes you through some spectacular scenery which is a good cross-section of the mountain country. You cross the Susten Pass at the 7,299-foot level, catch a glacier just near there, and then climb to the St Gotthard Pass at nearly 7,000 feet (as long as you can get a ride over the pass, rather than through the tunnel). On the other side of the St Gotthard Pass in **Ticino** everything is different: the climate, vegetation, colour of the landscape, and the language (Italian). It's an exhilarating trip, especially if you do it on a blue-sky day. (It usually rains!)

Geneva, which is where most hitchers enter Switzerland after a French tour, is a good introduction to the country – and a hint of what to expect pricewise. It is slick, 100% modern, and beautiful the way a jetplane is. It's no place for us cheapskate hitchers. The youth hostels are usually full during the summer, so if you're thinking of staying it's worth booking in advance. Sights to see include the *Jet d'eau* on the lake (not in winter), a fantastic spout which hurls water 400 feet into the air; the Palais des Nations, the United Nations European home; and the Museum of Art and History which contains a beautiful display of Impressionist and post-Impressionist work. Music buffs may like to visit the Museum of Old Musical Instruments. Philosophers shouldn't miss the Rousseau Museum.

The YOUTH HOSTEL is on rue des Plantaporrets (tel: 29 06 19) but is closed from mid-December until late February. If you don't have your hostel card it'll cost you nearly double. The YMCA-YWCA is at av. Sainte-Clotilde 9 (tel: 28 11 33). Ask for the dormitory and if you can do without sheets you'll save a couple of francs. The SALVATION ARMY (*Armée de Salut*) have a hostel at Ch. Galiffe 4 (tel: 44 91 21), and a women-only hostel at rue de l'Industrie 14 (tel: 7336438). Another good deal for women is HOME ST PIERRE, right by the cathedral at cour St Pierre 4 (tel: 3283707). The CENTRE MASARYK at av. de la Paix 11 (tel: 33 07 72) is cheap enough, as is the CENTRE ST BONIFACE at av. du Mail 14 (tel: 3218844). There's cheap eating at the YMCA-YWCA and at the UNIVERSITY MENSA at av. du Mail 2, CITÉ UNIVERSITAIRE at av. de Miremont 20, the INTERNATIONAL STUDENT CLUB at rue de Saussure 6 and at RÉSIDENCE INTERNATIONALE at rue des Paquis 63.

Lausanne, just a hop, step and jump from Geneva along the fast autoroute, is a city of 128,800. Like Geneva, it sits on Lake Léman. But for me it offers more charm than many other Swiss cities because it is not a big international or business centre. The cathedral is worth a visit, as is the old Episcopal Palace of the Bishops of Lausanne. Check out the incredible *Collection d'Art Brut* (literally 'raw art'), a collection of pictures painted by non-professional artists, some of them down-and-outs, some mentally disturbed. It's like no art collection you've ever seen. The prettiest area of Lausanne is the lakefront at Ouchy. Plenty of parkland for discreet dossing out around the International Olympic Headquarters, about a 20-minute walk west along the lake.

Just outside of town is the village of **Vevey**, a pretty lakeside spot which has seen more than its share of famous people. Courbet, Byron, Hugo, and Rousseau all made visits or lived there at one time or another. A few kilometres further on is **Montreux**, famous for its international music festivals, the Festival of Jazz, beginning on the second Friday of July, and the Festival of Classical Music held each September. Nicknamed the 'Swiss Riviera', Montreux and its surrounds have been on and off with the international set for a century – and that, along with the casino in town, should give you an inkling of the sort of money that's floating around. But outside of town, the Castle of Chillon is worth a visit. The castle is one of Switzerland's most photographed spots, but hard to hitch to. Could be best to take a train from Montreux.

After Montreux you have a choice of travelling north to Berne, or south to **Valais**. Valais is the valley of the upper Rhône and great mountain walking country with numerous side valleys worth exploring. (**Sion** is the capital. It has two castles and great grapes.) For me, **Zermatt**, the tourist resort at the foot of the Matterhorn, is the best destination. You can't hitch the last few kilometres because private cars are not allowed in the town, but must walk or take the train from **Täsch**. Don't miss the Gonergrat with its spectacular mountain views. If you're well-heeled you can take the cog-wheel train (from a special station in front of the main station. Or you can hike up and back in one day along well-marked trails. On the way, stop and see the reflection of the Matterhorn in the Riffelsee. Take food and a jacket if you're hiking. Good maps available from the tourist office in town. Wander through the Zermatt cemetery beside the church and see the graves of scores of climbers who have lost their lives on the peaks. See **Derborence**, a lovely lake surrounded by mountains, try hitching from **Pont-de-la-Morge**, just out of Sion or walk a few hours up from **Ardon**. There are numerous other possibilities; just go exploring. You can even walk over **Col de Balme** into France. At the top of Valais is the **Rhône Glacier**, and from there you can connect up with the mountain trip from Interlaken.

If you're making your way between Lausanne and Berne consider stopping over in **Fribourg**. Lots of people miss out Fribourg in their rush to get to the capital, which is a shame, as there aren't many more charming towns in Switzerland. Built on a hill rising up from the River Sarine, one of the town's main attractions is the variety of views you get of the old town as you wander around. Be sure to cross over the Sarine and stroll up towards the Loreto Chapel – the view from there is excellent. You can't fail to notice some of the colourful old fountains which are dotted around town: the Barbarian and Good Samaritan fountains are particularly striking.

Berne, the capital of Switzerland, is a small city of 154,000 people, but is has enough to keep you amused for a day. The clock tower is the principal attraction, one of those jobs which put on a complete stage-show each hour. Don't miss the bear pit for a show of a different type (real bears). You get a good view over the attractive Old Town from the tower of the cathedral or from the public park called the Rose Garden. In here you may also find a place to lay your head (and if you can't, try down by the river). On the edge of Berne is a hill known as the Gurten. You reach the top on foot or by rack-railway. Walk along the top and, on a clear day, you'll be rewarded by views of the Bernese Oberland.

From Berne you can head south to Interlaken (Highway 6), then on to Lucerne or the mountain trip previously mentioned. From Berne, Lucerne is more easily accessible by thumb via the motorway (Highways 1 and 2), but the scenery is not so good.

Lucerne, on Highway 10 from Berne, is small (62,400) and perhaps the prettiest of all Swiss cities. It is the site of another international music festival, in late August, and also of the Great Lakeside Evening Festival, in late June. Two things to see, if the subjects interest you, are the Swiss Transport Museum, which features wheeled monstrosities from all ages, and the Tribschen, a house where Wagner lived and worked. Glacier Garden is a favourite with the tourists but, without a doubt, the nicest thing to do in Lucerne is wander across the covered wooden Chapel Bridge, meet people on the Rathausquai and explore the old section.

Basel, north of Berne and north-west of Lucerne, is Switzerland's second largest city. Situated exactly on the junction of France, Germany and Switzerland, you have a nice choice of direction after you've seen the sights. The ancient cathedral, surrounded by medieval houses and standing beside a beautiful square, is nice to wander around. If you look closely at the outside of the cathedral you'll see where it was reinforced after it (and the rest of Basel) was largely destroyed by an earthquake in the 14th century. The strange animals on the outside at the river end of the building are supposed to be elephants, but the sculptor had never seen an elephant! Basel is famous for its innumerable museums. The Art Museum (Kunstmuseum) holds one of the world's outstanding collections of Holbein as well as a superb display of modern works. The Basler Papiermühle is a paper and printing museum where you can even have a go at making your own paper. The Zoo is considered one of the world's best. Check out Jean Tinquely's fantastically imaginative mechanical fountain near the City Theatre (the park alongside can be a good place to meet people).

St Gallen, in the north-eastern corner of the country, is about the same size as Lucerne. St Gallen is one of Switzerland's most beautiful towns, but its sights are of a specialist nature. It is built around a huge baroque cathedral which contains the famous Abbey Library, a collection of 2,000 ancient manuscripts and nearly 2,000 more very old printed books. St Gallen was founded by an Irish monk, Gallus, in the 7th century.

Hitching in Switzerland is no great problem although you might find it slow in the backwood areas. Major cities are well linked by fast highways, and the student population is flush enough to own its own transport – and they seem to be helpful in offering rides. In some countries it won't break the bank if you get stuck and have to catch a bus or train. In Switzerland it *will.*

Remember that many of the high passes are closed during the winter months. If travelling between October and May, be sure to check ahead of yourself. Good maps like Michelin tell which passes you can expect to be closed, and the Swiss National Tourist Office in London hands out a leaflet called *Switzerland by Car* which offers complete information on alpine passes.

● **Warning!** The Swiss hit hard on drug users. In their eyes there is no difference between hard and soft drugs. Offenders face a maximum of 20 years in prison and/or a SFr1 million fine. Nevertheless, if you need help with a drug problem (support that is, not supply), talk to the people at *Drop-In* at Asylstrasse 23, Zurich (tel: 252 54 55), open 8 a.m.–8 p.m.

● **Buying money** You can find good rates of exchange in Switzerland on most 'soft' currencies, e.g. Turkish lira, Moroccan dirhams. Sometimes you can buy up to 20% cheaper so it's a good investment if you expect to be spending time in the soft currency countries. But remember that most of those places have a limit on the amount of money you are permitted to carry across their borders . . . in fact, most of them practically force you to break the law.

Zurich: where to sleep

Try to keep out of hotels in Zurich or, for that matter, anywhere in Switzerland. They are fantastic places, clean, comfortable, with all mod-cons, but at an average of 50–65SFr a night for a single, they're budget-wreckers. Unless you're fairly well-heeled you should try to sleep rough or at least stick to hostels or other special facilities. And even then, student hostels can cost you as much as 30SFr. Most of the ones listed below are bargains by Swiss standards, but try to ring before you go to the place you choose. Because of the high prices of normal hotels the budget places are often booked up.

Youth Hostel at Mutschellenstrasse 114 (tel: 482 35 44). Ask for dormitory, because there are also double rooms (at double the price per person).

Foyer Hottingen at Hottingerstrasse 31 (tel: 261 93 15). Girls or married couples only. You must be in by midnight.

YMCA at Sihlstrasse 33 (tel: 221 36 73). Men only.

YWCA (Marthahaus) at Zähringerstrasse 36 (tel: 251 45 50). Men and women.
Hotel Hinterer Sternen, Freieckgasse 7 (tel. 251 32 68).
Justinusheim at Freudenbergstrasse 146 (tel: 361 38 06).
Hotel Dufour at Seefeldstrasse 188 (tel: 55 36 55).
Hotel Regina at Hohlstrasse 18 (tel: 242 65 50).
Hotel Italia at Zeughausstrasse 61 (tel: 241 05 55).
Hotel St Georges at Weberstrasse 11 (tel: 21 11 44).

At the Tourist Office, Bahnhofplatz 15 (at the main station), you can get a free *Hotel Guide*, which includes maps and prices, and sort out any hotel problems. The same office can also give you information on locations and costs of half a dozen camping grounds in the area – which, in summer, can help you save a packet. **Campingplatz** at Seebucht, Seestrasse 557 (tel: 482 16 12), reach by taking Bus 161 or 165 from Bürkliplatz to Grenzsteig, is open May to September and costs around 8SFr per tent, 5SFr per person. Showers extra. Believe me, it's as good a deal as you'll find in the city.

For roughing it, you might find a spot by the Zurich-See at Seefeld Quai. Otherwise, best bet is out around the Dolder sports park.

Zurich: where to eat

Swiss food is fantastic, but it's also expensive. In fact, Switzerland is a great place to visit if you want to lose weight. As in most countries, keep an eye open for chain restaurants, supermarket restaurants, buffets and cafés. In Zurich, best bets are: **Migros Coop, Manora** Silberkugel, and especially the **Stadtküche Zurich** (or Zurich's People's Kitchen). These, for anyone on a limited budget, are perfect but they open between 11.30 a.m. and 12.30 p.m. only! There are 13 of them and the addresses are:

Selnaustrasse 46
Untergraben 4
Schipfe 16
Nordstrasse 101
Neunbrunnenstrasse 4
Dorflindenstrasse 4
Bederstrasse 130
Luggwegstrasse 27
Sihlquai 332
Zentralstrasse 34
Dufourstrasse 146
Hofwiesenstrasse 9
Kernstrasse 11

Other places to consider are:
Mensa der Universität Zurich at Rämistrasse 71.

Mensa Polyterrasse at Rämistrasse 101.
Rheinfelder Bierhaus at Marktgasse 19. Cheap luncheon plates.
Culmann at Culmannstrasse 1. This one is a student haunt.
Catalana at Glockengasse 8. Spanish restaurant.
Kantorei at Spiegelgasse 33. Popular with student types.
Cafeteria Freischütz at Freischützgasse 1.
Restaurant 1001 at Niederdorfstrasse 4.
University Restaurant at Künstlergasse 10.
Cafeteria of the Institute of Dentistry (Zahnärztliches Institut) at Plattenstrasse 11. Closed mid-July to mid-August.

Another excellent chain where you can eat for 11 or 12SFr if you choose carefully is run by the **Zurich Women's Association**. Branches are located as follows:

Karl der Grosse at Kirchgasse 14.
Rütli at Zähringerstrasse 43.
Seidenhof at Sihlstrasse 7–9.
Olivenbaum at Stadelhoferstrasse 10.

Zurich: what to see and do

SWISS NATIONAL MUSEUM on Museumstrasse, near main station. No entrance fee. Good rundown on the history of Switzerland.

RIETBERG MUSEUM in the Rieterpark. One of Europe's great collections of non-European art.

KUNSTHAUS on Heimplatz. Includes good collection of Swiss art. Entrance charge but Wednesdays and Sunday afternoons free.

GROSSMÜNSTER CATHEDRAL near City Hall. The largest Romanesque church in Switzerland, built between 1100 and 1300. In the 9th century Charlemagne founded a church on the same spot.

OEPFELCHAMMER at Rindermarkt 12 is one of the city's oldest beerhalls. Prices are OK (though avoid the expensive restaurant next door). Good place to meet people. For jazz, *Casa Bar* at Münstergasse 30 is fine (no cover charge but the drinks are expensive), while for dancing try *Joker* in the Kongresshaus. If you want to meet up with local students go to the *International Student Club* at Augustinerhof 1, but you'll have to show a student ID card to get in.

CINEMA Anything made in English will probably be shown in English

– with up to three (German, French, Italian) subtitles on the screen. For programme info from cinemas, theatres and concert halls ask for the bi-weekly *Bulletin*, available free at the Tourist Office (Bahnhofplatz 15). Each cinema has complete listings for Zurich posted outside.

MARKETS A flea market is held every Saturday between 8 a.m. and 4 p.m. on Bahnhofstrasse towards the lake. There's also a curiosity market every Thursday from 9 a.m.–9 p.m. in the Rosenhof, the small square between Limmatquai and Niederdorf.

Transport in Zurich
You must have a ticket before you board trams or buses. There are vending machines for these at all stops. At the major stops you can also buy 12-ride tickets and day tickets. Trips cost between 1.90 and 3.30SFr depending on distance. Best way, for a day of sightseeing, is to buy the special day ticket for 7SFr which allows you unlimited travel for 24 hours, including trips on the ferries which ply the River Limmat.

Student discounts
Discounts for some concerts, cinemas and theatres. Reduced admission to galleries and museums. Discounts in many large stores. For information, contact:

Swiss Student Travel Office, Leonhardstrasse 10, 8026 Zurich (tel: 242 30 00). SSR publish a handy book, complete with colour maps, called *Switzerland the Cheap Way*. The latest edition is a bit dated (1978) but if you remember to ignore the prices quoted it's still very useful and, what's more, they seem to be giving them away now.

Addresses

Post office (for poste restante) at Sihlpost, Kasernenstrasse 95–9.
American Express at Bahnhofstrasse 20, 8022 Zurich (tel: 211 83 70).
Schweizerischer Studentenreisedienst at Leonhardstrasse 10, 8026 Zurich (tel: 242 30 00). Closed Monday mornings.
Tourist Office at Bahnhofplatz 15 (tel: 211 40 00).
US Consulate at Riedtilstrasse 15 (Tel. 363 06 44).
British Consulate at Dufourstrasse 56 (Tel. 47 15 20).

Hitchers' Tips and Comments . ..

BASEL: Signposting for getting out of the city is terrible. I walked in a complete circle, wasting two hours. When you reach the Football Stadium, keep right ahead for Lucerne road – don't turn left!

MALCOLM FRANKLAND, GLASGOW, SCOTLAND

I agree with *Malcolm Frankland*. Hitching out of Basle isn't helped by the terrible signposting. If you're heading north don't follow the Deutschland signs or you'll spend ages going nowhere. Instead follow the Karlsruhe A5 signs from Basel Bad train station.

TOMMY 'THE BONNY BAIRN' JOHNSTONE, FALKIRK, SCOTLAND

If you're down on your luck hitching and have to take buses, don't try to jump fares, particularly in Switzerland. Inspectors are numerous and come down heavily. On-the-spot fines.

GRAHAM CURRY, RETFORD, ENGLAND

Hitchers and van vagabonds leaving Switzerland should beware of Swiss customs. They seem to be taking a lot of time searching packs and vans. Seems to take longer getting out of the country than getting in. JOHN PURNELL, BIRMINGHAM, ENGLAND

To hitch from Basel to Berne, Lucerne or Zurich, you have to hitch on the slip-road in town. Don't try it on the main highway. It's hopeless. Traffic speed is fast and there's nowhere cars can pull over.

In university towns (like Berne) the student halls are normally empty during the vacation and sometimes the caretaker allows you in.

To hitch from Lausanne to Geneva, start in town. The lake route is very, very slow and hitching is forbidden on the motorway, and the law is strictly enforced. JEZ, HEMEL HEMPSTEAD, ENGLAND

Hitching from Lausanne to Geneva I would recommend trying between the roundabout and the petrol station on av. du Mont d'Or. JOHN MEHERS, LEEDS, ENGLAND

Warning! Our Swiss friends tell us they are clamping down on tents in parks, etc., especially in the Italian part, with fines of up to 200SFr.

SIMON WADSWORTH, SHIPLEY, WEST YORKSHIRE, UK

The obvious thing to eat in Switzerland that wasn't mentioned in your book is fondue – melted cheese which really fills! Does make you really thirsty though, so drink lots of water, not wine, with it.

If in Switzerland, don't skip Winterthur, near Zurich, with a very active alternative scene such as the Schwarzer Café.

ANNA LISS, AMSTERDAM

Austria

population	7,620,000
size	83,857 square kilometres
capital	Vienna, population 1,700,000
government	Federal republic
religion	Roman Catholic
language	German; some English spoken
currency	*Schilling* (AS) One *Schilling* equals 100 *Groschen*. Coins of 5, 10, 50 *Groschen*; and of 1, 5, 10, 20 *Schillings*. Notes of 20, 50, 100, 500, 1,000 and 5,000 *Schillings*

A pleasant morning's walk through Liechtenstein (see **The Small Countries**) and then a quick hitch and you're in **Feldkirch**. That's as nice a way as any of entering Austria. Feldkirch is an old-world kind of town. Her 17,000 inhabitants move slowly and don't seem to give a damn about anything. See the 10th-century Schattenburg Castle. There is a wine festival in the second week of July.

A few kilometres north is **Dornbirn**. On the edge of town you get good alpine views from the top of the Karren Gondola. If you continue up the road from the base of this, you come to the **Rappenlochschlucht** and the **Alplochschlucht**, two narrow gorges which walkers will enjoy.

A little further north is **Bregenz** on the shores of Lake Constance (the Bodensee). Have a look at the Vorarlberger Museum, which gives a good idea of the history of Vorarlberg Province, and wander through the Altstadt, the old section.

The Innsbruck road takes you through some really great country (*Sound of Music* all the way). If you manage a ride over the 5,000-foot Arlberg Pass, instead of through the expensive tunnel, you'll pass through **St Anton**, a famed ski-resort with Europe's oldest ski-school.

Innsbruck is 700 years old and, many say, Austria's most beautiful city, though in my opinion Salzburg could lay a pretty solid claim to that title. Innsbruck was Winter Olympics city in 1964 and 1976. Those interested in snow sports might like to see the Olympic speed skating oval, the Bergisel Olympic ski-jump, and the Olympic bobsleigh and toboggan runs in **Igls**. Anyone heading down into

Italy from Innsbruck will go over the famous Europe Bridge, the highest in Europe, 897 yards long and standing 624 feet above the river bed. In the city itself see the Imperial Palace, the Museum of Tyrolese Art, and the Alpine Museum at Emperor Maximilian's Arsenal.

The fastest way to **Salzburg** (population 139,000) is along the E17 which cuts briefly across Germany at **Bad Reichenhall** (a town with a local reputation for its healing mineral springs and a good base for hiking in the Alps). Sitting beautifully on a plain and backed with huge mountains, Salzburg's focal point is the 12th-century Hohensalzburg Castle. The Franziskanerkirche Cathedral is worth a look, as is the superbly presented Carolino Augusteum Museum. Mozart fans will know that the musician was born in Salzburg and will want to see his house and museum. They should note that the city holds a Mozart Week each January (exact dates may vary from year to year) which features the Vienna Philharmonic Orchestra. Then, of course, there's the fantastic Salzburg Music Festival which is held every July and August. Some 30 or 40 km north of Salzburg is the quite pleasant frontier town of **Braunau** – Adolf Hitler's birthplace.

Hallstatt is a tiny village of about 2,000 people a few kilometres off the Salzburg–Graz highway. Most of the village lies perched along the lake, with the road running behind it through tunnels in the cliff. Apart from being the ideal place to get a whiff of rural Austria it offers the added attractions of the Hallstatt Museum which features prehistoric objects found in various tombs, and the Dachstein Caves which you reach by cable railway. It's a great area for hiking. If you've had some experience you can climb up to the Hallstatt Glacier. It's quite a long way, so it's best to stay in Simony-Hütte for the night – bedding and food are provided. Hallstatt is in the Salzkammergut, and athletic hitchers will find dozens of lakes to swim in and mountains to climb.

The road now takes you through the lushness of Styria, over the 2,500-foot Schober Pass, through the towns of **Leoben** and **Bruck** (and precious few others) until you arrive in **Graz** which, with 250,000 people, is Austria's second largest city. Things to see include the fantastic Arsenal with the world's largest collection of medieval armour (30,000 pieces in all), the ornate mausoleum of Emperor Ferdinand II, the castles which you reach by cablecar, and several important galleries and museums.

Two main roads run south of Graz. The 67 leads you into Yugoslavia (only 40 km away) and the 70 goes to **Klagenfurt**, with side roads into Yugoslavia. The 70 then becomes the 100 and joins up with **Lienz**, a small Tyrol city crowned by a castle and as typical as they come. Here's the ideal place for any hitcher who has enough spare cash to take a few days off for some skiing. Thirty kilometres south of Lienz and you're in Italy.

The romantically minded could enter Austria from Germany at **Passau** and follow the Danube right down to Vienna. First stop would be the **Abbey of St Florian**. Lots to see, including a magnificent library of books and manuscripts. Music fans will want to visit the church. Anton Bruckner, who was born near St Florian, is buried in the crypt beneath the organ. Further along the route – just to put a dent in your romanticism – drop in to **Mauthausen** and visit the Nazi concentration camp. About 200,000 people died here, many from exhaustion after being forced to struggle up the infamous Stairway of Death carrying as much as one hundred pounds of stone from the quarry below. Imagine walking up a couple of times with your pack! A more pleasant stop is **Melk**, perhaps the most beautiful area in the entire Danube Valley; the river meanders between vine-covered hillsides. Take time off to visit **Stift Melk**, the Benedictine Abbey, once a castle and handed over to the monastic order in 1106. Medieval **Dürnstein** is the site of the castle where Richard the Lionheart was held prisoner for ransom on his return from the Third Crusade in 1192. Blondel the Minstrel sang beneath these very walls!

Hitching tends to be rather erratic compared to Switzerland. There's no problem on routes such as Salzburg to Vienna but in some parts of the country it can be quite slow. For example, if you head north of **Linz** to Czechoslovakia, you might as well resign yourself to catching a train, or catching a bus from **Freistadt** (a lovely old walled town) to the border, no matter what your map says about this being an 'E' route.

Vienna: where to sleep

Prices fairly high. Student and hostel accommodation is generally about 200–250AS for one of the cheapest singles.

Hostelling International hostels:

Jugendgästehaus Wien-Brigittenau, Friedrich Engelsplatz 24 (tel: 33282940/3300598).

Jugendherberge Myrthengasse, Myrethengasse 7/Neustifgasse 85 (tel: 52363160/52394290).

Jugendherberge Lechnerstrasse, Lechnerstrasse 12 (tel: 7131494).

Hostel Ruthensteiner, Robert Hamerlinggasse 24 (tel: 8934202/ 8932796).

Jugendgästehaus der Stadt Wien (Hütteldorf), Schlossbergasse 8 (tel: 8771501/8770263). Long way out.

Schlossherberge am Wilhelminenberg, Savoyenstrasse 2 (tel: 458503700). Also far from the centre.

Other youth/student accommodation:

Hostel Zöhrer, Skodagasse 26 (tel: 430730).

YMCA Inter-Rail Point, Kenyongasse 25 (tel: 936304). Mid July–mid Aug. only.

Believe-It-Or-Not, Myrthengasse 10 (tel: 5264658/964658).

Katholisches Studentinnenheim, Servitengasse 3 (tel: 343409). Open 1 July–20 Oct. For female students only.

For help with student accommodation talk with the people at **Austrian Student Travel Office** at Reichsratstrasse 13 (tel: 4087821), who operate a student accommodation service.

For sleeping out try the golf-links on Hauptallee and the Prater Park, or Donaupark on the east side of the canal.

Vienna's camping grounds are all a fair way out but they'll save you money on accommodation. Two of them, **Wien-West I** and **Wien-West II**, are close to each other in Hüttelbergstrasse. Take the U4 underground westwards to the end of the line (Hütteldorf), then change to bus 52B. Wien-West I is open July to end of August; Wien-West II open all year.

Vienna: where to eat

Count on paying 60–120AS in a cheap restaurant. But if you're a student, try the first two listings below and you'll eat dinner for around 30–50AS:

Mensa der Osterreichischen Hochschülerschaft at Führichgasse 10. Students only. Dinner served from 6–10 p.m. Open during student holiday periods only.

Mensa des Hauptausschusses at Universitätstrasse 7. Open all year except Easter and Christmas. Dinner served from 6–10 p.m.

Also try eating at any of the wine houses and cellars. Prices will usually be a bit more than 100AS, but the food is great. Don't forget to buy Vienna pastry from the *Konditoreien*. Cheap enough and great breakfast food, especially if you have a sweet tooth. Only rich hitchers will be able to buy anything there, but the rest of you bums can torture yourselves for free by taking a look at the marzipan displays in the window of **Demel** at 1010 Wien Kohlmarkt 14.

Vienna: what to see and do

SCHLOSS SCHONBRUNN is a huge baroque palace containing more than 1,400 rooms. It was the modest summer residence of the Habsburgs from 1695. Costs about 50AS for a guided tour in English, but less if you're a student.

KUNSTHISTORISCHES MUSEUM at the Ring. Fine collection of old masters. Works by Rembrandt, Brueghel, Vermeer, Velázquez, etc. Closed Mondays. Admission fee.

HOFBURG was the official residence of the Habsburgs. Lots to do. You can see the imperial rooms where Emperor Franz Josef lived, or the SCHATZKAMMER which contains the royal treasures, including the insignia of the Holy Roman Empire and the sword of Charlemagne. Then there's the famous SPANISH RIDING SCHOOL (check with tourist office for performance times, closed July and August) and the BURG KAPELL where the Vienna Boys Choir perform each Sunday except in summer. It'd take you days (and some expense) to get through the place if you wanted to see everything.

ST STEPHAN'S GOTHIC CATHEDRAL at Stephansplatz. Climb the tower for a tremendous view over the city and head down into the crypt and have a look at some skulls. Admission charge for both tower and crypt. Organ concerts.

MUSICIANS' MUSEUMS are essential visits for music lovers. The BEETHOVEN MUSEUM at Moelkerbastei; the HAYDN MUSEUM at Haydngasse 19; the MOZART MUSEUM at Domgasse 5 (in the Figarohaus); the SCHUBERT MUSEUM at Nussdorferstrasse 54.

SIGMUND FREUD MUSEUM at Berggasse 19. Freud, the man who invented psychoanalysis, lived in this house for 47 years until the annexation of Austria by the Nazis in 1938 forced him to leave the country. (He died in London the following year.) If you don't get offered one, ask for the guide to the museum in English. Admission cheaper with student card. If you find the opening hours too short, you can return without paying again if you keep your ticket.

KELLERS AND HEURIGE are wine cellars and wine gardens and were once – not so much now – an integral part of the life of the Viennese. But still good fun. Costs depend on how thirsty you are. One good keller, though rather hot in summer, is Esterhazykeller at Haarhof. The Heurige are out in the north-western suburbs – try to avoid the touristy ones, especially the Grinzing area.

PRATER is an amusement park featuring the world's largest ferris wheel. No entrance charge to the grounds.

THEATRE for those who want a taste of the Vienna of old. Try the **Theater an der Wien** at Linke Wienzeile 6 (standing room is cheapest).

BURG KREUZENSTEIN is a moated medieval castle thirty minutes from the centre of Vienna. Take a train from Landstrasse.

Transport in Vienna
Single tickets for the public transport system are expensive, so it makes sense to look at the special deals on offer. After only three trips you've got your money's worth out of a day ticket. The 3-day and 7-day passes are even better value (bring a passport photo if you want a 7-day pass).

Student discounts
Reductions to museums. For information contact the Austrian Student Travel Office in Vienna (see below).

Addresses

Main post office (for poste restante) at Fleischmarkt 19, 1010 Vienna.
American Express at Kärntnerstrasse 21–23, Vienna (tel: 515400).
Austrian Student Travel Office at Türkenstrasse 4–6, Viena (tel: 401480). The Salzburg branch is at Hildsmannplatz 1a (tel: 84 67 69); the Innsbruck branch is at Erlerstrasse 19–25 (tel: 29 997).
Vienna City Tourist Office Kärntnerstrasse 38 (tel: 513 88 92).
US Embassy at Gartenbaupromenade 2, Vienna (Tel. 31 55 11).
British Embassy at Jauresgasse 12, Vienna (Tel. 713 15 75).
Info centres at Damböckgasse 1 (tel: 57 95 21); Rötzergasse 29 (tel: 46 86 69); and Pragerstrasse 20 (tel: 30 33 89).

Hitchers' Tips and Comments . . .

In Austria and Switzerland, good places for a night's kip are in the little huts you see in fields or on mountains. They're usually open and keep you 100% dry when it rains.

TRUE BRIT, CHELMSFORD, ENGLAND

Ask permission if the place is obviously on someone's land, and – thinking of hitchers who'll pass that way in the future – leave things exactly as you find them. K.W.

Visit Vienna flea-market on Saturdays between 8 a.m. and 6 p.m. Come early for bargains and haggle like mad. Avoid vendors with tables. They have a one-year concession and out-of-your-mind prices.

Worth hitching down to Baden (about 26 km south-west of Vienna). It's a beautiful spa town dating from Roman times. Lots of sulphur springs and baths. Also, a large 'cure' park which features free classical music concerts in summer. Baden is expensive, but you can save if you shop at *Eisenberger's Supermarket*. I found food cheaper there than in Vienna. TOBIAS WILLIAMS, VIENNA, AUSTRIA

In Salzburg we couldn't afford an hotel and crashed in the entrance hall of the railway station. There were dozens of other hitchers there, too, and the police didn't worry anyone.

A. BROWN-GRANT, OXFORD, ENGLAND

In Vienna, the Prater Park is a bit of a walk out of town, so if you're tired and want to crash right away try the small parks near the Rathaus (town hall). PHILIP ATTWOOL, ORPINGTON, UK

In Innsbruck, try dossing out at the deserted green hut near the Olympic ski-jump, It's well hidden, waterproof and has an inside lock. We stayed two nights and had no bother.

GREGOR MURPHY, PAISLEY, SCOTLAND

Getting out of Vienna (West). Ride the U4 train west to Ober St Veit, get off and cross over the railway footbridge to the McDonald and Services. There is a lay-by. Linz and Salzburg rides every 10 minutes or you are doing it wrong, mate!

District 16: the place in Wien to find cheap hotels, student bars, other English and Americans, lots of jobs and flat shares changing hands by word of mouth. Great food markets – try Thalia Strasse and Kilchstetten G. And all 15 minutes' walk from the rip-off city centre! DAVE COLLARD, CANTERBURY

Italy

population	57,576,400
size	301,277 square kilometres
capital	Rome, population 4,000,000
government	Republic
religion	Roman Catholic
language	Italian
currency	*Lira (L)* Coins of 50, 100, 500, 1,000 *lire*. Notes of 1, 000, 2,000, 5,000, 10,000, 50,000 and 100,000 *lire*

The four most common entry routes into Italy are (1) along the French Riviera to **Genova** (Genoa, birthplace of Columbus), with its fantastic harbour area, (2) in over the French Alps to **Torino** (Turin) where you can catch the important Egyptian Museum and Museum of Ancient Art, (3) from Switzerland through the Swiss-Italian town of Lugano to **Milano** (Milan), or (4) through the Mont Blanc Tunnel.

Winter travellers coming in on the Turin route should note that the Col du Mt Cenis on the French side of the border may be impassable between December and May. Most of the passes in Switzerland (No. 3 route or any near it), like Simplon, Lukmanier or Splugen may be closed during the same months. Summertime travellers should remember that the Riviera route is blanketed with family holiday cars from June through August and that the hitching can sometimes be very, very slow.

Milan is not my favourite city. With a population of more than one and a half million it's big, dusty, noisy, and industrial, but there are many things to see, notably the church of Santa Maria delle Grazie which houses Leonardo da Vinci's famous *Last Supper*. The Gothic Duomo cathedral stands 357 feet high and has (if you're interested in such facts) 4,400 statues serving as decoration. A trip to the roof gives you a fantastic view over the city and allows you to wax poetic to gargoyles if you feel so inclined. La Scala is the big stop for opera lovers. It's a superb theatre and features the best singers in the world. Cheapest way to view a show is to buy standing room.

Museum fans will have a ball in Milan. Right near La Scala is the Museo Teatrale which relates the history of the 150-year-old theatre, while the National Museum of Science and Technology (free on Sundays and Thursday mornings) has a Leonardo Gallery in which you can see models of da Vinci's fascinating inventions. Then there's the Pinacoteca di Brera (free on Sundays) which Milan claims as the second gallery in Italy after Florence's Uffizi. Finally, drop in on the 13th-century Castello Sforzesco, and the strange, ornate cemetery known as Cimitero Monumentale.

Halfway between Milan and Venice (Venezia) is **Verona**, used by Shakespeare as the backdrop to *Romeo and Juliet*. See a well-preserved Roman amphitheatre, Italy's largest outside Rome. Don't miss the fruit market at the Piazza delle Erbe, nor the Old Castle or the church of St Zeno Major. But most of all, enjoy the centre of the old town with its jigsaw of squares, alleys and stairways: a photographer's delight.

Venice may be the world's weirdest city. Built on a lagoon 4 km from the mainland (but with a road connection) it spreads over 118 tiny islands. It is criss-crossed by more than 160 canals and, as no cars are allowed into the city, you either walk from place to place or jump a *vaporetto*, a canal boat. Take a tip that Lines 1 and 3 might be slower than Lines 2 and 4, but they are cheaper. Also remember that though *vaporetti* are fun – and certainly not to be missed for at least one ride – they aren't essential; the city is small enough to cover on foot.

Venice vies with Florence as the most expensive city in Italy. To keep the budget intact, consider eating and sleeping in neighbouring **Mestre**, particularly around the station area. From Mestre you can bus or train into Venice each day. The centre of Venice – and some would claim of the world – is fabulous St Mark's Square, or, as Venetians call it, the *Piazza*. St Mark's is one of *the* great squares of Europe. Don't miss it! But don't do what one hitcher did and take a drink at Florian's (or indeed at any of the other posh sidewalk cafés lining the square. His extravagance cost him about half his food budget for the day. Things could have been worse – if the orchestra had been playing at the time all his day's allowance would have been out the window!

Big sights in Venice, apart from the city itself, include the Basilica of St Mark's (climb into the gallery for a closer look at the incredible mosaic ceiling) and the neighbouring Palace of the Doges; the Gallery of Modern Art (great collection, free on Sundays) and the Guggenheim Collection (outstanding collection of 20th-century paintings). Take the lift to the top of the 98 metre high Campanile for a view over Venice's rooftops and down into St Mark's Square. The original Campanile, which was originally a lighthouse and look-out tower, collapsed in 1902. The one you see now was rebuilt by 1912 to the exact specifications of the old plans. For a look at Venetian glass-blowers in action jump *vaporetto* no. 5 at Fondamente Nuova, which will take you to the island of **Murano**. Another interesting island trip (leaving from the same place) is to **Torcello** with its old, old churches. For one of the best overall views of

Alps
L. Como
Milan
Turin
Verona
Venice
Po
Ferrara
Genoa
Bologna
FORMER
Florence
Pisa
San Marino
Siena
Tiber
ITALY
ADRIATIC SEA
Ajaccio
CORSICA
Rome
Naples
Mount Vesuvius
Pompeii
Sorrento
Capri
SARDINIA
Apennines
Cagliari
TYRRHENIAN SEA
Cantanzaro
Messina
Reggio di Calabria
SICILY
MEDITERRANEAN SEA
MALTA
0 Miles 200
0 km 200

Belgrade
YUGOSLAVIA
Sofia
BULGARIA
T U R K E Y
Istanbul
Souflion
Thessaloniki
ALBANIA
Mount Athos
Pindus Mountains
CORFU
GREECE
AEGEAN SEA
Lamia
IONIAN SEA
Marathon
Athens
Piraeus
Corinth
Olympia
Hydra
Spetsia
Messini
Sparta
RHODES
SEA OF CRETE
CRETE

Venice, take the boat to nearby **San Giorgio** island and the lift up the tower of San Giorgio Maggiore church.

If you want to find yourself a little company, try the Lido beach. To get there you take another boat ride. Once on the beach you must make sure you avoid paying several thousand lire for a dressing room. Lonely souls can also search for mates (only in summer) at the nearby tourist resort of **Lido de Jesolo**, reached by boat or bus. Your friend found, tempt the romantic in yourself by walking together on the Rialto Bridge around ten or eleven in the evening and listening to the music coming from the gondolas. The people *in* the gondolas are paying a small fortune for the privilege (like enough to keep you on the road for two or three days!).

Go back to the Rialto, which is the centre of Venice's commercial centre, at around eight or nine in the morning and watch the city go to work. At this hour the Grand Canal is seething with vessels of all kinds, including Coca-Cola delivery boats! The bridge leads to Venice's main fish and vegetable market which has been operating since the 11th century.

Heading back across the country, you pass through **Ferrara** with its marvellous moated Castello Estense and its 12th-century cathedral, and then through gracious **Bologna**, perhaps the best place in the country to try some good Italian home cooking. See the Fountain of Neptune and climb the 320-foot Asinelli Tower for a great view over this ancient town. East of Bologna the coastal town of **Ravenna** is famed for the mosaics which decorate its many ancient churches.

Heading south from Bologna the next big stop (there are plenty of nice villages in between) is **Florence** (Firenze). Considered *the* great art city of the Western world, it's a natural target for thousands of students from all over the globe. Consequently, you have an excellent chance of finding someone who'd just love to accompany you on a tour. Good meeting places are all around the central Piazza della Signoria and the Uffizi, and on the steps of the Duomo (the Cathedral), which the youth of Florence have used as a rendezvous point since the Renaissance.

All museums and galleries in Florence are free on certain days which seem to change constantly (check tourist office), otherwise they will set you back a hefty entrance fee (less on student cards, of course). With something like 50 places to visit in the city, you have to choose carefully what you want to see. The Piazza della Signoria with the Loggia della Signoria and the copy of Michelangelo's *David* standing in front of the Palazzo Vecchio are absolute musts and, in my opinion, should be visited at least twice, once in the day, once at night. Most people consider the Uffizi Galleries and the Pitti Palace indispensable. What else? Try the Baptistry opposite the Duomo with its unparalleled *Door of Paradise* by Ghiberti. Climb the Campanile, which was designed by Giotto. From the top you can see all of Florence and at the same time admire Filippo Brunelleschi's 42-metre-diameter dome which crowns the Duomo and is larger than the dome of Rome's St Peter's. Take Bus 13 to the Piazzale Michelangelo where you can see yet another copy of *David* and look out over Florence and the Arno Valley. Visit Santa Croce, badly damaged during the 1966 floods, but now restored. If you're particularly interested in Michelangelo, see the Casa Buonarroti, bought by the artist for his family, and stuffed with paintings and letters relating to the man himself. Drop in on the Medici Chapel where you can see Michelangelo's work adorning the tombs of the famous family. Try – well, work it out for yourself – free literature from the tourist office at Via dei Tornabuoni 15. There is so much to see and you will be surrounded by the masterpieces of so many famous artists that you may end up wondering if perfection isn't a trifle claustrophobic.

For me, the absolute knock-out visit in Florence is to the Galleria dell'Accademia (usually open mornings only) to see Michelangelo's original *David*. People stand in front of this statue as if they are hypnotized. Check out the sculptor's unfinished works as you wander down the aisle towards *David*. For me, they give an idea of what goes into creating a concept from a block of marble and make me appreciate David's power and presence even more.

For a pleasant break, visit **The Paperback Exchange** at Via Fiesolana 31, just a five-minute walk from the Galleria dell'Accademia. The Paperback Exchange offers 10% discount off cash sales on secondhand books to hitchers who show this guide.

Pisa stands just an hour or two west of Florence. Here you can see the famous Leaning Tower. Ask for Il Campanile. It was begun in 1173 and leans 14 feet out of plumb owing to land or foundation subsidence after construction. Galileo used this very tower when making experiments before formulating his laws of gravity and when studying the acceleration of falling objects. In the same square (Piazza del Duomo) see the 12th-century cathedral and the dome-shaped Baptistry, built between the 12th and 14th centuries. On the side of the square opposite the kilometre-long line of souvenir stalls (can you live without a Leaning Tower of Pisa lamp base?) is the Cemetery (Campo Santo) with 600 tombstones and a chapel with 15th-century Old Testament frescoes. The dirt of the Campo Santo is said to be mixed with earth from the Hill of Calvary brought from Jerusalem by crusaders.

Heading south, make for Siena via **Volterra** (cathedral, palaces,

1st-century Roman ruins, etc.) and then try and get to **San Gimignano**, a 14th-century hill-top town famed for its 14 soaring stone towers – all that are left of 72 which once dominated the skyline. San Gimignano seems scarcely changed since the day it was built . . . if you ignore the tourist junk on sale. A stroll through the streets – particularly just after sunrise – truly evokes a sense of the past.

Siena, about 30 km south-east, is the most important town in Tuscany after Florence. Once again, there are galleries and churches enough to keep you busy. But, with a population of only 55,000, this beautiful medieval city is small enough to wander in at leisure. Maybe a nice resting place before hitting the bustle of Rome. If you're in the area in July or August, try to catch the Palio, a wild horse race around the Piazza del Campo with riders wearing medieval costume. (Exact dates from tourist office, and be warned that there's not a bed to be had during the festival.) Climb the 409 steps of the 102-metre-high Torre de Mangia (*without* your pack because it won't fit) for tremendous views across the rooftops and green, rolling Tuscan countryside. Another superb view back on to the Piazza del Campo and the city can be seen from the tower of the museum beside the black and white striped Gothic cathedral (once again, packs don't fit!).

You're probably getting the idea by now that you'll never see all of Italy, or even most of Italy, in one trip, but if you've still got the strength and the time try continuing south-east through **Perugia** (yep, great square, great palaces, great galleries, great cathedral) and on to **Assisi**, home of St Francis, mystic and poet (he is said to have written the first poems in the Italian language). The value of the visit is in the sheer beauty of the town. Long, narrow streets, ancient houses and a lifestyle apparently undistorted by the excesses of the 20th century make it worth the detour. And, for such a small place (population about 25,000), there's plenty to see. The local tourist office can supply a free brochure devoted to Assisi and nearby villages.

After Rome, the next big 'must' is the Bay of Naples. **Napoli**, a city of one and a quarter million, has for centuries been subjected to earthquakes and volcanic eruptions, but the place just keeps on going. It is a marvellous town in which to wander – so Italian that it's almost a cliché. The two big things to see are the Castel Nuovo, dating from 1282, and the National Museum with its collection of ancient sculpture and important finds from Pompeii.

Pompeii is the greatest standing remnant of the Roman world. Once an important city of 20,000 people, it was completely buried by an eruption of Mount Vesuvius in AD 79. The memory of the place died in the succeeding centuries until the name became a mere legend. Then, late last century, it was rediscovered, and for decades the work of digging it out of millions of tons of dirt has continued. Now you can wander for hours in a complete Roman city – and it's weird. In some streets you see ruts in the cobbles from chariot wheels. In doorways you see grooves scraped into floors by the doors which once opened across them. And you can see the stone-entombed bodies of some of the citizens. (If you're not heading as far south as Pompeii and still want to see the ruins of a Roman town, try **Ostia Antica**, 22 km south-west of Rome. Founded in the 4th century BC, Ostia Antica served as Rome's trading port with her colonies and at its zenith was the home of 100,000 citizens.)

Herculaneum, close to Pompeii, is another city which was buried in the same eruption. Not as fascinating as Pompeii, but OK.

The villain of the piece, Mount Vesuvius, is a volcano 3,984 feet high, and it's still active. You can walk up to the top, if you're feeling fit, or take the expensive chair-lift if you're not, and then descend into the actual crater amongst the fumes drifting out from crevices. Interesting stuff.

Also in the Bay of Naples area is the famous resort town of **Sorrento** (beautiful and expensive) and the fabulous island of **Capri**, once the favourite haunt of old Emperor Tiberius (you can see the ruins of his palace). Don't miss the Blue Grotto if you can afford the dollars that the excursion will cost you. To get to Capri, the cheapest way is to take a steamer from Naples. It's a $1^1/_2$-hour trip each way and makes for a fascinating day. If you want to hitch out to Sorrento (difficult because it's a built-up area), you can buy a return fare to Capri from there, but you get a much better look at the bay by leaving from Naples.

The island of **Ischia** is a rich man's place, but apart from private yachts and bikini'd kittens, it's laden with plenty of sights to see. Take a return trip by steamer from Naples.

South of Naples and you're into Calabria which, though progressing fast, still tends to prefer a lifestyle unchanged for centuries. See, too, the Greek temples at **Paestum**.

You can cross into **Sicily** from **Reggio Calabria** to **Messina** quite cheaply. Once there, forget the Mafia. Just remember that Sicily (pop. 5,000,000) is the largest island in the Mediterranean (10,000 square miles) and home of some of its richest archaeological finds.

Capital and chief port **Palermo** (pop. 700,000) is an Arab-Norman-influenced city of baroque squares, running fountains and Florentine statues (plus odd gentlemen wearing pink ties who try to sell you contraband watches which may not even work). See the

12th-century Palace of the Normans with its marble-floored Palatine Chapel and dazzling mosaics.

At **Segesta**, 56 km west of Palermo, a desolately beautiful but unfinished Doric temple dates back to the 5th century BC. Further south, at **Agrigento's** Valley of the Temples, a clutch of imposing temples overlooks a labyrinthine on-site museum containing a superb collection of Greek art.

Syracuse (pop. 100,000), 128 km south of Messina, was the birthplace of Archimedes, who discovered the theory of water displacement whilst taking a bath. Syracuse was once the most important city in the Western world after Athens; half a million people lived there. Today it's a stylish town, with baroque palaces, beautiful piazzas, and a 7th-century cathedral. The massive archaeological zone includes a Roman colosseum, well-preserved Greek theatre and interesting caves and catacombs.

Don't miss **Etna**, at 10,725 feet the highest volcano in Europe. You reach it by bus, funicular and foot from **Catania**, Sicily's second largest city, on the east coast. The walk from the funicular terminal to the summit takes one hour. (If you're lucky enough to see Etna erupt when you hit town, keep your distance. When she last blew, in the summer of 1979, several tourists who disobeyed police orders and went too close won free cremations.)

Hitching

Hitching in Italy is generally OK. There are a tremendous number of *autostradas*, but I find I've always had more luck on the smaller roads. You're allowed to hitch on the *autostradas*, but the rules are the same as anywhere else in Europe. Namely, you can only pick up rides on entrance roads; hitching on the actual *autostrada* is a no-no and will result in you being turfed back to where you belong by the scores of patrolling *polizia*.

● **Warning!** The Italians are tough on drugs and the word is out that they're using undercover cops. So choose your friends carefully. If you're copped out and you're lucky, you'll only get three years.

● **Crossing to Sardinia** Ferries to Cagliari cost about 50,000L from both Naples and Civitavecchia (north of Rome), and about 80,000L from Genoa.

Rome: where to sleep

In Rome expect to pay between 22,000 and 35,000L for student accommodation. Hotels and *pensiones* – cheap ones – will take as much as 40,000L from you unless you find a real bargain. Doubles and triples, of course, give you a good saving per head. Make sure you don't land in a place which insists that you pay full pension (bed and all meals) – they may offer a good deal, but it won't be as much fun as eating out. Incidentally, when you're arranging for your room or buying a meal you'll find that speaking Spanish (if you've got some) will solve most problems (unless you can speak Italian, in which case that will solve *all* your problems).

Del Foro Italico Youth Hostel at Viale delle Olimpiadi 61, Flaminio, Rome (tel: 3236279). Fair way out of town.
Casa dello Studente, Città Universitaria at Via Cesare de Lollis 24 (tel: 49 02 43). Ask for dormitory. Open 25 July–7 September.
Albergo del Popolo at Via Apulia 41 (tel: 4465236).
Protezione della Giovane at Via Urbana 158. Hostel run by nuns. Women only. Non-religious. (tel: 4880056).
YWCA Via Cesare Balbo 4 (tel: 4880460). Women only. Prices from 30,000–40,000L depending on the type of room.

For cheap *pensiones* head for Via Principe Amedeo which is bang in the middle of town and two blocks to your left as you stand at the front of and with your back to the Terminal Station (in Piazza dei Cinquecento). The Terminal Station (Stazione Termini), by the way, is *the* nerve centre in Rome for travellers. You can change money, post mail, store bags and wash up. There are always scores of travellers from all over the world. And there are plenty of bad types, as well. Watch out for them! The Via Palestro, a couple of blocks to the right of the station, is another good area. For help in finding accommodation go to the EPT information office in the Terminal Station.

For sleeping rough, head into the gardens of the Villa Borghese, *but only if there are four or five of you*! Gangs hang around waiting to rob loners. Second choice is the park at Colle Oppio, near the Colosseum. Third choice, the slopes leading up to and also around, Piazza Garibaldi (behind and above the Trastevere) but, again, *only in groups* and, even then, don't let anyone see you bedding down. (When sleeping rough never let anyone see you bedding down *anywhere*!)

● **Warning!** See hitch-hiker's letter in **How to survive** chapter (page 63).

Rome: where to eat

Expect to pay around 15,000–20,000L for a filling meal. To cut costs, remember that in Italy, as in Spain, Greece and France, bar-owners usually don't object if you bring in a pile of food you've bought elsewhere to make a meal – as long as you buy a drink or two in the process. In the Colosseum/Colle Oppio area there are plenty of cheap food shops where you can buy in small quantities. The *Rosticcerie* and *Tavole Calde* are eating places which feature cheap, quick meals ideal for travellers low on lire.

In most Roman bars, sitting down for a coffee or drink costs double. Note that more and more Italian restaurants are charging extra for *servizio* (service) or *coperto* (cover charge) or both. These additions can bump your bill 20% above the food price! Look for places that offer a tourist menu (usually three courses) with service and cover charge included. Even then, drink may not be included and this can add substantially to costs. Try and hold off and have a drink later, preferably from your own pack bottle. Make sure that VAT is included in the price of dishes offered on the menu.

Da Peppino at Via Castelfidardo 35 (couple of blocks to the right of the Terminal Station) is one of the cheapest places in town – but it's closed on Fridays. All around that area to the right of the station is dead cheap.

Mario's at Via del Moro 53. Just over the river near Ponte Sisto. Cheap!

La Fieramosca at Piazza de Mercanti, Trastevere. Excellent, but for splurgers only!

Osteria con Cucina de Andreis Luciano at Via Giovanni Amendola 73–5.

L'Archetto at Via Germanico 105.

Filleto di Baccalà at Largo dei Librari 88.

Rome: what to see and do

THE ROMAN FORUM AND THE PALATINE Open every day except Tuesday. Entrance charge, but half-price on Sundays. Ticket gives entrance to both sites. The FORUM was the heart of the Roman Empire, the place from which all roads started and the market and meeting place of Rome's citizens. It is said that the site was first built upon, in wood, as far back as the 6th century BC. The PALATINE is a low hill between the Forum and the Tiber and was the first of Rome's seven hills to be inhabited. At night (check the tourist office for times) a *son et lumière* display is held in the Forum. It costs a lot to enter, but from the back of the Capitoline Hill (or Campidoglio) once the sacred hill of Rome, you can watch the display (even if you can't hear it all) for nothing. Also, on Campidoglio is the CAPITOLINE MUSEUM (entrance charge) which contains a fine antique collection, much of it related to Imperial Rome. In the summer try visiting the Forum late in the afternoon – say 6 p.m. It's cooler, there are fewer people and it's much more evocative. If you can't afford the stiff entrance fee, you can see the Forum and Palatine (and the Colosseum and Circus Maximus) by taking a long walk. Start at the Campidoglio, make your way down the Via dei Fori Imperiali, along St Gregorio, up Via dei Cerchi and complete the circuit by wandering up Via di San Teodoro. It won't be any fun at all if you're carrying your pack.

COLOSSEUM The Colosseum was built between AD 70 and AD 80. The big inauguration show lasted 100 days during which 5,000 wild animals were slaughtered. Not too long after, the Romans graduated to watching people being killed. The Colosseum could hold 50,000 spectators.

THE PANTHEON at Piazza della Rotonda is the best preserved of all Rome's ancient buildings. It was built in AD 27 and then, after being burned down, rebuilt by Hadrian in the 2nd century AD. Various Italian kings, as well as the painter Raphael, are buried there.

THE PIAZZA NAVONA was built in the 1st century AD as an athletics stadium by the Emperor Domitian. In the Middle Ages it was used for jousting tournaments. On special occasions in the 19th century the square was flooded and the city's rich drove their coaches through the water. (No, I *don't* know why!) Now the square is amongst Rome's most popular strolling spots. Good place to meet people. See Bernini's fanciful *Fountain of the Four Rivers* in front of Borromini's church of SANT' AGNESE IN AGONE. Don't take a drink at the cafés unless you've recently received an inheritance.

THE VATICAN CITY The Vatican became an independent state ruled by the Pope as the result of a treaty signed on 11 February 1929 between the Papacy and the Italian State. The city covers an area of 109 acres and has a population of 1,000. It has its own newspaper (*Osservatore Romano*), its own postal service, radio station, railway station, court of law, and its own diplomatic representatives. It imports food and exports a nebulous hope which affects the lives of millions around the world. It is an indispensable stop on a Roman tour. Principal sights in the city are the fabulous ST PETER'S BASILICA, the SISTINE CHAPEL, the VATICAN MUSEUM and the RAPHAEL ROOMS. (About 30% discount off entrance charges to holders of student cards.) Tickets for papal audiences can be picked up at several points around Rome and in the Vatican – check at the tourist office about this. If you just want a quick look at the Pope, at noon most Sundays he gives a sermon from the balcony overlooking St Peter's Square. In St Peter's, walk up the centre aisle and see marked on the floor the comparative sizes of other cathedrals around the world. If you can afford it, take the lift to the roof for a great view across the square. From there it costs nothing to enter the gallery and look down over 100 foot into the cathedral. Then climb up and around inside the dome (packs definitely don't fit!) to the very top for a stunning view over all of Rome. Back in the church again, don't miss Michelangelo's *Pietà* (first chapel to the right of the main doors), now unfortunately protected by a glass wall after some nutter tried to smash it several years ago.

CHURCHES St Peter's is the main church to see, but others, all of artistic or historical interest, include SANTA MARIA DEGLI ANGELI, SAN PIETRO IN VINCOLI (which houses Michelangelo's *Moses*), and SANTA MARIA MAGGIORE.

CATACOMBS Bus no. 118 from the Colosseum takes you out along the Old Appian Way and passes the CATACOMBS OF ST SEBASTIAN and the CATACOMBS OF ST CALLISTUS. Both are worth seeing. The Catacombs of St Callistus are considered the most important in Rome. Entrance charge to both.

MUSEUMS AND GALLERIES Amongst the many to be seen are the GALLERIA BORGHESE, the LATERAN MUSEUM, the NATIONAL MUSEUM OF ROME, the NATIONAL GALLERY OF MODERN ART and the NATIONAL GALLERY OF ANTIQUE ART. If you only have time for one museum, then the Vatican Museum is considered amongst the most important.

THE TREVI FOUNTAIN at Via del Muratte. This is the place where, if you're romantically inclined, you toss a coin into the water and make a wish that you will soon return to Rome. If you're a hitch-hiker, you'll notice that a lot of young Italians have figured out how to get the coins back on dry land without getting their feet wet. They use magnets on a fishing line, hurl them into the water and slowly drag them back along the bottom. Guys using bigger and better magnets – I saw one a foot long and about an inch wide –

bring in as many as five coins at a time. The fishing takes place just after dark and about an hour after it starts there aren't many coins left – so if you want to try it get there at the right time. (Beware of two things: the locals who don't like foreign competition, and the police who think it's all illegal.) Incidentally, I haven't seen fountain-dragging done anywhere else in Europe. Perhaps it hasn't caught on. It might be a good way of picking up pocket money. If you don't want to make money, go to the Trevi after dark during summer anyway. It's a great meeting place.

THE SPANISH STEPS These 137 steps lead off the Piazza di Spagna up to the church of TRINITÀ DEI MONTI. Nearby is KEATS' HOUSE, where the poet died in 1821. The Piazza, and the steps, which in the 18th and 19th centuries were the centre of the English colony in Rome, are now the meeting place of American travellers visiting American Express for their mail. Good place to meet people and dig out information. Keep away from cafés in this square (or any other important square in Italy). A simple cappuccino can cost you four times what it costs standing up in a backstreet bar.

SECONDHAND BOOKS Check out the **Economy Book Centre** at Via Torino 136 (nearest Metro stop is Republica on Line A). They stock new and used titles and offer 10% discount on cash sales of secondhand books to hitchers who flash the *Hitcher's Guide*. You can trade in or get cash for your paperback books. Another English-language bookshop (dealing only in new books) is the **Anglo-American Book Co.** at Via della Vite 57, just a short walk from the Piazza di Spagna. They also have a Technical and Scientific shop on the first floor at no. 27 (just in case you're feeling guilty about lost study time).

MARKETS There's a flea market at Porta Portese every Sunday morning. It's considered one of the best in Europe. Campo de' Fiori (south of the Piazza Navona) is the site of Rome's most famous fruit and vegetable market. The statue in the centre commemorates the philosopher-priest Giordano Bruno who was burned by the Inquisition in 1600 for claiming that the universe was infinite.

CINEMAS Several cinemas around town show original version films. For information, buy the daily paper or a copy of the English-language publication *This Week in Rome*.

CONCERTS Check with tourist office for dates of concerts held outdoors in the Basilica of Maxeusis. Great setting with the cheapest seats around 1,000L.

Transport in Rome

There are two Underground (*metropolitana*) lines. Line A goes from Stazione Termini up to Via Ottaviani near the Vatican. Stops include Piazza di Spagna. Line B runs from Stazione Termini to the south and includes a stop at the Colosseum. Buses operated by ATAC cover the rest of the city. Bus and metro tickets cost 900L. Once validated a bus ticket can be used for any number of journeys in the next $1^1/_2$ hours. For 3,000L you can get a 24-hour pass valid on the *metropolitana* and the bus system. Eight-day bus passes cost 12,000L. Monthly transport passes are available, though the scope of these is restricted. Further details are available at any ATAC booth: the one on Piazza Cinquecento in front of the Termini train station is your best bet for English-speaking staff.

● **Warning!** When buying tickets for public transport in Rome or anywhere in Italy be careful of short-changing. Because you are dealing in hundreds, thousands and even tens of thousands of lire it is easy to get confused when someone thrusts a handful of change at you. Some ticket sellers know this and take advantage. If you suspect it has happened, stay in the queue, and make a big show of counting the money. If the ticket seller *has* cheated, he'll just slide the extra notes over and shrug.

Student discounts

Reductions in some museums and art galleries, some theatres and cinemas, to some *son et lumière* spectacles, and for goods purchased in some department stores. For information contact:

Ministry of Public Instruction at Viale Trastevere 76A, Rome.

● **Warning!** Watch out for gangs of street urchins who haunt tourist areas. Four or five will approach you, one with a square of cardboard. The one with the cardboard will thrust it against you and ask for money. While you react they will go for your wallet or bag. Best thing is to let them understand you know what they're up to *before* they get close. If they *do* get close, shout at them, but loudly. Remember: they are little kids, they are poor and they need help, but they are also professionals and more interested in *all* your money than the bit you might voluntarily give them. And, boy, can they run fast . ..

Addresses

Main post office (for poste restante) at Piazza S. Silvestro, Rome.
American Express at Via Due Macelli 79 (tel: 678 5981).
State Tourist Office in Termini train station (tel: 487 1270/475 0078).
Centro Turistico Studentesco (CTS) Via Genova 16 (tel: 46791).
US Embassy at Via Vittorio Veneto 119a, Rome (tel: 46741).
British Embassy at XX Settembre 80a, Rome (tel: 475 5441).

Hitchers' Tips and Comments . . .

Travellers catching Italy to Greece ferries should remember to save some lire to pay port tax. I didn't, and had to accept a lousy rate of exchange on a travellers' cheque in the port office in order to pay the tax. TINI WILLIAMS, CHILWELL, ENGLAND

If you're crossing to Sicily, take the ferry from Villa San Giovanni, which is much cheaper than the one from Reggio Calabria.
HUGH DUNNE, DUBLIN, IRELAND

If you're sleeping out in Rome, be careful of the gardens outside the Terminal Station – lots of rip-offs happening. Also, in Italian trains, careful of police in civilian clothing looking for dope.
PAUL ROUSE, SION MILLS, N. IRELAND

In Italy, soft drinks with restaurant meals cost the earth. Eat dry, then buy a drink elsewhere. AVRIL HORTON, LEEDS, UK

I followed suggestions in the *Hitcher's Guide* and slept in the grounds of the Villa Borghese in Rome. But I disregarded the warnings in the *How to Survive* chapter and was robbed of money, passport and camera. Please advise readers *not to crash out alone in Italian parks*! Sensible people were sleeping out at the Termini railway station, *in groups*! PHILIP ATTWOOL, ORPINGTON, UK

People wearing shorts and/or with bare shoulders are not allowed into St Peter's, Rome and many other Italian churches.
DAVID MCGONIGAL, LEEDS, UK

Here I sit locked in a hotel room in Fabriano, Italy, pretending to be brave while the porter keeps calling through the door. I was going to see more of Italy, but this is the last straw. I have only spent two days in Rome, two in Pompeii and now one here and it's been a continuous hassle. I am not particularly pretty, am short and round, and am sick of being pawed. Other girls I've spoken with have had the same problem. Spain was as you warned us, but there, at least, the men weren't persistent and neither did they manhandle. *Please* warn girls about Italy! It must be the deadliest place ever. I'm well able to look after myself, but this is getting me down. I'm shooting through. I'm heading to Austria. If I survive one more day of Italy to get there, I can survive anything! JANE, NEW ZEALAND

In Rome beware of the old gypsy trick of holding a tray of trinkets up to your chest. While they're trying to convince you to buy, their kids are going through your pockets, and you'll never even know!

FRANK BAUROTH, UNIVERSITY OF DALLAS, USA

Beware of the little gypsy kids on buses in Rome – pickpockets extraordinaire. Rucksacks with back and side pockets are very accessible – keep your backs to the wall.

When sleeping rough, use your spare laces to tie yourself or your sleeping bag to your rucksack and other possessions. Easily cut or untied but, at least, it's another insurance policy.

SIMON AND GEOFF, SHEFFIELD, ENGLAND

Where to crash in Venice. First hitch as far as Mestre, which is where the road to Venice begins. Find the railway station. Cross the lines using the bridge. As you cross, you can see the flyover beneath you. Just crash out under the flyover. In the morning dump your gear at the railway station, and get a day return to Venice. Then, when you leave, the toll stations for the autostradas going west are only about a 4 km walk.

Why no mention of the most famous balcony in history? Just off the market square in Verona is Juliet's house with the balcony where she heard Romeo do his thing.

A. R. BRZOZOWSKI, KETTERING, NORTHANTS, ENGLAND

Italian theft is getting silly. You can be approached by someone asking the time who then snatches your necklace, bag, watch, etc., even if you are wearing it. One bloke had his sleeping bag cut open, his trouser pocket cut open and his wallet stolen while he was asleep.

If hitching from Bari (southern Italy) further south, get bus 12 from the central station to the Mobil service station.

SIMON WADSWORTH, SHIPLEY, WEST YORKSHIRE, ENGLAND

In Rome try Pension Esedre, Pension Eureka and Pension Terminus, all in the same building at Piazza della Republica 47.

C. HOPPER, BRIGHTON, SUSSEX, ENGLAND

For camping near Venice take vaporetto 14 from St Mark's to Punta Sabbioni. Once there, turn right and after a 5-minute walk you arrive at the campsite.

Also, in Venice, a 24-hour go-anywhere vaporetti ticket is a sound deal. CREB AND WEZ, BIRMINGHAM, ENGLAND

For a safe, convenient outdoor spot to crash in Florence, try the Palazzo dello Congresso's Park right beside the station. Its grounds are surrounded with an iron fence and they lock the gates about 10 p.m. You can easily climb the smaller cement fence portion if you have to. Once in there, you're safe from the thugs and loonies that everyone else is complaining about.

MARK QUAIL, ST GEORGE, CANADA

From Florence take the no. 7 bus to Fiesole, a beautiful village with an amazing view. If you walk up the hill along the main road, and down the next small road you come across, you'll find some Etruscan graves, that, though not much to look at, you can kip in!

ANNA LISS, AMSTERDAM

To get clear across Italy in one day, check the locations of Motorway Service stations on maps and then hitch from one to the next, asking for rides. It helps if you speak Italian.

ROBERT A. H. PRINS, IPSWICH, ENGLAND

Spain

population	39,952,000
size	194,883 square miles
capital	Madrid, population 3,250,000
government	Constitutional monarchy
religion	Roman Catholic
language	Spanish is the official language but vernacular languages have official status in many of the autonomous communities. Variants of Catalán are spoken along the east coast and in the islands, Basque is spoken in the Basque provinces on the northern coast, and Gallego in Galicia
currency	*Peseta* (pta) Coins of 1, 5, 10, 25, 50, 100, 200 and 500 *pesetas*. Notes of 1,000, 2,000, 5,000, 10,000 *pesetas*

Unless you have unlimited time, travelling in Spain presents one big problem – where to go! The cities in Spain which have become household words outdo those of any other country: Madrid, Barcelona, Pamplona, Segovia, Toledo, Sevilla, Granada, Salamanca, Málaga, Valencia, Alicante, Cartagena, Córdoba, Zaragoza, Bilbao,

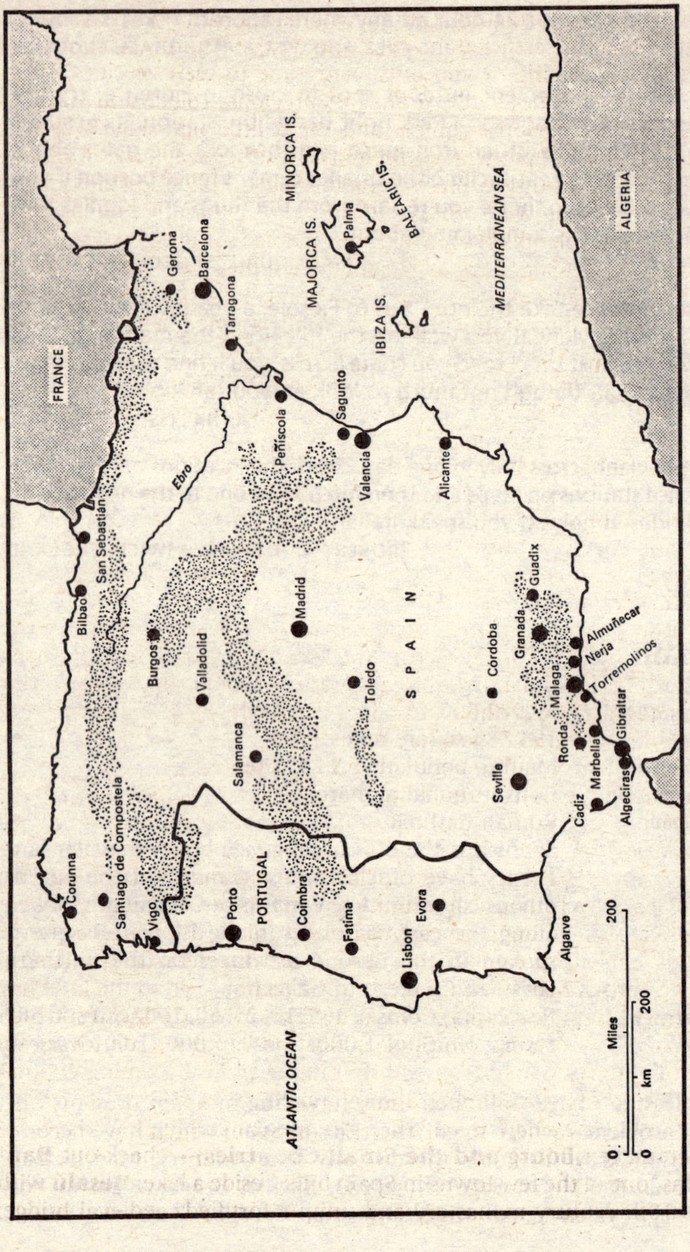
FRANCE
ALGERIA
MEDITERRANEAN SEA
ATLANTIC OCEAN
SPAIN
PORTUGAL
MINORCA IS.
MAJORCA IS.
IBIZA IS.
BALEARIC IS.
Palma
Gerona
Barcelona
Tarragona
Peñiscola
Sagunto
Valencia
Alicante
Ebro
San Sebastián
Bilbao
Burgos
Valladolid
Madrid
Toledo
Salamanca
Córdoba
Granada
Guadix
Almuñecar
Nerja
Torremolinos
Malaga
Gibraltar
Ronda
Marbella
Algeciras
Cadiz
Seville
Corunna
Santiago de Compostela
Vigo
Porto
Coimbra
Fatima
Lisbon
Evora
Algarve
Miles
km
0
200
0
200

San Sebastián, Tarragona, Gerona. All names with which the mind has some vague association.

But after Madrid, if you only have time to see five cities, they should probably be Seville, Granada, Barcelona, Toledo and Málaga. They are my personal choices and I'm a little one-sided when it comes to Spain. I particularly prefer the southern region of Andalucia, the land of tiny white mountain villages, old and smelly bars and cafés, cheap wine, bullfights, and a to-hell-with-it philosophy which leaves plenty of scope for tomorrow to look after itself. Sevilla, Granada and Málaga are all part of the south.

The two main north-eastern entry points into Spain are **La Junquera** (with most traffic, though horribly jammed in summer) and **Port Bou** (less traffic, but a better introduction to Spain – or rather, Catalonia, where, incidentally, the locals prefer to speak Catalán; but don't worry, 95% of the population will understand your Spanish).

Any number of Catalán towns and villages are worth a visit if you have time. **Gerona** offers an attractive medieval section, with a cathedral begun in the 11th century, a museum of city history and an archaeological museum within the beautiful 12th-century Monastery of San Pedro de Galligans. Lines on walls with dates beside them in some riverside bars celebrate the height reached by the river Oñar during its regular floodings! The cathedral is one of the best examples of Catalan Gothic, despite the fact that it has a Romanesque cloister and a tower. Nearby, at the foot of the wide exterior stairway leading to the church, are the Arab baths. Before leaving the area try some of the specialities of the region. Fish and shellfish in general are great (better than chips!); sample lobster à la Catalan, snails, Buñuelos (cream filled buns), crema catalana (a sort of pudding) and – an absolute must – wine from El Ampurdán. Delicious!

Figueras is the home of the Dali Museum, not to be missed by art freaks – a truly psychedelic collection of Don Salvador's wildest fantasies, including a room which when viewed through a mirror hung beneath a camel becomes a three-dimensional comic strip caricature of Mae West. To see the artist's house go to the little bay of **Port Lligat**. It's a couple of kilometres north of **Cadaqués**, which remains one of northern Spain's most beautiful seaside towns (in spite of thirty years of tourist infiltration) and is becoming popular with hitchers and other well-known unsavoury types.

West of the *autopista* – if you're going to or coming from Andorra (see **Luxembourg and the Small Countries**) – check out **Bañolas**, one of the few towns in Spain built beside a lake; **Besalú** with its 10th-century monastery and unique fortified medieval bridge;

and **Ripoll**, with yet another monastery – this one featuring an incredible stone doorway with more than 200 carved figures representing characters from the Bible. Unfortunately, the carvings are 'dying' of stone cancer. If you need relief from churches, cathedrals and the like, pay a visit to Ripoll's Arms Museum to see one of Europe's best collections of old-fashioned handguns.

To visit a true political anachronism while in this area, go to the 'lost' town of **Llivia**, Spanish to the core and part of the province of Gerona, but actually in France, and reached by a 'neutral' road from **Puigcerda** 3 km away in Spain. In 1659 Spain was forced to cede 33 Pyrenean villages to France. Llivia won its claim that it was a town and thus remained Spanish – in French territory!

Further south and on the coast again, **Tossa de Mar** is a pleasant spot to rest your bones, while just a few kilometres away is the place Spaniards call 'The Tourist Factory', **Lloret de Mar**. Lloret in high summer is not exactly a poet's heaven on earth, but here you could find company or a little work in one of the scores of foreign-run bars. (Be warned that in Spain it's illegal to work without a work permit or residency permit for Europeans – so watchit!)

Barcelona is Spain's second city, but vies with Madrid in its claim to be the most dynamic. It is the largest seaport in the Mediterranean and that, along with a population of two and a half million, contributes to its reputation of being the liveliest city in the country. The port is a good place to start wandering. Stroll down the Ramblas to the 190-foot-high Columbus Monument. The 25-foot-high statue of the explorer is heroically pointing to the Americas – unfortunately he is pointing the wrong way. Moored close by is a replica of Columbus' ship *Santa Maria*, a full-sized, completely fitted reconstruction from the original plans. To see an even more dramatic piece of reconstruction work, visit the Maritime Museum (diagonally across the square from the Columbus Monument) which houses a meticulously built copy of an oared galley, the *Real*, flagship of the Christians in the 1571 Battle of Lepanto. Back on the portside again, rich hitchers can lighten their bulging wallets by buying a ticket on the cablecar which will take them across the port or up to Montjuich mountain. Views across the city during the ride are truly stupendous. Destitute travellers can forget the cablecar and take the 57 bus from the railway station up to Montjuich. Visit the castle which houses a military museum, and check out what is claimed to be the world's largest amusement park. The mountain also offers good views over Barcelona. While up there see the **Pueblo Español** – the Spanish Village – built in the 1920s and containing examples of every type of regional architecture in the country.

Back in the city, wander through the famous Barrio Gótico (check the cathedral and the Placa del Rei), and if you're into art see the Picasso Museum with many works from the artist's blue period, and the Museum of Modern Art which has more works by Picasso and some by Dali. Don't miss Gaudí's still unfinished La Sagrada Familia church (you'll love it or hate it, but you've got to see it!) and the apartment buildings he designed on the Paseo de Gracia. To meet people try the Placa Reial (off the Ramblas) where you should also find cheap *pensiones*, and for more cheap food and accommodation try Barceloneta, the fisherman's and workingman's suburb (see below for further details of eating and sleeping possibilities).

Just off Highway N11, 40 km north-west of Barcelona, is the famous old monastery of **Montserrat**. This 11th-century Benedictine building sits in a tremendous mountain location and, if you feel like fighting it out with the 500,000 tourists who visit each year, it's worth going up. The monastery is home to La Moreneta, a 12th-century wooden image of the Virgin.

The coast road is the quickest way down south and goes through some good places. **Tarragona** is one of them. It's small enough (45,000 people) to wander around easily and it's one mass of monuments and ruins. It's one of the oldest cities in Spain and St Paul is said to have visited it during its Roman period and converted the locals to Christianity. A few kilometres away are the seaside resorts of **Salou** and **Cambrils**.

Heading further south, towns worth seeing include **Peñíscola**, a small place of only 3,000 but amongst the most beautiful villages in Spain, which sits dramatically on a promontory jutting into the sea. **Sagunto**, 22 km south of Castellón, is a fortified town and historically one of the most interesting on the coast. Greeks, Romans, Carthaginians and Moors all paid business calls. **Valencia** and **Alicante** are both cities which would take a couple of days of anyone's time (and between the two is **Benidorm**, one of Spain's biggest resort towns), but if you have to keep moving then Granada is next stop. On the way, you will pass through **Guadix** and **Purellena** and see weird troglodyte dwellings.

Granada is where the Alhambra is, but it is more than that. It's the sort of city which is good to return to or to tell yourself you will return to one day. It dates back to at least the 5th century BC and its crumbling age is one of its fascinations. Old streets twist and turn, weeds grow from the roofs, and it is commonplace rather than unusual to look through a door or an archway to find a courtyard left over from Moorish days. It was the Moors who built the Alhambra and to look over this reconstructed Arabian relic takes at least half a day, even for a swift visit. If you plan to visit the neighbouring Generalife – the summer palace – the whole tour will take most of a day. Tickets are expensive, but valid for a couple of days. Student cards will get you in for half-price. Historians should visit the Royal Chapel behind the 16th-century cathedral, where they can see the tombs of Ferdinand and Isabella, the Catholic monarchs who drove the Moors from the country and created a united Spain. See also Sacromonte (go at night), one of the world's best-organized tourist traps, where gypsies operate flamenco dives from the depths of all-mod-con cave-houses. If you want to sample what they're offering, be prepared to pay too much.

Málaga is the next stop if you decide to have a look at the Costa del Sol. Whichever route you choose, the trip down to the coast can be a rough one so don't move too far after you've found a prime hitching spot. The road is bend-ridden with bad edges – which doesn't encourage motorists to stop. Villages worth looking at if you're travelling along the N340 include **Almuñecar** and **Nerja**. Nerja is the site of a recently discovered cave which has traces of human habitation dating back 20,000 years, and a 195-foot stalactite, the world's largest.

In Málaga there is not much in the way of specific sights to see, apart from the beautiful old Arab fortifications, but the whole city is a trip in itself. There are literally hundreds of bars, for instance, in which you can go berserk trying to taste the dozens of famous sweet wines which Málaga province produces. At about 60ptas a glass it's a pleasant way to kill yourself.

About 14 km west of Málaga is the much-written-about tourist resort of **Torremolinos**. Twenty years ago it was a not-very-attractive fishing village. Now it's a not-very-attractive city of skyscrapers packed with package tourists. For the hitcher its main advantage is that all year round there are people in town looking for partners. Best place to start the hunt is down on the Carihuela beach. Plenty of bars there with like-minded souls. Also great fish restaurants. Best place to eat in the centre of Torremolinos is the LANJARÓN RESTAURANT in the old section called Calvario. They also have cheap rooms.

Another good thing about it is the TORREMOLINOS SECONDHAND BOOK MARKET where you can pick up something to read real cheap. It's upstairs at Calle San Miguel 26 (the main shopping street). They have a free noticeboard where people advertise for rides all over Europe, things to buy and sell, etc. They offer a 10% cash discount on secondhand books to any hitch-hiker who flashes his copy of the *Hitcher's Guide*.

From Torremolinos, the N340 continues straight down to **Algeciras** for ferry connections with Morocco (see **Morocco and North**

Africa) and from Morocco to Gibraltar (see **The Small Countries**). The ancient city of **Tarifa** lies 25 km beyond Algeciras. Once it marked the end of the known world. Nowadays it bills itself as the windsurf capital of Europe and the beaches at **Punta Paloma** and other points north-west of the city are the destination for hundreds of windsurf fanatics who live in campsites and on the shoreline, for up to months at a time, waiting for the steady, strong winds the area is famed for. Great place to meet interesting people. If time is available, a detour to **Ronda**, 50 km into the Sierra de Ronda along the C339, is a nice trip. The city perches on the edge of a 600-foot-high cliff.

Seville can be reached by continuing along the N340 past **Cádiz** and then going north via **Jerez de la Frontera**, the sherry-producing area where there's plenty of free wine-tasting, or by going north-west from Málaga and meeting up with the N334 at **Antequera**. Seville with its population of half a million is the fourth city of Spain and so old that legend tells it was founded by Hercules. Like many other southern Spanish cities, it reached its zenith during the long Arab occupation and today one of the best things to see is the 320-foot-high Giralda Tower and the beautiful cathedral alongside. In the cathedral is a tomb said to contain the remains of Christopher Columbus. But the really big thing to see in Seville, apart from the city's own lifestyle, is the three-day-long *feria*, or fair, which is held each year around April when the entire population goes mad with bullfights, flamenco, and all things Spanish. The *feria* is heavily attended by tourists, but the Sevillanos tend to disregard them and keep to the business in hand. Check local or international Spanish tourist offices for exact dates of the fair and also of the *Semana Santa*, or Holy Week Fiesta, which precedes it. The processions are considered the best in the country.

If you have gone as far as Seville, you might as well continue to **Córdoba**, just 140 km away. The old section of Córdoba is more than worth the effort. Particularly, see the 10th-century Mezquita, the largest mosque in the world after the one in Mecca. It covers 22,000 square metres and contains 850 columns, and a complete Roman Catholic church. See also the superb Archaeological Museum and check the display of Spanish handcrafts at the government-run shop Artespaña, which is housed in a magnificent 15th-century inn not too far from the mosque.

Toledo, 70 km south of Madrid, is said by the Spaniards to be the city which most perfectly includes all the most important elements of Spanish history. It is an historical and architectural monument to all that Spain has been, and in 1937 the entire city was declared a national monument. Toledo was the home of El

Greco and a house said to have belonged to the artist has been refurnished to imitate the style of his period. A gallery next door contains many important works. Around the corner from the house is the tiny church of Santo Tomé which contains what many experts consider his best painting, *The Burial of the Count of Orgaz*. Other points of interest include the Gothic cathedral which is claimed as the best in Spain, and the huge Alcázar, scene of a tremendous siege during the civil war.

South of Toledo is **La Mancha**, Don Quixote country, and fans of the sprightly gentleman can pick up a free pamphlet from tourist offices describing a trip through villages associated with his adventures. Best place to see those famous windmills is at **Consuegra**.

From Seville, the E52 leads into Portugal for those heading for Lisbon, and the N630 leads north, joining with the E3 for those travelling to France. (The cheap living ends at the border! Load up with cigarettes and wine before crossing into France!) The four major cities on this route are all worth time if you can spare it: **Salamanca, Valladolid, Burgos** (home of the legendary El Cid) and **San Sebastían**. For me, Salamanca is the pick of the bunch. Start at the superb Plaza Mayor, one of Europe's most beautiful squares, then wander through the nearby university area (the university was founded in the 13th century). See the House of Shells and choose between the Old (12th-century) and New (16th-century) cathedrals.

However, I would not suggest that you completely ignore **Valladolid**, a city of 325,000 inhabitants. The city is set in the heart of the plateau called the Meseta Central, and has an altitude of 2,270 feet. Valladolid figures prominently in Spanish history. From the beginning of the *Reconquista* (reconquest) of Spain from the Moors, it gained more and more significance, until it became the Capital of an immense empire. Because of this preponderant role in Spain's history, a great number of magnificent castles were built to defend it. Try to see the following: LA MOTA, Medina del Campo, one of the most beautiful castles in Spain; SIMANCA, a Moorish castle which was reconquered by the Christians in the 11th century. The Tourism Office in the Plaza de Zorrilla (tel: 35 18 01) will tell you of many more sights to see. On the eating side, you must try the local stews, roasts and special sauces accompanied by *lechuguino*, an excellent local bread. *Bacalao al ajo arriero* (cod – but what cod!) is another delicacy, but pride of all must go to *lechazo* (suckling pig). The city has some great cheap hotels – try the Mayoraga.

North of Portugal is the region of Galicia, a beautiful and rewarding part of the world, but completely impossible in the summer when every coastal road is clogged and every seaside campground overflowing. Unfortunately, most of the rest of the year it rains in Galicia. However, once in the region, make your way around the truly spectacular *rías*, or fjords, and try and visit **Santiago de Compostela**, a city of 90,000, third city in Christendom after Jerusalem and Rome, and named after Spain's patron saint, San Yago, or St James (whose remains are said to be in a silver urn in the crypt beneath the cathedral). Because of James, during the Middle Ages the city became the destination of hundreds of thousands of pilgrims a year. Visit the cathedral and take a long look at the Obradoiro façade, and the Door of Glory. With luck you will see modern-day pilgrims doing what pilgrims have done for centuries – pushing their fingers into the notches of 'The Tree of Life' and praying for protection. On either side of the cathedral are the plazas de España and de la Quintana, both beautiful and both good meeting places.

● **Bullfights** Tickets are expensive. Generally, a seat in the shade (*sombra*) will cost 2,500ptas. Seats in the sun (*sol*) are cheaper, while standing room is cheapest of all. But as the fight takes about two hours it's worth investing in sitting space.

● **Fiestas** There's nothing quite like a Spanish fiesta, and you should try to visit one if you're anywhere near it. Here's a list of some of the more important fiestas, including the months they are usually held. You'll have to check with the Spanish Tourist Office to get exact dates, as they change from year to year. *Cabalgata de Reyes*, the Fiesta of the Kings, is a parade held in most Spanish cities on the Eve of Epiphany in January. *Moros y Cristianos*, mock battles between Moors and Christians, are especially popular in the Levante area. Some of the best known are at Bocairente (province of Valencia) in February; Alcoy (Alicante) in April; Villajoyosa (Alicante) in July; Villena (Alicante) in September. *Fallas de Valencia* is one of the most spectacular shows in Spain. Don't miss it if you're a firework freak. Huge firework-filled statues are burned in the streets. Held in Valencia on Saint Joseph's night in March. (Alicante has a similar show on Saint John's Eve.) *Semana Santa*, Holy Week, features vast Easter parades; best places to see them are Sevilla, Málaga, Valladolid, Granada. Also, during Holy Week, Passion Plays are held in various towns. Most outstanding are Esperraguera (Barcelona), Ulldecona (Tarragona), Moncada (Valencia). The Passion Plays are relics from the medieval theatre, as are certain other plays held during the year in Spain, namely the *Misterio de Elche* in Elche (Alicante) in August, and the *Misterio de San Quillén y San Felicia* in Obanos (Navarra) in August. *Ferias*: all cities have their *ferias* (or fairs). Amongst the best: Sevilla's Spring Fair, in April, and Madrid's

San Isidro in May. *Feria del Caballo*, the Horse Fair, is held in Jerez de la Frontera in May. *Corpus Cristi* in June, especially in Granada, Sevilla and Toledo. In Sitges (Barcelona), the roads are paved with magnificent flower carpets. *Romería del Rocío* in Almonte (Huelva) in June: the most famous *romería* in Spain. But you need about a week to spare and a horse to join in properly. *San Fermín*, in Pamplona, in July: the famed running of the bulls. (Be warned: statistics show that more foreigners than Spaniards get gored!) The *International Festival of Music and Dance*, at Granada in July, is held in the fabulous Alhambra. You have to book well in advance. *Human Castles*: you have to see it to believe it. People on top of each other, up to nine high; popular in the north. Try Vilafranca del Penedés (Barcelona) in August. *Batalla de las Flores* in Laredo (Santander) in August: parade during which those taking part and the spectators pelt each other with flowers. *Fiesta de la Vendimia*: the grape-harvest fair in Jerez de la Frontera in September.

● **Wine** Many, many villages in Spain make a small supply of local wine. So when roaming through the back areas, drop into local bars and ask for *vino del terreno* (the wine of the land). Some of it is remarkably good. It's usually cheap.

● **Cigarettes** They come as cheap as 60ptas for 20 and you can buy a first-class cigarette for 85ptas a pack. English or American-style filter-tips cost about 100ptas. Imported cigarettes over 165ptas. Worth stocking up to carry you through more expensive countries.

● **Piropos** If you're a lady hitcher, don't be surprised if a Spaniard suddenly walks up and starts whispering passionate sounding phrases to you. Keep your nose in the air and keep walking. It's purely the Latin manifestation of hairy-chestedness, like a harmless wolf-whistle in London or New York. The *piropo*, or compliment, is usually of a very personal nature and if you don't speak Spanish you're going to miss out on some wildly endearing pieces of Don Juanism, like: 'If only I was worthy to be the father of your children,' or 'Your body is a flower to be plucked by the grateful.'

● **Drugs** Don't be tempted to bring drugs into Spain from Morocco via Algeciras (or anywhere else). The Algeciras customs post uses specially trained dogs to sniff out the goodies. Even if you arrive in Algeciras from Ceuta, or in Málaga from Melilla, you may still be searched by mainland customs. Ceuta and Melilla are Spanish territories on the Moroccan coastline, but people entering the mainland from these cities are subject to a second customs hassle.

● **Warning!** Australians, New Zealanders and South Africans cannot enter Spain without a visa granted in a Spanish consulate outside Spain. *You cannot get the visa at the border or at a Spanish airport!* The visa is cheap, nearly always granted and can usually be obtained on the day of application. All non-EC members should check with Spanish consulates before attempting to enter Spain, just in case the rules have changed even further.

The Canaries and Balearics

● **Crossing to the Canary Islands** The seven main islands of the **Canaries** lie about 1,500 km from Spain's southern tip and just off the Saharan coast. (The nearest, Lanzarote, is only 112 km from Africa.) They're blessed with year-round springtime temperatures and thus are popular with hitchers heading south to escape the annual northern freeze. There's no way of hitching there, unless you catch a yacht from Gibraltar or one of the harbours on the Costa del Sol (try Puerto José Banús just west of Marbella and the Estepona harbour), but regular ferry services run from Cádiz.

Here's a rundown on the islands, starting with the biggest:

● **Tenerife** (area: 790 square miles, pop. 500,000)

Chief town **Santa Cruz de Tenerife** (pop. 180,000) is one of the world's busiest shipping ports, but a surprisingly quiet and pleasant town to walk through. Apart from the relaxed colonial atmosphere it has nothing special to offer, but check out the archaeological museum if you want a little local history.

Puerto de la Cruz, 35 km west across the island, is where the action is. A former fishing village turned high-rise resort, it's filled with bazaars, hotels, bars, restaurants and discos; yet the old centre still retains genuine charm. Plenty of chances to meet the opposite sex. **Warning!** Meals and rooms are expensive here. This is Charter-flightsville and priced accordingly. (Avoid the Tenerife wine, too. It's more expensive than mainland plonk and tastes worse.)

The **Botanical Gardens** just outside Puerto de la Cruz are worth a look. Founded in 1788, they are famed for a collection of trees brought from all over the world. Don't miss the monkeys.

La Orotava, 6 km inland, is a typical Canary town. Houses with traditional wooden balconies overlook the banana-filled valley below. Further inland, after crossing giant pine-woods, you reach **Las Cañadas National Park**, square miles of lava fields and exploded volcanoes, which stand as stark, terrifying and beautiful monuments to nature's power. The centrepiece of the park is

Mount Teide. At 12,000 feet it's the highest mountain in Spain – mainland or islands. A cablecar takes you to the peak. The views are worth the price of the ticket. (You can see several islands on a clear day.)

West of Puerto de la Cruz, the town of **Icod de los Vinos** boasts the world's oldest dragon tree. This monstrous 60-foot-high shrub is said to be 3,000 years old, but is almost certainly not.

Two of Tenerife's best beaches are at **Los Cristianos**, a fishing village tourist resort and **Playa de las Americas**, a custom-built seaside package holiday town. To reach them, hitch down the 100-kilometre coastal highway from Santa Cruz. The inland route is more interesting but can be tough going.

● **Gran Canaria** (area: 600 square miles, pop. 550,000)

Capital **Las Palmas de Gran Canaria** (pop. 275,000) is a raucous, bustling wide-open port, full of duty-free shops (most things are cheaper in England and America: watch out for tricks like seemingly cheap cameras which are mounted with third-rate, unheard-of lenses), bars, restaurants and dives. You name it, you can usually get it. La Vegueta is the town's old quarter. Amongst its historical buildings is the Casa de Colón (Columbus' house, where the famous explorer lived during a stay on the island). Now it's a fine arts museum and home of the island's historical archives. Nearby, the Canary Museum has nine galleries devoted to the culture of the Guanches, Gran Canaria's original inhabitants. The Canary Village, in the beautiful Ciudad Jardín (Garden City), has a museum of local paintings, traditional Canary architecture and a folklore show. Worth a visit if you don't mind tripping over a few tourists. For cheap restaurants and rooms in Las Palmas, nose around behind the old fishing port and 'Muelle de la Luz' (literally, Jetty of Light). Swimmers should head for the long, wide sandy beach of Las Canteras, shielded by an offshore reef. It's right in the town.

Caldera de Bandama is the island's biggest extinct volcano. It's about 1 km across and tomatoes grow like weeds on the fertile valley floor. From the lookout point on top you can see Las Palmas in the distance.

Teror, the island's prettiest village, is peaceful in spite of its name. It's full of medieval houses lined with delicately carved wooden balconies. In September it celebrates Gran Canaria's greatest religious festival, when each village on the island brings a float to participate in a massive procession. It's all in honour of the patron saint, Our Lady of the Pines. Teror's 15th-century church stands on the spot where she is supposed to have appeared.

● **Lanzarote** (area: 310 square miles, pop. 45,000)

Here is a desolated volcanic landscape of craters, caverns and weird lava formations. The island's last eruption occurred in 1736.

Capital **Arrecife** (pop. 20,000) is a simple port with little going for it, but you can find cheap restaurants and pensions. Watch out when the wind blows the wrong way from the fish-canning factory.

You can find not-so-cheap accommodation in nearby **Puerto del Carmen**, a fishing village whose good beaches have turned it into the island's main tourist area.

Playa Blanca, down south, is an unspoilt little port with beach tavernas and a couple of bars. On clear days you can see both Fuerteventura Island and the African coast 112 km away. Quiet, white-sanded beaches offer ideal free accommodation.

For the full tourist bit in Lanzarote, ride a camel over orange-black dunes near the **Fire Mountain** and feel the heat coming out of live volcanoes. If you walk or hitch into Fire Mountain, don't wander too far off the road into the lava fields. Seemingly sturdy lava rocks chip when stood upon and the surface of the rocks is incredibly abrasive. A fall could do you real damage.

Up north try not to miss **Jameos del Agua**. It's a massive cave, complete with tiny lake, formed from a volcanic bubble. On Saturday night it doubles as a nightclub with a folklore show one end and a disco the other.

Interesting villages inland are **Haria**, with its palm oasis, and **Yaiza**, which must be the most immaculate 'pueblo' in Spain. Try the local green-white Malvasia wine – 15% proof and truly volcanic.

● **Fuerteventura** (area: 780 square miles, pop. 20,000)

This looks like a giant chunk of the Sahara which landed in the sea. Tourism is well rooted now, but you can still get away from it all. Head for the marvellous sandy beaches that seem to cover half the island. The island's first capital, **Betancuria** (pop. 950), is a simple village that has seen few changes since Jean Bethancourt, a Norman adventurer, founded it in the 15th century. The present capital is **Puerta del Rosario**, which has little to offer. But you might find some action at nearby **Playa Blanca** with its excellent beach. **Corralejo**, in the north, is the main tourist resort. Hitchers carrying masks and snorkels should set out for **Isla de los Lobos** (Wolf Island) 3 km offshore from Corralejo. You'll find the best underwater fishing in all the Canary Islands.

● **La Palma** (area: 280 square miles, pop. 100,000)

This lush, pear-shaped island is famous for its cultivated craters. Capital **Santa Cruz de la Palma** (pop. 20,000) is quiet and quaint with several pensions and a seafront promenade lined with neat old houses.

La Cumbrecita, in the centre of La Palma, is one of the world's biggest craters. It's 25 km across, 58 km around, and over 7,000 feet deep. The valley floor is planted with subtropical vegetables and citrus fruits. Visit **Fuencaliente**, scene of the 1971 San Antonio volcanic eruption. Best swimming and best chance of finding company is at **Tayacorte** on the west coast.

● **Gomera** (area: 146 square miles, pop. 25,000)
On this rugged island of fertile valleys and mountains, locals communicate with each other by a remarkable whistling language known as *silbo*. Capital **San Sebastián de la Gomera** (pop. 7,500) has a few pensions and not much else. But this town was Columbus' last stop before heading into the unknown Atlantic in search of the new world and San Sebastián offers several memorials to his visit. Wandering through the few island villages is relaxing and rewarding (hitching can be slow!). Gomera has no airport and few tourists, except those coming across with you on the Tenerife ferry (from Los Cristianos).

● **Hierro** (area: 107 square miles, pop. 7,500)
This wild island counts over a thousand volcanic mountains. It's the most westerly of the Canary Islands. Capital **Valverde** (pop. 5,000) is 2,000 feet above the tiny port of **La Estaca** where boats arrive from Tenerife. Few tourists visit the island; out here you really can find a spot to get away from it all. Hierro was once considered by geographers as the 'official' end of the world.

● **Crossing to the Balearic Islands** Ferries from Valencia, Alicante or Barcelona to Palma. Don't believe all that newspaper claptrap about the **Balearics** being spoilt. Of course, they're popular. You only have to read travel brochures to see that. But there's a lot more to them than that clichéd world of concrete and fish 'n' chip signs harped on by journalists who seldom stagger beyond their hotel bar.

The archipelago includes four islands which lie halfway between the Spanish Mediterranean coast and Algeria. Boats from Barcelona, Valencia and Alicante visit them all, except Formentera which you reach from Ibiza:

● **Mallorca** (area: 1,405 square miles, pop. 581, 564)
Capital **Palma de Mallorca** (pop. 300,000) crams in nightclubs, sophisticated shops, a big yacht harbour and fishing port, and an

old Gothic quarter. A great city for walking. Don't miss the Gothic cathedral, begun in 1230 and finished over 300 years later. Four Majorcan kings are buried here, and the treasury, with its gold plate and jewelled candelabras, is worth visiting. In nearby Terreno suburb see the well-preserved Moorish castle of Bellver and the Pueblo Español not far away (same as Barcelona's, only smaller). Plaza Gomila, below, is the Pigalle-like nightclub area. Good spot for meeting up with the opposite sex, though expensive. Rooms in many of the *fondas* behind Pio XII Square at the top of the Borne (Palma's central boulevard) are cheap. For eating out try the cheap but simple restaurants at the far end of the gaudy Apuntadores alleyway off the Borne.

Take the little train from the station in the Plaza España across the mountains to the French-looking **Soller**. It's easier than hitching, and cheap. Notable hill villages nearby are **Deya**, for thirty years home of English author Robert Graves, and claimed by many to be the prettiest village in Spain; and **Valldemossa**, where Chopin passed a lousy winter with George Sand in the Carthusian Monastery. A mass of island caves (Drach, Arta, Campanet, Genova) are worth viewing. The best is **Drach**. But be warned: in summer up to 1,000 visitors at a time are stumbling through. Good unspoilt beaches are **Alcudia** and **Cala Ratjada** in the north.

● **Menorca** (area: 250 square miles, pop. 62,000)

Nicknamed the 'blue and white island', the most northerly Balearic island sports neat white villages and blue-watered coves. It also has green fields with cows, wet, windy winters and a few Georgian-fronted houses to remind you the British occupied it for 50 years.

The capital, **Mahon** (pop. 22,000), is a sleepy, rather staid town huddled around the longest inlet in the Mediterranean. They say that 200 years ago Nelson dallied here with Lady Hamilton in Villa San Antonio (just across the inlet from the town), thereby scandalizing the local populace. By day Mahon is pleasant enough, but at night it's a crock. So after sundown try one of the lively open-air bars in the neighbouring harbour town of **Villa Carlos**. Someone's usually playing a guitar. Soloists are welcome – in any language. **Cala Fonts** at Villa Carlos is tempting, particularly at night. Enjoy a drink on the waterfront there but not a meal, unless you're well heeled. You pay for the view!

Ciudadela, at the other end of the island, is a quiet Moorish town that suddenly goes crazy during the wild San Juan horseriding *feria* on 24 June.

For archaeological buffs, the island is dotted with *taulas* and *talayots,* huge Stonehenge-type constructions that date back to the Bronze Age. They're the oldest traces of previous inhabitants to be found in any of the islands. There are a hundred different sites to visit. The most convenient is the *taula* at **Trebalugar**, just behind Villa Carlos. The beaches of **Arenal d'en Castell** (in the north) and **Santo Tomás** and **San Jaime** (in the south) provide some of the best swimming in the Balearics. Cross-country trekkers can find beaches which are empty even in the middle of summer (don't break your neck scrambling down to them). Behind **Son Bou** beach are caves which were inhabited thousands of years ago.

Don't leave without trying the local gin, another legacy of the British. It's good value at 300ptas a bottle, and a dash of soda and lemon gives you the favourite Menorquin apéritif, *pallofe*.

● **Ibiza** (area: 220 square miles, pop. 70,000)

Capital **Ibiza Town** (pop. 27,685) was once a haven for hippies. Now you mostly find put-ons who can safely play the Bohemian because they have big bank accounts to back their independence. Still, there are plenty of good types around and in the cobbled Dalt Vila (old quarter) above the town strange dives are full of local artists and eccentrics. At the top of the Dalt Vila see the 15th-century Gothic cathedral and fine views of the bay and town. The Archaeological Museum opposite the cathedral contains a unique collection of Punic relics excavated from Puig, the nearby Phoenician burial ground. You can find low-budget restaurants and pensions behind the waterfront. (And a joint called Johann Sebastian Bar.)

Santa Eulalia del Río, 12 km up the coast, is a relaxed town, popular with artists and writers, but the area is fast sinking beneath hotels and apartments.

On the other side of the island, 16 km from Ibiza Town, the one-time small fishing port of **San Antonio Abad** staggers under an avalanche of package tourists. But, amongst the sea of high-rises, you can still find cheap bars and eating-spots (mainly at the back of the town). If you avoid July and August, boat trips to the half-dozen beaches outside San Antonio Bay are pleasant and cheap.

● **Formentera** (area: 45 square miles, pop. 4,800)

This tiny sickle-shaped island has white beaches and a bleached port, **La Sabina**, that looks as if it's a leftover from the old Spanish Sahara.

Tiny capital **San Francisco Javier** (pop. 794) is a dusty one-horse town with an 18th-century church which used to have a cannon on the roof to repel pirates.

Es Pujols is the island's single diminutive resort. Its handful of apartments and restaurants are filled mainly by German tourists. Just beyond it, the simple village of **San Fernando** provides the best-value meals and rooms on the island, and is a good place to meet fellow-travellers.

The island is lined with unspoilt beaches which provide ideal free accommodation in summer. **Playa Mitjorn**, in the south, is the longest.

Addresses

Palma de Majorca:

Tourist information centre at av. Jaime III (tel: 71 22 16). There is also a branch located at the airport (tel: 26 08 03).
Police headquarters at San Fernando (tel: 28 16 00).
Passport office at Ruiz de Alda 1 (tel: 28 04 00).

Ibiza:

Tourist information centre at Paseo Vara de Rey 13 (tel: 30 19 00).
Police headquarters at Vicente Serra 25 (tel: 31 58 61).

Menorca:

Tourist information centre at Plaza Explanada 40 (tel: 36 37 90).

Barcelona: where to sleep

Barcelona has four good Hostelling International Youth hostels. Prices for a bed are in the 1,300–1,700ptas range. Double rooms in the pensions below work out cheaper per person.

Hostels:

Hostal Montserrat, Mare de Deu de Montserrat, Passeig de Nostra Senyora del Coll 41–51 (tel: 4051166). Bus 28 stops outside. The Vallcarca (L3) metro stop is a short walk away.
Hostal de Joves, Passeig Pujades 29 (tel: 3003104). Bus 29 or 41. Metro: Marina (L1).
Hostal 'Pere Tarrés', Numancia 149–51 (tel: 4102309). Bus 7, 15 or 34. Metro: Les Corts (L3).
Hostal 'Studio', Duquesa d'Orleans 58 (tel: 2050961). Bus 22, 64 or 66. Metro: Sarria or Reina Elesenda.

Pensions:
La Paz, Argentera 37 (tel: 3194408).
Rio, Sant Pau 119 (tel: 2410651).
Figueras, Pasaje San Pablo/Sant Pau 2 (tel: 2550594).
Galerias, Carre del Pi 5 (tel: 3173002).
Mari-Luz, Palau 4 (tel: 3173463).

Prices at the campsites around the city start at around 500ptas per tent and per person in the third-class sites. All the sites are a fair distance out, so the constant commuting can make camping an expensive proposition. But if you'd like to be close to a beach the following sites may appeal to you:

Cala-Gogo El Prat (tel: 3794600). Towards the airport in Prat de Llogerat. Good shade, and its own beach. Bus 605 from Pl. España to Prat, then bus 604 to the beach. Open Mar.–Nov.
El Toro Bravo (tel: 6581250), with its own nudist section, and **Filipinas** (tel: 6582595) are two year-round sites just south of El Prat in the Vildecans area. Both sites can be reached on bus 93 from Pl. Universitat or bus 90 from Pl. Goya.

Barcelona: where to eat

Most Barcelona restaurants serve lunch from 1–4 p.m. and dinner from 8–11 p.m. Average prices for a two-course à la carte meal are about 900–1,000ptas. There are also plenty of restaurants serving up decent three-course set menus for about the same price. Unusually for Spain, though, set menus are normally only available at lunchtime. In and around the Ramblas and Ronda Sant Antoni is the place to look for cheap meals. Try:

Restaurante Riera, Joaquim Costa 30 (off Ronda Sant Antoni near Pl. Universitat).
Restaurante Bidasoa, Serra 21 (off Josep Anselm Clavé).
Restaurante Biocenter, Pintor Fortuny 24. Vegetarian eatery off the Ramblas.

Getting around
Although walking is the best way to see Barcelona, there is a good public transport system (bus and metro). Placa de Catalunya is the main terminus. With single tickets for the bus and metro costing 120ptas, buying 10-trip tickets (600ptas) can cut costs dramatically.

Addresses

Barcelona Information Round-the-clock information service (tel: 010). English speakers available.
Viajeseu at Avenida José Antonio 615, Barcelona 7 (tel: 2313462).
Emergencies Municipal Police (tel: 091) National Police (tel: 092). Station specializing in tourist-related cases at Ramblas 43 across from Placa Reial.
Ambulance (tel: 300 20 20).

Madrid: where to sleep

Spain is one of the few countries where you can relax and let your hair down moneywise. It's amongst the even fewer countries – Portugal, Greece, Turkey, Morocco – where youth or student accommodation can be just as expensive as what you can find in the streets. In Madrid, for example, the two local hostels charge 1,200ptas each, but here it's no great thing to find a single for 1,400ptas, or doubles for 2,000–2,300ptas. Watch out, though – taking a bath or shower in a pension can cost extra. Try any of the following pensions, all central:

Suiza Española, Carrera de San Jerónimo 32 (tel: 4296814).
Josefina, Gran Vía 44 (tel: 5218131).
Vives, Barquillo 25 (tel: 2325263).
Marbella, Plaza de Isabel II 5 (tel: 2476148).
Mori, Plaza de las Cortés 3 (tel: 4297208).
Iserte, Fuencarral 16 (tel: 2315212).

Youth hostels:

'Richard Schirrmann', Casa de Campo (tel: 4635699).
Hostal Marcenado, Santa Cruz de Marcenado 28 (tel: 5474532).

Madrid: where to eat

Eat where you like. Just avoid anything with chrome or plastic trimmings. In the warren of streets between Plaza Mayor and Puerta del Sol you can find little bars which will serve small omelets for 300ptas and a *caña* (draught beer) for 130ptas a glass. Choose your place well and you can treat yourself to a good meal, wine included, for 1,000ptas. Avoid the 3-course tourist menus you will see advertised all over the place. Most of them offer a good deal but you can eat cheaper by just ordering yourself one big special course. Calle del Barco, which is off Avenida José Antonio, has half a dozen really cheap and good restaurants. Don't be frightened to drop in on some bars before you eat to have a few *vinos* and *tapas* (tiny appetizers) – they'll set you up well for your meal and usually won't cost you more than 150ptas a go. Spaniards, incidentally, don't eat their evening meal until 9 or 10 p.m.

Try one of the capital's specialities called *cocido madrileño* (sausage, chickpea and potato stew) or *chorizo* (spicy sausage). The student quarter (Argüelles Metro: Argüelles or Moncloa) is worth hunting around for cheap eats. Plenty of budget eating places between Calle San Bernardo, Fuencarral and Gran Via.

Ledesma, San Vicente Ferrer 78. Metro to Noviciado.
La Sanabrasa, Leon. Metro to Anton Martin.
El Bierzo, Encomienda 19. Metro to La Latina.
El 5, Andres Mellado 5. Metro to Argüelles.
La Biótica, Amor de Dios 3. Vegetarian restaurant. Metro to Alonso Martín.
Los Pesqueros, Arriaza 18. Metro to P. España.
Sotillo, Claudio Coello 2. Metro to Retiro.
Casa Basilio, Luna 26. Metro to San Bernardo.
La Gata Flora, Calle Dos de Mayo 1. Metro to Noveciado or Tribunal. Good pasta and sangria.
Bar Macchu Picchu, Calle Infantas 10. Metro to Gran Via. As name suggests, it's Peruvian. Serves great meals.
El Barabatu, Calle Echegaray 5. Famous for onions stuffed with tuna. Yummy!

Madrid: what to see and do

THE PRADO One of the really great art galleries of the world. Unbelievable collection of Goya, just about everything that Velázquez ever put on canvas, rooms full of El Greco and four or five fantastic works by Bosch – and that's just part of it. Visit the nearby Prado annex Casón del Buen Retiro in Calle Felipe IV to see Picasso's wrenching *Guernica*. Admission charge to both.

EL RASTRO This is the flea market along Ribera de Curtidores. Open every morning, but at its best on Sundays. (It's too crowded to carry a pack comfortably.) Costs nothing and it's great fun. If you want to buy something, haggle like mad – but you'll be haggling against experts, because half of the stallholders are gypsies. Watch out for pickpockets.

THE PLAZA MAYOR One of the most beautiful squares in Europe and a good place from which to start exploring the 'old' Madrid. Don't eat or drink in the plaza – too expensive. Move to the streets behind.

STAMP MARKET for philatelists who want to try to pick up a bargain, or people who want to watch some expert haggling. Plaza Mayor from 11 a.m.–2 p.m. every Sunday.

BULLFIGHT TICKETS To buy a ticket (May is one of the most active months), and to get a glimpse of the Madrid Hemingway wrote about in 'The Undefeated', go to Calle Victoria – a small street on your right as you walk up Carrera de San Jerónimo which leads out of the Puerta del Sol. Streets in this area, like Calle Echegaray, have great bars.

BULLFIGHT MUSEUM at the Las Ventas bullring. This shows the history of bullfighting in paintings, engravings and models. Small admission fee. Open from 10.30 a.m.–1 p.m. and from 3.30–6.30 p.m.

PALACIO REAL (Royal Palace) at Plaza de Oriente. A huge and richly decorated palace probably of interest to architectural fans. Stiff entrance fee.

REAL FABRICA DE TAPICES (Royal Tapestry Factory) at Calle Fuenterrabia 2. Founded in the 18th century by Felipe V. Fascinating creaky old building where you can watch artisans working on tapestries originally designed by Goya.

PLAZA DE ESPAÑA Centrepieces of this skyscraper-surrounded garden plaza are two massive and evocative bronzes of Don Quixote and Sancho Panza presided over by a stone monument of Cervantes, their creator. Usually plenty of travellers to talk to.

Transport in Madrid

Metro and bus tickets cost 120ptas per ride. For 600ptas you can get a 10-trip ticket (Metro – *billete de diez*; bus – *bonobus*). If you're in a group, say four people, don't be scared of taxis. Fares are far from prohibitive. Trouble is that the vehicles are driven by hell-drivers.

For help with youth-related problems from travel to food and lodgings contact **Comunidad de Madrid**, Direccion General de Juventud (tel: 521 95 11). If you want to visit them you will have to get a ticket on to the Metro at the Puerta del Sol Station where they are situated.

Student discounts

Theoretically, in Spain you should get reduced admission to various places like the Prado and the Alhambra. Practice and theory in Spain, however, are two different things. If you have an ISIC card try your luck by flashing it everywhere. Details from:

TIVE, José Ortega y Gasset 71, Madrid (tel: 401 95 01).

Addresses

Main post Office (for poste restante) at Plaza de Cibeles, Madrid.
American Express at Plaza de las Cortes 2, Madrid (tel: 222 11 80).
TIVE, see **Student discounts**, above.
Tourist Information Office at Plaza Mayor 3, Madrid (tel: 266 48 74).
US Embassy at Serrano 75, Madrid (tel: 276 34 00).
British Embassy at Fernando el Santo 16, Madrid (tel: 419 02 00).

Hitchers' Tips and Comments . . .

No problem dossing in Algeciras when you're waiting for the Ceuta or Tangier ferry. Police seem friendly enough. But if you're kipping in the seafront garden, beware the mad gardener who insists on hosing down the grass around 8 a.m. DAVE P., LEEDS, ENGLAND

Stuff Dave P.'s advice to doss in Algeciras. Too many (hard) drug dealers. Two German tourists suffered car break-in plus mugging. Gibraltar's Catalan Bay is preferable MICHAEL GRAHAM, SCOTLAND

For cheap accommodation in Barcelona, try Casa de Huéspedes Mari-Luz, Calle Palau 4 (tel: 317 3463). Walk down Ramblas, turn left on Calle Fernando, then right at Hotel Rialto. (You have to climb about 80 stairs.) Also try Pension Fernando, Calle Fernando 31 (tel: 301 7993) run by Mari-Luz's husband. For good cheap food try Casa José, Plaza San José Oriol 10, off the Ramblas. The paella is good value for money. STEVE, HECKMONDWIKE, ENGLAND

At La Junquera, just across the Spanish border where the A17 and N11 intersect, there are usually about 50 trucks pulled over and waiting to clear customs. Ask around and you can often pick up a ride to major Spanish cities.

JOHN OTIS, MANKATO, MINNESOTA, USA

Hitchers sleeping out on beaches in Spanish tourist resorts should be warned that they're in danger of being mugged and/or robbed. I heard several nasty stories from Benidorm and Torremolinos.

PAUL JOHNSON, PARK RIDGE, ILLINOIS, USA

Try never to sleep rough alone. Get a group of four or five together. To protect yourselves from sneak-thieves who try and spirit away backpacks, tie all luggage together with rope or belts. K.W.

Paper-napkin dispensers in just about all Spanish bars supply unlimited quantities of (thin) toilet paper.

J. D. BOYLE, TOPEKA, KANSAS, USA

Ceefax pages are a boon – I found a £45 flight to Malaga. It's cheaper than the Plymouth–Santander ferry and saves the trouble of hitching through Spain. Malaga isn't as bad as Katie Woods makes out in *Europe by Train*, but it's a hell of a night-time hike along the N340 to get to the city from the airport. Forget Hostal Residencia Chinitas – cheap but crap, and they insist on advance booking. A better bet is Hostal Residencia Buenos Aires on calle Bolsa. It's more pricey, but it's a nice place. OLLY DAVIES, HARROGATE, ENGLAND

There's a good trick for dossing in Spain. Go to a fiesta at the weekend, stay up drinking and dancing all night, and crash in a park during the day, when it's warmer and safer. It's not too expensive: you can carry cheap litre bottles of beer (*litronas*) around with you, and, 'cos it's so crowded, most bars don't even seem to notice. There are loads of wild little fiestas in villages every weekend in July and August. Tourist information in cities should be able to tell you where they are.

If you dress up, you can do the same thing at the weekend in Madrid, but the booze is more expensive (a *copa* in a posh club could set you back 1,000 pesetas). All the discos have *invitaciones* that get you in free. You can find them in the trendy/gay clothes shop in the triangle between the metro stations Alonso Martinez, Bilbao and Gran Vía. To get pissed on the cheap, go to Bar 21 (21 Toledo Street, near the Plaza Mayor) and ask for 'un diablo'. The area called Malasaña (near metro stations Bilbao, Tribunal and San Bernardo) is good for all-night drinking. WILL THOMPSON, LEEDS, ENGLAND

Portugal

population	10,421,000
size	35,404 square miles
capital	Lisbon, population 2,128,000
government	Republic
religion	Roman Catholic
language	Portuguese
currency	*Escudo* ($) One *escudo* equals 100 *centavos*. Coins of 50 *centavos*, and 1, 2$^1/_2$, 5, 10, 20, 50, 100 and 200 *escudos*. Notes of 500, 1,000, 2,000, 5,000 and 10,000 *escudos*

Oporto, Portugal's second city, with a population of 325,000, lies just 150 km across the Spanish border. If you have a nose which enjoys tracking the smell of the grape, this could be your idea of heaven because the city lends its name to port wine, and the Douro River which it straddles is the waterway which carries barge-loads of grapes down from the vineyards. Much of the final product ends up stored in vats holding as much as 100,000 litres in the wine *adegas* near the bridges at Vila Nova de Gaia. Some *adegas* offer free tastings. If you're sober enough after finding the ones that do, don't miss the cathedral and the cathedral square, and visit the Soares dos Reis Museum in the 18th-century Carrancas Palace, which features Portuguese painting. (Interesting to note that in Roman times there were two towns, Portus – the harbour – on the right bank, and Cale on the left bank. The twin cities were known as Portucale – thus Portugal.)

If you're in a wandering mood head inland to the province of Trás-os-Montes. **Bragança** is a good destination. The trip can be slow and the landscape is not exactly lyrical, but I like the austereness of it. It's a slice of the country the tourists usually miss. In Bragança head for the old section, completely walled and fortified. From the keep of the 12th-century castle you enjoy a great view over the town.

South-west towards Coimbra lies the **Buçaco Forest**, a 250-acre national park containing over 700 varieties of trees and plants. Several trails offer planned walks. One takes you by the Fonte Fria – the Cold Fountain – a cascade tumbling down a 144-step staircase. If you're interested in Portuguese history, check the Military Museum which commemorates Wellington's victory over the French in the Battle of Buçaco in 1810.

Coimbra (population 60,000) is the seat of an ancient university founded in Lisbon in 1290 and transferred to the city in 1308. I hitched in and out of town with students and found them open and friendly. You'll notice that some male students wear torn black cloaks. The rips commemorate successful amorous adventures! Nearly all the main sights are in the photogenic old section, a frustrating but beautiful maze of narrow alleys and time-worn stairs. Visit the Old University, the cathedral and the Machado de Castro Museum. About 15 km south-west of Coimbra stand the Roman ruins of **Conimbriga**, considered to be among the most important in the entire Peninsula.

Further south again and you come to the Monastery of **Batalha** (the word means battle), built in the 14th and 15th centuries to commemorate the Battle of Aljubarrota (1385) when an ill-equipped Portuguese army defeated a superior Spanish force. Henry the Navigator is buried in the Founder's Chapel, and the Unknown Soldiers are buried in the Chapterhouse. The multi-turreted building is among Portugal's most popular sights. Just a few kilometres down the road is **Alcobaça** where there's another monastery built to celebrate another battle. The complex, comprising the church, the exquisite Cloister of Silence and various peripheral buildings, makes it Portugal's biggest church. Check the 18th-century kitchens just off the cloister.

Inland a few kilometres lies the sanctuary of **Fátima**, where in 1917 the Virgin Mary is said to have made a series of appearances to three shepherd children. If you are interested in religion, or in the phenomenon of crowd psychology, visit Fátima on the 13th of any month, when pilgrims flock there to worship. On 13 May, the anniversary of the first apparition, up to a million people congregate on the esplanade. Whatever your beliefs, it's really something to see. And so is the gross commercialism which has turned a sacred place into a gigantic supermarket full of tin and plastic religious trivia. Continue inland to **Tomar**, wonderfully situated on the Nabaõ River and presided over by a 12th-century Knights Templar castle. See the Convent of Christ with its famous Templars' Rotunda, modelled on Jerusalem's Holy Sepulchre.

Should you want to enjoy a more down-to-earth experience, head in the other direction, to the coast and the fishing town of **Nazaré**. This is undoubtedly the most photographed town in Portugal, and in summer is inundated by tourists. Some of the gnarled fishermen the tourists line up to photograph after paying their escudos aren't even fishermen but old-timers who have realized that *looking* like a fisherman can be a profitable sideline. But Nazaré is still a real fishing village. Try to visit in winter when things are quieter. The famous Nazaré scene of fishing boats being hauled from the water and up the beach by oxen is rare now – tractors are much more efficient. Camera-toting hitchers should try for a shot from the Sitio quarter which perches on a 300-foot cliff north of the town.

If you fancy a spot of fishing yourself, head south again and make a detour over to **Peniche**, from where you can take a boat (in calm weather!) to **Berlenga Island**, about 10 km offshore. The island offers superb line and underwater fishing (got your spear in your pack?).

Approaching Lisbon via the N8 you can choose between several detours on or near the Estoril coast. **Sintra**, a few kilometres inland, is a town of magnificent buildings, and the surest way to see one for free is to get picked up for vagrancy or some other dastardly deed because the town jail is in a castle. Sintra's fame as a summer resort began centuries ago when it was favoured by Portugal's kings as a retreat. See the Royal Palace, the whimsical Palácio da Pena and the dramatically situated but skeletal Moorish castle. If you're in Sintra on the second or fourth Sunday of the month, catch a bus to neighbouring **São Pedro de Sintra** for the town market. Stock up on genuine, old-fashioned, homemade bread and cheese and fresh country produce. Back on the coast, **Cascais** is pleasant for an overnight stay. Like Sintra, it owes its beginnings as a tourist destination to royalty who started using it as a summer resort in 1870. You won't find anything truly old in Cascais because it was wrecked in the earthquake of 1755, but you'll enjoy the beach and the bay which it shares with neighbouring **Estoril**. Visit the Castro Guimarães Museum where you can examine archaeological exhibits tracing the history of the area which was first settled by Palaeolithic man and then by Romans, Visigoths and Moors. Try to make it down to the **Boca do Inferno** (the Mouth of Hell), just 2 km south of Cascais. The 'Mouth' is a geological freak which sucks in the sea and spits it out in huge spouts of spray along with a great booming accompaniment. Best on a day when the sea is really wild.

South-east of Lisbon the indispensable visit is to **Evora**, capital of the Upper Alentejo province. The town of 40,000 has been declared by the government to be a 'museum city'. It's a fair description of the place. Though its white walls and narrow streets give it a completely Moorish feeling, within an hour you can stroll by the 2nd-century Roman temple of Diana, a 12th-century cathedral, the 15th-century Dos Lóios Monastery and a gruesome 16th-century chapel called the Capela dos Ossos (the Chapel of Bones), which has 5,000 skulls decorating the walls. If you feel like wandering off the beaten track, try a sidetrip towards the Spanish border to the ancient fortified town of **Monsaraz** which seems hardly to have changed for centuries. From Monsaraz it's easy enough to find your way into Spain via any one of several inland routes.

The usual coastal route into Spain is via the **Algarve; Sagres, Lagos, Albufeira** and **Faro** are the principal towns. All can be suffocatingly busy in summer, to the point where it is nearly impossible to move a car in the crowded streets, much less park it within a kilometre of where you want to go, so you can guess what the hitching is like! Winter is the time to visit. Cold wind can sweep in from the Atlantic, it may rain, but at least you will be able to see what you came to visit.

● **The Madeira and Azores islands** The volcanic, subtropical Madeira Archipelago, 850 km from Lisbon in the Atlantic Ocean, comprises the island of **Madeira** itself, the island of **Porto Santo** and two uninhabited groups, the **Desertas** and the **Selvagens**. The Azores Archipelago comprises ten major islands totalling 902 square miles spread across 500 km of the Atlantic, the nearest island lying 1,100 km from Portugal's Cape Roca. The Azores are divided into three main groups, the Eastern, Central and Northwestern. **São Miguel** in the eastern group is the largest island. The Madeira and Azores islands, which belong to Portugal, are most easily reached by plane or ship from Lisbon.

● **Bullfights** If you find the Spanish version of the bullfights bloody, you may prefer the Portuguese fights which come into the category of sport rather than ritual. The bull is never killed. All good, clean fun (as long as you are not the bull). Check at the tourist office for dates. Students can buy half-price tickets through the student travel bureau (see p. 263).

● **Festas** Festivals and fairs in Portugal are great fun. You should check with Portuguese national tourist offices for exact dates, as they tend to change. Try some of the following: *Mardi Gras Carnivals* in Estoril-Cascais, Torres Vedras, Loulé and Ovar during the four days up to Shrove Tuesday. *Holy Week* – Easter religious processions in Braga. *Festivals of the Popular Saints*, Lisbon in June. *Festival of St John* in Porto features funfair, fireworks, handicrafts, regional cooking; in June. *Festival of the Red Waistcoats* at Vila Franca de Xira (Lisbon) with bullfights, amusements; in July. *International Music Festival* in Sintra, during second fortnight in August. *Festa of Our Lady of Nazaré* in Nazaré in September with fair and bullfights.

Oporto: where to sleep

West of av. dos Aliados is usually the most fertile ground for room-hunters, but in the summer months pensions throughout the city, and the local youth hostel, are often full by mid-afternoon. Cheaper options in Oporto include:

Youth Hostel, Rua Rodrigues Lobo 98 (tel: 6065535). Buses 2, 20 or 52 from Praça Liberdade direction Rua Julio Dinis. 1,100–1,400$ depending on the season.
Estoril, Rua de Cedofeita 193 (tel: 2002751).
Astória, Rua Arnaldo Gama 56 (tel: 2008175).
Brasil, Rua Formosa 178 (tel: 310516).
Grande Oceano, Rua da Fábrica 45 (tel: 282447).

There are three good campsites well priced for hitch-hikers' pockets, and near beaches. The tourist office can advise you which bus to take:

Salguieros-Canidelo (tel: 7810500). Open May–Sept.
Madalena, Lugar da Mariñha (tel: 714162). Open June–Sept. Bus 50 from Rua Mouz, near Porto São Bento railway station.
Marisol, Rua Alto das Chaquedas 82, Canidelo (tel: 7125942).

Oporto: where to eat

For cheap and basic meals you must try the workers' cafés, situated mostly around Praça Carlos Alberto, Rua da Picaria and Rua do Almada. They are open six days a week (usually from 11 a.m.–7.30 p.m.) with the busiest time around midday.

Kinary Snack Bar at Rua Dom João 8. Good choice of meat and fish dishes at prices to suit the pocket.
King Long at Largo Dr Tito Fontes 115. Superb Chinese food. Cheap.
Brasa Churassqueria, Praça Batalha 117. Chicken dishes.

Addresses

Tourist office at Rua Clube dos Fenianos 25 (tel: 312740). From São Bento station, follow Avenida dos Aliados to the Town Hall and you will find the tourist office over to the left.

American Express at Star Travel Service, av. dos Aliados 210 (tel: 2003637/2003689). Closed at lunchtime.
Medical Assistance: Hospital de Santo Antonio, Rua Prof. Vicente Jose de Carvalho (tel: 2007354).
Emergencies: Police or Ambulance (tel: 115). Police Station is situated on Rua Alexandre Herculano (tel: 2006821).
UK Consulate at av. de Boãvista 3072 (tel: 684789). Not open at weekends.

Coimbra: where to sleep

The area around Coimbra *A* railway station has the least expensive accommodation in town, particularly Rua da Sota and the streets running off it. Although outside appearances could be off-putting the pensions themselves are perfectly acceptable and safe. Here are some suggestions:

Vitoria, Rua da Sota 9 (tel: 24049).
Lorvanese, Rua da Sota 27.
Flor de Coimbra, Rua da Poco 8. Good inexpensive meals are available to residents. Singles 1,500$ per night.

Hostels:
IYHF Youth Hostel, Rua Henriques Seco 12–14 (tel: 22955). B&B from 1,300–1,600$ depending on the season. From Coimbra *A* take bus 7, 8, 29 or 46 to Praça Republica. From the square walk up Rua Lourenço de Almeida Azevdo along the side of the park until you see Rua Henriques Seco.

Camping:
Parque de Campismo Municipal de Coimbra, Praça 25 de Abril (tel: 712997).

Coimbra: where to eat

There are a few student refectories (*cantinas*) around the University, where you get good value cafeteria meals for 250$, and no shortage of small, dingy side streets where you can get good, cheap tucker. Try Rua Direita which is just off Praça Ocho de Maio or Beco do Forno and Rua dos Gatos.

Churrasqueria do Mondego, Rua Sargento Mor 27 (tel: 23355), off Rua Sota, and a few minutes walking from Portagem. The barbecued chicken (*frango no churrasco*) is magic!

Cafe Santa Cruz, Pr. 8 de Maio (tel: 33617). A good place to meet Portugese students, 'cos this is one of their favourite haunts.

Addresses

Tourist office at Largo Portagem (tel: 23886). From Coimbra *A* station, walk 2 blocks east along av. Emidio Navarro, keeping the River Mondego on your right.

Medical Assistance at Hospital da Universidade de Coimbra (tel: 723211). This is reputedly the best hospital in the country. I hope you don't have to prove this!

Emergencies: (tel: 115) Police (tel: 22022). Police Station: Rua Olímpio Nicolau Rui Fernandes.

Sintra: where to sleep

Here, as in most other beautiful places in Portugal, accommodation is pretty thin on the ground after midday so arrive early. Fortunately the tourist office (tel: 2931157) is very helpful and may be able to fix you up with private rooms at reasonable rates. Here are some of the cheaper *pensãos*:

Economica, near the Palacio Real. One of the cheapest.

Casa Adelaide at av. Guilherme Gomes Fernandes 11–1 (tel: 9230873). Near the Town Hall, roughly halfway between the railway station and the Palacio Real.

Nova Sintra, Largo Alfonso de Albuquerque 25 (tel: 9230220), through Largo D. Manuel I.

Bristol, close to the Palacio Real.

Hostels:

Pousada de Juventude de Sintra, Sta. Eufémia S Pedro de Sintra 2710 (tel: 9241210). B&B 1,100–1,400$ in dorms according to the season. Other meals available.

Sintra: where to eat

Casa da Avo. This inexpensive eatery is very close to the fire station.

Pensão Bristol, Rua Visconde de Monserrate. Here you can get huge, very cheap, meals.

Lisbon: where to sleep

Accommodation-wise, Portugal is not as cheap as Spain, but it tries hard. Count on paying about 15–20% more for a bed. The best place to search for a *pensão* is in the maze of streets on the hill leading up to the Castle of St George, but on the *west* side. The southern side, the real Alfama, caters to the tourist types, and prices are correspondingly higher. The next best place is on the west side of the Rossio, the big main square, or failing that, in the area called Bairro Alto which is to the west of Rua da Misericórdia. All of these places are right in the main commercial area of town. Make sure you hire a bed only, and don't get quoted a price which includes all meals.

Here is a list of some of the really cheap places:

Pensão Imperial at Praça dos Restauradores 78, 4th and 5th floors (tel: 342 01 66).
Pensão Madeirense at Rua da Glória 22, 1st floor (tel: 342 58 59).
Pensão Pérola da Baixa at Rua da Glória 10, 2nd floor (tel: 34 628 75).
Pensão Norte at Rua dos Douradores 159, 4th floor (tel: 87 89 41).
Pensão Ninho de Aguias at Costa do Castelo 74 (tel: 86 81 51)

Lisbon has two youth hostels, one is in the city, whilst the other is a 20 minute train ride away – but easy to get to:

Pousada de Juventude de Lisboa, Rua Andrade Corvo 46, 1000 Lisbõa (tel: 532696). Top quality hostel. B&B 1,700–2,000$ depending on the time of year. Full board also available. Bus 2, 90, 44, 45, 46 for Picoas or take Metro to Cidade Universitaria ap Picoas and the hostel is only 50 m away.

Catalazete, Estrada Marginal, 2780 Oeiras (tel: 4430628). B&B 1,100–1,500$ according to the season. Full board also available. Frequent trains from Cais do Sodré to Oeiras. On leaving the station, go through the underpass to the right beneath the Praia sign. Look for the sign pointing to the hostel, 3/4 mile but the way is well sign-posted.

Lisbon: where to eat

Pick your place carefully and you can eat well for 1,000$, and feast for 1,500$. Happy hunting grounds for cheap meals are in the Rua das Portas de Santo Antão (parallel to the Avenida da Liberdade), the Rua da Madalena and in many of the small streets leading off those two. Here are some suggestions:

Adega Triunfa, Rua dos Bacalhoeiras. If you like seafood, this is the place for you. Located in the Baixa area.
O Barriga, Travessa da Queimada 31. This is in the Bairro Alto. Good deal, good tucker!
Bizarro, Rua da Atalaia 133. Also in the Bairro Alto. You won't have to wait long for your meal, which will cost you less than 1,500$. Great value.

At the time of writing the days of foreign students devouring 250$ meals in the local student *cantinas* are no more. Rule changes mean you must now hold a local student ID card. Ask the Tourist Office if there have been any further changes.

Lisbon: what to see and do

THE CASTLE OF ST GEORGE begun by the Visigoths in the 5th century, offers stunning views of Lisbon, the harbour and Tejo River. Walk up through the Alfama or ride up on Bus 37 (from Praça do Rossio).

THE ALFAMA is the oldest section of Lisbon and for most visitors the essence of the city. A memorable and insoluble maze of narrow, winding streets, crumbling steps, multi-coloured house fronts; an amazing tangle of drying washing between the houses and a forest of TV aerials above them; street vendors, suspicious characters, and scruffy kids being chased by their mothers. A poor place, but a nice place.

THE CATHEDRAL was built in the 12th century but remodelled after the earthquake of 1755. See the sacristy and the cloisters.

PRAÇA DO COMÉRCIO the big square down by the waterfront, is the hub of the city, and a good place to run into fellow hitchers. Street vendors and fish sellers work there most mornings.

THE MONUMENT TO THE DISCOVERIES was built in 1960 to commemorate the 500th anniversary of the death of Henry the Navigator. It's shaped like a ship's prow and decorated with dozens of carved figures. Henry himself, model caravel in hand, stands on the very end of the bow staring out over the river.

THE BELÉM TOWER on the waterfront near the Coach Museum was built in the 16th century to guard the river approach to Lisbon. It was the first sight of home after long years at sea for generations of Portuguese explorers.

JERÓNIMOS MONASTERY and the Tower of Belém were two of the few important buildings to survive the 1755 earthquake which killed 40,000 citizens and left Lisbon in ruins. Built in the 15th and 16th centuries, it's considered a masterpiece of Manueline (after King Manuel I) art. Even if you're up-to-here with churches, take a look at the cloister. Worth the effort.

THE '25TH OF APRIL' BRIDGE is the longest suspension bridge in Europe. It's 2 km across and the foundations go down 259 feet to bedrock beneath the river. Try to get a ride across. You'll be 230 feet above the water and looking down over the city. Nearest thing to an aerial view of Lisbon without being in an aeroplane.

STATUE OF CHRIST THE KING If you *do* get that ride across the bridge, watch for the 90-foot-high statue – reminiscent of the one in Rio de Janeiro – which dominates the other side of the river. Better still, take the lift to the balcony up top which gives a great view over river and city.

MUSEUMS Among the many: the NATIONAL MUSEUM OF ANCIENT ART, known locally as 'Janelas Verdes' (green shutters), a treasure trove not to be missed; the COACH MUSEUM in Belém, considered to hold the world's best collection of non-motorized vehicles; the GULBENKIAN MUSEUM, Praça da Espanha, houses an amazing collection of just about everything from Egyptian antiquities to Rembrandts and Impressionists; the MUSEUM OF FOLK ART in the Avenida Brasília, Belém, home of the country's largest collection of traditional art.

NIGHTCLUBS Best districts for Portuguese-style nightclubs are the Alfama and Bairro Alto districts. It's there that you can find the *fado* singers. Well worth seeing, but it'll cost you at least 3,000$ for a drink even if you play it on the cheap.

MOVIES are nearly always shown in original language with Portuguese subtitles. Plenty of English-language shows around, most quite recent. Seats are reasonably priced even in the city centre.

THE FLEA MARKET at Campo Santa Clara on Calçada de São Vicente is in full swing Tuesdays and Saturdays.

Transport in Lisbon
The subway is the quickest method of getting around Lisbon and the cheapest. City buses are just as cheap, but slower. Taxis, as in Madrid, are among the cheapest in Europe. If you're in a group they're the ideal way of moving around.

Student discounts
For information contact the Departamento de Turismo Universitário, R. Gonçalves Crespo 20–2°, 1100 Lisboa (tel: 53 87 02/56 12 23).

Addresses

Main post office (for poste restante) at Praça dos Restauradores, 1200 Lisbon.
American Express at STAR, Avenida Sidónio Pais 4a, Lisbon (tel: 53 98 71).
Tourist Office at Palácio Foz, Praça dos Restauradores, Lisbon (tel: 34 636 43/58).
US Embassy at Avenida das Forcas Armadas, 1600 Lisbon (tel: 726 66 00/726 10 81).
British Embassy at Rua de São Domingos à Lapa 37, 1200 Lisbon (tel: 396 11 91).

Hitchers' Tips and Comments . . .

For cheap eating in Lisbon, buy take-away food at the Expresso Supermarket near the youth hostel. To crash out, take a train to Cascais, a really nice little place with lots of possibilities. Get off at Cais do Sódre station. For sightseeing, don't miss Sintra. Take the train from Rossio.
LUIS MOURAO, LISBON, PORTUGAL

Unlike in Spain where the hitching is reasonable (away from the coastal areas), in Portugal it's really bad. The locals just aren't into it. Be prepared for long waits. But the country is marvellous.
JON MORE O'FARRALL, TRINITY, JERSEY, CHANNEL ISLANDS

Greece

population	10,264,156
size	131,957 square kilometres
capital	Athens, population 3,500,000
government	Republic
religion	Greek Orthodox
language	Greek. Some French understood, English widely spoken
currency	*Drachma* (dr) Coins of 1, 2, 5, 10, 20, 50, and 100 *drachmas*. Notes of 50, 100, 500, 1,000, 5,000 *drachmas*

If you enter Greece from Bulgaria, **Thessaloniki** will probably be your first stop. It is the country's second city (after Athens) and was founded in 315 BC on the site of an even older city – Thermai. As guardian of such a long history, you'd think the city would offer a rich selection of ruins to visit. Unfortunately, a devastating fire in 1917 burned out much of the city centre and, consequently, the choice is limited. But the old Turkish quarter in the upper part of the city survived and remains one of the most fascinating sections to wander through. To really appreciate the age of Thessaloniki you should visit the Archaeological Museum. Amongst its exhibits see the fantastic treasure of gold jewellery found in tombs as recently as the late 1970s. Also worth a visit: the city's ancient churches, particularly the 5th-century Basilica of St Demetrius and the 3rd-century church of St George.

About 150 km south-east of Thessaloniki, on the tip of the easternmost of the three peninsulas of Chalkidiki, is the strange place called **Mount Athos.** This is an autonomous region, in effect a state unto itself, and run by monks. There are 20 monasteries, many of them around 1,000 years old. Known as the 'Holy Mountain', Mt Athos cannot be visited unless you arrange for your embassy or consulate to get authorization on your behalf from the Greek Ministry of Foreign Affairs or from the Ministry for Northern Greece. According to a law made in 1060 by a monk called Constantine the Gladiator which is still in force, no woman is permitted to approach the monasteries. And that goes for all female creatures – dogs and cats included.

At 150 km north-west of Athens is **Delphi**, situated at 2,000 feet on the slopes of Mount Parnassus. This is the place where the famous Oracle lived – he who was known as the 'Holy of Holies'. See the Temple of Apollo and plenty of other excavated ruins.

The plain of **Marathon** traditionally lies 42 km from the centre of Athens. It was here that the decisive battle of 490 BC took place between the Athenians and the Persians. Outnumbered ten to one the Greeks nevertheless won and sent a messenger named Pheidippides to tell the people of Athens the news. The guy made it in record time, gave the message, and died on the spot. Exhausted. The Olympic Marathon honours the event. It's hardly worth hitching out to see the field – it's marked only by the grave of the Greeks who fell – but if you do, continue on an extra few kilometres to **Ramnous** where there are two temples, one of them to Nemesis, the goddess of divine vengeance. (She still wreaks it – the road to Ramnous is rotten.)

About 72 km due south of Athens, on the tip of the peninsula and at **Sounion**, is the beautiful temple of Poseidon, one of the best sights in the country.

Corinth is one of a cluster of important sites on the Peloponnese Peninsula. Modern Corinth, a city of 16,000, is 7 km from the ancient city which was once the largest and most powerful in Greece. It was razed by the Romans in 146 BC, then again by the Goths, and then hit by an earthquake in AD 521. Understandably there are plenty of ruins to see.

Some 50 km on from Corinth are the ruins of **Mycenae**, a city inhabited as far back as 3000 BC. It was the German businessman/archaeologist Heinrich Schliemann – the man ridiculed by popular opinion when he set out to find Troy – who excavated here and found skeletons of men and women adorned with gold masks and crowns. Schliemann believed them to be the bodies of Agamemnon and his companions, though this has yet to be proven. You can see the treasure he unearthed in the Mycenaean Room of the Archaeological Museum in Athens. At the site itself, you can see the Gate of the Lions, the Treasure of Atreus and the Royal Tombs. All in all Mycenae counts as one of the most exciting archaeological spots in Greece.

Further south again and you come to **Epidaurus**, which in ancient times was a famous health centre – perhaps the first ever – and which was visited by ailing people from all over the civilized world. The main sight is the old theatre, the most perfect in Greece, which can seat 16,000 people and is still used each year at the annual Epidaurus Festival (July-mid-August).

There's not much left of **Sparta**, the capital of Laconia, to tell you what the place once was. These days it's a deadly boring town of 11,000 with only a few identified ruins surviving from the days when it was the most powerful city in the world. (The Pass of Thermopylae where Leonidas and his handful of Spartans held the Persians at bay in 480 BC is just a few kilometres south of **Lamia**.)

Seven kilometres west of Sparta, on one of the slopes of Mt Taygettus is the ruined city of **Mistra**, which dates from AD 1249. Even though by Greek standards the place is a 'modern' ruin, it's worth looking over because it's a treasure house of Byzantine art.

Whatever you do, try not to leave the Peloponnese without getting up to **Olympia**, site of the ancient Olympic games, first held in 776 BC. (Not to be confused with Mt Olympus, south of Thessaloniki, and home of the ancient Greek gods.) The sacred flame of the Olympics is still kindled at Olympia every four years and carried by relays of runners to whichever city is staging the spectacle. Plenty to see, including the museum and the stadium; best of all, though, is the rare beauty of the setting.

Hitching in Greece, on the main highways, is about the same as anywhere else, but if you get off the beaten track – easy to do in Greece – it can be very slow. If you're stuck on the way to some mountain village, don't hesitate to grab the local bus. It'll be cheap enough.

● **Language** Greek is not the sort of language you conquer overnight. For most of us it's not the sort of language which is conquered at all. But a few odd words can be picked up without too much trouble.

Try these:

yes – *neh*	no – *Oh-yee*
please – *pah-rah-kah-lo*	thanks – *ef-ha-ree-stoh*

Good day, good evening, goodnight and goodbye are all covered by *yas-sou*.

● **The evil eye** The Greeks are still a little superstitious. The Greek Orthodox Church has a special prayer to ward off the evil eye and many people, women especially, carry special little blue stones to help them in their fight against evil. Shy girls secretly pin the stones to their bras – though God knows which evil eye *they* are trying to divert. You can buy these stones very cheaply. Nice souvenir.

● **Important** Greek authorities will ban entry to the country to any traveller who has visited North Cyprus since 15 November 1983, and carries in his passport the stamp 'Turkish-Cypriot Federal State' or 'Republic of Northern Cyprus'.

The Greek Islands

The main tip where trips to Crete and the islands are concerned is always to go 'deck class', which is the cheapest. The best place to find out about costs (and also to check if your student card will get you a fare reduction) is ISYTS at 11 Nikis Street, Athens. This is a student outfit and not a regular travel bureau.

● **Crete** (area: 3,245 square miles, pop. 440,000)

Iraklion (pop. 80,000) is an untidy, bustling town founded by the Saracens in MD4ad 823. Visit the daily market to buy cheap food. Low-budget pensions in town are near Daidolou Street. Don't miss the Archaeological Museum, which covers Crete's 4,000-year-old Minoan civilization in fascinating detail. See the Venetian fortress at the port.MD1

Five kilometres inland is **Knossos**, the ancient Minoan capital lovingly restored by British archaeologist, Sir Arthur Evans, in 1900. Among its best sights are the throne room (oldest in Europe) and the well-preserved central court. See the wall paintings of bull-vaulting.

Rethymnon, 72 km west of Iraklion, has a Turkish-Venetian waterfront, and a skyline of minarets and turrets proclaiming the town's Ottoman past. Low-priced spots are on Makedonia Street. If you're in town in July don't miss the wine festival in the municipal park.

Chania, 72 km further west, has a crescent-shaped Venetian harbour promenade lined with taverns and open-air restaurants.

Inland, the rugged Sfakia mountains form a natural stronghold which centuries of Venetian, Turkish and German invaders failed to crack. You understand why when you tackle the arduous mountain paths leading to the Sfakians' hospitable but fiercely independent villages. Try *raki*, the local firewater. It'll blow your head off.

An energetic five-hour walk there (locals do it in three!) is along the 19-kilometre **Samaria Gorge**, largest in Europe. Cliffs rise as high as 2,000 feet, while at its narrowest the gorge is only 16 feet across. In Spring, streams run along the valley bottom. Starting point is the inland village of **Omalos**. At the end of the gorge you catch a boat round to the tiny fishing village of **Chora Sfakion**, where British troops made their final escape from the island in 1941. From here you can hitch or bus your way back to Chania.

Phaestos, on a hill overlooking the Messara plain 60 km south of Iraklion, houses the well-kept ruins of Crete's second largest Minoan city. Worth the trip for the evocative location.

Aghios Nikolaos, 70 km east of Iraklion, is the island's top resort, an Aegean St Tropez with expensive bars and a self-consciously attractive harbour setting. But a great place to meet people. Boats run from here in summer to the Cyclades islands and Rhodes.

Try not to miss the fertile inland **Lassithi** plain with its 10,000 windmills and **Cave of Dikte** where legend says Zeus was born.

THE ARGO-SARONICS

The four main islands of this group run closely parallel to the Greek Peloponnese mainland as it descends south from the Saronic into the Argive Gulf. But hitching is difficult in the Peloponnese because of lack of cars, so only try it if you have plenty of time to spare. All (except Spetsai and Hydra) are easy to reach from Piraeus if you can only spare a day for island tripping. You need two days to enjoy Spetsai at leisure, due to the travelling time involved.

● **Aegina** (area: 35 square miles, pop. 12,000; 1½ hours from Piraeus)

Capital **Aegina Town** has plenty of cheap waterfront rooms and restaurants. But be warned: at weekends the place is packed with day-trippers from Athens.

Aghia Marina, 15 km across the island, is a popular beach resort stacked with tavernas. A short walk up through orchards of pistachio trees brings you to the impressive Doric temple of Aphaia, with its Parian marble sculptures and limestone columns, standing evocatively above the sea.

● **Poros** (area: 25 square miles, pop. 5,000; 3½ hours from Piraeus)

The island capital of **Poros** is a tumbling white port with lively harbourside cafés facing the Peloponnese town of Galata only 400 yards away. Here the channel between island and Greek mainland is so narrow that it resembles a large river. The caique (boat) crossing only takes three minutes. Caiques also run regularly up the island coast to Monastiri, an 18th-century monastery.

Inland, among Poros' pinewoods, is the ruined Temple of Poseidon (the Greek god of the sea) where the Athenian orator Demosthenes poisoned himself.

● **Hydra** (area: 21 square miles, pop. 4,000; 4 hours from Piraeus)

Hydra Town boasts 18th-century Venetian houses (symbols of its seafaring past) and a waterfront array of fashionable boutiques and restaurants. Once a backwater for artists, it's now inundated by international trendsetters and hourly cruise ships. So avoid that incredibly expensive harbourside. Cheaper rooms and meals can be found at the back of the town.MD1

Because of the island's barren and mountainous terrain local transport is still by donkey. (The island also has *one* taxi.) Hike up to the hilltop monastery of **Aghia Triada**. Its views over the Peloponnese mainland and sea are out of this world.

● **Spetsai** (area: 10 square miles, pop. 5,000; 5½ hours from Piraeus)

Spetsai Town is a stylish port popular with Athenians. The waterfront Dapia Square is a stage set of bars and open-air restaurants. Ask at Takis Tourist Office near the jetty for cheap rooms in town.MD1

Spetsai's so small you can walk round the pine-wooded coastline in six hours. Take a caique (very cheap) to **Anarghiri**, the island's best beach. As few cars are allowed on the island, main transport is by horse and buggy. (**Warning!** They are expensive.) Spetsai was the setting for John Fowles' book *The Magus*, wherein he called the island Phraxos.

SPORADES

Our word 'sporadic' is taken from the Greek word used to describe these green isles which are strewn haphazardly offshore from Euboea, a large island attached by drawbridge to the eastern Greek mainland at Chalkis. Boats run to most of them from Kymi, Aghios Konstantinos and Volos. Here's some basic information about the three largest:

● **Skiathos** (area: 25 square miles, pop. 4,000)

Capital **Skiathos Town** is a white, red-roofed port surrounded by pines. It's a favourite with writers and artists. Inland, the ruins of **Castro** are worth a visit. **Koukounaries**, fringed by stone pine groves, is the pick of the island's fine beaches.

● **Skopelos** (area: 35 square miles, pop. 5,000)

Skopelos Town, the capital, has a rising amphitheatre of multicoloured houses, and low-priced, waterfront pensions. Two cliff-top churches guard the harbour entrance. Inland Episkopi boasts the medieval ruins of a bishop's palace. Several nearby 7th-century monasteries have been converted into hotels. Visit the southern village Agnonda for the island's best beach.

● **Skyros** (area: 75 square miles, pop. 3,000)

You'll find rooms to let in the white, flat-topped houses which climb the precipitous slopes behind the capital of **Skyros**. At the town's entrance stands a statue erected in the name of the British poet Rupert Brooke, of a nude youth symbolizing 'immortal poetry'. Brooke died of fever on board a hospital ship in Tris Boukes, or Trebuki Bay, during the First World War and is buried in an olive grove near the fishing village of **Linaria**.

Skyros' barren and isolated villages are depositories of folk arts like woodwork, weaving and embroidery. The coast offers unspoilt beaches and dozens of caves ideal for underwater exploration. (Got a mask and snorkel in your pack?)

CYCLADES

These barren islands surround the holy island of Delos in the centre of Homer's 'wine-dark' Aegean Sea. Altogether 211 islands (yes, 211!) form this group, though only 24 are inhabited.

Boats regularly make the five-hour run from Piraeus to Mykonos. Connections to other islands from here are frequent and cheap. (**Warning!** Avoid August for two reasons: the *meltemi* wind can give you a rough ride, and room prices on the islands rocket.)

● **Mykonos** (area: 30 square miles, pop. 3,863)

Capital **Mykonos Town** (pop. 5,000) is picture-postcard Greece, all windmills and white cube houses set against the blue sea. The place brims with open-air cafés, crowded shopping stalls and lively tavernas, popular with tourists and locals alike. Seven of the island's 365 churches are situated in Paraportiani Square, and the little museum on the quay contains religiously significant tombs from Delos. Private houses and a youth hostel provide cheap lodgings, and outside of town there's a camping site. For good beaches try **Aghios Stephanos** and **Ornos**.

Visit **Delos** for the day. Four thousand years ago this was the religious centre of the Greek world. Now, the 10 square miles of rock are inhabited only by a few goatherds and their animals. The archaeological site includes a museum, shrine and mosaic ruins. Most impressive remains include the Sanctuary of Apollo and the Terrace of Lions.

● **Santorini** (area: 30 square miles, pop. 6,400)

Santorini, previously called Thira, is the capital and her brilliant white houses stand on an ash-grey pumice cliff, the outer rim of a vast volcano which disappeared in a cataclysmic explosion 4,000 years ago. You can walk up the 2km zigzag path to the town from the harbour, but it's easier to use the donkey transport or the recently installed funicular. Local houses have low-priced rooms to rent.

The island is dotted with small ruins: Minoan, Doric, Roman and Venetian. Best are the Minoan excavations near **Akrotiri** on the south coast. Inland, tomatoes and vines grow miraculously out of the multi-coloured rock landscape. Try the strong Santorini wine – famous since the Middle Ages.

● **Naxos** (area: 180 square miles, pop. 15,000)

The largest Cyclades island lives from agriculture, not tourism, and is full of vineyards, lush valleys and citrus orchards. Capital **Naxos Town** offers cheap rooms, tavernas and a beautiful old Venetian quarter called the Castro. Across the island the unspoilt village of **Apollon** lies beside a near-deserted beach. If you want to see what real Greek life is like, stay here in a private house. It's idyllic and easy on the pocket.

IONIAN ISLANDS

These six cypress-and-olive-green islands lie off the coast of north-west Greece. Boats run regularly to Corfu, the most important, from Brindisi in southern Italy and Igoumenitsa on the Greek mainland.

● **Corfu** (area: 225 square miles, pop. 100,000)

Capital **Corfu Town** beautifully blends its past cultures. French colonnades overlook an English cricket pitch, and Venetian back-streets merge with a market wafting smells of Oriental spices. You'll find cheap pensions near the Old Harbour. Worth a look is Mon Repos, the former Greek royal summer residence where Britain's Prince Philip, Duke of Edinburgh, was born.

The fishing village of **Benitses**, 12 km south, is popular with both expatriate artists and tourists. Lively tavernas line the waterfront, and in summer spontaneous street dancing often brings traffic to a standstill. At nearby **Gastouri** see Kaiser Wilhelm's monstrous Achilleion. Built in 1891 in mock-Florentine style, it's a museum by day and a casino by night.

● **Paxos** (area: 20 square miles, pop. 3,000)

This is a mini-island of olive trees and coves and only three hours by boat from Corfu Town. Prices in **Gaios** (pop. 600) have boomed since the arrival of the yacht-set.

● **Cephalonia** (area: 300 square miles, pop. 70,000)

The modern port of **Argostoli** was totally rebuilt after an earth-quake in 1953. Worth visiting on the island are the **Necropolis of Mazaracata**, with its 83 Mycenaean tombs, and the fishing village of **Assos**. Inland are vast unspoilt pine forests, and mountains rising to 5,000 feet.

● **Zante** (area: 180 square miles, pop. 45,000)

Zante Town, once known as the 'Flower of the Levant', now nestles under a solitary ruined Venetian castle. The 1953 earthquake robbed the island of any architectural glory, but there are beautiful Italianate gardens and vineyards to visit. Porta Roma boasts one of the island's many fine beaches.

● **Levkas** (area: 110 square miles, pop. 6,000)

In August **Levkas Town** hosts an international folklore festival which gobbles up every free bed on the island. But it's worth visiting if you don't mind sleeping on the beach (which the tourist office says is forbidden). See **Vliko**'s beautiful bay, and the Temple of Apollo in the south, where 7th-century-BC poetess Sappho jumped to her death from the cliffs.

● **Ithaca** (area: 40 square miles, pop. 2,500)

This is Homer's 'precipitous isle', home of Ulysses. Capital **Vathy** is a tiny modern port with an inlet and a beach. Above it stands the ruined medieval Parachorion. Mount Aetos' 2,600-year-old Alaleomenae castle offers incredible views of the island.

DODECANESE

Greece's most easterly islands, the Dodecanese, lie just a few kilometres off the Turkish mainland. The trans-Aegean boat trip from Piraeus to Rhodes takes 20 hours. Of the group's twelve islands, try these three:

● **Rhodes** (area: 550 square miles, pop. 70,000)

Capital **Rhodes Town** (pop. 35,000) is an international tourist town of bars, hotels and restaurants. The busy harbour is guarded by two statues of deer which mark the spots once straddled by the 100-foot-high Colossus of Rhodes, one of the seven ancient wonders of the world, which was destroyed by earthquake in 227 BC. In the walled medieval quarter Turkish minarets and the Suleiman Mosque vie with the Christian-built Grand Master's Palace and the Street of the Knights. Cheap rooms and restaurants are in Apellou Street. There's a youth hostel nearby.

Don't miss beautiful **Lindos**, 60 km south, a white village of cobbled lanes overlooking a sandy bay. No cars are allowed here: only donkeys, which carry tourists up to the superb clifftop acropolis behind the village. Avoid summer if you want a room. They're all booked by travel agencies.

Also worth a look here are the 3rd century BC ruins of ancient **Kamiros** on the west coast, and **Petaloudes**, where giant plane trees shade a gorge filled by millions of butterflies. Catch superb island views from **Mount Philerimos**, with its nearby Byzantine monastery.

● **Kos** (area: 115 square miles, pop. 15,000)

Mosques remind you of the Turkish heritage lurking in the modern port capital of **Kos**. (Look for cheap pensions near the harbour.) Hippocrates, the famous physician, was born here; outside the town see the ruins of the 4th-century-BC Asclepeion, sanctuary and site of his medical school.

Inland Kos is green farming country, full of citrus and vegetable orchards. The coast is lined with unspoilt sandy beaches, which solve accommodation problems.

● **Patmos** (area: 15 square miles; pop. 3,000)

Capital **Chora** rears above the harbour village of **Skala**. See the medieval, fortified monastery built as a memorial to St John the Divine, who is supposed to have written his Apocalypse in a grotto between Skala and Chora. The monastery perching above the town houses a library containing precious manuscripts and ecclesiastical relics. Well worth the climb if you're in the mood.

Caiques run along the wild barren coast to beautiful coves and beaches.

Athens: where to sleep

The local Hostelling International hostel charges 1,600dr for a dorm bed. With a bit of luck you might find a single for 1,800–2,000dr, though 2,500–3,000dr is more realistic. At some hotels you can sleep on the roof for about 1,000dr: in this climate this is as good a deal as any.

Youth Hostel at 57 Odos Kypselis Street (tel: 8225 860).
Residence Pagration at 75 Damareos Street, Pagrati (tel: 751 95 30).
Hotel Orion at 105 E. Benaki Street (tel: 362 84 41).
YWCA (*XEN*) at 11 Amerikis Street (tel: 36 26 180). Ask for dormitory. Women only, but the cafeteria is open to both sexes.
Athens Connection at 20 Ioulianou Street (tel: 821 39 40). Near the train station. Doubles, dorms, free luggage storage, and a multilingual staff.

For help with all student accommodation, drop into **ISYTS** at 11 Nikis Street. They know it all and probably won't insist that you be a student (as long as you look like one) before helping you.

If sleeping rough, check with the local kindred souls before bunking out. Athens is one place to keep right away from the cops. In fact, a note from the polite and very efficient Greek Tourist Office informs me that: 'Greece has a police force of a high standard. Camping . . . is not permitted other than on authorized camp sites. Drugs, nude bathing/sunbathing and other well-known infringements of the law are also not permitted.'

Athens: where to eat

Cheap eating in Athens presents no problem. 1,000–1,500dr should see you through a fairly big meal. Stick to the tavernas rather than restaurants and keep away from where the tourists eat.

Which may leave the problem of figuring out a Greek menu, which is no easy task. The following are some standard dishes which are OK:

Dolmades rice and minced meat wrapped in vine leaves. A traditional dish.
Souvlaki shishkebab – spiced meat and vegetables on a skewer. Buy them from street stalls for cheap eating.
Moussaka casserole of aubergines, meat and spices.
Kalamaraki squid.
Retsina a local wine which has a resin flavour.
Ouzo a killer drink just right for setting you on your ear.

Athens: what to see and do

THE ACROPOLIS For many people this hill in Athens will be the climax of their European wanderings. It's beautiful. You can spend half a day up there without even knowing it. What to see? The PARTHENON, first of all. Then the ACROPOLIS MUSEUM, the TEMPLE OF ATHENA NIKE, the ERECHTHEUM, the PROPYLAEA, the THEATRE OF DIONYSUS, the THEATRE OF HEROD ATTICUS, etc.

THE AGORA to the west of the Acropolis. This was the old city centre. Don't miss the museum.

TEMPLE OF OLYMPIAN ZEUS on Leoforos Amalias. Also, nearby, the ARCH OF HADRIAN.

NATIONAL ARCHAEOLOGICAL MUSEUM in Pattission Street. Entrance charge. Closed Mondays. Very important museum of Greek sculpture and objects discovered during digs all over Greece.

MUSEUM OF POPULAR ART in Kydathineon Street. If you're into the handicrafts scene, drop in here for some ideas. Good collection of handicrafts from all over the country.

FLEA MARKET on Ifestou Street near Monastiraki Square. Best days, Saturday and Sunday. Good place to go to find items of equipment you want to replace. (Remember to bargain!) Also a big underground book market with secondhand books in most languages.

GREEK MUSIC AND BAR LIFE Go into the *boîtes* in the area known as Plaka which is just below the Acropolis. Try the following streets – Mnisikleous, Erechteous, and Tholou. This is where you can hear the *bouzouki* music and watch the *sirtaki* danced. And good luck to you: the *retsina* and *ouzo* will kill you!

MOVIES Most Athens cinemas show up-to-date films in original-language versions with Greek subtitles. Prices are OK.

Transport in Athens

Subway and buses are the best way to get around. If operating in a group, you can save money by taking a taxi. They're cheap.

Student discounts

Large reduction on entrance to museums, galleries and archaeological sites; also fare reductions on inter-island ferries. For information contact ISYTS at the address shown below.

Addresses

Main post office (for poste restante) at 100 Eolou Street, Athens.
American Express at 31 Panepistimions, Athens (tel: 3234 78 14).
ISYTS (for students) at 11 Nikis Street (2nd floor), Athens 10557 (tel: 322 12 67 and 323 37 67).
National Tourist Information Office at 2 Karageorgi Street, Athens and at Syntagma Square, Athens (tel: 322 25 45).
US Embassy at 91 Vasilissis Sophias Boulevard, Athens (tel: 72 12 951).
British Embassy at 1 Ploutarchou, Athens 10675 (tel: 72 36 211).

Hitchers' Tips and Comments . . .

In Thessaloniki the gardens on the waterfront are good for kipping, but watch your gear. M. PICKERSGILL, SOUTH AFRICA

The rundown on Greece doesn't cover the route Thessalonika–Istanbul. Hitchers hitting this trail should stop off at Kavala, it's a beautiful place, the sort worth a promise for a return trip one day.

Athens train station is OK to bed down for a night or two, cops wake you about 7 a.m., but no pressure to move on. Dunno what it's like from Piraeus to the Greek Islands but from Volos to the three eastern islands (Skopelos, Skiathos and Skyros) make sure you take the *same* boat back as you went on. The situation is that they promote one boat company out to the islands, and once there another company covers the advert boards for the run back. Those that aren't informed (and deciphering a Greek boat ticket is like deciphering a Greek anything else) get it all explained on the way back, stating that they've got to pay again, with no refund on the first ticket. I noticed a lot of travellers were getting caught out this way – me included! MARCEL THOMAS, HORNDEAN, ENGLAND

Loads of cheap places to eat and sleep in the Plaka district of Athens, at the base of the Acropolis.

RICHARD WALFORD, READING, ENGLAND

Athens still no good for dossing out. Particularly, forget National Park. Some real nasties hanging around there.

Lots of half-completed villas on Greek and Italian coastlines. They provide ideal cover and ideal surroundings for a quiet night's kip.

DAVE P., LEEDS, ENGLAND

When kipping in half-finished houses or buildings, remember that many of the bigger projects have a nightwatchman who may have a dog, and that construction workers are on the job at 7 or 8 a.m. So (unless you have permission to be where you are) that means no fires, and an early morning start. K.W.

Athens flea-market great for selling unwanted objects or clothing.

PATRICK HINE, OXFORD, ENGLAND

If you're camping out in Greece, consider buying the green mosquito coils which burn slowly during the night and suffocate the wretched creatures. MICHAEL PICKER, SHEFFIELD, ENGLAND

I hear the Greek police are clamping down on people sleeping on the beaches. RALPH HUNT, CHESHUNT, ENGLAND

I've heard that Greek authorities now demand an address in Greece before they'll let you in. The way around it is to get a hotel or campsite address out of a guide book and stick that down on the immigration form. Then forget all about it.

JOHN PILKINGTON, BRISTOL, UK

In Crete, don't try the Samaria Gorge walk during winter because some parts are flooded and impassable and *very* dangerous! El Greco freaks will want to visit the tiny village of Fodele (a couple of kilometres inland along the Iraklion to Rethymnon route), where the painter is said to have been born. Booze and cigarettes much cheaper at duty-free counter of Iraklion airport. Great pleasure for me in Crete was absolute honesty of the Cretans. They might try and take you for a few extra drachmas when you're buying souvenirs (that's biz, after all), but you could leave your rucksack in the main street of a village and return two hours later and it'd still be there. (But that doesn't mean some *tourist* wouldn't rip it off!)

'JOHNNY THE WONK', LIVERPOOL, UK

Plaka area in Athens pretty touristy, but you can still find places which are cheap even by Greek standards. Nikis Street is a good bet for accommodation and also for travel bargains.

Check the ISYTS, notice-boards in hostels and travel agencies for special offers. PAUL, LONDON, UK

Try Elena's Guest House at 14 Apollonos Street, Athens. Clean, cheap, and friendly management. SYLVIA SMITAS, MISSISSAUGA, CANADA

Dossing in Athens really good. Try sleeping just outside the Agora (Plaka district: just follow the signs to the Acropolis). If you want total safety, climb the fence and sleep inside.

TONY MILLER, NEWCASTLE-UPON-TYNE, ENGLAND

If your budget is tight, avoid Syntagma Square in Athens. Drink prices can be double what you'll pay elsewhere. Also, girl hitchers should note that the square is happy hunting ground of the *kamaki* (fishermen), the nickname for men out after tourist girls.

CLAIRE BETTINGTON AND SUSAN COOPER, LEDBURY, UK

Dasia and Barbati beaches on the north of Corfu are ideal for sleeping out as they are right off the roadways and you don't get disturbed by anybody. JANET PAWLTER, CHELMSFORD, UK

On the backroads of Greece, most of my rides came from tractors. Don't be proud! It's a great way of viewing the countryside, and you'll get there eventually. On Crete, a nice place to rest up is Matala. There are lots of caves in the surrounding hills where you can crash out free. But go over the hill to the south of the village because the caves by the village beach are periodically raided by the cops.

ALAN THATCHER, NEW ZEALAND

Cheap place to stay in Athens is: Hotel Larissiakon, corner of Philadelphia and Liosion Streets.

K. M. FITCHET, JOHANNESBURG, SOUTH AFRICA

Try to get a coach back to London from Athens, rather than from Istanbul, thus avoiding a change at Thessaloniki, where we had to wait three days for a bus. MARK SHEPHERD, BAILRIGG, LANCS, UK

The former official youth hostel (500 metres from Fira on the right) on Santorini has lost its official recognition, but in spite of this it is still a lot better and a bit cheaper than the former unofficial one (300 metres on the left), which is now the official hostel. Membership card is not needed, no curfew, good meals, cheap bar and if you don't want to go out in the evening you can watch movies on video.

ROBERT A. H. PRINS, IPSWICH, ENGLAND

When taking a taxi to the airport make sure that the meter is on. Don't chat with the driver 'cos he'll take his time AND your money.

CHRIS 'DOC STRANGE' TAYLOR

8 · SCANDINAVIA, FINLAND, AND ICELAND

For the hitcher from Australia or North America, the big wastelands of Norway and Sweden will spur a memory of the endless, brooding countryside typical of their homelands. Think of Nevada or the Nullarbor and take away the heat but keep the distance. The sort of distance where you can drive all night and by dusk of the next day be only halfway to where you're heading. The scenery is different, vastly so, but the distances hold the same mood because Norway and Sweden are big lands. Malmö to Kiruna, for instance, is about 2,000 km.

The physical beauty of Norway, Sweden, and Finland is legendary (Denmark is flat, not very interesting visually) and the beauty of the female inhabitants of the four countries has entered the spectrum of legend. It's all true. The fjords and mountains and tundra plains are exciting. The women are unbelievable.

But apart from such physical aspects, Scandinavia is exciting sociologically. It is in these countries that the finer ideas of socialism have been put into practice. Poverty is practically unknown, education is an experimental science, medicine is available to all, prison reform is a reality, the arts are encouraged by the governments, and the housing problem – in places like Oslo – is treated as a problem. Taxation, of course, pays for all this and it's high, but the money seems to be put to fair use.

Scandinavia seems to have reached the level of balanced affluence craved by the rest of the world. Its citizens nevertheless are the first to point out the many failings of their governments. They gripe and groan until you nearly believe they are getting a bad deal. Well, a bad deal is a relative thing, I suppose, and perhaps the Scandinavians aren't getting all that they should. But you only need to look around some place like Helsinki's Tapiola Garden City or a couple of Denmark's experimental schools or consider that neutral Sweden hasn't been involved in a war since 1814 to know that whatever the failings of the governments, their achievements are not only many, but bright.

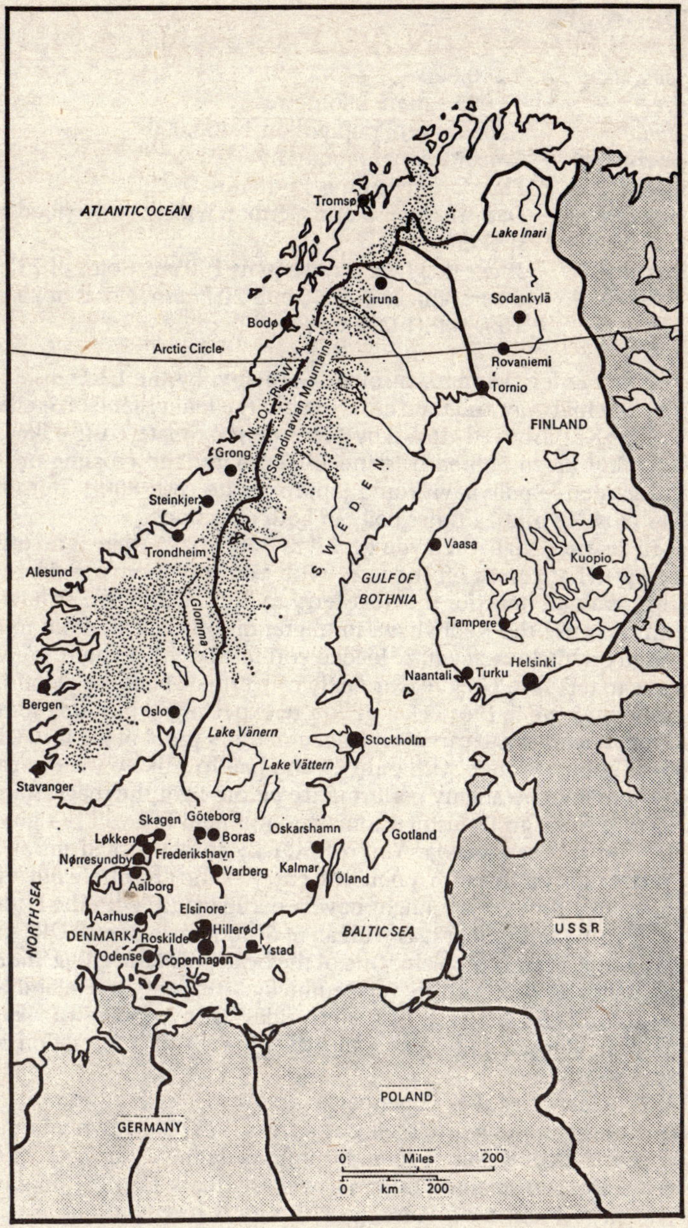
ATLANTIC OCEAN
Tromsø
Lake Inari
Kiruna
Sodankylä
Bodø
Arctic Circle
Rovaniemi
Tornio
NORWAY
Scandinavian Mountains
FINLAND
Grong
SWEDEN
Steinkjer
Trondheim
Vaasa
Alesund
Kuopio
GULF OF BOTHNIA
Glomma
Tampere
Helsinki
Naantali
Turku
Bergen
Oslo
Lake Vänern
Stockholm
Lake Vättern
Stavanger
Skagen
Göteborg
Løkken
Boras
Oskarshamn
Gotland
Frederikshavn
Nørresundby
Varberg
Kalmar
Öland
Aalborg
NORTH SEA
Aarhus
Elsinore
Hillerød
DENMARK
Roskilde
BALTIC SEA
USSR
Odense
Ystad
Copenhagen
POLAND
GERMANY
0 Miles 200
0 km 200

Denmark

population	5,200,000
size	43,093 square kilometres
capital	Copenhagen, population 1,400,000
government	Constitutional monarchy
religion	The state religion is Lutheran
language	Danish: English and German widely understood and spoken
currency	*Krone* (kr) One *krone* equals 100 *øre*. Coins of 25 and 50 *øre*, and of 1, 5, 10 and 20 *kroner*. Notes of 20, 50, 100, 500, 1,000 *kroner*

You can enter Denmark through Germany, by the E3 Flensburg–Kolding highway and then cross over to the main island of Sjælland by the Knudshoved–Halsskov ferry (approximate cost: 45kr), or by going up to Fehmarn Island in Germany and crossing on the Puttgarden–Rødbyhavn route (approximate cost: 80kr). Both ferries cross 18 and 14 times daily in both directions.

Be warned that when you get off at Rødbyhavn there is no traffic except what comes off the ferry with you. If you miss a ride, you must wait an hour for the next ferry to dock. Often you *do* have to wait because the Rødbyhavn immigration officials are notoriously rough on hitchers. If you're loaded you're all right, if you're not you have to talk fast. They're extremely concerned about the amount of cash you have in the pocket. If you're expecting to pick up funds in Copenhagen, try to carry some documentary proof of the fact. Once I was going through with only £5 and had to strike up with nearly an hour-long Academy performance before I got the magic stamp.

Once through Danish customs and immigration you're right for the rest of Scandinavia. You're unlucky to get picked up at the Norwegian or Swedish points of entry – they're often not even manned – though you might have a performance with the Finns.

Hitching in Denmark, as with all of Scandinavia, seems OK. After two visits, I can't complain. One of the beauties of travelling in these countries is that you're very unlucky – except in Finland – if you don't get at least half your rides with people who speak English. Consequently you can pick up a lot of information in a very short time.

Principal cities after Copenhagen are Århus, Aalborg and Odense. One of the things worth seeing at **Århus** is its 'Old Town' museum, which is a collection of some 60 houses dating as far back as 400 years and transplanted from all over Denmark into the one area. The city's Prehistoric Museum is the most recent resting place of the Grauballe man. He lay in a bog for 1,600 years and remains in an excellent state of preservation.

Aalborg, the chief city of North Jutland, is a gourmet's paradise. This city of 155,000 boasts something like 170 restaurants. It's worth picking one for a splurge meal! For those interested in Vikings, the remains of a Viking village and a 682-grave cemetery can be seen at **Nørresundby** just outside Aalborg. The site of the village is known as **Lindholm Høje**. If you're American and passing through Aalborg on 4 July, head on out to Rebild National Park, 30 km south of the city. Each year since 1912 they have held Independence Day celebrations there.

Although primarily visited by tourists to see the monuments and museums connected with Hans Christian Andersen (1805–75), **Odense** has plenty more to offer. It's one of the oldest towns in Denmark. St Canute's Cathedral – King Canute was killed in Odense 900 years ago – is one of the most important Gothic buildings in the country. The Funen Village, 2 km from the centre of town, is a museum of peasant culture and an operating farm. At **Ladby**, 20 km north-east of Odense, you can descend into an underground mound and see a 10th-century Viking ship. The 72-foot ship was the coffin of a Viking chief who was buried with his weapons and jewellery, four hunting-dogs, and eleven horses.

Hillerød, some 40 km north of Copenhagen, is famous for its Frederiksborg Castle. Built originally between 1602–20 in Dutch Renaissance style, much of it was destroyed by fire in 1859. A fair lump of the money used for its restoration came from J. C. Jacobsen, the famous Carlsberg brewer.

Castle fiends will also want to see Kronborg Castle at **Helsingør,** 30 km north-east of Hillerød. It is the setting of Shakespeare's *Hamlet.* Unfortunately, there is a confusion of dates. Hamlet was a 12th-century gentleman and Kronborg is a 16th-century castle. Nevertheless, worth seeing, especially as the castle contains the Danish Museum of Trade and Shipping.

About 10 km west of **Roskilde**, at **Lejre**, is an Historical Archaeological Experimental Centre which is working on the reconstruction of an Iron Age village – not just the house, but the crafts and farming techniques as well.

Finally, for summer wanderers of both sexes who are yearning for a little company, the beach resorts of North Jutland might provide the answer. Towns like **Skagen, Lønstrup** and **Løkken** (the largest resort) are where the summertime action is: but remember that they're tourist towns and expensive (though beach-sleeping is obviously in) and that they're inundated by suburbia on the loose.

Copenhagen: where to sleep

In Copenhagen's hotels you're looking at paying at least 250kr per person in singles or doubles. Private rooms are a cheaper option. The **Copenhagen Tourist Association** in Kiosk P at the Central Railway Station charge 150kr and upwards for lodgings in a private house, plus a 15kr commission for the service. **USE IT** at Radhusstræde 13 (tel: 33 15 65 18) and **H.A.Y.4U** at Kronprinsengade 10 (tel: 33 33 08 05) find rooms at the same rates, and don't charge a commission. Youth hostels and student accommodations are usually about 90kr, though the YMCA and YWCA hostels are a good bit cheaper.

Hostelling International hostels:
'Amager', Vejlandsallé 200 (tel: 32 52 29 08).
'Bellahøj', Herbergvejen 8 (tel: 31 28 97 15).

Other hostels/student accommodation:
City Public Hostel, Absalonsgade 8 (in the Vesterbro Ungdomsård) (tel: 31 31 20 70).
KFUK (YMCA) Interpoint, Store Kannikestræde 19 (tel: 33 11 30 31). July–mid Aug.
KFUM (YWCA) Vesterbros, Valdemarsgade 15 (tel: 31 31 15 74). Mid July–mid Aug.
Sleep-In, Per Hendrik Lings Allé 6 (tel: 31 26 50 59). July–Aug.

Cheaper hotels:
Søfolkenes Mindehotel, Peder Skramsgade 19 (tel: 33 13 48 82).
Skt. Jørgen, Julius Thomsengade 22 (tel: 35 37 15 11).
Amager, Amagerbrogade 29 (tel: 31 54 40 08/31 54 50 09).
Hebron, Helgolandsgade 4 (tel: 31 31 69 06).
Jørgensen, Romersgade 11 (tel: 33 13 81 86).

At about 50kr per person (tent included) camping is the best deal in Copenhagen. Try:

Strandmølle, Strandmølleveg 2 (tel: 42 80 38 83).
Absalon, Kordalsvej 132 (tel: 31 41 06 00).
Bellahøj, Hvidkildevej (tel: 31 10 11 50). June–Aug.

Failing all that, head out to Langelinie and sack out on the grass. Find a quiet spot and play it cool. Needless to say, sleeping in Langelinie is absolutely and completely forbidden.

For all sorts of info about Copenhagen contact **USE IT** at

Radhusstræde 13 (tel: 33 15 65 18). Ask for the excellent *Playtime* magazine, which is free and contains a useful city map plus pages of facts about accommodation, food, entertainments, etc. in the capital. At the USE IT office you can check the board for offers and messages, get free use of a locker (for a returnable deposit) and even arrange a ride. Use It also allows you to use their address as a poste restante address.

Copenhagen: where to eat

For breakfast try Danish pastry; for snacks *smørrebrød* (the tasty open sandwiches) or *pølser* (the Danish hotdogs sold at street corners). *Pølser* can save your life here. All but the one-potato-more-than-a-pig types amongst us can't put more than four away, which means you can stuff yourself for about 75kr. Sit-down meals anywhere in Scandinavia can be a frightening proposition, and you'll only appreciate Danish prices if you've arrived from points north. Hopefully you have, because the 50–70kr meals at the places below are as good as things get.

Universitetskafeen, Fiolstræde 2.
Alexander's Original Pizza House, Lille Kannikestræde 5. All-you-can-eat pizza and salad.
Riz Raz, Kompagnistræde 20. Vegetarian Mediterranean buffet.
Den Gronne Kælder, Klarehoderne 10. Vegetarian restaurant.
Vista Self-Service Restaurant, Vesterbrogade 40 (upstairs).
Cafe Sorgenfri, Brolæggerstræde 8.

In high-priced Scandinavia remember that Chinese restaurants are amongst the best deals you can find – rice is cheap and fills you up quickly.

Copenhagen: what to see and do

TIVOLI GARDENS The fun-park to end all fun-parks. Entrance fee around 35kr. Open from 1 May–13 Sept. Plenty of opportunity to meet people.

BREWERIES The two great Danish breweries, **Carlsberg** at Ny Carlsbergvej 140 and **Tuborg** at Strandvejen 54, offer a tour of their premises and plenty of free beer at the end of the walkabout. Visit

Carlsberg at 9 a.m., 11 a.m. or 2.30 p.m. weekdays, and Tuborg between 8.30 a.m. and 2.30 p.m. weekdays.

LIBERTY MUSEUM OF DENMARK (also called the Danish Resistance Museum). Fascinating collection of objects used by the Danes in their underground fight against the German occupation forces during the Second World War. On Esplanaden. No admission fee.

LANGELINIE A pleasant walk – if you like that sort of thing – along the favourite promenade in Copenhagen. High spot for those over forty is the famous LITTLE MERMAID sitting on her rock. Those under forty – like Copenhagen students – have a bad habit of painting her a variety of colours and, once, even knocked her head off. But she's OK. Good sleeping-out area.

FIOLSTRÆDE This, apart from being a pleasant street, is where the university is. Good place to meet up with students or get information about whatever is worrying you.

THE GLYPTOTEKET MUSEUM This houses the national art collection. Free on Sundays and Wednesdays. Some good works by Degas, Renoir, Manet, and Cézanne, and also Rodin's *The Citizens of Calais*. The museum was founded last century by Carl Jacobsen who also founded the Carlsberg breweries. At Dantes Plads.

THE ROUND TOWER at Købmagergade. Costs to get in but it gives you a good view of Copenhagen from the top. There are no steps, but a spiral ramp all the way up. Legend tells that Peter the Giant galloped up to the top on his horse followed by his queen in a carriage.

CIRCUS BENNEWEIS World-famous circus and well worth seeing. Bit of a hit to get in. Cheapest seat over 45kr. Open 1 April to end of October.

BAKKEN AMUSEMENT PARK Not as flamboyant as Tivoli, but free admission and plenty of chance to meet the opposite sex. Open April through August. Twenty-minute train ride from Central Station to Klampenborg Station, so probably cheaper to go to Tivoli anyway.

BELLEVUE A beach between Copenhagen and Helsingør. It's also known as *Fluepapiret* which means 'fly-paper', meaning it has a great attraction to bikini'd blondes which in turn means it's an attraction to bearded Danes. Draw your own conclusions – and the best of luck.

LOUISIANA This is Denmark's museum of contemporary art. It's on the coast at Humlebæk, about 40 km out of Copenhagen and beyond Bellevue. Worth a trip for the art freaks and architecture students.

CINEMA Movies in Copenhagen are usually shown in the original language with Danish subtitles. All the latest American and British movies are showing. Prices reasonable. Much cheaper in the suburbs, of course.

NYHAVN This seamen's quarter is worth a couple of hours one night. Maybe they'll hit your pocket if you step inside for a drink (you can usually spot the clip-joints), but it's a trip just digging the characters – tourists included – in the streets.

Transport in Copenhagen

Best way of getting around Copenhagen is by bus or train. Tickets are interchangeable and can be used on as many buses and/or trains as you like within a set time and zone. Cheapest way to buy rides in the central area is to invest in a 10-ride ticket for around 90kr. Single-ride tickets start at 10kr, with prices rising the further you travel. If you're broke and want to go somewhere, stand at the appropriate bus or train stop and watch people getting off. If they throw away their ticket, grab it. It may be valid for a few minutes more, in which case you can jump aboard for free. Conversely if you're finished with a ticket which has time left on it, pass it to any waiting types who look like they could use it.

Another possibility is the **Copenhagen Card**, which provides free and unlimited travel by bus and train throughout the metropolitan region, including North Zealand. The card also offers free admission to a wide range of sights, attractions and museums as well as 50% discount on crossings to Sweden.

Cycling is a great way to see Copenhagen. To rent a bike try the **DSB Cykelcenter** at Reventlowsgade 11 (tel: 33 14 07 17) or the slightly cheaper **Dan Wheel** at Colbjørnsengade 3 (tel: 31 21 22 27). Be ready to leave a hefty deposit for your wheels.

Student discounts

Half-price admission to museums and art galleries for card-holders. Also possible to buy certain goods on discount. Check with the **Danish International Student Committee** at the address shown below.

Addresses

Main post office (for poste restante) at Vesterbro, Tietgensgade 37, DK-1500 Copenhagen.
American Express at Amagertorv 18, DK-1146, Copenhagen K (tel: 33 12 23 01).
Danish International Student Committee at Skindergade 28, DK-1159 Copenhagen K (tel: 33 11 00 44).
Danish Tourist Board at H. C. Andersens Boulevard 22A, DK-1553 Copenhagen V (tel: 33 11 13 25).
US Embassy at Dag Hammarskjöldsallé 24, DK-2100 Copenhagen Ø (tel: 31 42 31 44).
British Embassy at Kastelsvej 36–40, DK-2100 Copenhagen Ø (tel: 31 26 46 00).

Hitchers' Tips and Comments. . .

Many apartment houses in Scandinavian countries have no flats on the garret, or attic, floor. Stairs continue up under the roof. Usually there's no door. Such places offer free, dry, warm places to sleep. Great in winter weather. Some German apartments are built the same. KLAUS KRUGER, GERMANY

Plain-clothes police search and frisk suspicious types on trains heading into Denmark. DUNCAN SMITH, BOURNEMOUTH, ENGLAND

Head for the YMCA in Helsingør. They do a fantastic breakfast.
CRAIG SEATON, WORKSOP, NOTTS, UK

Many of the most beautiful places are only accessible by ferry, the ferries are fairly expensive for a hiker, but don't despair. Catch a lorry on the waiting area. They can carry a free passenger on each trip.

Almost all ferries have facilities for taking a bath, free! It is not exactly permitted, but nobody will stop you. No soap or towel is provided. HANNE MARK, DENMARK

If you want to tour the Tuborg brewery be sure to go on the last tour, then at the end choose an emptyish table. All the beer on the table is there to be drunk, so this way you get more. Go for the 'Gold Label' beer – it's better stuff than the 'Green Label'.
JOHN MEHERS, LEEDS, ENGLAND

When going from Copenhagen up to Sweden take the train to Helsingør and get the ferry from there. You'll save hours, and the train only costs around 30kr. Going south towards Berlin it takes hours

longer hitching than the way I do it. Go on a shopping daytrip to Rostock. It costs about 12kr, and will get you on the Gedser–Rostock ferry, on which you're bound to get a hitch all the way to Berlin.

LARS PETER SVANE, COPENHAGEN, DENMARK

Sweden

population	8,590,600
size	449,964 square kilometres
capital	Stockholm, population 1,600,000
government	Constitutional monarchy
religion	Lutheran
language	Swedish; English widely understood and spoken; some German and French
currency	*Krona* (Skr) One *krona* equals 100 *öMDRV.* Coins of 50 *öre*, and 1, 5 *kronor*. Notes of 10, 20, 50, 100, 500, 1,000, 10,000 *kronor*

Presuming that you'll be crossing into Sweden from Denmark you have several ferry crossings to choose from. Among them:

Dragör to Limhamn, costing about 25 Danish kronor.
Copenhagen to Malmö, by hydrofoil costing about 30 Danish kronor.
Helsingør to Hälsingborg, costing about 22 Danish kronor.

If you're entering Sweden from Norway, the two fastest routes are the E18 if you're heading for Stockholm, or the E6 if you're going to Göteborg and the south for a crossing into Denmark.

Göteborg, along with Kiruna, Visby, Kalmar and Ystad (and Stockholm, of course) can give you a pretty fair picture of Sweden. But remember that Sweden is a summertime place if you want to do it on the cheap. With the high cost of hotels in Scandinavia, sleeping out when you're on the road is just about mandatory unless you're loaded, and you can't sleep out in the Scandinavian winter! The Swedish law, *Allemans Rätt*, or Everyman's Right, allows you to camp out anywhere for one night without the landowner's permission, except public parks (see introduction to this chapter) or in someone's front garden, as long as you don't cross ploughed fields, leave rubbish lying about, or light fires where they can be dangerous.

Göteborg is a city of 693,000. Things worth seeing include the Guldhedens Vattentorn, the 400-foot water tower, the Röhss

Museum of Arts and Crafts which will give you a rundown on the best of Swedish design, the Maritime Museum, the Archaeological Museum (featuring finds back to 2000 BC), and the Military Museum in Kronan Fortress. The best museum in this city of museums, though, is the Göteborg Art Gallery which features dozens of good pictures by Pissarro, Rousseau, Matisse, Picasso, Van Gogh, and Braque. Also sculptures by such greats as Rodin and Moore, and a superb representative collection of Scandinavian painters. For stage buffs there is even a Theatre Museum – something you don't find in many cities.

At **Borås**, 70 km east of Göteborg on Route 40, is the Freedom Zoo in Borås Park, something really worth seeing if you're one of those people who likes looking at animals but hates the conventional method of caging them. These beasts – elephants, giraffes, rhinos, and all the rest – roam in wide open spaces.

If you're heading south to Ystad, you might want to drop into **Varberg**, 80 km from Göteborg, where in the Varberg fortress you can see the remains of Bocksten Man, another gentleman, this time medieval, who was recently hauled from a bog. He was preserved so well that his clothing is claimed as the only complete set of medieval clothes in existence.

Ystad, right on the southern tip of Sweden, in the province of Skåne, is interesting because of its Middle Ages aspect. Ancient winding streets, half-timbered houses, and old churches dot the town, while in the surrounding countryside you find castles, manor houses, and also a medieval monastery.

Visby, on the **Island of Gotland**, is another leftover from the old Sweden. Unfortunately, it costs a packet to get there. The trip from Oskarshamn or Nynäshamn (about four hours) costs 190kr at weekends, 150kr during the week (student ID can knock about one-third off these prices). Known as the City of Ruins and Roses, Visby, population 16,000, was once an extremely important seaport, but after being captured in the 1300s it drifted out of history and towards oblivion. It remains today the only walled city in northern Europe. To see? Everything. Just walk around – the Maiden's Tower, where a girl was entombed alive for helping an enemy king, Gallow Hill, the ancient Powder Tower. Catch 22: you'll get your money's worth if you've got some money.

Kalmar, 80 km south of Oskarshamn and on the E66 east coast road up to Stockholm, is a worthwhile place. A city of 52,000, it is the sister city of Wilmington, Delaware. This international handshake salutes the first Swedish emigrants to America who came from Kalmar and went to Wilmington in the 1600s. The main sight is Kalmar Castle and its museum.

If you can't afford the Gotland Island trip, you may like to compensate with a trip to **Öland Island**, which is a fantastic area for amateur archaeologists interested in the Iron Age. A fair percentage of the Swedes in America, incidentally, must have Ölander ancestors, because about 25% of the island population emigrated. You cross to the island via Europe's longest bridge – nearly 6 km long.

Kalmar is in the middle of an area containing about twenty of Sweden's famed glass factories. For a free visit to the best-known glass factory in the world, visit **Orrefors**, which is easy to hitch to, being 45 km west of Kalmar on Highway 31. The factory is open all year and conducted tours are available Monday to Friday from 8 a.m. to 3 p.m.

Kiruna, in northern Lapland, is the big trip. It is 1350 km north of Stockholm and 150 km into the Arctic Circle. From Stockholm you have a choice of routes: the east coast E4 up to Luleå and then a swing inland on Highway 97, connecting with the 98 outside Gällivare; or the E4 up to Sundsvall and a swing west along the E75 to Östersund, followed by a straight northern route to Kiruna along road numbers 88, 343, 97 and 98. If you're working against a time limit, then you're better off on the eastern sea-road to Luleå. The inland route takes you through a cross-section of Swedish geography – really great country – but the population is spread thin and so are the cars. Although it hosts only 31,000 citizens, area-wise Kiruna is the world's largest city, containing within its distended limits an expanse of plains, lakes, Lapp camps, 30,000 reindeer, and two mountains of iron totalling some two billion tons of ore.

The town itself is not wildly interesting, but it's a good stopping place after a long haul from Stockholm, and it's the ideal place to watch the midnight sun between 31 May and 14 July. For those six weeks there is continual daylight and you can enjoy the unique experience of watching the sun beginning to rise again without first sliding below the horizon. Mosquitoes, incidentally, are really bad in mid-July.

- **Canoeing** If you're in the forest areas of Dalsland and Värmland (north of Göteborg), you might want to try a two-or three-day canoe trip. Check at lakeside towns. At **Dals Langed**, just off Highway 172, a canoe costs about 130Skr a day. A rich hitcher's sport, but great fun!

- **Prospecting** For semi-precious crystals and stones and alluvial gold, the Kopparberg district of Örebro country is the place (Örebro is 200 km west of Stockholm). Check for precise details from the tourist office in Stockholm or Örebro. I've never done it myself, but have heard of people making the odd pound. Don't count on it, though!

Stockholm: where to sleep

Hotelcentrallen at the Central Railway Station have an efficient accommodation service finding hostel beds for 12kr, hotel beds for 25kr. Read on before rushing to them! The good news is that the Swedes buck the European trend and actually drop hotel prices in the summer. The bad news is that this brings the cheaper doubles down to about 250kr per person. Once again in Scandinavia it's the hostels and dormitories which save the day. Well, not really – at about 100–110kr per head they're still exorbitantly expensive, but if you've got this far the shock of Scandinavian prices should be wearing off a bit. Unless there are a few of you don't think escaping to the campsite will save you lots of *kronor*. The Swedes charge a large fee per tent (any tent – from a one-person tent to a family-sized monster), and not a lot per person. Count on paying about 80kr just to put your tent up in one of the sites around Stockholm.

Hostelling International hostels:

'af Chapman', Skeppsholmen (tel: 679 50 15). Stockholm's famous floating youth hostel, the 'af Chapman' being a fully rigged late-19th-century sailing ship.
Zinken, Zinkensväg 20 (tel: 658 29 00).
Vandrarhem, Skeppsholmen Västra Brobänken (tel: 679 50 17).

Other hostels/student accommodation:

Columbus Hotell-Vandrarhem, Tjärhovsgatan 11 (tel: 644 17 17).
Brygghuset, Norrtullsgatan 12N (tel: 312 424).
Sleep Inn, Dobelnsgatan 56 (tel: 612 31 18).
Gustaf af Klint, Stadsgårdskajen 153 (tel: 640 40 77). In an old navy ship.

Camping:

Bredäng (tel: 977 071). T-bana: Bredäng (line 13 or 15).
Ångby (tel: 370 420). T-bana: Ångbyplan (line 17 or 18).

For sleeping rough, try around Kaknäs Tower (take Bus 69). Sleeping out should present no problems – as long as it's warm enough

– because just about all of the many islands upon which Stockholm is built are bordered with trees and parks.

Stockholm: where to eat

Be warned. . . eat at student restaurants, department store cafeterias (such as Domus), at self-service joints, or hit restaurants at lunchtime when most do a *Dagens rätt* (fixed three-course menu) Mon.–Fri. That way you might emerge with some change (some, but not a lot) out of 55kr. Obviously anywhere doing a reasonably cheap all-you-can-eat buffet breakfast/lunch should be investigated with a view to stuffing yourself, and surreptitiously putting together a doggy bag for later. That apart it's buy at the supermarket time. Fruit isn't too bad a buy – about UK prices.

Stockholm: what to see and do

GRÖNA LUND'S TIVOLI on Djurgården. Entrance charge. Super amusement park, not as pretty as the Copenhagen Tivoli, but OK if you like that sort of thing. Mainly of interest because there are plenty of friendly people of the right age floating around and because on the grounds are two clubs. The **Dance In** is more expensive than the **Dance Out**, but there's a better class of people. All in all, not very exciting, but it might amuse a sad hour. Open April through September.

THE VASA on Djurgården. This warship which sank moments after being launched in 1628, was rediscovered in 1956 and lifted from the seabed in 1961. The story of the recovery is told in a film shown at the museum. One of the best examples in the world of an ancient sailing vessel. Admission charge.

SKANSEN Also at Djurgården. Open all year round. An open-air museum with examples of farms, town sections, etc., from all over Sweden, and demonstrations of arts and crafts. Mostly 18th century. Entrance fee.

THE NATIONAL MUSEUM OF ART on Södra Blasieholmshamnen. Fairly good collection. Admission charge.

MUSEUM OF MODERN ART on Skeppsholmen. Reasonable collection

of modern European masters and good collections of Swedish stuff. Closed Mondays. Entrance charge.

MILLESGARDEN on the island of Lidingö. Home and works of the famous sculptor Carl Milles. Closed during winter season. Admission charge.

SAUNA BATHS Saunas are usually fairly expensive.

CLUBS Some clubs and discotheques require membership but try the **Glädjehuset**, Kungsgatan 55. For jazz try **Fashing** at the corner of Kungsgatan and Vasagatan. Also try the pubs. The **Engelen** at Kornhamnstorg 59B is in the old town and OK.

BLUE MOVIES If you want to see one, go to the street called Klara Norra Kyrkog. There are quite a few porn shops and blue cinemas there. (Make sure you don't cop an American-made show. The product isn't up to standard.)

Transport in Stockholm

The Stockholm Card (*Stockholmskortet*) can be a good deal depending upon what you have in mind sightseeing-wise. The card allows visitors to wander around on the bus, Underground (*T-bana*) and local trains for up to three days, and also includes a bus tour of the city and free entrance to the TV tower, the Skansen, the Gröna Lund amusement park, and almost all of the city's museums. The Stockholm Card costs 160kr for each 24-hour period. Available at the Tourist Centre, or from *Pressbyro* kiosks.

Addresses

Main post office (for poste restante) at Vasagatan 28–34, Stockholm.
American Express at Birger Jarlsgatan 1, Stockholm (tel: 6795200).
Sveriges Forenade Studentkarer (Student Travel Department) at Kungsgatan 4, Stockholm (tel: 34 01 80).
US Embassy at Strandvägen 101, Stockholm (tel: 789 53 00).
British Embassy at Skarpögatan 6, Stockholm (tel: 6 67 01 40).
Swedish Travel Centre at Stureplan 8, Stockholm (tel: 6117430).

Hitchers' Tips and Comments. . .

The phenomenal cost of travelling in the Nordic countries is no secret. But, while in Stockholm, I discovered that by trying to pay for a ticket with a 100Skr note, explaining in my best English that it was all I had, the result was a free ride every time. For two weeks I rode the Tunnelbana saving the price of a cup of coffee with every ride. BRUCE ALAN WHITHAM, NEWCASTLE, CANADA

In some large shops in Sweden the food halls (often in the basement) have free left luggage lockers. (You have to pay a deposit for the key.) Useful if you want to ditch your pack for a couple of hours. KEVIN BILKE, SOUTHAMPTON, UK

To eat cheap in Sweden, note that most restaurants do a daily special Monday through Friday, usually served between midday and 2 p.m. The special includes a main dish, often with as much side salad as you can eat, a glass of milk, beer or mineral water and sometimes coffee as well. The dish and price are advertised outside restaurants as Dagens Rätt (Today's Dish).

If you're a student, try the Student Reception Service in university towns. You'll get information about all sorts of things, plus the bars are much cheaper (though expensive by British standards). Sweden has universities in Lund, Linköping, Göteborg, Stockholm, Karlstad, Uppsala and Umea.

Finally, when getting off the ferry in Hälsingborg, go to the main truck depot just 500 metres from the ferry station and try for a ride from the truck drivers. The depot is called Asg-Centralen.

MATS RÖNNE, LONDON, UK

If you're stuck in Stockholm without a ticket home, try busking on the main street. When the police ask what you're up to just say you're broke. I did and got a night in jail, food and a free flight back to London. PAUL DOWRICK, ANDOVER, ENGLAND

More often in these circumstances the local police pass you over to the British Consul who, if he loans you funds to get home, also arranges for your passport to be confiscated until the loan has been repaid. Avoid desperate moves – like the one suggested by Paul – except as an absolute last resort. K.W.

STOCKHOLM: if you want to catch up on the news in Stockholm you can read all sorts of foreign newspapers for free in the library in the Culture House of Sergelstorg Square.

ALAN BARLOW, CHEADLE, UK

Norway

population	4,249,800
size	323,877 square kilometres
capital	Oslo, population 465,000
government	Constitutional monarchy
religion	Lutheran
language	Norwegian; English widely understood and spoken; some French and German
currency	*Krone* One *krone* equals 100 *øre*. Coins of 50 *øre*, and 1, 5 and 10 *kroner*. Notes of 50, 100, 500, 1,000 *kroner*

The cheapest way of reaching Norway is through Sweden (see Swedish section for ferry fares from Denmark) and then hitching along the E6 to the Norwegian-Swedish border. If you have more money and/or less time, two other ways of getting there are:

Copenhagen to Oslo ferry. A 16-hour journey, costing from 420 Danish kroner (one way).
Frederikshavn (Jutland) to Larvik ferry. A 6-hour journey, costing about 300 Danish kroner (high season).

Top towns in Norway, after Oslo, are Bergen, Stavanger, and Trondheim. **Stavanger**, some 584 km from Oslo, is Norway's fourth city and one of the best from the point of view of seeing what the old Norway was like. The wooden houses in Old Stavanger and the narrow, winding, cobbled streets are a sight for eyes glazed by the dazzle of metal and plastic. Two sights in one are the cathedral at the marketplace. The market swings every day, except Sunday, until 2 or 3 p.m. The cathedral, a 12th-century structure, is an outstanding example of Middle Ages architecture in Norway. For a cheap sightseeing trip, jump bus Number 8 at St Olavsgarden. It covers most parts of Stavanger. For a good look at the fjords, particularly if you're not heading up further north, try a trip on one of the ferries which sail between Stavanger and Bergen. At 185kr it's not cheap, but you do see some fantastic sights on the six-hour trip. Highly recommended – especially when you consider that hitching between the two is tough. Even so, if you do hitch, it would be a shame not to stop off on the way to see the huge Folgefonn Glacier and Laatefoss Waterfall near the town of **Odda**.

Don't miss **Bergen**'s colourful harbour. It's a pleasure just to walk in the area. Right on the waterfront is the Fish Market – a sight and a smell in itself – while on your right as you face the water is the beautiful street called Bryggen, a row of timbered houses built in 1702 to recreate a slice of medieval Bergen after a fire destroyed much of the city. Also on Bryggen is the Hanseatic Museum which is devoted to life as the German merchants who traded in Bergen centuries ago lived it. The Rasmus Meyer and the Stenersen collections are worth seeing because they contain many of Edvard Munch's works. For a display of a different sort, try the Fishery Museum, which gives a rundown on Norway's most famous industry. All are at the Permanenten on Olav Kyrresgate. For getting around the city, the Tourist Information Office, and most hotels, sell a special tourist ticket which allows unlimited bus and tramcar travel for 48 hours within the city limits. If you can afford it and want to see a great view over this Viking city with its seven hills, you should invest a few kroner and take the funicular up the 1050 feet of Mount Fløien. Along the water-front you'll find dozens of fjord boat trips advertised and costing anywhere from 50 to 250kr. All are good because the scenery around Bergen is spectacular. It's just a matter of figuring if you want to pay out – and if so, how much. Not far from Bergen is **Troldhaugen** (Troll's Hill) which was the home of Edvard Grieg.

If you're heading further north, **Alesund** is Norway's greatest fishing town and its large fleet, which operates from Baffin Bay, heads out after seals as well as smaller fry. There might be the possibility of odd jobs in Alesund.

Trondheim, Norway's second largest city and the principal city of the north, was founded nearly a thousand years ago. A pleasant place with an ancient cathedral and a very interesting Museum of Music History, it has been known as the Royal Town since the days when Norway's monarchs were crowned there. When the Norwegian Royal Family visit Trondheim these days they stay at Siftsgarden which is claimed to be the largest wooden building in Europe.

Near the city is the village of **Grong** which sits on the Namsen River, just one of Norway's 200 salmon-filled streams. Hitching fishermen may be interested in knowing that there are a quarter of a million lakes in Norway, most of which play host to trout. Fishing licences cost money but, if you can figure a way of rigging some light tackle, you should be able to haul a cheap meal out of most stretches of water in the backwoods without much trouble. (Fishing with a licence does not mean that fish bite better.)

Once above Trondheim, you're heading for the Arctic Circle. **Bodø** is the most popular place for viewing the midnight sun (5 June–9 July and *no* sun from 19 Dec.–9 Jan.) and there's plenty of traffic to that point. After Bodø the roads can be lonely and the people scarce. Most of the time you have no proof you're on a civilized planet. Once in Finnmark you're in an area bigger than Denmark but inhabited by only 78,000 people. It's wild and its beautiful and it's lots of other appropriate clichés – but don't find yourself 20 km from the nearest town at night at the wrong time of year. You might catch a cold.

On the way up to the North Cape, **Tromsø** is worth stopping at if only to see its fabulous Arctic church. (The wreck of the German battleship, *Tirpitz,* which was bombed there by the RAF during the Second World War, can no longer be seen.) The Tromsø Museum will give you an idea of how people – particularly the Lapps – have managed to live in the Arctic.

After **Steinkjer**, the road, National Highway 6, is mostly gravel, but as you get further and further north you'll notice more and more tourist facilities because the North Cape is slowly becoming the place to have been. Finally, when you reach **Honningsvaag** (ferry from Käfjord – 25kr), you've made the northernmost village in the world! About 40 km further on is the barren North Cape – the end of Europe – a rocky plateau on a latitude of 70° 10′ 21″ N which rises 1,000 feet straight out of the Arctic Ocean.

Oslo: where to sleep

If the prices in Denmark or Sweden brought a tear to your eye, the bad news is that Norway is reckoned to be the most expensive country in mainland Europe, and that is certainly reflected in accommodation prices. B&B at Oslo's Hostelling International hostels costs 150kr! Local *pensjonater* are often not much more expensive if there are two or more of you, but these are thin on the ground. Check also to see if the overnight price at a *pensjonat* includes breakfast – the buffet breakfast at the hostels at least lets you stuff yourself with grub (eating is another expensive proposition in Norway). **Innkvartering** in the main train station find hotels and private rooms for a 20kr fee. Reckon on paying at least 200kr per person for a double in someone's home. Hotel prices don't bear thinking about!

Hostelling International hostels:
Haraldsheim, Haraldsheimveien 4 (tel: 22 22 29 65/22 15 50 43).
Holtekilen, Micheletsveien 55 (tel: 67 53 38 53).

Other hostels:
KFUM (YMCA), Møllergata 7 (tel: 22 42 10 66). Mattresses on the floor. July–mid Aug.

Pensjonater:
Ellingsen, Holtegata 25 (tel: 22 60 03 59).
Coch, Parkveien 25 (tel: 22 60 48 36).

Camping:
Ekeberg, Ekebergveien 65 (tel: 22 19 85 68). No bargain if you're on your own. 90kr to pitch a tent. No charge per person. June–Aug.

Oslo: where to eat

Norwegians are in the habit of eating only two meals a day. A big breakfast and a big dinner – with maybe a snack somewhere along the line. As with most places in Scandinavia, expect to pay out between 70 and 120kr for a meal.

Christiana Dampkjokken at Torggt. 8.
Expressen Cafeteria at Fred. Olsensgt. 11.
Frogner Baths Cafeteria at Middlethungst. 28.
Glasmagasin, Stortorget. 10.
Vegeta Vertshus, Munkedamsvn 3B.

Oslo: what to see and do

EDVARD MUNCH MUSEUM Open all year. Admission 10kr. At Tøyengate 53. Munch (1863–1944) is considered a leading European contemporary painter. The work is interesting, giving a clue to the psyche of the Northerner. The man had a phenomenal output, creating over 1,000 paintings and 4,000 drawings. The museum exhibits about 300 paintings, plus sketches and some sculpture.

THE VIGELAND SCULPTURES Admission free. At Frogner Park. Gustav Vigeland, another great Norwegian artist, was financed by the city of Oslo to create the 192 pieces of work on display in this park. The work took him thirty years.

NATIONAL THEATRE Behind the theatre used to be a good meeting place for kindred spirits.

AKERSHUS CASTLE Small admission charge. Open April to October. Used to be the strongest castle in Scandinavia. Used as office space by the Germans during the war. See its Resistance and Defence museums in the castle grounds.

KON-TIKI MUSEUM Admission charge. In the Bygdøy peninsula. This houses the balsa raft in which Thor Heyerdahl and his crew sailed 4,300 miles across the Pacific in 1947. Apart from proving his theory that pre-Inca Indians might have travelled the same way to reach Polynesia, Heyerdahl made around a million pounds out of the adventure and had his book, *Kon-Tiki*, translated into more than eighty languages. Also see a copy of the reed boat *Ra II* which Heyerdahl and his multinational crew sailed and drifted 3270 nautical miles across the Atlantic to Barbados in 1970.

THE VIKING SHIPS Admission charge. At Huk Aveny 35 (within walking distance of the *Kon-Tiki*). You can see three Viking ships in fair state of preservation, along with a display of artifacts found with them. One ship is 1100 years old.

HOLMENKOLLEN SKI JUMP The oldest in the world and the site of Olympic competitions. Twenty minutes or so by train. A very interesting Ski Museum (for snow-sport fans) is situated next to the jump tower. Admission charge to the museum and tower.

FRAM MUSEUM This museum, built in the style of an ancient Norwegian boat-house, exhibits the polar exploration ship *Fram*, used by several famous Norwegian explorers. Amundsen started his celebrated South Pole dash in the *Fram* in 1910. The museum is in Bygdøy. You reach it by taking a ferry from Pier 3 or Bus 30 from the National Theatre.

NORWEGIAN FOLK MUSEUM at Museumsveien 10, Bygdøy. (Bus 30 or Pier 3.) Over 150 wooden buildings have been dismantled and shifted from their original sites and taken to Bygdøy where they have been re-erected to form a nearly complete collection of Norwegian rural architecture. All are complete with their original furnishings. All that – and more – is in the outdoor section of the museum. Indoors you'll find over 100,000 exhibits including playwright Henrik Ibsen's study and a section on the culture of Lapland.

TOWN HALL Town halls aren't usually recommended in this book. But have a look at this one! It's as much a gallery of contemporary Norwegian art as a red-tape machine.

Transport in Oslo
The tram and bus system in the city charges about 16kr a ride. A Dagskort allows unlimited travel for a day and costs 40kr. There is also a 7-day ticket which costs 140kr.

Student discounts
For details contact the **Universities Travel Bureau**, Universitetssentret, Blindern, Oslo 3 (tel: 45 50 55).

Addresses

Main post office (for poste restante) at Dronningensgate 15, Oslo. Entrance from Prinsensgt.
American Express at Winge Reisebureau at Karl Johansgt 33, Oslo (tel: 42 91 50).
Studentenes Reisekontor at Universitetssentret, Blindern, Oslo 3 (tel: 45 50 55).
Studentenes Reisekontor at Parkveien 1, Bergen (tel: 33 191).
Tourist Information Centre at City Hall (entrance from the port) 0037, Oslo 1 (tel: 33 43 86).
US Embassy at Drammensveien 18, Oslo (tel: 44 85 50).
British Embassy at Thomas Heftyesgate 8, Oslo 2 (tel: 55 24 00).

Hitchers' Tips and Comments. . .

If you're out of money in Oslo, don't sleep in the parks or at Bygdøy. Take the tram to Frognerseteren or a bus (No. 41) to Sorkedalen and walk ten minutes into the woods. JOHS ANKEN, OSLO, NORWAY

The carnivorous insect life in western and northern Scandinavia, Norway especially, can be terrifying from June to August. It makes you wonder what the beasts eat when fresh Englishman is unavailable. British repellents don't seem to work. Local ones are better. You can't emphasize this insect plague enough. I've known people made quite ill by mosquito and horsefly bites up there.

Also, if you're up in those parts in early summer when the sun shines strongly but there's still plenty of snow about, *you must wear sunglasses*. The reflections are blinding, and dangerous to your eyes.
ADRIAN PARK, PRESTON, ENGLAND

The E6 is now surfaced much further north, but beware – in places there's road, but no roadside! Watch it if you're stuck out there at night! AIDAN MURRAY, ATHLORE, ENGLAND

In Oslo they use the same ticket system as in Copenhagen. You can transfer to another bus or tram within the hour.

ALAN BARLOW, CHEADLE, UK

Note: this is only valid for clip-cards and NOT valid for single tickets.

K.W.

Nothing wrong with sleeping in Bygdøy, except for the wildlife. A fox stole one of my friend's training shoes and kept on coming back for the other one. Generally, I found Oslo easy to crash out in.

PHILIP ATTWOOL, ORPINGTON, UK

In Oslo go to the top of the hill overlooking Oslo – up past the Olympic ski-slope. Spectacular view and free binoculars. When everyone's gone (about 9 p.m.), you can pitch your tent for free and camp.

A. P. KIK, MIDDLESBROUGH TEESSIDE, UK

Norway's quarter of a million lakes aren't full of fish. As a matter of fact, 90% of the lakes south of Dovre are empty of fish due to air pollution.

Cheap places to eat (good food and large helpings) in Oslo are the Spisestedet in the 'working commune' (an underground leftover from the hippy era) at Hjelmsgt 3.

Oslo's latest and most international disco is Barock, Universitetsgaten 4. JOKER, BAERUM, NORWAY

Finland

population	5,000,000
size	338,145 square kilometres
capital	Helsinki, population 500,000
government	Republic
religion	Evangelical Lutheran and Greek Orthodox
language	Finnish and Swedish are the official languages: some English spoken
currency	*Markka* (mk) One *markka* equals 100 *penniä*. Coins of 5, 10, 20 and 50 *penniä* and 1 and 5 *markkaa*. Notes of 10, 50, 100, 500 and 1,000 *markkaa*

Getting to Finland can be an expensive proposition. You have to spend a lot of days on the road and enter at the Swedish-Finnish border at Tornio on the E12 highway (fine if you're travelling south after the Kiruna trip) or pay a fair wallop on the ferry boats. Typical fares are:

Stockholm to Helsinki, costing about 200–300mk and lasting around 14–16 hours. Daily.
Stockholm to Turku, costing about 110–170mk and lasting about $9^1/_2$–11 hours. Daily.
Kapellskär to Naantali, costing about 100mk and lasting about 8 hours. Daily.
Umeå and Sundsvall to Vaasa (if you're a long way up north in Sweden), costing about 150–170mk and lasting about 4–8 hours.

Prices vary according to season, and between different companies, shop around.

The port of **Turku** is Finland's second city, with 165,000 people. It is the oldest city in the country and the former capital. (Åbo is its Swedish name, as Helsingfors is the Swedish name of Helsinki.) Resurrection Chapel is considered a masterpiece of modern Finnish architecture, while for something a little older, the cathedral and Turku Castle date from the 12th century. Music fans will be interested in the Sibelius Museum, while sports nuts might want to see the Turku Sports Park running track, reputed to be the fastest in the world and on which Olympian Paavo Nurmi set many of his world records. Of more general interest is Scandinavia's biggest open-air marketplace at the old trade hall in the city.

Tampere, 180 km north-west of Helsinki, is about the same size as Turku. It is known as the City of Sapphire Lakes. Twenty-two lakes are within its city limits, as are the Tammerkoski Rapids. At Pyynikki, the National Park, is the famous summer theatre, which was the first in the world to operate with a revolving auditorium. Watching a production as you move around the stage is quite something. For details of plays check with the tourist office – but it's generally expensive – 20–30mk a ticket. The university, a nice piece of architecture, is the best place to meet up with people.

For those in Finland only briefly, Helsinki, Turku and Tampere are probably the best bets for a quick look around. For those with time and money and who are heading north into Lapland, **Kuopio** (population 75,000) is a good stopping place. This city, 400 km north of Helsinki, is one of the centres of lake shipping. (In Finland there are 60,000 lakes, comprising 9% of the country's total area and resulting in another 30% being marshland.) The big thing at Kuopio is to climb the 700-foot Puijo Hill and the 225-foot tower on top of it for one of the best views of Scandinavia. From the top you can gaze over 18,000 square miles of the lake country! If you're in the Market Square, try the *kalakukkos*, hard-crusted fish pasties native to the province.

Vaasa, on the west coast, where many cross to from Umeå in Sweden, is a pleasant city of 55,000. There are actually two towns, Old Vaasa and New Vaasa. The Old was destroyed by fire in 1852 and is now a place of ruins and monuments. Worth visiting is the fishing village of **Björkö**, 10 km north of Vaasa.

If you've crossed the Swedish-Finnish border up north, the first town you'll come to is **Tornio**. It's an island, accessible only by bridges and a good town to meet people. Population 22,000. Try to get out to the salmon weir at **Kiviranta**.

Just a few kilometres below the Arctic Circle and 850 km from Helsinki is the capital of Finnish Lapland. **Rovaniemi** was completely destroyed during the Second World War but has been rebuilt and is now three times as large, with 30,000 inhabitants. There are only a few thousand Lapps left in Lapland, but many of them work around Rovaniemi. Here you can learn about Lapp handcrafts and their nomadic lifestyle. If you're up there before or after summer when the snow is down, try the Pohtimolampi Sports and Excursion Centre (28 km out plus a 3 km walk) where they run the only reindeer-driving school in the world. For the midnight sun you have to go further north. Try **Sodankylä**.

Beyond Rovaniemi is a strange wilderness of frozen lakes, rivers, and tundra plains – and very few people.

● **Language** *Minä rakastan sinua! Ymmärrätko? Minä rakastan sinua!* It doesn't matter how sincere you are, you won't get away with it. It means, 'I love you! Do you understand? I love you!' Try English or French, or even Swahili. It's easier. The language is of Finno-Ugrian origins, related to Hungarian and Estonian. (Wouldn't hurt to try *kiitos*, meaning thank you.)

● **Pori Jazz Festival** Second week in July at Pori, a coastal town in West Finland. Finnish and international names. Details from: Pori Jazz Festival, Mikonkatu 30, 28100 Pori 10.

● **Turku Music Festival** 10–17 August, includes a whole spectrum of music – classical through rock and jazz. For further info on this or any other festival, write to Finland Festivals, Aleksanterinkatu 19, PB56, 00100 Helsinki 10.

● **Rock Festivals** There's at least one every weekend during the summer. Best ones are Provinssirock in Seinäjoki (first weekend in June), by the Laituri in Turku (second weekend in June), and Ruisrock in Turku (late June/early July).

● **Reindeer Joring** Exclusively a Lapland winter sport. You get in a *pulkka* – a one-seated chariot fitted with skis – have a quiet word with your power source, which is a frisky reindeer, hang on tight and wish yourself *bon voyage*.

Helsinki: where to sleep

Helsinki just doesn't have hitchers at heart. The average year-round temperature of 5° C/41° F (minus° C/below 20° F most of the winter, though it averages around 21° C/70° F in July) makes it hard to sleep out and hotel prices are astronomical, with the cheapest singles going for about 150mk. Hostels are probably the best deal if you're on your own. Prices for dormitory beds start at 45mk, while 70mk sometimes gets you a bed in a double, though you can also pay close on hotel prices in some hostels where singles and doubles are available. **Hotellikeskus** (tel: 171 133) in the main train station finds beds in hotels and hostels for a small fee.

Hostelling International hostels:

Hostel Academica, Hietaniemenkatu 14 (tel: 402 02 06). June–Sept. only.

Satakuntatalo, Lapinrinne 1A (tel: 694 22 26). Late May–Aug. only.

Stadium Youth Hostel, Pohj Stadiontie 3B (tel: 496 071).

Eurohostel, Linnankatu 9 (tel: 664 452).

Other hostels:

Kallio Youth Hostel, Porthaninkatu 2 (tel: 70 99 25 90). June–Aug. only.

Camping:

Rastila (tel: 316 511). Miles from the centre. Solo travellers pay 40mk, but the price per person falls progressively for 2–5 people sharing the same tent. Open 15 May–15 Sept.

An ancient law allows you to pitch a tent anywhere providing you first obtain the landowner's permission. It is polite to camp out of sight of people's houses. Don't leave any litter lying around.

For sleeping out (and God help you) try Hietaranta Beach, Sibelius Park or find a place in the parks around Olympia Stadium.

Helsinki: where to eat

Don't expect to eat cheaply in Finland – even hostel breakfasts cost 25mk! All things considered, though, these can be very good value, as they are usually all-you-can-eat buffets. For other meals head for university cafeterias, or any eatery called Baari, Grilli, Krouvi or Kahvila, and you should emerge with some change from 50mk.

University Cafeterias. At Fabianinkatu 33 and Hallituskatu 6 (Fabianinkatu).
Hotelli Satakuntatalo, Lapinrinne 1A. Open year round. Lunch 11 a.m.–2 p.m.; dinner 5–8 p.m.
Palace Café, Eteläranta 10 (2nd floor).
Café Engel, Aleksanterinkatu 26.
Green Way, Kaisamenkatu 1. Vegetarian meals. Student reductions.

Helsinki: what to see and do

HELSINKI DESIGN CENTRE Kasarmikatu 19. Free. Displays the best in crafts and design in the country. Particularly interesting are the fabric designs.

ATENEUM ART GALLERY Kaivokatu 2. Fair collection of European masters, but fine collection of Finnish art from the last few centuries.

NATIONAL MUSEUM Mannerheimintie 34. It contains three sections. Prehistoric, historic, and ethnographic. It's also free on Tuesdays if you're looking for somewhere dry and warm.

TAPIOLA GARDEN CITY This is one of the best-designed living centres in Scandinavia. It shows you what suburbia can be like when someone puts his mind to creating a livable-in situation. Much better than anything you'll see in England or America. Take a bus from the bus station, or walk – but it's 9 km from the centre of Helsinki.

SAUNAS The cheapest sauna bath in town seems to be at the Olympia Stadium at Eläintarha. (Tram 3T or 3B from Central Station.) Costs about 20mk. Also a swimming pool at the stadium and in summer it's as good a place as any to meet people.

LINNANMÄKI Fun fair. Admission charge. Open May to mid-September. Get there on streetcars 7 or 8. For a little movement, try *Tivoli*, the discotheque in the middle of the park, open May through August. (Extra admission, but it may be worth it if you're looking for something.)

Transport in Helsinki

The Helsinki bus and tram system is the way to get around. There are various ticket options. A single ticket costs 10mk and allows unlimited transfers on the system for one hour. Ten trip tickets are available for 85mk. Travellers' cards for the whole network are available for one, three and five days, costing 25, 50 and 75mk respectively. Another possibility is the **Helsinki Card** which, as well as offering unlimited travel on public transport also gains the holder free entry into museums, and other offers such as a free city tour by bus and discounts at many local restaurants. The Helsinki Card costs 80mk for one day; 105mk for two days; and 125mk for three days. The card is available from the city tourist office.

A useful introduction to the city is the no. 3 tram service which whisks you past a number of the principal sights during a round trip of 45 minutes.

Student discounts

Various museums, art collections, and theatres offer discounts to card holders. For full information check with the **Finnish Student Travel Service** (FSTS), Travela Ltd, at Mannerheimintie 5C, 00100 Helsinki 10 (tel: 90 624 101).

Addresses

Main post office (for poste restante) at Mannerheimintie 11, 00100 Helsinki 10.

American Express at TRAVEK Travel Bureau, City Passage Aleksanterinkatv 21, 00130 Helsinki 13 (tel: 66 14 53).

Finnish Student Travel Service (FSTS) at:

Kauppakatu 12, 40100 Jyräskylä 10 (tel: 941 17507).

Hallituskatu 33, 90100 Oulu 10 (tel: 981 222 720).

Tuomiokirkonkatu 36, 33100 Tampere 10 (tel: 931 309 95).

Hämeenkatu 14, 20500 Turku 50 (tel: 921 335 815).

Helsinki City Tourist Office at Pohjoisesplanadi 19, 00100 Helsinki 10 (tel: 169 3757 and 174 088).

Finnish Travel Association at Mikonkatu 25, 00100 Helsinki 10 (tel: 170 868).

US Embassy at Itäinen Puistotie 14A, 00140 Helsinki 14 (tel: 171 931).

British Embassy at Uudenmaankatu 16–20, Helsinki 12 (tel: 647 922).

Hitchers' Tips and Comments. . .

If you're really hungry and down and out, go for the dried kippers which you can buy in supermarkets very cheaply. You can eat them straight away because they're precooked. Very nutritious.

If you want to spend a while in Lapland, walking around (the only real way to see it), buy a map or two in Rovaniemi to show you the many little country huts. Only the scale maps show them, but you need scale maps for walking anyway. The cost of the map is cancelled out by the fact it shows you where to get free accommodation and basic facilities, in return for which you are only asked to chop firewood and leave the place clean. If you've got good boots and gear you can have a real 'back to nature' trip inside the Arctic Circle.

DUNCAN S. GREY, DURHAM CITY, ENGLAND

In-season fruit can be ridiculously cheap in Finland and Norway. You can fill yourself up for next to nothing.

Finnish forests abound with wild mushrooms and toadstools. Many varieties make ultra-cheap and highly nutritious eating. *But take care – some are lethal! Check with the locals!*

Rural chain-stores like *Sokos* or *Osuuskauppa* in Finland (or *Slaget* in Norway), run a bargain of the week. The discount can be as much as 50%. Keep your eyes open for some really good offers.

ADRIAN PARK, PRESTON, ENGLAND

When in Helsinki, find out about the '3T' tram. It does a figure-of-eight about the city and the tourist office publishes a good guide that goes with the route. Rich types can actually take the tram, but the rest of us just walk the route. It's only 5 or 6 miles and takes in most sights.

PHILIP ATTWOOL, ORPINGTON, UK

Re your ferry points. The difference in the Finnish language between a/ä is rather important! For example: Älä means 'don't', but ala means 'start'. Sälli means 'kid' and Salli is the woman's name 'Sally'. Näin is 'I saw', but Nain means 'I made love'.

By the way, there are two other ferry routes to Finland: from

Travemünde (Germany) to Helsinki (22 hours); from Gdansk (Poland) to Helsinki (36 hours).

Some tips: worth seeing and visiting are Åland Islands between Sweden and Finland. It is part of Finland, but everyone speaks Swedish there. The ferries during daytime go via Åland between Naantali-Kapellskär and Turku-Stockholm. It's cheap and the ferries are luxurious. FINNISH READER FROM SAVONLINNA

Sorry mate, couldn't read your name. K.W.

Cheap good meals can be obtained in the Helsinki University Hall.
K. M. FITCHET, JOHANNESBURG, SOUTH AFRICA

Those 'Lapp' handicrafts in Rovaniemi are tourist crap – you can get the same stuff on the market square in Helsinki. All the Lapps in Finland live far to the north of Rovaniemi.
SAMULI SCHIELKE, TAMPERE, FINLAND

If hitching in winter, never let the driver let you off in the middle of nowhere at night. In summer this might be frustrating; in winter the cold weather means it can be very dangerous.
ANNA KULJU, TAMPERE, FINLAND

Iceland

population	253,500
size	103,000 square kilometres
capital	Reykjavik, population 100,000
government	Republic
religion	Lutheran
language	Icelandic: English widely understood
currency	*Krona* (kr) Coins of 1, 5, 10 and 50 *kronur*. Notes of 100, 500, 1000 and 5000 *kronur*

Getting there can be expensive because of the distance. If you're rich you can fly, but most people take the ferry to **Seydhisfjordhur** from Scrabster, near Thurso, Scotland (about 800 km) or from Bergen, Norway (about 1,000 km). The boat calls at Torshavn on the Faerøe Islands.

Alternatively, if you've got a cast-iron stomach, try hitching a lift on an Icelandic fishing boat. Best ports to try are Bremerhaven, Germany, or Grimsby, England. At Grimsby docks ask at Danbrit, who are the agents for Icelandic vessels, if any Icelandic boats are in port. While in the docks keep a close eye on your stuff or it'll disappear. At the boat, chat up the watchman who'll know if there's any chance of getting a ride. If so, it's between you and the skipper. Things may be a bit primitive aboard; dirty, smelly, horrible food (the cook is the one who knows how to boil water!) and the showers used to store nets. But the fishermen are all good blokes. (Don't try to keep up with their drinking!) It depends on the skipper as to whether you'll be asked to pay towards your passage or work. Those boats that have sold their catch in Europe will probably be heading straight home which means there won't be much work to do anyway.

Anyone wanting to hitch home can try at either Grindavik or Vestmannaeyjar, the two main Icelandic fishing ports. But be warned that this could mean a six-week fishing trip in the Arctic ocean with back-breaking work (like 36 hours at a stretch) with maybe a storm thrown in. But as a deckhand you'd get a percentage of the profits.

On arrival in Iceland you'll be confronted by immigration officials who will insist that you have a return ticket to your country of origin. If you don't have one, you'll be taken around to the airline office to buy one. The ticket can usually be cashed in if you decide to make other arrangements.

What to take

Plenty of money. Iceland is *very* expensive.
Warm clothing. All the tourist blurbs say how warm it is in Iceland. What they mean is, it's warm for the latitude, which is just below the Arctic Circle. The weather is often wet and cold, particularly in the mountains. If there is a summer it will be in June-July, but even summer doesn't mean good weather. With luck you'll get so warm you have to take off one of your coats!

MD1A tent, and good sleeping bag. Because of costs, weather and the fact that you may be miles from civilization when night falls.

MD1Bottle of vodka. Booze is extremely expensive, about four times the UK price. Icelanders like vodka. Scope here for good profit.

Where to sleep

Iceland has several youth hostels, but two are so remote you can't reach them by hitching. Avoid hotels because of high prices, but do look for hotels which offer *svefnpokaplass* (sleeping-bag accommodation), which is a cheap deal (little more than a youth hostel) providing you bring your own sleeping bag. The Edda Hotels, usually open only in summer, also sometimes offer svefnpokaplass. The Icelandic YHA distributes a leaflet listing these places.

If you don't have a tent, you may be able to sleep in farmers' barns. Most don't mind if you ask permission first, and guarantee not to smoke or use a stove (because of the hay).

In remote areas you find orange-coloured emergency huts for stranded travellers and shipwrecked sailors, complete with food, stove, fuel, bedding and radio transmitter. If you sleep in one of these places, *don't touch the supplies* unless you yourself are in a bad way, or you will be depriving someone else of his means of survival.

Where to eat

You will be on bread and cheese or cooking for yourself because restaurants are so expensive. Always carry plenty of food because it's often a couple of days' hitching between villages. Shops close during the weekends so stock up on Fridays. If you want to eat out, try cafeterias, but even they are expensive.

What to see and do

In **Reykjavik**, don't miss the art galleries and museums, particularly the National Museum, which will give you an idea of Icelandic history, and the open-air Arbaer Folk Museum. At weekends the capital (and the whole island) is dead, so the citizens compensate by indulging in a certain amount of drinking. The deadliest drop is called *brennivin* (firewater) and you can consider yourself lucky if you can't afford it.

Thingvellir, 50 km east of the capital, is where the Althing, the Icelandic parliament, was founded in AD 930. It's the oldest parliament in the world. Until 1800 the Althing met at the Logberg, where speakers stood on the clifftop to address the assembly below. See the Drowning Pool where adulteresses were thrown, and the Money Chasm where for decades idiots have thrown coins into the water. **Lake Thingvallavatn** is the largest in Iceland.

To the north is **Reykholt** where you can see steam springs. (Any place name with 'reyk' in it indicates that steam is present.)

In the north-west the **Vestfirdir Peninsula** boasts wild, untamed scenery, while at **Latrabjarg**, the most westerly point in Iceland, you can admire some of the highest cliffs in the world. Locals lower themselves on ropes down their faces to collect eggs. The northernmost part of Vestfirdir is uninhabited, the landscape untouched by man.

Akureyri, in the north, is Iceland's second largest town with 14,500 people. To the east is **Myvatn**, Iceland's fourth largest lake, famous for its volcanism, hot springs, boiling mud and weird rock formations that look so much like the moon that American astronauts were trained here. Careful where you put your feet because the mud is hot enough to cause severe scalds. Further on is **Dettifoss**, Europe's highest waterfall, which is up a minor road and difficult to thumb to (a day's walk if you don't get a lift), but it's worth the trouble getting there.

In the south-east is **Vatnajokull**, Europe's largest glacier which takes up an eighth of Iceland. Immediately to the south is **Skaftafell National Park**, while south-west is **Hekla**, Iceland's most famous volcano, which last erupted in January 1991.

Near **Lake Laugarvatn** is the original Geysir, now inactive. But nearby is another, called **Strokkur**, which spouts twice an hour. While in the area, try and see **Gullfoss Waterfall**.

The **Vestmann Islands** can be reached by ferry from the port of **Thorlakshofn**. The trip takes three hours. There is only one inhabited island called **Heimaey**. Here stands the Vestmanns' only village, **Vestmannaeyjar**, which was partially destroyed in 1973 when a volcano erupted out of the ground at the edge of town. The new volcano is now about 600 feet high. It is still steaming and its rocks are hot to touch. If you climb to the crater, wear good boots as the cinders will cut shoes to pieces. Watch out for poisonous gas. You can't see it, but if you have trouble breathing, turn back. The neighbouring volcano is extinct and as it's the highest point on the island it affords a good view of the new island of **Surtsey** which rose from the sea during 1963–6.

Hitching

Hitching is pretty bad because the population is thinly spread and 40% of Icelanders live in Reykjavik.

On the main road around the island the second car to come by will stop if the first didn't, but you may wait three hours for the *first* car. You do get long rides lasting all day, but more likely you'll get a ride 10 km to the next farm. On minor roads, just start walking and hope somebody decides to use that road that day.

● **Warning!** The interior of Iceland is pure wilderness and totally uninhabited. It's not advisable to go there unless you mount a full-scale expedition or join a (high-priced) tour which takes the proper equipment. If anything goes wrong you could be three days from the nearest telephone. If you plan a hike, leave details of your itinerary with the Tourist Office and report to them on your return so they know you're OK.

● **Warning!** Don't buy any more kronur than you need at the time. Most European banks won't touch them and even in Iceland itself you may have trouble converting them back to hard currency.

Addresses

Main post office (for poste restante) at Pósthusstraeti 5, Reykjavik.
American Express at Utsyn Tourist Agency, Austurstraeti 17, Reykjavik (tel: 26 611).
Tourist Information at Bankastraeti 2, Reykjavik (tel: 623045).
US Embassy at Laufásvegur 21, Reykjavik (tel: 29 100).
British Embassy at Laufásvegur 49, Reykjavik (tel: 15 883 and 15 884).

Hitchers' Tips and Comments. . .

You failed to mention the beautiful scenery of the Snaeffels Peninsula and also the famous Snaeffels Volcano, which was the starting point for Jules Verne's *Journey to the Centre of the Earth*. The volcano can be seen, on a clear day, from Reykjavik, even if you can't visit it.
MARK NAISBITT, DARLINGTON, DURHAM, UK

You did not mention the Blue Lagoon in Iceland, which is situated about 20 minutes drive from Reykjavik. It's a natural bath place made of mud and is believed to have healing powers. It's very popular both with Icelanders themselves and tourists.

People travelling to Vestfirdir can take a ferry that goes from the village Stykkisholumur over the bay. The journey takes about three hours and the scenery is beautiful with hundreds of small islands and magnificent birdlife.
EDDA EIRIKSDOTTIR, REYKJAVIK, ICELAND

9 · EASTERN EUROPE

Compared to the West, Eastern Europe is, with a few exceptions, a tricky prospect for hitchers. The basic problem is that hitching tends to be downright difficult, added to which there is often the hassle of having to buy visas in advance, sometimes at a prohibitive cost. It's not all doom-and-gloom though. Public transport is cheap, so if you are keen to see these countries you can get about by train and bus without spending a fortune, unlike in Western Europe. Secondly, the last few years have seen travel restrictions eased considerably, and the coming years will probably see things getting easier still.

Note: The information on visa requirements given in the following country sections was correct at the time of going to press in 1995, but may well have changed by 1996. Be sure to check out the up-to-date details with travel agents or embassies.

A few hints:

- **Photography** Remember to keep your camera pointed right away from military installations or anything which could be interpreted as such.

- **Drugs** If they catch you in the Eastern bloc countries it can be goodbye world for a long, long time.

Albania

population	3,208,00
size	27,398 square kilometres
capital	Tirana, population 300,000
government	parliamentary democracy
religion	predominantly Moslem with Orthodox and Roman Catholic minorities
language	Albanian. Little English, French or German spoken
currency	*Lek* One *lek* equals 100 *qindarkas*

Tourist sights in the Albanian capital **Tirana** are few. The city is never likely to become a highpoint of a European tour in the way that Prague, Cracow or Dresden have become. However, once you realize that the main attraction here is the inquisitive and friendly people there's no reason why you shouldn't leave the city with fond memories.

The best of all the sights is the NATIONAL HISTORICAL MUSEUM which has a fine collection dating from the Stone Age up to present-day Albania. An unexpected bonus are the guides, who speak a variety of languages and are delighted to fill you in on the exhibits. One of the more unusual is the bust of Apollo. Look at the bust from various angles, and don't be surprised if the Greek god begins to look a bit girlish at some points. This remarkable effect earns the bust its other name – the Goddess of Butrint.

The PALACE OF CULTURE dominates Skanderbeg Square in the same way that its namesake dominates Warsaw. Both were a gift from the USSR, but whereas the Poles never had any choice in the matter, the Albanian version was still not completed at the time of the Albanian–Soviet split of 1961. The Albanian government decided to finish the job. Judge for yourself!

On the square stands an equestrian statue of the national hero Skanderbeg. Trained by the Turks, who honoured him with the name Skanderbeg, Gjergj Kastrioti formed the League of Lezhe in 1444, uniting the Albanians in revolt against Turkish rule, and he remained undefeated throughout the 25 battles he fought.

As might be expected, the cult of personality surrounding the former dictator, Hoxha, ensured a statue of him was placed on the square near the national hero. Hoxha's statue was torn down in 1991. A new statue may soon be in place, dedicated to the world's most famous living Albanian: Mother Teresa.

At one corner of the square stands the 19th-century clock tower and the Mosque of Ethem Bey, the most important mosque in Tirana. Not far from the square is the former palace of King Zog, a chieftain from the north who took the throne in the 1920s, bled his countrymen dry, then signed their fate over to Mussolini before departing with his ill-gotten gains. Near the palace is one of Tirana's more endearing attractions, the excellent puppet theatre.

After the revolutions which swept Eastern Europe in 1989–90 a number of museums celebrating the Communist movements and their luminaries (invariably excruciatingly boring) were hastily converted into equally boring new museums. Albanian good sense avoided this scenario in the case of the ENVER HOXHA MUSEUM. The glass pyramid which housed Hoxha's remains and assorted paraphernalia cost US$70 million to build – it's now a discotheque!

Durres, the country's main port, lies to the east of Tirana. Durres dates back at least as far as the 7th century BC. Several remains from that long history make a visit worthwhile. The Archaeology Museum is small, but what it lacks in quantity it makes up for in quality. Each exhibit is absolutely unique. Not being confronted with rows of objects only experts could tell apart keeps your interest high. The town's 6th-century Byzantine walls are just to the rear of the museum. A short walk away is the town's main sight, a 1st/2nd-century Roman amphitheatre. Excavations have also uncovered a small 10th-century Byzantine church on the site with contemporary wall mosaics.

North of Tirana the towns of **Kruje** and **Lezhe** are intimately associated with Skanderbeg. Kruje was Skanderbeg's power base from 1443 until 1468 when he died of fever. Three times during that period the Turks laid siege to the citadel you can still see today, each time without success. It finally fell on the fourth siege, ten years after Skanderbeg's death. The citadel now contains a museum which documents the long struggle against the Turks quite superbly, plus the 16th-century Turkish baths, and the Bektashi tekke which was used by one of the mystical Islamic sects. Skanderbeg actually died in the town of Lezhe from which he had initiated the revolt. His tomb is in the ruined Church of St Nicholas. See also the old citadel above the town.

Gjirokaster, in the far south of the country, is the best preserved old town in Albania. Gjirokaster is an easy stopover on the way to or from Greece, but worth going out of your way to see in any case. The main attraction is simply wandering around the twisting, cobbled streets, but there are sufficient sights to keep you occupied for a while. Gjirokaster's 14th-century citadel now houses an impressive Armaments Museum. You can't miss one of the star exhibits – the US spy plane the Albanians intercepted in 1957. The Muzeu Historik Cercis Topulli tells the story of two local brothers who led a revolt against the Turks in 1908. The view of the town from just outside the museum is hard to beat. The town's most famous son was born in the Palorto part of town in 1908 – one Enver Hoxha, later to be ruler of Albania for 40 years. You can still see the house Hoxha was born in. Be sure to see the tall houses just below the citadel. You'll notice that there are no ground-floor windows. They were built without a door on the lower level as well; access being gained by a ladder. These features were due to the need for protection during the blood feuds which were rife a few centuries ago.

● **Visa requirements** Prior to travelling to Albania citizens of the UK, Ireland, Canada, USA, New Zealand and Australia must obtain a visa from an Albanian embassy or consulate as these are not sold at the Albanian border.

Hitching
Hitching is very difficult in Albania as there are few private cars. Locals do hitch rides from trucks. If you do the same and get a lift you will be expected to pay about half the fare for the trip by bus or train. It's best to save yourself the frustration of waiting and get the bus or train in the first place. They're dirt cheap in any case.

Hitchers' Tips and Comments . . .

Forget about any black-marketing here, there's no chance of selling anything to anyone. The locals are so unused to foreigners that they will stare at you in the street as if you were a man from Mars. When leaving, load up on cigarettes which are dead cheap.

ALAN BARLOW, CHEADLE, UK

Bulgaria

population	9,300,000
size	110,994 square kilometres
capital	Sofia, population 1,000,000
government	parliamentary democracy
religion	Mainly Eastern Orthodox with small Roman Catholic and Moslem minorities
language	Bulgarian. Russian is widely spoken; some German, French and English is understood
currency	*Lev* One *lev* equals 100 *stotinki*. Coins of 1, 2, 5, 10, 20 and 50 *stotinki*, and of 1, 2 and 5 *leva*. Notes of 1, 2, 5, 10, 20, 50, 100 and 200 *leva*

Entering Bulgaria on the main highway from Bucharest the first major halt is the city of Ruse. From Ruse, Sofia is 327 km away by the E85 and E83; Veliko Târnovo is 107 km away straight down the E85; Plovdiv 299 km by the E85 and E772; and the Black Sea city of Varna 203 km away along the E70 and A2. An alternative to entering Bulgaria from Romania via Ruse would be to hitch via Craiova to cross the border at the town of Vidin in the far north-western corner of the country. This leaves you much closer to Sofia (199 km away), and much further from the rest of the main towns.

Ruse has a history dating back to AD 70, but there really isn't very much to see in the city. A notable exception is the Transportation Museum, set in what was Bulgaria's first train station, and including the country's first train amongst the exhibits. Highlight of **Vidin** is the Baba Vida Fortress – the most important and impressive of its kind in Bulgaria. Originally built by the Bulgarians between the 10th and 14th centuries the fortress was then rebuilt in the 17th century by the Ottoman Turks.

Hitching from Ruse to Sofia you might find yourself breaking your journey in the city of **Pleven**, 149 km along the route. Like Ruse, Pleven is a bit short on things to see. Perhaps because the locals don't see their city as a major tourist attraction they are unusually friendly towards those who do spend some time there, so you might find yourself staying a little longer than planned. If you are in town one sight not to be missed is the 1877 *Panorama*, one of relatively few 360° murals still in existence. The painting depicts the third assault made on the city during the five month battle of Pleven between the Turkish army and a combined Russian and Romanian force seeking to drive the Turks out of the Balkans. To get the most from your visit either buy a brochure, or request a guide you can converse with.

Built on four hills rising above the River Yantra **Veliko Târnovo** is one of the most spectacularly sited cities in Europe, and the one place in Bulgaria which definitely should not be missed. Veliko Târnovo was capital of the Second Bulgarian Empire (1185–1393) and you can see the ruins of the Tsaravets Citadel which was destroyed when the Turks took the town in 1393. The remains are impressive, and there are some great views from the citadel as well. Amongst the town's churches see St Dimitar of Salonika which has some interesting frescoes. There are more frescoes in Holy Forty Martyrs Church, but restoration work may keep the doors closed for a few years yet. The quaint, winding streets of the old town are full of houses from the period of the Bulgarian National Revival in the 19th century. For an unrivalled view of the city head for the terrace of the restaurant in the Sveta Gora Park.

There are several worthwhile trips in the vicinity of Veliko Târnovo. About 10 km to the north-west is the village of **Arbanasi**, originally an Albanian settlement. In the Birth of Christ Church are some stunning mid-17th-century frescoes in which the artists crammed about 3,500 figures into 2,000 different scenes. The entrance fee also includes admission to the 17th-century Konstantzaliev House which has exhibits on the traditional life of the region. Some 7 km north of Veliko Târnovo stands **Preobrazhenski Monastery**, built in the 19th century only 500 m away from the ruins of the original monastery destroyed by the Turks five centuries earlier. On the opposite side of the valley from Preobrazhenski is the Holy Trinity Monastery dating from the same period.

Bulgaria's second city **Plovdiv** is an altogether more attractive place than the national capital. As in Veliko Târnovo the narrow streets of the old town contain many fine houses from the time of the National Revival. Especially worth seeing is the house of the merchant Stephen Hindlian which has been meticulously restored to its original state. Two of the city's museums are set in a couple of houses from the same period – the Ethnographic Museum with its collection of traditional costumes in the Koyumdjioglu House and the National Revival Museum in the Georgiadi House. The Imaret and Friday mosques are reminders of the Turkish occupation, while from the Roman period you can see the remains of the forum and the amphitheatre, plus the fully restored 3,000-seat theatre. Even older are the remains of the Thracian town of Eumopias.

Koprivstica, 77 km north-west of Plovdiv, has great significance to Bulgarians as the place where the 1876 uprising against Turkish rule began. From a tourist point of view the great attraction is that Koprivstica is an almost perfectly preserved example of a town built in the style of the Bulgarian National Revival (the result of the town having been destroyed in the early 19th century).

Sightseeing isn't likely to be top of your priorities on the Black Sea coast, but there are a few things worth seeing if you get bored soaking up the sunshine. In **Varna** see the St Anastasius Orthodox Church and the adjacent Roman baths (which are much more impressive than the town's other baths). Down the coast towards Burgas is **Nesebar**, one of the country's prime tourist attractions. Amidst the picturesque, twisting streets of the old town are numerous medieval churches built in the characteristic local style of alternating layers of white stone and red brick. Be sure to see St Stefan, an 11th-century church extensively decorated with 16th-century frescoes. **Burgas** itself has a pleasant enough old quarter, but nothing really worth going out of your way to see. The thing to see in **Sozopol** is the old town, the streets and houses of which are every bit as attractive as those of Nesebar, but without the abundance of medieval churches. Depending upon how you feel about arty types you might (or might not) want to be in town for the annual arts festival in early September.

Perched high in the Rila Mountains 120 km south of the capital is **Rila Monastery**, the most important monastery in the country, and something of a must on any tour of Bulgaria. The monastery played an invaluable role in preserving Bulgarian culture during the long and oppressive Turkish occupation. Highlights of the monastery complex are the church with its frescoes and fabulous gilded iconostasis, and the amazing wooden cross of Brother Raphael which bears some 1,500 human figures less than one centimetre tall (the cross is in one of the museums). If you fancy doing a bit of walking the **Rila Mountains** are as good a spot as any in Bulgaria – great scenery, a well developed system of mountain huts (bring your own food though), and usually plenty of company at the end of a day's walking. The favourite walk of all is from Complex Malyosita to the Rila Monastery. It's possible to do the walk in a day, but unless you are a really keen walker it's probably more enjoyable to spread it over two days.

Just before the Greek border a small deviation from the E79 will take you to the town of **Melnik**. Stunningly located in the midst of the surrounding hills, the town is just as easy on the eye as the location. It's best just to wander around and enjoy the place – sooner or later you'll come to the main sights such as the Kordupulov House, the ruins of the ancient Bolyar House, and the numerous mansions built in the National Revival style. Whilst in town you'll probably want to try the potent Melnik red wine, a favourite amongst Bulgarians. From Melnik you can follow a footpath over the hills to the Rozhen Monastery, 7 km away. This is worth it to see the monastery itself, but even more so for the superb (and sometimes bizarre) scenery en route.

● **Vias requirements** Nationals of the UK, Ireland, Canada, Australia and New Zealand all require visas to visit Bulgaria. These must be purchased in advance as they cannot be bought at the Bulgarian border. Citizens of the USA do not need a visa to enter Bulgaria.

Hitching
Hitching is permitted in Bulgaria, but not easy. Your best bet are long-distance lorries. It's against the law to sleep or camp rough. If you do decide to sleep out don't light a fire.

Sofia: where to sleep

Hotel rooms can be difficult to find throughout most of the tourist season. Private rooms are a better bet, though even these have been known to run out in peak season. Book these through **Balkantourist** or **ORBITA** (addresses below). Alternatively you might consider offers made by touts at the train station, though these are usually poorer options in terms of location and quality compared to those booked through an agency. Unless you have booked hostel accommodation in advance you'll just have to visit the **Bulgarian Youth Hostel Federation** or ORBITA offices to see what is available – don't expect much success in summer.

There are four campsites around Sofia, all open May/mid May –

October. The Vrana and Cherniya Kos sites are both about 10 km out, off the E80 (Plovdiv direction) and the road to Pernik respectively. The Bankya site is 16 km out, off the E80 on the way to the Serbian border. Lebed is a similar distance out off the road to Samokov: this site has chalets only.

Sofia: where to eat

The **Dunav** on Knyaz Dondukov is about as cheap as you get, and does vegetarian options as well as meat-based dishes. You'll find similarly priced self-service establishments dotted all over town. Count on paying about £1 for a couple of courses. £3–4 will buy you a good meal at a mid-range eatery. The **Mehana Koprivshtitsa Restaurant** is a good place for sampling Bulgarian specialities. Go down the stairs from the arcade at Vitosha blvd 1/3. Along the street at Vitosha blvd 34 the **Bulgarska gozba Restaurant** is another place which regularly features a good choice of national dishes.

Sofia: what to see and do

ST SOPHIA CHURCH A three-naved basilica built in the 5th and 6th centuries. The city takes its name from this church.

ALEXANDER NEVSKY MEMORIAL CHURCH Built in the neo-Byzantine style in 1912, the church is a memorial to the 200,000 Russian soldiers killed in the fight to liberate Bulgaria from the Turks.

NATIONAL ARCHAEOLOGICAL MUSEUM Probably the best of the city's museums, with a first-rate collection of ancient sculpture.

BANYA BASHI MOSQUE The doors of this 16th-century mosque are usually closed, but the highpoint is the superb minaret, so it's not too disastrous that you can't see inside.

NATIONAL MUSEUM OF HISTORY A huge complex with some great exhibits, such as the 4th-century Panagjurishte gold treasure, but descriptions of displays are in Bulgarian only which is a great shame.

BOYANA CHURCH A UNESCO-listed monument in the suburb of Boyana, the church has superb frescoes from the mid-13th century. The portraits of the church's patrons are especially noteworthy. Note the depiction of The Last Supper with the disciples rigged out in the typical Bulgarian garb of the period.

Transport in Sofia
The city and its suburbs are covered by an excellent public transport system comprising buses, trolleybuses and trams. A (low) flat fare is charged no matter how far you travel. Buy tickets beforehand, and then punch your ticket in the machines on board.

Addresses

'Pirin' Tourist Agency at blvd Stambolijski 45a, Sofia (tel: 879552).
Bulgarian Youth Hostel Federation at blvd Vassil Levski 75, Sofia, (tel: 883821).
Balkantourist and the State Tourist Information Office at Knajaz Dondukov 37, Sofia (tel: 884430).
ORBITA (Student Travel Office) at blvd Stambolijski 45a, Sofia (tel: 801812).
British Embassy at 65–67 blvd Marshal Tolbukhin, Sofia (tel: 885361). Provides embassy services to citizens of Canada, New Zealand and Australia.
US Embassy at blvd Stambolijski 1, Sofia (tel: 884801).

Hitchers' Tips and Comments . . .

Head gestures in Bulgaria are the reverse of ours – a nod means 'no', a shake of the head means 'yes'. ALAN BARLOW, CHEADLE, UK

The villages and provincial towns in Bulgaria are really cheap. I got my boots polished, bought a packet of crisps and a round of beers for less than a quid! Official hotels are really expensive, though. I got offered rooms by locals a few times, but, obviously, you can't gamble on it. Sofia is more like a Western capital, price-wise.

When I was leaving the country, a border official tried to rip me off by applying the old Communist visa rules. I didn't say anything or give him any money or my passport and he went away!

JON BANKS, LONDON, ENGLAND

The Czech Republic

population	12,000,000
size	78,862 square kilometres
capital	Prague, population 1,500,000
government	parliamentary democracy
religion	Roman Catholic with a substantial Protestant minority
language	Czech. Most Czechs have some knowledge of Russian. Increasing numbers are learning English, but German has been reinstated as the second language. Older people tend to speak German
currency	*Koruna* One *koruna* equals 100 *haléřu*. Coins of 10, 20 and 50 *haléřu*, 1, 2, 5, 10, 20 and 50 *korun*. Notes of 100, 500 and 1,000 *korun*

The most popular entry point into the Czech Republic for people hitching from Britain is the region of West Bohemia, a part of the country noted for the famous spa towns of **Karlovy Vary**, **Mariánské Lázně** and **Františkovy Lázně**, and for the brewing town of **Pilsen** (Plzeň). The walks in the forests surrounding the three spas (prescribed as part of the 'cure') are great, but otherwise, once you've sampled the waters there isn't really a lot to do in these towns which attract an older crowd. Certainly, unless you're a real architecture buff, you probably won't want to visit more than one of them. Two specialities to watch out for are the highly distinctive herb liqueur *Becherovka* which is made in Karlovy Vary, and the wafers filled with chocolate or sugar (*Lázeňské oplatký*) sold in Mariánské Lázně. Both are grand for killing off the foul taste of the waters.

Heading south-west from the spa towns brings you to **Pilsen**, home of the famed Pilsner Urquell beer, and also of the Škoda engineering works (recently bought out by Volkswagen). The brave little Škoda has been the butt of a thousand jokes over the years such as 'The only thing worse than getting a ride in a Škoda is actually owning one'. By way of contrast you won't hear many jokes being cracked about the town's beer. To most people this will mean Plzeňsky Prazdroj (better known abroad under its export name Pilsner Urquell), but the town's other brewery, Gambrinus, knocks out some great stuff as well. Definitely not to be missed is the excellent Brewing Museum on Veleslavínova.

Going south-west from Pilsen takes you into the region of South Bohemia. This part of the country, characterized by rolling hills and a host of attractive small towns is arguably the Czech Republic at its best. Near the Austrian border is the regional capital of **České Budějovice**, founded in 1265. Overlooking the impressive main square with the Samson Fountain, the Town Hall and St Nicholas' Cathedral is the 72-metre-high Black Tower. Climb the tower for a great view over the old section of town. České Budějovice is another must for beer lovers – the famous Budvar beer has been brewed here since 1894.

About 9 km north of České Budějovice on the Vltava River stands **Hluboka Castle**. It looks like a cartoonist's idea of a castle, or something built specifically for tourists to visit, but its extraordinary history dates back to the 13th century. The castle has since been rebuilt several times, so that the version you see today owes most to a 19th-century remodelling along the lines of Windsor Castle.

Whatever you do, don't miss the town of **Český Krumlov**, 22 km from České Budějovice. The town's castle is ranked second in importance only to that of Prague and would in itself be reason enough to visit this small town on the Vltava. However, the most interesting aspect of Český Krumlov is the remarkably intact historic core of the old town which is so impressive that UNESCO has classified it as a World Heritage Site.

On the main road from České Budějovice to Prague stands the town of **Tábor**, founded in 1420 by the Hussites (followers of the Czech reformer Jan Hus who was burned as a heretic in 1415). Tábor's old town is notable for its twisting streets which were specifically designed to slow down any invaders. At the centre of town is a particularly appealing main square with the gabled town hall, the parish church, a renaissance fountain and a statue of the Hussites' military leader Jan Žižka. The most remarkable sight in town is the warren of underground passages hewn out by the Hussites to help defend the town against their Roman Catholic enemies. Guided tours of the tunnels begin in the town hall.

Around the capital Prague are several places of interest, including the castle at **Karlštejn**, 28 km to the south-west. This was built with 6-metre-thick walls in the 14th century to house the Bohemian crown jewels and assorted saintly relics. The tiny village of **Lidice**, 22 km north-west of Prague, was liquidated in reprisal for the assassination in Prague in 1942 of Reinhard Heydrich, Hitler's representative in occupied Bohemia and Moravia. Prior to the village being razed to the ground 192 men were shot dead, and 196 women and 105 children despatched to concentration camps. There is a small museum run by some of the few survivors.

In the Middle Ages **Kutná Hora**, 65 km east of the capital, was the second most important town in Bohemia, and a royal seat. Its wealth was founded on silver deposits, which in turn led to a mint being founded in the town which was run by Italian craftsmen. In the old section be sure to see St Barbara's Cathedral with its unique frescoes of miners and minters at work, the Italian Court and the richly decorated Stone House. If you're into the macabre, a more unusual and gruesome attraction is the charnel house in the Sedlec part of town near the train station.

There is no shortage of things to see and do in Moravia's second city, **Olomouc**, but especially worthy of mention are the town hall and the elaborate plague column (the largest in the Czech lands). Between Olomouc and the Polish border lies the industrial city of **Ostrava**. Even the locals will think you are mad if you are in town for any reason other than to see the football or ice hockey. A far better place to break a journey between Olomouc and Poland would be the small town of **Nový Jičín**. As well as a picturesque main square Nový Jičín has the more unusual attraction of the country's one and only hat museum.

The Moravian capital, **Brno**, lies south-west of Olomouc. Visit the twin-spired Cathedral of Saints Peter and Paul which looms above the old town. On another hill nearby stands the Špilberk Fortress dating from the 13th century. During many stages of its history the castle has served as a prison and you can still see the torture chamber and cells. Many of the town's oldest buildings are grouped around Zelný trh (often called the Cabbage Market) which is about as old as the city itself. As in Kutná Hora there are plenty of old bones to look at in the church of the former Capuchin Monastery just off Zelný trh. Here the mummified bodies of monks and patrons of the church are displayed in the crypt.

North-west of Brno is **Pernštejn Castle**, the finest in Moravia. To the north of the city is the **Moravský Kras** (Moravian karst), a limestone area 25 km long and 6 km wide full of weird limestone formations, caves, canyons, underground rivers and forests. If you're interested in exploring the Moravský Kras consider basing yourself in Blanski. **Slavkov**, east of Brno, has entered our history books as Austerlitz, scene of Napoleon's great victory against the combined forces of Russia and Austria.

South-west of Brno, near the Austrian border, is the town of **Znojmo**, which is famed for its gherkins. Znojmo is an attractive enough town with a few fine old buildings and some great walks around the outskirts. Plus visitors can at last see Znojmo's main cultural attraction – the 11th-century rotunda of St Elisabeth with its 12th-century frescoes of the Premysl dynasty who ruled over the country. The rotunda stands within the grounds of the local brewery – and for that reason was off-limits to tourists for years! Just don't turn up on a Monday or you'll be as disappointed as many who went before you (rotunda open Tues.–Sun.).

About 75 km west of Brno is the splendidly preserved town of **Telč**. Even in a country where picturesque main squares are remarkably common Telč's square stands out. In truth Telč is one of the most attractive small towns in Europe. Not quite as grand as Telč, but stunning in its own right is the small town of **Slavonice**, only 21 km south of Telč on the Austrian border.

● **Visa requirements** British, Irish and US nationals do not need a visa to visit the Czech Republic. Citizens of Canada, Australia and New Zealand must buy a visa in advance as these are not issued at the Czech border.

Hitching

Hitching is tolerated throughout the country, but it is not that easy because of the small size of the usually full cars. So it follows that it is easier to hitch alone, and with as small a pack as possible. If rides are hard to get remember that public transport is very cheap.

Prague: where to sleep

Accommodation can be a hassle – especially in summer. Youth hostels, many of which are open only in the peak of summer, are frequently full by midday. Prices range from about £3–5 per person. Hotels in the capital are expensive compared to elsewhere in the Czech Republic, but the cheaper B and C graded hotels are affordable if there are two of you sharing. Count on paying £7–10 per person for a double. Beware of extra charges for showers as these can cost you a fortune. **Pragotur**, **Čedok** and a number of other organizations (look for adverts at the bus and train stations) will find you a room in a private house. Prices of £9–11 for a single, £6–7 per person in doubles are fairly standard.

Camping could be your best bet as prices are low and there are lots of sites in the city (even so the sites can fill up in peak season – get there as quick as possible in the day). There's a good atmosphere in the campsites in summer with lots of Czechs and Germans sitting around campfires drinking and singing. Many campsites also have bungalows for hire.

You are allowed to sleep in the open, but it is not permitted to light a camp fire outside a campsite. If you do, and get caught, you will most likely be hit with a heavy fine.

Prague: where to eat

Prices are high compared to the rest of the country, but still very cheap by European standards, provided you don't get ripped off (cheating customers is quite common in Prague but almost unheard of outside the capital). Prague eateries can get crowded, so it can be a good idea to reserve restaurants in advance. Menus should be posted outside, or sometimes just inside the door. Be suspicious of any establishment which doesn't have a menu displayed. If you're not too fussy about what you want to eat, your best bet may be to go to a self-service buffet (there are plenty around Wenceslas Square) and choose the shortest queue. If there are two of you, one can queue for the drinks while the other queues for the food!

A fairly typical meal is soup (*polévky*) followed by pork (*vepřový*) with dumplings (*knedlíky*) and Czech cabbage (like sauerkraut). And don't forget Czech beer – the best in the world and the cheapest drink you can buy. Prague's favourite is Staropramen 12° which you can find all over town, but it's worth making a trip to U Flekå on Křemencová to sample Flek 13° which is brewed on site, or to U supa on Celetná to try Braník 14°.

Cukrárna (cakes and sweets) tempt you virtually wherever you turn, and the local ice cream (*zmrzlina*) is delicious.

Prague: what to see and do

OLD TOWN SQUARE (Staromestske Namesti) is the hub of *Stare Mesto*, the Old Town. Admire the 14th-century OLD TOWN HALL, climb the tower for a fine view down into the square; see the famed 15th-century ASTRONOMICAL CLOCK – on the hour Christ and his Apostles appear at windows above the clock and Death in the form of a skeleton tolls the hour. (Don't go until the cock crows!) In the centre of the square is a monument to 15th-century theologian Jan Hus whose reformist ideas led him to the stake. Most warm nights students and other worthies gather beneath the statue. TUN CATHEDRAL on the east side of the square is an important example of Prague Gothic. The white church behind the Old Town Hall is ST NICHOLAS. Fanciful architecture on the north side of the square is worth a long look. Best thing about the square is the amazing diversity of the people who wander through it.

FRANZ KAFKA'S BIRTHPLACE at the corner of Kaprova and Maislova streets, just behind St Nicholas Church. For literature freaks only. Pay homage!

WENCESLAS SQUARE (Vaclavske namesti), centre of the *New Town,* was once a market place. Now it's a long boulevard lined with shops and hotels. But it's still a meeting place. In recent years the square has witnessed political events which will enter Czechoslovakia's history books. See the STATUE OF KING WENCESLAS.

NATIONAL MUSEUM in Wenceslas Square. History, natural science. Library of over one million volumes.

PRAGUE GHETTO The OLD JEWISH CEMETERY was used from the 15th century until 1787. Because of lack of space graves were built one on top of the other. There are 12,000 headstones. In the STATE JEWISH MUSEUM, which is housed in an old synagogue on the edge of the cemetery, there is a permanent exhibition of haunting artwork made by children while they suffered in Nazi concentration camps. Nearby is the JEWISH TOWN HALL. Try telling the time from the clock with the Hebrew figures. It runs backwards.

CHARLES BRIDGE is one of sixteen which cross the Vltava River, and links the *Stare Mesto* (Old Town) with the *Mala Strana* (Lesser Town). Is it Europe's most beautiful bridge? The first stones were laid in the 1350s; it is over half a kilometre long between the two towers at either end and is lined by thirty statues. Climb the tower on the Mala Strana side for a terrific view over the city (and a great photo). In the right light you see why the city is known as Prague the Golden. Buskers, artists, musicians, poets, pick-pockets, villains and tourists from East and West mingle on this architectural gem. You can spend half a day on Charles Bridge without ever looking at your watch.

PRAGUE CASTLE or *Prazsky Hrad* is the noble architectural panorama you admire when crossing Charles Bridge from the Old Town. The steep walk up to the castle is best made without your pack. From the ramparts (east of the castle) you can look back at a stunning view over the city. Enter the castle precinct through the Gate of the Battling Giants into the First Courtyard. In the Second Courtyard is the office of the Czechoslovakian President. Check the treasures in the Chapel of the Holy Rood. In the Third Courtyard stands ST VITUS CATHEDRAL, Prague's biggest church. Architecture freaks will love the cathedral because it incorporates examples of most architectural styles the city has known. A church has existed on this site since around AD 900. In the ROYAL PALACE, visit the 62-metre-long Vladislav Hall which in the Middle Ages was used amongst other things for jousting matches. Don't miss quaint GOLDEN LANE with its minute 16th-century artisans' houses.

Transport in Prague

Public transport is so cheap you don't have to think twice. The fast, efficient, spotlessly clean three-line Metro system is an eye-opener. Buy tickets in entrance halls. You can ride as far as you like and cross from one line to another on one ticket.

Addresses

Pražská Informačni služba (PIS) at Na Příkopě 20, Praha (tel: 544444) Tourist information office.

Čedok at Na Příkopě 18, Praha (tel: 2127111). Tourist information office.

Čedok at Panská 5, Praha (tel: 225656/227004). Accommodation service – hotels and private rooms.

Pragotur at U Obecniího domu 2, Praha (tel: 2317200/2317281/2317234). Accommodation service – hotels and private rooms.

Top Tour at Rybná 3 (tel: 2296526/2321077/2320860). Private rooms.

AVE Ltd at Wilsonova 80 (tel: 2362560). Private rooms. The company have two offices in the main train station, and one at the airport.

British Embassy at Thunovská 14, Praha 1 (tel: 533347). Also provides the usual embassy services to citizens of Australia and New Zealand.

US Embassy at Tržište 15 (tel: 536641). Address mail to: US Embassy Prague, c/o Amcongen (PRG), APO New York 09213, USA.

Hitchers' Tips and Comments . . .

Hitching is OK, and for short distances usually faster than by train or bus. I found youth hostels filled with school groups, so you must book in advance, whatever the Hostelling International handbook says. You're allowed to camp in forests, but not in state parks.

RAY LAMPERT, CALGARY, CANADA

The centre of Prague is full of private exchange offices, but don't use them if there's a bank open. These exchange offices offer decent rates, but then they take huge commissions.

SAMULI SCHIELKE, TAMPERE, FINLAND

If you don't find a place to sleep in Prague try Petrin Hill. Don't try the main railway station. I did, and the next night in the Petrin Park felt like being in a hotel, even although it was April and the nights were still a bit cold. ANNA KULJU, TAMPERE, FINLAND

You are as well to spend all your Czech cash before leaving the country, unless you are moving on to Poland or Hungary where you will get a fair rate of exchange. You'll lose out dramatically if you change Czech money in Austria or Germany. Note that the small exchange bureaux will only convert crowns into hard currency for Czech citizens, so if you want to change your cash get to the bank before it closes. RONNIE LISTER, CROOK, ENGLAND

Slovakia

population	5,310,154
size	49,104 square kilometres
capital	Bratislava, population 480,000
government	parliamentary democracy
religion	Roman Catholic with Protestant and Orthodox minorities
language	Slovak. Knowledge of Russian is widespread. Increasing numbers of Slovaks are learning English, but German is generally much more useful at present
currency	*Koruny*

The good news for anyone hitching through Slovakia is that it is possible to take in the main sights whilst sticking to a more or less direct line of travel between the national capital, Bratislava, in the far west and the second city, Košice, close to the country's eastern border.

Heading eastwards from Bratislava the first obvious stop is **Trnava**, the oldest royal town in Slovakia, frequently referred to as the Slovak Rome. This description is fair enough in as much as Trnava was the seat of the Hungarian archbishopric between 1541–1820, after the Turks had taken Buda and gone on to ravage Esztergom, but it can lead visitors to expect far more in the way of architectural attractions than there actually is. Nevertheless the Church of St Elizabeth and the sumptuous Jesuit Church are well worth seeing, as are the remarkably intact town walls. The highlights of the nearby town of **Nitra** are the medieval castle and one of the more striking plague columns in Slovakia.

Heading into Central Slovakia there are several places to see around the regional capital Banská Bystrica. From Nitra the first logical target is the old German mining settlement of **Banská Štiavnica**, a strong contender for the title of the most beautiful town in Slovakia. The sloping main square is lined with many fine mansions from the town's heyday in the 16th century. A short walk away is the old castle and an interesting structure known as the **Klopačka** which served to rouse the local silver miners for the day's work.

Like Banská Štiavnica, **Kremnica** reached its peak in the 15th and 16th centuries, though Kremnica's wealth was derived not from silver but from gold, and the establishment of a mint in the town. Again there are some very fine houses lining the main square, the centrepiece of which is the most ornate plague column in the country. One of the houses on the square contains a small museum with examples of coins minted in Kremnica over the years.

Banská Bystrica itself has some noteworthy old buildings, but the main tourist attraction is the Museum of the Slovak National Uprising chronicling the unsuccessful revolt against Nazi rule which began in Banská Bystrica in 1944. The controversial building housing the museum is well worth seeing even if you don't fancy going inside.

Pushing on into East Slovakia the first major stop is **Poprad** on the fringes of the Spiš region. Poprad is the most obvious starting point for excursions into the High Tatras where there are plenty of opportunities for mountaineering, hillwalking and skiing. The town itself is basically modern and unappealing, but because there are plenty of visitors about you might find yourself staying a few days to enjoy the company you are likely to miss in some of the other Slovak towns mentioned here. Whilst in Poprad don't miss (most people do) **Spišská Sobota**. Only 2 km from central Poprad this small village was only recently incorporated into the city. Here, grouped round the church, belfry and plague column are houses with the overhanging gables and thatched roofs which are typical of the Spiš region. More examples of these traditional houses, plus one of Slovakia's best castles, can be seen in the town of **Kežmarok** to the north-east of Poprad.

East along the E85 from Poprad is the town of **Levoča**, a definite must on any tour of Slovakia. At the centre of the main square are the town hall and the Church of St James. The town hall is perhaps the finest in the country, while St James' Church contains a gothic altar by the local master Pavol of Levoča which is ranked amongst the greatest in Europe.

About 10 km east of Levoča are the ecclesiastical citadel of

Spišská Kapitula and the incredibly photogenic ruins of **Spišský Hrad**, the largest castle in Slovakia. Some 8 km south-west of Levoča lies the district capital **Spišská Nová Ves**. Here you can see some lesser works by Pavol of Levoča in the gothic church, but that apart there isn't really much reason to visit the town, unless you are planning to use it as a base for exploring the **Slovenský Raj** (Slovak Paradise) 10 km to the south-west. This area of narrow limestone gorges, waterfalls and strangely eroded rocks offers walkers a completely different environment from that of the High Tatras. Particularly interesting are the Kysel', Velký Sokol and Suchá Belá canyons (the latter has a beautiful waterfall). But the real highlight of the area is the Dobšiná Karst cave – don't miss it.

From Levoča the E85 runs through Prešov to Košice, the capital of East Slovakia. **Košice** (population 200,000) may not be the biggest or liveliest city, but if you arrive here after spending a bit of time exploring small Slovak towns and the countryside it will seem like you have arrived in Las Vegas. The main sight is the Cathedral of St Elizabeth, generally reckoned to be the most important historical building in the country. Within the Cathedral is the tomb of the Hungarian national hero Ferenc Rákoczi. **Prešov**, the cultural centre of the Slovak Ukraine, is itself worth a stopover for its historical buildings, especially some of the restored burghers' houses.

About 30 km north of the Prešov is **Bardejov**, the one Slovak town which can stand comparison with Banská Štiavnica. The main square looks pretty much the same as it must have done about 400 years ago. Standing alone in a central position towards the foot of the square is the town hall, beyond which is the Church of St Aegidius – a combination which seems made for photographers. Be sure to see inside the church itself as the collection of gothic altarpieces rivals that of virtually any church in Europe. Another must is the Šariš Museum just off the main square, which, in addition to some interesting displays on local history, has an excellent collection of over 300 icons.

● **Visa requirements** Visitors from the UK, Ireland and the USA do not need a visa to enter Slovakia. Citizens of Canada, Australia and New Zealand must obtain a visa in advance as these are not issued at the border.

Bratislava: where to sleep

Cheap hotels are thin on the ground in the Slovak captial. Pensions/private rooms are a better option. Book through **Satur** (see

Addresses below). Hostels spring up all over town in summer, usually in student residences. These are often advertised at the bus and train stations. In recent years **BIPS** (see **Addresses** below) have operated some temporary hostels. Ask for details at their office. The one year-round hostel is the **Juniorhotel Sputnik** at Drienová 14 (tel: 238000) run by CKM (though Satur, the new Slovak equivalent may have taken over by 1996). As the name suggests, it's actually a hotel, and whereas Hostelling International members used to be able to stay there for about £4 (a great bargain), a recent price hike means they'll now pay about £8 a night (still less than half the normal price).

There are two campsites out at Zlaté Piesky which are open from mid-May–mid-Sept. Reasonably priced two- and four-bedded bungalows can be hired, though you'll be very lucky to get one if you arrive without having booked in advance.

Bratislava: where to eat

Eating out in the Slovak capital won't put a strain on your budget. In fact, if you've got a bit of spare cash, this is a fine place to indulge yourself a bit – especially if you like cream cakes and pastries. There are plenty of cheap self-service restaurants around town where a 2-course meal will set you back as little as 60p. Some aren't very good though. Two which are worth seeking out are the **Dietna Jedalen** down the passage at Laurinska 8, and the **Mliečne Speciality** at Rybárska brána 9. The **Stará Sladovňa** at Cintorínska 32 is basically a beer hall, but it turns out good meals at around £1.50–2.50. For an enjoyable meal in a less raucous setting try the **Slovenská Restauracie** at Štúrova 3 which offers a wide choice of traditional Slovak fare, or the **U Zlatého Kapra** at Prepoštská 6, which specializes in fish dishes. A meal in either of these will set you back £2.50–4.

Bratislava: what to see and do

ST MARTIN'S CATHEDRAL One-time coronation church of the Hungarian royalty. Be sure to see the lead statue of St Martin by Donner.

BRATISLAVA CASTLE The castle looks better seen from a distance than it does strolling about the castle grounds. There are some good views of the old town from Castle Hill.

'AT THE GOOD SHEPHERD' A tall, rococo-style house at the foot of Castle Hill, so called because of the small statue of the Good Shepherd set in a niche on the wall. Houses an interesting collection of antique clocks.

BRIDGE OF THE SLOVAK NATIONAL UPRISING An undeniably imposing structure spanning the not-so-blue Danube. Unfortunately a large chunk of the old town was torn down to make way for the bridge. Ascend to the observation platform for great views over the town and beyond.

SLAVIN On a hill overlooking the city is this colossal memorial honouring the Red Army soldiers killed in the fight to liberate Bratislava from the Nazis.

SLOVAK NATIONAL THEATRE An impressive neo-Renaissance building from the mid-1880s, in front of which stands the Ganymede fountain.

NAMESTIE 4 APRILA One of the city's oldest squares, with its medieval statue of the Knight Roland, and the OLD TOWN HALL. The courtyard of the Old Town Hall is particularly attractive, Sometimes it is used as a concert venue, so it's tough luck if you turn up when it's full of temporary seating.

'AT THE RED CRAYFISH' Just down from the Michael Tower is this old pharmacy with a baroque interior and a small pharmaceutical museum on the premises. Unusual, and well worth a visit.

Transport in Bratislava

The public transport system of trams and buses is cheap. It's also comprehensive, unless you find yourself staying in the monstrous Petrzalka housing estate across the Danube. Buy tickets in advance, then cancel them on boarding. There are automatic ticket machines at the main termini; otherwise you can buy them from some of the small stands selling newspapers and the like.

Addresses

BIPS (Bratislava Information & Publicity Service) at Panská 13, in the old town centre (tel: 333 715/334 325). BIPS publish a leaflet *Kam v Bratislave* (Where to Go), with English information sections.

Satur, Miletičova 1 (tel: 82472) will deal with postal enquiries. The office at Jesenského 5–9 (Tel. 427 36724) deals with personal visitors.

MD1Student agency at Hviezdoslavovo námestie 16 (tel: 331 607)

MD1**US Embassy** at Hviezdoslavovo namestie 16, Bratislava (tel: 331607).

British Embassy. Opened in 1994. The British *chargé d'affaires*, Mr Bates, can also be contacted at Panska 17 – the same address as the British Council (tel: 331261/331185).

Hungary

population	10,709,000
size	93,033 square kilometres
capital	Budapest, population 2,200,000
government	parliamentary democracy
religion	Mostly Roman Catholic and Protestant
language	Hungarian; some German and English understood in tourist areas
currency	*Forint* One *forint* equals 100 *fillérs*. Coins of 10, 20, 50 *fillérs*, and of 1, 2, 5, 10 and 20 *forints*. Notes of 10, 20, 50, 100, 500, 1,000 and 5,000 *forints*

Many hitchers combine Austria and Hungary in the one trip. If you enter Hungary after a look at Vienna, try and make your first stop at the walled town of **Sopron**, close by **Lake Ferto**. The town is amongst Hungary's most beautiful. In Roman days it was an important link on the trade route to Byzantium. For great views (and photographs) of the city centre climb the more than a hundred steps of the *Tuztorony* (or Fire Tower). Several churches and museums will help you spend a pleasant half-day in this old town. Music fiends should visit the Liszt Ferenc Museum. When he was still a child Liszt made his debut as a pianist in Sopron and part of the museum's exhibits are devoted to his life.

At **Fertöd**, 27 km east of Sopron, visit the Esterházy Palace. This baroque palace, with its 126 rooms, was rebuilt in its present-day form in the 1770s. Like Sopron, Esterházy offers special musical associations as Haydn was the resident musician at the court of the Esterházy family. The palace is sometimes called the 'Versailles of Hungary'. It's certainly the finest palace in the country by a long chalk, but don't expect anything on the scale of Versailles or you're doomed to disappointment. Heading south from Sopron you should really try to see the small border town of **Köszeg** as it's pretty much unique in Hungary. While other Hungarian towns were being remodelled in the baroque or later architectural styles Koöszeg retained its medieval core. You won't see such a fine collection of renaissance buildings as those lining the main square anywhere else in the country. One of them contains a baroque-style pharmacy which is worth a look. Just off the square are the churches of St Emmerich and St James. See the frescoes in St James'. A short walk away is Koöszeg's castle which dates from the 13th century. The castle had a major role in European history. In 1532 the castle garrison resisted a Turkish army of 200,000, allowing time for the Austrians and their allies to prepare for the ultimately successful defence of Vienna which was the Turks' main target.

A day's hitching south (if you're lucky) brings you to **Szombathely**, said to be the oldest town in Hungary. (The Roman settlement of Savaria was founded nearby in AD 43 by Claudius I). In 1957 archaeologists dug up a Temple of Isis which now serves as a backdrop for summer concerts. See also the 4th-century Basilica of Quirinus and the 15-metre-long mosaic pavement in the Romkert, or Garden of Ruins. Art students should check the Savaria Museum with its collection of Hungarian paintings. Rest up and stock up in the main square, Koztarsasag tér.

South again to **Lake Balaton**. At 78 km long and 15 wide at its widest point, with 197 km of shoreline and covering 596 sq.km, this is Central Europe's largest lake. Several million people a year visit and you, like most foreigners, will have great fun sorting out where you are going and where you have been because nearly all the names of the lake resorts use 'Balaton' as their prefix. Did you hitch from Balatonfuzfo to Balatonalmadi yesterday, or was it from Balatonszepezd to Balatonfenyves via Balatongyorok with a stop for a sandwich in Balatonszentgyorgy? Balaton is a linguistic disaster area, a place where through one slip of the tongue a rendezvous with one you love can turn into a police hunt for a missing person. Apart from all that Balaton is OK as long as you aren't visiting in high summer. If hitching is tough, use the train which circumnavigates the lake. There are many places to visit. Don't miss **Fonyod** on the southern side which dates back to the Stone Age: in the evening try for some free dinner by tossing in a line from the pier for one of the lake's forty varieties of fish. At **Buzsak** 16 km further south you can see some folk art (pretty touristy now, but still attractive). **Tihany**, which occupies a tiny peninsula on the north shore, has been declared a national park and is amongst the best known of the Balaton resorts: see the 18th-century Abbey Church built atop a 900-year-old Romanesque crypt and, next door, the Tihany Museum which gives you a rundown on the lake since the Romans used it as a resort area.

Just a few kilometres north-east of the lake on the route to Budapest lies **Szekesfehervar**, founded in AD 972 and claiming for itself the title of the oldest *Hungarian* settled town, as opposed to, for instance, Roman. (Needless to say the Romans were here too.) Hungarian kings were crowned and sometimes buried here until 1527. See the Garden of Ruins, Liberty Square, City Hall, the Bishop's Palace and lots more. But the real beauty of the town is that though it is only minutes from the main road you get the feeling you are right off the tourist track.

Pecs, capital of Baranya County in the south-west and site of Hungary's first university (founded in 1367), was known to the Germans as *Fünfkirchen*, or five churches. But the surprise in the town's main square is a 16th-century Turkish Mosque (now a church), a remnant of the Turkish occupation of 1543–1686. And in Rákoczi Street stands another mosque, now a museum – the only one in all of Hungary still with its minaret. See the ceramics collection in the Janus Pannonius Museum. Across the road the collection of 'op art' works by world famous Victor Vasarely are exhibited in the house in which he was born. Nearby is a gallery of the neo-surrealist works of the not-so-well-known Tivadar Csontvary Kosztka which for my money are a knockout.

North of Budapest, along the Duna (as the Hungarians know the Danube), don't miss **Szentendre**, quaint to the point of eye-popping and touristic to boot but worth the visit. After a stroll amongst some of Europe's prettiest village streets which include a Greek-Orthodox, a Serbian-Orthodox, and a Baroque church, you could hoist your thumb and move on another 5 km to the open-air Ethnographical Museum and enjoy the display based around 19th-century Hungarian peasant life. Following the Duna north and then west brings you to the cathedral city of **Esztergom**, formerly the capital and royal residence of the early Hungarian kings; Stephen I, first king of Hungary and considered founder of the State was born here in 977. See the Great Cathedral, modelled on Rome's St Peter's, which is the largest church in Hungary, the Royal Palace, the Museum of Christian Art and the pretty 18th-century buildings in the main square. Directly across the river is Czechoslovakia. The bridge which linked the two countries at this point was destroyed in the Second World War; a ferry makes the connection now.

Heading east, don't miss **Eger**. For Hungarians the town is a symbol of Christianity's centuries-long battle with Islam. In 1552 the defenders of Eger routed a Turkish army; in 1596 the town was lost again and in 1687 won back. A magnificent 35-metre-high minaret stands today in the city like an exclamation mark accenting the long success of the invaders. In the Castle Museum, named after

Istvan Dobo who led the defenders of 1552, are mementos of those terrifying days. The Minorite Church, one of over 150 in the city, is considered one of Hungary's more important monuments. After a day of hard sightseeing and the rigorous contemplation of history, you can reward yourself by enjoying the other thing Eger is famous for: *Egri bikaver*, the Bull's Blood wine of Eger (try it, but preferably with a meal!).

Miskolc, second largest town in Hungary, may not immediately endear itself to you, but if you are heading east you'll probably hit it. Check the view from the lookout point below the TV mast on Avas mountain and also the man-made caves used as wine cellars. Liberty Square is pleasant enough. Some 55 km north of Miskolc, close to the Czech border, is the **Aggtelek region** featuring a cave system which spelunkers from the world over come to admire. Visit **Baradla Cave**, 23 km long. Various trips taking from one to five hours guide you through huge chambers full of wondrous stalactites and stalagmites. Be warned that even in summer it's cold down there! East of Miskolc, by the Tisza river, lies **Tokaj**, another famous wine town. A distinctive golden wine has been produced in and around Tokaj for over 700 years. However hard they try, vineyards from other countries cannot imitate it. Check the wine cellars and the wine museum.

There are places in the Hortobagy, on Hungary's Great Plain or *puszta*, which stretches all the way from Budapest to the eastern borders and covers 52,000 sq.km, where you can truly imagine the ancient Magyars riding hard through thigh-high grass to take possession of the country. Wander through the **Hortobagy National Park**, visit **Hortobagy** itself and admire its stone bridge of nine arches.

● **Visa requirements** British, Irish, US and Canadian nationals do not require a visa to enter Hungary. Citizens of Australia and New Zealand should obtain a visa in advance from a Hungarian embassy as visas are not issued at the border.

Hitching
Hitching is officially not permitted in Hungary, but those who need to do it or simply appreciate the art form of doing it do it would be unlucky to be stopped.

Budapest: where to sleep

Rooms in cheap hotels and pensions are difficult to find at most times of year. One possibility is the hotel at the **Citadella**, which offers rooms and also much cheaper dormitory-style accommodation.

A room in a local's home is a less expensive option. Book through **Budapest Tourist**, **Coopturist**, at the **Express** office in Keleti train station or at any **IBUSZ** office. Many hostels only open July or mid-July through till August or mid-August. Fortunately the accommodation scene isn't nearly as bad as it was a few years ago, so that even if you arrive in the afternoon in peak season you have a chance of getting a hostel bed. It does make sense to book in advance though – see the *Hostelling International* (HI) handbook for the latest details on how to do so. HI hostels are highly recommended; no curfews, friendly staff, locked baggage rooms and great places for meeting up with people – all for about £3.50–4.

There are plenty of campsites in the city. Standards are OK, but a solo traveller will pay about £2.50–3.20 for an overnight stay. Add on another £1 if you want to leave your pack at the station and you might begin to think that camping in Budapest is an option to be taken up only if you can't pin down a hostel bed. It's worth noting that **Budapest Tourist** book two- and four-bedded bungalows at the city's campsites. These can be great value, but you'll have to be really lucky to get a bungalow on arrival in summer.

Budapest: where to eat

Restaurants are cheap. Around Keleti station they are *really* cheap. Eat where locals eat. Keep away from anything featuring gypsy music (the reason the violinists have the little finger of their bow hand crooked is to snatch banknotes from you). Self-service restaurants offer exceptional bargains. Soups (*levesek*) are excellent. Note that what we call Hungarian goulash is called *porkolt* or *tokany* in Hungary. Their goulash or *gulyasleves* is a soup. You won't find much English spoken, or any English menus in cheaper restaurants. Sympathetic waiters will let you check the plates in the kitchen.

Budapest: what to see and do

THE CASTLE DISTRICT is the heart of the city's major sights and is on the hilly western side of the Danube, in Buda. On the eastern side of the river lies Pest, flat as far as you can see. The walk up is no fun with a pack. If you have a few forints spare treat yourself to a ride up in the cable tram leaving from Clark Adam tér by the Chain

Bridge. Lose yourself for a while amongst beautiful streets before making your way to the 13th-century MATTHIAS CHURCH. During its long life it has been both the coronation church for Hungarian kings and, during the Turkish occupation, a mosque. Behind the church see the bronze STATUE OF ST STEPHEN, Hungary's first Christian king. Wander the ramparts of fanciful FISHERMEN'S BASTION for great views over the river to the Hungarian PARLIAMENT BUILDING (the huge domed building left of the Chain Bridge) on the Pest side. The Bastion is as new as it looks: it was built this century. It takes its name from the Fishermen's Guild which used to defend this section of Castle Hill. Check the reflection of the Bastion in the glass wall of the ultra-modern Hilton Hotel behind.

THE ROYAL PALACE dominates the southern end of the Castle Hill plateau. It was begun in the 13th century by Bela IV, the same king who founded St Matthias Church, added to over the centuries, destroyed during the Turkish era, rebuilt and then so badly damaged during the Second World War that it had to be completely rebuilt yet again. It now houses the NATIONAL GALLERY and the BUDAPEST MUSEUM OF HISTORY.

ST GELLERT'S MONUMENT above the Elizabeth Bridge stands at about the same spot from which the Italian saint who tried converting the Hungarians to Christianity was launched in a nose-dive towards the river by not so playful pagans. Views over city, river and bridge make it worth the climb. (If you decide to sleep up here, make sure you have one or two others for company – some days there are lots of loitering weirdos.)

THE CITADELLA high above St Gellert's Monument is a 19th-century fortification still bearing Second World War shrapnel scars received when it was wrested from the Germans by the Russians. A LIBERATION MONUMENT to those same Russians crowns the hill.

MARGARET ISLAND is a little get-away-from-it-all traffic-free wonderland in the middle of the river between Buda and Pest.

THE MILLENIUM MONUMENT on Hosok tere (Heroes' Square) tries to impart the drama and romance of a thousand years of Hungarian history through groups of statues of kings, Magyar tribal chieftains and heroes. In the square is the MUSEUM OF FINE ARTS. The collection includes fine examples from most European Schools.

THE CITY PARK (Varosliget) behind Heroes' Square is another hideaway from city pressures. See VAJDAHUNYAD CASTLE, a reproduction castle built between 1904 and 1908. It houses the AGRICULTURAL MUSEUM. In the courtyard stands the STATUE OF ANONYMOUS. The moated castle is particularly evocative when it is floodlit at night. Don't miss the nearby SZECHENYI BATHS. You can drop in for a look at Europe's largest public medicinal baths or pay a small fee and swim in them yourself.

Addresses

Tourinform at Sütoö u. 2 (tel: 1179800). Tourist information service, and impartial advice on accommodation possibilities in the city as Tourinform doesn't make any bookings itself.

Express Youth and Student Travel Bureau at Szabadság tér 12 (tel: 1179800), Semmelweis utca 4 (tel: 117860), and in Keleti train station.

Coopturist at Bajcsy Zsilinszky út 17 (tel: 1310992).

IBUSZ at Tanács körút 3c (tel: 1186866); at Felszabadulás tér 5 (tel: 1186866); at Petoöfi tér 3 (tel: 1185707); and in the three main train stations.

Budapest Tourist at Roosevelt tér 5–6 (tel: 1186000).

US Embassy at Szabadság tér 12, 1054 Budapest V (tel: 1126450, after normal office hours 1530566).

British Embassy at Harmincad utca 6, Budapest (tel: 2182888). Also provides embassy services to citizens of New Zealand.

Hitchers' Tips and Comments . . .

I found hitching in Hungary OK, but if you get off the main roads take a train. They're cheap. But don't take an express. They're twice the price, half as interesting, and only marginally faster.

ALAN THATCHER, NEW ZEALAND

Hitching is OK in Hungary. The cars aren't fast, the drivers are a bit crazy, but the people are friendly. There's often competition from the locals, so you increase your chances if you use a gimmick. It's important to get hold of the excellent free motoring map published by the Tourist Board, if only to show your driver where you want to go, because sure as hell he isn't going to understand your pronunciation.

'THE WIBBLER', LEEDS, ENGLAND

In summer the queues of cars crossing into Hungary from Austria can be lengthy. BRENDA SCOTT, DUMFRIES, SCOTLAND

If hotels and campsites are full at popular Hungarian destinations, you can try for accommodation in private houses. Some are registered with travel agencies, some simply have notices up outside the actual house. The rooms are reasonably priced.

JOZSEF BOROCZ, BUDAPEST, HUNGARY

The pastry shops are as good as Austria's and one-sixth of the price.

PETE FRASER AND MAGGIE WILCOCK, HARLOW, ENGLAND

Budapest's Keleti railway station is a good place to kip. It's clean and the police don't move you on until 4.30 a.m.

MIKE LOWRY, EDINBURGH, SCOTLAND

It's fairly difficult to find a student hostel in Budapest in summer. But you can get a private room for ten dollars a night.

A. ZALE, BUDAPEST, HUNGARY

Change money at a bank or at IBUSZ and keep your receipt. That way you can change forints back at a bank or IBUSZ office and get a decent rate. Changing forints privately, or at a bank in Austria, you lose out dramatically.

JAN DE VONK, LEEUWARDEN, THE NETHERLANDS

Poland

population	38,200,000
size	312,683 square kilometres
capital	Warsaw, population 1,700,000
government	Parliamentary democracy
religion	Roman Catholic
language	Polish; a little German and English understood
currency	*Zloty* Notes of 50, 100, 500, 1,000, 2,000, 5,000, 10,000, 20,000, 100,000, 500,000 and 1,000,000 *Zloty*

If you enter Poland from the south, your first major stop should be **Cracow**, population 700,000, the country's third largest city after Warsaw and Lodz. From 1320–1609 Cracow was the capital of Poland. In the 1800s it was even capital of an independent republic. The Nazis occupied the city during the Second World War and only a surprise attack by the Russians in 1945 saved it from destruction.

Consequently medieval Cracow still stands to take its place amongst Europe's most beautiful towns.

Cracow tourist department claims the city offers 'more than one thousand buildings and monuments of historical and architectural interest'. A dozen or so should see you through. Not to be missed is *Rynek Glówny*, the Old Market Place, known locally as Cracow's Drawing Room because of the number of people who meet to chat or drink tea at the outdoor cafés. The arched arcades of the 100-metre-long Cloth Hall makes the square reminiscent of St Mark's in Venice. See St Mary's Church, the most important of the city's 60 old churches. Check out the altar piece. Stroll a couple of hundred metres west of the square to the Jagiellonian University established in 1364 and amongst the oldest in Europe. South of the square climb Wawel Hill for a great view over the old city and to visit Wawel Castle and museum, once home to Polish kings, and Wawel Cathedral, See of the Archbishop of Cracow and thus, recently, of Cardinal Wojtyla, who became Pope John Paul II.

Some 15 km from Cracow are the still working **Wieliczka Salt Mines**. A 2 km route along a section open to the public takes you through weird chambers, some with salt carved statues, some with mini-lakes. About 54 km from Cracow is the town of **Oswiecim**, known in English as **Auschwitz**, site of the huge extermination camp of **Auschwitz-Birkenau**, where the Nazis systematically murdered and incinerated over 4 million men, women and children from 29 countries. See the gas chambers and the crematoria and let it sink in that some first-class pricks actually *planned* all this. You will never forget what you see in Auschwitz.

After Venice and Leningrad, **Wroclaw** has more bridges than any other European city – 84 of them which cross the Oder River and canals and lend the city a special atmosphere. Theatre freaks will know all about Wroclaw. It is the home of the innovative Jerzy Grotowki's Laboratory Theatre and the Henryk Tomaszewski Pantomime Theatre. Like so many Polish cities, Wroclaw was wrecked in the Second World War (the country suffered 6 million dead, about 20% of the population!), but has been completely rebuilt. See the beautifully reconstructed Old Town, particularly the Gothic Town Hall which houses the Historical Museum, and visit *Ostrow Tumski* (Cathedral Island) to see the cathedral which was built during the 13th to 15th centuries. (Plenty of parks for emergency dossing.)

North takes you to **Poznan**. (If you are heading to Warsaw from Berlin, this may be your first major stop.) Like Cracow, Poznan has also enjoyed moments as the country's capital. Citizens still proudly point out that Poland's first two kings lived here and that in AD 968 it was the site of Poland's first cathedral. This century its fame rests on being a meeting place for businessmen; the Poznan International Trade Fair is known throughout the world. See the renaissance Town Hall in the Old Market Square. Check out the goats on the town hall clock at noon. Visit the History Museum inside the town hall and the Museum of Musical Instruments nearby at number 45. Take a stroll to Cathedral Island (*Ostrow Tumski*) on the Warta river which was Poznan's earliest inhabited area and where the first cathedral was built. (The cathedral standing now has been rebuilt since the war.) Poznan hosts several important music festivals. Check exact dates with Polish tourist offices before your trip.

About 14 km south-west of Poznan is **Wielkopolski National Park**. The beach at Lake Rusalka (one of 16 in the park) is a great place to meet young Poles at weekends. Travelling south-east from Poznan you come to **Kornik**, an ancient town complete with moated castle and a park exhibiting over 2,000 varieties of trees and shrubs. At **Swarzedz**, 10 km along the E8, those who are seriously interested in such things can visit an open-air beehive museum!

North-west of Warsaw on the road to Gdansk lies **Torun**, home of the famed 16th-century astronomer Nicolaus Copernicus. (He proved that the planets revolve around the sun.) His birthplace is open to the public. Don't miss the Leaning Tower of Torun. Not as precarious as that of Pisa, but worth a look. At **Malbork**, further north, see the tremendous Castle of the Teutonic Knights.Since its foundation in AD 997 **Gdansk** (the German Danzig) has found itself woven into the fabric of history like few European cities. This century has continued the tradition: Poland's refusal to give Gdansk to Germany was one of the excuses Hitler used for precipitating the Second World War; and of course Gdansk is the home of Solidarity. The author Günter Grass, who was born in Gdansk in 1927, wrote about the city in his famous novel *The Tin Drum*. Centre of town is *Dlugi Targ*, the market square. Check out the town hall with its Historical Museum and climb the tower for an overall view of the city. There's another great view from the steeple of the Mariacki Cathedral. Like everywhere else in Poland most of the old town has been reconstructed since the war. For a glimpse of what things were like in another age stroll down Mariacka Street. The politically motivated should check the monument to Solidarity workers killed in the 1970 uprising at what was then known as the Lenin Shipyard. August is festival time and accommodation can be hard to find.

When you have finally had enough of cities, treat yourself to a few days by the rivers and lakes and in the forests of the **Mazurian Lake District**, east of Gdansk. Amongst a number of places worth a visit are **Frombork** (cathedral town by a lagoon, many associations with Copernicus), **Olsztyn** (castle, Gothic cathedral,

Archaeological Museum, main town in area) and **Nidzica** (14th-century Gothic castle used by Teutonic Knights). Just 6 km east of the 14th-century city of **Ketrzyn**, Second World War buffs can visit the **Wolf's Lair** which was where, in 1944, Colonel von Stauffenburg narrowly missed assassinating Hitler.

Lublin, 175 km south-east of the capital, is the most important city in Eastern Poland, and worth a stopover on account of its compact old town. There are some especially fine buildings around the Rynek, and down Grodzka. Whilst walking down the latter keep your eyes peeled for some of the small reminders of the thriving Jewish community which lived in this part of the city before the arrival of the Nazis. On the outskirts of Lublin stands **Majdanek**, the second largest of the Nazis' extermination camps (after Auschwitz-Birkenau). In fact what you see is only a small part of the planned development on the site as the Red Army swept over the region before work on Majdanek was anywhere near complete. Nevertheless some 360,000 people met their death in Majdanek. The vast size of the camp is actually easier to appreciate than at Birkenau as Majdanek was built on a gentle slope, with the result that you can see all over the camp from the upper end. At this point is an enormous dome covering the ashes of many of those who perished in Majdanek.

Kazimierz Dolny, 40 km west of Lublin, can justifiably claim to be Poland's most picturesque small town. Fine renaissance houses line the main square, at the centre of which is an old wooden well. Rising above one end of the square is the parish church, beyond which are the ruins of the castle.

Continuing south-east from Lublin brings you to **Zamość**, one of Poland's real gems, but so far out of the way that few foreigners other than Ukrainians or Russians in transit actually pass through the town. Zamość was founded in the late 16th century by the Polish chancellor Jan Zamoyski who commissioned the Italian architect Morano to plan an ideal new town. Apart from the staircase in front of the town hall the main square is just as Morano planned it. A short walk away is St Thomas' Collegiate Church, another work by Morano, and the palace built for the chancellor himself. Dotted about the fringes of the old town are remains of the impressive system of fortifications which ensured that Zamość fulfilled Zamoyski's desire for a bulwark against attacks from the east. You can also see the synagogue that was part of the original town plan, though it now serves as a public library; the Jewish community, so important in pre-war Zamość, is now little more than a memory. There isn't much about town nowadays to commemorate Zamość's most famous (Jewish) citizen, the communist theorist Rosa

Luxemburg who was born in the house at ul. Staszica 37. In Zamość, as in Poland as a whole, history is being re-written again, and Luxemburg's criticisms of Lenin are dismissed as an irrelevance.

● **Visa requirements** British, Irish and US nationals do not require a visa to visit Poland. Citizens of Australia, New Zealand and Canada must obtain a visa in advance from a Polish embassy as these are not issued at the border.

Hitching
There are few places better to hitch than Poland. Hitchhiking is actually officially encouraged here. Travel any distance and you'll be sure to see locals standing waiting for a lift. Drivers stop to ask where people are headed as a matter of course.

Warsaw: where to sleep

The **Centrum Informacji Turystycznej** on plac Zamkowy (tel: 6351881) doesn't take bookings, but will give impartial advice on accommodation possibilities, including info on cheap hotels which you won't get anywhere else. You can book private rooms through **Syrena** at ul. Krucza 17 (tel: 287540/257201), or through the considerably more expensive **Romeo and Juliet** at Emilii Plater 30 (3rd floor) where you will have to pay in hard currency.

The **Polish Youth Hostels Association** (PTSM) run two hostels. One is at ul. Smolna 30 (tel: 278952), the other at ul. Karolkowa 53a (tel: 328829). **ALMATUR** at ul. Kopernika 23 (tel: 263512) can advise on beds in International Student Hostels during the summer.

There are a number of campsites in the city, the best of which is **Gromada** on ul. zwirki i Wigury (tel: 254391). The Centrum Informacji Turystycznej will fill you in on details of the other sites.

Two places to doss out: walk over the Slasko-Dabrowski bridge (the one by the Old Town) and turn left into the wild park area by the river; in Zazienki Park make sure you're well hidden. Don't use tents or light a fire in either place.

Warsaw: where to eat

Go where working-class Poles eat and you'll eat cheap and well. Be careful if you order beer (*piwa*) – some places give you imported stuff instead of the local brew. Local beer is cheap and good; wine is mostly imported and expensive. Tea (*herbata*) is dead cheap in most cafés but comes without milk. Coffee (*kawa*) is a bit more expensive. Street kiosks sell cheap, filling slabs of pizza with hot sauce for snacks.

Warsaw: what to see and do

THE OLD TOWN'S hub is *Rynek Starego Miasta* (Old Market Place), quaint, colourful, cobbled and evocative of another era. But the square (like most of the city) was systematically destroyed by the Nazis and has been rebuilt from the ground up since the war. If you have trouble grasping the idea drop into the HISTORICAL MUSEUM on the north side of the square and see a short film which documents the events. Also check out the fascinating material on display about the Polish Resistance. North of the square see the BARBICAN, built in 1548 to guard a city gate, and now a popular spot for souvenir sellers. Beyond is Freta Street leading to *Rynek Nowomiejski* (New Town Market Square). At 16 Freta Street see the MARIE CURIE MUSEUM, where Poland's famed scientist (the discoverer of radium) was born.

THE ROYAL ROUTE is a pleasant 4 km walk which starts at Castle Square and takes you down the connecting streets of Krakowskie Przedmiescie, Nowy Swiat and Aleje Ujazdowskie to end at Lazienki Park. You'll need a map to identify the 25 or 30 important points on the route. In the centre of Castle Square (Plac Zamkowy) see the 30-metre-high 17th-century COLUMN OF KING SIGISMUND III VASA and on the Vistula River side the completely rebuilt ROYAL CASTLE, in 1791 site of the ratification of Europe's first constitution, now a museum of interior decoration. On your left is the entrance to lovely Piwna Street. Like the Old Market Place, Castle Square is a meeting place for travellers and locals alike. Wandering up the Royal Route look for the statue to poet Adam Mickiewicz and KASIMIERZOWSKI PALACE (behind the University), which once housed the Knight's School where Tadeusz Kosciuszko was educated. Kosciuszko, who is a national hero of Poland for his leadership of national insurrection, and famed in the United States for his role in the US War of Independence, also has Australia's highest mountain named after him. At the ACADEMY OF FINE ARTS, visit Chopin's drawing room. At the nearby HOLY CROSS CHURCH fans can pay homage to the great musician – the ashes of his heart are entombed in a column. Diagonally opposite the church see the statue to Polish astronomer Copernicus. On Jerozolimskie Avenue, just around the corner from Nowy Swiat, take a look at the POLISH ARMY MUSEUM. The gardens look like a military hardware car-boot sale.

LAZIENKI PARK at the end of the Royal Route is a forest park, built in the 18th century as the summer residence of King Stanislaus Augustus. Stately trees and shady walks conceal – amongst other things – BELVEDERE PALACE, and THE PALACE ON THE WATER. Chopin fans can pay homage at a weird and flamboyant statue to the composer. Nice place to scoff a picnic lunch after a hard morning's walk down the Royal Route. Keep a mouthful for the tame squirrels.

WILANOW PALACE stands 10 km from the centre of town at Wilanow. Grab Bus 180 which travels down Marszalkowska Street before cutting across to Belwederska via Spacerowa Street at the southern end of Lazienki Park. The Baroque palace built in the 17th century by King Jan Sobieski is sometimes described as a mini-Versailles. Inside is the MÚZEUM PLAKATU housing one of Europe's largest poster collections. Pleasant gardens. Good place to observe locals in relaxed mood.

WARSAW MERMAID (Pomnik Syreny) by the Syreny Bridge at the end of Tamka Street (take Bus 128 from Forum Hotel near Culture Palace). The symbol of Warsaw and mother of the city. She came out of the river and told two children, Wars and Szawa (Warszawa – get it?) to establish a city. Apparently they did.

MEMORIES OF THE WAR It's impossible to escape memories of the Second World War in Warsaw. The murderous excesses of the Nazis have imprinted themselves into the soul of this city which has had to rebuild itself from the ground up since 1945. Amongst the memorials: MONUMENT TO THE HEROES OF THE GHETTO at Zamenhofa Street, once the heart of the Warsaw Ghetto, which remembers the hundreds of thousands of Jews murdered there or transported to death camps, and the insurrection of the Jewish fighters in April 1943; MONUMENT TO THE HEROES OF WARSAW in Teatralny Square which commemorates all citizens who died in the city; MONUMENT TO THE WARSAW UPRISING at the corner of Dluga and Miodowa streets where statues of heroic figures emerging from city sewers recall an episode during the Warsaw uprising of September 1944. But perhaps the most touching reminders of those evil days are plaques all over the city remembering people who were murdered in a particular spot. Nearly half a century after the events, Warsaw folk still lay flowers by them.

PALACE OF CULTURE AND SCIENCE 37-storey-high Russian neo-Gothic blot-on-the-landscape looming over DAILY MARKET in Defilad Square and detested by locals. Butt of many a joke like: 'Why is it so nice to be on the roof of the Culture Palace?– Because then you can't see it.' What you can see is a stunning view over the city which makes the elevator trip worthwhile.

CINEMA Many foreign-language films are shown undubbed. Check local papers.

Transport in Warsaw
Buses and trams in the local transport system are so cheap you don't have to worry about your budget. Buy tickets at a *Ruch* stand and cancel them at the machines on the vehicles after you board.

Addresses

Polish Association of Youth Hostels (PTSM) at Chocimska 28, Warsaw.
Harctur Scout Travel, Niemcem'cza 17, Warsaw.
Juventur, Youth Travel and Information, Jerozolimskie 32, Warsaw.
Tau Travel, Tvzech Krzyzy Sq. 16, Warsaw.
Almatur (Travel and Tourism Office of the Polish Students' Association) at ul. Kopernika 23, Warsaw (tel: 26 35 12).
US Embassy at Aleja Ujazdowskie 29–31, Warsaw (tel: 28 30 41).
British Embassy at Aleja Roz 1, Warsaw (tel: 28 10 01).

Hitchers' Tips and Comments . . .

In Krakow see the marketplace, called Rynek Glówny (Main Square). And don't miss the Wawel on its hill above the Vistula River. Up there you can see castles, churches, the tombs of the Polish kings and museums.

Canteens, which are common in Polish cities, are highly recommended. You can have a hot, decent meal much cheaper than in a restaurant.

Hitching in Poland is great. Everybody does it: housewives, whole families, the lot. They don't put out a thumb, they just stand there, or wave at the cars. On the Warsaw to Krakow road there were about sixty people hitching, and in the 45 minutes we waited we saw one guy turn down five lifts! Not speaking Polish is a disadvantage in the rush to a car which stops, but we hitched a lift on a public bus with fare-paying passengers aboard. Poland is the place where all good hitchers go when they die!

JEFF HOYLE AND MIKE FULLEN, BURY, ENGLAND

Don't take Polish money into the Czech Republic thinking you can change it there. The Czech banks just don't want to know, and you'll lose out substantially changing it anywhere else.

TERI THOMPSON, SHORT, UK

Cashing a travellers' cheque in Poland can make you feel like you're being punished for something you did in a past life. Finding a bank to carry out the transaction is tricky enough. Getting the transaction completed before your short back-and-sides is flowing down your back is another matter. Take a book – and a sandwich or two.

CHARLIE CLARK 'THE KELSO ONION MAN', BARROW, ENGLAND

In Poland it's normal to offer to pay for a ride – a little bit more than half the bus fare is the going rate. Since you're a foreigner the drivers will rarely take your money, but it's polite to try.

SAMULI SCHIELKE AND ANNA KULJU, TAMPERE, FINLAND

Romania

population	23,190,000
size	237,500 square kilometres
capital	Bucharest, population 2,300,000
government	parliamentary democracy
religion	mainly Romanian Orthodox with small Greek Orthodox, Roman Catholic and Protestant minorities
language	Romanian. English and French are the foreign languages taught in schools. German and Hungarian can be useful in Transylvania and the Banat
currency	*Leu* One *leu* equals 100 *bani*. Coins of 25 *bani*, 1 *leu*, 3, 5, 10 and 100 *lei*. Notes of 100, 200, 500, 1,000 and 5,000 *lei*

Hitching in from Hungary the first major town on your route is likely to be Oradea (on the main road from Budapest), or Arad if you have made your way via Szeged. **Arad** is a pretty uninspiring place as a whole, and its one main sight, the citadel, is closed to the public on account of its military role. **Oradea** is a much better introduction to Romania. Overall it's a more pleasant town than Arad, there are a few churches worth seeing, and the old episcopal palace, built along the lines of Vienna's Belvedere Palace, is quite impressive.

About 60 km south of Arad is **Timişoara**, a city best known in Western Europe as the place where the revolt against the dictator Ceauşescu began. The Reformed Protestant Church from which Father Tökés condemned Ceauşescu is off blvd 6 Martie, across the canal from the Orthodox Cathedral. The church is used by members of the local ethnic Hungarian community. Timişoara's position at the meeting point of several countries and cultures is reflected in the three main churches of the town – the 18th-century Serbian church, the baroque Roman Catholic cathedral (used mainly by ethnic Hungarians), and the 20th-century Romanian Orthodox Cathedral.

Cluj-Napoca, 153 km east of Oradea, is famous as the birthplace of two of Hungary's greatest kings: Matthias Corvinus and his father, János Hunyadi. You can see the house Corvinus was born in 1440. The Botanical Gardens are excellent, and there are a couple of decent museums in town. The Ethnographical Museum has a fine collection of traditional Transylvanian costumes. Nearby is the History Museum of Transylvania. It's worth remembering that the Romanian and Hungarian versions of Transylvania's history are markedly different, and that the almost permanent state of tension between the two countries can occasionally rise to the surface where there are sizeable Hungarian communities within Romania. In the wake of the 1989 revolution there were clashes in Cluj-Napoca between Romanians and ethnic Hungarians.

Deva, 149 km east of Oradea, has a 13th-century citadel built on top of an extinct volcano, but otherwise not much to commend a stopover apart from its brandy. You can't really avoid Deva though if you want to see the castle at **Hunedoara**, 13 km to the south. Built in the Gothic style in the 14th century the castle was the stronghold of the Hunedoara family which included János Hunyadi (in Romanian Iancu de Hunedoara) and Matthias Corvinus. Hunedoara looks just like the sort of castle you might have drawn when you were young: all battlements and towers, with a huge drawbridge.

Continuing east from Deva you reach **Sibiu**, a town almost universally acclaimed as the most beautiful in Romania. In truth it's one of the finest sights in Europe: towns which have preserved their medieval core virtually intact aren't exactly ten-a-penny. Don't miss the Evangelical Church which contains a huge 18th-century organ and a superb mid-15th-century fresco of the crucifixion, but otherwise simply enjoy wandering round the old town rather than looking for specific sights. What you see may disorientate you a bit though, for Sibiu is actually a classic example of an old German settlement, one of the original seven towns founded in Transylvania by German settlers (hence Siebenburgen – the German name for the region). In recent years there has been a steady flow of Transylvanian Germans back to the homeland (where most have to be taught to speak modern German), but it's still not unusual to hear Sibiu called by its German name: Hermannstadt.

Sighişoara (Schässburg) to the north-east of Sibiu is just as easy to fall in love with as Sibiu. Again the centre of town is very much the same as it would have been centuries ago. For some people Sighişoara actually scores over Sibiu in having more 'sights', and in having kept its old walls almost intact, including eleven walltowers. Of these the most striking is the 14th-century Clock Tower with its mid-17th-century clock. There's a fine local museum in the tower, but even if you don't fancy the museum it's worth paying the admission for the chance to ascend the tower to enjoy a great view over the town. Not far away is the one-time residence of the infamous Vlad Dracul, known in Romania as Vlad Tepes (the Impaler) due to his habit of mounting his enemies arse-first on stakes, but better known in English-speaking countries as one of the sources of inspiration for Bram Stoker's *Dracula*. The mid-14th-century Bergkirche is reached by the 17th-century Covered Staircase. The tombstones in the church and the cemetery are lasting evidence of the Germanic presence which has now all but vanished from Sighişoara.

East of Sibiu and south-east of Sighişoara is **Braşov**, the second largest city in Romania. At the centre of the soulless post-war development is a fine historic centre. Again the feel is one of being in a German town, never more so than when looking at the Gothic Black Church on the main square, still used by the local German community who call the town Kronstadt. The old town hall now houses the Historical Museum which is fair enough, though a trip to the First Romanian School Museum with its collections of religious artefacts is a bit more rewarding.

You'll see more tourists in Braşov than in any other town in the country. For most the attraction isn't the town itself, but its proximity to **Bran Castle**. Forever touted as Dracula's castle, in fact it's highly doubtful if Vlad Tepes ever stayed in Bran, though he may have attacked the castle at one point. Laying history aside for the tourists (why should Romania be any different from most countries?) there are plans afoot to turn Bran into a sort of Dracula theme park, which is a real shame because it's well worth seeing in any case without being spoiled by such garbage. Near the castle is an open-air museum of old farm buildings collected from all over Transylvania. The ticket to enter the castle also allows you into the *skansen*.

You don't need to go far from Braşov to sample the various attractions of the Bucegi Mountains which include a number of spectacular cable-car rides, skiing, walking and climbing (walkers and climbers can make use of a well developed system of mountain huts known as cabanas). The alpine resort of **Poiana-Braşov**, only 10 km out of Braşov, offers ski runs to suit all levels of competence. **Sinaia**, 46 km from Braşov, is very much the main resort in the area, and the starting point for one of the most popular walks in the mountains. All told the walking involved takes about $2^1/_2$ hours. Begin by catching the cable car from Sinaia to Cabana Mioriţa, then hike via Cabana Piatra Arsá to Cabana Babele, from where you can catch a cable car down to Buşteni, just along the main road and train line from Sinaia.

Compared to Transylvania the region of Wallachia around the capital is a bit short on tourist attractions, though you only have to go 34 km north from Bucharest to reach the monastery church on the island in **Lake Snagov**. The church has some bona fide associations with Vlad Tepes. Not only was he a patron of the church, and commissioned some building projects in the vicinity, but the man himself is almost certainly buried here. After being betrayed and murdered Vlad Tepes was decapitated (it's said his head was later presented to the Turkish sultan). In 1935 what had always been thought to be Vlad's grave was exhumed, and the corpse within was found to be headless.

The other great sight in Wallachia is the town of **Curtea de Argeś**, 38 km from the mining town of Piteşti. The town's fame derives from two stunning churches; the mid-14th-century Prince's Church which is smothered in contemporary frescoes, and the early 16th-century Bishop's Church. The latter is an extraordinary combination of Orthodox and Islamic architecture which will almost certainly become one of the star features in Romanian tourist literature once the industry gets itself organized.

The same will no doubt be true of the fortified monastery churches of the northern province of Bukovina. The five most famous– **Putna**, **Suceviţa**, **Moldovita**, **Voronet** and **Humor** – were all erected between the mid-15th century and the late 16th century, and rank amongst the finest medieval monuments in Europe. The churches are renowned principally for their superb frescoes, many of them adorning the exterior as well as the interior walls. Each monastery has its own particular attractions, but the fresco of the Last Judgement at Voronet is generally thought to be the finest of all the works. From a practical point of view (assuming you've abandoned your hitching principles) all the monasteries except Suceviţa are relatively easy to reach by train.

Romania's greatest source of tourist revenue at present is the

Black Sea coast with its miles of beaches and warm summer climate. Those who visit come primarily for the beachlife, but if you fancy a change there are a couple of museums worth seeing in **Constanţa**. The Archaeological Museum has many exhibits found locally which date back to ancient Greek times; highlights include the statue of the Goddess Fortuna and that of a mythical creature known as a Glykon. Just over the road is another museum built around a huge Roman mosaic from the 3rd century which was found on the site in 1959.

● **Visa requirements** Citizens of the UK, Ireland, Canada, USA, Australia and New Zealand all require a visa to visit Romania. Although visas can be bought at the border the authorities recommend that you obtain a visa in advance from a Romanian embassy or consulate.

Hitching
Hitching is permitted in Romania, but is far from easy. The official I spoke with said that 'the population is not very familiar with the custom, so things might be a little slow'. If you do get a lift it's quite probable the driver will expect some payment. Bear in mind how badly off Romanian workers are, and remember that they have done you a favour. If possible find out in advance how much the trip might have cost by public transport and offer half that amount – the driver will probably be more than happy. All things considered though, you're probably better off using the cheap public transport wherever possible.

Bucharest: where to sleep

A fair number of the city's cheapest hotels are in the area around the Gara de Nord. There are a few singles for under £10, but your chances of getting one on arrival without prior reservation are next to zero. Private rooms are a safer bet – generally about £10 per night. Private rooms, and hotels, can be booked through the **ONT** office at Bd. Magheru 7 (tel: 145160). You may be able to negotiate a cheaper deal on private rooms with the touts at the train station, but be warned that the quality of your room, or of its location (or both), will probably fall well below those available through ONT. For hostel accommodation approach **CATT** at Str. Mendeleev 7–15 (tel: 144200), but don't get your hopes up. In the past CATT have been less than anxious to help independent travellers, and their hostels have been more expensive than private rooms in any case.

Camping Bănasea is out by the airport, reached by bus 205 or trolleybus 81 from the Gara de Nord. From the airport bus 149 (Sundays bus 358) will drop you at the site, while bus 148 leaves you a 10-minute walk away (the road is unlit).

Romanians catching an early morning train often sleep in the waiting room at the Gara de Nord. If you decide to join them check your pack in at the left luggage before crashing out.

Bucharest: where to eat

You'll find dirt cheap self-service joints scattered all over town, but the quality of the food is generally lousy. Basically you can cut corners too much here. The **Salon Spiniol** at Calea Vitoriei 116 is a decent pizza restaurant where a meal still costs under £2. As little as £5–6 will buy a meal at the famous **Hanul Lui Manuc** at Str. 30 Decembrie 62. These old-style inns (known as *han*) are the best places to find traditional Romanian cooking, which is very good indeed. Otherwise you're probably better sticking to the restaurants of the B-class hotels.

Bucharest: what to see and do

HOUSE OF THE PEOPLE The building at the heart of Ceauşescu's plan for a new city centre fit for the Romanian capital. As usual much ado was made in the West about a few historic buildings destroyed to create the new urban dream, and very little about the forced labour, including the many workers who for one reason or another never returned home.

HANUL MANUC A typical old inn which you should check out even if you don't have a meal there.

STAVROPOLEOS CHURCH An early 18th-century church, typical of churches found throughout the city.

PALACE OF THE REPUBLIC Built in 1937 for the king, there was much fighting in and around the palace in 1989.

CENTRAL COMMITTEE OF THE COMMUNIST PARTY BUILDING Ceauşescu made his last speech from the balcony. His visible shock at the dissent from the crowd was one of the great TV moments of 1989.

PATRIARCHAL CATHEDRAL and the nearby PATRIARCH'S PALACE.

MUSEUM OF HISTORY Excellent collection starting with the prehistoric period. Superb treasury.

VILLAGE MUSEUM Next to the Herăstrău Park is this collection of nearly 300 buildings brought here from all over the country.

CISMIGIU GARDENS Bucharest may not be the most attractive of cities, especially in its present run-down condition, but rowing about the small lake fringed with weeping willows on a sunny day is very pleasant indeed.

Transport in Bucharest
The public transport system of trams, buses, trolleybuses and the three-line metro is cheap, but, apart from the metro, a bit unreliable. With a decent street map you can see all the sights quite easily by sticking to the metro and walking a little from the nearest station.

Addresses

ONT (National Tourist Office) at blvd Magheru 7 (tel: 145160).
US Consulate at Strada Tudor Argezhi 9, Bucharest (tel: 104040). Send mail to: American Consulate General BUCH, APO New York 09213.
British Consulate at Strada Jules Michelet 22–4, Bucharest (tel: 145211/111635).

Hitchers' Tips and Comments . . .

Hitching in Romania is extremely hard and drivers who give lifts expect payment. Everyone I know who's been there says the same. Try the train. It's dead cheap.

MALCOLM CLARKE, LONDON, ENGLAND

Food supplies are still a bit unpredictable, and sometimes you'll struggle to find much in the local shops. Try and build up a store of food whenever you have the chance, but at the same time try to show some sensitivity by not buying a pile of goods all at once.

AARON COHEN, LONDON, ENGLAND

Russia

population	147,386,000
size	17,075,400 square kilometres
capital	Moscow, population 9,000,000
government	parliamentary democracy
religion	Mainly Russian Orthodox
language	Russian. Little English, French or German spoken
currency	*Rouble* One *rouble* equals 100 *kopecks*

Even if they have never visited **Moscow** there are two sights that most Westerners would instantly associate with the Russian capital – ST BASIL'S CATHEDRAL and the KREMLIN. The former, with its nine richly coloured onion domes looking like Christmas tree decorations, regularly appears on TV as the backdrop to an earnest looking reporter. It's undoubtedly one of the great buildings of Europe, albeit one with a somewhat unreal quality; almost as if it had been built specifically for the benefit of camera clicking tourists and news teams. Apparently the architect who produced this masterpiece lived to regret it – he was blinded on the orders of his patron, Tsar Ivan the Terrible, to prevent him ever surpassing St Basil's.

The Kremlin is the highlight of the city, an incredible complex of buildings which includes the Grand Palace, the Bell Tower, the Church of the Twelve Apostles, the Annunciation Cathedral, the Archangel Cathedral and the superb Armoury. The ANNUNCIATION CATHEDRAL was the coronation church of the Russian tsars. You can still see Ivan the Terrible's throne. The ARCHANGEL CATHEDRAL was where the tsars were laid to rest. Amongst other tombs, you can see that of the notorious Ivan. In case you've never watched TV news programmes, the classic view of the Kremlin for your photographs is from across the river.

Near the Kremlin stands the TOMB OF THE UNKNOWN SOLDIER, with an eternal flame burning in memory of the staggering 25 million citizens of the then USSR killed during the Second World War. And a trip into the GUM department store is a must if only to see the interior decoration. Another unusual sight is the Moscow metro, where each station is decorated with original artwork. If you're not the museum type you could do worse on a rainy day than have a tour around the metro.

Back above ground, of Moscow's churches three deserve special mention: the SMOLENSKY CATHEDRAL; the YELOKHOVSKIY CATHEDRAL; and the much smaller TRINITY CHURCH in Nikitniki. Around town are various museums set up in the one-time residences of great Russian authors. Even if you're not a fan of the likes of Chekhov, Gorky, Tolstoy or Dostoevsky a visit will show you how the relatively well-off Russian of the day lived. Art lovers are well catered for by the TRETYAKOV GALLERY which contains some of the very best of Russian and Soviet works, and the PUSHKIN MUSEUM OF FINE ARTS which is particularly strong on European Renaissance and Classical works. Curiosity value apart, the EXHIBITION OF ECONOMIC ACHIEVEMENTS is likely to be a bit dull for all but economists and engineers.

Moving north 71 km from the capital you reach the town of **Zagorsk**. The attraction here is the superb 14th-century Troitse-Sergiyeva Monastery which boasts no fewer than nine churches.

Vladimir, 126 km north-east of Moscow, has three great 12th-century monuments: the Golden Gate; St Dmitry's Cathedral; and the Assumption Cathedral, within which lie the rulers of the principality of Vladimir-Suzdal. The principality, which was a power to be reckoned with in the 12th and 13th centuries, is also noted for the unique style of painting which developed there.

If you only see one town outside Moscow and St Petersburg make it **Suzdal**, 26 km north of Vladimir. The highlights are the 15th-century Archbishop's Palace, the 13th-century Church of the Nativity in the Kremlin, and the 18th-century wooden churches, but all told there are in the region of 100 historic monuments in a town surrounded by countless windmills. Bring plenty of film.

The greatest monuments in **Yaroslavl**, 241 km north-east of Moscow, date from the 17th century, though the town itself (named after its founder Prince Yaroslav the Wise) dates back to the early 11th century. See the Church of the Epiphany, and the Church of the Prophet Eliah which has striking contemporary frescoes.

Novgorod, 531 km to the north-west of Moscow, was a major trading centre doing business with the Vikings at the same time as the rulers of England were fighting with them or trying to buy them off. The town contains the oldest surviving stone monument built by the ancient Rus, the mid-11th-century Cathedral of St Sophia. The cathedral is also noted for its golden dome in the shape of a battle helmet, and for a set of 12th-century Byzantine bronze doors which serve as a reminder of the city's trading past. Of the many other churches in the old town by the River Volkhov, St Nicholas' is especially worth seeing.

St Petersburg was built for Tsar Peter the Great who wanted a new capital that looked like a European capital (Moscow obviously didn't). Consequently there is an orderliness about St Petersburg that sets it apart from other Russian cities. The major sight is the HERMITAGE MUSEUM in the 18th-century Winter Palace. Masterpieces by the likes of Da Vinci, Michelangelo, El Greco and

Rembrandt are all present amongst a stupendous collection of French, Spanish, Italian, Dutch and Flemish works. Nowhere near as overwhelming in terms of size is the collection of the RUSSIAN MUSEUM, but for a look at the development of Russian art the exhibits here are hard to beat.

There's some fine work by some of the foremost artists of 19th-century Russia in ST ISAAC'S CATHEDRAL, one of the biggest churches in the world. In summer you can ascend to the huge dome for a panoramic view over the city. Nearby stands a suitably grandiose equestrian statue of the city's founder, known as the BRONZE HORSEMAN.

The HISTORY OF ST PETERSBURG MUSEUM catalogues the horrendous suffering of the great siege of 1944 when 650,000 died. Unfortunately, in the new Russia the crucial role that St Petersburg played in the workers' movements may now be brushed over.

Within the grounds of the immense FORTRESS OF THE SAINTS PETER AND PAUL stands the 18th-century cathedral of the same name. Buried in the cathedral are Peter the Great and many later tsars of Russia, some of whom used the fortress as a prison for political radicals. Amongst those executed here was Lenin's older brother, Alexander Ulyanov. If you feel a sense of *déjà vu* when confronted with the KAZAN CATHEDRAL don't be surprised. It's modelled on St Peter's in Rome.

In the vicinity of St Petersburg are three palaces worth a detour if you have the time; **Petrodvorec**, **Pavlovsk** and **Pushkin**. If you have to pick one, go for Petrodvorec which is by far the grandest. This palace was planned as Peter the Great's Versailles.

● **Visa requirements** Citizens of the UK, Ireland, USA, Canada, Australia and New Zealand all need visas to visit Russia. These must be fixed up in advance as they are not available at the Russian border.

Hitching

Despite attempts to obtain clarification as to whether or not foreign nationals are allowed to hitch in Russia I can't say whether or not you can do so. The following extract from *Alexei Alexandrovich*, a student at Novosibirsk University, is as much useful information as I have at the time of writing 'To judge from your book hitching in Russia is not so easy as in Europe. People are getting more and more unfriendly, and in some areas of our country hitching is sometimes dangerous'. If you are planning a trip check out the latest details for yourself. I hope you have more luck than I did!

Hitchers' Tips and Comments . . .

Vital for a trip is a phrasebook, because nobody speaks English apart from the Intourist guides!

SANDRA BRADLEY, S. HUMBERSIDE, ENGLAND

Try Berlitz's Russian for Travellers. K.W.

Customs officials are nowhere near as pernickety as they once were, but it's still a good idea to remove the film from your camera before entering or leaving the country just in case they open up your camera. AGNIESZKA ZDANOWSKA, WARSAW, POLAND

The Ukraine

population	52,000,000
size	603,700 square kilometres
capital	Kiev, population 2,500,000
government	parliamentary democracy
religion	Orthodox, with a Uniate minority
language	Ukrainian. Little English, French or German spoken
currency	*Kupony*

Entering the Ukraine from Poland the first logical stop is the city of **L'viv**. Since it first became apparent that the Soviet Union might just crumble L'viv has been the centre of Ukrainian nationalism. This is a bit of a curiosity, as pre-Second World War L'viv was a Polish city (Lwow), with an overwhelmingly Polish population. With the post-war shifting of borders, the Poles were booted out. Ironically, most of them ended up in Breslau (now Wroclaw), a German city cleared of its Germans once it fell under Polish control.

L'viv is a city with enormous tourist potential. Parallels have been drawn with Prague and Cracow, which isn't too far-fetched as L'viv has the same mix of quaint old streets and superb monuments. The charming main square (*Rinok*) centred on the old town hall is a grand place for relaxing while you watch the locals going about their business. Attractions include a Pharmacy Museum located in the old city pharmacy; an excellent collection of weaponry in the old arsenal; and an Ethnographical Museum with informative displays on traditional Ukrainian dress. For a great view over the town climb up Castle Hill. Not to be missed are the Gothic Roman Catholic cathedral, the Usspenskiy Cathedral and St Andrew's Church. The latter is as good a place as any to witness a Uniate ceremony. The Uniates maintain an Orthodox style of service, but in all other matters follow Rome. For that reason you'll often hear of them referred to as Greek Catholics.

The Ukrainian capital, **Kiev**, is a very old city, chronicled as the stronghold of the Kievan Rus as early as 882. Over the next 250 years Kiev became one of the great trading centres of Europe. Surviving structures from that period include the Golden Gate and the fantastic St Sophia's Cathedral. The cathedral was built on the order of Prince Yaroslav the Wise, whose body lies in a marble tomb within. See also St Andrew's Church (named after the country's patron saint), and the Kievo-Pecherskaya Monastery. Not only are the monastery buildings visually stunning, but there's also the more macabre attraction of mummified monks' remains to be seen in the catacombs.

The Black Sea town of **Yalta** has gone down in history as the place where Stalin, Roosevelt and Churchill sat down and carved up post-war Europe. You can see the Livadia Palace in which the negotiations took place. The cliffside Swallow's Nest looks out of place here. It's a mock-up of a traditional German castle built early this century by a German oil tycoon.

● **Visa requirements** To visit the Ukraine nationals of the UK, Ireland, Canada, USA, New Zealand and Australia must be in possession of a visa. These are not available at the Ukrainian border.

Hitching

As with Russia, I haven't been able to get any information from the authorities as to whether hitching is allowed. Check out the latest details before setting off. Public transport is cheap, but getting tickets out to Poland can be a nightmare. It makes sense to buy a return ticket from some Polish station to L'viv if you do decide to train it.

Lithuania

population	3,690,000
size	65,200 square kilometres
capital	Vilnius
government	parliamentary democracy
religion	Roman Catholic
language	Lithuanian. Russian is widely spoken. Knowledge of English and German is increasing
currency	*Litas*

Close to the present-day capital, Vilnius, is **Trakai**, the old capital of the Grand Duchy of Lithuania. Little more than a small town nowadays, it's difficult to believe Trakai could ever have been the seat of some of the most powerful rulers in Eastern Europe – until you clap eyes on the castle. Set on an island in Lake Galve, the Grand Duke's stronghold is one of the most imposing castles in Europe.

The second city, **Kaunas**, is a pleasant, compact old town, devoid of the bustle of the old quarter of Vilnius. Notable buildings include the Kaunas Basilica, the old town hall and the 19th-century Russian Orthodox Church. Outside the Kaunas Historical Museum stands the Freedom Statue. Removed by the Soviets during their occupation of the city, the statue made a re-appearance in 1989. Nearby is the highly unusual Devil Museum. Most of the 200 or so exhibits are traditional folk carvings, but the piece showing Hitler and Stalin running around amongst piles of human bones is a telling comment on recent Lithuanian and European history.

If you're in **Klapeida**, the country's main port and third city, the Museum of Lithuanian History is worth a visit. That apart, the city is short on things to see as a result of heavy wartime bombing. By way of compensation the nightlife far outshines that of any other Lithuanian town, including the capital. There's also the fine Smilsine beach if you fancy a bit of sunbathing. Swimming isn't to be recommended though, as cleaning up this part of the Baltic after 40 years of unfettered industrial pollution is going to be a long and expensive job.

● **Visa requirements** The governments of Lithuania, Latvia and Estonia operate a common visa policy whereby possession of a valid visa for one country allows entry into the other two. Citizens of the UK do not need a visa to visit Lithuania. Citizens of Ireland, USA, Canada, Australia and New Zealand must be in possession of a visa issued in advance by one of the three countries' embassies or consulates as visas are not issued at the Lithuanian border.

Vilnius: where to sleep

The **Youth Hostel** at Filaretu 17 (tel: 260606) has beds at £3.30 – the cheapest in town. The **Baltic Accommodation and Travel Service** at Geležinio Vilko 27 (tel: 661692/667680) charges twice as much, but is still a bargain by local standards. Cheapest hotel rooms are in the annexe (*corpus*) of the **Hotel Vilnius** where singles cost £10, doubles £16. Book through the reception of the main hotel building at Gedeminio 20/1 (tel: 624157/623665).

Vilnius: where to eat

In all but the most expensive restaurants attached to luxury hotels a 3-course meal will cost under £2. There are plenty of fine restaurants to choose from, but the **Viola** at Kalvarijû 3 serves excellent Armenian food, and the **Literatû Svetaine** at Gederimo 1 is also worthy of mention. At the latter, beer and wine can be purchased in hard currency only. Establish the price before ordering as this can add a substantial amount to the cost of your meal. Also worth a visit is the **Blyniné** at Pilies 8 which specializes in filled pancakes.

Vilnius: where to go and what to do

At the heart of Vilnius is MUSEUM SQUARE. The LITHUANIAN ART MUSEUM is housed in the old town hall. A short stroll will take you to the old university buildings, the highlight of which is the 17th-century astronomical observatory. The most beautiful of the city's churches is the ST ANNE CHURCH of the Bernardine Monastery. Napoleon was so taken by this Gothic marvel that he considered having it transported back to France. The cathedral contains the tombs of some of the Grand Dukes of Lithuania, the country's rulers during its medieval heyday. For a grand view over the city climb the GEDIMINAS TOWER on Castle Hill. On Bernardinu you can see the house that was once the home of Mickiewicz, the great Polish poet. The LITHUANIAN STATE MUSEUM deals with various Soviet acts directed against the Lithuanian people, including those immediately preceding independence. Even more sobering is the LITHUANIAN STATE JEWISH MUSEUM which is spread over two locations; one at

Pamenkalnio 12, the other at Pylimo 6. Around the turn of the century Vilnius was recognized as the cultural and intellectual centre of East European Jewry, and boasted no fewer than 96 synagogues. Nowadays the synagogue at Pylimo 39 is the sole surviving synagogue in the city once known as the 'Jerusalem of Europe'.

Transport in Vilnius
Public transport is cheap and efficient. Tickets should be bought in advance from *spaudos* kiosks, then validated on boarding.

Addresses

Main post office at Gedimino 7, Vilnius.
US Embassy at Akmenû 6, Vilnius (tel: 223031).
British Embassy at Antakalnio 2 (tel: 222070).

Latvia

population	2,700,000
size	64,600 square kilometres
capital	Riga, population 870,000
government	parliamentary democracy
religion	Protestant
language	Latvian. Russian widely understood. Increasing numbers of Latvians are learning German and English
currency	*Lat*

The Latvian capital, **Riga**, has a striking old town which bears many resemblances to other old Hanseatic settlements found around the Baltic. There is no shortage of beach resorts in the vicinity of the capital, of which **Majori** and **Jurmala** are the best. The sands are fine, but don't come here for a swim. Decades of pumping out pollutants willy-nilly have rendered this part of the Baltic absolutely filthy.

If you fancy doing some walking the **Gauja National Park** is the most obvious destination. The park, covering some 920 sq.km, is full of lakes, streams, caves and ancient woods, plus the ruins of Krimulda Castle. From Riga the easiest point of entry into the park is the town of Sigulda, 60 km to the north-east.

In the far south-west of the country, just up the coast from the Lithuanian port of Klapeida, is **Liepaja**. It's one of the oldest towns in Latvia. There are a few sights worth seeing, such as the Trinity

Lutheran Church and St Joseph's Cathedral, but Liepaja lacks the intact old town which makes Riga so attractive.

● **Visa requirements** The governments of Latvia, Lithuania and Estonia operate a common visa policy whereby possession of a valid visa for one country allows entry into the other two. Visas are not required by UK, Estonian, Lithuanian, Polish and Hungarian passport holders. All other nationalities must obtain a suitable visa prior to travelling to Latvia as these are not issued at the Latvian border. Latvian visas are issued free of charge to US nationals.

Riga: where to sleep

The **Riga Youth Hostel** at Kalnciema iela 10/12 (tel: 226463) and the **Laine Hostel** at Skolas iela 11 (tel: 287658/288816) both charge £6.60 per night. Cheap hotels are almost non-existent. Try the **Victoria** at A Caka 55 (tel: 276209/272305) where rooms with shower and TV run £8.50 for singles, £12.50 for doubles. The hotel also has some very basic doubles for £4. Private rooms are available from **Patricia**, Elizabetes iela 22–4a (tel: 284868) and the **Tourist Club of Latvia**, Skunu 22 (tel: 227680/212377).

Riga: where to go and what to do

For an overall view of the town's layout climb the tower of ST PETER'S CHURCH. Near St Peter's you can visit St John's Church and, on Peitavas iela, the only one of the city's synagogues still in use. The CATHEDRAL on Doma Laukums is the largest church in the Baltic States. It contains the biggest pipe organ in the world – make an effort to attend a recital while you're in town. Other historical landmarks to watch out for are the old GUNPOWDER TOWER and the CASTLE. Inside the latter you'll find the MUSEUM OF FOREIGN ART (mainly reproductions), the LATVIAN HISTORY MUSEUM and the RAINIS MUSEUM OF LITERATURE (named after the national poet). The MUSEUM OF LATVIAN ART has a particularly good selection of local art from the 19th and 20th centuries.

Transport in Riga

The public transport network of trams, buses and trolleybuses is dirt cheap and efficient. Buy tickets from newspaper kiosks, and then validate them on boarding by punching them in the machines.

Addresses

Main post office at Stacijas laukums 1, Riga.
US Embassy at Raiņa blvd 7 (tel: 227045/210006/222611).
British Embassy at Elizabetes iela 2 (tel: 320737/325287).

Estonia

population	1,600,000
size	45,100 square kilometres
capital	Tallinn
government	parliamentary democracy
religion	Protestant
language	Estonian. Russian is widely spoken. Increasing numbers are learning English and German
currency	*Kroon* One *kroon* equals 100 *senti*

Tallinn, the Estonian capital, is a busy port with considerable tourist potential on account of the charming old town. Its quaint streets are great for simply wandering round, but there are some impressive monuments to see on the way. Worth a detour is the Estonian Open-air Museum at **Rocca-Al-More**, 25 km west of the capital. Open from May to October, the museum contains a fine collection of farm buildings and mills from around the country which were originally built between the 17th and 19th centuries.

Tartu, south-east of the capital, certainly merits a visit, though, in contrast to Tallinn, not a lot remains of the old town. The architectural highlight is the university, the oldest surviving university in the Baltic states. The Museum of Classical Art has a small, but surprisingly good collection of Greek and Roman exhibits. Two churches to see – even though they're in ruins – are the impressive St John's and the hilltop Church of Saints Peter and Paul.

South of Tallinn **Parnu**'s main attraction is its beach. Think twice before jumping into the sea, though: if you could read Estonian you'd realize that there is no shortage of signs warning that high pollution levels make bathing unsafe. Other than the Museum of the City of Parnu and the museum devoted to the 19th-century poetess Lydia Koidula there's nothing much to do here on a rainy day.

One of the country's principal attractions is the Episcopal Castle in the town of **Kuressaare** on the island of Saaremaa. This picturesque moated fortress was built in the 16th century when Kuressaare was the stomping ground of the bishops of Saare-Laane. There's nothing else of importance to see in the town, but Kuressaare is a good base for a relaxing few days. The lovely beaches of Mändjala and Júarre are just a short trip away, and, unusually for the Baltic States, it's safe to go swimming off the beaches. To appreciate the gentle pace of life on the island, hire a bike from the outlets at Pikk tr. 4 or Rohu tn. 5 (about £1.50 per day).

● **Visa requirements** The governments of Estonia, Latvia and Lithuania operate a common visa policy whereby possession of a valid visa for one country allows entry into the other two. UK nationals do not require a visa to enter Estonia. Citizens of Ireland, USA, Canada, New Zealand and Australia must be in possession of a suitable visa prior to travelling as visas are not issued at the Estonian border.

Tallinn: where to sleep

At the time of writing there was a distinct shortage of cheap hotel rooms in the Estonian capital, but, thankfully, the hostels operated by the **Estonian Youth Hostels Association** and a recently established network of private rooms were managing to cope with the increased demand for inexpensive lodgings.

Hostels:
'Agnes', Narva maantee 7 (tel: 438870). June–Aug. only. £5.
Youth Hostel, Kuramaa TN (tel: 327781). Closed Sun. £5.

Private rooms:
Family Hotel Service (Hua Ai Trade Ltd), Mere puistee 6 (tel: 441187). £6.60–10.00 per person.

Tallinn: where to eat

Eateries are being opened, closed and renovated at an astonishing rate just now, but, overall, eating out in Tallinn remains a tremendous bargain. It's still possible to have an excellent 3-course meal for under £3. Try the **Rüütlibaar** at Kohtu 2.

In all restaurants beware of ordering wine or imported beer as this can bump up the bill substantially (an imported beer can cost two or three times the price of the meal).

Tallinn: where to go and what to do

In front of the late 14th-century Town Hall on Raekoja plats is the figure of Old Thomas (*Vana Toomas*), the legendary protector of the city. The finest of Tallinn's churches are the OLEVISTE KIRIK and the NIGULISTE KIRIK. The former is more imposing from the outside, but the latter scores in interior decoration, largely because of its superb medieval *Dance of Death* painted by Nothe. TOOMPEA CASTLE is now the seat of the Estonian parliament (no admittance). For an unbeatable view of the city climb the late 15th-century tower known as KIEK IN DE KOK. The local museums are interesting enough, but nothing to go out of your way to see on your first day. The SEA MUSEUM (Meremuseum) deals primarily with the role of the city as a port through the ages, and this long time-span makes it more enlightening than the TALLINN CITY MUSEUM where the focus is on 19th-century Tallinn. The old city jail behind the town hall houses a collection on early Estonian photography. The FINE ARTS MUSEUM is housed in the old Kadriord Palace.

Transport in Tallinn

The same tickets are valid on the city's buses and trams. Buy them in advance from newspaper kiosks and cancel them on boarding. Prices are so cheap that a monthly pass costs the equivalent of £1. Single rides cost about 3p.

Addresses

Main post office (for poste restante) at Narva mnt. 1, Tallinn.
Estonian Youth Hostels Association at Liivalaia 2, Tallinn EE0001 (tel: 445853).
US Consulate at Kentmanni 20, Tallinn (tel: 455005).
British Consulate at Kentmanni 20, Tallinn (tel: 455328).

The former Yugoslavia

At the time of writing, of the republics which made up the former Yugoslavia only Slovenia and Macedonia (see the following sections) were stable and not involved in the war which broke out in 1991.

This section seeks merely to point out some of the places you might want to consider visiting in Yugoslavia (Serbia and Montenegro), Croatia and Bosnia-Hercegovina in the event that peace has been declared by 1996. Bear in mind that war damage may mean that little remains to be seen in what were once some of Yugoslavia's main attractions. While the historic centre of Dubrovnik emerged relatively unscathed from the fighting, it seems highly unlikely that Sarajevo will do the same. The old Turkish bridge in Mostar, photos of which used to appear in most of Yugoslavia's tourist brochures, has been the most notable monument destroyed during the conflict.

In Yugoslavia the main attractions include the Serbian capital, **Belgrade**; the cities of **Niš** and **Novi Sad**; the Montenegrin towns of **Kotor**, **Budva** and **Sveti Stefan**; and the famous Serbian monasteries. For hitchers, Ravanica and Mansija are the most obvious monasteries to head for as both are easily reached from Ćuprija on the main Belgrade to Niš highway.

In Croatia try to see the capital, **Zagreb**; the historic cities of **Split** and **Dubrovnik**; **Pula** and the **Plitvice Lakes**.

Sarajevo, **Mostar** and **Jajce** were the three main draws in Bosnia-Hercegovina prior to the outbreak of war.

Addresses

Ferijalni savez Jugoslavije (Yugoslavian Youth Hostel Association), Moše Pijade 12/V, 11000 Beograd (tel: 339802).

Ferijalni savez Hrvatske (Croatian Youth Hostel Association), Savska cesta 5/1, 41000 Zagreb (tel: 411847).

Slovenia

population	2,100,000
size	20,251 square kilometres
capital	Llubljana, population 330,000
government	parliamentary democracy
religion	Mainly Roman Catholic
language	Slovenian. German is widely spoken throughout the country; Italian is understood along the coastline. Some English understood
currency	*Tolar*

Slovenia packs a lot into a small area. Every few days you can be doing something different, yet be only a short distance from your last stop. It's a great place to relax if you're suffering from a cultural overdose picked up in Italy, Austria or Hungary.

Entering Slovenia via the Austrian city of Villach the main

highway runs right to the national capital Llubljana. En route the road passes through Jesenice; 10 km from the alpine resort of **Bled**. There's something wrong with you if you aren't captivated by **Lake Bled**; the clear blue lake is overlooked by a castle, there's a little island complete with onion-domed church, and the magnificent Julian Alps provide a stunning backdrop. It's worth strolling round the lake to see it from all possible angles. Skiing, climbing and hill-walking are just a short hop away. Local buses run to the entrance to the Vintgar Gorge where an easy walk is rewarded with some splendid scenery.

Bohinjske Jezero, 31 km south-west of Bled, offers much the same delights as Bled, but is less developed. The village church overlooking the lake seems to have been built with photographers in mind. A $1^1/_2$ hour walk will take you to the Savica Waterfalls – highly recommended. The cable-car ascent of Mt Vogel (1,540 m) is not to be missed either. On a clear day the views over the Julian Alps are superb.

Llubljana is a pleasant city that retains the air of the provincial Austrian city that it once was when the Habsburgs held sway over Central Europe. It isn't really a city for sightseeing; the historic buildings and monuments are interesting without being outstanding, and the local museums are fairly nondescript. The city's main attraction is its easy-going atmosphere. Have a squint at the sights by all means, but above all plan on idling the time away, perhaps over coffee and cake, or with a glass of the local Union beer.

The **Postojna Caves**, 56 km south-west of Llubljana, are a must. Four million years old, the caves are a veritable extravaganza of stalactites, stalagmites and strange rock formations. You'll also see a weird-looking relative of the salamander known as *Proteus anguineus* who resides in the caves. Postojna's caves are by no means unique as there are plenty of smaller complexes in the area, including one, **the Škocjanska Cave**, that can stand comparison with Postojna. An added bonus is that the Škocjanska Cave, 33 km south-west of Postojna, is much less touristed than the more famous caves at Postojna. The drawback is that because Škocjanska receives relatively few visitors you'll have to trek back to Postojna if you want a bed for the night.

Along Slovenia's little strip of the Istrian coastline are a couple of old Venetian settlements that merit a detour. In **Koper** the cathedral contains a number of works by the painter Carpaccio, who may – or may not – have been a native of the town. The Venetian influence is clear in the loggia, and in the Praetor's Palace (former residence of the Venetian governor) with its Lion of St Mark. The chequered history of the region is reflected in the buildings on the charming main square of **Piran** where a very Austrian-looking town hall rubs shoulders with an array of Venetian *palazzos*. If the bell tower of the Church of St Jurij looks familiar that's because it's a copy of the one on St Mark's Square in Venice. Piran's medieval walls are impressive – the views you get of the town whilst walking along them no less so.

Slovenia's second city, **Maribor**, lies to the north-east of the capital. The old centre has just about everything you would expect in a small city once under Habsburg rule, right down to the plague column. With a bit of restoration work Maribor's historic centre will no doubt be very attractive, but as things are it probably isn't the sort of place you'll want to spend much time in.

In stark contrast to Maribor, you might find yourself staying longer than intended in the beautiful, small town of **Ptuj**, 25 km to the south-east. Ptuj's most unusual sight is the Roman funerary monument standing on Slovenske trg. Other than that there's nothing exceptional about the town's monuments, yet the castle, Priory Church, town hall and municipal tower all fit in rather nicely with the quaint houses of the old town.

The village of **Ptujska Gora**, 12 km from Ptuj, does contain an exceptional sight. Not only is the Gothic church of Sv Marika one of the most striking in the country, but it houses what is arguably Slovenia's greatest work of religious art – a relief showing the Virgin Mary as the Protectoress of the World. Assembled under the shelter of the Virgin's cloak are 80 individually identifiable sculpted figures.

● **Visa requirements** Citizens of the UK and Ireland do not need a visa to enter the country. Citizens of the USA, Canada, Australia and New Zealand can acquire a visa at the border.

Hitching

Hitching is not permitted on the small motorway (*autocesta*) network. On other roads hitching can be difficult, so overall it isn't really to be recommended for getting around a country where public transport is cheap and efficient.

Llubljana: where to sleep

As well as booking private rooms, the **Turisticno-Informacijski center** (TIC) at Slovenska 35 (tel: 215412) will give advice on cheap hotels such as the **Park** at Tábor 9 (tel: 316777), and on any hostels in the city. In 1994 the **Youth Holiday Association of Slovenia** operated a hostel from mid June–mid Aug. at Vidovanska 7 (tel:

321067/321060). The year-round hostel at Kardeljeva ploščad 28 which emerged in 1993 promptly disappeared in 1994. Ask around – who knows, it may re-appear in 1996! The **Ježica** campsite is at Titova cesta 260a (tel: 372901). Twin-bedded bungalows are also available at the site.

Llubljana: where to eat

There are cheap self-service restaurants dotted around the town where you can pick up a 2-course meal for about £1, and a number of decent pizzerias which cost just a little bit more. Even the restaurants along the waterfront are unlikely to break your budget. Count on paying £2.50–4 for a meal with a beer.

Llubljana: what to see and do

ST NICHOLAS' CATHEDRAL Notable mainly for its frescoes by Quaglio and Langus.

LLUBLJANA CASTLE The views over the city on the way up more than compensate for the rather disappointing climax to the climb.

FRANSISCAN CHURCH Overlooking Presernov trg and the Triple Bridge.

BRIDGE OF DRAGONS Built across the River Llubljanica in 1900, the bridge is the symbol of the city. The name comes from the four dragons who guard the ends of the bridge.

TOWN HALL AND THE ROBBA FOUNTAIN The figures on the mid-18th-century fountain represent the Sava, Krka and Llubljanica rivers.

NATIONAL MUSEUM The saving grace is the only complete skeleton of a mammoth found in Europe.

NATIONAL GALLERY A none-too-inspiring collection. The Slovene Impressionists are acclaimed for their role in forging a national consciousness, but unless you are familiar with the works of their mentors the French Impressionists, or with Slovene national history, you won't get much out of these paintings.

Addresses

Turisticno-Informacijski center (TIC) at Slovenska 35, Llubljana (tel: 215412).
Youth Holiday Association of Slovenia at Parmova 33, Llubljana (tel: 312150).

Hitchers' Tips and Comments . . .

You might be whisked to your destination by an Austrian or German tourist in a BMW. More likely you'll get there eventually courtesy of lots of locals giving you short lifts in their little cars. Save on hassle – take the bus or train.

TAM 'THE VICAR' VICKERS, PERTH, SCOTLAND

Slovenia is OK for hitching, but finding accommodation can be a problem. WILL KELSO, LANCASTER, ENGLAND

Macedonia

population	2,100,000
size	25,713 square kilometres
capital	Skopje, population 310,000
government	parliamentary democracy
religion	Orthodox Christian and Moslem
language	Macedonian. Little English spoken
currency	*Dinar*

Macedonia's main tourist attraction is the town of **Ohrid**, situated on the shore of Europe's deepest lake, Lake Ohrid. The highly picturesque old town, enclosed by its medieval walls, offers a wealth of monuments dating back as far as the Roman period. The Roman amphitheatre is just a short walk away from the old North Gate. Many fine churches remain from the time when Ohrid was the seat of the Macedonian archbishopric. Of these, special mention should be made of the 13th-century Sveti Kliment and the 11th-century Sveti Sofija. Both shelter exquisite frescoes, whilst the latter also retains the *mimbar* (pulpit) from the time the Turks converted the church into a mosque. The citadel affords great views out over the town and the lake, and nearby are the ruins of the Early Christian basilica.

As a tourist attraction the Macedonian capital, **Skopje**, can't compete with Ohrid, but there are still plenty of things to see, and Skopje has the advantage of being a real live town instead of one increasingly given over to tourism.

Skopje: where to sleep

You can forget about finding a cheap hotel bed in the Macedonian capital. Private rooms are a better option, but even these are no bargain at £15 for singles, £11 per person in doubles. Book through the **Turistička Agencija** (tel: 223429) near the bus station and the Orthodox Church. The **Dom Blagov Šošolčev** (HI Hostel) near the train station at Prolet 25 (tel: 233866) offers beds in six-bedded dorms for about £6 (plus a £1.30 supplement for non-members). In July and August similarly priced beds are usually available in converted student dorms such as the **K. J. Pitu** at Ribar 58 (tel: 235360) and the **Goce Delčev** at Taftalidze 11 (tel: 253021).

The **Feroturist Autocamp Park** (open April to mid-October) charges about £2.90 per person and per tent. Beds are also available in caravans (about £6.30 per person). The site is conveniently located between the stadium and the Vardar river, about 15 minutes' walk from the centre of the city.

Skopje: where to go and what to do

Reminders of the days of Turkish rule are dotted around the city. Near the Turkish bridge stand the 15th-century DAUD PASHA BATHS, the largest of their kind outside Turkey. The three caravanserai still in existence (the Kursumli Han, Kapan Han and Suli Han), are all located in the old market quarter. The dome of the late 15th-century MUSTAFA PASHA MOSQUE was cracked during one of the many earthquakes which have struck the city. You can ascend the mosque's minaret for a fine view. A different perspective can be had by climbing up to the ruins of the castle.

The most interesting of the city's Christian churches is SVETI SPAS with its elaborate iconostasis. The MUSEUM OF MACEDONIA features a potentially very interesting display, but one which suffers from the lack of labelling in anything other than Macedonian, and the absence of guidebooks in other languages.

10 · MOROCCO AND NORTH AFRICA

Morocco

population	25,208,000
size	451,684 square miles
capital	Rabat, population 1,472,000
government	Constitutional monarchy
religion	Moslem
language	Arabic; Spanish and French also official languages; some English and German spoken in tourist centres
currency	*Dirham* (dh) One *dirham* equals 100 *francs*. Coins of 5, 10, 20, 50 *francs*, and of 1, 5 *dirhams*. Notes of 5, 10, 50, 100 *dirhams*

Cheapest way to Africa is from Algeciras, in Spain, to Ceuta, which is the tiny Spanish colony just across from Gibraltar. The Algeciras–Tangier ferry is more expensive.

Tetouan, just a few kilometres from Ceuta, with a population of 856,000 is becoming a favourite stopping place for hitchers on their way south. At the moment it's not particularly tourist-minded and is a good place to enjoy your first glimpse of a Moroccan city. Plenty of mosques, a fairly good market section, and OK people.

Tangier, 72 km away, is an out-and-out tourist town and every Arab in it is chasing the fast buck. Nevertheless it's worth a day and if you go down into the *medina*, go to the Petit Socco (the small square) where you can sit in the cafés and talk with Arab students and other hitchers.

Ketema, up in the Rif Mountains, is promoted by the Moroccan tourist office as the ideal area for nature-lovers. So it is. But it's also where a great proportion of Morocco's hash is grown. To anybody thinking of buying a kilo, this book warns you strongly about the dangers of exporting the stuff. The Spanish officials at Algeciras do spot-checks on every boatload of tourists arriving. They do a lot of their checking on hitch-hikers. The ones they catch out get locked away for a few years.

Fez is an indispensable stop. One of the four imperial cities – the other three are Marrakesh, Rabat, and Meknes – it is actually three cities in one. The old city, Fes El Bali, is the one to head for. Here is one of the best market areas you'll find anywhere in the world; a tiny winding street some 3 km long which probably hasn't changed much since the city was founded in AD 808. Scores of side streets lead off it creating such a maze that you can get lost by turning two corners. Deep in the *medina* you'll see people working at trades with implements as old as time; men hand-beating copper pots, sewing fine embroidery to kaftans, turning wood on string lathes worked with the toes, workers splattered with dazzling colours from the dye pots. Lots to see. Don't miss Fez!

Meknes, population 750,000, 60 km west of Fez, although interesting, is a let-down. After Fez anywhere with the exception of Marrakesh is an anti-climax. But just north of the city are the ruins of the old Roman town of **Volubilis**.

Rabat population 1,472,000 is the capital of Morocco and has a fair amount to offer the wanderer. Linked by a bridge over the Bou Regreg to its sister city of **Sale** (once a pirate port), it has a good market area. See also the famous Tower of Hassan which was to have been part of the largest mosque in Islam, but was never finished, and the Mechouar, the Royal Palace.

Casablanca, like staid old Tangier, population 3,210,000 is no longer as rough as it was in the 1930s and 1940s when they made the great Humph Bogart movie. Nowadays it's a big bustling modern city and the main commercial centre in Morocco. But the old *medina* area is still intact and a delight to wander through.

Ask most people which is their favourite city in Morocco and you'll find it's a toss-up between Fez and **Marrakesh**. Marrakesh, called the 'pink city' because of the light which reflects from its ochre walls, has one great attraction which keeps visitors amused day after day and which has kept the Arabs amused for centuries. It's Djemma el Fna – the Place of the Dead – the great marketplace which in the morning handles most of the city's trading and where in the late afternoon jugglers, acrobats, snakecharmers, and storytellers come to entertain the crowds. See also the Koutoubia Mosque, with its 221-foot-high minaret and, just north of Djemma el Fna, the *medina* area which is nearly as good as the one in Fez.

Goulimime, way, way down south of Marrakesh, is where you see the famous Blue Men – desert nomads who have permanently blue-stained skin as a result of dye running from the robes they wear.

Beyond Goulimime, the roads get very rough and if you're hitching on for any great distance (and the distances between towns can be very great) try to get aboard a truck. They go longer.

Hitching

Hitching in Morocco is OK – particularly if you're a man and woman travelling together. The Arabs – a happy, easy-to-get-on-with bunch at any time – are very much taken by Western ladies, especially if they have long blonde hair.

For people who want to head east across towards Egypt, the coastal road is good most of the way, though you'll probably have trouble entering Algeria and Libya. Check on formalities *before* you try the trip.

● **Warning!** Because of tense political situations in some parts of North Africa, particularly Libya, it is advisable to be well informed before you enter those areas. Also, in Egypt, Algeria, and Libya, don't even pretend to point your camera at anything which looks vaguely military.

● **Haggling** It can't be stressed too much that a price asked in Morocco is merely a manner of beginning a discussion as to the true value of the object. That goes for beds too. In the *souks* (the markets) the general rule for bargaining is to offer slightly less than one half of what the seller is asking and then act like crazy until you've agreed to pay slightly over half, and even then that will be too much. If you don't get a 30–40% reduction, you can be sure that you're *really* being done! One of the best haggling techniques is to enter a shop in league with someone else. One of you expresses interest in the article, the other is non-committal. As the bargaining progresses, the non-committal one becomes more and more bored, insisting it's time to go. At crucial moments during the bargaining the one who's doing the buying pretends that he has to go to keep his friend happy. This act, if well performed, gets the price down with a speed which is in exact proportion to the amount of concern felt by the seller that he may lose his sale altogether.

Morocco: where to sleep

Finding a cheap bed for the night rarely presents any problems in Morocco. Even though prices in the likes of Fez and Marrakesh have risen sharply as more and more tourists visit these cities, you can still find excellent rooms there for as little as 75dh. One hint about towns like these: the usual maxim of rooms in the *medina* (old town) being the cheapest doesn't always hold true. Tourist-oriented hotels in the *medina* are quite often *more* expensive than comparable hotels in the *ville nouvelle* (European-built quarter). Out on the roads, in the smaller towns such as Ouezanne and Tetouan, you can find clean, first-class accommodation for 45dh a head. Cheap and dirty places, of which there are plenty all over the country, rarely charge more than 20dh – though even this is negotiable! I've stayed in plenty of 20dh hotels and, although sometimes they're fine, mostly they stink. I've heard of beds going for a lot less – but they're not for me.

Morocco: where to eat

How cheaply you can eat depends upon how strong your stomach is. Eat in the *casbah* where it is cheaper, of course, but you should take a little care in choosing your café. Go into something which doesn't look *too* filthy. Plenty of guys you meet in Morocco will tell you that *they're* never sick, but they might neglect to say that they've been living there for six months and that their stomachs are used to whatever it is stomachs get used to. Odds are that whatever you eat you're going to get a touch of diarrhoea, especially if you have a pampered American or English belly. Moroccan hygiene and European hygiene are two different things.

Prices are cheap. 25–30dh should get you a good plateful of couscous with bread and a coke to wash it down. Out on the streets the little shishkebab braziers sell one or two kebabs with bread for a few dirhams. If you're really broke, buy a couple of those and get yourself some fruit from the market and you can eat for around 10dh.

Other local dishes you may like to try include: *Harrira*, a rich peppery soup; *Bastilla*, chicken or pigeon meat in a flaky pastry flavoured with almonds, saffron herbs and spices then decorated with cinnamon and icing sugar; *Tajine*, a slowly simmered stew of meat or chicken and vegetables served piping hot under a glazed earthenware cover which (should) keep the aroma of the meat; *Mshoui*, lamb roasted and basted; *Hout Tajini*, another stew, this time with fish as the main ingredient; *Djaja Maamra*, steamed chicken stuffed with couscous, almonds and raisins; and, for sweet, try *Cornes de Gazelle* (gazelle horns), croissant-shaped pastries with almond paste. Meals are usually finished off with fresh fruit and mint tea.

In the big cities the water is generally OK to drink, but out on the road, in the small villages, you can't be too sure. Why take a chance anywhere? Bottled water is cheap.

Transport in Morocco

In Moroccan cities, don't worry about jumping a bus! They're cheap! If you decide to take inter-city transport, buses are cheaper than trains, but as with everything else in Morocco it's hard to establish the correct price. I once checked around Tangier to find how much a bus ticket was to Fez. I asked at three different places; the tourist office, the bus station, and at the bus itself. Each price quoted was different. I ended up hitching. If you do take a bus, try to get one of the 'peasant' buses. They're loaded with chickens, goats, and God-knows-what – and the Arabs are great travelling companions!

Tetouan: where to sleep

Pension Iberia, Place Moulay el Mehdi. It's on the 3rd floor above the BMCE bank. 28–40dh for a single/double. Cold showers available; hot ones you pay 3dh.

Hotel Regina rue Sidd Mandra 8 (tel: 2113). 48–60dh. All rooms have a bathroom with hot water.

Tangier: where to sleep

Hotel Palace, rue Mokhtar Ahardan 2 (tel: 93 61 28). Singles 50dh, doubles 100dh per night. Showers are available. Clean, spacious and secure.

Down the same street there are many other establishments similar in price and cleanliness. Shop around and take your pick – then you can't blame anyone!

Youth Hostel, rue El Antaki 8 (tel: 94 61 27). 20dh per night. 100 m from bus station and 800 m from railway station. Advance booking is essential summer or winter.

Fez: where to sleep

Hotel Central, rue Nador 50 (tel: 62 23 33). Singles 55dh per night, doubles 75dh. Showers and baths increase the cost.

Hotel du Jardin Publique, Kasbah Boujeloud 153 (tel: 63 30 86). Singles 30dh, doubles 60dh per night.

Hotel du Commerce, pl. des Alaouites (tel: 62 22 31). Said to be the cleanest in the area. Singles 30dh, doubles 60dh.

Youth Hostel, rue Abdeslam Seghrini 18, Ville Nouvelle Fes (tel: 62 40 86). All meals are available. 15dh per night. 150 m from bus station.

Meknes: where to sleep

Hotel Maroc, rue Rouamzine. Singles 40dh, doubles at 80dh. Toilets and showers are clean.
Youth Hostel, Boulevard Okba Ben Nafii (near Transatlantique Hotel) (tel: 52 46 98). 15dh per night. Meals are available.

Rabat: where to sleep

Youth Hostel, rue Marassa 43, Bab El Had, BP 488 RP Rabat (tel: 72 57 69). About 1.2 km from the railway station. 25dh per night.

Hotels:
Hotel Maghrib El-Jadid, 2 rue Sebbahi (tel: 73 22 07). Singles 40dh, doubles 70dh per night.
Hotel Marrakesh, rue Sebbahi 10 (tel: 27703). Singles 40dh per night, doubles are 70dh.

Camping:
Camping de la Plage (tel: 78 23 68). This campsite is on the beach. It has running water, toilets store/restaurant all for 10.50dh per person plus 5dh per tent.

Casablanca: where to sleep

Hotel Geneve, rue du Marché aux Grains 44. Singles are 35dh per night, doubles 45dh per night.
Hotel Candide, rue du Marché aux Grains 33. 30dh for a single, but there are no showers.
Youth Hostel, Amiral Philibert 6, Ville Ancienne, Casablanca (tel: 22 05 51). Close to both the railway station and the bus terminal. 30dh per night. Members' kitchen; meals are also available.

Marrakesh: where to sleep

Hotel de France, rue Riad Zitoune el-Kedim 197 (tel: 44 30 67). Singles 30dh, Doubles 60dh, Hot showers 5dh. Clean bathrooms.
Youth Hostel, rue El Jahed, Quartier Industriel (tel: 44 77 13, 328–31). 20dh per night. This is a very clean hostel where you have a members' kitchen, or meals if you wish.

Goulimime: where to sleep

Hotel Salam. They charge like wounded bulls here: 70–80dh for a single per night.

Addresses

Main post office (for poste restante) at Poste Principale, Rabat.
American Express at blvd Mohammed El Hansali 26, Casablanca (tel: 636 61). Boulevard Pasteur 54, Tangier (tel: 334 59). Avenue Mohammad V 173, Marrakesh (tel: 328 31).
Student Union of Morocco at rue Zayanes 55, Agdal, Rabat.
Morocco Tourist Agency at rue el Jazair 22, Rabat (tel: 212 52 53 54).
US Embassy at avenue de Marrakesh 2, Rabat (tel: 662 65).
British Embassy at blvd Tour Hassan 17, Rabat (tel: 209 05).

Hitchers' Tips and Comments . . .

Take an extra watch or two if you're heading for Morocco, especially the very cheap but flashy kind you can pick up in the UK. It's a good investment. Just walk around with the watch you want to sell on your wrist. Eventually you'll be approached by a buyer who, after a lot of haggling, will give you double what you paid.

Watch out for thieves in Morocco. Once a Moroccan's set his sights on your wallet or something, he'll sit up all night, if need be, to pinch it. Lots of tales of people having sleeping bags delicately cut open during the night and all possessions taken from inside. It's a way of life. CLIVE GILL, BIRCHINGTON, ENGLAND

Unless you look like an Arab I reckon you ought to stay out of Tangier. Hustler hassles are getting to be a real problem. But Fez is recommended to everyone. In fact, anywhere south is OK. Once away from tourist areas the Arabs are really nice and not out to screw you. JOHN OTIS, MANKATO, MINNESOTA, USA

Fez is a hassle these days, too. But you've still got to see the place. K.W.

I was the victim of a rip-off in Casablanca and I want to warn all hitchers. A Moroccan kid approached me with 800 French francs, spun some story about not being able to change them at a bank because he didn't have a passport, and asked me to change them for him. To keep it short, I fell for it, and cashed about £90 in travellers' cheques to meet the required amount of dirhams. I gave him the dirhams and then watched closely as he counted my 800 francs into my hand – seven 100-franc notes and two 50s. Without any thanks he then pissed off. A few minutes later, in a café, I checked the francs. You've guessed! The two 50-franc notes were OK, but the other seven notes were worthless rubbish from some Central African country, valued at about a quid each. The bastard did me out of £75! It didn't make me feel any better to learn that plenty of travellers who think they're doing someone a favour are being ripped off in the same way. Take care, folks!

J.L.T. TOO EMBARRASSED TO GIVE MY NAME, UK

Watch those friendly 'guides' in Morocco. A lot of them are professional pickpockets. RICK TOOHEY, ATLANTA, USA

There is a great deal of traffic crossing the Sahara. Be sure to get lifts in vehicles with lots of passengers (more people to dig and push when you get stuck in the sand).

BARRY SIMMONDS, BLACKPOOL, UK

I thought I'd just regale you with a little story about an incident that happened to me in Morocco last November.

The Algeciras to Ceuta ferry now costs 1740ptas. Don't bother haggling: they're the same price right the way along the front. Don't panic (unlike me!) if you arrive on the night ferry. Get directions to the Ceuta police station. I got driven at high speed in a patrol car to a local landlady who put me up for the night. The cops were really friendly and fed me endless biscuits.

Now for the bad news: over the border to Tetouan. Not ten minutes off the bus, some local crazy had knocked me to the ground. A bit shook up, I headed for Place Moulay. Pension Iberia is really crap. There's no water, let alone cold, and the owner tried to hit me for 90dr a night. Haggling got nowhere, so I made my excuses and left.

Ahmed – the man who claimed to be the owner of the hotel – came too, saying he'd help me find a bureau de change and some food. We went into the souk. I started getting a bit wary when he mentioned he'd take me to see his college professor – call me a cynic, but I don't know of that many tutors who live in covered markets – so I hot-footed it. He caught up with me and gave me a sound kicking for my trouble.

My next mistake was to cross the forecourt of King Hassan's old palace. This place was roped off and deserted so I thought it'd be a good move to nip across the square. Bad move. An armed guard appeared. It seems that there's a mandatory jail sentence for going anywhere near it.

After failing to find any hotels under £8, I returned to Ceuta to rethink. I was detained at the border for nearly two hours by the border guards. Three of them stripped my pack, convinced that I'd just done a dope run. The leap from 'You are a heroin addict' to 'You homosexual, English' took some imagination. It took a photo of my girlfriend to convince them I wasn't gay. Don't even think of fighting the civil liberties corner here: these guys were about as enlightened as the dark side of the moon.

OLLY DAVIES, HARROGATE, ENGLAND

I was travelling with £10 a day in Morocco. It's perfectly possible, but you end up feeling terrible – there are loads of unemployed guys trying to work as guides, polish your boots, sell you things, etc, who assume all Westerners are loaded. If you go with a bit more cash, you get less hassle – just hire a guide. Once, I lost my temper and it made things worse. The trick is to ignore all attempts at conversation. It's harder on your own.

JON BANKS, LONDON, ENGLAND

If you hire a guide in Morocco, don't buy anything with them, since they get a commission from the shopkeeper. Tell them at the beginning that you don't want anything. I heard about one guy getting a knife pulled on him by his guide in Marrakesh for refusing to buy a carept. One scam is for Moroccans to hang around outside shops. They go in with Westerners and tell the shopkeeper they are their guide, so they can get the commission.

Irish speakers can really freak them out when they come up testing out ten languages on you! SIAN, DUBLIN, IRELAND

There's loads of hash rip-offs in Morocco. One of them: they sell you some gear, go round the corner and tell the cops (or their mates with cop uniforms). Result: they get the pot back, you have to bribe your way out of jail. Don't buy off anyone who comes up to you in the street or who knows where you're staying.

WILL THOMPSON, LONDON, ENGLAND

Algeria

population	25,324,000
size	2,380,444 square kilometres
capital	Algiers, population 1,483,000
government	Single party independent republic
religion	Moslem
language	Arabic; French almost universally spoken; Spanish and Berber used in some regions
currency	*Dinar* (AD) One *dinar* equals 100 *centimes*

Algeria can be entered by road or rail from Morocco or Tunisia, or by boat from Marseilles.

The country offers many of Morocco's attractions – plus some special to itself – with less hassle but more cost. The big bonus is a friendly, hospitable and generous people. As with most Moslem countries, to be a visitor is to be a guest.

Many hitchers' first stop will be **Algiers** which is a pity because much of the city, particularly the *casbah*, is in bad shape; beggars, slums, sewage in the streets, the whole bit. Nevertheless the *casbah* is worth a visit, particularly if you want an idea of what Algeria's War of Independence against the French must have been like. This maze of claustrophobic, narrow alleys frustrated French forces during eight years of guerrilla fighting.

The country's troubled economy is best illustrated by a visit to the main square by the Grande Poste – itself a magnificent building, built in the Moorish style, and decorated with gold leaf. City life used to centre on the square's view over the harbour area. Now the view is dominated by the square itself, which was ripped out to make way for a new metro system, but unfortunately, oil money ran out in the late 1980s, and it was left a derelict building site. Today the square is a national joke.

Places to visit in the capital include the Place des Martyrs, the Grand Mosque, the Museum of Popular Arts, the Mosque of Sidi Abd Er Rhamane (all sited around the *casbah* area) and, further out, the Jardin d'Essais, and the neighbouring Museum of Fine Arts. Take a stroll around the Bois des Arcades, the lavish shopping thoroughfare, which features a statue of a *moudjahid* (holy fighter).

A pleasant 400-kilometre trip east of the capital takes you to the country's third largest city, **Constantine**. The city has been described as an eagle's nest. It sits on a plateau 2,100 feet above sea level, and is surrounded by the 500–1,000-foot deep Rhumel Gorge. Check out the Sidi M'Cid suspension bridge, one of the highest and most dramatic in the world. The *souk* area is much as it was centuries ago. Visit the Palace of El Hadj Ahmed and the Place de la Breche. In many cafés and restaurants you can eat and drink while looking out over spectacular views. It is one of the Arab world's most beautiful cities.

Constantine is also the gateway both to the amazingly complete Roman remains of eastern Algeria, and to the vast Sahara desert. Heading south from Constantine takes you to **Batna**, which is not worth the stop, but the road takes you by the impressive salt lakes at **Les Lacs**. Just 35 km outside Batna is **Timgad**, which is among the most complete Roman town remains anywhere. Timgad was covered for centuries by protective desert sands, and as a result has withstood time amazingly well. Roads, pillars and underground dwellings remain in good condition, as do the impressive triumphal arch and tombstones with carved pictures of their occupants. Few tourists visit the site.

Head south through **Rhoufi** and you touch the desert when you reach **Biskra**. The 160 km journey is stunning, with roads cutting through a mountain range and canyons of varying reds, browns and greys. For part of the trip the road runs alongside the El Abiod canyon, a riverbed of uncharacteristic greenery, which in parts is host to gigantic palm groves. Biskra itself is a large oasis town, sandy and spacious, with a more central African mood than its neighbouring towns to the north.

A genuine sense of the desert can be gained by visiting **Ouargla** or **Ghardaia**. However, even these more accessible desert towns involve trips of over 400 km each way! (It can never be said strongly enough: when hitching in desert regions take sufficient food supplies for at least 24 hours and *lots* of water; dying of thirst is a serious possibility round here. Local buses are a cheap and safer alternative than hitching.)

Ouargla is surrounded by half a million palm trees. See the Museum of the Sahara and the nearby ruins of Sedrata. If you're there at the right time check out the Spring Festival of music and dance. If you only have time for one of these trips, perhaps Ghardaia is the best visit. Arcaded streets, a large market, the 12th-century Djemaa Chaaba – an underground mosque where prayers are held on the roof – and one of North Africa's largest and most ornate cemeteries make it one of the most interesting towns in the area.

Those adventurous souls amongst you who are *really* serious about seeing and understanding something of life in the Sahara should head for **Tamanrasset**, a market town at the foot of the Ahaggar (or Hoffar) Mountains, which is a traditional stopping-off place for travellers heading into the heart of Africa, to Niger and

Mali. But be warned that Tamanrasset is a full 1,000 km south of Ghardaia (and also be warned that some of the world's highest shade temperatures have been recorded there, so best leave the trip for the cooler months).

If you do make it to Tamanrasset, treat yourself to a side-trip into the mountains to **Assekrem**, a hermitage founded in 1905 by the French Count Charles-Eugène Foucauld. Foucauld – explorer, ascetic and linguist – was befriended by the Tuaregs and compiled a Tuareg dictionary. Admirers of his way of life continue to maintain the hermitage, and a hostel on the site provides food and beds for overnight stops.

The trip takes about a day each way, and you'll drive through villages scarcely touched by the 20th century. Roads are little more than tracks. Try and pick up your ride from Tamanrasset but make sure you choose someone with a four-wheel drive. The odds of a regular car making it are slim. On the way keep an eye out for rock drawings, some dating back to 400 BC and, like Timgad, preserved by sand burial. You can guess where they are by parking tracks left by previous vehicles.

The **Tassili n'Adjjer** mountains, further east, towards Libya, are dubbed 'the world's finest open-air museum'. They contain tens of thousands of ancient rock paintings, some of these dating from 6000 BC! The area can only be visited in the cooler months, such as October and November.

Wherever you go after Tamanrasset requires a long journey which will remind you that Algeria is gigantic. In fact, it's the second largest country in Africa and the tenth largest in the world.

If you have got plenty of time when heading north from Tamanrasset, try to arrange a hitch to the beautiful oasis town of **Timimoun**. The town is built on the fringe of the Grand Erg Occidental. On nights when there is a moon the views from the escarpment, on which the town lies, are fantastic.

After making your weary way north-west, take a break in the ancient city of **Tlemcen**, not far from the Mediterranean, or from the Moroccan border. In fact, the narrow streets of this walled city, which has its origins in a 4th-century Roman settlement, are reminiscent of Morocco. The city is important to Algerians as it is the setting of the mosque and shrine of the national and Moslem hero Sidi Bou Mediene. In his honour, Mohammed Boukharouba, who became President of the Algerian Republic, adopted the name Bouhemedienne during the War of Independence. Apart from the Sidi Bou Mediene mosque from which you have a great overall view of the city, see the Place du Mechouar, Place Emir Abdelkader, the Sidi Bel Hassen mosque, and if you're still in the mood for mosques, the Sidi al-Haloui mosque outside the new city to the west.

North of Tlemcen is **Oran**, Algeria's second city. Oran was founded by Andalusian traders in the 10th century, in the 15th became the adopted home of Moslem refugees from Spain and in the 16th and 18th centuries was occupied by Spain. The Spanish influence remains. The palm tree-lined avenues could be in Seville. The mosaic promenade overlooking the bay could be in Málaga. In a country where alcohol is hard to come by Spanish-owned bars, often decorated with bullfight posters, are full of customers speaking Spanish and drinking beer. The city is unique in Algeria, a quirky mixture of happy-go-lucky Latinism and strict Islamic morality.

Oran is a good place to buy souvenirs. Under pleasant arcades in the city centre you can find things cheaper than anywhere else in the country. Even Saharan rugs can cost less in Oran than in Tamanrasset, especially after the obligatory haggle.

Check out the Plaza Mayor and its old cathedral, the Place de la Perle, and take a stroll out to the Santa Cruz citadel. If at the end of the day you've earned it, wander down to the fishing harbour, find a cheap seafood restaurant and buy yourself a plate of fresh fish.

● **Warning!** The Algerian-Moroccan border area with the old Spanish Sahara – just north of Mauritania – is still the object of armed clashes between Polisario guerrillas and the Moroccan army. The area is potentially dangerous, even to harmless hitchers. Best keep away. Entry to Morocco is not possible in this area.

● **Changing money** There is no limit to the amount of foreign currency you can bring into Algeria. Theoretically, that amount is supposed to be declared. Theoretically, you can export up to the amount you declared. In practice, you are expected to buy dinars for day-to-day expenses and are obliged to keep official receipts for all money changed. If you don't have receipts, when you leave the country you may be asked to justify how you lived without changing money. The black market is strong and some traders will offer good rates against hard currency for goods or services. Both practices are illegal. And as you don't get receipts for illegal deals you may have trouble if you are spot-checked when you leave the country.

● **Language** French is widely spoken but remember that as far as the Algerians are concerned it is the language of colonialism. You will win more friends if you try to speak a few words of Arabic.

● **Photos** Don't even think about pointing your camera at anything vaguely military (that includes soldiers or army vehicles).

Algeria: where to sleep

Head for the back streets and sleep in the hotels that Algerians use – about £2 a night for one star or worse. There are 39 Youth Hostels. The cheapos are basic, and you may be sharing with the odd cockroach or two, but you'll get by. For a good wash, search out public showers in the back streets.

Algeria: where to eat

Like everything else, prices are more expensive than elsewhere in North Africa, but the quality is usually better. But, avoid drinking tap water, especially further south.

Many small cafés offer good deals. In big cities you can splash out on European food, especially pizzas. Bear in mind that the country closes down by 9 p.m.

Transport in Algeria
Hitching is generally OK, but for long lifts ask around in the main tourist areas, especially if you are heading for the south. Buses and trains are cheap by Western standards. If you have more money than time, consider a plane – it costs £100 return from Algiers to Tamanrasset.

Algiers: where to sleep

You could try the **Hotel de Palais** or the **Central Touring Hotel** both on rue Ramdane Abane, but here are a few real cheapos:

Hamman, rue Arbadgi Abderrahman 15 B. AD13 per night.
Hotel el Badr, rue Amar el Kamar 31. Doubles AD70 per night, breakfast included. Just off Square Port Said in the direction of the medina.
Hotel Tunis, rue Amar el Kamar 38. AD70 per night for a double.
Hotel es Saada, rue des Tanneurs 1. AD60 per night for a double.
Hotel Club, rue des Tanneurs 2. Doubles cost AD60 per night.
Hotel Bearn, rue Larbi Ben M'Hidi 13. AD60 per night or, for long stays, AD50.

Algiers: where to eat

Restaurant la Pizzerie at rue Ramdane Abane. For something slightly up-market.

Restaurant Couscous at Square Port Said. For good cheap tucker, you can't beat this.

Restaurant le Saigon at rue Valentin 10. Top quality Chinese food at top quality prices. Expect to pay AD50 per person, but if you look around, you may meet some useful people.

Constantine: where to sleep

Hotel Central, rue Hamloui 19. Singles and doubles cost AD50–70 per night. A clean place.

Hotel Grand, rue Larbi Ben M'Hidi 2. Singles and doubles AD80–120 per night.

Youth Hostel at M. J. Cite Filali (tel: 69 54 61).

Constantine: where to eat

For budget eateries, try the area around the lower end of rue Hamloui, same street as Hotel Central, **Restaurant el Baraka** at rue Hamloui 23 gives good value: main course AD20, salads AD6.

Ghardaia: where to sleep

Hotel Napht. Pretty popular with travellers. Doubles cost AD100 per night. Has an air-conditioned lounge.

Hotel Atlantide at rue Ahmed Talbi. Doubles AD70 per night. Just round the corner from the Hotel Napht.

Youth Hostel at Mj. Emir Abdelkader, Ghardaia Centre BP (tel: 89 44 03). AD40 per night.

Youth Hostel at Mj. Dahane Brahim a Metili, Wilaya de Ghardaia (tel 89 76 68). AD40 per night.

Ghardaia: where to eat

Places to eat are hard to find, budget or otherwise. Best bet:

Restaurant el Hoggar. The food is acceptable, and prices about the same.

Tamanrasset: where to sleep

Apart from finding a bed, you will also be looking for a hitch/lift to get to Assekrem, which is about 75 km away. So why not kill two birds with the one stone and stay at the Hotel Dassine (see below). That's where all the tourists hang out, and they come here for one thing – to see Assekrem.

Hotel Dassine (also known as Camping Zerib) costs AD15 per person. Cold showers and toilets are available. Great place to fix up your lift for next morning to Assekrem.
Hotel Ilamane in the centre of town. AD65 per night.
Hotel Tinhinane. AD120 per night for doubles. Breakfast included. It also has a bar.
Auberge Jeunesse ex-centre culturel, Quartier Tahagart (tel: 73 40 47). Members' kitchen. 500 metres from bus station.

Tamanrasset: where to eat

Restaurant le Palmier. AD20 will get you a main meal; a bowl of soup is AD10 extra. If this sounds too expensive, there are others.

Timimoun: where to sleep

Hotel Ighzer on the main street just past the mosque. Doubles will cost you AD80 per night. Camping in the backyard might cost you only AD10.
Hotel Rouge de l'Oasis. A bar that has been known to let rooms for AD120 per night – worth enquiring.
Camping le Palmeraie. Just to the left as you come into town. AD25 per person. Hot showers.

Tlemcen: where to sleep

Hotel Majestic, place Cheikh Bahir Ibrahimi. Singles and doubles cost from AD80 per night.
Hotel Moderne rue 1 Novembre 20. Doubles AD70 per night.
Camping Municipale situated inside the walls of Mansourah amongst olive groves, but 20 minutes walk from town. AD10 per person plus AD15 per tent or vehicle.

Hostel:

Auberge Jeunesse Sidi-Chaker, Tlemcen 13000 (tel: 26 32 26). AD40 per night. 500 m from the bus station.

Tlemcen: where to eat

There are a few cheap eateries on rue Larbi ben M'Hidi; worthwhile shopping around. Try the **Hotel Olympia**, just 10 minutes' walk from the bus station.

Oran: where to sleep

Hotel Riad, blvd Mellah Ali 46. Singles and doubles with bath AD75–100.

Hotel Melliani, blvd Mellah Ali 14. Doubles, breakfast included, AD87–125 per night. Cold showers only.

There are many others, particularly cheap ones on the rue Ozanam and again just off blvd Emir Abdelkader. Shop around and you might get one to suit. Hostels include:

Auberge de Jeunesse, rue Benadjila Lahouari 3, Seddikia, Wilaya d'Oran (tel: (6) 35 02 45). Members' kitchen. 2 km from the railway station; 200 m from bus station. AD40 per night.

Auberge de Jeunesse, rue Maoued Ahmed 19 (tel: (6) 39 82 99). AD40 per night. About 1 km from the railway station and 500 m from the bus station.

Addresses

Main post office (for poste restante) at La Grande Poste, 5 blvd. Mohamed Khémisti, Algiers.

US Embassy at BP 549, 4 Chemin Cheikh Bachir El-Ibrahami, 16000 Alger-Gare, Algiers (tel: (a) 601 186; fax: 603 979).

British Embassy at Résidence Cassiopée, Bâtiment B, 7 Chemin des Glycines, Algiers (tel: 60 56 01; fax: 60 44 10).

Hitchers' Tips and Comments . . .

Pickpockets in Algeria are after passports. They sell them to forgers who then tailor them to the needs of would-be illegal immigrants.

The pickpockets work in teams of three or four, often at crowded bus stations. Be *particularly careful* when getting on buses. Money belts are the only answer, and even they mightn't stop these bastards. GEORGE TURNER, HUDDERSFIELD, UK

Tourists (except students) now *must* change 1,000 dinar when entering Algeria and at inflated official rates.

RICK TOOHEY, ATLANTA, USA

I haven't been to North Africa (except Morocco) in some time, so can't attest to what's happening at borders re visas, compulsory money changing, etc. Can't get much sense out of tourist offices either. Most don't even bother to answer my queries. But I can tell you this: hitchers' letters are contradictory. Someone will write in with a piece of info and then another letter will arrive dated two months later with a completely different description of what's going on. All you can do is find the latest information before leaving your base, and then update with other hitchers as you near your destination. The bureaucratic bullshit puzzle applies not only to North Africa, but also to Middle Eastern and Eastern European countries.

K.W.

I found hitching good in Algeria. In the south you can get long lifts due to the great distances between main towns. Best lifts are on the trans-Saharan trucks. I managed to make it to Tamanrasset. At the service stations there, in the early morning or late afternoon, you can sometimes get a lift down to Niger, or even to the coast. Once you head inland in Algeria it is *important* that you carry at least two litres of water in a refillable container!

SIMON LINGLEY, UPPINGHAM, UK

Nowhere in Algeria could we change Eurocheques! We had been misinformed by our bank in England. This proved to be a real nightmare. Also worth knowing: you cannot buy water unless you have an empty bottle to exchange, and you need loads of water, especially in the south. Q. PAGE AND GIDEON COLES, LONDON

Tunisia

population	8,200,000
size	164,078 square kilometres
capital	Tunis, population 1,500,000
government	Independent republic under one-party presidential regime
religion	Moslem
language	Arabic, with French widely spoken
currency	*Dinar* (TD) One *dinar* equals 1,000 *millimes*. Coins of 5, 10, 20, 50, 100 *millimes*, and of $^1/_2$, 1 *dinar*. Notes of 5, 10, 20 *dinars*

Ferries connect Naples, Palermo and Marseilles to Tunis. Ferry bookings *out* of Tunisia can be heavy. Try and book passage back to Europe well in advance.

In **Tunis**, the capital, the most interesting area is in and around the ancient *medina*. Enter at the Porte de France. See the Djama ez Zitouna mosque (you are allowed on to the arcaded verandah of the mosque but not permitted inside unless you are Moslem), wander through the various *souks* which specialize in specific products: the Attarine for perfume, the Orfevres for gold and silver, the Koumach for clothing and material. The Bardo National Museum is about 3 km from the centre, but worth the effort of getting there to gain insight into Tunisia's history and to see the knock-out collection of Roman mosaics.

A few kilometres out of Tunis (try the cheap train ride from the station at the end of the main street, av. Habib Bourguiba) are the ruins of **Carthage**, the city which was defeated and destroyed by the Romans in 146 BC. About 3 km further on is the village of **Sidi Bou Saíd** which for my money is the prettiest in Tunisia. Not a great deal to see, but it's great for photographers and a must if you're exploring northern Tunisia in depth.

The Roman ruins of **Dougga**, 100 km inland from Tunis, are the best preserved in Africa, and perhaps the most evocative in all the Roman world (including those of Rome!). You'll have to find a bed in the country town of **Teboursouk** and walk or hitch to the ruins some 9 km away and 2,000 feet up in the mountains. The ruins cover 62 acres. Highlights are the theatre which seated more than 3,000 people and the Capitol. In the streets you see ruts from chariot wheels and also get a good idea of how sophisticated Roman drainage systems were. Great stuff for history buffs and ruin freaks.

South of Tunis, **Hammamet** is a pleasant tourist town with little to offer apart from a beach, a fort once garrisoned by the French

Foreign Legion and a small, touristy *medina*. On the other hand, you may meet someone there. North is **Nabeul** which is worth a visit if you're in the area for the Friday morning market. Further north, beyond the fishing port of **Kelibia**, and near the tip of **Cape Bon**, are the ruins of **Kerkouane**, a well-preserved Punic village (check out the 2,400-year-old bathrooms!).

Heading south along the coast you reach **Sousse**, Tunisia's third largest city and one of its oldest: it dates back to the early Phoenicians. Climb the tower in the Ribat (fortified monastery) for a great overall view, visit the courtyard of the Grand Mosque in front of the Ribat, then wander uphill through the *medina* to the museum in the casbah. From the walls you get another view down on to the city. (Be warned that throughout Tunisia, you pay one price for an entrance ticket to a monument and a 200% supplement if you wish to photograph within the monument, and even then you are not allowed to use tripod or flash.)

Next to Sousse is **Monastir**, revered amongst Tunisians as the home town of Habib Bourguiba, who led Tunisia to independence from the French occupation. The Ribat here is the most fascinating in the country and well worth the price of the ticket to enter and explore. Climb the tower for a great view of the Bourguiba mausoleum over the Moslem cemetery. The walled *medina* is worth stopping for only if you have time.

Inland from Monastir and Sousse stands the holy city of **Kairouan**, which is amongst the most important in Islam. Visit the courtyard of the Grand Mosque after buying your ticket from the Syndicat d'Initiative (Tourist Office), and with the same ticket the Sidi Sahab Mosque, also called The Barber's Mosque. Check the wonderful carpets made in the city (someone will try and sell you one small enough to fit your pack) and wander the endlessly fascinating streets of the city.

South of Monastir **El Djem**, stark and alone on a plain, is the home of yet another of Tunisia's fabulous historical sights. This one is a 3rd-century 30,000-seat Roman amphitheatre. You can see it for miles before you reach the humble village which in its present state offers no clue (apart from the amphitheatre and semi-excavated ruins nearby) of its past importance.

Sfax, Tunisia's second city, is hardly worth the stop if time is short, but **Gabès**, 133 km south, is. This oasis town on the edge of the desert is surrounded by 300,000 palm trees. Tiny villages within the palm tree forest, for instance the handicraft town of **Chenini**, are great to wander in to sense the pulse of Tunisian rural life. If you have time try and find the Roman dam and the waterfall.

Djerba claims it is Homer's 'island of the lotus eaters' (so do

Majorca and Menorca in the Balearics) and also Ogygia the home of Calypso (as does the Maltese island of Gozo). Visit **Houmt-Souk** with its pleasant but touristy *medina*, the Museum of Folklore and Popular Arts and the impressive Bordj el Kébir, the 15th-century waterfront fort. **Adjim** is where the famed Djerba divers plunge 50 feet down for sponges. **Guellala** is the island's pottery centre. A causeway connects the island to the mainland at **El Kantara**, or you can take a cheap ferry from **Djorf**.

Inland again, **Matmata** (best reached by detouring back through Gabès) is a troglodyte town with many people still living underground. Matmatans dig 20- or 30-foot-deep pits and then dig their homes into the walls of the pit. Friendly touts offer to show you a cave-dwelling for a small fee.

Next best stop is **Douz**, right on the edge of the great eastern Saharan desert. But to get there do not try the direct route from Matmata to the old Foreign Legion and slave town of **Kebeli**. The route looks simple on the map but there's little traffic on it because the road is all but impassable except for four-wheel-drives. Much safer to retreat again to Gabès and take the **El Ksar, Limaguess** route. Try and reach Douz in time for the Thursday morning market when people come in from surrounding villages and the desert by foot, on camels and donkeys and in 4 × 4s to buy up supplies and sell and trade animals. The general market is in the square, the animal market a couple of streets off the square. Not to be missed!

Sabria, 30 km from Douz, is about as far into the desert as you can go without a proper vehicle (it's a hard-top road). You'll probably be picked up without any trouble because desert people tend to look out for each other. But best not to try this trip (or any other trip in desert regions in North Africa) without carrying three things: enough water for at least a day (minimum one litre), snack food for at least a day and warm clothing to protect you against cold desert nights in case you get stuck.

If you've come this far you'll want to cross the **Chott el Djerid** which, with an area of 2,000 square miles, is the Sahara's largest salt lake. Pick up a ride from around Kebeli. Try and stop at one of the cafés on the bitumen road across so you can wander a few hundred yards over the dry salt skin of the lake.

Tozeur is a good stop-over place. Distinctive, ochre brickwork decorates houses and mosques. Many designs on Tozeur's famed rugs copy the brickwork theme. About 23 km further on stands **Nefta** in its artificial oasis of hundreds of thousands of palms watered by wells almost 2,000 feet deep. From Nefta it is only half an hour's drive to the Algerian border. Check formalities *before* you try and cross the border.

Hitching
Hitching in Tunisia is good, but the competition is fierce because Tunisians hitch in droves, preferring to try their luck on the road rather than depend on erratic bus services. But the Tunisians are friendly and also curious about and anxious to speak to foreigners, so you should get around OK. You should, however, remember that in some countries in North Africa, *use of the thumb in an upward direction is considered to be an obscene gesture*. Be discreet also about taking photographs of people.

● **Haggling** Same rules apply as for Morocco. Hotels and restaurants are fixed price. Always establish the price of any service before you use it.

Tunisia: where to sleep

Standards vary widely in budget and sub-budget establishments. Some dirt cheap places are just that: dirty and cheap. Others offer excellent value including hot water. In small towns you may only find one hotel and be stuck with it. In larger places you'll have a choice and it's worth comparing prices and conditions. TD4 or 5 should get you a decent single. If you can afford TD7–9 you will probably have your own bathroom with shower.

Tunisia: where to eat

In working-class restaurants you eat for TD3 or 4, often with no menu choice. In better class places you'll have a menu choice and pay TD6 or 7 for salad, main dish and fruit and eat very well. Tunisian salad is excellent. Couscous is different from the excellent Moroccan version (drier and the meat isn't as good), but is healthy and filling. Making up your own meal from the markets is dead cheap, particularly if you buy seasonal fruit. Tap water in major towns is OK, but elsewhere stick to mineral water. Mineral water is only sold in glass bottles which are hard to carry so it's worth investing in a water bottle or plastic container.

Transport in Tunisia
Buses and trains are cheap, but heavily used and the service is erratic. Taxis in Tunisia are within hitchers' budgets, when shared by three or four, and in Tunis, at least, are charged on the meter price. Make sure the meter is on.

Teboursoux: where to sleep

Maison des Jeunes (tel: 08 65095). TD3 per night. It's a small hostel so best book in advance.

Hammamet: where to sleep

Hotel Benilla (tel: 02 80356). TD10 per night, breakfast included.
Maison des Jeunes (tel: 02 80440). All meals are available. TD3 per night.

Best bet is to head along to the **Tourist Agency**, av. Habib Bourguiba (tel: 08 44 491) and ask them about other budget digs.

Nabeul: where to sleep

Nabeul is a tourist trap like Hammamet (above) and in the summer the visitors *and* the prices increase. Here are a few good cheapos:

Hotel Les Jasmins (tel: 02 85343). TD9 per night.
Pension les Oliviers (tel: 02 86865). TD4–9 per night.
Pension les Roses (tel: 02 85570). TD4–6 per night (off season).
Pension les Hafsides (tel: 02 85823). TD8–10 per night.

Hostels:
Maison des Jeunes (tel: 02 86689). All meals are available. TD3 per night.
La Gazelle, centre de sejour et de vacances, Dar chaabane el fehri, Nabeul (tel: 02 21366). TD4 per night.
Town Centre (tel: 02 85547). TD4 per night.

Sousse: where to sleep

Hotel Medina (tel: 03 21722). Next to the Grand Mosque. TD10–14 per night with shower and breakfast.
Hotel Emira (tel: 03 26325). TD10 per night, breakfast and shower included.
Hotel Claridge, av. Habib Bourguiba (tel: 03 24759). TD11.500–16 per night.
Hotel Paris, 12 rue de Paris. TD5 per person. Clean and quiet with free hot showers.

Hostel:

Souse Hostel, place Boujaafar (tel: 03 27548). TD4 per night. About 2 km from the railway station.

Sousse: where to eat

The best of all the restaurants are situated on the av. Habib Bourguiba. Try seafood at the **Restaurant le Bonheur**. (Meals are also available at the youth hostel.)

Monastir: where to sleep

Hotel Yasmin, Route de la Falaise (tel: 03 31511). TD10 per night, with shower. It also sports a restaurant.
Hotel Mourabou (tel: 03 61585). TD4 per night.

Hostel:

Maison des Jeunes, Monastir town centre (tel: 03 61216). This is a fairly small-capacity hostel, so book in advance, particularly in summer when the joint is jumping.

Kairouan: where to sleep

Hotel Sabra, rue ali Balhaouane (tel: 07 20260). TD4–7 per night with shower and breakfast.
Hotel Marhala Souk el Belaghija 35 (tel: 07 20736). TD4.500 per night.

Gabès: where to sleep

Hotel de la Poste, av. Habib Bourguiba (tel: 05 70718). TD7 per night. There's a café down below with the same name.
Hotel Marhaba, blvd. Farhat Hached, opposite the bus station, is much cheaper but a bit more noisy.

Hostel:

Centre de Stages et de Vacances, rue de l'oasis (tel: 05 20271). TD3.500 per night.

Gabès: where to eat

Restaurant a la Bonne Table, av. Habib Bourguiba. Try their *farci chicken*, and other dishes. Good tucker.

Addresses

Tourist bureau, av. Hedi Chaker (tel: 05 70254).

Djerba: where to sleep

In olden days Djerba was a recreational centre. Nowadays, it is a very popular place with package tours, because of its great beauty spots.

Hotel Marhala, rue Moncef Bey 11, Houmt Souk (tel: 05 50619). This is a good-sized hostel. TD4.500 per night including breakfast (off-season prices).
Hotel Arischa, Houmt Souk (tel: 05 50384). TD4 per night.
Hotel Sable d'Or, Houmt Souk (tel: 05 50423). TD4 per night including shower.

Addresses

Tourist office at blvd H. Bourguiba, Houmt Souk (tel: 05 50915).

Douz: where to sleep

December is a great time to be in Douz when the *Oases Festival* is held. But the town is really buzzing with people – so be prepared.

Hotel 20 Mars. TD2 per night.
Hotel Marhala (tel: 05 95315). TD7.500–11.900 per night, singles and doubles breakfast included.

Addresses

Tourist office at rue Farhat Hached (tel: 05 90930/90940)

Tozeur: where to sleep

Hotel Essaada, right in the centre of town (tel: 06 50097). At TD2–4 per night, you can't grumble.
Residence Warda (tel: 06 50514). TD6.300–9.600 per night. Showers are available but there may be a extra charge.
Hotel Khalifa, av. Habib Bourguiba (tel: 06 50068). TD5 per night. Showers are available. Price includes breakfast.

Nefta: where to sleep

Hotel Marhala (tel: 06 57027). This is good value at TD5–6.900 per night, breakfast included.
Hotel de la Liberté, on the far side of the corbeille. TD3 per person. There's no sign, so ask around.

Tunis: where to sleep

Most of the cheaper hotels are situated between the old town (*medina*) and the railway station.

Hotel Cirta, rue Charles de Gaulle 42 (tel: 241 582) Very clean place – recommended. TD5–7 per night.
Hotel Agriculture, rue Charles de Gaulle 25 (tel: 246 394). TD5–7 per night.
Hotel de Suisse, rue de Suisse 5 (tel: 243 821). TD4.500 per night.
Hotel de Bretagne, rue de Grèce 7 (tel: 242 146). TD6.500 per night.
Hotel Central, rue de Suisse 6 (tel: 240 433). TD4.500 per night.
Hotel Bristol, rue Lt. Med. Aziz Taj 30 (tel: 244 836). TD7–10 per night.
Hotel Salammbo, rue de Grèce 6 (tel: 244 252). TD10 per night with shower.

The youth hostel, although a good one, is so far out of the city, that it is perhaps better spending a few more shekels in a hotel than spending your time catching buses for a 20-minute ride each way. But for what it's worth:

Maison des Jeunes de Rades at banlieue Sud, Tunis (tel: 483 631). TD3–4 per night. Meals available.

There are two more hostels in the city, but they are usually very crowded and very hot:

Centre d'hébergement, Jelili ez Zahra, Oued Meliane Ezzahara, BP 1140 Tunis RP (tel: 481 547) Take a 26A bus from la Place Barcelone. TD4 per night. Meals available.

Tunis Medina, Auberge de la Jeunesse Tunis, rue Saida Ajoula 25 (tel: 567 850). About 500 m from La Place du Governement la kasbah in the old city. TD4 per night.

Tunis: where to eat

Here are a few good eating places:

Restaurant Carcassonne, av. de Carthage 8 (near to the Café de Paris in the av. Habib Bourguiba. 4-course set menu sets you back only TD3. When you take into account the free bread, it is very filling.

Restaurant Abid, rue de Yougoslavie, near the corner of rue Ibn Khaldoun. Good eating for around TD3.50.

Restaurant Le Cosmos, rue Ibn Khaldoun 7, has the best seafood in Tunis. You may pay a little more, but it is well worth it. The price of TD10 includes a half-bottle of red wine.

Restaurant l'Etoile, rue Ibn Khaldoun 3. The menu here is every bit as good as Le Cosmos, price much of a muchness.

For much cheaper snacks, try the heaps of pâtisseries around the area between av. Habib Bourguiba and the Post Office, on the rue Charles de Gaulle. Especially good for croissant and coffee breakfasts; they also serve chicken, chips, pizzas and, *naturellement*, cakes – after all it is a pâtisserie. However, I cannot imagine anyone coming to Tunisia for a feast of chicken & chips or pizzas.

Tunis: what to see and do

SOUK DES CHECHIAS They make the little red fez caps here, which in this day and age no one except old people wears. Good for souvenirs.

BARDO MUSEUM Houses a fantastic collection of Roman mosaics and statues of marble. Take a no. 3 bus from opposite the Africa Hotel on av. Habib Bourguiba and stay on till the terminus.

CARTHAGE: PUNIC AND ROMAN RUINS a must-see. The ruins are spread over a large area, but include an amphitheatre, which is used today as a very attractive setting for musical festivals. The Antonine Thermal Baths were the largest in the Roman Empire.

SIDI BOU SAID as mentioned previously, this is only a few stops on the TGM line from the ruins of Carthage. The village is a confection of domes, arched doors, balconies and grilles in dazzling blue and white – you could almost be on the French Riviera.

Addresses

US Embassy at av. de la Liberté 144, Tunis (tel: 232 566).
British Embassy at place de la Victoire 5, Tunis (tel: 245 100).
American Express at Carthage Tours, av. Habib Bourguiba 59 (tel: 254 605).

Hitchers' Tips and Comments . . .

The *medina* in Tunis is very touristy and it's getting harder to find bargains. Watch out for the following rip-off: you haggle with a dealer for something you like and agree on a price; then he produces a similar item and wraps it, saying (if you catch him at it) that the one you saw is a slightly damaged display item; later you find you've been given an inferior item.

Note that it's very easy to sell watches, blue jeans, etc. to the local boys.

Hitching is pretty good in Tunisia. Some drivers demand money for lifts but most don't, so there's never any need to pay.

HUGH DUNNE, DUBLIN, IRELAND

Libya

population	4,000,000
size	1,806,157 square kilometres
capital	Tripoli (population 990,697) and Benghazi (population 500,000) are co-capitals
government	Proclaimed as the Libyan Arab Republic
religion	Moslem
language	Arabic; Italian widely understood; English normally understood in shops, hotels, etc.
currency	*Dinar* One *dinar* equals 1,000 *dirhams*

Tripoli ('the shores of Tripoli' is relevant to the US Marines' action against the Libyan pirates) is a city of 600,000 people. Several good mosques to see, several interesting museums, plus the Arch of Marcus Aurelius which dates from AD 163. See the castle and the market of Suk-el-Mushir.

Close by (90 km east along the coast road) is the ancient Roman city of **Leptis Magna**, one of the least-visited but best-preserved Roman cities in existence.

About 300 km inland, through a stark desert landscape, you come to the oasis city of **Ghadames**, which sits right at the point where the territories of Tunisia, Algeria and Libya converge. This is a Tuareg city, focal point of desert caravans, and one of the most fascinating in Africa. Strongly recommended to anyone searching for *real* Arab flavour.

As a startling contrast, **Benghazi**, population 219,317 which was savagely mauled in the Second World War, is a city of wide streets and with a completely modern aspect. Any students of the military (are there any left?) might like to visit the battlefields in the area surrounding the city or drop in on **Tobruk**, near the Egyptian border, which was the scene of a siege and terrible fighting during the desert war. In Benghazi itself, however, you can see the Royal Palace and the cathedral and search out shops which sell the famous Benghazi rugs.

● **Visa requirements** Libya is hard to enter. To even attempt to get a visa, you must have your passport translated into Arabic, a smallpox vaccination certificate and two passport photographs. Visas are not, repeat not, issued at the border. Full details from Libyan embassies or consulates.

Addresses

US Embassy at Garden City, Shari 'al Nsr, Tripoli (tel: 34 021 or 320 26). (American hitchers take note: as we go to press the US Embassy is closed.)

British Embassy at Sh. Gamal Abdel Nasser 30, Tripoli (tel: 31 191). The British Embassy is closed at this moment, too! Try British Interests Section, c/o Embassy of the Italian Republic, PO Box 4206, Sh. Uahran 1, Tripoli (tel: (21) 31 191).

Egypt

population	53,153,000
size	1,001,017 square kilometres (including Sinai Peninsula)
capital	Cairo, population 14,000,000 (20,000,000 might be more realistic)
government	Independent state under one-party presidential regime
religion	Moslem
language	Arabic, with English widely understood
currency	*Egyptian pound* (E£) One *pound* equals 100 *piastres* (pt)

Egypt, along with three other regions – China, the Indus Valley and Mesopotamia – was one of the first centres of civilization in the world. Its recorded history goes back as far as 6,000 years to the time of the Pharaohs. It has some of the finest displays of antiquity to be seen anywhere – and on a grand scale. So, if the opportunity presents itself to visit Egypt, grab it with both hands; you will not regret your visit, and you can make it cheap. The people are visitor-friendly; the climate is dry and warm in the summer (but desert nights in the winter can be cold).

Getting into Egypt through Jordan has distinct advantages; apart from an interesting ferry trip from Aqaba, it rules out all the hassles you might encounter about having an Israeli stamp on your passport or an Egyptian stamp at a border point between Israel and Egypt, which would also rule out travelling to another Arab country. There are boats daily to Nuweiba or Suez. Other possibilities are coming from Cyprus or Rhodes to Alexandria or Port Said, but it is reported that the ferry costs are quite high. Bucket shops in Athens might get you a cheap flight – in some cases, cheaper than the ferry – but make enquiries. Hitching on Egypt's extensive network of roads is good. There are excellent roads along the length of the Canal to the Red Sea coast, and also from Alexandria to Cairo and the Nile Delta.

Cairo – the big focal point of any Egyptian trip – is a capital city of astonishing diversity and vitality uniting elements of Africa, the Orient and Western Europe. This city of nearly 14,000,000 was founded in the 10th century but **Giza**, just a few kilometres out, is considerably older and the site of the famed Pyramids and the Sphinx. The Pyramid of Cheops is the largest of the three at Giza, standing 446 feet tall and having a 740-foot base on each side. It covers 12 acres and contains more than 2 million blocks of stone, each weighing around $2^1/_2$ tons. Visit the Tomb of Cheops, right in the centre of the mammoth. The Sphinx, near the Pyramids, was built at about the same time – 2700 BC. See, in Cairo itself, the Alabaster Mosque which has one of the most startling interiors you'll find in any religious building anywhere. Also in the Citadel area you can see the City of the Dead, a cemetery built like a miniature town. The Egyptian Antiquities Museum has the best collection of its type in the world, including the fantastic treasure removed from the tomb of Tutankhamun.

Alexandria (population 2,917,327) was founded in 331 BC by Alexander the Great and was once the centre of both Greek and Egyptian culture. It is more modern than Cairo, but still retains some Hellenistic and Roman relics as a reminder that it once was the cultural capital of Europe (as we know it now). These days it's a busy port city. See Pompey's Pillar, the catacombs of Kom Al-Shoqafa (only rediscovered 75 years ago), the Greco-Roman Museum and the Ras-at-Tin Palace. West of Alexandria are the battlefields of **Alamein**, and east, **Rashid**, where the famous Rosetta Stone which gave scholars the clue to translating hieroglyphics was discovered in 1799.

Port Said is the northern exit into the Mediterranean for Canal shipping. It has a population of approx. 400,000 and is a bustling port in terms of volumes of shipping. Its entrance is guarded by the large statue of M. de Lesseps who conceived the idea of the Canal in the 19th century. The country reaps benefits in revenue from users of the Canal to the tune of about £1,000 million annually. Not so well known, however, is the fact that a navigable canal was built in 2100 BC by the Pharaohs, stretching as far as **Lake Timsah (Ismailiya)** but it fell into disuse in AD 8. (The rate of unemployment must have been at record lows for 2,108 years!) Some canals in Britain could benefit from that technology! It's worth the trip, particularly if you aim for Port Said and Ismailiya. After that it's all straight, narrow and boring until you finish up in **Suez**. That said, there are a couple of good watering holes en route. **Port Fuad**, which is a sort of suburb of Port Said, is very affluent. It can be reached by a short ferry ride across the canal from Port Said. It has excellent, clean beaches, and some very good budget hotels. More important to the budget traveller, however, is the Yacht Basin/Marina/Club. You may be told that you need a pass to enter; if you have your passport you should be OK. At the Yacht Club you can enquire about the possibility of working your way to a number of destinations. You might just strike it lucky and get a boat trip for free. Should you have to wait a few days, there are also some good cheap hotels in the area.

Ismailiya is HQ of the Suez Canal Company, a Pilot station, and a canal traffic junction half-way between Port Said and Suez. It lies on Lake Timsah; has the University of Suez Canal, faculties of Science and Medicine. A pretty city of 544,400 people, with its shady avenues and flower lined promenades, lush parks and gardens. Midan El Gumhuriya is a good shopping street.

Suez, at the most southerly end of the canal, does not have a lot to offer; except to watch passing water traffic. It could be interesting for people wishing to travel to Jordan. Boats leave every three days, and Jordanian visas are available on board.

Instead of backtracking to reach Cairo, it is quite a good idea to continue to **Hurghada** (if time permits) then cross to **Qena**, **Luxor** and **Aswan**. Hurghada on the Red Sea blossomed as a travellers resort during the period Sinai was in Israeli hands. There are excellent coral reefs around the islands offshore. If you have to overnight at Qena, there is a good hotel, El Salam. It only costs E£3, communal H&C showers. Take mosquito repellent.

Returning towards Cairo, **El Balyana** is a pleasant little place if you have to stay the night. A Youth Hostel there charges you 60pt per night. Worth a look at the Temples of Abydos there; you can walk, if you don't mind sweating a bit.

Asyut, further down the Nile, has the Coptic Monastery which is worth a look. **El Minya**'s main attractions are the Hatshepsut Temple and the noble tombs of Beni Hasas.

The **Nile** trip is one of the most exciting you can undertake. There is plenty of traffic all the way down to **Luxor** and there's also the possibility of hitching rides on river transport.

The beautiful Abu Simbel Temple, which was built by Rameses II 3,000 years ago, is situated 256 km south of **Aswan** which is 240 km south of Luxor. The 400,000-ton temple has been cut into sections and relocated 200 feet up a mountainside to save it from being submerged in the Nile as a result of dam works. The area can only be reached by plane or boat. The return boat trip takes four days. Take your own food.

● **Visa requirements** You must buy a visa before you enter Egypt. Full details from Egyptian embassies or consulates.

Cairo: where to sleep

Most of the cheap hotels are situated near Talaat Harb, between there and the Opera Square. If you have earplugs, you might need them! It's quite noisy. Here are a few cheapos:

Pensione Suisse, 26 Sh. Bassiouni (tel: 746639). Singles E£10 and doubles E£15 per night, breakfast included.

Tulip Hotel, 3 Midan Talaat Harb (tel: 758433). Variety of rooms costing between E£12 and E£25.

Golden Hotel, 13 Sh. Talaat Harb (tel: 742659). Singles E£5, doubles E£10 per night. A bit of a flop house.

Hotel Beau-Site, 27 Talaat Harb (tel: 747877). Singles E£10 and doubles E£12 per night. They sell beer.

Grand Hotel, 17 26th July Street (tel: 757700). Somewhat more upmarket, but great value for outlay of E£20–40 for single with shower, doubles E£40–50 per night with air-conditioning and TV.

Pensione Roma, 169 Sh. Mohammed Farid (tel: 3911088). Entrance is at the side of a department store called Gatttegno. Immaculate, and recommended, therefore book in advance. Singles E£14, doubles E£28 per night.

Hotel Select, 19 Sh. Adly (tel: 3933707). Singles and doubles for E£5–8. Mattress on floor for E£2.

Cairo: where to eat

In central Cairo, there are many thousands of *fuul* and *felafal* cafés and teahouses, where you can buy a meatless meal for less than E£1.

In the evenings, try the **Khan el Khalily** bazaar, and sample the wonderful old teahouses.

Felfela's, 15 Sh. Hada Sharawi (tel: 3922751). Good evening meal for E£4–5. Not far away they also have a sandwich bar; filled rolls cost 60 pt.

Café Riche, 17 Sh. Talaat Harb, is popular for a cheap meal, a beer and a good bit of people-watching.

Hotels Hilton, **Sheraton** and **Meridien** used to sell breakfasts on an all-you-can-eat basis from around E£4. Worth checking out – and bring your doggie bags.

Fatatri el Tahriri, 166 Sh. Tahrir. Excellent place for *fiteer* – E£3 for medium ones, E£4 for large.

Cairo: what to see and do

THE PYRAMIDS OF GIZA & THE SPHINX Entry about E£10 unless you possess an antiquity pass.

MEMPHIS & THE PYRAMIDS OF SAQQARA 20 km south of Cairo. Get a bus from Tahrir Sq. to Giza Sq. Costs about E£4.

EGYPTIAN MUSEUM Contains one of the best collections of ancient Egyptian artifacts, including the famous mummies and the sarcophagus of Tutankhamen.

ISLAMIC MUSEUM has excellent displays of artifacts going back to when Cairo was the cultural capital of the Islamic world.

KHAN EL KHALILY This bazaar is well worth a day's wandering.

CAMEL MARKET takes place every Friday morning. Get a no. 99 bus from Tahrir Sq. to Suq al Gimaal.

CAIRO WATER BUS Try a ride on them. They are dirt cheap. CAIRO TOWER is recommended for a great view over the city. Entrance fee is E£3. Don't go when it's raining.

MOHANDISEEN is a suburb built originally to house Egypt's technocrats. You would think you were in America in this boulevard bursting with discos, boutiques, fast-food outlets. Get a 99 bus from the Arab League Bldg south of Opera Square.

EGYPT FREE STORE Diplomatic Section. Situated beyond *Atlas Zamalek Hotel* on Arab League Street in *Mohandiseen*. Show your passport and enquire about the regulation which permits foreigners to purchase up to 4 litres of imported alcohol at duty-free prices within one month of arrival in Egypt.

Transport in Cairo

You can get around Cairo pretty well by the Metro which is both pristine and efficient. A *No Litter* and *No Smoking* ban exists in all parts of the facility.

Alexandria: where to sleep

Hotel rooms are very hard to come by during the high season (June–Sept.), so if you intend staying in Alexandria book in advance. Here are some budget places:

Hyde Park Hotel, 8th Floor, 21 Sh. Amin Fikry (tel: 35666/7). Comfortable and single rooms at E£10 per night, doubles E£15 without breakfast.

Hotel Acropole, 4th Floor, 1 Sh. Gamal al Din Yassin, Alexandria (tel: 805980). Singles E£6 and doubles E£10 per night.

Hotel Ailemma, 7th floor, 21 Sh. Amin Fikry. E£11–13 for single with breakfast, E£17–20 for double with breakfast.

Hostel:

Alexandria Youth Hostel, 32 Port Said Street (tel: 5975459). About 2 km south-east of the city centre. E£4.50 per night. Meals available. Pity they do not have lockers – there is no place to secure your pack.

Alexandria: where to eat

Fuul Mohammed Ahmed, 317 Sh. Shakar. You'll get a good meal for around E£2.

Restaurant Denis, 1 Sh. Ibn Bassam (tel: 483 0457). Serves fresh seafood by weight – fish for around E£8–15, salad E£1.

Alexandria: what to see and do

CATACOMBS OF KOM EL SHOGAFA located in the south-west part of the city. They date from the 2nd century AD.

Port Said: where to sleep

Holiday Hotel, Sh. Gomhoria (tel: 220 711). E£25 per night with air-conditioning, bathroom and breakfast.

New Regent Hotel, 27 Sh. Gomhoria (tel: 223 802). E£14 per night includes air-conditioning and bath.

Hotel Abu Simbel, 15 Sh. Al Gumhuriyyah. Singles E£17 per night, doubles E£26 per night includes fan, fridge TV and shower.

Hotel de la Poste, Sh. El Gumhuriyyah (tel: 229 994). E£13 singles, E£20 doubles. Good bar and restaurant.

Ismailiya: where to sleep

Ramses Hotel, just off Midan Orabi. Value for money at E£15 per night, which includes air-conditioning, TV and a phone.

Hotel Isis, Midan Orabi (tel: 227 821). Singles E£10 per night including shower. Doubles E£17 per night.

Hostel:

Sea Scout Building, Lake Timsah (tel: 322 850). E£2 per night. It has limited capacity so book in advance.

Ismailiya: what to see and do

On the shores of LAKE TIMSAH there are several excellent beaches. They are owned by resort clubs who charge admission – in some cases the cost of a buffet, E£5–10. Well worth it if the mercury starts to melt.

Hurghada: where to sleep

Happy House, Midan El Dhar Mosque (tel: 44 0540). E£4–5 per night. Clean place. Cooking facilities are available.

Luxor Palace (tel: 44 1458). E£3 breakfast included.

Hurghada: where to eat

Happy House Restaurant, Mosque Square. Great meals for E£1.50.

Red Sea Restaurant. Meals here cost E£8 but are excellent.

Hurghada: what to see and do

The owner of **Happy House** runs trips to coral reefs, as do a number of other operators. Trips last from 8 a.m.–6 p.m. and cost about E£8–10, which includes a fish supper and the use of masks and snorkels.

Luxor: where to sleep

New Karnak Hotel, Sh. Abdel el Maneim el Adasi (tel: 38 2427). Near the railway station. E£3 for a single. E£6–8 for a double, breakfast included. Has a good restaurant.

Horus Hotel (tel: 38 2165). E£25–35 for a double. Cheapest beers in town E£1.60. Also has a built-in alarm call: the *muezzin* commences at 3.50 a.m.

Grand Hotel (tel: 38 4186). E£5–10 per night. Hot showers and a washing machine are available for guests.

New Home Pension (tel: 38 3059). Singles/doubles cost E£10–20. It has a washing machine, kitchen, fridge and stove, but not a particularly good reputation for female travellers.

Hostel:

Luxor Hostel (tel: 382139). E£3 per night. Meals are available.

Luxor: where to eat

New Karnak Hotel. 80pt gets you omelette, bread and fruit juice.

Mensa. As you come out of the station, this is on the right. Rice, tomato sauce and spinach for 50pt.

Limpy, opposite the station. You can get kebabs or fish for around E£4–5.

Luxor: what to see and do

If you are into ruins, then this is the place for you. In and around Luxor there are a number of archaeological sites dating back to 1500 BC, many of them still in first-class condition even down to the paint on their walls.

Don't miss the Valley of the Kings and the Valley of the Queens, the Karnak Temples, the Temple of Luxor, the Tombs of the Nobles, and the Funerary Temples of the Kings.

At night you can listen to great Egyptian folk music played live at the **Nile Casino Bar**; the drinks are, however, a little more expensive than other places.

The **Tourist & State Information office** is the only place to obtain a comprehensive booklet covering the many things to see in Luxor. It is on the El Bahr El Nil road on the way to Aswan.

Aswan: where to sleep

Hotel Continental, Corniche el Nil (tel: 32 2311). E£1.75 for a bed in a dorm. Good place for contacts.

Hotel Marwa, Abtaal El Tahrir Street. This is a clean place, and E£10 will get you a double room with a fan and a shower.

Aswan: where to eat

El Shati Terrace, opposite the Continental Hotel, gives good breakfasts and set menus for E£2–4.50.

Try also a small café immediately opposite the youth hostel in Abtaal el Tahrir Street, for a great meal which costs only 85pt.

Aswan: what to see and do

THE ASWAN DAM is the sight everyone wants to see. It is the largest modern structure in Egypt and that's about all you can say – you look at it, take a photograph and, bingo, it's all over. However, if you have a concession card, either student or IYHA, you can get to Saad el Ali for 15pt and then take a shared taxi across the dam for 60pt per person, plus a E£1 fee to cross the dam wall.

PHILAE TEMPLE on Philae Island. Worth visiting.

ELEPHANTINE ISLAND Museum is good value for a 50pt entrance fee.

TOMB OF THE AGHA KHAN, MONASTERY OF ST SIMON and tombs of the MIDDLE KINGDOM NOBLES are all worth seeing.

MOSQUE in Aswan town is worth the E£1 which is charged for a guide to lead you on the climb up the minaret.

CULTURAL CENTRE Nile Street. Most nights you can watch Nubian dancing which costs you E£1.10 with a concession card.

ABU SIMBEL This world-famous temple is worth the visit, so budget for it. A bus leaves Aswan at 8 a.m. (returning at 5 p.m.), and a return ticket costs E£16.

El Minya: where to sleep

Palace Hotel on Sh. Gumhorria (tel: 32 4071). French colonial style; extremely clean. E£7 per night without bathroom. Breakfast is an extra E£2.

Hotel Savoy. If the above is full, try here. E£5–8 for singles/doubles.

Addresses

Tourist office at 5 Aldi Street, Cairo (tel: 391 3454)
US Embassy at North Gate 8, Kamal El-Din Salah Street, Cairo (tel: 355 7317).
British Consulate at Sh. Ahmed Raghab, Garden City, Cairo (tel: 354 0852).
Egyptian Youth Hostels Association at 1 El-Ibrahimy Street, Garden City, Cairo (tel: 3550329/3540529).
Youth Travel Bureau at the Travel Section, 7 Abdel Hamid Saiid Street, Maarouf, Cairo (tel: (2) 758099).

Hitchers' Tips and Comments . . .

I've just returned from a hitching trip in Egypt. Here are a few hints which might help fellow hitchers:

Hitching down the Nile is an unforgettable experience, but about two-thirds of all cars are registered as taxis – identifiable from the front by their yellow-and-orange licence plates. I got plenty of rides with private car owners, but many expected *baksheesh* for the service. You can feign incomprehension and walk off, or cough up the usually small sum they ask for. If you agree to pay you can decide if you're being had by remembering that the per capita income is around $500 per year. (If you get fed up with the endless demands for money, just take the train, which is unbelievably cheap.)

The most pleasant way to visit the Valley of the Kings is not on an exorbitantly overpriced coach tour, nor by renting a bike (the area is like a furnace all year round), but by hiring a donkey and a guide. To do this just go to the ferry that takes you across the Nile and look like a tourist. The donkey-men will pick you up quick enough. Bargain furiously and make sure there are no hidden extras.

Water-purification tablets are an absolute must in Egypt. Outside large towns the water usually comes straight from the Nile. Nile waters are supposed to have life-giving properties, but the stuff is lethal! [*Stick to bottled water everywhere in Egypt, even in the cities. K.W.*]

Re currency, there's a rule that you must exchange a certain amount of money every day you spend in Egypt, but it seems to be a random amount depending on whether officials like the look of your face. I found only two places where one could exchange piastres back to foreign currency: Cairo airport (but only if you have receipts to prove you changed it in the first place); or on the black market at a loss of 10%.

To enter Egypt from Israel, first check that the border is open! As a rough guide, it's supposed to be open from 8 or 9 a.m. to 6 p.m. Monday through Thursday, and 9 a.m. till noon on Fridays. But there are religious holidays and other events which can leave you kicking your heels by the border for 36 hours or more. [*These times could change from month to month. As Philip suggests, check before you get there. K.W.*] Once you do get by the barbed wire allow three hours for the processes of Israeli bureaucracy to take their sluggish course.

This is *very* important: if you go to Israel and you want to visit another Arab country (apart from Egypt) you should ask the Israelis *not* to stamp your passport with an Israeli visa!

PHILIP GODDARD, CAMBRIDGE, ENGLAND

When entering Egypt from Israel, there's a wide no-man's-land between the two borders which is crossed by a special bus, so you have to hold back some Israeli money to pay the fare or try your luck bribing the driver with cigarettes. Keep your cool at all times on the Egyptian border. They try and railroad you into changing $150 at very unfavourable rates. Say you are only staying a few days and sometimes you can get away with changing $100 or less. I saw one guy talk his way through without paying anything by insisting he was catching a boat from Alexandria the next day.

If you're taking a taxi to Cairo ignore the people who first approach you. There's a proper taxi stand where you can buy a ticket for around E£6. Ignore any further demands from the driver for money. Pick a driver who doesn't look stoned. A burst tyre or two on the way is routine.

Egyptians will go to extraordinary lengths to get hold of your cash. Remember, a few quid to us is a week's wages for them. Never flash your money. Keep most of it hidden and only have a few pounds in your wallet.

It's OK to exchange your foreign currency in big shops in Cairo – they all offer about the same rate – but be careful you don't get ripped off.

When visiting the pyramids it's worth staying for the sound and light show in the evening – but make sure you go on a day when it's in English.

If you have a student card you get 50% off train fares. Because of heavy bookings it's nearly always worth buying your ticket a few days before you wish to travel.

If you're going from Cairo to Luxor or Aswan it's a long journey and worth travelling 'second-class air-conditioned'. There's a big difference between plain second class and second-class air-conditioned. I travelled second class from Aswan to Cairo. The windows didn't shut, lights kept going out, people slept in the luggage racks, the train stopped at every station and we were pestered by beggars. (It was a 24-hour journey!) Third class is worse!

At the Valley of the Kings in Luxor, don't hire a bloody bike! I did, and apart from getting lost, having a flat tyre, sunstroke, fighting loose handlebars and suffering from exhaustion, I had a good time. You must buy your entrance tickets to the Valley when you first cross the Nile or you'll travel miles to some temple and they won't let you in because you haven't got a ticket. You also risk being sold tickets to temples or tombs closed for restoration. I reckon it's best to go by donkey with a guide. PHILIP NEWSON, LONDON, ENGLAND

When you're hot and tired in Cairo, go sit in the beautiful air-conditioned lounge of the Cairo Hilton. No one asks you to leave. At the equally luxurious Meridian Hotel you can taste the high life by spending about E£4 and then sunbathe by their pool all day in perfect peace. This tip is mostly for girls who want a little privacy from ogling Egyptian eyes.

You can save lots of money when travelling in Egypt by buying a vacuum flask and sterilizing your own water – saves spending money on drinks.

Take something to combat mosquito bites, especially if you're allergic to them. Boy, did I suffer!

CAROL LYONS, NORTHERN IRELAND

Mosquito bites can cause you hell. Check at chemists or with doctors as to good insect repellents. Mosquitoes tend to bite at night when you're still and defenceless, so, if you're travelling in North Africa or in the Middle East it's worth taking a mosquito net. It doesn't weigh much. K.W.

Best place to look for cheap rooms in Cairo is the Tahrir Square/Talaat Harb Street area. I found US dollars the best currency for changing on the black market. ALAN THATCHER, NEW ZEALAND

Girls hitching in Egypt should be prepared. Egyptians think Western women are easy and that even married girls will bed-hop. They offer dinner, music, wine and hash and they expect favours in return!

ESTER, AUSTRALIA

Don't bother hitching – the trains are dead cheap. I travelled third class which, although a bit uncomfortable, was great fun. The Egyptians are really friendly and hospitable, especially if you try learning some Arabic. You have to buy your ticket within half an hour before the train leaves.

Abu-Simbel: a boat (barge) leaves Aswan High Dam every Saturday morning bound for Abu-Simbel. It's mainly for Egyptians taking supplies to the Nubian village of Simbel (hence a bit rough), but there were plenty of young tourists. It takes around four days – remember to take food and especially water. The temples are really worth the visit. MILTON STUBBS, NORTH BAILEY, DURHAM, ENGLAND

For International Student Cards try the Medical Faculty at the University of Cairo. You will need two passport-size photographs and £6. No proof that you are a student seems required. With these cards there are reductions on just about everything.

ROD SINCLAIR, SCOTLAND

To get from Jordan to Egypt, take a ferry from Aqaba to Nuweiba. The ferry costs $28 and you can pay with dinars; in the opposite direction you must pay in dollars.

In Egypt you don't have to change any money on the border any more. The currency market is free now, so especially in Cairo look for good rates before you change your money. National Bank of Development was my favourite one. SAMULI SCHIELKE, FINLAND

Don't miss Dahab on the Red Sea. It's dirt cheap, has the best snorkelling and diving on this side of the planet, and there are lots of other travellers there to swop info. with.

JILL & TONY, LAKE DISTRICT, ENGLAND

11 · TURKEY AND THE MIDDLE EAST

Turkey

population	60,000,000
size	301,381 square miles
capital	Ankara, population 3,500,000
government	Republic
religion	Moslem
language	Turkish; some English, French and German understood in large cities
currency	*Turkish lira* Coins of 50, 100, 500 *lira*. Notes of 1,000, 5,000, 10,000, 20,000, 50,000 and 100,000 *lira*

When you cross the Bosphorus at Istanbul which, incidentally has a population of 7,400,000 or the Dardanelles at Eceabat on the Gelibolu (Gallipoli) Peninsula, you've reached Asia: another continent, another world. You'll curse because there is so much to see and so little time in which to see it.

After Istanbul, the main city on Turkey's European side is **Edirne**. Amongst other sights check out the Selimiye Mosque, designed by master architect Sinan when he was in his eighties and built in the late 16th century, and the 15th-century Eski Mosque, the oldest building in the city. (Non-Moslems can enter any Turkish mosque, except during prayer time. Dress properly: no shorts or bare arms. Leave shoes at the mosque door. Lady hitchers should wear a scarf over their heads.) If you're lucky enough to be in Edirne in June try and catch a wrestling match. To make an already tough sport tougher, competitors are covered with oil.

If you cross to Asia by ferry at **Eceabat** you may decide to spend an extra day in the area to visit the Gallipoli battlefields. They have been declared an historical national park in memory of the tens of thousands of Turkish, French, British and Dominion soldiers who lost their lives in the savage First World War battle. Australians and New Zealanders particularly may want to visit Anzac Cove (Anzac Koyu), where the ANZACs made their landing.

First important visit on the Asian side is to **Troy** (Truva), a few kilometres south of the ferry port of **Canakkale**. Troy was discovered in the 19th century by Heinrich Schliemann who used the

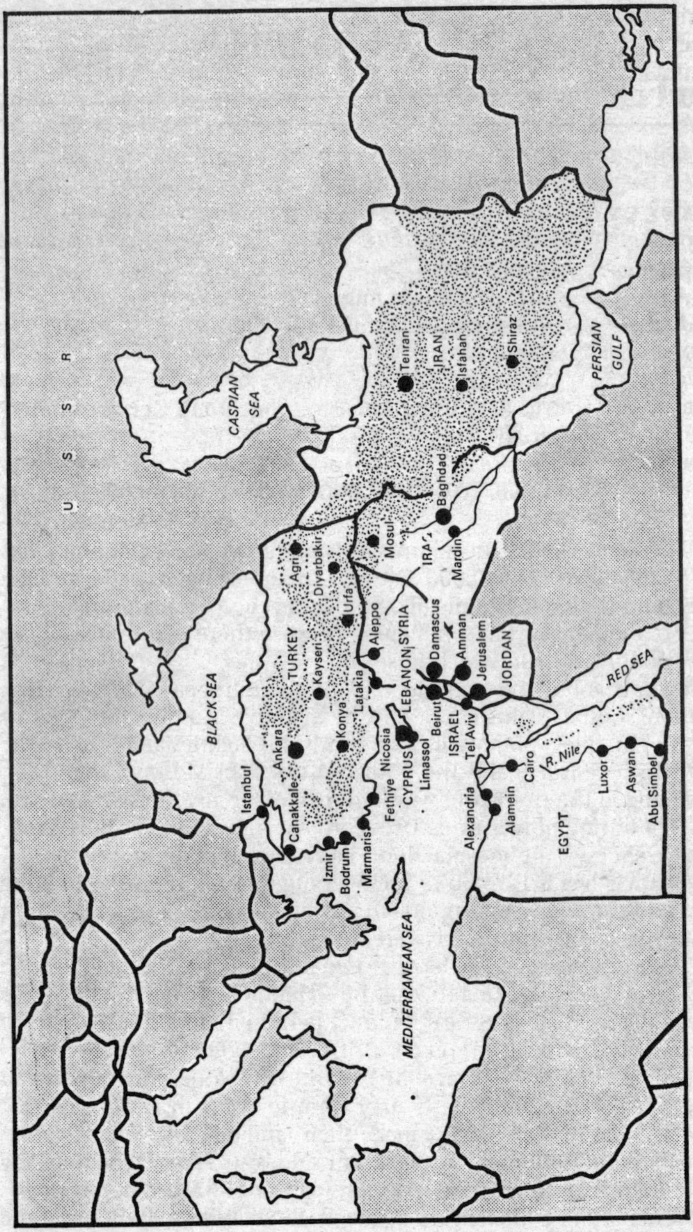
U S S R
CASPIAN SEA
BLACK SEA
MEDITERRANEAN SEA
PERSIAN GULF
RED SEA
TURKEY
IRAN
IRAQ
SYRIA
LEBANON
JORDAN
ISRAEL
CYPRUS
EGYPT
R. Nile
Tehran
Isfahan
Shiraz
Baghdad
Mosul
Mardin
Agri
Diyarbakir
Urfa
Aleppo
Damascus
Amman
Jerusalem
Kayseri
Latakia
Konya
Beirut
Tel Aviv
Ankara
Nicosia
Limassol
Istanbul
Canakkale
Izmir
Bodrum
Marmaris
Fethiye
Alexandria
Alamein
Cairo
Luxor
Aswan
Abu Simbel

writings of Homer to locate it. Before Schliemann the city and the events of Homer's *Iliad* and *Odyssey* were considered fiction. Excavations have now revealed nine successive settlements on the site, the oldest dating back 5,000 years, the most recent lasted from 350 BC to AD 400. Homer's Troy was on the seventh level. The visit is fascinating (and the site is particularly beautiful in spring) but there are no great buildings to be seen here and you'll be surprised at how small the city was. Troy is a specialist visit for hitchers with a particular interest in archaeology and those who are incurable dreamers.

A site with more to offer the non-specialist wanderer is the ruins of **Pergamum** at **Bergama**. See the Asclepion, one of the ancient world's most important medical centres (take a drink from the cold, sweet water of the Sacred Fountain), wander along the Sacred Way, make your way back to town and find a ride up the steep hill (and I mean steep – leave your pack in Bergama if possible, because if you have to walk, it's 5 km to the Akropolis. See the theatre, the Altar of Zeus, the Temple of Trajan, and, though there's not much left of it, the library, one of the most important in antiquity. Once it held 200,000 manuscripts, which Antony presented to Cleopatra after the Alexandria library was burned. It was at Pergamum that books were first bound into page form.

Izmir, Turkey's third city (population 2,700,000) is beautifully situated on the Aegean Sea, but personally I don't count it as an essential visit in Turkey unless you have plenty of time. If you find yourself there make your way up to Kadifekale Castle for an overall view, wander down to the Roman Agora, check out the Archaeological Museum south of Konak Square, cross the bridge over the highway from the square and into the bazaar. In Konak Square itself you can always find someone to talk to.

About 70 km south of Izmir is **Ephesus**. If you only have time to visit one ancient city in Turkey, try this one. The ruins stand just a few kilometres outside **Selcuk**. On the way you can see the pitiful remains of the Temple of Artemis, once four times bigger than the Parthenon in Athens and counted amongst the Seven Wonders of the World. Looming behind it is Selcuk Castle. Ephesus dates from 2000 BC. Greeks, Romans and Turks have all left memories of their stay, though what you see now is mostly Roman. Climb to the top of the Great Theatre which seated 25,000 people for a bird's eye view down Marble Street to your left and Harbour Street directly in front of you (Ephesus was on the sea until the harbour silted up). Walk up Marble Street by bas-reliefs celebrating famed gladiators and take in the exquisite façade of the superbly restored Celsus Library. Directly opposite the library is a building reputed to have been the brothel. (Tag on to a tour to hear the endless jokes about a tunnel connecting the library to the brothel.) Behind the brothel, check out the (very) communal latrines. Wander up Curetes Street for an endless feast of ruined temples and fountains. If you have a camera try a shot back down Curetes Street to the library.

Selcuk and Ephesus have several sites important to the history of early Christianity. Close by Ephesus's Magnesia Gate is a tomb where Luke is said to have been buried. In Selcuk, the Basilica of St John commemorates the apostle who wrote his gospel in Ephesus before dying there and who is believed to have accompanied the Virgin Mary to Ephesus after the death of Christ. You can see the Virgin's house (Meryemana), where she is said to have died, 7 km from Selcuk on Mount Aladag.

After the heavy dose of culture, you might need a rest. Try hitching down to **Bodrum** further down the Aegean coast. Plenty of tourists in this area, but it's a pleasant enough place. Climb the towers of the museum-castle of St Peter for great views. Bodrum was the site of King Mausolus's Mausoleum, yet another of the ancient Seven Wonders of the World before it was destroyed in an earthquake.

Yet a third Wonder of the World, the Colossus, stood on the Greek island of Rhodes, just a couple of hours by sea from **Marmaris**, on the Mediterranean coast. You'll find good beaches around Marmaris and a nice atmosphere in town. There are even better beaches around **Fethiye**, particularly the one at **Olu Deniz**, 25 km away. (Don't try sleeping out on the Olu Deniz promontory because it is a park. For sleeping out take the coast road to your right as you face the promontory.) In Fethiye climb up to the 2,500-year-old rock tombs behind town.

All along the Mediterranean coast lie dozens of pleasant towns, villages and ruins worth a visit. **Antalya**, though it has a population around 1,100,000 and is a tourist area, is particularly beautiful. Mosques, museums, fascinating back streets and a harbour make it a good place to rest up for a while.

Turkey's largest port on the Mediterranean is **Mersin**, But unless you're planning to sail to Northern (Turkish) Cyprus – and it is quite cheap – don't bother visiting the town. Should you go there, make a point of calling at the Tourist Office (tel: (741) 163 58); they can give you all the guff you require for the boat trip. Then, for a couple of quid, you can always kip down at the Hotel Kent, 51 Istikal Caddesi (tel: 1165), very clean, but spartan accommodation – still, at that price you can't grumble.

Inland north-west and a solid day's hitch away lies **Pamukkale** (the Cotton Castle), one of Turkey's most unusual natural wonders.

Warm thermal springs, their waters laden with calcium, have tumbled over a rocky mountainside for thousands of years leaving white calcium bicarbonate deposits in their wake and carving basins which are now amongst the country's most famous tourist attractions. Stash your pack and join hundreds of bathers for a unique dip. As a bonus, directly behind the glistening white mountainside lies ancient **Hierapolis**, a sprawling expanse of ruins which are a delight to wander through. Particularly fascinating is the kilometre-long necropolis with over 1,000 tombs. If you take a bed at Pamukkale, don't accept the first price offered. Polite and judicious conversation may reduce the price by 10–15%.

A full day's hitch east (maybe two) brings you to **Konya**, Turkey's oldest city. Top sight is the Mevlana Museum and Tomb. Mevlana means 'our master', and was the name given to the 13th-century mystic Celaleddin Rumi who created a philosophy of love and tolerance and with his friend Schemsi Tebrizli founded the order of the Whirling Dervishes. The brotherhood of the dervishes was dissolved by government order in the 1920s, but if you are lucky enough to be in Konya in December (the month of Mevlana's death in 1271) you can see special demonstrations of the strange, hypnotic dance which carries the dervishes into a trance. Other sights in Konya include important mosques, the archaeological museum and the 13th-century Agzikarahan Caravanserai (one of the stopping-places for the caravans travelling the ancient Silk Route).

Another couple of hundred kilometres east brings you to the region of **Cappadocia** in Central Anatolia which, Istanbul aside, is my favourite place in Turkey. This is the weirdest landscape I have ever seen. Prehistoric volcanic activity covered the area in ash which, mixed with mud, formed a soft rock called tuff. Hundreds of thousands of years of erosion have carved the tuff into cracked valleys and free-standing conical formations. But the real fascination of Cappadocia is the way man has adapted himself to this un-worldly landscape by digging into it rather than building on top of it.

Perhaps the most sensible place for a hitcher to make a base is in the troglodyte town of **Goreme**. From here you can easily reach many of the main sights of Cappadocia. The nearby Goreme Open-air Museum is a wonderland of churches (mostly 11th-century) which were carved into the soft rock and decorated with frescoes. A few kilometres along from Goreme on the road to **Avanos** (an important pottery town), at **Cavusin**, is the 8th-century rock church of St John the Baptist, the oldest in the region. A few kilometres more towards Avanos a road branches to the right. Halfway along is **Pasabag**, an area with fine examples of 30- and 40-foot 'fairy chimneys', fancifully shaped rocks carved by the wind, many wearing 'hats' so that they look like huge mushrooms. Hermits and stylites (ascetics who forsook the world to live on top of pillars) haunted this area in medieval times. Just 1 km further on is the open-air museum of **Zelve**, a deserted village chipped into the sides of hills and covering many acres. This is a 3-star visit when it comes to weird. Particularly check out the huge monastery in the first valley (there are three valleys, each signposted). The monastery can only be described as a beehive which has been carved into the mountain. Zelve was lived in until 1950 when erosion and dangerous rockfalls put the villagers in danger and the government moved them further down the valley to another town.

Time permitting try and make it to the underground cities of **Kaymakli**, 20 km south of **Nevsehir**, and, 10 km further on, **Derinkuyu**. The cities, built between the 6th and 10th centuries, were used as hide-outs during invasions. Kaymakli has eight underground levels, about 30 km of passages and probably housed around 15,000 people. Derinkuyu descends to a depth of 55 metres. It could have housed 10,000 people. A tunnel once joined the two cities.

North-west of Cappadocia is Turkey's capital, **Ankara**, a city of some 3,500,000 people. Compared with the rest of the country Ankara has only a few highlights to offer the wanderer. If you do visit, see the Anit Kabir, the mausoleum of Mustafa Kemal, known as Atatürk (Father of the Turks), who was the Republic's first president and the man who forced Turkey to turn her face to the West. Amongst other achievements he latinized the Turkish alphabet, secularized the government and introduced emancipation for women. See also the Museum of Anatolian Civilizations and the superb and recently completed Kocatepe Mosque.

Heading into the east the roads get emptier, but the sense of excitement builds. North-east takes you to the border with Russia. Due east to Iran, south-east to the borders of Syria and Iraq.

● **Warning!** Take great care in Turkey's far south-east! More than 2,500 people have been killed since the Marxist Workers' Party launched a campaign for secession in 1984. The government has responded with a get-tough policy. The area bristles with guns. Areas bordering Middle Eastern countries – particularly Iraq – have been dangerously sensitive since the 1991 Gulf War and there have been several kidnappings of Westerners in recent years.

Of the many fascinating spots to visit in the east, 2,159 m **Nemrut Dagi**, north-east of **Adiyaman**, tops the bill. Fifty metres from the summit is the hill tomb of the 1st-century-BC King, Antiochus I. In his attempt to be remembered for ever (so far he's succeeded)

Antiochus reshaped the top of Nemrut Dagi and built three terraces. One faces north. The other two face east and west, to catch the rays of the rising and setting sun, and are populated with 10-metre-high limestone statues of gods seated on huge thrones. These days their heads lie on the ground. Nemrut Dagi is a summer visit. Best to try it only from May to October. If you decide to sleep on the mountain to catch the scene at sunrise you will need a high quality sleeping bag – it can get bloody cold up there at night, even in summer. Access is by a road from **Karadut** which takes you to within about a kilometre of the statues. (Hitching it is not easy. If you have bad luck you may decide to take a tour from **Kahta**. If you do, keep away from professional tour operators, make a group of similar thinking travellers and use your imagination. For example, take a hire car for the day; ask at the tea house for anyone willing to take on the job of driving you all up; check if any *dolmus* is making the run.)

Hitching

Hitching in Turkey is a common way for locals to get around. Because most Turks are gentle and generous souls you normally don't have to wait too long. (I've heard reports of Turkish truckies expecting payment from hitchers. If it happens, haggle like hell.) The only real problem is that the further east you go the fewer cars there are and a lot of rides you do get will only be between villages. But, so what? Turkey is a great country to travel through slowly. And if speed is essential, public transport is so cheap that the occasional long-distance bus ride won't break the average hitcher's budget.

● **Camel wrestling** For one of the oddest sights you're likely to see anywhere, try to find yourself a real, live, genuine camel-wrestling match (in Turkish, *deve guresi*). Best places are the Aegean villages in January. The animals are separated before they do themselves any harm.

● **Languague** Oh boy! Turkish belongs to the Ural-Altaic language group and, lucky us, has an affinity with Finnish and Hungarian. But you gotta have a go, right? So try these few words:

Hello – *Merhaba*	Goodbye – *Hosca Kalin*
Please – *Luften*	Thank you – *Tesekkur ederim*
Yes – *Evet*	No – *Hayir*

Do you speak English? – *Ingilizce biliyor musunuz?*

● **For lady hitchers only** European or American clothing

standards don't work in Moslem countries. You'll feel much more comfortable in Turkey – particularly in outback areas – and be more readily accepted, if you follow the dress style of modern girls in those areas. Basically, cover as much skin as possible without suffocating yourself. Jeans and a blouse would be acceptable in most places. Shorts and T-shirt with no bra underneath would not be. No topless sunbathing except in areas heavily populated by tourists.

● **Money** With rampant inflation and the lira's tendency to fall in value against hard currencies it doesn't make sense to change lots of money at once. Change money as you need it and you won't lose out. The lira is actually so unstable that some shops and hotels quote their prices in US dollars. American dollars and German marks are particularly good currencies to carry in Turkey. **Remember**: keep your currency exchange slips or you won't be able to change excess lira back to hard currency before leaving the country.

● **Maps** Turkish tourist offices give away superb maps complete with descriptive information about Ankara, Istanbul and Izmir. Their country road map is good enough to hitch on and includes distances between main cities and towns.

● **Warning!** Turks, like most Moslems, are (with the obvious few exceptions) honest people. So are most of your fellow hitchers. But some are not. Watch your stuff in hostels and hotels. Some people keep themselves on the road by stealing from anyone stupid enough to leave valuables unguarded. **Another warning!** Keep away from drugs, keep away from unofficial money changers. In Turkey, either enterprise can land you in deep shit.

Bodrum: where to sleep

During the months of July and August late arrivals can expect to find it difficult to find a bed. There are some private homes who offer rooms. Look for the sign *'Oda Var'* or *'Ev Pansiyon'*.

Here are some good cheap places:

Yenilmez Pansiyon, off Neyzen Tevfik Caddesi (tel: 2520).
Bahçelu Ağar (tel: 6141/1648). Situated behind the Marina.
Belmi, Yangi Sokaği 6 (tel: 6141/1132).
Menekşe, (tel: 6141/3416).

The latter two are both just off Neyzen Tevfik Caddesi.

Bodrum: where to eat

The place is famous for its seafood restaurants; but look out – they are not cheap!

Orhan's, in an alley off Kale Caddesi, which is the main shopping area away from the tourist office.
Uslu Büfe, Neyzen Tevfik Caddesi.
Cakir Ali, Cevat Sakir Caddesi.

Bodrum: what to see and do

Although Bodrum has no real beach, it has real good value in boat trips, especially to Kos. Contact **Motif**, Neyzen Tevfik Caddesi 72 (tel: 6141/2309) and check out the cost of a cheap day return.

About 3 km west of the town you will find GÜMBET, a resort of sorts. TURGUTREIS is another resort with plenty of pansiyons; north of there is a very pleasant little resort called KADIKALESI which has a large expensive hotel, a few pansiyons, and a brace of eateries; it might be worthwhile visiting to get away from the hustle of Bodrum.

Marmaris: where to sleep

Pensions:
Dilek, Haci Mustafa Sokak 108 (tel: 612 13591). Right behind the marina.
Isiksal, Haci Mustafa Sokak 89 (tel: 612 11391).
Can Pansiyon, 53 Sokak 17 (tel: 612 11233).
Kordon Pansiyon, Kemalpasa Sok 8 (tel: 612 14762). From the post office go inland and to the left. Good atmosphere and cheap.

Hostels:
Interyouth Hostel, Kemeralti Mah, Iyilktas Mevkii (tel: 612 16432). A very clean and cheap sleeping place. Meals are available. Singles £3.

Marmaris: where to eat

If you stay at the hostel try their meals, which are cheap. Otherwise try:

Han Kifte Salonu, close to the post office.
Can Restaurant (see Can Pansiyon above) or, on the opposite side of the road: **Istanbul Pide Salonu**.

Antalya: where to sleep

Over the past ten years, many townhouses in the old town (Kaleici), the area roughly bounded by Cumhuriyet Caddesi and Atatürk Bulvari, have been converted into guesthouses. Hidirlik and Hesapci Sok are particularly well supplied with guesthouses. There is a cluster of cheap hotels around the bus station, but this area is much noisier than the old town. Here are a few good places where £3–4 should get you a single, £6–8 a double:

Adler Pansiyon, Barbaros Mahalle, Civelek Sok 46 (tel: 17818).
Pansiyon Falez, Hidirlik Sok 48 (tel: 170985). Breakfast included.
Tunay Pansiyon, 7 Mermerli Sok (tel: 124677). From the Clock Tower by the junction of Kazim Caddesi and Cumhuriyet Caddesi walk towards the coast, and then look for the signs leading up to the guesthouse.
Aksoy Pansiyon, Kocatepe Sok 39 (tel: 126549). Just round the corner from the Adler (above).
Sabah Pansiyon, Hesapçi Sok 60a (tel 175345). Breakfast included.
The Garden, Hesapçi Sok 44 (tel: 110816). Most rooms have a shower. Breakfast included. Just across from Kesik Minare (Truncated Minaret).

Antalya: where to eat

Options are decidedly limited when it comes to budget eateries. If you are staying in one of the B&B's you will get directions to the places where the locals eat, like **Tektat** at Sarampol 84. In the Cumhuriyet Caddesi you will find a fair number of sidewalk cafés and restaurants. Make for the covered pedestrian precinct Eski Sebzeciler Ici Sokak; there is a proliferation of good eating places here.

Addresses

Turizm Danişma Bürosu, Cumhuriyet Caddesi (tel: 111747). They offer you small plans of the city; also lists of local accommodation.

Tourist Information Antalya, Ozel Idare Ishani alti no 2 (tel: 15271).

American Express, Pamfilya Travel Agency, 30 Agustos Caddesi 57B&C (tel: 121401).

Goreme: where to sleep

Goreme is but one of three towns worth visiting in the Cappadocia region. The others are Nevsehir and Urgup. Many travellers choose to make Goreme their base because it has some very interesting accommodation. Prices are more or less standardized at £3 per person for rooms without baths. Try one of the following:

Pansiyon Ufuk Pansiyon and **Halil Pansiyon**. Some of the rooms are built into the rock and, as a result, stay cool. They also offer good food.

Eski Goreme Pansiyon, Goreme Village.

Tan Pansiyon, Goreme Village.

Peri Pansiyon (tel: (4857) 1136). The rooms are carved out of rock.

Rock Valley Pansiyon, Goreme Village. Good restaurant.

Ankara: where to sleep

The largest concentration of cheap hotels is located in the streets off Atatürk Bulvari between the Opera and Ulus Meydani. Hotels in this area have the advantage of being centrally located and close to both the bus and train stations. Cheap hotels proliferate along this stretch of Atatürk Bulvari. Less conveniently located, but nevertheless still within walking distance, are Gazi Mustafa Kemal Bulvari and the Maltepe district where cheap sleeperies and eateries abound. Here are some places with singles in the £3–5 price range:

Otel Savas, 3 Altan Sok (tel: 3242113).

Beyrut Palas Oteli, 11 Denizciler Caddesi (tel: 3108407).

Terminal Oteli, right beside the bus station (tel: 3104949).

Pinar, Hisar Caddesi (tel: 3118951). £4.60 for doubles with shower. Ulus district.

Babil, Gazi Mustafa Kemal Bulvari 66 (tel: 2317877).

Buhara, Sanayi Caddesi 13 (tel: 3245245/3245246). Good value for money. Ulus district.

Sipali, Itfaiye Meydani, Kosova Sok 1 (tel: 3240235/3240236).

Simple clean rooms. Recommended. Across from the Opera, take the road leading off Atatürk Bulvari to the junction of Derman Sok and Kosova Sok.

Hisar, Hisarparki Caddesi 6 (tel: 3101988/3108128). Particularly good. Ulus district.

Zümrüt Palas, Posta Caddesi 16 (tel: 3103210/3103211). One of the best hotels listed here.

Coruh, Denizciler Caddesi 47 (tel: 3124113/3124114).

Avrupa, Posta Caddesi Susam Sok 9 (tel: 3114300). Ulus district.

Cumhuriyet Ogrenci Yurdu Cebeci, Siyasal Bilgiler Fakultesi Arkasi (tel: 3193634). This student residence is converted into a youth hostel from July–end Aug.

Ankara: where to eat

You would think that the part of Ulus between the Hisar and the post office would offer good eateries. It doesn't! Your best bet is to go north of Ulus Meydani and walk along the Çankiri Caddesi to compare prices.

Cumhuriyet Yildiz Lokantasi, Çankiri Caddesi. Here you will be invited into the kitchen to choose your own meals.

Rema Lokantasi, Posta Cad/Sanayi Caddesi, Ulus. This is a very basic cafe, but it is the cheapest in the area.

Korfez Lokantasi, Bayindir Sok 24. Few people will argue that this is the best eatery in town. The prices are moderate; the servings are huge.

Kebabistan, Karanfil Sok/Yüksel Caddesi Kizilay. This is a quality restaurant which has got 'Heinz' variety in kebabs. Try the mushroom *şiş*.

Uğrak Piknik, Çankiri Caddesi, Ulus. a cafeteria with meals costing from £1.75.

Turkish wine from the Anatolian Plain is worth trying. Make sure to sample the *Kavakidere, Doluca* and *Kavalleros* brands. The word for wine is *sarap*.

Addresses

British Embassy, Sehit Ersan Caddesi 46A, Cankaya (tel: 1274310).

British Council, Kirlangic Sokak 9, Gazi Osman Pasa (tel: 1283165). They keep a list of reliable doctors.
US Embassy, 110 Atatürk Bulvari (tel: 1265470).
Tourist Information, 33 Gazi Mustafa Kemal Bulvari, Demirtepe (tel: 2301911). They dish out a pretty fair map.

Pamukkale: where to sleep

Halley Pansiyon (tel: 6218 1204).
Kervansaray (tel: 6218 1209).
Ziya (tel: 6218 1195).

Pamukkale: where to eat

Kervansaray (tel: 6218/1209).
Ünal Restaurant. Tripe soup is their speciality.

Istanbul: where to sleep

Cheapest areas are found on the European side of the city. Sultanahmet and Eminonu (behind the railway station) are good bets for centrally located and affordable beds. Don't immediately accept the first price on a room offered to you. Try and judge if the hotel or *pansiyon* (which is usually cheaper) needs your business. (If you arrive at night and there are a lot of keys hanging by the desk, business may be bad.) If you decide you are in a buyer's market, a very polite and reasonable discussion may bring the price down 10% or more. Always ask to see the room and communal toilet and bathroom before final agreement to terms. In some cheapo hotels even a hitch-hiker's minimal expectations may not be fulfilled. Expect to pay about £3.30 for a hostel bed; and £5–6 for singles, £7–9 for doubles in the hotels and pensions listed:

Hostels:
Yücelt Hostel, Caferiye Cad 6 (tel: 5136150/5136151).
True Blue Hostel, Akbiyik Cad 2.
Sultan Tourist Hotel II, Cankurtaran Akbiyik Cad 3 (tel: 5169260).
Orient Youth Hostel, Akbiyik Cad 13 (tel: 5179493).

Pensions and hotels:

Hacibey Pansiyon, Özbekler Sokak.

Optimist Pansiyon. Contact the Optimist Guesthouse (tel: 5162398) on the Hippodrome.

Hippodrome Pansiyon, Öçler Sok 9 (tel: 51609002).

Hotel Merih, Zeynep Sultan Camii Sok 25 (tel: 5228522).

Hotel Park, Utangac Sok 26 (tel: 5223964).

Hotel Anadolu, Salkim Söğüt Sok 3 (tel: 5121035).

Istanbul: where to eat

Turkey provides the cheapest eating in Europe. Many restaurants have their food laid out in full view so you can simply point to what you fancy. The ones that don't will let you into the kitchen to see what's cooking. Kebabs are filling, lamb is excellent, salads good value. Fish will leave your budget in shreds. Bottled water is cheap, beer and Coke affordable, wine expensive. Tea (*cay*) is cheap, Turkish coffee affordable, Nescafé exorbitant.

The best eating houses in the city are in the Laleli, Aksaray, Taksim and Galata areas.

Here are a few good cheapos:

Ahtapot, Köyiî Kilise Meydani 50, Beşiktaş. Good fish restaurant.

Altin Sofrasi, Suleymaniye Caddesi 33. If you are walking around this area, don't miss this place.

Aksu Oçakbaşii, Aksaray Caddesi Azìmkar Sok 5, Lâeli. Good food, reasonably priced.

Haci Abdullah, Sakizagaci Caddesi 19, Beyoğlu. Small place frequented by locals; it is cheap and good.

Han Restaurant, Kartcinar Sok 16, Karaköy. In the Galata Tower area. Particularly good at lunchtime.

Istanbul: what to see and do

THE MOSQUES There are dozens of mosques in Istanbul, but try and visit these four: SULTANAHMET MOSQUE, known as the Blue Mosque. It was built in the 17th century. The exterior is under repair. The restoration will take longer than it took to build it. Don't miss a visit to the courtyard or to the interior. AYA SOFYA, directly opposite Sultanahmet, was declared a museum in 1935 by Atatürk. Aya Sofya was built as a church by the Emperor Justinian in the 5th century on the site of an older church which had been built by Constantine the Great. When the Turks conquered Constantinople they converted the building into a mosque and added the minarets you see today. From the nave, look up (and up and up) into the cupola of the 180-feet-high dome. In the gallery, admire the mosaics and look down into the nave to grasp the huge proportions of this incredible building. SULEYMANIYE MOSQUE is one of the landmark buildings which has made Istanbul's skyline famous. It's the one you see on the hill on your right as you return across the Galata Bridge from Karakoy. Suleymaniye was built in the 1550s by Suleyman the Magnificent, the sultan who brought the Ottoman Empire to the pinnacle of its power and influence. It was designed by the architect Sinan, whose bronze statue now sits in the gardens beside the Golden Horn on the Karakoy side gazing back at his masterpiece. KARIYE MOSQUE (known as the *Chora*). The mosque was formerly a church and is now a museum housing mosaics and frescoes, some of which date from the 11th century, though most are 14th-century.

YEREBATAN SARAYI (Just off Sultanahmet Square.) Known as the Sunken Palace, Yerebatan Sarayi is one of Istanbul's ancient water cisterns. This one is 140 metres long and 70 metres wide and boasts 336 columns topped by ornate capitals. Look for the head of Medusa which was found on the base of a column during recent cleaning.

THE HIPPODROME (Just off Sultanahmet Square.) This was built in the 2nd century as a chariot-racing stadium. Originally it was about 400 metres long and 150 metres wide. You can still see the basic shape. Now it's a pleasant walking area (and a great place to meet people). The three main monuments on the Hippodrome are the Column of Constantine, probably dating from the 9th century, the Greek Serpentine Column dating from 500 BC and the Egyptian Obelisk dating from 1500 BC.

THE PALACES The two most famous are Topkapi and Dolmabahce. TOPKAPI, just a short walk from Sultanahmet, is considered one of the great buildings of the world. It was started in the 15th century and continually added to until the 19th, and was the official residence of the sultans. Particularly look at the Harem, the fabulous collection of riches in the Treasury (which includes the dagger with emerald-studded handle made famous in the film *Topkapi*) and the fascinating collection of holy Islamic relics, which includes possessions of the Prophet Muhammad, amongst them his sword, a letter written by him on gazelle skin, and, mounted beneath a magnifying glass, a hair from his beard. In the mid-1800s the sultans moved to DOLMABAHCE PALACE, which sits right on the Bosphorus about a 15-minute walk down from Taksim Square. The palace is a fine example of Turkish architecture mixed with European. It is a place of pilgrimage for Turks. The last sultans of the Ottoman Empire lived here and Atatürk died here in 1938. You'll notice that all the palace clocks read 9.05, the time of his death.

KAPALI CARSI (The Covered or Grand Bazaar) is one of the world's most famous markets. Really, it is an entire town, covering some 60 acres and with more than 4,000 shops. It's fascinating to wander through and you'll meet plenty of shop owners willing to chat, and probably a few who'll buy you tea. But asking prices in this market are high. If you see something you like, make sure you know what the asking price for a similar object is *outside* the market before you start bargaining, because bargain you must . . . Ask for the Book Market (Sahaflar Carsisi) if you need cheap reading matter.

THE ARCHAEOLOGY MUSEUM (behind Sultanahmet) is worth a visit to see the first-rate collection of sarcophagi and a bust which is reputed to be that of Alexander the Great.

BOAT TRIP ON THE BOSPHORUS Don't take advertised tours. Go to the Galata Bridge and pick your own on a regular ferry route. Plenty to choose from and affordable. Try the run towards the Black Sea taking you by Rumeli Hisari and Anadolu Hisari, the old forts on the European and Asian sides respectively.

Transport in Istanbul

It's all cheap. Cheapest are buses, which at rush hour (which is most hours in Istanbul) can also be crowded, uncomfortable and often beyond the physical endurance of even road-toughened hitchers. The *dolmus* offers a compromise. It's a communal taxi which costs about 25% more than a bus, is 50% faster and 100% more comfortable, and like a bus runs along fixed routes. They are usually big old limousines or mini-buses, and are often painted blue. *Dolmus* stops have a 'D' painted on a blue sign. Taxis are cheap by European standards but are good value only if there are three or four to share. All taxis run on meters. Taxi sharks at tourist sites quote a price instead of running the meter. The price is always double or more what the meter price would be. Just walk to the nearest road and catch a cruising cab. Cabs throughout Turkey have a red light system on their meters. One red light means you are on the normal fare rate. Two red lights means you are on night fare (which should only be turned on after midnight and until dawn) and are paying double. Always check the light! A small percentage of taxi drivers in Turkey, like a small percentage in the rest of the world, are arseholes. A 10% tip is normal.

Student discounts
I quote from a handbook on Turkey supplied by the Turkish Tourist Office:

> Some Turkish organizations, such as Turkish Airlines, recognize the ISTC card and accordingly grant reductions to holders of these cards. The price reductions offered to students are as follows:

Turkish Maritime Lines	International line 10% Domestic lines 10%
Railways	10% June–Nov, 30% Dec–May
Cinemas and Concerts	505
Coach	10% may be available from some companies

Theory and practice in Turkey are two different things, but try your luck anyway. Plus, *always* flash your Student Card when buying a ticket for entry into any tourist site or museum. You never know.

Addresses

Main post office (for poste restante) at Buyuk Postahane, Sirkeci, Istanbul.
American Express at Hilton Hotel, 91 Cumhuriyet Caddesi (near Taksim Square), Istanbul (tel: 1329558).
Tourist Office at Sultanahmet, Divanyolu Caddesi 3, Istanbul (tel: 5224903).
British Consulate at Mesrutiyet Caddesi 34, Tepebasi, Istanbul (tel: 1447540).
US Consulate at Mesrutiyet Caddesi 147, Tepebasi, Istanbul (tel: 1436200).

Hitchers' Tips and Comments . . .

When entering Turkey your driver will get a special stamp in his passport which shows he brought in a car. Make sure you don't get the same stamp! If you do, you won't be able to leave because customs officials will think you've sold an imported car in Turkey.

PETER NASH, CHELMSFORD, ENGLAND

In Istanbul, avoid snapping photos of men with bears unless you want to pay a 'fee' under threat of a bear hug.

JOHN PILKINGTON, BRISTOL, UK

Don't doss anywhere in Turkey unless you're *sure* you won't be seen by the police or the army. They're strict about dossing. Even beaches are often searched. If caught you could be arrested which means a load of hassles, Turkish jails being no joke. On the other hand, camping sites are good and cheap in Turkey. If you're in Bodrum, try *Camping Ayaz* just outside town. Cleanest camping I've ever seen. Good place to recuperate if you've got food poisoning.

TONY MILLER, NEWCASTLE-UPON-TYNE, ENGLAND

A lifesaver for me in Turkey was a simple roll of toilet paper. Turks don't seem to use it. Also take a couple of dozen anti-diarrhoea tablets. Odds are you're going to need them.

JIM STAFFORD, DUBLIN, IRELAND

I recommend fellow hitchers to consider a trip to the Black Sea Coast. It's unaffected by the evils of mass tourism. People don't seem to mind picking up hitchers, but there aren't that many cars. Buses and mini-buses are really cheap, though, and travelling on them is a great way to get to know the Turks. I've often been offered a meal and a bed. One last thing. The political situation in Turkey is more often than not unstable. Be very, very careful. Stay away from police, soldiers and drugs. I've heard sad things about people in trouble in Turkey. Take care with everything you do, even with things like talking about politics or wearing shorts outside of tourist areas!

ALFRED BLAAK, KOEKANGE, HOLLAND

The Londra Trucking Camp is the place to hitch out of Istanbul. This is where the lorries to and from Europe stop.

SIMON LINGLEY, UPPINGHAM, UK

Several people had horror stories about what happened when they had a Turkish stamp in their passport. One West German had his rucksack turned inside out at the borders of Greece, Yugoslavia, Austria, Switzerland and his own country!

ERIC THE HIPPO, LONDON, ENGLAND

We thought Turkey a great place, especially once out of Istanbul. The people are really friendly and just wouldn't stop helping us – giving us free food and drinks (and accommodation on many occasions) simply because they love to speak to foreigners.

CREB AND WEZ, BIRMINGHAM, ENGLAND

Hitching is very easy in Turkey but, if you get stuck, it's dark or the weather is bad, take the bus. They're dirt cheap, stop anywhere and go everywhere. If going south from Istanbul, get the boat to Yalova from the pier near the Galata Bridge. Don't let *Midnight Express* put you off from visiting Turkey. The Turks are the friendliest of people. I've even had the police set up a road block for me so I could get a lift and another policeman persuaded a bus driver to take me for a four-hour ride for nothing. Just keep away from drugs.

ALAN BARLOW, CHEADLE, UK

Cyprus

population	747,000
size	3572 square miles
capital	Nicosia, population 171,000
government	Republic
religion	Greek Orthodox and Moslem
language	Greek and Turkish, with English widely used
currency	*Cypriot pound* (C£) One *pound* equals 100 *cents* (previously 1,000 *mils*)

Cypriot history is a succession of foreign invasions and domination. Current problems have arisen from the Cypriot mix of Greek and Turkish blood. To simplify a complex situation, Cyprus became independent after the British left in 1960. In 1974 the military junta ruling in Greece promoted a coup in Cyprus which provoked an invasion by Turkey, and resulted in a de facto division of the island between Turkish and Greek Cypriots. In 1983 the north declared itself an independent Turkish Federated State of Cyprus but, so far, only Turkey has recognized the state. *At the time of writing you may not cross from one part of the island to the other. Best check the situation before you visit.*

By air, Cyprus is easily accessible from the Middle East and Europe. There are various shipping lines operating to Cyprus, connecting it with Piraeus (Greece) and the Middle East. In summer the service is frequent, but not in winter. For examples of fares, the Black Sea Shipping Company charges about C£60 from Piraeus for the cheapest class cabin, and the trip takes 38 hours. From Latakia in Syria it's around C£25 (cheapest class again), and takes about eight hours. Sol Lines charge about C£45 from Piraeus to Limassol in spring and autumn, and about C£55 in summer, both deck class.

● **Visa requirements** No visa is required for visitors from the British Commonwealth, USA and most of Western Europe. No jabs or malaria tablets needed. You're supposed to declare foreign currency if you have over £650, and you may be asked to show that you have enough money for the time of your stay. Officially you can only take C£50 worth of Cypriot currency in or out of the country.

Cyprus: where to sleep

Upon arrival immigration may insist that you have booked accommodation. So, if you know your arrival date, make a booking before you come for at least one night to satisfy them. If not, make a one-night booking when you arrive. Once you're over this hurdle, there are no official hassles and you can sleep where you like.

There are a few youth hostels for around C£3 per night (sheets extra). Note that Troodos hostel is open only in summer. Hotels are generally fairly expensive, but if you get the free hotel booklet from the tourist office and hunt around in it, especially in the 'Hotels without Star' and 'Guest Houses' sections, you'll find some singles for around C£6 to C£8, or half this price in Limassol. Larnaca is short on anything cheap. If you get stuck there, ask at the taxi office as they know a few crash pads, but bargain over the inflated prices.

There are three organized campsites, listed under 'Hotel Apartments' in the hotel booklet, which charge around C£1.50 per tent and C£1 per person per day.

Sleeping out is no problem, and seems to be accepted. As long as you're sensible and discreet you shouldn't have any hassles with anyone. The warm sunny weather suits the exercise (it rarely rains), except in the mountains where it can be cold.

Cyprus: where to eat

Food is a bit more expensive than in Turkey. Hunt out local haunts and avoid tourist traps, and you'll find good food at a realistic price. Cheapest dishes are usually things like moussaka, but be cautious with such meals as they are normally prepared once a week for the whole week. Try and find out how fresh the dish is and how it has been stored. Try the delicious fresh grapes in season. Local wine is cheap and plentiful.

Cyprus: where to go and what to see

Nicosia, with a population of 171,000, is the capital of the island. It is also, now, a divided city. See the excavated treasure in the Cyprus Museum. Through the middle of the town runs a line of barricades, guards and empty buildings.

Limassol is the second city of the island with a population of 135,000, and although most of the old town is gone there is just enough left to give a whiff of what it must have been like. In the castle, Richard the Lionheart married Berengaria, and it was the same castle which was the headquarters of the Knights Templar and the Knights of St John. (There is a small zoo in the public gardens.)

Larnaca, population 62,000, is said to have been founded by the grandson of Noah and has many religious associations, including the tomb of Lazarus who, according to legend, came to Cyprus after having been resurrected by Christ. About 5 km outside Larnaca there is a very important monument of the Islamic world – the shrine of Hala Sultan who was a female relative of the prophet Mohammed.

Paphos and the west coast are less travelled than other parts. There are some fine mosaics in the House of Dionyssos. North of Paphos you find beaches, including Coral Bay and Polis. Between Paphos and Limassol is the birthplace of Aphrodite, **Petra tou Romiou**.

Inland are the mountains which offer, along with cooler temperatures, walking in summer and skiing in winter. There are numerous monasteries around the island. When the going gets hot, as it does in summer, check out the swimming beaches along the coast. The following beaches are worth a look-see when the mercury soars: **Cape Greco**, **Agia Napa**, and **Paralimni Protaras**, which all lie about 25 miles east of Larnaca – a very easy hitch.

Turkish Cyprus Turkish Cyprus is accessible only from Turkey, or by direct flight from London. There are ferries all year round between Famagusta and Mersin, and in the high season there are additional ferries from both Mersin and Tasucu to Kyrenia. The Mersin–Famagusta ferry costs about C£80 one way, including the steep port taxes. (Student discount available.)

According to the Cyprus government, it is illegal to enter Cyprus through any of the Turkish-controlled ports of entry though, of course, they have no means of stopping you. But, having entered Turkish Cyprus, you cannot cross to the rest of Cyprus.

Famagusta has a population of 38,000 and until 1974 it was the island's main port. Visit the old city and see the huge citadel identified with Othello's tower in Shakespeare's play.

Kyrenia is a small and very attractive seaside town with a beautiful old harbour fringed with cafés. It also boasts three castles. **St Hilarion**, which stands high above the city, is spectacular and worth climbing up to see.

A really worthwhile expedition is to the ruined Gothic abbey of **Bellapais**, 5 km from Kyrenia and open, in summer, from 7 a.m.–6 p.m., in winter, from 8 a.m.–5 p.m.

Nicosia (Turkish sector) In the fine old section visit the former Cathedral of Santa Sophia, now the Selimiye Mosque.

Hitching

Hitch-hiking is easy here. Beware of being picked up by mini-buses then charged for the ride. If you are relying on the tourist office map, be warned that it hasn't been updated for some years during which time the road network has changed partly because the cease-fire line cuts through pre-existing roads.

Nicosia: where to sleep

Make sure that before checking in to any establishments you state quite clearly what you wish to pay for i.e. B&B, half-board or full-board. VAT of 5% is over and above the prices quoted. In the establishments below expect to pay C£7–8 for B&B; C£5–6 without breakfast.

Hotel Denis, 19 Diagoras Street Eylenja (tel: 02 330267).
Delphi Hotel, 24C. Pantelides Ave (tel: 02 475211).
Royal Hotel, Corner Aeschylos & 17 Euripides Street (tel: 02 4632455).
Sans Rival, 7G Solon Street (tel: 02 474383).
Femina Guest House, 114 Ledra Street (tel: 02 465729).
Gardenia Guest House, 23 Rigaena Street (tel: 02 463416).
Peter's Guest House, 5 Solonos Street, PO Box 2099 (tel: 02 448519).

There is also a **Youth Hostel** at 5 Hadjidakis Street (tel: 02 444808). Off Them. Dezvis Street. Open 24 hours. C£3 per night.

Nicosia: what to see and do

BYZANTINE MUSEUM Houses a superb collection of icons covering a period of 1,000 years.

CATHEDRAL OF ST JOHN Near the Laiki Yitonia. Within its walls are the busy pedestrian shopping streets of Ledra and Onasagorou crammed with stores and roadside stalls.

Limassol: where to sleep

Expect to pay C£3–4 in singles or doubles at the places below:

Acropole Hotel, 21 George Malikides Street (tel: 362706).
Astoria Hotel, 13A George Malikides Street (tel: 362708).
Kallithea Guest House, 12 Simos Menardos Street (tel: 362127).
Excelsior Guest House, 35 Anexartisia Street (tel: 353351).
Luxor Guest House, 101 Agios Andreas Street (tel: 362265).

For camping, try **Governor's Beach Camping** Pentakomo (20 km east of Limassol) (tel: 05 632300). C£1.50 per day per tent, plus C£1 per person.

Limassol: what to see and do

RUINS OF ANCIENT CITY KINGDOM OF ARMATHOUS Legend has it that mythological Ariadne visited the kingdom.

AGIOS GEORGIOS ALAMANOS CONVENT where the nuns spend most of their time painting icons.

GERMASOGEIA DAM This is a beauty spot. Great place for walking and fishing.

Larnaca: where to sleep

Harry's Hotel, 2 Thermopylon Street (tel: 654453).
Larnaca Youth Hostel, 27 Nicolaou Rossou Street. Near Agios Lazaros church. C£3 per night.

Larnaca: what to see and do

CHURCH OF PANAGIA ANGELOKTISTI Contains a 6th-century life-size Byzantine mosaic of the Virgin Mary.

LEFKARA VILLAGE To the west of Larnaca. Tourists come because of its famous lace – well, it is said that Leonardo da Vinci admired the lace from here, so it must be good.

STAVROVOUNI MONASTERY Perched on top of a mountain, access is by way of a winding hillside road. Built by St Helena – the monastery – not the road! The AGIOS MINAS CONVENT is worth seeing.

Paphos: where to sleep

The **Paphos Youth Hostel**, 37 Eleftherios Venizelos Avenue (tel: 06 722338), has beds for C£3 per night. Or you could try:

Trianon Guest House, 99, Makarios Avenue (tel: 06 232193). Singles C£5.

Lazaros Omirou, 25 Ayiou Kendia (tel: 06 232909). C£5 per person.

The nearest campsites are:

Feggari Camping, Pegaia, Coral Bay (tel: 06 621534). About 11 miles north of Paphos. C£1 per day per tent, plus C£1.50 per person per day.

Geroskipou Zenon Gardens Camping, Geroskipou 8 (tel: 06 242277). C£1 per tent, plus C£1 per person per day.

Paphos: what to see and do

APHRODITE ROCKS Birthplace of the goddess, promontory juts out of the sea some 16 miles east of the town.

GEROSKIPOS VILLAGE lies on the south-east side of Paphos. Today, amongst other things, it is famous for its *loucoumi* or Turkish Delight.

AGIOS NEOFYTOS MONASTERY Built above Paphos, it is complete with exquisite 12th-century frescoes and icons.

CHRYSORROGIATISSA MONASTERY from here there is a wonderful panoramic view. They also make good wine. Worth a visit!

POLIS VILLAGE which lies about 23 miles north of Paphos is well worth the trip to see. There is a great camping site right on the beach. The BATHS OF APHRODITE with their great view over the bay is another worthwhile trip.

Addresses

American Express at A. L. Mantovani & Sons, 35–7 Evagoras Avenue, Nicosia (tel: 02 443777/8/9).
Tourist Bureau at Laiki Yitonia, Nicosia (tel: 02 444264).
Tourist Bureau at 15 Spyrou Araouzus Street (tel: 62756).
US Embassy at Therissou Street and Dositheos Street, Nicosia (tel: 02 465151).
British Embassy at British High Commission, Alexander Pallis Street, PO Box 1978, Nicosia (tel: 02 473131).

Hitchers' Tips and Comments . . .

If you go to Cyprus, it is impossible to cross from North Cyprus (Turkish) to South Cyprus (Greek) or vice versa. Also, if you go to North Cyprus, do not allow your passport to be stamped, otherwise you will not be allowed to enter Greece. This happened to us and we were deported from Rhodes when we arrived there from Marmaris, Turkey. That then causes problems getting back to Europe, unless you go through the former Communist countries.

In Kyrenia, northern Cyprus, if going to the St Hilarion Castle (and it's worth a visit), get a lift all the way to the top. There is a military checkpoint half-way up the mountain road which stops walkers and only allows vehicles up to the castle. The soldiers there, though, are friendly and helped us to get a lift to the castle on a NATO bus.

CREB AND WEZ, BIRMINGHAM, ENGLAND

● **Warning!** War and revolution are rife in the Middle East. If you are contemplating a trip to the area, keep yourself well informed on what is happening. The best way to do this is through your embassy or consulate. Visas are needed in many countries.

Following is a brief summary of what there is to see in the Middle East countries.

Syria

population	12,259,000
size	185,100 square kilometres
capital	Damascus, population 2,800,000
government	Republic
religion	Moslem
language	Arabic, French and English
currency	*Syrian pound* (S£) One *pound* equals 100 *piastres*

There is a malaria risk from May through to October, and it's a good idea to have a cholera jab. Don't drink the tap water.

You can take up to S£200 into the country, and unlimited foreign currency which you are supposed to declare on arrival. You can take out local and foreign money up to the amount imported and declared.

● **Visa requirements** Visas are necessary for everyone except those from Arab countries. Some nationalities (e.g. Australians and New Zealanders) may get their visas at the border but others (e.g. Americans and British) must obtain them from a Syrian consulate abroad. If intending to stay more than 15 days, you must report to the 'Direction de l'Immigration des Passeports et de la Nationalité' within 15 days of arrival. South Africans, Israelis, or people with an Israeli stamp in their passport, are refused entry. The border with Israel is closed and since 1967 Israel has occupied the Golan Heights.

Where to sleep

Syrian youth hostels cost about S£12 a night, including sheets and cooking facilities (no meals are provided). Damascus Youth Hostel is at Saleh el Ali Street 66, Mazra'a Square (tel: 45 95 40), which is also the address of the Syrian Youth Hostels Association. There are also hostels in Aleppo, Bosra, Der'a, Homs, Latakia and Zabadani.

Cheap hotels are quite affordable, e.g. a double for around S£48. For cheap hotels in Damascus start your search from the Place des Martyrs and work towards the old city.

If you sleep out, be wary. It may be OK in some places, but risky in others.

Where to eat

Eating in Syria is cheap compared to Jordan, so if you're heading in that direction, eat out while you can afford it. When you sit down for a meal, bread, olives, salad and pickles are free, so don't order too much. If you have a sweet tooth you'll enjoy Syrian pastry shops. Syria has nice fruit juice places where you can buy freshly squeezed juice.

Hitching

Hitching is okay on the main roads. Sometimes, you even get free rides in service cars. But hitching is not recommended for women without a male companion. If you get stuck, buses are cheap (e.g.

Hama-Damascus, $3^1/_2$ hours, about S£12). But be warned that they can get overcrowded and there may be a rush for the bus when it pulls up. Hitching may be slower but it might be more comfortable, too! Women hitchers may prefer to pay a bit more for a less crowded bus. If not, be prepared to fight off wandering hands.

What to see

Damascus (population of nearly a million), which dates back to 4000 BC, is the oldest continually inhabited city in the world. Its Grand Bazaar is one of the great visits in the Middle East. See also the Omayad Mosque with the tomb of St John the Baptist, the Azem Palace, the National Museum and the tomb of Saladin. Narrow back alleys around the old city are interesting. Much of the old wall and gates still stands. Everything to see in Damascus is within walking distance of the cheap hotel area and the youth hostel.

In **Aleppo**, second city of Syria, see the bazaars, the Museum of Aleppo, the Great Mosque and the Aleppo Citadel. Also, the ruined Convent of Simeon. There, fifteen centuries ago, St Simeon lived on the top of a pillar for twenty-seven years.

Palmyra, once the most important city in Syria, is now only a village. But there is much to be seen, including the ancient cemeteries with their weird decorations, and the Citadel of the Ma'anites.

Hama has huge old Roman waterwheels (*norias*) along the river Orantes, and a museum. Check out the back alleys and the sleazy Roman baths, but careful you don't get dragged inside – you may find *baksheesh* forcefully demanded from you.

Krak des Chevaliers – the Castle of the Knights – is the best-preserved Crusader castle in the Middle East. It saw tremendous battles before the Arabs took it in 1271. Complete with moat, dungeons (take a torch), drawbridge and all the rest, it's worth going out of your way to see it. But be warned that it's situated several kilometres off the main Tartus to Homs highway and difficult to reach by hitching. There is sporadic public transport, so best leave early so you can get back. The village below the castle seems unfriendly. Watch out for kids hurling rocks. If you miss the last bus down to the highway and someone offers to give you a ride down, they may expect payment.

Tartus is worth a visit if you want to check out a museum and a 12th-century cathedral built by the Crusaders.

Latakia is a very ancient city which is now Syria's main port. As well as beaches, there are many ruins to see, including a Roman triumphal arch. North of the city is **Ras Shamra** where important excavations are being made.

Near the Jordanian border is **Bosra**, a 2nd-century Roman city which later became an important Christian centre. Visit the 6th-century Byzantine cathedral, the Roman baths, and Trajan's Palace.

Addresses

American Express at Chami Travel, Mouradi Building, Rue Fardons, Damascus (tel: 11 16 52 or 11 95 53).

Student Office at IAESTE (Syrian committee), University of Aleppo, Aleppo.

US Embassy at BP 29, Abu Roumaneh, rue Al-Mansur 2, Damascus (tel: (11) 333 052 or 332 557).

British Embassy at PO Box 37, Quartier Malki, 11 rue Muhammed Kurd Ali, Immeuble Kotob, Damascus (tel: (11) 712 561/2/3).

Hitchers' Tips and Comments . . .

In Damascus, you find cheap hotels in the El Mardja area near the Grand Bazaar. Lots of military movement on the Homs–Palmyra road. I don't advise hitching along it. Palmyra worth the visit, even if you have to reach it by bus. Six square miles of Roman ruins. Stay at the Camp Zenobia, or even in the ruins. Aleppo was my favourite Syrian city. You find cheap hotels in the area opposite the Tourist Office. SIMON LINGLEY, UPPINGHAM, UK

Syrian visas can be bought at any consulate and the cost depends on where you get it. You may need a letter of introduction from your embassy. British embassies charge S£6 at their rate of exchange for such letters. Some nationalities are allowed to get their visas at the border (the British are not among them). If you're in Syria for more than 15 days, you have to get an exit visa from the police. When applying for a visa, don't let on if you are Jewish or you'll be turned down. People with 'obviously' Jewish names probably won't get the visa anyway. Make a point of learning Arab numbers, or shops and banks will cheat you. In Damascus you can change money at the Souk el Hamadiyeh (US dollars preferred) and in Aleppo on Al Ayoubi Street at the clock tower, near the museum, and the tourist office. Don't bother trying to hitch out of Damascus to the south. It's a long walk and you'll end up among military installations.

Instead, take a bus to Dera'a for S£4 from Bab Moussalla Square.

In Aleppo see the Citadel, the biggest in the Middle East. Krak des Chevaliers is hard to hitch to and badly signposted. Best to get a bus from Homs. The Arabic name of the Krak is Kalet Al Hosen which the locals are more likely to understand. Lastly, be careful in Syria about what you say. Don't ever admit to anyone that you have been in Israel or that you're going there, or even give mild approval of the place. Do not bring into the country any goods of Israeli manufacture, or Israeli money. If you do, it will be regarded as implicit evidence of having visited Israel or having Zionist sympathies. If they find you out, you'll be refused admittance to the country or deported. In line with this paranoia, do not hitch near anything military. Remember that the official line is that President Assad is the greatest man who ever lived, and you will be advised not to disagree with it at any time, including when talking with someone who slags the government. It's no exaggeration to say that there are secret police everywhere. ANONYMOUS

Buses are dead cheap in Syria.

The Syrian border is a real rip-off. You must change US$100 to Syrian pounds at a rate which is a quarter of the tourist rate and a tenth of the black market rate. There's no way to avoid it.

In hotels and hostels you must pay in cash dollars too, although the very cheapest hotels accept Syrian pounds.

There's a new motorway from Damascus to Amman under construction. When it's finished the old border crossing might stay out of use. Check before you head to the frontier.

SAMULI SCHIELKE, TAMPERE, FINLAND

Iran

population	57,730,000
size	1,647,305 square kilometres
capital	Teheran, population 6,042,584
government	Republic
religion	Islamic
language	Persian
currency	*Rial* One *rial* equals 100 *dinars*

● **Warning!** I have *no* information about the attitude of Iranian officials towards hitch-hikers since the revolution. If you get there, tread warily!

Teheran, with a population of over 6,000,000 and at an altitude of 4,000 feet, is the capital of Iran. See the bazaars and the museums. Visit the Mesjedeh Sepahsalar Mosque, the only one still in use which non-Moslems may visit. See the Crown Jewels collection, including the largest uncut diamond in the world and the famous Peacock Throne. Just outside town, visit the ancient city of **Rai**, once the capital of Iran.

Isfahan is the home of the Mosque of Madreseh, the Palace of the Shahs and another good bazaar area.

Shiraz is known as 'the city of roses, nightingales and poets' and is just 64 km south-west of **Persepolis**, which is the ruined capital of ancient Persia. Here you can see the tombs of Darius and Xerxes and the ruins of fantastic palaces. One of the big archaeological sites of the world.

Iraq

population	17,250,000
size	434,738 square kilometres
capital	Baghdad, population 4,868,000
government	Republic
religion	Moslem
language	Arabic
currency	*Dinar* One *dinar* equals 1,000 *fils*

● **Warning!** As a result of the 1991 Gulf War, Iraq is not a country to be visited by any except the most experienced travellers. Reports of armed conflict between factions within the country are common.

Baghdad is your genuine Arabian Nights city. See (from the outside unless you're a Moslem) the Kadhimain Mosque with its pure gold dome, the Abbassid Palace with its tremendous collection relating to the history of Islam, and visit the carpet market in the Covered Bazaar.

Babylon, ancient capital of the Babylonian empire and site of the Hanging Gardens of Babylon, one of the Seven Wonders of the World, is 88 km south of Baghdad. See Nebuchadnezzar's Procession Street, the Lion of Babylon and the throne room.

Mosul once had a much better-known name – **Nineveh**. It sits on the west side of the Tigris River and has a million inhabitants. The ruins of Nineveh, which was destroyed in 612 BC, are on the east bank.

Addresses

US Embassy at PO Box 2447, 929/7/57 Hay Babel, Masba, Alwiyah, Baghdad (tel: (1) 719 6138/9 or 719 3791 or 718 1840).
British Embassy at Zukak 12, Mahala 218, Hay al-Khelood, Baghdad (tel: (1) 537 2121/5).
Both of these are closed at present owing to the current political situation.

Lebanon

population	2,897,000
size	10,452 square kilometres
capital	Beirut, population 1,500,000
government	Republic
religion	Half Moslem, half Christian
language	Arabic, but English widely spoken
currency	*Lebanese pound* One *pound* equals 100 *piastres*

● **Warning!** Check things out carefully before trying to enter Lebanon. It's a dangerous place. For full information contact Lebanon embassies or consulates.

Lebanon can be reached from Istanbul by sea, for about £50.

Beirut with a population of over 1,000,000 is the capital, and can be very expensive if you're not careful. Things to see include the Al-Khodr Mosque where it is said St George slew the dragon, the National Museum and the Pigeon Grotto. To meet people, try the American University, the largest American educational complex outside the States. People from all over the world study there.

Baalbek, 56 km north-east of Beirut, was the Heliopolis of the Greeks and Romans. Many of the ruins are equal to anything you can see in Rome. The Temple of Bacchus, built around AD 150, is outstanding.

Byblos is another ancient town, one so important to archaeologists that they have been excavating there since 1921, discovering successive layers of settlement dating back 7,000 years. Plenty to see if you like examining rocks and ruins.

Addresses

US Embassy at avenue de Paris, Immeuble Ali Reza, Beirut.

British Embassy at PO Box 60180, Middle East Airlines Building, Tripoli Autostrade, Jal el Dib, East Beirut (tel: 417 007 or 410 596 or 416 112). There is also another British Embassy at Shamma Building, Roouché, Ras Beirut (West Beirut) (tel: 812 849 or 812 851 or 804 929).

Israel

population	4,821,700
size	21,946 square kilometres
capital	Jerusalem 468,900. The diplomatic capital is Tel Aviv population 1,094,700)
government	Republic
religion	Jewish
language	Hebrew, with English widely spoken
currency	*Shekel* One *shekel* equals 100 *agorots*. Coins of 10, 50 *agorots*, and of 1, 5, 10, 50 *shekels*. Notes of 5, 10, 20, 50, 100 *shekels*

Israel can be reached by sea from Piraeus (Greece), to Haifa for around £45 one-way. It is possible to come by land from Egypt and from Jordan via the Allenby Bridge (the latter is possible if you have a permit issued in Amman but, due to the political instability of the region, the bridge may be closed at any time).

When you arrive in Israel, ask for the border stamp to be put on a separate piece of paper because most Arab and Moslem states will not allow entry if there's evidence of a visit to Israel in your passport. The initial stamp is valid for three months after which you're supposed to register. If you're going to Egypt and intend visiting other Arab states afterwards, don't get your Egyptian visa in Israel. It will say it was issued in Tel Aviv (a dead giveaway), and remember that the Egyptian stamp you'll receive at the border, if going overland, will also ban you from certain countries as it will state the name of the crossing point and show that you crossed from Israel.

Your luggage will very likely be searched on entry for bombs and guns. If entering from Jordan, you will definitely be searched. Do not leave your pack unattended anywhere. This is not so much a precaution against thieves but because it's all too easy to start a bomb scare.

Israel is expensive but you can save money on food by buying in the supermarkets where prices of basic food are heavily subsidized. With inflation at over 200% at the last count, don't change more money than required for immediate needs. Your shekels will lose

5% of their value every week. Keep all exchange receipts in order to change your shekels back to hard currency. Prices on consumer goods, such as cassette recorders, radios and most electrical appliances, are high so a profit can be made on such goods if you bring them into the country to sell.

Accommodation prices quoted within this section do not include *Value Added Tax* which, in Israel, runs at **18%**. To avoid paying it, try to pay for your accommodation in foreign currency – foreigners who pay in foreign currency are exempt from VAT.

Hitching

Hitching is very good in Israel, particularly if you wear a green uniform and carry a gun. There are always lots of soldiers on the road and drivers always give them priority. Your chances of getting a lift are vastly improved if you are a woman, or a man travelling with one. When hitching, don't use your thumb as in Europe. The gesture means 'fuck off'. Usually, the locals hitch by pointing at the ground with their forefingers. Unlike hitchers in other countries, Israelis do not spread themselves along the roadside but bunch together, usually at a bus stop. When a car stops, there'll be a free-for-all to get the seats. Just push your way in, though it may be difficult when carrying luggage. Remember, it'll be soldiers first. If you get stuck, buses are cheap.

Everything closes on the Jewish Sabbath, Friday sunset to Saturday sunset. All shops shut, buses stop running, museums close and there's little traffic on the roads. It's advisable not to doss out near borders or in the former Occupied Territories (Gaza, West Bank, and Golan).

Jerusalem with its 468,900 inhabitants is the religious centre of Israel, and during its 4,000-year history it has become a holy city for Jews, Moslems and Christians. The Jewish part of the Old City is the only place on earth where you can see a *Hassid* (wearing a fur hat in the middle of summer and speaking Hebrew into a mobile phone) standing alongside an Arab who is selling Turkish carpets to two nuns. It is a city that lives the past; you can't be unmoved by Jerusalem. A religious city, it holds something sacred for members of all sects. A city with a soul. Everything in it is cooler, slower, more human – and expensive.

Just to the south of Jerusalem is **Bethlehem** where Christ is said to have been born. The Church of the Nativity marks the site.

Beersheba, the principal city in the Negev desert, is a good place to see Bedouins. Every Thursday morning they hold a market. **Tiberias** is a resort town on the western side of the **Sea of Galilee**

where there are some great beaches; the climate is pleasant and warm.

Masada is best reached from Beersheba. This great rock, which rises 1,700 feet above the western shores of the Dead Sea, was the site of Herod's Palace and where the Zealots made their last stand against the Romans in AD 73. When the Romans finally took the fortress they found every man, woman and child had killed themselves rather than go into slavery.

The **Dead Sea** is the lowest point on earth (1,312 feet below sea level). You'll have trouble swimming in it, let alone sinking, because of the high salt content. Don't swallow any of the water, it'll make you very sick. If you have any cuts, you'll soon know about them. Several beaches have showers to rinse off the salt.

Way down south, on the Red Sea, is the resort of **Eilat**. The town isn't much, but offshore are superb coral reefs. The best are some kilometres south of town in the Egyptian Sinai. (The Egyptian consulate in Eilat issues visas good for the Sinai.) Scuba equipment can be hired but, if you can't afford that, visit the Aquarium, which includes an underwater observatory 15 feet under the surface of the sea where marine life can be seen in its natural surroundings. There are several hostels in Eilat (official and otherwise) and a campsite, or you can doss on the beaches (watch out for thieves and rats).

Tel Aviv–Jaffa combined make Israel's largest city, population 1,094,000. Jaffa, where Jonah is said to have been spewed out by the whale, was founded in 1500 BC. Adjoining Tel Aviv was founded in 1909. See the bazaars in the old city and the fine modern museums and galleries in the new.

Haifa, which lies about 90 km north of Tel Aviv, is a seaside resort with beautiful beaches and caters for the holidaymaker and tourist. As a result, it is expensive. North of Haifa is the old town of **Acre** (or Akke). Here you can see the city walls; the El-Jazza Mosque ('the Mosque of the Butcher') with Roman columns in the courtyard; 15 other mosques; the Crusaders' Subterranean City; and the Turkish Citadel which is now a museum of the Jewish Irgun resistance.

For details of working on *kibbutzim*, see the chapter **Working in Europe**.

Distance Chart
(in miles)

	JERUSALEM	TEL AVIV	HAIFA	TIBERIAS
JERUSALEM	–	39	99	97
TEL AVIV	39	–	56	82
HAIFA	99	56	–	43

TIBERIAS	97	82	43	–
ACRE	112	73	14	35
ARAD	65	98	158	144
ASHDOD	41	26	86	109
ASHKELON	45	39	99	122
BEERSHEBA	52	70	130	147
BETT SHE'AN	70	73	42	23
ELIAT	194	220	280	250
HAMMAT GADER	97	86	55	13
JERICHO	24	63	92	73
MASADA	66	104	161	113
MITZE RAMON	104	122	182	198
NAZARETH	97	63	22	18
NETANYA	58	18	41	64
SAFED	120	104	45	22

Jerusalem: where to sleep

Accommodation here is not what you would call cheap. Here are a selection of the best and least expensive options:

Hotel New Imperial, Jaffa Gate (tel: 272400). £6–£8 per night.
Savoy, Jerusalem (tel: 283366). £7.80–£10 per night.
Zion, 4 Lunz, Jerusalem (tel: 232237). £9.50–£11.50 per night.

Hostels:

Moreshet Hayahadut, the Jewish Quarter (tel: 288611). £5–£11 per night. Includes breakfast.

Louis Waterman Wise Hostel, 8 Hapisgah Street, Bayit Vagan Quarter (tel: 423366). 1.5 km from the central bus station. This hostel has everything. Open gardens, library, information about tours etc. From £4.50 per night. Breakfast costs £2.

Beit Shmuel Hostel, 13 King David Street (tel: 203456). £5–£11 per night.

Beit Bernstein Hostel 1 Karen Hayesod (tel: 228286). £5–£11 per night. Approx 1 km west of the city, take any of the following buses from Jerusalem Bus Station: 7, 8 or 14.

Then there are Christian Hostels, which cost £6.50–£15 per night for a bed in a double room, which is good value when breakfast is also thrown in. In some, full-board is standard, so enquire in advance:

St Charles Hospice, Roman Catholic, German Colony (tel: 637737).
Rosary Convent Hostel, Catholic, 14 Agron Street (tel: 228529).
Dom Polski, Catholic, 8 Hamom Hashlishit Street (tel: 285916).
Dom Polski, Catholic, Old City, by Jaffa Gate (tel: 282017).
St George Hostel, Anglican, 20 Nablus Road (tel: 283302).
Lutheran Hostel, German Lutheran, Old City (tel: 282120).
Maison d'Abraham, Ras al Amud (tel: 294501).
St Andrew's Hospice, Church of Scotland. Near the railway station (tel: 717701).
Casa Nova, Franciscan (tel: 292791).
Rumanian Hostel, 46 Shivtei Israel (tel: 287355).
American Hostel, Catholic, 41 Via Dolorosa Third Station (tel: 284262).
Foyer de Florence, Greek Catholic (tel: 282023).
Fraternité Dominican de Bethsade, French, 22 St Mark Street (tel: 285587).

Then we have the Arab Hostels which are the cheapest of all at £2 and £3.50 per night. They are all located in the Old City. Their disadvantage is that they are not considered to be very clean and it is also difficult to recommend them because of their lack of security.

Olivette House, Azhara Street.
Aharam, Hagai Street.
El Hashami, 73 Khan el Zeit.
El Arab, Haketzavim Street (Damascus Gate).
Jock Inn, 12 Henchke.
Mister A. Jirjis Street.
Palace, 15 Hanevi'im.
Feisal, 22 Hanevi'im.

Jerusalem: where to eat

You will find that eating out is quite expensive compared, say, to Egypt. If you can find digs where the kitchen can be used, then that's your best bet. Failing that, camp out. A few cheapo eateries do exist:

Misadonet, 74 Kerekh Bethlehem.
Mishkenot Shaananim. Yemin Moshe, above the Cinematheque. Ask for Chef's salad at £3.50.

Jerusalem: what to see and do

JAFFA GATE, CITADEL OF DAVID The only gate on the west side of the city.

THE CITADEL, TOWER OF DAVID One of the most important and famous sites in the city. Part of it date back 3,000 years.

DAMASCUS GATE The Roman square was the main entrance to Jerusalem during Roman times; this was the northern gate in the walls.

LIONS' GATE (or St Stephen's Gate). It is said that this was the gate through which St Stephen was led on his way to be stoned to death.

VIA DOLOROSA One of the most sacred streets in Christendom, as it was the path where Jesus walked bearing the cross.

THE WESTERN WALL Jews from all over the world come to place scraps of paper containing written requests in the Wall.

ABBEY OF THE DORMITION According to tradition, this is where Mary, Mother of God, fell into eternal sleep.

GREAT SYNAGOGUE New City. Built in 1982, the synagogue is richly adorned and can seat 1,500; it has a roll-back roof so that couples can marry here under the open sky according to custom.

HEBREW UNIVERSITY The campus covers an area of 50 hectares. There are over 1,500,000 volumes in the Library.

THE KNESSET BUILDING The Israeli Parliament building, where 120 members of the Knesset convene in the Plenum, which can be seen from the visitors' gallery.

CHURCH OF THE ASCENSION It is believed by Christians that this was the spot where Jesus ascended into heaven.

MAHANEH YEHUDA MARKET Important place for the backpacker. This is the best place to buy fruit and vegetables.

Addresses

Israel Students Tourist Association at 5 Eliasmar Street (tel: 02 225258)

Tourism Police, at the Kisleh, Old City (tel: 273222)
Government Tourist Information Office at 24 King George St., Jerusalem (tel: 02 241281)
Black Market money-changers at Jaffa Road, near Zion Square.

Bethlehem: where to sleep

Budget sleeping places are very thin on the ground here: one solution could be sleeping rough, but it is not recommended: here are three of the cheapest digs:

St Joseph's Pension, Syrian Catholic (tel: 742 483). Around £5 upwards per night.
Bethlehem Star, El Baten Street (tel: 743 249). From £11 per night.
Al-Andalus Hotel, Manger Square (tel: 741 348). From around £9 per night.

Bethlehem: what to see and do

CHURCH OF THE NATIVITY Built on the site of Jesus's birth by Emperor Constantine in AD 325. It is one of the oldest churches in the world.

HERODION 8 km from Bethlehem. A fortified mountain palace built by King Herod about 1,500 feet above sea level. The building served as a palace, fortress and a monument – it is said that Herod is buried here.

SOLOMON'S POOLS About 3 km south of Bethlehem. The large pools are from the Second Temple and trap rain water. They have provided Jerusalem with water since ancient times.

Beersheba: where to sleep

Beit Yatziv Youth Hostel, PO Box 7 (tel: 77444). £4.50 per night.
Arava Hotel, 37 Histadrut (tel: 78792). £10 per night.
Aviv Hotel, 48 Mordei Hagetaot (tel: 78059). £10–£12.50 per night.

Beersheba: what to see and do

ABRAHAM'S WELL Hevron Road.

MUSEUM OF THE NEGEV Old Town Hall building.

ABRAHAM BROWN GALLERY Exhibitions of paintings and sculptures.

Tiberias: where to sleep

There are many beaches where you can kip down. **Maagan, Kinar Holiday village, Hailanot** cost £3, **Tsedafim Beach** £2, **Hawai Beach** £1.50. For one night only.

Hostels:

Meyaihas Hostel, Ha Yarden Street (tel: 790350/721775). Close to the beach. £5 per night, including breakfast.

Tiber Youth Hostel, at Poriah (tel: 750050). £5 per night includes breakfast.

YMCA, on the Tiberias/Ginosar road (tel: 720685). £5 per night includes breakfast.

Karei Deshe at Tabha. Rooms with bath, gas refrigerator. £5 per night (tel: 720601).

Hospices:

Terra Sancta, Catholic Franciscan (tel: 720516 – ask for Father Faraji). £2.80 per night, bed only. Kitchen facilities.

Franciscan Casa Nova Guest House, Catholic (tel: 754071). B&B or full-board, for singles, doubles, or groups. £9.50 per night per person.

Tiberias: where to eat

Ein Gev. Popular fish restaurant which serves 140,000 every year (300 fish are fried each hour). Not cheap – but good tucker.

Tiberias: what to see and do

HAMMAT GADER On the south-eastern shore of the Sea of Galilee, the 2,000 year old Roman bath houses have been restored and are in operation today.

BETHSAIDA Native residence of the apostles Philip, Simon and Andrew. Here, Jesus fed the 5,000.

CAPERNAUM On the northern shore, it is said the Jesus preached and lived in the home of Simon Peter. Well-preserved ruins of a 3rd-century synagogue.

THE MOUNT OF BEATITUDES It was here that Jesus is said to have appointed the twelve apostles.

TABGHA Site of the miracle of the Loaves and Fishes.

MAGDALA Home of Mary Magdalene.

Eliat: where to sleep

Eilat Youth Hostel, opposite the Red Rock Hotel (tel: 72357). Take a bus 5, 13 or 15 from the bus station because it is a climb of about 1 kilometre. Hot showers and lockers are available. B&B will knock you back £5; full-board is available – but enquire about the price.

Shalem Hostel on Hativat Ha Negev Street (tel: 76544). Kitchen, bar, feature film nightly. Open 24 hrs. £3.50–£16 per night.

Max and Merran's Fawlty Towers Hostel at 116/1 Ofarim Street (tel: 72371). Dorm bed will cost around £3. Very friendly, easy-going place.

Best beach is between the **Blue Sky Caravan** to **Sun Bay** at the edge of **Coral Beach**.

Eliat: where to eat

Eliat has around 160 restaurants offering anything from fish and chips, to chicken chow mein. Take your pick!

Egged Self-Service Restaurant at the bus station provides the usual inexpensive meals. Open from 4 a.m. till 4 p.m. but closed Saturdays.

Fisherman House at Coral Pier (tel: 71330) offers self-service fish, chips, salad and bread for around £2. You can eat as much as you like.

Addresses:

Government Tourist Office. Worth visiting to enquire about charter flights. They are at Rechter Commercial Centre, Hatemarim Blvd (tel: 76737/72268).

Tel Aviv: where to sleep

Youth Hostel, 32 Bnei Dan Street (tel: 5460719). Some rooms with shower – so enquire. £3.50–£10 per night.
Joseph Motel, 15 Bogroshov (tel: 280955). £3.65 per night. Dorm rooms.
Moma's Hotel, 28 Ben Yehuda (tel: 297421/287471). £3.50 per night in dorm rooms.
No. 1 Hostel, 84 Ben Yehuda (tel: 5237807). £3.50 per night.
Nes Tziona Hotel, 10 Nes Tziyona Street (tel: 5103404). Near the sea. £5.50–7.80 per night. Recommended by Ministry of Tourism.
Dizengoff Hostel, 11–13 Dizengoff Square (tel: 5242024). Dorm rooms from £4, singles/doubles from £10.

Tel Aviv: where to eat

Workers' Restaurants are located in the industrial streets of south Tel Aviv, behind the Diamond Exchange in Ramat Gan. They open in the afternoon and serve meals of Bulgarian, Polish, Romanian, Hungarian.

Siba Lemesiba at 77 Ben Yehuda Street serves a variety of plain oriental dishes from around £1.
Domino Pizza on the corner of Ben Yehuda and Bagrashov Streets makes excellent, reasonably priced pizzas.

Addresses:

Government Tourist Information Office, 5 Shalam Aleichem Street (tel: 660258/9).
Police: (tel: 100)

Haifa: where to sleep

Carmel Youth Hostel, Mobile Post, Hof Hacarmel (tel: 04 531944). Meals are available. £8.50 per night.

Beit El Hostel, 40 Hagefen Street (Hadar) (tel: 04 521110). £4.50 per night.

St Charles Hospice, 105 Jaffa Road (tel: 04 523705). Dorm beds around £6, singles/doubles from £10. Breakfast included.

Haifa: what to see and do

THE BAHAI TEMPLE AND GARDENS One of the most beautiful temples in Haifa. No entry for those wearing shorts. Situated on Zionism Blvd.

CARMELITE MONASTERY Founded by Christian hermits who had to leave their homes after the Moslem conquest 1192.

ELIJAH'S CAVE Allenby Road. Legend has it that Elijah the Prophet lived here after fleeing from the Kings of Israel.

Acre: where to sleep

Gate Hostel, 24/12 Salah Ah Street (tel: 910410). Private hostel in the Old City. Showers. £3 per night. £1.25 buys you breakfast.

IYHA Acre (tel: 911982). Near the lighthouse at Pizani Port. Dorm rooms. Showers on each floor. Lockers. £5.50 per night. Meals are available. Bus to Haifa takes about 30 mins.

Addresses

Main post office (for poste restante), Tel Aviv-Yafo Post Office, 7 Mikve Yisrael Street, Tel Aviv.

American Express c/o Meditrad Ltd, 16 Ben Yehuda Street, Tel Aviv (tel: 294654).

Israel Students' Tourist Association at 109 Ben Yehuda Street, POB 4451, Tel Aviv (tel: 247164).

Israel Information Office at 5 Shalam Aleichem Street (tel: 660258/9).

US Embassy at 61 Hayarkon Street, Tel Aviv (tel: 654338).
British Embassy at 1 Ben Yehuda Street (tel: 5100166).

Hitchers' Tips and Comments . . .

Warning! People are coming to Israel without a return ticket and with prices high and jobs hard to find they're getting stuck here. Also, it seems that the British Embassy isn't feeling so charitable nowadays. CHRIS CLARKE, LONDON

A word of warning to anyone who wants to work in a kibbutz. Beware of some of the agencies who promise to fix everything up for you. If you're unlucky you may meet a shady operator who screws as much as he can out of you and when you arrive in Israel nobody wants to know about you. HUGH DUNNE, DUBLIN, IRELAND

In Israel try working on a moshav – like a kibbutz but you work for a farmer and you get paid a wage.
CREB AND WEZ, BIRMINGHAM, ENGLAND

Very expensive country. A cheap place to stay in Jerusalem is 'Mr A's Hostel', Old City, near Jaffa Gate.

It's preferable to work on a kibbutz as the life is easier. On the moshav you'll be working 10–11 hours per day and many of them are dead at night.

Eat self-service Felafel – pitta bread stuffed with salad and pickles. Don't get caught on the road or in a small place on the Sabbath day. No buses run and cars are few. The Sabbath is approximately 3 p.m. Friday to 3 p.m. Saturday.
K. M. FITCHET, JOHANNESBURG, SOUTH AFRICA

In Israel don't take your camera into a cinema. Security people may want to open it to check for hidden bombs – goodbye film!
THEO VAN DRUNEN, OOSTERHOUT, HOLLAND

There is a weekly magazine called *This Week*, available from Information Offices. It gives information on where to eat, museums to see and maps of the large cities.
MARTIN GREEN, NOTTINGHAM, ENGLAND

Always keep enough money handy to pay the airport or port tax which is levied on departures from Israel.
A. CHAPLIN, HATFIELD, HERTS, UK

Sleeping out in Jerusalem is very unwise, especially in Arab areas. I found the Hotel Zefonya great value. In Tiberias on the Sea of Galilee the Swiss Motel was the best value I've had anywhere.

ANDREW WARMINGTON, CAMBRIDGE, ENGLAND

If you intend to spend some time in Israel and your initial visa expires, your renewal visa must be stamped in your passport. Therefore, if you had any future plans of visiting Arab countries (except Egypt) forget it! You cannot enter them with the Israeli stamp.

The best area to look for work is Eilat. It's a tourist trap with hotels that nearly always need staff: chambermaids, kitchen staff, etc.

If you cannot get work in the hotels, go to the 'Peace Café' in the evening. It's a focal point for fellow travellers, the cheapest beer in town, and you often hear of work that's going. BLONDIE, UK

Jordan

population	4,009,000
size	97,699 square kilometres
capital	Amman, population 1,160,000
government	Monarchy
religion	Moslem
language	Arabic, some English and French spoken
currency	*Dinar* (JD) One *dinar* equals 1,000 *fils*. Coins of 5, 10, 20, 50 and 100 *fils*. Notes of 500 *fils* and 1, 5, 10, 20 *dinars*. *Piastres* sometimes referred to instead of *fils*: 10 *fils* equal 1 *piastre*

At present Jordan seems pretty safe to travel in but on the West Bank sporadic violence erupts, so keep an eye on the situation!

The only relatively hassle-free way to thumb into Jordan is from Syria. The two countries are often not on the best of terms, but the border is normally open.

Part of Jordan, the West Bank, has been occupied by Israel since 1967. If you want to cross between Israel and Jordan, check out the constantly changing situation before you arrive in the Middle East, where it can be difficult to obtain reliable information.

● **Visa requirements** Visas are best obtained in advance from a Jordanian embassy or consulate. The validity period varies.

The following is roughly the situation at the time of writing: if you have an Israeli stamp in your passport, you cannot enter Jordan. The Israelis used to put a stamp on a piece of paper into your passport instead of stamping the actual passport, but they seem to refuse to do this now. In Jordan you can apply for a permit to visit the West Bank, in Amman. This takes about a week to get and the only place you can cross is Allenby Bridge. Once on the West Bank there is nothing to stop you travelling anywhere in Israel but, if you want to re-enter Jordan, it may not be possible. Check it out first. If you get your Jordanian visa before entering Israel, it *may* be possible to enter Jordan but not to re-enter Israel.

● **Warning!** Tap water should not be drunk. Hygiene is not as good as the modern surroundings may lead you to believe. There is still malaria in some parts. Obtain malaria tablets before you arrive, as they are difficult to obtain locally.

Where to sleep

There are no official youth hostels. Cheap hotels cost around JD3,000 a single or JD4,500 a double. In Amman these are found in the Balad or downtown area. It's cheapest to sleep on the roof, but this is not recommended for females, as even European males (especially those with blond hair) are sometimes groped during the night. There are government rest houses near some tourist sites but these are expensive. At Petra the Bedouins sometimes offer to put you up in their caves. There is no accommodation at Jerash, which is best visited as a day trip from Amman.

Jordan is not geared for camping, though there are some places where you could pitch a tent. Sleeping out shouldn't be too much of a problem, but it's not a good idea for women, nor in the north from November to March when it rains.

Where to eat

Eating out is none too cheap in Jordan, especially when compared to Syria. A lot of Jordan's food is imported. Search out the local bakery for good, cheap bread, then hunt around the markets for something to go with it. A cooker is worthwhile.

Alternatively, try the cheaper takeaways: *falafel* – small balls of ground chickpeas served with salad in a sandwich (about 450 fils each); *shawarma* – delicious slices of spitted spiced lamb. Pieces are sliced off and wrapped in bread and cost about 350 fils each. Two should fill you up.

Don't miss the fruit juice stalls in Amman.

Hitching

Hitching is generally good, though not recommended for women without a male companion. Couples move fastest but, in the front of a vehicle, make sure the man sits between the driver and the woman. It's cheap to catch a local bus from the centre of Amman to a better hitching spot in the suburbs. The Desert Highway offers easy hitching but the King's Highway, which is a more interesting route, is difficult. (Petra can be time-consuming to get in and out of from the Desert Highway.) People are generally friendly and hospitable but, occasionally, ask for money. Buses are not a viable alternative here. They are few and they are expensive.

The best map of the country is the Oxford, which includes a plan of Amman.

Carry your passport with you in the vicinity of Aqaba, where there are checkpoints on the roads.

What to see

Amman is built on seven hills. It can be a confusing place to find your way around. Sixty years ago it was a desert village; now it is a modern town. Many businesses have moved from Beirut to Amman because of the war in Lebanon, which has caused a fast expansion of the city and spiralling prices. As is the case all over Jordan, a large proportion of the population are Palestinian refugees.

See the Roman Theatre which seats 6,000 spectators, and the Costume and Folklore Museums beneath it. Go up to the Citadel to see the ruined Temple of Hercules, visit the Jordan Archaeological Museum and see the Circassian Guards outside the Basman Palace.

Jerash, just 30 km north of Amman, has been called the Pompeii of the Middle East. Founded around 330 BC by Alexander the Great, it reached prominence in Roman times. Then, slowly, the sand piled up and it was all but forgotten until the 1920s when archaeologists went to work on the site. Plenty to see, including three theatres, two baths, innumerable churches and the remains of the huge Temple of Artemis.

Swimming in the **Dead Sea** is a unique experience. You cannot sink. In fact, it can be difficult to get your feet back on the bottom if you start floating. Best stick to the popular swimming spots – in places, the retreating level of the Dead Sea has exposed quicksand.

About 30 km south of Amman is **Madaba**, known for its mosaics. East of Amman and out in the desert are quite a few castles, but for the hitcher they are difficult to reach. If you have the time to risk some slow hitching, the **King's Highway** south of Madaba offers spectacular scenery, a Crusader castle at **Kerak** and the Crusader fortress of **Shoubak**.

Petra, halfway between Amman and Aqaba, is a weird sight and, for 700 years – between the 12th century and 1812 when it was accidentally rediscovered – it was truly a lost city. 'Rose-red Petra' (and it really is) was founded in 300 BC by the Nabataean Arabs who took 500 years to carve it out of the solid rock of the mountains. Access is only by foot or hired horse from **Wadi Musa** through the dramatic **Siq**, a narrow chasm which made Petra so eminently defendable. After you've seen Petra you won't regret the desert journey you had to make to get there.

Aqaba is Jordan's port and was also doubling as a backdoor port for Iraq during its war with Iran. The town itself is unattractive – lots of litter, ships, hotels and development. The best parts of the beach are fenced in by the big hotels. Just across the bay is Eilat in Israel, so for security reasons swimming is not permitted after 6 p.m. It's worth travelling down the coast towards Saudi Arabia (you'll need your passport) and snorkelling among the fantastic coral reefs. In this direction you'll also find the Aqaba Marine Science Station. On the other hand if you must hang around Aqaba (possibly to think about getting to Egypt – Suez or Nuweiba), then why not hike along to the Corniche Hotel which will cost you JD3 for a double for one night. It's a clean place with fans and is good for making contacts.

Addresses

Main post office at Prince Mohammed Street in Amman is reliable for poste restante. Security check at door. No mail service to Israel.

American Express at International Traders, Abdal-Karimal-Khattabi Street, Amman (tel: 661014).

Student Office at IAESTE Office, Faculty of Engineering, University of Jordan, Amman (tel: 843 555 ext. 1789).

US Embassy at PO Box 354, Jabal, Amman (tel: 644 371).

British Embassy at PO Box 87, Abdain, Amman (tel: 823 100).

Hitchers' Tips and Comments . . .

Hitching good in Jordan due to friendly people. About 80% of traffic on 'Desert Highway' are trucks. Petra *must* be visited. You can sleep with the Bedouins in the valley there – amazing experience. Not much in Amman. Cheap hotels are downtown near the Hasimi Mosque. SIMON LINGLEY, UPPINGHAM, UK

It's possible to cross from Jordan to Israel (though not the other way unless you have already come from Jordan and your visa is still valid) via the Allenby Bridge (King Hussein Bridge in Jordan). The trick is to ask to visit the West Bank which is part of Jordan under Israeli military occupation. To do this you must get a permit from the Ministry of the Interior in Amman, which is at the far end of King Hussein Street, a 40-minute walk from the centre. You must be there before 1 p.m. and you need a 50 fils revenue stamp (not a postage stamp) from the post office and one photo. Fill out some forms and wait between one and four days. It costs nothing, but don't say you are visiting Israel proper, only the West Bank, which includes East Jerusalem (the Old City). It's not possible to cross by foot. You must take a bus for 1 dinar or take a JETT bus from Amman for 2½ dinars. The checkpoint closes at 1 p.m., so it may be best to take the bus from Amman which starts at 6 a.m. From the Israeli side you may only take a taxi out of the customs post to either Jericho or Jerusalem. The price is negotiable. Anyone walking around in the Israeli border zone may be shot on sight, if he doesn't tread on a mine first. The Jordanians will let you back as long as there's no evidence of having visited Israel proper, but the Israelis may not let you cross back. And, of course, the whole thing may shut down at any time due to the tense situation in the Middle East. ALAN BARLOW, CHEADLE, UK

There is a cheap restaurant in the centre of Amman, close to the central post office, called the Jerusalem (known locally as the Ma'atem Kudz). It sells 'traditional' dishes, including mansaf, a dish of rice, pine nuts and lamb, covered in a sauce made from dried sheep's milk, normally served at feasts. Meat is generally of poor quality and expensive; fortunately you can eat well on vegetable dishes alone. Locally produced okra (ba'amia) and aubergines (ba'idinjan) are cheap.

If in Petra, remember that the ticket you receive when hiring a horse to take you down the Siq is also for a return ride on the same horse. When you alight in front of the Treasury, make sure that your horse-owner stays put until you have been around the site, or comes back for you if you intend to stay several hours or overnight. If you get on any other horse to take the return journey, expect to be hassled for a second payment all the way back up.

ANGELA BURNS, LONDON

To get from Jordan to Egypt take a ferry from Aqaba to Nuweiba which costs $28 (and you can pay with dinars). From Egypt to Jordan the ferry ticket costs $25 – only dollars accepted. The ferry runs twice a day. There are exact departure dates, but nobody cares about them. Morning ferry is more full than evening ferry.

Jordan is one of my favourite countries. Hitch-hiking is great. Roads are good, people are very friendly and the price level is affordable. Although there's not much of tourists sights in Amman, it's a very nice place to stay for a few days. Petra just can't be missed. You have three ways to hitch there. You can come all the way from Amman on the King's Highway, or you can get on the desert highway which is faster. Or you can go via Shaubak or via Ma'am. When you go via Shaubak, you leave your lift at a junction in the middle of nowhere, from where you've got 30 km to Shaubak. In half an hour a car will come and pick you up (if the first car doesn't, the second will). From Shaubak there are few cars, but lifts are possible. If you get stuck, the bus to Petra goes twice a day. In Petra you can stay at the Student's Rest House. SAMULI SCHIELKE, TAMPERE, FINLAND

12 · WORKING IN EUROPE

With the establishment of the European Economic Area (EEA) between the countries of the EC (Belgium, France, Germany, Greece, Italy, the Netherlands, Luxembourg, Denmark, Ireland, the United Kingdom, Spain and Portugal) and Sweden, Norway, Finland and Austria from EFTA, citizens of all these countries can now work anywhere else in the EEA without a work permit, except in areas of public administration. Residence permits may be required in some instances: check the situation with the embassy. It should be noted that the theory and practice of a national of an EEA country working in another EEA country are usually two very different things. Even assuming you are sufficiently competent in a foreign language, and theoretically should have equal rights to a job, employers invariably favour their fellow countrymen.

Those who are not nationals of one of the EEA countries will almost certainly require a work permit anywhere in Europe. Sometimes this permit has to be obtained by the visitor before he enters the country in question, other times it must be obtained by the visitor's employer after he has found a job. The rules and regulations are generally so wound up in red tape, and change so often, that the only sure way of finding out complete details on the subject, as they apply at any particular time, is to write to the nearest tourist agency in your own country or the country in which you hope to work.

Presuming that most English-speaking people would be seeking a job in England, the following addresses are offered. These tourist agencies will give you the information you need or put you in touch with the people who have the information.

Americans should write to the British Travel Offices at:

680 Fifth Avenue, New York, NY 10019.

John Hancock Center, Site 2450, 875 N. Michigan Avenue, Chicago IL 60611.

612 South Flower Street, Los Angeles, Calif. 90017.

Canadians should write to:

151 Bloor Street W, Suite 460, Toronto, Ontario M5S IT3.

602 West Hastings Street, Vancouver 2, BC.

Australians should write to:

171 Clarence Street, Sydney, NSW 2000.

New Zealanders to:

Box 3655, 97 Taranki Street, Wellington.

And South Africans to:

Union-Castle Building, 36 Loveday Street, PO Box 6256, Johannesburg.
Union-Castle Building, 1st Floor, 51–5 St George's Street, Cape Town.

Every day people arrive at English points of entry, hoping to find work but without enough money in their pockets to support themselves. Many of those people, unless they have a work permit in their hands, are sent right back from where they came. These work permits are getting harder and harder to find and generally are only available to people who can fill jobs which British workers can't. If you do get one it applies only to one specific job.

Check it all out before you leave home!

Useful guides published by Vacation-Work, 9 Park End Street, Oxford OX1 1HJ, England, are: *Summer Jobs in Britain* and *Summer Jobs Abroad.*

● **Warning!** Beware of job-finding firms, particularly those which guarantee you work in the world's most exotic corners after they've received your £10 registration fee. Obviously not all – or even most – job-finding firms are crooked, but during the last few years there have been reports of fly-by-night operators who advertise heavily for a week, rake in the loot and are never heard of again.

The position – at the time of writing – is roughly this.

Austria

Work or resident permits are not required by citizens of the EC and other EEA countries. Nationals of any other countries need work and resident permits for all types of work, including *au pair* positions. Permits can only be applied for by the prospective employer in Austria. On principle, work permits are not granted to those on a visit to Austria. An excellent command of German is essential for any type of employment, apart from *au pair* work. Even then, work is very difficult to find as preference is given to locals, and to workers from neighbouring countries.

Students can obtain further information from:

OKISTA, Türkenstrasse 4, 1090 Wien, Austria.

Belgium

Work permits are not required by citizens of the EC and other EEA countries. Nationals of all other countries should possess a work permit before entering Belgium. Your employer must obtain the permit on your behalf, and then send it to you to present on your arrival in Belgium. For non-EEA nationals, work is hard to find.

Denmark

Work permits are not needed by nationals of the EC and other EEA countries, though they do require a residence permit for stays of longer than three months. Work permits are rarely issued to nationals of any other countries. Students can try writing to:

Danish International Students' Committee, 36 Skindergade, 1159 Copenhagen K, Denmark.

Egypt

Work permits are required if you wish to work in Egypt. However if you are in the country as a visitor, and you would like to stay for a longer period, working would certainly help to buy bread and butter. Teaching is a possibility, because so many people in Egypt wish to learn both conversational and business English. It is well worth contacting the following for fuller and further information:

British Council at 192 Corniche El Nil, Aquza, Cairo (tel: 345 3281).

Although this organization recruit their employees in the UK, vacancies do occur locally in Cairo and Alexandria with good rewards (by Egyptian standards) of E£1600 per month for a 24-hr week.

Another place worth a try, and also in Cairo, is:

International Language Learning Institute, c/o Mr Nadr Yechya, 9 Orman Villas, Dokki, Cairo. A second branch is located at Borg el Giza, El Kebly, Giza, Cairo (tel: 720431). It is believed that Mr Yechya can probably arrange a work permit for you.

There is also a possible opening in journalism with the English-language media in Egypt. *Cairo Today* (travel and photos) and the *Egyptian Gazette* (feature stories and sub-editing work).

Finland

Work permits are not required by nationals of the EC and other EEA countries, but citizens of all other countries should be in possession of a work permit before entering the country. Jobs are limited. For students, however, there is a fair chance of *au pair* work and also of entering the 'Family Scheme' programme where you live with a family, help with their daily work and also tutor them in the English language. For the latter there is free board and pocket money. Contact:

International Trainee Exchange of the Ministry of Labour, Kalevankatu 16, PL 524,00101 Helsinki 10, Finland.

France

Work permits are not needed by the citizens of the EC and other EEA countries, but are required by all other foreign nationals. You can take it as a basic rule that non-students *and* students must have a work permit before they enter France. However, occasionally this rule is relaxed and students (*only* students) are permitted to enter the country, seek employment and after having found it make application to the local Department of Work for a work permit. When you make this application you will need the following documents: (*1*) valid passport; (*2*) student identification card; (*3*) a letter from your university or college establishing your *full-time* student status; (*4*) a letter from your proposed employer which will state his intention to employ you; (*5*) (if you are a minor) a written permission from your parents allowing you to enter France and work, witnessed by a member of a French consulate or French embassy. Jobs are not easy to find but there is some work available.

Germany

Work permits are required by all those who are not nationals of the EC or other EEA countries. You may find jobs available on factory assembly lines, on building projects, in the hotels and catering trades . . . in short, in unskilled areas. If you are bilingual you may find office work, but this is rarer. *Au pair* work is available. To find work you should get in touch with:

Zentralstelle für Arbeitsvermittlung, Feuerbachstrasse 42, D-6000 Frankfurt am Main, Germany.

This is a government labour agency through which trades and businesses channel staff requests. The agency can put you in touch with possible employers. It will also give you full information on applying for a work permit.

Greece

Citizens of the EC and other EEA countries do not need a work permit. Nationals of other countries should be in possession of a work permit from their prospective employer before travelling to Greece. Further information from any Greek National Tourist Office or, in Greece, from:

Ministry of Labour, 45 Piraeus Street, Athens.

Ireland

Work permits are required by those who are not citizens of the EC or other EEA countries. You are supposed to find a job and have your employer apply for the work permit on your behalf before arriving in Ireland.

Israel

As we go to press, work permits must be obtained by your prospective employer before you enter the country, but contact the nearest Israel Tourist Office to make sure this remains true. The main work for young people is available on *kibbutzim*, or collective farms, for which you receive bed and board, the loan of work clothes and, maybe, about £10 per month pocket money. You may also receive free newspapers, cigarettes, aerogrammes, etc., depending on the *kibbutz*. You are expected to stay for at least a month. The work is, of course, mainly agricultural but sometimes in factories. The work will be boring, or dirty, or both, and basically you will do the work the *kibbutzniks* don't like but, in general, it is not too hard. You will meet volunteers from all over the world and probably make lasting friendships.

For full information, you should write before going to the Israeli government/*kibbutz* representative office in your country or, when applying in Israel, contact any of the following *kibbutzim* organizations:

Ichud Hakevutzot Vehakibbutzim, Hayarkon Street 53A, Tel Aviv.
Hakibbutz Hameuchad, Soutin Street 27, Tel Aviv.
Hakibbutz Ha'artzi, Leonardo da Vinci Street 13, Tel Aviv.
Hakibbutz Hadati, Dubnov Street 7, Tel Aviv.

Or try the Israel Student Tourist Association, Ben Yehuda Street 109, Tel Aviv, Israel.

People with letters of recommendation from the *kibbutz* representative in their own country will get preference at the *kibbutz* offices. The offices will place you only on *kibbutzim* belonging to their own organization, so, if one office can't fix you up, try one of the others. You will have to pay a registration fee/insurance premium of about £10, or show an insurance policy that covers you for accidents at work. Applying direct to a *kibbutz* is less certain. You will probably only get in if you know someone already there or if there is a shortage of volunteers.

For a whole book on *kibbutzim*, try: *Kibbutz Volunteer* by John Bedford, published by Vacation-Work, 9 Park End Street, Oxford OX1 1HJ, England.

An alternative to *kibbutzim* is the *moshav*, or cooperative farm. Work is harder and the hours are longer than on a *kibbutz*. You get paid about £140 worth of shekels a month, out of which you have to meet living expenses, so you won't get rich. The shekels are a drawback because it is difficult to convert them to hard currency. Your shekels rapidly lose their value with inflation in Israel at a couple of hundred per cent (and rising). How hard you work and your living conditions in general will depend on your farmer, and you will have more contact with the farmer than with other volunteers (it's the other way around on a *kibbutz*).

In Israel contact the Workers Moshavim Movement, Leonardo da Vinci Street 19, Tel Aviv.

There are opportunities for black work in the hotels and bars of Eilat, Jerusalem and Tel Aviv. But there is a lot of competition from West Bank Arabs and the pay is bad, so you'll probably just make enough to live on.

Italy

Work permits are not required by nationals of the EC and other EEA countries. For others it is very difficult and you almost certainly can't take a job which could be satisfactorily filled by an Italian citizen. If you manage to find something your employer will have to get you a permit before you actually start working. For *au pairs* things are brighter. One address to contact with enquiries about *au pair* work is:

Au Pairs–Italy, 46 The Rise, Sevenoaks, Kent TN13 1RJ.

Luxembourg

Work permits are not needed by citizens of the EC and other EEA countries. Others who hope to work in Luxembourg should find a prospective employer, who in turn will obtain the necessary work permit from the Administration de l'Emploi before you enter the country.

Netherlands

Citizens of the EC and other EEA countries do not require work permits. For others it is difficult. Also, you must have your work permit in hand as you enter the country. Not much work available, though some *au pair*, and picking and packing bulbs. Students might manage to find something temporary by contacting:

Studenten Werkbureau Amsterdam, Koniginneweg 184a, Amsterdam.

Norway

Work permits are required by all foreign nationals, except those from the EC and other EEA countries. Those needing work permits must get them prior to arriving in Norway. After finding a job you must apply to your nearest Norwegian embassy for the permit, which can take up to three months to come through. Embassies can't find a job for you, but they may be able to supply lists of companies looking for staff. The best employment prospects are in the fish-processing and hotel and catering sectors. Students interested in working on Norwegian farms for bed and board with some pocket money should contact:

Norwegian Committee for International Information and Youth Work, Akersgate 57, Oslo 1, Norway.

Portugal

Citizens of the EC and other EEA countries do not need a work permit. They do need a residence permit, but once you have the documentation confirming employment this is issued as a matter of course. Nationals of all other countries must obtain a work permit from the Ministry of Labour for all jobs intended to last longer than 30 days. For shorter term jobs the written permission of the Ministry of Labour is necessary. Because of the low wage scale, if you do get a job you can't expect to earn enough to more than tick over, so don't expect to fund a few months travelling from working in Portugal.

Spain

While citizens of the EC and other EEA countries do not require work permits, nationals of all other countries must obtain these through their prospective employers who will make the necessary arrangements with the Ministry of Labour. Work permits are rarely issued if the job could just as easily be done by a Spaniard. Given the current high rate of unemployment in Spain this means that work opportunities for non-EC nationals are severely restricted. Outside of jobs teaching English or some jobs in the tourist industry there isn't much on offer.

Students requiring information on vacation work should write to:

Spanish Union of Students, Bolsa Universitaria de Trabajo, Glorieta de Quevedo 8, Madrid 8.

Sweden

Citizens of the EC and other EEA countries do not require a work permit, but a residence permit must be obtained for stays of longer than three months. Nationals of other countries should obtain a work permit before entering the country, for which you will need documented proof that you have a job, and somewhere to live.

For information on job possibilities, write to:

International Association for the Exchange of Students for Technical Experience, Imperial College, London SW7, UK.

or:

Arbetsmarknadsstyrelsen, Fack, S-17199 Solna, Sweden.

Switzerland

Unlike the other EFTA countries, Switzerland is not part of the recently established European Economic Area (EEA), which means that foreign nationals still need work permits for all types of work. Work permits must be obtained prior to travelling to Switzerland. Job opportunities for foreigners are limited. Best bets are hotels, *au pair* work, and temporary grape-picking jobs.

For good information about working in Europe you should buy the annual *Directory of Summer Jobs Abroad*, published by Vacation-Work, 9 Park End Street, Oxford. This excellent book gives up-to-date work permit and visa information plus long lists of companies and organizations seeking staff.

For people who want good, steady (rather than casual) work outside the British Isles, the best thing to do is to check the classified advertisements in London newspapers like the *Observer* and *The Times* or an international paper like the Paris edition of the *Herald Tribune*.

If you are in a particular country and in need of a job, one trick is to check out the local English language papers. They flourish where there are big tourist populations. For instance, in Spain there are at least four, all of which carry classified advertisements, some of which offer work. They are *Lookout* magazine which covers the Costa del Sol, and a rather strange little daily paper called the *Iberian Sun* which is available in most large cities, the *Costa Blanca News* covering the Costa Blanca and the *Majorca Daily Bulletin* covering the Balearics.

The type of work offered by advertisements in these papers is usually for secretaries or translators. Anyone who can type, take shorthand and who is completely fluent in a second language stands a chance of finding a job on the Continent. Anyone who is fluent in a second language and who is a qualified professional worker also stands a chance.

It's a good idea, when coming to Europe, to bring any documents you have proving your qualifications and experience in your field.

Many hitchers find their way into the movies as extras. Pay may be as much as £25 a day (considerably more if you can con someone into giving you a line to speak) and you might get work in a crowd scene for five to six days.

The main centres for film work at the moment are Madrid, Rome and London (London being well tied up by the unions).

You never know when this type of work is coming up. If you're interested, keep your ears open – there's usually someone in the hostels who knows what's happening.

Of course it's possible to find odd jobs in just about any European country if you're in the right place at the right time and if the employer takes a liking to you. For instance, in the summer there is limited (repeat *limited*) bar work available for pretty girls in most of the tourist resort areas – the Costa del Sol and Costa Brava in Spain, the Algarve and Costa do Sol area in Portugal, the French and Italian rivieras, etc. Also there is grape harvesting in southern France (Hérault) and southern Germany (Mosel valley) in September and October. Most of this work is of a very temporary nature and badly paid. You'll make enough to live on but not enough to build up your roll. You and your employer may be breaking the law, but you'll probably get away with it. (Don't write to me if you don't.)

There are other ways of picking up money. Plenty of hitchers make a living with their guitars either playing in the street or in clubs or restaurants where they receive food, a percentage of the take on drinks and/or tips.

Another way, particularly in Paris where the cops seem to be fairly easygoing towards down-and-outs, is to join up with pavement artists. Get yourself a packet of chalks and make a huge abstract on the pavement and wait hopefully for the pennies to fall. Of course if you're a trained artist who is capable of making really good chalk drawings, your chances of making some bread are tripled.

Some people carry silver wire and pliers in their pack and make simple jewellery to sell on sidewalks or in outdoor markets. Plenty of hitchers pick up objects in one country (e.g. beads in Morocco) to sell in the next. One hitcher makes £1 a time by cutting paper silhouettes of people or animals. Another makes simple puppets out of scrap found on the side of the road which he sells for as much as £3. I've seen a hitcher stage a quick magic show with handkerchiefs and lengths of rope while his wife passed a hat and kept an eye out for the police.

Straight-out begging is another way but the cops from any country are hard down on that. But if you're really broke you might be forced to do it. If so, be persistent and expect plenty of abuse. You might get enough for a feed which will fortify you enough so that you can think of another idea.

Hitchers' Tips and Comments . . .

If you're down in Greece and Italy and in need of money or food make for a big port and approach one of the charter boats. They're always after crew, and even if you don't know about boats you can usually bluff your way to a job. You get free food, a lot of nautical miles, a few quid a week and a handful of blisters. Appearance isn't very important, but too much hair can lose you the better jobs.

It's nearly always possible to get a very temporary job as a kitchen porter (glorified pot washer) in both France and the UK without a permit. In small French cafés, you usually get just food. In big hotels, a lot more work, but food *and* pay. In UK seaside towns in peak summer season cafés and hotels aren't too particular who works for them. You get money, food and sometimes a bed, which is good for a week's recuperation. Also in the UK fruit and potato picking jobs are available. Badly paid but good for a laugh and a kip.

Cheers and good hitching. CLIVE GILL, BIRCHINGTON, ENGLAND

By profession I am a charter boat skipper. My boat is moored at Monte Carlo. I noticed in your book a couple of references to working on charter boats. I'd like to point out to would-be 'sailors' that unless they have papers, work is very hard to find. Bluffing your way into a job, like Clive Gill did, will nine times out of ten lead to a black eye from an irate skipper who suddenly finds himself shorthanded because he's carrying a man who knows nothing about boats. Some skippers I've known have been so mad they've dumped the offender on deserted coastlines miles from civilization!

Anyway, if any readers are qualified and seriously interested, best places to hunt jobs are Antibes, Cannes, Beaulieu-sur-Mer, Monte Carlo (both old and new ports), Cros-de-Cagnes, Villeneuve-Loubet-Plage and La Napoule. April and May are the best times of the year, but also check with skippers during summer. Gibraltar is good from September onwards for boats sailing to the Caribbean and then on to the United States.

CAPTAIN M. J. WIATER, RNR, MONTE CARLO, FRANCE

For grape-picking in Germany, go to Bingen, a small town on the Rhine, south of Koblenz, and report to the local job centre.

GREGOR MURPHY, PAISLEY, SCOTLAND

Since I've taken to tramping these last few years I can give a couple of hints on how to keep going financially. Winter – December until

April or May – is no time for travelling. But in Switzerland you can work these months in hotels or for ski-lifts. You get good sleeping quarters, time enough for a bit of skiing and you can save enough to tramp the other months of the year. The Swiss newspaper *Hotel-Revue* lists all open hotel jobs in the country . . . jobs like porter, chauffeur, etc. For ski-lift work it's a good idea to ask at ski-lift offices in each resort town. It's best to locate your job and sign a contract around October. (Then you can move down to Greece and lap up some sun before winter sets in and you have to start work.) Hotels and ski-lifts will arrange work permits – but step one is to find the job.

Aside from tramping it's fun and exciting to crew along on sail-boats (if you've got a good stomach). It's possible to go to ports on the south coast of England (Ramsgate, Gosport, Cowes, Plymouth, Lymington) on weekends and bum rides.

Or for the more adventurous, boats often leave Gosport for France, Spain and other Mediterranean ports. Often this leads to a job as a paid hand. A few summers ago I bummed lifts on boats for four months and ended up fifty quid ahead!

STEVE BLUME, CHICAGO, USA

I've found if you're really broke a travelling circus is usually happy to pick you up. You get great food, a little money (lots of hard work!) and the chance to mix with truly fantastic people. I've done it twice and both times I just hated to leave.

JAMES DALY, DUBLIN, IRELAND

For grape-picking work in Germany, go to Altzey, not far from Mainz, during the season. I got a fair wage plus free food and lodgings.

TRUE BRIT, CHELMSFORD, ENGLAND

The address you give for working in Germany is no good unless you're a student writing from abroad. If you're already in Germany it is best to go to the local Arbeitsamt (Employment Office), the address of which can be found in the phone book. These offices have severely restricted opening hours and are staffed with hostile civil servants who are rude and unhelpful, and very often they don't like foreigners. Some will refuse to deal with you unless you speak in German. If your German is poor or non-existent you will probably get washing-up jobs, though you will do better if you have some sort of trade. Having got your job your problems are just beginning as you have to tackle the bureaucracy involved in getting a residence permit, without which you cannot have a Lohnsteuerkarte (tax card), without which you will pay the top rate of tax. At all stages deny having a religion unless you want to pay an extra church tax. If you find black work, you will have none of this trouble.

ALAN BARLOW, CHEADLE, UK

Regarding work in Norway. Plenty of fruit-picking jobs around the Hardanger Fjord region. You can begin with strawberries in July, and continue with cherries, plums, apples and pears through September.

Some work on Crete, picking olives and oranges. Head up to the smaller villages around early November and start asking around.

SUPERTRAMP SCHWARM, EAU CLAIRE, WISCONSIN, USA

AMSTERDAM: If stuck for work try the Heineken Brewery – mostly donkey work.

ROTTERDAM: Try the dockyards. It stinks, it's smelly and bloody hard graft. But pay is amazing, depending on hours.

A. P. KIK, MIDDLESBROUGH, TEESSIDE, UK

13 · PHOTOGRAPHY

Whether you're a serious amateur with a £200 SLR or a happy snapper with a £5 secondhand Instamatic, you'll probably be putting up with the extra weight of a camera in your pack to record your European hitch-trip.

For better pictures – especially if you've taken very few before – there are some simple hints you can follow:

1. Make sure you remove the lens cap before shooting. (If you don't you don't get any pictures!)
2. Keep your picture edges straight. Do this by lining up some vertical in the scene with the side of your viewfinder.
3. Don't jerk your camera when you shoot a picture or the snap will be blurred. You can avoid camera-shake by keeping one foot forward of the other and by holding the weight of the camera in the left hand so that the right is free to squeeze the shutter carefully. Practise squeezing the shutter when your camera is empty.
4. If you own a non-automatic camera with a built-in lightmeter and you know nothing about the operation of cameras and lightmeters, here are some very basic rules. *(a)* If you are snapping a general view with the sky in it, point your camera slightly down towards the ground so that you eliminate *most* of the sky from the meter eye. *Now* set your camera according to the maker's instructions. You do this because there is more light reflected from the sky than there is from the ground and, presumably, you want a correct exposure for the landscape. *(b)* If you want to photograph the sky (a sunset or cloud formation) or make a silhouette, then you disregard rule *(a)* and take your reading from the sky, usually to one side of the sun in case of sunrise and sunset pictures. *(c)* If you are taking pictures in the whitewashed villages of Spain, Italy, Greece, etc., then remember that the white walls reflect more light than the rest of the scene. If you aim your camera at an old lady sitting by a white wall, your meter will read the brightness of the wall and your old lady will come out too dark. What you must do is always take a reading from the subject you wish to photograph. If you can't go close enough to someone to measure the light on them, place your hand between six and nine inches in front of the camera meter eye so that the same light falls on your hand as on your subject, and take a reading from your own skin-tone.
5. If you own an automatic camera with no manual override, the

only control you have over exposure is via the ASA (or DIN) rating ring. If you think the general scene is reflecting more light than the subject you want exposed correctly, then try under-rating your film. For example, if you are using 100 ASA film and your ASA ring is set on 100 ASA, simply turn the ring back until it reads 50 ASA. The trick *might* work. (Don't forget to put it back in the right place for subsequent shots.) Only try it if you are using transparency film which needs critical exposure. If you're using negative film just leave the ring where it's supposed to be. The laboratory will probably make an automatic adjustment when they print your pictures.

6. If you're photographing sports, like skiing, car-racing, etc., remember that unless you have a sophisticated camera with very high speeds $^{1}/_{500}$th of a second or better), you cannot stop action going directly across your viewfinder – it will be blurred. Try to position yourself so that the car or skier is travelling at an angle towards you. If you can't, pan your camera with the action as you take the picture.
7. If you're photographing people, don't be afraid to approach them for a close-up. Most people don't mind, or if they do they'll simply say no. (But Moslem Arabs have a habit of getting very angry about cameras. They believe that the camera is capturing their spirit as well as their image.)
8. Don't keep film in your pocket for any length of time. Your body warmth can affect its colour balance. Keep the film in its container and keep the container in a side-pocket of your pack where there is some air circulation. Keep colour film away from the sun.
9. Always load and unload your camera in the shade. If there is none, turn your back to the sun and unload in your own shadow. This is to minimize the chance of light getting to the film and fogging it.
10. If you carry your camera in your pack, wrap it in a dry towel or shirt to protect it as much as possible from knocks and from car vibration which can loosen screws.

● **Film** Colour film prices in some countries are exorbitant. In Spain and France, for instance, they'll break your budget. Switzerland, Andorra and Britain are good places to buy film. In Britain, make sure you go to a discount place. Boots (the chemist shops) seem to offer a good deal. Major photo-shop chains are usually cheaper again. Always try and buy all the film you need in a large city where prices are competitive – outside the cities you can pay 20% more. In Mediterranean countries never buy film anywhere except in a photo shop – if you do you'll be paying too much and it may have been sitting in the window in sunlight thus altering its colour balance. If you're broke buy out-of-date film *from camera shops only* (because they store film correctly). You can usually get it at half price! Look for the expiry dates on the side of the boxes and buy the films which have just gone over their dates. Always look at the date when you buy a film. If the film is out of date tell the salesman and ask for a discount.

14 · WEIGHTS AND MEASURES

Miles/kilometres

A kilometre is roughly 6/10ths of a mile, so for a quick estimate multiply the number of kilometres by 6 and move the decimal point one place to the left (212 kilometres × 6 = 1272. Insert decimal point one place to left = 127.2 miles).

km	*miles/km*	*miles*
1.609	1	0.621
16.093	10	6.214
160.930	100	62.136
804.650	500	310.680
1609.300	1000	621.360

Pounds/kilograms

There are roughly 2.2 pounds to a kilogram.

kg	*lb/kg*	*lb*
0.453	1	2.205
0.907	2	4.409
1.360	3	6.614
1.814	4	8.818
2.268	5	11.023

Litres/gallons

For a rough calculation figure $4^1/_2$ litres to the British imperial gallon. The American gallon is slightly less than 4 litres.

litres	*gallons/ litres*	gallons
4.55	1	0.22
22.73	5	1.10
45.66	10	2.20

Pounds per square inch/kilograms per square centimetre

lb per sq in	*kg per sq cm*	*lb per sq in*	*kg per sq cm*
18	1.266	35	2.461
20	1.406	36	2.531
22	1.547	39	2.742
25	1.758	40	2.812
29	2.039	42	2.953
32	2.250	43	3.023

Pounds per square inch/kilograms per square centimetre

lb per sq in	*kg per sq in*	*lb per sq in*	*kg per sq cm*
45	3.164	50	2.515
46	3.234	60	4.218

Equivalent sizes

women's clothing sizes

British	36	38	40	42	44	46
American	34	36	38	40	42	44
Continental	42	44	46	48	50	52

men's suits and overcoats

British and American	36	38	40	42	44	46
Continental	46	48	50	52	54	56

shirts

British and American	14	14½	15	15½	16	16½	17
Continental	36	37	38	39	41	42	43

stockings

British and American	8	8½	9	9½	10	10½
Continental	0	1	2	3	4	5

socks

British and American	9½	10	10½	11	11½
Continental	38/39	39/40	40/41	41/42	42/43

shoes

British and American	3	4	5	6	7	8	9	10
Continental	36	37	38	39	41	42	43	44

Continental glove sizes are the same as in Britain and America

Fahrenheit/Centrigrade

The general rule for the conversion of Centigrade into Fahrenheit is to multiply by 9/5ths and add 32. To translate Fahrenheit into Centigrade, subtract 32 and multiply by 5/9ths.

15 · LANGUAGE

The vocabulary in this language section has been kept as concise as possible for a very simple reason. When you can't speak a language and have no intention of learning it, the fewer words you have to play with the better. All you need are the basic words of survival and politeness. ('Thank you' is undoubtedly the first phrase you should memorize in any language.)

Even this ultra-simple list could cause you problems. Example? You're in Toledo and you want to go to Madrid, so you walk up to a fellow and say: '*Por favor, dónde está la carretera para Madrid?*' You say it so nicely that the fellow thinks you can speak Spanish, so he rattles off his answer: '*Pues, tiene que andar por la carretera unos dos kilómetros y medio más o menos, entonces tome Usted la primera bocacalle a la derecha . . . mire! si quiere le llevo en mi coche, es más sencillo*!' From there on in you'd better think awful fast because if this guy is in a hurry, odds are you're going to miss out on the ride up to the Madrid road which he just offered you!

The list has also been designed to help you on your way with emergencies and, as well, I hope you'll find enough words in here to allow you to carry on a bit of 'pidgin' smalltalk with just about anyone. Be patient!

Rich hitchers should check out electronic translators. They are the same size as calculators and come in several language configurations. Some have, say, 15,000 words of Spanish and English. Others have 3,000 words of English, French, German, Italian and Spanish. Others have Dutch thrown in. Many have calculator functions, a small data storage bank (for telephone numbers, passport numbers etc), and currency, weights and measure converters.

Bi-lingual machines are best if you plan to spend all your time in one country, but if you are wandering, obviously the more languages your machine has the better. You can enter a word in any language and then have instant access to that word in all languages. Fantastic way to learn the essentials. And you have your own portable language laboratory to amuse you when you're waiting for that ride that never comes.

1 'ch' is guttural, from the back of the throat, as in the Scots 'loch'.

2 To persistent beggars asking for money

French

English	*French*	*pronounced*
thank you	merci	*mair-see*
please	s'il vous plaît	*sil voo play*
good morning	bonjour	*bon-joor*
goodbye	au revoir	*oh re-vwahr*
yes	oui	*wee*
no	non	*noh*
I am . . .	je suis . . .	*jer swee*
are you going to . . . ?	allez-vous vers . . . ?	*allay voo ver*
where is . . . ?	où est . . . ?	*oo eh*
the road to . . .	la route pour . . .	*la root poor*
the toilet	le lavabo	*lu la-va-boh*
the youth hostel	l'auberge de jeunesse	*ohberge de-jerness*
the station	la gare	*la gar*
I would like . . .	je voudrais . . .	*jer voo-dray*
to eat	manger	*mon-zhay*
a room	une chambre	*oon shombre*
how much?	combien?	*kohm-biyen*
when?	quand?	*kon*
left	gauche	*gohshe*
right	droit	*dwar*
straight ahead	tout droit	*too dwar*
yesterday	hier	*ee-yeh*
today	aujourd'hui	*oh-joor-dwee*
tomorrow	demain	*derman*
1	un	*urn*
2	deux	*der*
3	trois	*twah*
4	quatre	*catre*
5	cinq	*sank*
6	six	*sees*
7	sept	*set*
8	huit	*weet*
9	neuf	*nerf*
10	dix	*dees*
11	onze	*onz*
12	douze	*dooz*
13	treize	*traiz*
14	quatorze	*ka-torz*

English	*French*	*pronounced*
15	quinze	*kanze*
16	seize	*seyz*
17	dix-sept	*dees-set*
18	dix-huit	*dees-weet*
19	dix-neuf	*dees-nerf*
20	vingt	*van*
30	trente	*trarnt*
40	quarante	*kar-rarnt*
50	cinquante	*san-karnt*
60	soixante	*swah-sant*
70	soixante-dix	*swah-sant dees*
80	quatre-vingts	*catre van*
90	quatre-vingt-dix	*catre van dees*
100	cent	*sonn*
1000	mille	*meel*

Shopping
Apples – *pommes*. Aspirins – *aspirines*. – Bananas – *bananes*. Bandages – *pansements*. Beer – *bière*. Biscuits – *biscuits*. Blouse – *chemisier*. Boots – *bottes*. Bread – *pain*. Cheese – *fromage*. Chocolate – *chocolat*. Coffee – *café*. Dress – *robe*. Egg – *oeuf*. Fish – *poisson*. Fruit – *fruit*. Jacket – *veston* (men's), *veste* (ladies'). Meat – *viande*. Milk – *lait*. Mineral water – *eau minérale*. Oranges – *oranges*. Potatoes – *pommes de terre*. Salt – *sel*. Sandwich – *sandwich*. Sausage – *saucisse*. Shirt – *chemise*. Shoes – *souliers*. Skirt – *jupe*. Soup – *potage*. Socks – *chaussettes*. Sticking plaster – *sparadrap*. Sugar – *sucre*. Sweater – *tricot*. Tea – *thé*. Trousers – *pantalon*. Vegetables – *légumes*. Water – *eau*. Wine – *vin*.

German

English	*German*	*pronounced*
thank you	danke schön	*dan-ker-shun*
please	bitte	*bit-teh*
good morning	guten Tag	*goo-ten-targ*
goodbye	auf Wiedersehen	*ouf-weeder-zen*
yes	ja	*yah*
no	nein	*nine*
I am . . .	Ich bin . . .	*ik bin*

English	*German*	*pronounced*
are you going to . . . ?	gehen Sie nach . . . ?	*gay-en-see nark*
where is . . . ?	wo ist . . . ?	*vo eest*
the road to . . .	der Weg nach . . .	*der veg nark*
the toilet	die Toilette	*de twarlet-tuh*
the youth hostel	die Jugendherberge	*de you-gend-er-berga*
the station	der Bahnhof	*der barn-hof*
I would like . . .	Ich möchte	*ik mersh-ta*
to eat	essen	*ess-en*
a room	ein Zimmer	*ein tsimmer*
how much?	wie viel?	*vee-feel*
when?	wann?	*varn*
left	links	*leenks*
right	rechts	*reckts*
straight ahead	geradeaus	*gay-ray-day-ous*
yesterday	gestern	*guess-tern*
today	heute	*hoy-tuh*
tomorrow	morgen	*mor-gen*
1	eins	*eintz*
2	zwei	*tzvai*
3	drei	*dry*
4	vier	*feer*
5	fünf	*funf*
6	sechs	*zex*
7	sieben	*zee-ben*
8	acht	*arkt*
9	neun	*noyn*
10	zehn	*tzain*
11	elf	*elf*
12	zwölf	*tzwuhlf*
13	dreizehn	*drytzain*
14	vierzehn	*feertzain*
15	fünfzehn	*funfzain*
16	sechzehn	*zextzain*
17	siebzehn	*zeebtzain*
18	achtzehn	*arktzain*
19	neunzehn	*noyntzain*
20	zwanzig	*tzvahntzig*
30	dreissig	*dry-tzig*
40	vierzig	*feer-tzig*
50	fünfzig	*funf-tzig*
60	sechzig	*zex-tzig*

English	*German*	*pronounced*
70	siebzig	*zeeb-tzig*
80	achtzig	*ark-tzig*
90	neunzig	*noyn-tzig*
100	hundert	*hoon-dert*
1000	tausend	*tow-sent*

Shopping
Apples – *Apfel*. Aspirins – *Aspirin*. Bananas – *Bananen*. Bandages – *Verbandszeug*. Beer – *Bier*. Biscuits – *Plätzchen*. Blouse – *Bluse*. Boots – *Stiefel*. Bread – *Brot*. Cheese – *Käse*. Chocolate – *Schokolade*. Coffee – *Kaffee*. Dress – *Kleid*. Egg – *Ei*. Fish – *Fische*. Fruit – *Obst*. Jacket – *Jacke*. Meat – *Fleisch*. Milk – *Milch*. Mineral water – *Mineralwasser*. Oranges – *Apfelsinen*. Potatoes – *Kartoffeln*. Salt – *Salz*. Sandwich – *Belegtes Brötchen*. Sausage – *Wurst*. Shirt – *Hemd*. Shoes – *Schuhe*. Skirt – *Rock*. Soup – *Suppe*. Socks – *Socken*. Sticking plaster – *Heftpflaster*. Sugar – *Zucker*. Sweater – *Pullover*. Tea – *Tee*. Trousers – *Hosen*. Vegetables – *Gemüse*. Water – *Wasser*. Wine – *Wein*.

Spanish

English	*Spanish*	*pronounced*
thank you	gracias	*grar-thee-ahs*
hello	hola	*hola ol-ah*
goodbye	adiós	*ah-dee-os*
yes	sí	*see*
no	no	*noh*
I am . . .	yo soy . . .	*yo-soy*
are you going to . . . ?	va usted a . . . ?	*vah-oosted a*
where is . . . ?	dónde está . . . ?	*donday estah*
the road to . . .	la carretera para . . .	*lar car-ray-tera parah*
the toilet	el retrete	*el raytraytay*
the youth hostel	el albergue juvenil	*el-al-ber-goh hoovay-neel*
the station	la estación	*la ay-star-thee-on*
I would like . . .	querría . . .	*kerr-eeya*
to eat	comer	*com-mayr*
a room	una habitación	*oona ahbee-tah-thee-on*

English	*Spanish*	*pronounced*
how much?	cuánto?	*kwon-toe*
when?	cuándo?	*kwon-doe*
left	izquierda	*eeth-key-air-dah*
right	derecha	*day-ray-cha*
straight ahead	todo derecho	*toh-doh day-ray-choh*
yesterday	ayer	*a-yer*
today	hoy	*oy*
tomorrow	mañana	*marn-yar-nar*
1	uno	*oo-no*
2	dos	*dos*
3	tres	*tress*
4	cuatro	*kwat-tro*
5	cinco	*thin-ko*
6	seis	*sais*
7	siete	*see-ay-tay*
8	ocho	*o-choh*
9	nueve	*noo-ay-vay*
10	iez	*dee-eth*
11	once	*on-thay*
12	doce	*do-thay*
13	trece	*tray-thay*
14	catorce	*ca-tor-thay*
15	quince	*keen-thay*
16	dieciseis	*dee-eth-ee-sais*
17	diecisiete	*dee-eth-ee-see-ay-tay*
18	dieciocho	*dee-eth-ee-o-choh*
19	diecinueve	*dee-eth-ee-noo-ay-vay*
20	veinte	*vain-tay*
30	treinta	*train-ta*
40	cuarenta	*kwa-renta*
50	cincuenta	*thin-kwenta*
60	sesenta	*say-senta*
70	setenta	*say-tenta*
80	ochenta	*o-chenta*
90	noventa	*no-venta*
100	cien	*thee-en*
500	quinientos	*keen-nee-entos*
1000	mil	*meel*

Shopping

Apples – *manzanas*. Aspirins – *aspirinas*. Bananas – *plátanos*. Bandages – *vendajes*. Beer – *cerveza*. Biscuits – *galletas*. Blouse – *blusa*. Boots –

botas. Bread – *pan*. Cheese – *queso*. Chocolate – *chocolate*. Coffee – *café*. Dress – *vestido*. Egg – *huevo*. Fish – *pescado*. Fruit – *fruta*. Jacket – *chaqueta*. Meat – *carne*. Milk – *leche*. Mineral water – *agua mineral*. Oranges – *naranjas*. Potatoes – *patatas*. Salt – *sal*. Sandwich – *bocadillo*. Sausage – *Salchicha*. Shirt – *camisa*. Shoes – *zapatos*. Skirt – *falda*. Soup – *sopa*. Socks – *cálcetines*. Sticking plaster – *esparadrapo*. Sugar – *azúcar*. Sweater – *suéter*. Tea – *té*. Trousers – *pantalones*. Vegetables – *verduras*. Water – *agua*. Wine – *vino*.

Hebrew (Israel)

English	*Hebrew (pronounced as written)*
good morning	Boker Tov
hello/Goodbye	Shalom
how are you?	Ma Shlomcha[1]
thank you.	Toda Raba
please	Bevakasha
waiter	Meltzar
breakfast	Aruchat-boker
water	Mayim
knife	Sakin
egg	Beytza
sugar	Sukar
I want	Ani Rotze
to drink	Lishtot
juice	Mitz
jam	Riba
a roll	Lachmania
bread	Lechem
coffee	Kafe
tea	Te
table	Shulchan
chair	Kise
plate	Tsalachat
glass	Koss
cup	Sefel
bill (as in cafe)	Cheshbon
1	Achat
2	Shtayim

1 'ch' is guttural, from the back of the throat, as in the Scots 'loch'.

English	*Hebrew (pronounced as written)*
3	Shalosh
4	Arba
5	Chamesh
6	Shesh
7	Sheva
8	Shmone
9	Tesha
10	Esser
100	Mea
1000	Elef

Italian

English	*Italian*	*pronounced*
thank you	grazie	*grah-tzyeh*
please	per piacere	*pairr pee-ah-chay-ary*
good morning	buon giorno	*bwon-dior-no*
goodbye	arrivederci	*ar-reev-e-derch-ee*
yes	si	*see*
no	no	*noh*
I am . . .	io sono . . .	*yo sohno*
are you going to . . . ?	va lei a . . . ?	*vah lay-ee a*
where is . . . ?	dov'è . . . ?	*doh-vay*
the road to . . .	l'autostrada . . .	*l'otoh-stra-dah*
the toilet	il gabinetto	*eel ga-bee-naytoh*
the youth hostel	l'albergo per giovani	*l'albairgo per joh-vah-nee*
the station	la stazione	*la stah-tzyohnay*
I would like . . .	vorrei . . .	*vorr-ay-ee*
to eat	mangiare	*mahn-diah-ray*
a room	una camera	*oona kah-may-rah*
how much?	quanto?	*kwan-toh*
when?	quando?	*kwan-doh*
left	sinistra	*see-nee-strah*
right	destra	*dess-trah*
straight ahead	tutto diretto	*too-toh dee-ret-toh*

English	*Italian*	*pronounced*
yesterday	ieri	*ee-yay-ree*
today	oggi	*oh-djee*
tomorrow	domani	*doh-mar-nee*
1	uno	*oo-no*
2	due	*doo-ay*
3	tre	*tray*
4	quattro	*kwat-tro*
5	cinque	*cheen-kway*
6	sei	*say-ee*
7	sette	*set-tay*
8	otto	*aw-toh*
9	nove	*noh-vay*
10	dieci	*dee-ay-chee*
11	undici	*oon-dee-chee*
12	dodici	*doh-dee-chee*
13	tredici	*tray-dee-chee*
14	quattordici	*kwat-torr-dee-chee*
15	quindici	*kween-dee-chee*
16	sedici	*say-dee-chee*
17	diciassette	*deeh-cheeah-set-tay*
18	diciotto	*dee-chiot-toh*
19	diciannove	*dee-cheeah-noh-vay*
20	venti	*vayn-tee*
30	trenta	*trayn-ta*
40	quaranta	*kwah-rahn-ta*
50	cinquanta	*cheen-kwahn-ta*
60	sessanta	*sais-sarn-ta*
70	settanta	*set-tan-ta*
80	ottanta	*ot-tan-ta*
90	novanta	*no-van-ta*
100	cento	*chayn-to*
1000	mille	*mee-lay*

Shopping

Apples – *mele*. Aspirins – *aspirina*. Bananas – *banane*. Bandages – *fascia*. Beer – *birra*. Biscuits – *biscotti*. Blouse – *blusa*. Boots – *stivali*. Bread – *pane*. Cheese – *formaggio*. Chocolate – *cioccolata*. Coffee – *caffè*. Dress – *abito*. Egg – *uovo*. Fish – *pesce*. Fruit – *frutta*. Jacket – *giacchetta*. Meat – *carne*. Milk – *latte*. Mineral water – *acqua minerale*. Oranges – *aranci*. Potatoes – *patate*. Salt – *sale*. Sandwich – *panino*.

Sausage – *salsiccia*. Shirt – *camicia*. Shoes – *scarpe*. Skirt – *gonna*. Soup – *zuppa*. Socks – *calzini*. Sticking plaster – *cerotto*. Sugar – *zucchero*. Sweater – *maglione*. Tea – *tè*. Trousers – *calzoni*. Vegetables – *legumi*. Water – *acqua*. Wine – *vino*.

Dutch

English	*Dutch*	*pronounced*
thank you	dank U	*dahnk yu*
please	alstublieft	*als-too-bleeft*
hello	hallo	*hah-loh*
goodbye	daag	*dahk*
yes	ja	*yay*
no	nee	*nay*
I am . . .	ik ben . . .	*ick ben*
are you going to . . . ?	gaat U naar . . . ?	*haht yu nahr*
where is . . . ?	waar is . . . ?	*vahr iss*
the road to . . .	de weg nar . . .	*der veg nahr*
the toilet	het toilet	*het twa-let*
the youth hostel	de jeugdherberg	*der yugd-hair-berk*
the station	het station	*het sta-si-on*
I would like . . .	ik wil graag . . .	*ick vil grahg*
to eat	eten	*ay-ten*
a room	een kamer	*ayn ka-mer*
how much?	hoe veel?	*hu vehl*
when?	wanneer?	*wannair*
left	links	*links*
right	rechts	*rekts*
straight ahead	rechtdoor	*rekts-door*
yesterday	gisteren	*hist-erun*
today	vandaag	*fan-dak*
tomorrow	morgen	*morghen*
1	één	*ayn*
2	twee	*tvay*
3	drie	*dree*
4	vier	*feer*
5	vijf	*fife*
6	zes	*zess*
7	zeven	*zeh-ven*
8	acht	*ahkht*
9	negen	*neh-khen*

English	*Dutch*	*pronounced*
10	tien	*teen*
11	elf	*aylf*
12	twaalf	*twahlf*
13	dertien	*dehr-teen*
14	veertien	*feer-teen*
15	vijftien	*fife-teen*
16	zestien	*zess-teen*
17	zeventien	*zeh-ven-teen*
18	achttien	*ahkht-teen*
19	negentien	*neh-khen-teen*
20	twintig	*tvintihk*
30	dertig	*dare-tihk*
40	veertig	*fare-tihk*
50	vijftig	*fife-tihk*
60	zestig	*zess-tihk*
70	zeventig	*zeh-ven-tihk*
80	tachtig	*tahk-tihk*
90	negentig	*neh-khen-tihk*
100	honderd	*hohn-dert*
1000	duizend	*doy-zent*

Shopping

Apples – *appels*. Aspirins – *aspirines*. Bananas – *bananen*. Bandages – *verband*. Beer – *bier*. Biscuits – *koekjes*. Blouse – *bloes*. Boots – *laarzen*. Bread – *brood*. Cheese – *kaas*. Chocolate – *chocolade*. Coffee – *koffie*. Dress – *jurk*. Egg – *ei*. Fish – *vis*. Fruit – *fruit*. Jacket – *jack*. Meat – *vlees*. Milk – *melk*. Mineral water – *mineraal water*. Oranges – *sinaasappelen*. Potatoes – *aardappelen*. Salt – *zout*. Sandwich – *belegd broodje*. Sausage – *worst*. Shirt – *overhemd*. Shoes – *schoenen*. Skirt – *rok*. Socks – *sokken*. Soup – *soep*. Sticking plaster – *hechtpleister*. Sugar – *suiker*. Sweater – *trui*. Tea – *thee*. Trousers – *broek*. Vegetables – *groenten*. Water – *water*. Wine – *wijn*.

Swedish

English	*Swedish*	*pronounced*
thank you	tack	*tahck*
please	var snäll och	*vahr snel ok*
hello	hallo	*hal-loh*
goodbye	adjö	*ah-yuh*
yes	ja	*yaw*
no	nej	*nay*
I am . . .	jag är	*yawg air*
are you going to . . . ?	resar ni till . . . ?	*ray-sahr nee*
where is . . . ?	var är . . . ?	*vahr ehr*
the road to . . .	vägen . . .	*vay-gen*
the toilet	toaletten	*toh-ah-let-ten*
the youth hostel	ungdomshär-bärge	*ung-dums-hair-bahr-yeh*
the station	järnvägssta-	*yehern-vehgs-stah-*
tionen	*shoh-nehn*	
I would like . . .	jag vill ha . . .	*yawg veel hah*
to eat	att äta	*aht-air-tah*
a room	ett rum	*eht room*
how much?	hur mycket?	*huhr mew-keht*
when?	när?	*nehr*
left	vänster	*vehn-stehr*
right	höger	*huh-gehr*
straight ahead	rakt fram	*rakt fram*
yesterday	i g r	*ee gohr*
today	i dag	*ee dak*
tomorrow	i morgon	*ee mohr-gohn*
1	ett	*et*
2	tv	*tvoh*
3	tre	*treh*
4	fyra	*few-rah*
5	fem	*fem*
6	sex	*sex*
7	sju	*shew*
8	tta	*oht-tah*MDRV
9	nio	*nee-voh*
10	tio	*tee-yoh*
11	elva	*ehl-vah*
12	tolv	*tohlv*
13	tretton	*treht-ton*

English	*Swedish*	*pronounced*
14	fjorton	*fyohr-ton*
15	femton	*fem-ton*
16	sexton	*sex-ton*
17	sjutton	*shew-ton*
18	arton	*air-ton*
19	nitton	*nit-ton*
20	tjugo	*tshu-goh*
30	trettio	*treht-tyee*
40	fyrtio	*fur-tyee*
50	femtio	*fem-tyee*
60	sextio	*sex-tyee*
70	sjuttio	*shew-tyee*
80	ttio	*oht-tyee*
90	nittio	*nit-tyee*
100	ett hundra	*et hun-dra*
1000	ett tusen	*et too-sen*

Shopping

Apples – *äpplen*. Aspirins – *aspirin*. Bananas – *bananer*. Bandages – *bindel*. Beer – *öl*. Biscuits – *kex*. Blouse – *blus*. Boots – *stövlar*. Bread – *bröd*. Cheese – *ost*. Chocolate – *chokolad*. Coffee – *kaffe*. Dress – *klänning*. Egg – *ägg*. Fish – *fisk*. Fruit – *frukt*. Jacket – *jacka*. Meat – *kött*. Milk – *mjölk*. Mineral water – *mineralvatten*. Oranges – *apelsiner*. Potatoes – *potatis*. Salt – *salt*. Sandwich – *smörgås*. Sausage – *korv*. Shirt – *skjorta*. Shoes – *skorna*. Skirt – *kjol*. Socks – *strumpor*. Soup – *soppa*. Sugar – *socker*. Sweater – *sveater*. Tea – *té*. Trousers – *byxor*. Vegetables – *grönsaker*. Water – *vatten*. Wine – *vin*.

Arabic

English	*Arabic (spelt phonetically)*
I(me)	Ana/enta
Goodbye	Ma Salaam
please	minfudluk
thanks	shukran
Yes	aiwa

English	*Arabic (spelt phonetically)*
No	La
I want	ana ayz
Is it possible	mumkin
not possible	mish mumkin
yes, possible	aiwa mumkin
how much?	di bekam
good	kwoice (kuwayyis)
very good	kwoice ketir
fuck off !	imshee
stop! or stop	bus
bill (as in café)	el hesaab
tomorrow	bokra
no money[1]	ana mafeesh faloose[1]
May God give it to you	Allah Ya'tik
water	moyya
wash	ghasal
too much	ketir
trousers	bantalun
shoe	gezma
now	halan
illness	marad
rice	ghani
chicken	firakh
not clean	mish nadif
clean(verb)	naddaf

1 To persistent beggars asking for money

Calendar 1996

Jan	M	Tu	W	Th	F	Sa	Su
	1	2	3	4	5	6	7
	8	9	10	11	12	13	14
	15	16	17	18	19	20	21
	22	23	24	25	26	27	28
	29	30	31				

Feb	M	Tu	W	Th	F	Sa	Su
				1	2	3	4
	5	6	7	8	9	10	11
	12	13	14	15	16	17	18
	19	20	21	22	23	24	25
	26	27	28	29			

Mar	M	Tu	W	Th	F	Sa	Su
					1	2	3
	4	5	6	7	8	9	10
	11	12	13	14	15	16	17
	18	19	20	21	22	23	24
	25	26	27	28	29	30	31

Apr	M	Tu	W	Th	F	Sa	Su
	1	2	3	4	5	6	7
	8	9	10	11	12	13	14
	15	16	17	18	19	20	21
	22	23	24	25	26	27	28
	29	30					

May	M	Tu	W	Th	F	Sa	Su
			1	2	3	4	5
	6	7	8	9	10	11	12
	13	14	15	16	17	18	19
	20	21	22	23	24	25	26
	27	28	29	30	31		

June	M	Tu	W	Th	F	Sa	Su
						1	2
	3	4	5	6	7	8	9
	10	11	12	13	14	15	16
	17	18	19	20	21	22	23
	24	25	26	27	28	29	30

July	M	Tu	W	Th	F	Sa	Su
	1	2	3	4	5	6	7
	8	9	10	11	12	13	14
	15	16	17	18	19	20	21
	22	23	24	25	26	27	28
	29	30	31				

Aug	M	Tu	W	Th	F	Sa	Su
				1	2	3	4
	5	6	7	8	9	10	11
	12	13	14	15	16	17	18
	19	20	21	22	23	24	25
	26	27	28	29	30	31	

Sept	M	Tu	W	Th	F	Sa	Su
							1
	2	3	4	5	6	7	8
	9	10	11	12	13	14	15
	16	17	18	19	20	21	22
	23	24	25	26	27	28	29
	30						

Oct	M	Tu	W	Th	F	Sa	Su
		1	2	3	4	5	6
	7	8	9	10	11	12	13
	14	15	16	17	18	19	20
	21	22	23	24	25	26	27
	29	29	30	31			

Nov	M	Tu	W	Th	F	Sa	Su
					1	2	3
	4	5	6	7	8	9	10
	11	12	13	14	15	16	17
	18	19	20	21	22	23	24
	25	26	27	28	29	30	

Dec	M	Tu	W	Th	F	Sa	Su
							1
	2	3	4	5	6	7	8
	9	10	11	12	13	14	15
	16	17	18	19	20	21	22
	23	24	25	26	27	28	29
	30	31					

INDEX